TEACH Instructor Resource Manual

Leifer

Introduction to Maternity & Pediatric Nursing

Sixth Edition

Trena L. Rich, RN, PHN, MSN, APRN, CIC
Director, Quality Assurance
Patient Care Center
Western University of Health Sciences
Pomona, California

SAUNDERS
ELSEVIER

ELSEVIER
SAUNDERS

3251 Riverport Lane
St. Louis, Missouri 63043

TEACH Instructor Resource Manual for
Introduction to Maternity & Pediatric Nursing, Sixth Edition   ISBN: 978-1-4377-2713-5

Notices

Knowledge and best practice in this field are constantly changing. As new research and experience broaden our understanding, changes in research methods, professional practices, or medical treatment may become necessary.

Practitioners and researchers must always rely on their own experience and knowledge in evaluating and using any information, methods, compounds, or experiments described herein. In using such information or methods they should be mindful of their own safety and the safety of others, including parties for whom they have a professional responsibility.

With respect to any drug or pharmaceutical products identified, readers are advised to check the most current information provided (i) on procedures featured or (ii) by the manufacturer of each product to be administered, to verify the recommended dose or formula, the method and duration of administration, and contraindications. It is the responsibility of practitioners, relying on their own experience and knowledge of their patients, to make diagnoses, to determine dosages and the best treatment for each individual patient, and to take all appropriate safety precautions.

To the fullest extent of the law, neither the Publisher nor the authors, contributors, or editors, assume any liability for any injury and/or damage to persons or property as a matter of products liability, negligence or otherwise, or from any use or operation of any methods, products, instructions, or ideas contained in the material herein.

Vice President and Publisher: Tom Wilhelm
Executive Editor: Teri Hines Burnham
Developmental Editor: Tiffany Trautwein
Editorial Assistant: Kevin Clear
Publishing Services Manager: Deborah L. Vogel
Senior Project Manager: Deon Lee
Book Designer: Paula Catalano

Working together to grow
libraries in developing countries

www.elsevier.com | www.bookaid.org | www.sabre.org

ELSEVIER   BOOK AID International   Sabre Foundation

Printed in the United States of America
Last digit is the print number: 9 8 7 6 5 4 3 2 1

How to Use the TEACH Instructor Resource Manual

Welcome to TEACH, your Total Curriculum Solution!

The TEACH Instructor Resource Manual is designed to help you prepare for class lectures for *Introduction to Maternity & Pediatric Nursing*. We hope it will reduce your lesson preparation time, give you new and creative ideas to promote student learning, and help you to make full use of the rich array of resources in the Leifer teaching package.

Organization

The TEACH Instructor Resource Manual includes lessons that correspond with each chapter from your *Introduction to Maternity & Pediatric Nursing* textbook and includes the following two sections:

1. **Lesson Plans:** Includes several class preparation checklists and a 50-minute lesson that provide you with the building blocks for your curriculum.
2. **Lecture Outlines:** Consists of a 50-minute lecture outline that incorporates the PowerPoint® presentations.

Lesson Plans and Lecture Outlines are also available on Evolve at http://evolve.elsevier.com/Leifer.

Lesson Plans

The Lesson Plans are designed to promote active student learning and get students involved in class discussions and activities. They include preparation checklists for you, individual lesson(s), and performance evaluation tools to help you gauge your students' understanding of the course material and adapt lessons to their needs.

Checklists

The introduction of each Lesson Plan includes the following checklists to ensure that you are well-prepared for class:

- **Teaching Focus:** Identifies key student learning goals for the chapter
- **Materials and Resources:** Lists materials needed for each lesson
- **Lesson Checklist:** Includes instructor preparation suggestions
- **Key Terms:** Provides page references for each key term in the chapter
- **Additional Resources:** Lists instructor resources available for the chapter

Lessons

Each Lesson Plan includes one or more 50-minute lessons—building blocks that can be sequenced to fit your class schedule. The Lesson Plans are available in electronic format on Evolve so you can customize them to fit the requirements of your course. Every lesson includes a wide variety of teaching resources. In many cases, our subject matter experts have provided more resources and activities than can be covered in a 50-minute lesson. We encourage you to choose activities that match the needs of your students and your curriculum, and the materials and resources available at your school.

Lesson Plans can be a valuable tool for documenting how your curriculum covers learning objectives in compliance with accrediting organizations. Some accrediting organizations require that learning resources be integrated into a program's curriculum, to enhance students' learning experiences. The activities in this Lesson Plan Manual will help your students use available resources, such as the library or the Internet, to complement their textbook.

ELSEVIER

Each lesson includes the following sections:

- **Pretest** and **Background Assessment:** The first lesson in each chapter includes a Pretest and Background Assessment questions designed to help you gauge your students' readiness for the lesson. Depending on students' responses, you may wish to modify your lesson. Students who are comfortable with the topic may need more challenging activities. Students who have difficulty with the topic may need to start by addressing more fundamental concepts.
- **Critical Thinking Question:** Every lesson includes a Critical Thinking Question to motivate students by demonstrating real-world applications of the lesson content.
- **Lesson Guide:** The heart of the TEACH lesson plan is the three-column Lesson Guide that links Objectives and content from *Introduction to Maternity & Pediatric Nursing* with appropriate Teaching Resources. Teaching Resources reference all the elements of the ancillary package and include additional teaching tips such as class activities, discussion topics, and much more. This section correlates your textbook and its ancillary materials with the objectives upon which your course is based.
- **Homework/Assignments** and **Instructor's Notes/Student Feedback:** These sections are provided for you to add your own notes for assignments, for recording student feedback, and for other notes relating to the lesson.

Lecture Outlines

The Lecture Outlines include PowerPoint® slides to provide a compelling visual presentation and summary of the main chapter points. Lecture notes for each slide highlight key topics and provide questions for discussion—to help create an interactive classroom environment.

We encourage you to select material from the TEACH Instructor Resource Manual that meets your students' needs, integrate TEACH into your existing lesson plans, and put your own teaching approach into the plans. We hope TEACH will be an invaluable tool in your classroom!

Contents

1 The Past, Present, and Future 1

2 Human Reproductive Anatomy and Physiology 33

3 Fetal Development 52

4 Prenatal Care and Adaptations to Pregnancy 71

5 Nursing Care of Women with Complications During Pregnancy 101

6 Nursing Care of Mother and Infant During Labor and Birth 130

7 Nursing Management of Pain During Labor and Birth 157

8 Nursing Care of Women with Complications During Labor and Birth 174

9 The Family After Birth 202

10 Nursing Care of Women with Complications After Birth 229

11 The Nurse's Role in Women's Health Care 246

12 The Term Newborn 271

13 Preterm and Postterm Newborns 289

14 The Newborn with a Perinatal Injury or Congenital Malformation 312

15 An Overview of Growth, Development, and Nutrition 348

16 The Infant 378

17 The Toddler 399

18 The Preschool Child 419

19 The School-Age Child 444

20 The Adolescent 465

21 The Child's Experience of Hospitalization 488

22 Health Care Adaptations for the Child and Family 513

23 The Child with a Sensory or Neurological Condition 542

24 The Child with a Musculoskeletal Condition 578

25 The Child with a Respiratory Disorder 606

26 The Child with a Cardiovascular Disorder 637

27 The Child with a Condition of the Blood, Blood-Forming Organs, or Lymphatic System 658

28 The Child with a Gastrointestinal Condition 692

29 The Child with a Genitourinary Condition 724

30 The Child with a Skin Condition 744

31 The Child with a Metabolic Condition 773

32 The Child with a Communicable Disease 799

33 The Child with an Emotional or Behavioral Condition 822

34 Complementary and Alternative Therapies in Maternity and Pediatric Nursing 845

ELSEVIER

Introduction to Maternity & Pediatric Nursing, 6th ed.

Elsevier items and derived items © 2011, 2007, 2006 by Saunders, an imprint of Elsevier Inc.

Leifer

1 Lesson Plan
The Past, Present, and Future

TEACHING FOCUS

Students will have the opportunity to learn about past and present-day concepts of maternity and pediatrics, persons who have made significant contributions to the field, environmental stresses on the childbearing family and how culture affects childbirth and child care. Students will be introduced to the importance of vital statistics, the steps of the nursing process, the influence of international organizations, and federal programs concerned with setting standards for care and assisting mothers and infants. Students will have the opportunity to explore nursing care plans; clinical pathways; and the definitions of the Nursing Interventions Classification (NIC), the Nursing Outcomes Classification (NOC), and their respective influences on the nursing process. Students will have the opportunity to become familiar with the similarities and differences between the nursing diagnosis and the medical diagnosis frameworks. The chapter also covers the application of critical thinking skills as they relate to study challenges and lifelong learning tasks as well as to the nursing process. Students also will have the opportunity to examine the role of the school nurse and the expanding role of the community-based nurse.

MATERIALS AND RESOURCES

☐ Computer and projector (all lessons)

LESSON CHECKLIST

Preparations for this lesson include:

- Lecture
- Demonstration
- Guest speakers: Representative from the local department of public health, community health nurse
- Evaluation of student knowledge and skills needed to perform all entry-level activities related to understanding the past, present, and future of maternity and pediatric nursing, including:
  - ○ Comparing and contrasting contemporary concepts of maternity and pediatrics with those of the past and among various cultures
  - ○ Understanding the historical contributions of leaders in the fields of maternity and pediatric care and the development of international organizations and federal programs in these fields
  - ○ Understanding the classification systems used for diagnosis, research, reimbursement, nursing process, and patient outcomes
  - ○ Applying critical thinking to the nursing process
  - ○ Comprehending future trends in health care, including use of a computerized documentation process and developments toward community-based nursing

KEY TERMS

advanced-practice nurse (p. 10)
advocate (p. 10)
birthing centers (p. 5)
clinical nurse specialist (CNS) (p. 10)
clinical pathway (p. 12)
cost containment (p. 5)
critical thinking (p. 3)
cultural awareness (p. 6)
cultural competence (p. 6)
cultural sensitivity (p. 6)
culture (p. 6)
diagnosis-related groups (DRGs) (p. 9)
documentation (p. 6)
empowerment (p. 2)

evidence-based practice (p. 13)
family care plan (p. 16)
full inclusion (p. 10)
genomics (p. 6)
Health Information Portability and Accountability Act (HIPAA) (p. 4)
health maintenance organization (HMO) (p. 9)
Healthy People 2020 (p. 17)
labor, delivery, and recovery (LDR) room (p. 5)

mainstream (p. 10)
midwives (p. 5)
morbidity (p. 3)
mortality (p. 3)
nursing care plan (p. 11)
nursing process (p. 11)
obstetrician (p. 2)
obstetrics (p. 2)
pediatric nurse practitioner (PNP) (p. 10)
pediatrics (p. 2)
preferred provider organization (PPO) (p. 9)
puerperium (p. 2)
SBAR (p. 6)
statistics (p. 12)

Leifer

ADDITIONAL RESOURCES

TEACH PPT slide(s) Chapter 1, 1-67
EILR IC image(s) Chapter 1, 1-3
EILR OBQ question(s) Chapter 1, 1-10
EILR TB question(s) Chapter 1, 1-30
ESLR IRQ question(s) Chapter 1, 1-5
SG Chapter 1, pp. 1-6

Legend

PPT	**EILR**	**ESLR**	**SG**	**CTQ**
TEACH PowerPoint Slides	EVOLVE Instructor Learning Resources: Image Collection (IC), Open-Book Quizzes (OBQ), Test Bank (TB)	EVOLVE Student Learning Resources: Interactive Review Questions (IRQ) for the NCLEX® Examination	Study Guide	Critical Thinking Question in Nursing Care Plan (NCP CTQ) or Get Ready for the NCLEX! (GRN CTQ)

Class Activities are indicated in **_bold italic_**.

Leifer

LESSON 1.1

PRETEST

1. The branch of medicine that deals with child development and treatment of childhood diseases is
   a. obstetrics.
   b. pediatrics.
   c. gynecology.
   d. psychology.
2. The ability of a family to maintain control over the health care of family members is called
   a. empowerment.
   b. proactive.
   c. authority.
   d. inactivity.
3. The doctor who first initiated instilling 2% silver nitrate in the eyes of newborns to prevent blindness caused by gonorrhea was
   a. Louis Pasteur.
   b. Karl Credé.
   c. Ignaz Semmelweis.
   d. John Lister.
4. The first pediatric hospital in the United States (the Pediatric Hospital of Philadelphia) was founded in
   a. 1855.
   b. 1874.
   c. 1955.
   d. 1974.
5. Current legislation allows a mother who delivered by cesarean section to remain in the hospital for
   a. 24 hours.
   b. 36 hours.
   c. 48 hours.
   d. 96 hours.
6. The term describing patient progress that does not meet specific recovery goals is
   a. standard deviation.
   b. nonproductive.
   c. noncompliance.
   d. variance.
7. The Medicare system that determines payment based on diagnosis for a hospital stay is known as
   a. HMO.
   b. DRG.
   c. PPO.
   d. POS.
8. A systematic problem-solving approach used by nurses to identify, prevent, and treat health problems is called a
   a. care plan.
   b. nursing process.
   c. scope of practice.
   d. standard of care.
9. The organization that inspects the food supply, enforces proper garbage disposal, and inspects housing is the
   a. public health department.
   b. Department of Children and Family Services.
   c. Food and Drug Administration.
   d. American Academy of Pediatrics.
10. One of the most important documents addressing the needs of children in the areas of education, welfare, health, and protection is
    a. the Fair Labor Standards Act.
    b. the Child Abuse and Protection Act.
    c. the Children's Charter of 1930.
    d. *Healthy People 2020.*

Answers

1. b	3. b	5. d	7. b	9. a
2. a	4. a	6. d	8. b	10. c

BACKGROUND ASSESSMENT

Question: What are the components of the Fair Labor Standards Act?

Answer: This act was passed in 1938 and set the standard for child labor practices. It established 16 years of age as the minimum age for working, with the exception of work that involves hazardous material, in which case the child must be age 18 years of age. This law established national minimal standards for child labor and provided enforcement of the guidelines.

Question: What factors affect the health care delivery system?

Answer: The health care delivery system is affected by the need for providing adequate health care to patients while trying to contain the cost for the patients they serve. In an effort to minimize expenses, hospitals in some areas have benefitted by merging with other hospitals, which has led to reduced operating costs and duplication of services and increased buying power. Insurance reimbursements affect the health care delivery system. If health care providers (HCP) and hospitals do not receive sufficient reimbursement for the services they provide, they cannot remain financially viable and remain open. The federal Centers for Medicaid and Medicare Services (CMS) programs use diagnosis-related groups (DRGs), which determine the amount of time it typically takes to treat a specific illness and the rate of reimbursement a HCP or hospital will receive based on a patient's diagnosis. As a result, patients are discharged from the hospital earlier. Nurses are challenged to provide optimum care during these shorter hospital stays and within the constraints of cost containment. In addition, shorter hospital stays mean more patients will be cared for at home or in skilled or extended-care facilities.

CRITICAL THINKING QUESTION

A 17-year-old single pregnant adolescent comes to the clinic and informs the nurse that she is sick. The nurse determines that the adolescent views her pregnancy as an illness. How should the nurse proceed with obtaining needed information and outlining patient care?

Guidelines: This adolescent will most likely need medical, emotional, and financial support throughout the pregnancy and after the birth of her baby. The nurse should identify cultural influences and values that may affect the health of both the mother and the infant. The nurse also should assess the mother's understanding of pregnancy, labor, and newborn care to determine the appropriate amount of patient education. To determine what resources the young mother may need, the nurse should refer her to appropriate social service agencies within the community. The mother will need help to view her pregnancy as a healthy event. She will need ongoing education about the importance of prenatal care, the stages of pregnancy, preparation for birth, becoming a mother, and caring for her newborn.

OBJECTIVES	CONTENT	TEACHING RESOURCES
Recall the contributions of persons in history to the fields of maternity and pediatric care.	■ The past (p. 2) ☐ Obstetrics (p. 2) ☐ Pediatrics (p. 2) ☐ Obstetric and pediatric care in the United States (p. 3) – Government influences in maternity and pediatric care (p. 3) – Legislation (p. 3) – The Children's Bureau (p. 4) – White House conferences (p. 4) – International Year of the Child (p. 4) – Department of public health (p. 4)	PPT slides 13-36 *e* EILR OBQ questions 1-3 *e* EILR TB questions 2, 12, 13, 28, 29 SG Learning Activities, question 3 (p. 1) SG Review Questions, question 1 (p. 5) **BOOK RESOURCES** Box 1-1, The Children's Charter of 1930 (p. 5) Box 1-2, The United Nations Declaration of the Rights of the Child (p. 6) Review Questions for the NCLEX® Examination question 2 (p. 19) ▸ Discuss how contributions to the field of maternal and pediatric medicine (such as the importance of hand hygiene and nurse training programs) have helped advance the practice of medicine. ▸ Discuss how The Children's Charter of 1930 (Box 1-1, p. 4) continues to shape public policy for mothers and children today.

ELSEVIER
Elsevier items and derived items © 2011, 2007, 2006 by Saunders, an imprint of Elsevier Inc.   Leifer

OBJECTIVES	CONTENT	TEACHING RESOURCES
		Class Activity Assign students to conduct research on one of the following topics with an emphasis on how it influenced maternity and pediatric care today: – *Lillian Wald* – *Margaret Sanger* – *White House Conference of 1930 and the Children's Charter* – *Public health department* **Have students prepare a one-page report on the assigned topic and present it to the class.** *(For students to prepare for this activity, see Homework/Assignments.)*
Name two international organizations concerned with maternity and child care.	– International Year of the Child (p. 4)	PPT slide 34 **BOOK RESOURCES** Box 1-2, The United Nations Declaration of the Rights of the Child (p. 6) ▸ Discuss the effectiveness of the United Nations Declaration of the Rights of the Child (Box 1-2, p. 6) in ensuring child welfare throughout the world. *Class Activity **Lead a discussion in which students identify the contributions of the United Nations International Children's Emergency Fund (UNICEF) and of the World Health Organization (WHO) to improving maternal and pediatric health care worldwide.***
List the organizations concerned with setting standards for the nursing care of maternity and pediatric patients.	☐ Obstetric and pediatric care in the United States (p. 3)	PPT slide 55 *e* EILR TB question 1 SG Learning Activities, question 4 (p. 1) **BOOK RESOURCES** Review Questions for the NCLEX® Examination questions 3, 5 (p. 19) *Class Activity **Divide the class into three groups and assign each group one of the following organizations: ACNM, AWHONN, NAACOG, and ANA. Who are the members of each group? What is the group's stated purpose and function? Who benefits from its activities?***
State the influence of the federal government on maternity and pediatric care.	– Government influences in maternity and pediatric care (p. 3) – Legislation (p. 3) – The Children's	PPT slides 24-36 *e* EILR OBQ question 3 *e* EILR TB questions 6, 7, 20, 21, 29 SG Learning Activities, question 5 (p. 2)

OBJECTIVES	CONTENT	TEACHING RESOURCES
	Bureau (p. 4) – White House conferences (p. 4) – International Year of the Child (p. 4) – Department of public health (p. 4)	SG Applying Knowledge, question 1 (p. 5) ▸ Discuss the values reflected in government programs and legislation for mothers and children. How have these programs affected the welfare of our society as a whole? ▸ Discuss the contributions of the Sheppard-Towner Act of 1921, Title V of the Social Security Act, Fair Labor Act of 1938, and Title XIX of the Medicaid program to improving health care for mothers and children. **Class Activity** *Invite a representative from the local department of public health to discuss ways local agencies affect legislation on maternity and pediatric care. What recent activities are most important? How do federal rules and guidelines affect state nursing practice? How do reductions in funding or changes in legislation affect patient services?*
List three federal programs that assist mothers and infants.	– Government influences in maternity and pediatric care (p. 3) – Legislation (p. 3)	PPT slides 25, 26 *e* EILR OBQ question 3 *e* EILR TB questions 8, 14 *e* ESLR IRQ question 4 ▸ Discuss the influence of the Children's Bureau, White House conferences, and the International Year of the Child on the delivery of health care for mothers and children. **Class Activity** *Divide the class into three groups and assign each group one of the following programs that assist mothers and children: Head Start, Family Planning, Women's, Infant's, and Children's (WIC) program; and the Medicaid program. Have groups prepare a brief report about the benefits, drawbacks, and areas of improvement for each program. Invite class discussion and questions.*
Understand the legal responsibilities of the nurse to report certain diseases or conditions to the public health authorities.	– Department of public health (p. 4)	PPT slides 35-37 *e* EILR TB question 27 ▸ Discuss what a reportable disease or condition is within your state or county. **Class Activity** *Invite an infection preventionist to discuss reportable conditions and their importance to health and safety within your community. Invite class discussion and questions.*

1.1 Homework/Assignments:

1. Assign students to conduct research on one of the following topics with an emphasis on how it influenced maternity and pediatric care: Lillian Wald; Margaret Sanger; White House Conference of 1930, the Children's Charter; and the local public health department. Have students prepare a one-page report on the assigned topic and present it to the class.

1.1 Instructor's Notes/Student Feedback:

LESSON 1.2

CRITICAL THINKING QUESTION

Question: A 42-year-old woman delivers a 6 lb. boy who is diagnosed with Down syndrome. Her husband is visibly upset. How would you develop an appropriate nursing care plan using critical thinking and the nursing process for this family?

Guidelines: This family was expecting a "normal" baby and is now stunned at the diagnosis of their infant. The parents need time to assimilate this unexpected situation. The nurse acts as a support person to help them begin to understand the challenges they face in caring for a baby with Down syndrome. The family will need time to bond with the baby. An appropriate nursing goal is for the parents to accept the baby and care for him as a baby with special needs. Using the steps of the nursing process, the nurse assesses parental coping skills, determines the needs of the family upon discharge, and helps arrange support services. These may include a pediatrician who specializes in treatment of Down syndrome and medical supplies necessary for this newborn's specific needs. The nurse also can refer the family to sources of financial support and to support groups for parents of infants with Down syndrome and may suggest ways to incorporate family support for infant/child care and household tasks. The nurse can also assist in arranging for home health nurses to help after discharge and for continued family support.

OBJECTIVES	CONTENT	TEACHING RESOURCES
Contrast present-day concepts of maternity and child care with those of the past.	– Department of public health (p. 4) ■ The present (p. 5) □ Family-centered care (p. 5) □ Financial considerations (p. 6) □ Changing perceptions of childbearing (p. 6) □ Midwives (p. 6) □ Role of the consumer (p. 6) □ Cultural considerations (p. 7) □ Technology and specialty expertise (p. 7) □ Nursing care (p. 10) – Pediatric nurses as advocates (p. 10)	☒ PPT slides 38-52 𝒆 EILR IC images 1, 2 𝒆 EILR OBQ question 4 𝒆 EILR TB questions 3, 5, 16, 17, 22, 24, 25, 26 𝒆 ESLR IRQ questions 1, 2, 4 SG Learning Activities, questions 2, 6, 7, 8, 9 (pp. 2-4) SG Review Questions, question 2 (p. 5) SG Applying Knowledge, questions 3-5 (pp. 5-6) **BOOK RESOURCES** Figure 1-1, Fetal Surgery (p. 7) Figure 1-2, Gene Therapy (p. 9) ▸ Discuss how the concept of family-centered care has affected maternity and pediatric care. ▸ Discuss the ways environmental stresses affect the delivery of nursing care. What knowledge and considerations must nurses use during their assessment of childbearing families? *Class Activity **Divide the class into two groups. Have one group list key features of present-day concepts of maternity and child care. Have the other group list key features of past maternity and child-care practices. The groups should describe the nurse's role in each era.***

Introduction to Maternity & Pediatric Nursing, 6th ed.

OBJECTIVES	CONTENT	TEACHING RESOURCES
		Have each group present the advantages and disadvantages of each time, then discuss them as a class.
		Class Activity **Divide the class into small groups and assign each group one of the following stressors that can affect the childbearing family:**
		– *Early discharge after childbirth*
		– *Increasing cultural diversity*
		– *Changing family structure*
		– *Financial burdens*
		Have the groups brainstorm ways in which their assigned topic affects health care delivery and nursing practice. What challenges can arise for families? For nurses? What is the nurse's role in helping families address these problems?
Discuss how culture affects childbirth and child care.	☐ Pediatrics (p. 2) ☐ Cultural considerations (p. 7) ☐ Nursing care (p. 10) – Pediatric nurses as advocates (p. 10)	☒▦ PPT slides 42-46 ▣ SG Applying Knowledge, questions 3-5 (pp. 5-6) ▶ Discuss how the nurse's own cultural beliefs and ethnicity could affect care of patients. ▶ Discuss ways a patient's cultural beliefs and ethnicity could affect the nursing care plan. *Class Activity* **Have students describe individual cultural beliefs and practices regarding childbirth. What challenges does cultural diversity present to childbearing families? What are the implications for developing effective nursing care plans and interventions? What role can the nurse play in ensuring a positive outcome?**
Discuss common terms used in expressing vital statistics.	– Statistics (p. 12)	☒▦ PPT slide 47 *ℯ* EILR TB question 4 ▣ SG Review Questions, question 3 (p. 5) ▣ SG Applying Knowledge, question 1 (p. 5) **BOOK RESOURCES** Box 1-6, Common Vital Statistics Terms (p. 12) Table 1-2, Birth Rate Statistics in the United States from 2002-2006 (pp. 14-15) Review Questions for the NCLEX® Examination question 1 (p. 19) ▶ Discuss why understanding how to interpret statistical data is important for the nursing profession.

Introduction to Maternity & Pediatric Nursing, 6ᵗʰ ed.

OBJECTIVES	CONTENT	TEACHING RESOURCES
		Class Activity **Lead a question-and-answer session in which students correctly use the following terms important to vital statistics and data gathering: rank, number, percent, rate, and percent change. Refer to Table 1-2 (p. 11). What is the difference between morbidity and mortality?**
List four reasons why statistics are important.	– Statistics (p. 12)	⬛ PPT slide 47 📖 SG Review Questions, question 3 (p. 5) 📖 SG Applying Knowledge, question 6 (p. 6) **BOOK RESOURCES** Table 1-2, Birth Rate Statistics in the United States from 2002-2006 (pp. 14-15) Review Questions for the NCLEX® Examination question 1 (p. 19) ▸ Discuss the use of statistics in shaping prenatal care. Refer to Table 1-2, Birth Rate Statistics in the United States from 2002-2006 (pp. 14-15). ▸ Discuss the ways nurses might use Table 1-2, Birth Rate Statistics in the United States from 2002-2006 (pp. 14-15) to draw correlations and develop community education programs. *Class Activity* **Divide the class into small groups. Assign each group a different state and have them research the infant mortality rate and the birth rate for that state. Have each group present its findings and explain four ways the data can be used to optimize health care for the population. (For students to prepare for this activity, see Homework/Assignments.)**
State two types of health care delivery systems in the United States.	☐ Health care delivery systems (p. 9)	⬛ PPT slides 51, 52 𝒆 EILR OBQ question 5 📖 SG Learning Activities, question 1 (p. 1) 📖 SG Applying Knowledge, question 2 (pp. 5-6) **BOOK RESOURCES** Box 1-3, Health Care Delivery Systems (p. 9) ▸ Discuss the differences between these two systems and how they can impact the delivery of health care. *Class Activity* **Divide the class into small groups. Assign each group a health care delivery system. Have each group list the pros and cons of each type. Then present**

Introduction to Maternity & Pediatric Nursing, 6th ed.

OBJECTIVES	CONTENT	TEACHING RESOURCES
		the results to the entire class. What is different between the two in the delivery of health care (i.e., time for an appointment, referrals).
Discuss the role of the advanced-practice nurse.	– Advanced-practice nurses (p. 10)	PPT slide 53 SG Learning Activities, question 10 (p. 4) SG Review Questions, question 4 (p. 5) **BOOK RESOURCES** Box 1-4, Advanced-Practice Nursing Specialties (p. 11) ▸ Discuss the educational and certification requirements for each APN role. *Class Activity Divide the class into small groups. Assign each group a different APN role. Have them research the educational, licensing, and certification requirements for each. Present findings to the class. What is different and what is similar between each role?*
List the five steps of the nursing process.	☐ Nursing tools (p. 11) – The nursing process (p. 11)	PPT slide 56-58 EILR OBQ questions 6-8 ESLR IRQ questions 3, 5 SG Learning Activities, question 11 (p. 4) SG Review Questions, question 5 (p. 5) **BOOK RESOURCES** Table 1-1, Comparison of Medical and Nursing Diagnoses (p. 11) Box 1-5, Common Terms Used in Nursing Care Plans (p. 12) Box 1-7, Steps in Preparing a Care Plan (p. 13) ▸ Discuss the importance of incorporating a nursing diagnosis in the nursing process. Refer to Comparison of Medical and Nursing Diagnoses (Table 1-1, p. 11) *Class Activity: Lead a class discussion about the scenario below, then guide students to write an appropriate nursing care plan:* *A 28-year-old gravida 3 para 1 is in active labor with twins. Her last baby was delivered by cesarean section.* *Divide the class into small groups and have them identify each step of the nursing process in the care plan.*

OBJECTIVES	CONTENT	TEACHING RESOURCES
		Reconvene the class and have students compare their results.
Contrast a nursing care plan with a clinical pathway.	– Nursing care plans (p. 11) – Clinical pathways (p. 12)	PPT slide 57 EILR OBQ questions 6-9 EILR TB questions 9, 15, 30 SG Learning Activities, question 11 (p. 4) SG Review Questions, questions 5, 6 (p. 5) SG Applying Knowledge, question 7 (p. 6) **BOOK RESOURCES** Nursing Care Plan 1-1, Care of Childbearing Families Related to Potential or Actual Stress Caused by Cultural Diversity (p. 8) Box 1-5, Common Terms Used in Nursing Care Plans (p. 12) Box 1-7, Steps in Preparing a Care Plan (p. 13) ▸ Discuss the impact of cost-containment measures on clinical pathways. *Class Activity Divide the class in half. Have one half identify and discuss what is involved in a clinical pathway (also called* **critical** *pathway or* **care map***). Have the other half identify and discuss what is involved in a nursing care plan. Students should define key terms and should describe the purpose of their assigned topic. They also should discuss how the patient benefits and the roles of various health professionals (such as physician, RN, LPN/LVN, nursing assistants, advanced-practice nurses, and therapists). Ask each half to present its findings and then discuss as a class how a clinical pathway relates to a nursing care plan.*

1.2 Homework/Assignments:

1. Divide students into small groups. Assign each group a different state and have them research the infant mortality rate and the birth rate for that state. Have each group present findings in class and explain four ways the data can be used to optimize health care for the population.

1.2 Instructor's Notes/Student Feedback:

LESSON 1.3

CRITICAL THINKING QUESTION

The parents of a school-age child recently diagnosed with type 1 diabetes mellitus reluctantly tell the nurse that they have serious financial problems and don't know how they can pay for medication for their child once the basic necessities, such as food, rent, and utilities have been paid. How can the community health nurse help?

Guidelines: The community health nurse can assess the household situation, including social and financial needs, and develop a plan of care that uses available community resources such as WIC and Medicaid. The community nurse functions as an advocate for the patient and the family and also has the responsibility for educating the family about health maintenance and illness prevention. The nurse provides support and encouragement and can assist the family in problem-solving as the need arises. This family may need to be referred to a social service agency for long-term counseling and assistance.

OBJECTIVES	CONTENT	TEACHING RESOURCES
Define the Nursing Interventions Classification (NIC) and its relationship to the nursing process.	– NIC, NOC, and NANDA-I (p. 15)	PPT slide 58 EILR OBQ questions 6-8 EILR TB questions 10, 18 ESLR IRQ questions 3, 5 SG Learning Activities, questions 11, 12 (p. 4) SG Review Questions, questions 5, 6 (p. 5) **BOOK RESOURCES** Box 1-7, Steps in preparing a care plan (p. 13) ▸ Discuss the value of a standardized language to convey patient status and nursing activities. *Class Activity Lead a class discussion in which students define Nursing Interventions Classification (NIC). Provide them with the following scenarios and discuss how NIC can facilitate critical thinking to develop interventions to assist the following patients:* *1. A 16-year-old primigravida is admitted to the labor suite in early labor. She is in tears and anxious about labor and birth. She is undecided about parenting the baby.* *2. The parents of a 5-year-old boy bring him to the emergency department because he is having trouble breathing. The diagnosis is asthma.* *3. A 35-year-old woman who has gestational diabetes delivers an infant who is LGA (large for gestational age). The mother does not understand how her physical condition affects the newborn and what special care she and her child will need.*

Leifer

OBJECTIVES	CONTENT	TEACHING RESOURCES
Describe the Nursing Outcomes Classification (NOC) and its influence on the nursing process.	– NIC, NOC, and NANDA-I (p. 15)	☒ PPT slide 58 𝒆 ESLR IRQ questions 3, 5 [SG] SG Learning Activities, questions 11, 12 (p. 5) [SG] SG Review Questions, questions 5, 6 (p. 5) ▸ Discuss the importance of defining nursing outcomes that are directly influenced by nursing actions. *Class Activity **Pair students and assign each pair one of the clinical situations in the previous class activity. Ask student pairs to identify an appropriate Nursing Outcomes Classification (NOC) and its influence on the nursing process for their assigned situation. Ask volunteer pairs to present to the class for feedback and discussion.***
Compare and contrast nursing and medical diagnosis frameworks with focus on North American Nursing Diagnosis Association International (NANDA-I) taxonomy.	– NIC, NOC, and NANDA-I (p. 15)	☒ PPT slides 57, 58 𝒆 EILR OBQ questions 6-8 𝒆 ESLR IRQ question 5 [SG] SG Learning Activities, questions 11, 12 (p. 5) **BOOK RESOURCES** Nursing Care Plan 1-1, Care of Childbearing Families Related to Potential or Actual Stress Caused by Cultural Diversity (p. 8) Table 1-1, Comparison of Medical and Nursing Diagnoses (p. 11) ▸ Discuss the relationship among NIC, NOC, and NANDA-I. Refer to Nursing Care Plan 1-1 (p. 8) to identify specific examples. *Class Activity **Lead a discussion in which students define medical diagnosis and nursing diagnosis according to NANDA-I taxonomy. Have students match the nursing diagnosis with the correct medical diagnosis listed below.*** *Medical Diagnosis:* *1. Infant weight loss* *2. Acute asthma attack* *3. Exertional dyspnea* *Nursing Diagnosis:* *a. Ineffective airway clearance* *b. Risk for activity intolerance* *c. Ineffective feeding pattern*

OBJECTIVES	CONTENT	TEACHING RESOURCES

Define critical thinking.	☐ Critical thinking (p. 13)
	  – The nursing process and critical thinking (p. 13)
		PPT slides 57-59
		
		EILR OBQ question 9
		
		EILR TB questions 11, 23
		
		ESLR IRQ question 1
		
		SG Learning Activities, question 13 (p. 4)
		
		BOOK RESOURCES
		
		Box 1-8, Process of Critical Thinking (p. 15)
		
		▸ Discuss the role of critical thinking in problem-solving and problem prevention.
		
		*Class Activity **As a class, define critical thinking. Present the following clinical situation and ask students why critical thinking is important.***
		
		   The student nurse is assigned two patients in active labor. One is a gravida 3 who has experienced short labors in the past. The other is a primigravida.

Discuss the role of critical thinking in the nursing process and in clinical judgment.	☐ Critical thinking (p. 13) – The nursing process and critical thinking (p. 13)	PPT slides 59-61 EILR OBQ questions 7, 9 ESLR IRQ question 1 SG Learning Activities, question 11 (p. 4) **BOOK RESOURCES** Nursing Care Plan 1-1, Care of Childbearing Families Related to Potential or Actual Stress Caused by Cultural Diversity (p. 8) Nursing Tip (p. 13) Box 1-8, Process of Critical Thinking (p. 15) ▸ Discuss specific examples of critical thinking in Nursing Care Plan 1-1 (p. 8). *Class Activity **Using the clinical situation in the previous activity, lead a class discussion in which students apply the seven steps in the process of critical thinking to carry out appropriate tasks in the nursing process.***
Discuss the role of critical thinking as it relates to test-taking and lifelong learning.	– Using critical thinking to improve test scores (p. 15)	PPT slides 60, 61 EILR OBQ question 9 **BOOK RESOURCES** Box 1-8, Process of Critical Thinking (p. 15) ▸ Discuss the similarities and differences among the steps

OBJECTIVES	CONTENT	TEACHING RESOURCES
		used in critical thinking in the nursing process and critical thinking in lifelong learning. Refer to Box 1-8, Process of Critical Thinking (p. 15).
		*Class Activity **Lead a discussion in which students apply critical thinking to help them master school-related challenges such as taking tests. How can thinking critically help students solve problems in their professional and personal lives and contribute to lifelong learning?***
Discuss the objectives of *Healthy People 2020* as it relates to maternity and pediatric care.	■ The future (p. 17) ☐ Health care reform (p. 17) ☐ *Healthy People 2020* (p. 17)	⊠ PPT slides 62, 63 *e* EILR IC image 3 SG Learning Activities, question 14 (p. 4) **BOOK RESOURCES** Health Promotion, *Healthy People 2020*: Specific Contributions of Nurses (p. 11) ▸ Discuss ways nurses can influence community health. *Class Activity **Divide the class into small groups and assign each two or three of the 10 points listed in the Health Promotion box, Healthy People 2020: Specific Contributions of School Nurses (p. 11). Have each group discuss the benefits to maternity and pediatrics as well as the community at large. Have groups make presentations to the class.***
Examine the importance of documentation as a nursing responsibility.	– SBAR communication (p. 16)	⊠ PPT slides 64, 65 *e* EILR OBQ question 10 *e* EILR TB question 19 SG Applying Knowledge, questions 7, 8 (p. 6) **BOOK RESOURCES** Review Questions for the NCLEX® Examination question 2, 4 (p. 19) ▸ Discuss the pros and cons of paper versus electronic medical records. ▸ What security factors need to be considered with these two types of documentation? *Class Activity **Divide the class into small groups and have them practice documentation in the medical record for both paper and electronic charting. Have volunteers retrieve the information and discuss with the class.***
Describe the role of the community health nurse as	– Community-based nursing (p. 16)	⊠ PPT slide 66 ▸ Discuss a community health nurse's points of access to the general population, such as schools, churches, and

OBJECTIVES	CONTENT	TEACHING RESOURCES
a health care provider.		health fairs, and the potential influence on public welfare at each access point.
		▸ Discuss the trend among nurses who are branching out as private practitioners. What are the implications for public health?
		▸ Discuss the ways that technological advancements have facilitated the roles of community-based nurses.
		▸ Discuss the impact that community-based nurses make on cost-containment efforts.
		*Class Activity **Have students discuss the role and function of the community health nurse who provides care to mothers and children. What is the nurse's role in engaging other community agencies?***
		*Class Activity **Invite a community health nurse to speak to the class about the role of nursing in providing care to at-risk women and children in the community.***
		*Class Activity **Lead a discussion in which students identify the role of the community health nurse as a health care provider. What are the benefits for various members of the community? How can the community nurse advocate for the patient? In what ways can a community nurse contribute to containing health care costs?***
Performance Evaluation		⌧▤ PPT slides 1-67
		𝒆 EILR IC images 1-3
		𝒆 EILR OBQ questions 1-10
		𝒆 EILR TB questions 1-30
		𝒆 ESLR IRQ questions 1-5
		[SG] SG Learning Activities, questions 1-14 (pp. 1-4)
		[SG] SG Review Questions, questions 1-6 (pp. 4-5)
		[SG] SG Applying Knowledge, questions 1-8 (pp. 5-6)
		BOOK RESOURCES
		🔔 NCP CTQ 1, 2 (p. 8)
		Review Questions for the NCLEX® Examination, questions 1-5 (p. 19)

1.3 Homework/Assignments:

1.3 Instructor's Notes/Student Feedback:

1 Lecture Outline
The Past, Present, and Future

Slide 1

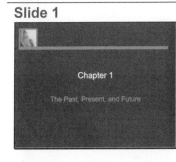

Chapter 1

The Past, Present, and Future

Slide 2

Objectives

- Contrast present-day concepts of maternity and child care with those of the past.
- Recall the contributions of persons in history to the fields of maternity and pediatric care.
- List the organizations concerned with setting standards for the nursing care of maternity and pediatric patients.

Slide 3

Objectives *(cont.)*

- Name two international organizations concerned with maternity and child care.
- List three federal programs that assist mothers and infants.
- State the influence of the federal government on maternity and pediatric care.
- Discuss how culture affects childbirth and child care.
- List four reasons why statistics are important.

Slide 4

Objectives *(cont.)*

- Discuss common terms used in expressing vital statistics.
- State two types of health care delivery systems in the United States.
- Discuss the role of the advanced-practice nurse.
- List the five steps of the nursing process.
- Understand the legal responsibilities of the nurse to report certain diseases or conditions to the public health authorities.

Leifer

Slide 5

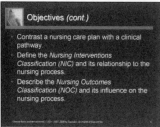

Objectives *(cont.)*

- Contrast a nursing care plan with a clinical pathway.
- Define the *Nursing Interventions Classification (NIC)* and its relationship to the nursing process.
- Describe the *Nursing Outcomes Classification (NOC)* and its influence on the nursing process.

Slide 6

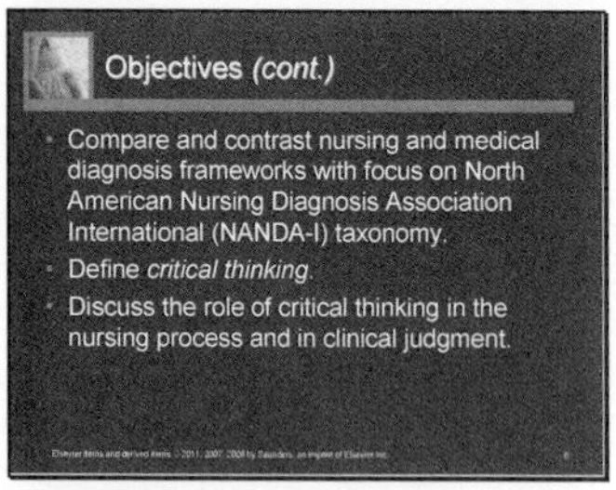

Objectives *(cont.)*

- Compare and contrast nursing and medical diagnosis frameworks with focus on North American Nursing Diagnosis Association International (NANDA-I) taxonomy.
- Define *critical thinking*.
- Discuss the role of critical thinking in the nursing process and in clinical judgment.

Slide 7

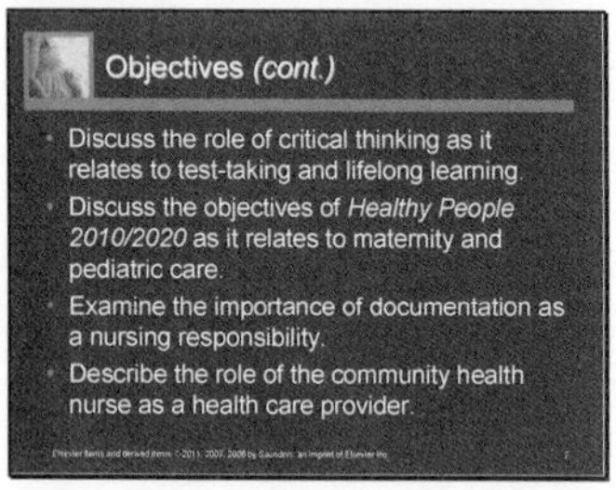

Objectives *(cont.)*

- Discuss the role of critical thinking as it relates to test-taking and lifelong learning.
- Discuss the objectives of *Healthy People 2010/2020* as it relates to maternity and pediatric care.
- Examine the importance of documentation as a nursing responsibility.
- Describe the role of the community health nurse as a health care provider.

Slide 8

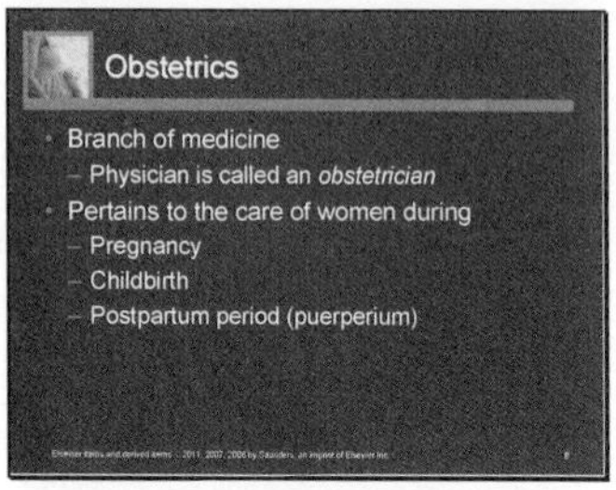

Obstetrics

- Branch of medicine
  - Physician is called an *obstetrician*
- Pertains to the care of women during
  - Pregnancy
  - Childbirth
  - Postpartum period (puerperium)

- Obstetrics is a Latin term meaning "stand by."
- What is the correlation between the Latin meaning and how obstetrics is viewed?

Slide 9

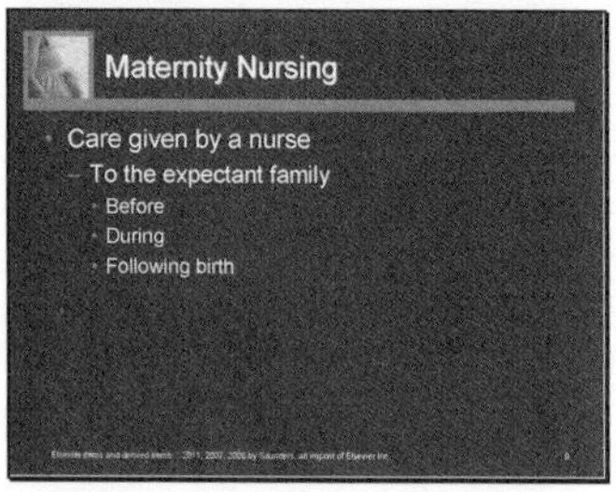

Maternity Nursing

- Care given by a nurse
  - To the expectant family
    - Before
    - During
    - Following birth

- The nurse plays an invaluable role in the care of the expectant family.
- Review each of the phases in which nursing care is provided to the expectant family.
- What are the roles of the nurse in each of the phases?

Slide 10

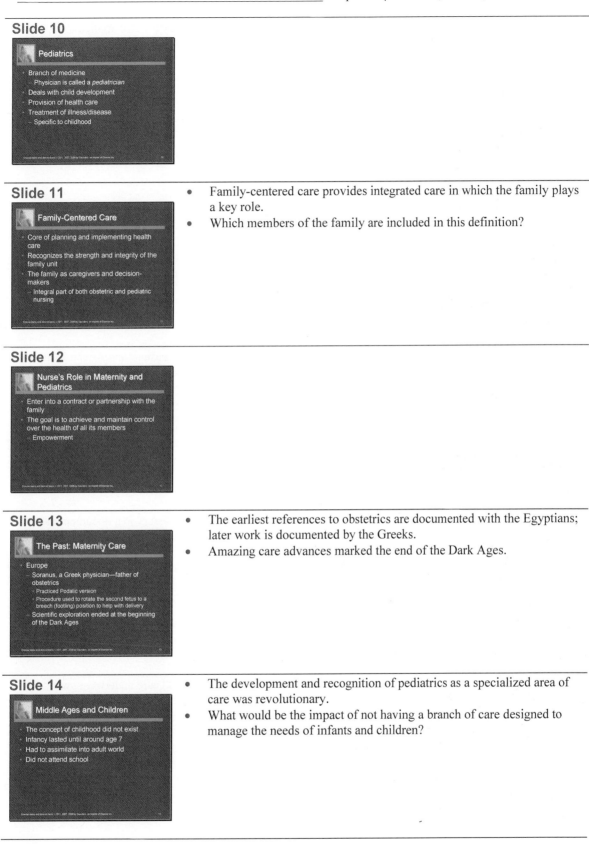

Pediatrics
- Branch of medicine
  - Physician is called a *pediatrician*
- Deals with child development
- Provision of health care
- Treatment of illness/disease
  - Specific to childhood

Slide 11

Family-Centered Care
- Core of planning and implementing health care
- Recognizes the strength and integrity of the family unit
- The family as caregivers and decision-makers
  - Integral part of both obstetric and pediatric nursing

- Family-centered care provides integrated care in which the family plays a key role.
- Which members of the family are included in this definition?

Slide 12

Nurse's Role in Maternity and Pediatrics
- Enter into a contract or partnership with the family
- The goal is to achieve and maintain control over the health of all its members
  - Empowerment

Slide 13

The Past: Maternity Care
- Europe
  - Soranus, a Greek physician—father of obstetrics
    - Practiced Podalic version
    - Procedure used to rotate the second fetus to a breech (footling) position to help with delivery
  - Scientific exploration ended at the beginning of the Dark Ages

- The earliest references to obstetrics are documented with the Egyptians; later work is documented by the Greeks.
- Amazing care advances marked the end of the Dark Ages.

Slide 14

Middle Ages and Children
- The concept of childhood did not exist
- Infancy lasted until around age 7
- Had to assimilate into adult world
- Did not attend school

- The development and recognition of pediatrics as a specialized area of care was revolutionary.
- What would be the impact of not having a branch of care designed to manage the needs of infants and children?

Slide 15

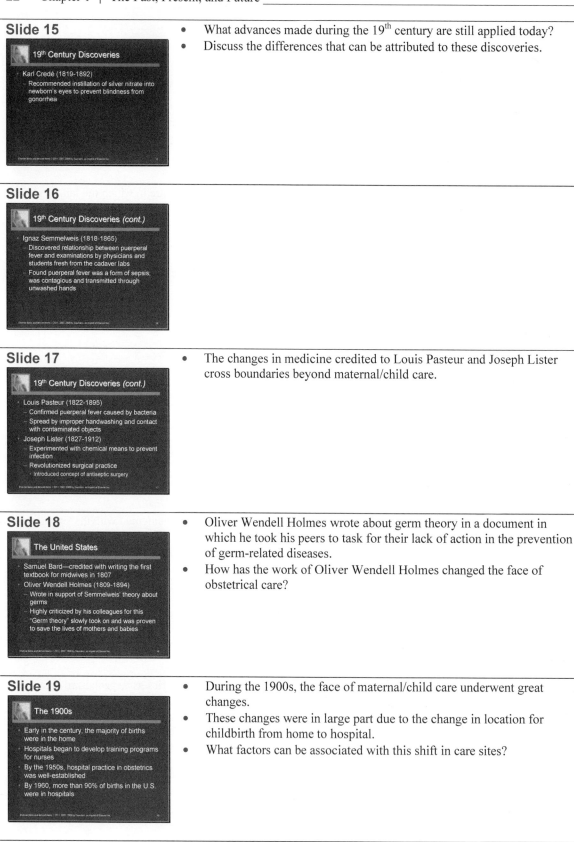

- What advances made during the 19th century are still applied today?
- Discuss the differences that can be attributed to these discoveries.

Slide 16

- The changes in medicine credited to Louis Pasteur and Joseph Lister cross boundaries beyond maternal/child care.

Slide 17

- The changes in medicine credited to Louis Pasteur and Joseph Lister cross boundaries beyond maternal/child care.

Slide 18

- Oliver Wendell Holmes wrote about germ theory in a document in which he took his peers to task for their lack of action in the prevention of germ-related diseases.
- How has the work of Oliver Wendell Holmes changed the face of obstetrical care?

Slide 19

- During the 1900s, the face of maternal/child care underwent great changes.
- These changes were in large part due to the change in location for childbirth from home to hospital.
- What factors can be associated with this shift in care sites?

Slide 20

> **The Birth Process in the 1960s**
>
> - Fathers waited outside of the delivery room
> - Mothers were placed in a "twilight sleep" and had little involvement in the delivery process
> - The infant was kept from parents for hours after birth, which delayed the parent-infant bonding process

- Reflect on your own deliveries and those of your children and grandchildren.
- Compare and contrast the stories shared.

Slide 21

> **Organizations that Advocated Change in the Mother-Infant Bonding Process**
>
> - American College of Nurse-Midwives (ACNM)
> - Association of Women's Health, Obstetric, and Neonatal Nurses (AWHONN)
> - American Nurses Association (ANA), division of Maternal Nursing

Slide 22

> **The Past: Pediatrics**
>
> - Abraham Jacobi (1830-1919)
>   - Father of pediatrics
>   - Established pediatric nursing as a specialty
>   - Founded children's hospitals
>   - Developed separate units for children in foundling homes and general hospitals

Slide 23

> **Culture**
>
> - Strong influence on the standards of child care
>   - Primitive tribes were nomads
>   - Strong survived and stayed with the tribe
>   - Weak were left behind to die
> - As time progressed, children were valued more on what they could produce
> - Today, as in the past, culture affects how a family perceives health and illness

Slide 24

> **Government Influences in Maternity and Pediatric Care**
>
> - Sheppard-Towner Act of 1921
>   - Funded state-managed programs for maternity care
> - Title V of the Social Security Act
>   - Provided funds for maternity care
> - Title V amendment of the Public Health Services Act
>   - Established maternal-infant care centers in public clinics

- Elevated mortality and morbidity rates spurred the interest and action of the government to intervene financially with programs designed to promote the health and wellness interests of children.

Leifer

Slide 25

Government Influences in Maternity and Pediatric Care *(cont.)*

- Title XIX of the Medicaid Program
  - Increased access to care by indigent women
- Head Start
  - Established to increase educational exposure of preschool children

- Medicaid, Head Start, and WIC are widely recognized and respected agencies that work to promote the health needs of women and children.
- Review the focus of each of these agencies.
- What are the implications of these agencies not being available to women and children today?

Slide 26

Government Influences in Maternity and Pediatric Care *(cont.)*

- National Center for Family Planning
  - Provides contraceptive information
- Women, Infants, and Children (WIC)
  - Provides supplemental food and education for families in need of assistance

Slide 27

Family Medical Leave Act (FMLA)

- Became law in 1993
- Allows for employees to take up to 12 weeks of unpaid leave to care for a newborn or family member
- Employee cannot lose benefits or pay status if they take FMLA

- In the mid 1990s, families gained the legal right to have time away from work to manage the health needs of their families.
- How many of you have been able to take family leave?
- How would the inability to have this time off have impacted your family?

Slide 28

HIPAA

- Healthcare Information Portability and Accountability Act (HIPAA)
  - Enacted in 2003
  - Set standards to protect a patient's health information
  - Allowed patients access and control over their health information

- HIPAA has become a driving force in health care today.
- Health care providers are educated about HIPAA.
- Failure to comply with regulations can result in hefty fines.
- How have you been personally affected by HIPAA?

Slide 29

HIPAA *(cont.)*

- Health care personnel are expected to maintain strict confidentiality
- Regulations mandate that the names and personal information of patients be kept in a secure and private place

Slide 30

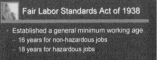

The Children's Bureau

- Established by Lillian Wald in 1912
- Focused attention on problems of infant mortality
- Was followed by maternal mortality
- Led to birth registration in all states
- In the 1930s, led to development of hot lunch programs in the schools

Slide 31

Fair Labor Standards Act of 1938

- Established a general minimum working age
  - 16 years for non-hazardous jobs
  - 18 years for hazardous jobs

Slide 32

White House Conferences

- First one in 1909, Theodore Roosevelt was president
- Continues to be held every 10 years
- 1930—Children's Charter was established
- 1980—involved all states in an effort to see what problems families were facing in various parts of the country

- White House Conferences were implemented as a means to review the health concerns of children.
- What impact do the location and participants have on this endeavor?

Slide 33

Federal Legislation Enacted to Protect Children

- 1974-75—Child Abuse Prevention and Treatment Act
- Education for All Handicapped Children
- 1982—Community Mental Health Center funded
- Missing Children's Act—provided for a national clearinghouse for missing children

- Children are afforded protection from abuse under the laws associated with the Child Abuse Prevention and Treatment Act.
- Under the law, handicapped children are entitled to education.
- What are your views on providing education to children who are profoundly handicapped?

Slide 34

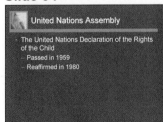

United Nations Assembly

- The United Nations Declaration of the Rights of the Child
  - Passed in 1959
  - Reaffirmed in 1980

Leifer

Slide 35

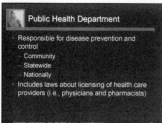

Public Health Department
- Responsible for disease prevention and control
  - Community
  - Statewide
  - Nationally
- Includes laws about licensing of health care providers (i.e., physicians and pharmacists)

- Where is your local health department located?
- What professions are found within the department?

Slide 36

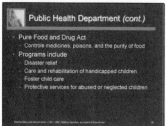

Public Health Department (cont.)
- Pure Food and Drug Act
  - Controls medicines, poisons, and the purity of food
- Programs include
  - Disaster relief
  - Care and rehabilitation of handicapped children
  - Foster child care
  - Protective services for abused or neglected children

Slide 37

Reportable Situations
- Nurse has legal responsibility to report certain diseases or conditions to local public health authorities
  - An illness that poses a health hazard to the public
- Suspected child abuse or suicidal behavior must be reported immediately to protect the child from further harm

Slide 38

The Present: Maternity Care
- Family involvement during pregnancy and birth
  - Necessary for bonding and support
- Three separate sections of the maternity unit
  - Labor-delivery
  - Postpartum
  - Newborn nursery
- Some facilities have merged all three areas into one

- Various facilities have modified the traditional settings.
- Review the division of care at local facilities.

Slide 39

Birthing Centers
- Provide comprehensive care
  - Antepartum
  - Labor-delivery
  - Postpartum
  - Mothers' classes
  - Lactation classes
  - Follow-up family planning

- A new trend in the care of the childbearing family is the emergence of freestanding birthing centers; these centers are separate from the rest of the acute care facility.
- What options are available in your community?
- Providing maternal/child-related classes is vital to the promotion of positive outcomes for families during this time.
- What potential topics are discussed in these classes?

Leifer

Slide 40

Clinical Pathways

- Collaborative guidelines define care within a timeline
- Expected progress of the patient
  - Becomes the standard of care
- Deviations easier to identify, called *variances*
- Use improves quality of care
- Reduces unnecessary hospitalization time

- Clinical pathways are utilized by numerous facilities.
- Does your local maternity center employ them?

Slide 41

Midwives

- First school of nurse-midwifery
  - Opened in New York City, 1932
- Certified Nurse-Midwife (CNM)
  - Registered nurse
  - Graduate from an accredited midwife program
  - National certification
  - Provides comprehensive prenatal and postnatal care
  - Attends uncomplicated deliveries

- The availability of a CNM will vary by geographic location.
- Are there CNMs in your community?
- The CNM manages uncomplicated deliveries, not cesarean deliveries.

Slide 42

Cross-Cultural Considerations

- Culture—socially inherited characteristics
- Becomes a patterned expression of thoughts and actions
  - Also called *traditions*
- Consists of
  - Values
  - Beliefs
  - Practices
  - Shared by members of a group

- The U.S. is recognized for blending numerous cultural groups.
- What is cultural awareness?
  Cultural awareness is the recognition of differing beliefs held by others.
- Providing quality nursing care requires the ability to be culturally aware and sensitive to those with different values.

Slide 43

Cultural Nursing Tip

- Cultural beliefs affect how a family perceives health and illness
- Holistic nursing includes
  - Being alert for cultural diversity
  - Incorporating this information into nursing care plans

Audience Response Question #1
It is important to be aware of a family's religious and cultural beliefs because:
1. reimbursement is based on cultural and religious beliefs.
2. patient care can be adapted to meet cultural and religious beliefs.
3. physician's treatment options must correspond to these beliefs.
4. caregivers' beliefs should be the same as those of their patients.

Slide 44

Awareness, Sensitivity, Competence

- Ask the patient what she considers normal practice
- Questions can include
  - How she views her pregnancy
  - If she views birth as dangerous
  - What kind of help she will need before and after delivery
  - The role her immediate or extended family plays in relation to the pregnancy and birth

- Determining the patient's beliefs and desires will help to ensure she and her family receive care that is unbiased and sound.

Slide 45

> The Pediatric Nurse as Advocate
>
> - An advocate is a person who intercedes or pleads on behalf of another
> - If the nurse believes the child's needs are not being met, the nurse must seek assistance
> - The nurse must also document his/her efforts to seek instruction/assistance, including from whom it was sought

- The role of advocate is a chief one for nurses.
- The nurse has legal responsibility to intervene when the needs of a child are not being met.

Slide 46

> Statistics
>
> - The gathering and analyzing of numerical data
> - The nurse can use statistics to
>   - Become aware of birthing trends
>   - Determine populations at risk
>   - Evaluate the quality of prenatal care
>   - Compare relevant information from state to state

- Refer to Table 1-2 on pages 14-15.
- Review the information listed for your state and bordering states.

Audience Response Question #2
Complete the analogy. Morbidity : Illness as Mortality : _____
1. Trauma
2. Death
3. Relapse
4. Wellness

Slide 47

> Technology and Specialty Expertise
>
> - Number of chronically ill children continues to grow
> - Increased need for technology now in the home setting
>   - Mechanical ventilators
>   - Tracheostomy
>   - Intravenous fluid administration

- What are some technological advances in the obstetrical and pediatric specialties?
- Review the ethical impact and dilemmas associated with these advances.

Slide 48

> Genomics
>
> - Study of the functions of all the genes in the human body
> - "Gene" therapy—used to replace missing genes or alter defective genes
> - Earlier diagnosis, intervention, patient education

- What is the Human Genome Project?
- Review its role in relation to maternal/child nursing.

Slide 49

> Health Care Delivery Systems
>
> - Cost-containment a driver for change
> - Diagnosis-related groups (DRGs): determine payment for a hospital stay based on the diagnosis
> - Push for early discharge
> - Established need for Nurse Case Managers and Utilization Review Nurses

- The cost for health care is a chief concern for all Americans.
- The growing health care related expenditures have spurred efforts to "manage" costs.
- One such means to manage health care costs and resources is the use of Utilization Review Nurses and Case Managers.
- Review the roles for these professionals.
- HMOs and PPOs are health care delivery systems. Compare and contrast HMOs and PPOs.

Slide 50

> ### Health Care Delivery Systems *(cont.)*
> - Two-tiered system
>   - First is for more financially stable (HMO/PPO)
>   - Second is for less financially stable (Medicaid and Medicare)

Slide 51

> ### Health Promotion
> - Preventing illness or disability—cost-effective
> - Chronically ill children live well into adulthood
>   - Increased need for complex medical care, in both hospital and home settings
> - Mainstreaming physically or mentally challenged children to assist them in becoming as independent as possible and integrated into society

Slide 52

> ### Older Children and Life-Threatening Illness
> - Nurse assists as an advocate to ensure that the older child is included in planning modified advance directives with their families and the medical team

Slide 53

> ### Advanced-Practice Roles in Maternity and Pediatric Nursing
> - Certified Nurse Midwife (CNM)
> - Clinical Nurse Specialist (CNS)
> - Neonatal Nurse Practitioner (NNP)
> - Pediatric Nurse Practitioner (PNP)
> - School Nurse Practitioner
> - Family Nurse Practitioner (FNP)

- What are potential sources of employment for each of the nurses listed on the slide?

Slide 54

> ### Developing Nursing Care Delivery
> - Steps of the Nursing Process
>   - Assessment/data collection
>   - Nursing diagnosis
>   - Outcomes identification
>   - Planning
>   - Implementation
>   - Evaluation

- The nursing process provides a means for nurses to take in and interpret data, and to make care decisions.
    - Assessment – the collection of patient data
    - Diagnosis – analysis of data in terms of NANDA-I
    - Outcomes identification – individualized expected patient outcomes
    - Planning – preparation of a plan of care designed to achieve stated outcomes
    - Implementation – patient care
    - Evaluation – review of the patient's progress

Leifer

Slide 55 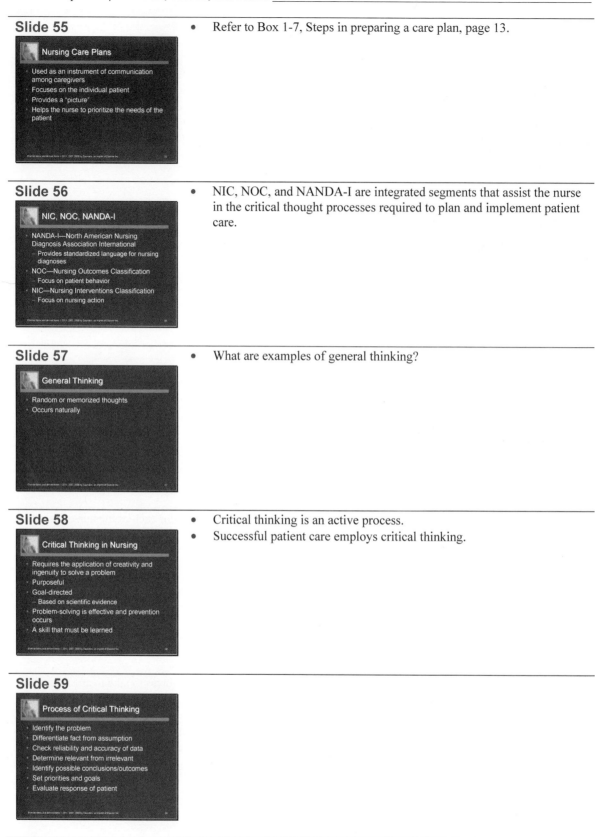 **Nursing Care Plans** · Used as an instrument of communication among caregivers · Focuses on the individual patient · Provides a "picture" · Helps the nurse to prioritize the needs of the patient	• Refer to Box 1-7, Steps in preparing a care plan, page 13.

Slide 56
NIC, NOC, NANDA-I
· NANDA-I—North American Nursing Diagnosis Association International
  – Provides standardized language for nursing diagnoses
· NOC—Nursing Outcomes Classification
  – Focus on patient behavior
· NIC—Nursing Interventions Classification
  – Focus on nursing action
	• NIC, NOC, and NANDA-I are integrated segments that assist the nurse in the critical thought processes required to plan and implement patient care.

Slide 57 **General Thinking** · Random or memorized thoughts · Occurs naturally	• What are examples of general thinking?
Slide 58 **Critical Thinking in Nursing** · Requires the application of creativity and ingenuity to solve a problem · Purposeful · Goal-directed – Based on scientific evidence · Problem-solving is effective and prevention occurs · A skill that must be learned	• Critical thinking is an active process. • Successful patient care employs critical thinking.
Slide 59 **Process of Critical Thinking** · Identify the problem · Differentiate fact from assumption · Check reliability and accuracy of data · Determine relevant from irrelevant · Identify possible conclusions/outcomes · Set priorities and goals · Evaluate response of patient	

Slide 60

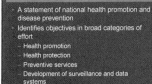

The Future: Health Care Reform

- Conflict exists between cost-containment and quality of care
- Having health insurance does not guarantee access to expensive care
- Those who cannot afford health care often do not seek preventive services

- The ever-increasing cost of health care, combined with the increasing number of citizens who do not have access to affordable care, has caused an outcry for health care reform.
- Access to desired health care is a concern being experienced by both the insured and uninsured.
- The insured patient might not be allowed by the insurance provider to obtain treatments deemed "excessive or too expensive."
- Uninsured patients might not be able to seek care due to a lack of financial resources.
- What are barriers experienced by the uninsured patient?

Slide 61

Healthy People 2020

- A statement of national health promotion and disease prevention
- Identifies objectives in broad categories of effort
  - Health promotion
  - Health protection
  - Preventive services
  - Development of surveillance and data systems

- *Healthy People 2020* is facilitated by the federal government.

Slide 62

Communication

- National patient safety goal
- One example—SBAR
  - Situation
  - Background
  - Assessment
  - Recommendation

Slide 63

Documentation

- It is the LEGAL responsibility of the nurse
- Facilities differ on the type of charting methods
  - Paper
  - Computerized
- Regardless of method, if you did not document the care you provided, medicolegally, you did not do it!

- What are the basic principles of documentation?

Slide 64

Community-Based Nursing

- Challenge is to provide safe, caring, cost-effective, quality care to mothers, infants, children, and families
- The nursing care plan must expand to a family care plan
- Therapeutic care is also provided in the home setting; therefore, educating family members on how to care for their loved one is essential

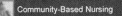

Slide 65

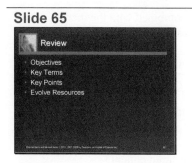

2 Lesson Plan
Human Reproductive Anatomy and Physiology

TEACHING FOCUS

In this chapter, students will be introduced to the anatomy and functions of the male and female reproductive systems. Students will explore the changes of puberty in males and females, including the menstrual cycle and hormones involved. Students will also discuss the importance of pelvic bones to the birth process.

MATERIALS AND RESOURCES

- ☐ Computer and PowerPoint projector (all lessons)
- ☐ Unlabeled copies of Figures 2-1, 2-2, 2-3, and 2-4 (pp. 21, 23-24) (Lesson 2.1)

LESSON CHECKLIST

Preparations for this lesson include:

- Lecture
- Demonstration
- Evaluation of student knowledge and skills needed to perform all entry-level activities related to human reproductive anatomy and physiology, including:
  - ○ Understanding the process of puberty and appearance of secondary sex characteristics in the male and female
  - ○ Identifying the anatomy of the male and female reproductive systems
  - ○ Explaining the functions of the external, internal, and accessory male and female organs in the process of human reproduction
  - ○ Describing the role of hormones in male reproduction and in the female menstrual cycle

KEY TERMS

bi-ischial diameter (p. 26)
climacteric (p. 29)
diagonal conjugate (p. 26)
dyspareunia (p. 23)
embryo (p. 24)
external os (p. 24)
follicle-stimulating
   hormone (FSH) (p. 27)
internal os (p. 24)

luteinizing hormone (LH)
   (p. 22)
menarche (p. 27)
menopause (p. 29)
obstetric conjugate (p. 26)
obstetrical perineum (p. 22)
oxytocin (p. 29)
ovulation (p. 27)
ovum (p. 25)

prostate gland (p. 22)
puberty (p. 20)
rugae (p. 23)
semen (p. 22)
smegma (p. 21)
spermatogenesis (p. 21)
transverse diameter (p. 26)
zygote (p. 25)

ADDITIONAL RESOURCES

TEACH PPT slide(s) Chapter 2, 1-45
EILR IC image(s) Chapter 2, 1-8
EILR OBQ question(s) Chapter 2, 1-10
EILR TB question(s) Chapter 2, 1-32
ESLR IRQ question(s) Chapter 2, 1-5
SG Chapter 2, pp. 7-14

Legend

PPT	EILR	ESLR	SG	CTQ
TEACH PowerPoint Slides	EVOLVE Instructor Learning Resources: Image Collection (IC), Open-Book Quizzes (OBQ), Test Bank (TB)	EVOLVE Student Learning Resources: Interactive Review Questions (IRQ) for the NCLEX® Examination	Study Guide	Critical Thinking Question in Nursing Care Plan (NCP CTQ) or Get Ready for the NCLEX! (GRN CTQ)

Class Activities are indicated in **bold italic**.

Introduction to Maternity & Pediatric Nursing, 6th ed.

Elsevier items and derived items © 2011, 2007, 2006 by Saunders, an imprint of Elsevier Inc.

Leifer

LESSON 2.1

PRETEST

1. The male hormone that causes boys to grow taller and develop secondary sexual characteristics is
   - a. follicle stimulating hormone.
   - b. estrogen.
   - c. progesterone.
   - d. testosterone.

2. Dyspareunia is defined as
   - a. painful sexual intercourse.
   - b. abnormal urine flow.
   - c. painful menses.
   - d. premature ejaculation.

3. The pelvic floor muscle that supports the internal and external reproductive organs is the
   - a. uterus.
   - b. levator ani.
   - c. abdominal muscle.
   - d. ischium.

4. The inner layer of the uterus that is functional during menstruation and implantation of a fertilized ovum is the
   - a. perineum.
   - b. myometrium.
   - c. endometrium.
   - d. perimetrium.

5. The pelvic shape that is most favorable for vaginal birth is the
   - a. anthropoid.
   - b. platypelloid.
   - c. android.
   - d. gynecoid.

6. The gland that secretes follicle-stimulating hormone (FSH) and luteinizing hormone (LH) is the
   - a. posterior pituitary gland.
   - b. thyroid gland.
   - c. anterior pituitary gland.
   - d. parathyroid gland.

7. In females, the ilium and the pubis form the
   - a. symphysis pubis.
   - b. pubic arch.
   - c. sacrum.
   - d. ischium.

8. In boys, hormonal changes usually begin between the ages of
   - a. 3 and 6.
   - b. 7 and 10.
   - c. 10 and 16.
   - d. 17 and 20.

9. Sebaceous glands in the areola that secrete a substance to lubricate and protect the breast during lactation are
   - a. pituitary glands.
   - b. Cowper's glands.
   - c. mammary glands.
   - d. Montgomery's glands.

10. The regular menstrual cycle is established within six months to one year of
    - a. maturation.
    - b. ovulation.
    - c. menarche.
    - d. menopause.

Answers

1. d	3. b	5. d	7. a	9. d
2. a	4. c	6. c	8. c	10. c

BACKGROUND ASSESSMENT

Question: What is the function of testosterone in the body?

Answer: Testosterone is the most abundant male hormone. Testosterone is produced when the anterior pituitary gland secretes FSH (follicle-stimulating hormone) and LH (luteinizing hormone). Both males and females have testosterone in their bodies, although it is much more abundant in males. The role of testosterone is directly related to male sexual maturation and reproduction. In males, testosterone increases muscle mass and strength, promotes long bone growth, increases basal metabolic rate, and enhances red blood cell production. Vocal cord enlargement, distribution of body hair, and development of acne are results of testosterone levels in adolescents.

Introduction to Maternity & Pediatric Nursing, 6th ed.

Elsevier items and derived items © 2011, 2007, 2006 by Saunders, an imprint of Elsevier Inc.   Leifer

Question: Where are the ovaries located? What are the two functions of the ovaries? What happens to the ova as a woman ages?

Answer: The ovaries are part of the female reproductive system. They are almond-shaped and are located in the lower abdomen on either side of the uterus. Ovaries are held in place by ovarian and uterine ligaments. Their functions are hormone secretion and ovum maturation; they primarily produce estrogen and progesterone, the two primary female hormones. Maturation of an ovum takes place in the ovaries during each reproductive cycle. Female infants are born with about 2 million oocytes that will be available during the reproductive years. There is a decline in the amount of available oocytes as a woman ages; the oocytes decrease in number to the thousands. Ova (oocytes) that remain in the ovaries after menopause no longer respond to hormonal stimulation.

CRITICAL THINKING QUESTION

The mother of 10-year-old fraternal twins brings her son and daughter for their annual physical. She asks the nurse what information she should give to her children regarding sexual maturation. What information should the nurse provide?

Guidelines: The nurse should explain the process of puberty and the development of secondary sexual characteristics to the mother. The nurse should also distinguish between the pubertal processes of boys and girls. In boys, puberty begins with the development of secondary sexual characteristics. These include enlargement of the penis and scrotum; a deepened voice; and growth of pubic, facial, and axillary hair. Nocturnal emissions, also referred to as "wet dreams," are also common. These changes are due to changing hormone levels in the body that typically occur between 10 and 16 years of age. Increase in height and musculature is due to increasing levels of testosterone, which is the primary male hormone. In girls, the first sign of puberty is breast development. Menarche (the first menses) typically occurs between 11 and 15 years of age. The female reproductive organs mature in preparation for sexual activity and childbearing, the hips broaden, the pelvis changes to a side basin shape, and fat deposits increase on the hips and thighs. Pubic and axillary hair also appear during this time.

OBJECTIVES	CONTENT	TEACHING RESOURCES
Describe changes of puberty in males and females.	■ Puberty (p. 20) ☐ Male (p. 20) ☐ Female (p. 21)	PPT slides 4-7 *e* EILR OBQ question 1 *e* EILR TB questions 6, 14, 19, 22, 25 *e* ESLR IRQ question 1 SG Learning Activities, questions 1-4 (p. 7) SG Review Questions, question 1 (p. 2) ▸ Discuss how the lack of a "universal rite of passage" has led to confusion for some contemporary adolescents. *Class Activity Divide the class into groups. Have students identify the hormones involved in puberty and discuss the functions and levels of each in boys and girls. Where is each hormone produced? Have each group share its conclusions with the class for discussion.*
Identify the anatomy of the male reproductive system.	■ Reproductive systems (p. 21) ☐ Male (p. 21) ☐ External genitalia (p. 21)	PPT slides 8-13 *e* EILR IC image 1 *e* EILR OBQ question 2 *e* EILR TB questions 1-3, 21

OBJECTIVES	CONTENT	TEACHING RESOURCES
	– Penis (p. 21)	SG Learning Activities, questions 5-6 (pp. 7-8)
	– Scrotum (p. 21)	SG Thinking Critically, question 3 (p. 14)
	☐ Internal genitalia (p. 21)	**BOOK RESOURCES**
	– Testes (p. 21)	Figure 2-1, The Male Reproductive Organs (p. 21)
	– Ducts (p. 22)	GRN CTQ 2 (p. 30)
	– Accessory glands (p. 22)	Review Questions for the NCLEX® Examination, question 1 (p. 30)
		▸ Discuss the various approaches to teaching male patients about the anatomy of their reproductive systems.
		▸ Discuss how the patient or nurse's ethnicity might affect teaching about male reproductive anatomy.
		Class Activity **Provide each student with unlabeled copies of Figure 2-1 (p. 21). In pairs, have students fill in the missing information without using their textbooks. Have students share their answers with the class.**
Explain the functions of the external and internal male organs in human reproduction.	■ Reproductive systems (p. 21) ☐ Male (p. 21) ☐ External genitalia (p. 21) – Penis (p. 21) – Scrotum (p. 21) ☐ Internal genitalia (p. 21) – Testes (p. 21) – Ducts (p. 22) – Accessory glands (p. 22)	PPT slides 9-13 *e* EILR IC image 1 *e* EILR TB questions 16, 21 *e* ESLR IRQ question 4 SG Review Questions, question 6 (p. 13) **BOOK RESOURCES** Review Questions for the NCLEX® Examination, question 1 (p. 30) ▸ Discuss why is it important for patients to understand the functions of the male reproductive system. *Class Activity* **Divide the class into groups and assign each either external or internal male genitalia. Have each group identify its relevant organs and explain the functions of each. Then have each group present its findings to the class.**

OBJECTIVES	CONTENT	TEACHING RESOURCES
Describe the influence of hormones in male reproductive processes.	☐ Internal genitalia (p. 21) – Testes (p. 21) – Ducts (p. 22) – Accessory glands (p. 22)	PPT slides 10-13 EILR OBQ question 3 EILR TB questions 4, 23, 29, 31 SG Learning Activities, question 8 (p. 8) SG Review Questions, question 2 (p. 12) **BOOK RESOURCES** Review Questions for the NCLEX® Examination, question 1 (p. 30) ▸ Discuss the ways that hormones may affect physical appearance. *Class Activity* **Divide the class into groups, and have them discuss the functions of testosterone as it relates to sexual and nonsexual processes. How does testosterone function in females? Have the groups share their findings with the class for discussion.**

2.1 Homework/Assignments:

2.1 Instructor's Notes/Student Feedback:

ELSEVIER

Introduction to Maternity & Pediatric Nursing, 6ᵗʰ ed.
Leifer

LESSON 2.2

CRITICAL THINKING QUESTION

A 16-year-old comes to the clinic for her annual physical. She asks the nurse to explain what happens in the body during menstruation. What information should the nurse provide?

Guidelines: The nurse should explain that certain hormones in the body control menstruation. The anterior pituitary gland secretes follicle-stimulating hormone (FSH) and luteinizing hormone (LH). FSH is responsible for the maturation of an ovarian follicle that contains a single ovum. The ovum is released from the follicle; the ovum and the empty follicle (corpus luteum) then begin to produce increased amounts of estrogen and progesterone, which build up the endometrium. This process is referred to as *ovulation*; it occurs about 14 days before the onset of menstruation. After ovulation, the corpus luteum turns yellow and secretes increased amounts of estrogen and progesterone to prepare the uterine lining for fertilization. If the ovum is not fertilized, estrogen and progesterone levels decrease, the corpus luteum deteriorates, and the endometrium breaks down. This is referred to as *menstruation*. A new cycle of ovulation/menstruation begins with the secretion of FSH and LH from the anterior pituitary gland.

OBJECTIVES	CONTENT	TEACHING RESOURCES
Identify the anatomy of the female reproductive system.	■ Female (p. 22) ☐ External genitalia (p. 22) – Mons pubis (p. 22) – Labia majora (p. 22) – Labia minora (p. 22) – Fourchette (p. 22) – Clitoris (p. 22) – Vaginal vestibule (p. 22) – Perineum (p. 23) ☐ Internal genitalia (p. 23) – Vagina (p. 23) – Uterus (p. 24) – Nerve supply (p. 24) – Anatomy (p. 24) – Fallopian tubes (p. 25) – Ovaries (p. 25) ☐ Pelvis (p. 25) – Types of pelves (p. 25) – False and true pelves (p. 26) – Pelvic diameters	PPT slides 14-35 EILR IC images 2-7 EILR OBQ questions 4-5 EILR TB question 4 ESLR IRQ question 5 SG Learning Activities, questions 9-11 (pp. 8-10) SG Review Questions, questions 3, 10 (pp. 12-13) SG Applying Knowledge, question 1 (p. 14) **BOOK RESOURCES** Figure 2-2, The External Female Reproductive Organs (p. 23) Figure 2-3, Side View of the Internal Female Reproductive Organs (p. 23) Figure 2-4, Frontal View of the Internal Female Reproductive Organs (p. 24) Figure 2-5, Four types of pelves (p. 25) Figure 2-6, Four important pelvic inlet diameters (p. 26) Figure 2-7, The Female Breast (p. 27) Review Questions for the NCLEX® Examination, questions 3-5 (p. 30) ▸ Discuss the various approaches to teaching female patients about the anatomy of their reproductive systems. ▸ Discuss how the patient or nurse's ethnicity might affect teaching about female reproductive anatomy.

OBJECTIVES	CONTENT	TEACHING RESOURCES
	(p. 26) – Pelvic outlet (p. 26) ☐ Breasts (p. 26)	*Class Activity* **Provide each student with unlabeled copies of Figures 2-2, 2-3, and 2-4 (pp. 23-24). In pairs, have students fill in the missing information without using their textbooks. Have students share their findings with the class for discussion.**
Explain the functions of the external, internal, and accessory female organs in human reproduction.	■ Female (p. 22) ☐ External genitalia (p. 22) – Mons pubis (p. 22) – Labia majora (p. 22) – Labia minora (p. 22) – Fourchette (p. 22) – Clitoris (p. 22) – Vaginal vestibule (p. 22) – Perineum (p. 23) ☐ Internal genitalia (p. 23) – Vagina (p. 23) – Uterus (p. 24) – Nerve supply (p. 24) – Anatomy (p. 24) – Fallopian tubes (p. 25) – Ovaries (p. 25) ☐ Pelvis (p. 25) – Types of pelves (p. 25) – False and true pelves (p. 26) – Pelvic diameters (p. 26) – Pelvic outlet (p. 26) ☐ Breasts (p. 26)	⊠ PPT slides 14-35 𝒆 EILR OBQ question 6 𝒆 EILR TB questions 10, 18, 20, 24, 27 SG Learning Activities, questions 13, 14 (p. 11) SG Review Questions, questions 7, 9 (pp. 13-14) SG Thinking Critically, question 2 (p. 14) **BOOK RESOURCES** Review Questions for the NCLEX® Examination, questions 4-5 (p. 30) ▸ Discuss why it is important for patients to understand the functions of the female reproductive system. *Class Activity* **Divide the class into small groups and assign each group one of the following organs: vaginal vestibule, vagina, uterus, fallopian tubes, ovaries, and breasts. Have students identify the structures relevant to their organ and explain its role in reproduction. Have groups present their findings to the class.**
Discuss the importance of the pelvic bones to the birth process.	☐ Pelvis (p. 25) – Types of pelves (p. 25) – False and true	⊠ PPT slides 28-33 𝒆 EILR OBQ questions 7, 8 𝒆 EILR TB questions 9, 12, 17, 26, 28, 30

OBJECTIVES	CONTENT	TEACHING RESOURCES
	pelves (p. 26) – Pelvic diameters (p. 26) – Pelvic outlet (p. 26)	SG Learning Activities, question 12 (p. 11) SG Review Questions, questions 4, 5 (p. 13) SG Applying Knowledge, question 2 (p. 14) **BOOK RESOURCES** Table 2-1, Average Pelvic Measurements (p. 27) Figure 2-5, Four Types of Pelves (p. 25) Figure 2-6, Four Important Pelvic Inlet Diameters (p. 26) GRN CTQ 1 (p. 30) Review Questions for the NCLEX® Examination, question 3 (p. 30) ▶ Discuss the reasons for delineating true and false pelves. ▶ Discuss average pelvic measurements and the implications of those measurements for vaginal births. Class Activity *Divide the class into groups. Have students identify the different pelvic measurements and explain the reason for obtaining each measurement. How are the measurements obtained, and what do the measurements signify?*
Explain the menstrual cycle and the female hormones involved in the cycle.	■ Reproductive cycle and menstruation (p. 27) ■ The human sexual response (p. 29) □ Physiology of the male sex act (p. 29) □ Physiology of the female sex act (p. 29)	PPT slides 36-38 EILR IC image 8 EILR OBQ questions 9, 10 EILR TB questions 5, 7, 8, 11, 13, 15, 32 ESLR IRQ questions 2, 3 SG Learning Activities, questions 15, 16 (p. 12) SG Review Questions, questions 8, 11 (p. 13) SG Thinking Critically, question 1 (p. 14) **BOOK RESOURCES** Figure 2-8, Female Reproductive Cycles (p. 28) Review Questions for the NCLEX® Examination, question 2 (p. 30) ▶ Discuss the different phases of the menstrual cycle. Class Activity *Have students research the hormonal influences on the process of menstruation. Divide students into small groups and have them discuss the*

Leifer

OBJECTIVES	CONTENT	TEACHING RESOURCES
		differences between the follicular and the luteal phase, then share their findings with the class. (For students to prepare for this activity, see Homework/Assignments #1.)
Performance Evaluation		PPT slides 1-45
		EILR IC images 1-8
		EILR OBQ questions 1-10
		EILR TB questions 1-32
		ESLR IRQ questions 1-5
		SG Learning Activities, questions 1-16 (pp. 7-12)
		SG Review Questions, questions 1-11 (pp. 12-13)
		SG Thinking Critically, questions 1, 2 (p. 14)
		SG Applying Knowledge, questions 1-3 (p. 14)
		BOOK RESOURCES
		Review Questions for the NCLEX® Examination, questions 1-5 (p. 30)
		GRN CTQ 1, 2 (p. 30)

2.2 Homework/Assignments:

1. Have students research the hormonal influences on the process of menstruation. Divide students into small groups and have them discuss the differences between the follicular and the luteal phase.

2.2 Instructor's Notes/Student Feedback:

ELSEVIER

Introduction to Maternity & Pediatric Nursing, 6th ed.
Leifer

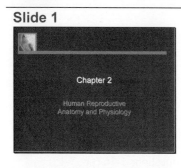

2   Lecture Outline
Human Reproductive Anatomy and Physiology

Slide 1

Chapter 2

Human Reproductive
Anatomy and Physiology

Slide 2

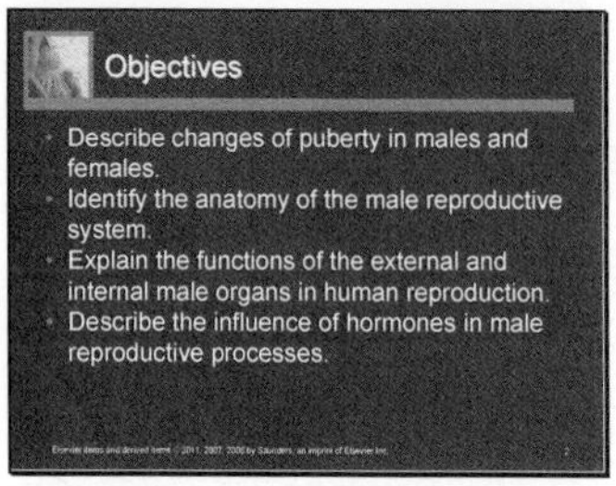

Objectives

- Describe changes of puberty in males and females.
- Identify the anatomy of the male reproductive system.
- Explain the functions of the external and internal male organs in human reproduction.
- Describe the influence of hormones in male reproductive processes.

Slide 3

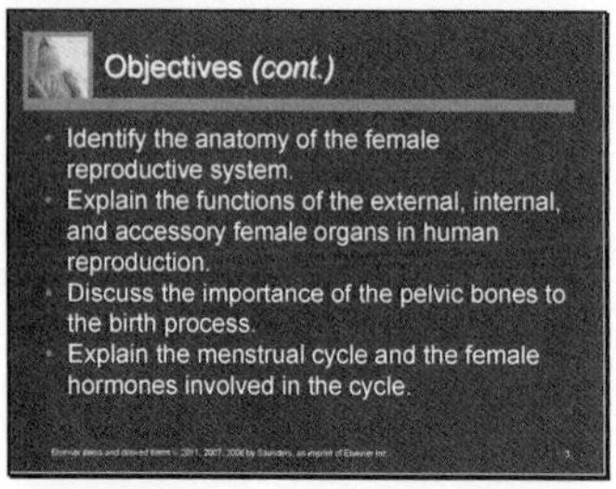

Objectives *(cont.)*

- Identify the anatomy of the female reproductive system.
- Explain the functions of the external, internal, and accessory female organs in human reproduction.
- Discuss the importance of the pelvic bones to the birth process.
- Explain the menstrual cycle and the female hormones involved in the cycle.

Slide 4

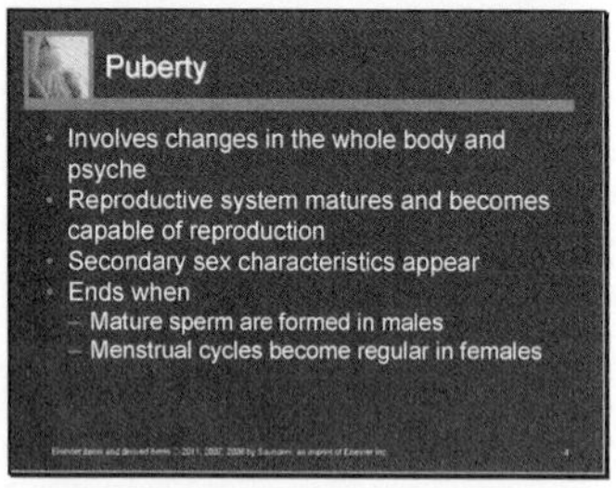

Puberty

- Involves changes in the whole body and psyche
- Reproductive system matures and becomes capable of reproduction
- Secondary sex characteristics appear
- Ends when
  - Mature sperm are formed in males
  - Menstrual cycles become regular in females

- Boys grow taller, more muscular, and develop pubic and facial hair and a deepened voice.
- Girls experience menarche, broadened hips, breasts, and pubic and axillary hair.

Introduction to Maternity & Pediatric Nursing, 6th ed.

Leifer

Slide 5	• Examples of celebrations include demonstrations of bravery, such as hunting or displays of self-defense.
Puberty (cont.) · Celebrated in many cultures as a rite of passage into adulthood · Other cultures lack this ritual – Has led to confusion for some adolescents in many industrialized nations	• Can you describe rites of passage in our culture?

Slide 6	• The hormone levels in the male are constant, not cyclic as in females.

The Male
 	
· Hormonal changes begin between 10 and 16 years of age
· Outward changes
  – Penis and testes increase in size
  – Grows taller, more muscular
  – Secondary sex characteristics
    · Pubic and facial hair
    · Deeper voice
· Testosterone levels become constant
· Nocturnal emissions ("wet dreams") may occur
  – They do not contain sperm
	Audience Response Question #1
	What is the first outward change of puberty in males?
	1. Development of pubic hair
	2. Nocturnal emissions
	3. Voice deepens
	4. Penis and testes increase in size

Slide 7	• Puberty and the onset of menstruation begin at younger ages today than in previous generations.
The Female · Development of breasts occurs first · First menstrual period (menarche) occurs approximately 2 to 2.5 years later (around 11 to 15 years of age) · Growth spurt ends earlier than the male · Hips broaden · Pubic and axillary hair appear	• To what can these changes be attributed?

Slide 8	
Male Reproductive System 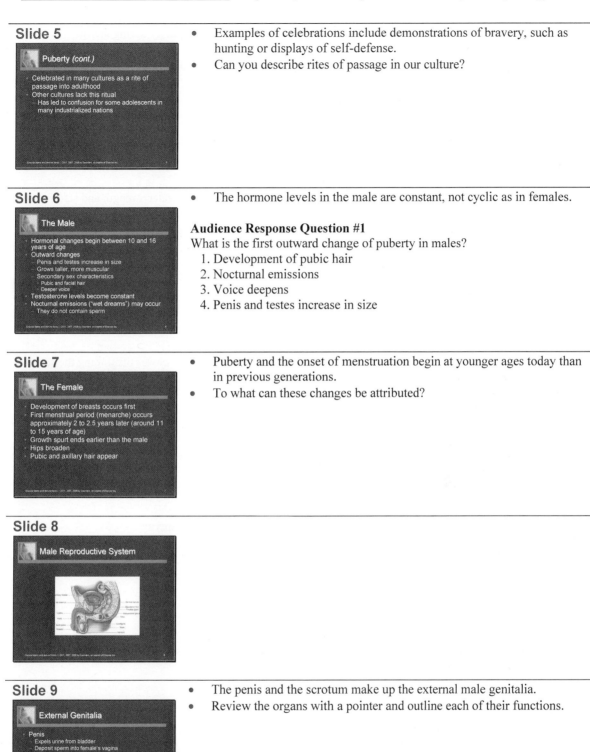	

Slide 9	• The penis and the scrotum make up the external male genitalia.

External Genitalia
 	
· Penis
  – Expels urine from bladder
  – Deposit sperm into female's vagina
  – Contains erectile tissue
  – Blood is trapped within the spongy erectile tissue to enable erection
· Scrotum
  – Sac that contains the testes
  – Suspended from the perineum
  – Helps keeps testes cooler than the rest of the body
  – Necessary for spermatogenesis
	• Review the organs with a pointer and outline each of their functions.

Slide 10 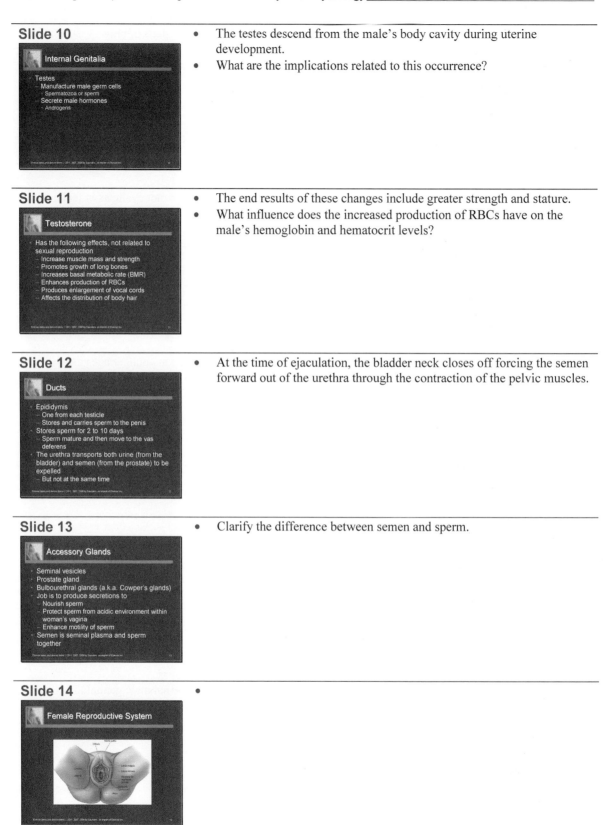**Internal Genitalia** Testes – Manufacture male germ cells · Spermatozoa or sperm – Secrete male hormones · Androgens	• The testes descend from the male's body cavity during uterine development. • What are the implications related to this occurrence?
Slide 11 **Testosterone** · Has the following effects, not related to sexual reproduction – Increase muscle mass and strength – Promotes growth of long bones – Increases basal metabolic rate (BMR) – Enhances production of RBCs – Produces enlargement of vocal cords – Affects the distribution of body hair	• The end results of these changes include greater strength and stature. • What influence does the increased production of RBCs have on the male's hemoglobin and hematocrit levels?
Slide 12 **Ducts** · Epididymis – One from each testicle – Stores and carries sperm to the penis · Stores sperm for 2 to 10 days – Sperm mature and then move to the vas deferens · The urethra transports both urine (from the bladder) and semen (from the prostate) to be expelled – But not at the same time	• At the time of ejaculation, the bladder neck closes off forcing the semen forward out of the urethra through the contraction of the pelvic muscles.
Slide 13 **Accessory Glands** · Seminal vesicles · Prostate gland · Bulbourethral glands (a.k.a. Cowper's glands) · Job is to produce secretions to – Nourish sperm – Protect sperm from acidic environment within woman's vagina – Enhance motility of sperm · Semen is seminal plasma and sperm together	• Clarify the difference between semen and sperm.
Slide 14 **Female Reproductive System**	•

Slide 15

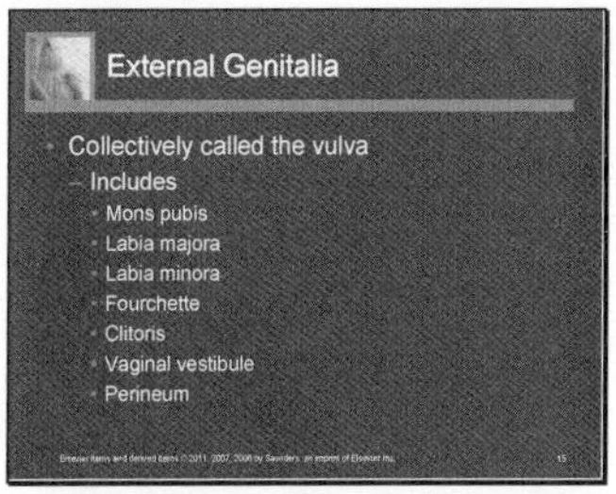

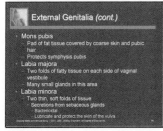

- The external genitalia have an extensive venous supply.
- In the event of sexual trauma, bruising and swelling are common.

Slide 16

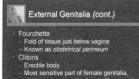

Slide 17

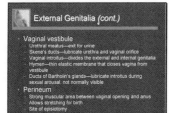

- The term *vulva* refers to the grouping of the external female genitalia.
- What is the clinical importance of the perineum?

Slide 18

- Discuss the "social" implications associated with the presence of the hymen.
- The hymen is not be a reliable indicator of sexual activity.
- The perineum can also tear during the delivery process.

Slide 19

Internal Genitalia

Leifer

Slide 20

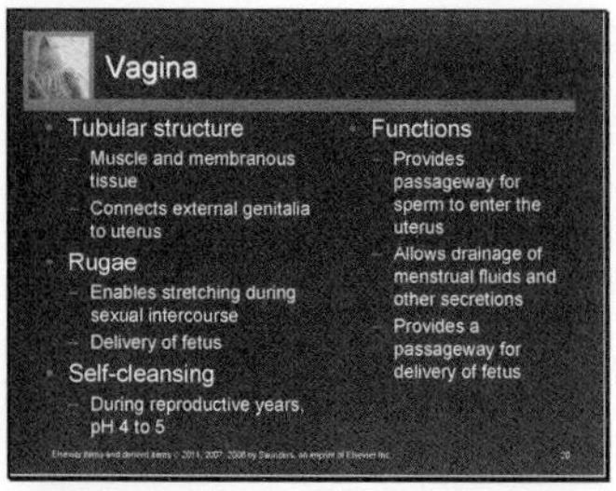

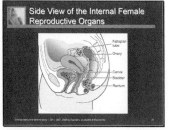

- The use of douches should be reviewed with female patients.
- Douching alters the normal chemical balance of the vagina.
- What are the physiological implications of frequent douching?
- Is douching is medically recommended?

Slide 21

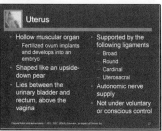

- Outline the internal female reproductive organs and their functions.

Slide 22

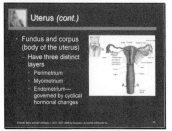

- The uterus is known as the *womb*.

Slide 23

Slide 24

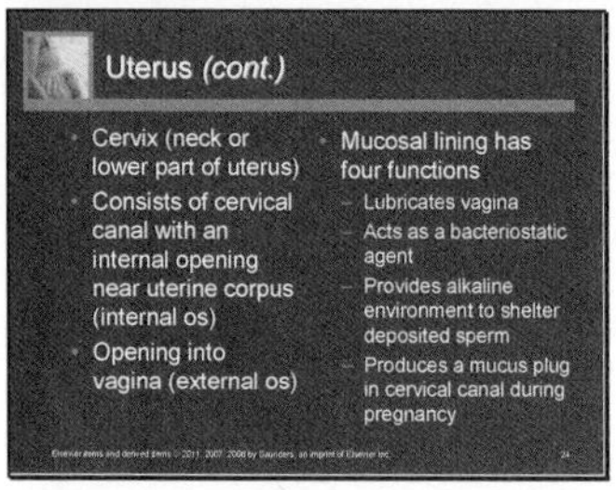

- The cervix provides a source of cells for the health care provider when performing a Pap test.
- What is the importance of the cervix in maintaining pregnancies?

Slide 25

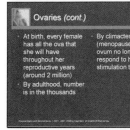

Fallopian Tubes

- Four sections
  - Interstitial
  - Isthmus
  - Ampulla
  - Infundibulum
    - Fingerlike projections called fimbriae capture the ovum (egg) as it is released from the ovary
- Four functions
  - Passageway for sperm to meet the ovum, site of fertilization
  - Safe, nourishing environment for the ovum or zygote (fertilized ovum)
  - Means of transporting ovum or zygote to the corpus of the uterus

- The fallopian tubes are the most common site for ectopic pregnancies.
- What features (location and size) are associated with the occurrence?
- Review the significance of untreated sexually transmitted infections on the fallopian tubes.

Slide 26

Ovaries

- Almond-shaped
- Size of a walnut
- Held in place by ovarian and uterine ligaments
- Two functions
  - Production of hormones
    - Mainly estrogen and progesterone
  - Stimulate maturation of an ovum during each reproductive cycle

Slide 27

Ovaries *(cont.)*

- At birth, every female has all the ova that she will have throughout her reproductive years (around 2 million)
- By adulthood, number is in the thousands
- By climacteric (menopause), the ovum no longer respond to hormonal stimulation to mature

Slide 28

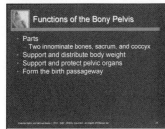

Types of Female Pelves

Gynecoid   Anthropoid   Android   Platypelloid

- Gynecoid most favorable for vaginal delivery
- Platypelloid is unfavorable for vaginal delivery

- Gynecoid is the classic female pelvis.
- Anthropoid is a long, narrow oval. Women can deliver vaginally, but the back of the fetus is likely to turn toward the pelvis.
- The android pelvis is typical of male anatomy.
- Platypelloid has a shortened anterior-posterior diameter and a flat, transverse oval shape.
- Which pelvis shape is best suited for vaginal birth? *Gynecoid*
- Which shape is least suited for a vaginal birth? *Platypelloid*

Slide 29

Functions of the Bony Pelvis

- Parts
  - Two innominate bones, sacrum, and coccyx
- Support and distribute body weight
- Support and protect pelvic organs
- Form the birth passageway

Slide 30

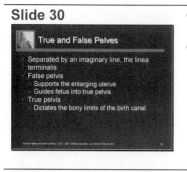

- The external size of the pelvis does not define the adequacy or size of the opening or shape of the internal pelvic diameter.
- Discuss the myth about the size of maternal hips being an indicator for vaginal delivery.

Slide 31

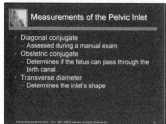

- During pregnancy, the health care provider will make inferences about the adequacy of the mother's pelvic opening.

Slide 32

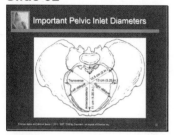

Slide 33

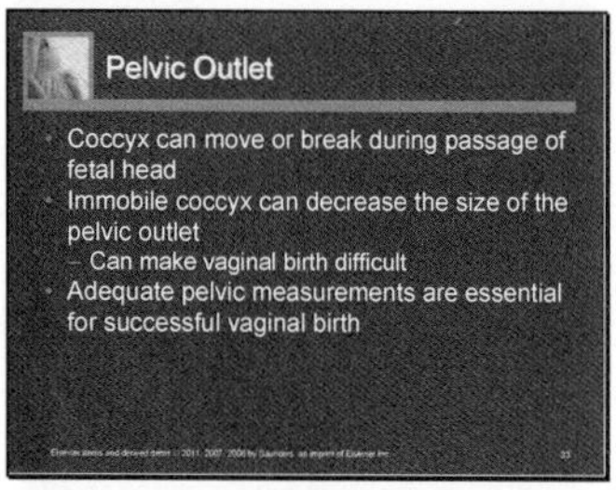

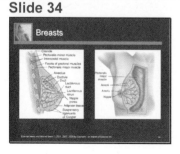

- In addition to pelvic size, what other phenomena can hinder a woman's pelvic size and ability to deliver vaginally?

Slide 34

- Using a pointer, review the primary structures and functions of the female breast.

Slide 35	

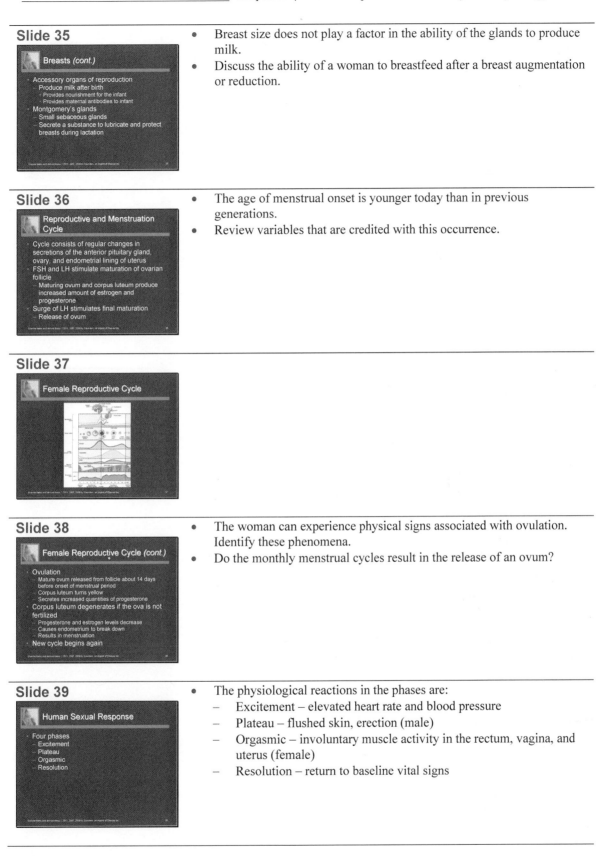 **Breasts** *(cont.)*
 	
· Accessory organs of reproduction
  – Produce milk after birth
    · Provides nourishment for the infant
    · Provides maternal antibodies to infant
· Montgomery's glands
  – Small sebaceous glands
  – Secrete a substance to lubricate and protect breasts during lactation
	• Breast size does not play a factor in the ability of the glands to produce milk.
	• Discuss the ability of a woman to breastfeed after a breast augmentation or reduction.

Slide 36	

Reproductive and Menstruation Cycle
 	
· Cycle consists of regular changes in secretions of the anterior pituitary gland, ovary, and endometrial lining of uterus
· FSH and LH stimulate maturation of ovarian follicle
  – Maturing ovum and corpus luteum produce increased amount of estrogen and progesterone
· Surge of LH stimulates final maturation
  – Release of ovum
	• The age of menstrual onset is younger today than in previous generations.
	• Review variables that are credited with this occurrence.

Slide 37	
Female Reproductive Cycle	

Slide 38	

Female Reproductive Cycle *(cont.)*
 	
· Ovulation
  – Mature ovum released from follicle about 14 days before onset of menstrual period
  – Corpus luteum turns yellow
  – Secretes increased quantities of progesterone
· Corpus luteum degenerates if the ova is not fertilized
  – Progesterone and estrogen levels decrease
  – Causes endometrium to break down
  – Results in menstruation
· New cycle begins again
	• The woman can experience physical signs associated with ovulation. Identify these phenomena.
	• Do the monthly menstrual cycles result in the release of an ovum?

Slide 39	

Human Sexual Response
 	
· Four phases
  – Excitement
  – Plateau
  – Orgasmic
  – Resolution
	• The physiological reactions in the phases are:
	  – Excitement – elevated heart rate and blood pressure
	  – Plateau – flushed skin, erection (male)
	  – Orgasmic – involuntary muscle activity in the rectum, vagina, and uterus (female)
	  – Resolution – return to baseline vital signs

Slide 40

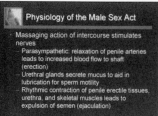

Physiology of the Male Sex Act

- Massaging action of intercourse stimulates nerves
  - Parasympathetic: relaxation of penile arteries leads to increased blood flow to shaft (erection)
  - Urethral glands secrete mucus to aid in lubrication for sperm motility
  - Rhythmic contraction of penile erectile tissues, urethra, and skeletal muscles leads to expulsion of semen (ejaculation)

Slide 41

Physiology of the Male Sex Act *(cont.)*

- After orgasm (resolution)
  - Erection ceases
  - Cavernous sinuses empty
  - Arteries contract
  - Penis becomes flaccid
- Sperm can reach fallopian tubes within 5 minutes
  - Can remain viable in female for up to 4 to 5 days

Slide 42

Physiology of Female Sex Act

- Female psyche can initiate or inhibit sexual response
- Local stimulation of breasts, vulva, vagina, and perineum increases sexual sensations
  - Parasympathetic nerves signal erectile tissue around vaginal introitus
  - Dilation and filling of arteries, leads to tightening of vagina around penis
  - Stimulates Bartholin's glands to secrete mucus (aids in vaginal lubrication)

Slide 43

Physiology of Female Sex Act *(cont.)*

- Posterior pituitary gland secretes oxytocin
  - Stimulates contraction of uterus and dilation of cervical canal
- Orgasm believed to aid in transport of sperm into fallopian tubes
  - Egg lives 24 hours after ovulation
  - Sperm must be available during that time for fertilization to occur

Slide 44

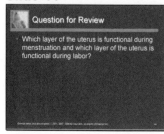

Question for Review

- Which layer of the uterus is functional during menstruation and which layer of the uterus is functional during labor?

Slide 45

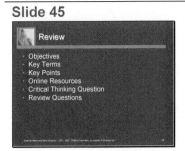

3 Fetal Development

TEACHING FOCUS

In this chapter, students will be introduced to fetal development from the division of a cell through birth. It includes a range of topics including gametogenesis, fertilization, and the identification of prenatal development milestones. The student will become acquainted with changes at various levels of fetal development as well as changes in circulation as the fetus completes prenatal life and prepares for birth. Other discussion points include the effects of environmental factors on a developing fetus, the importance of proper prenatal care, and the physiology of multifetal pregnancies.

MATERIALS AND RESOURCES

- ☐ Computer and PowerPoint projector (all lessons)
- ☐ 3-D model of developing embryo/uterus (all lessons)
- ☐ Videotape such as "From Conception to Birth" (Polymorph Films) (Lesson 3.1)

LESSON CHECKLIST

Preparations for this lesson include:

- Lecture
- Student performance evaluation of all entry-level skills required for student comprehension and application of knowledge of fetal development, including:
  - ○ An understanding of the key terms related to prenatal development
  - ○ An understanding of fetal development and maturation of body systems
  - ○ An ability to explain the functions of the placenta, umbilical cord, and amniotic fluid
  - ○ Knowledge of the effects of environmental factors on a fetus and an ability to convey those effects to patients

KEY TERMS

age of viability (p. 37)
amniotic sac (p. 35)
autosome (p. 31)
chorion (p. 34)
decidua (p. 34)
diploid (p. 31)

dizygotic (p. 41)
fertilization (p. 32)
gametogenesis (p. 32)
germ layers (p. 34)
haploid (p. 31)
monozygotic (p. 41)

oogenesis (p. 31)
placenta (p. 38)
spermatogenesis (p. 31)
teratogen (p. 31)
Wharton's jelly (p. 39)

ADDITIONAL RESOURCES

TEACH PPT slide(s) Chapter 3, 1-55
EILR IC image(s) Chapter 3, 1-8
EILR OBQ question(s) Chapter 3, 1-10
EILR TB question(s) Chapter 3, 1-28
ESLR IRQ question(s) Chapter 3, 1-5
SG Chapter 3, pp. 15-20

Legend

PPT	EILR	ESLR	SG	CTQ
TEACH PowerPoint Slides	EVOLVE Instructor Learning Resources: Image Collection (IC), Open-Book Quizzes (OBQ), Test Bank (TB)	EVOLVE Student Learning Resources: Interactive Review Questions (IRQ) for the NCLEX® Examination	Study Guide	Critical Thinking Question in Nursing Care Plan (NCP CTQ) or Get Ready for the NCLEX! (GRN CTQ)

Class Activities are indicated in **bold italic**.

Leifer

LESSON 3.1

PRETEST

1. The three germ layers of the embryo are the
   a. ectoderm, mesoderm, and endoderm.
   b. ectoderm, autosome, and endoderm.
   c. mesoderm, teratogen, and chorion.
   d. chorion, placenta, and amniotic sac.

2. Substances that can damage a growing fetus are called
   a. surfactants.
   b. autosomes.
   c. teratogens.
   d. chorions.

3. The process of mitosis in the sperm is called
   a. spermatogenesis.
   b. oogenesis.
   c. meiosis.
   d. foramen ovale.

4. Two arteries and one vein form the
   a. autosome.
   b. blastomere.
   c. oocyte.
   d. umbilical cord.

5. Chromosomes are made up of one pair of sex chromosomes and 22 pairs of
   a. DNA.
   b. chorion.
   c. autosomes.
   d. oocytes.

6. The point at which the fetus can survive outside the uterus is the
   a. in utero survival age.
   b. age of viability.
   c. age of maturity.
   d. 14th week of gestation.

7. The sac that is formed from the chorion and the amnion is the
   a. amniotic sac.
   b. synovial sac.
   c. lacrimal sac.
   d. air sac.

8. Twins formed from two separate ova and two separate sperm are
   a. identical twins.
   b. monozygotic twins.
   c. conjoined twins.
   d. dizygotic twins.

9. The moment when a sperm penetrates an ovum and unites with it is called
   a. embryonic development.
   b. implantation.
   c. fertilization.
   d. meiosis.

10. The deciduas basalis develops into the
    a. placenta.
    b. zygote.
    c. mesoderm.
    d. yolk sac.

Answer

1. a	3. a	5. c	7. a	9. c
2. c	4. d	6. b	8. d	10. a

BACKGROUND ASSESSMENT

Question: What are the three germ layers and how do they differ from each other?
Answer: The three germ layers are the ectoderm, the mesoderm, and the endoderm. They differ from each other in that each one develops into specific organs and tissues.

Question: Why are chromosomes important, and what is the difference between the body chromosomes and the sex chromosomes?
Answer: Chromosomes contain the genetic material, the "blueprint," that determines how organs will develop and grow. Body chromosomes are involved in the development of body organs and tissues that are specific to an individual. The sex chromosomes determine an individual's gender.

CRITICAL THINKING QUESTION

A patient wants to know why prenatal nutrition is important. In particular, she asks why she should take folic acid. In addition, the same mother wants to know why she should not smoke or drink alcohol during her pregnancy. What should the nurse tell her?

Guidelines: The nurse should explain that the mother's health and nutritional status directly affect the health of her developing fetus. The nurse should also explain that nutrition is very important during the first trimester because that is when the fetus is most vulnerable. Folic acid is important because it can prevent neural tube defects like spina bifida. In addition, the nurse should explain that nicotine and alcohol can pass through the placental barrier and into the fetal circulation. These substances, along with illicit drug use, can cause infection, congenital anomalies, fetal alcohol syndrome, and addiction in the fetus.

OBJECTIVES	CONTENT	TEACHING RESOURCES
Describe the process of gametogenesis in human reproduction.	■ Cell division and gametogenesis (p. 31)	⊠▤ PPT slides 4-6 **e** EILR IC image 1 **e** EILR OBQ questions 1-3 **e** EILR TB questions 1, 25 SG Learning Activities, question 1 (p. 15) **BOOK RESOURCES** Figure 3-1, Normal Gametogenesis (p. 32) ▸ Discuss the two types of cell division, mitosis and meiosis. Describe the terms *diploid* and *haploid*. *Class Activity **Distribute copies of the illustration on page 32 of the text and divide the class into two groups. Have one of the groups develop a mini lecture on the process of spermatogenesis, and have the other group develop a mini lecture about the process of oogenesis. Then have each group present its findings to the class as a whole.***
Explain human fertilization and implantation.	■ Fertilization (p. 32) ☐ Sex determination (p. 33) ☐ Inheritance (p. 33) ☐ Tubal transport of the zygote (pp. 33-34) ☐ Implantation of the zygote (p. 34)	⊠▤ PPT slides 7-17 **e** EILR IC images 2-5 **e** EILR OBQ questions 2-3 **e** EILR TB questions 2-3, 6, 18, 20-21, 26 **e** ESLR IRQ question 1 SG Learning Activities, questions 4-6 (p. 15) SG Review Questions, questions 1, 7 (pp. 18-19) SG Thinking Critically, questions 1-2 (p. 20) **BOOK RESOURCES** Nursing Tips (p. 33) Figure 3-2, Ovulation and Fertilization (p. 33)

OBJECTIVES	CONTENT	TEACHING RESOURCES
		Figure 3-3, Sex Determination (p. 34)
		Figure 3-4, Inheritance (p. 34)
		Figure 3-5, Maternal-Fetal Circulation (p. 35)
		Review Questions for the NCLEX® Examination, question 1 (p. 42)
		▸ Discuss the roles of the X and Y chromosomes in sex determination. How do the male and female each influence the gender of the child?
		*Class Activity **Review the processes of fertilization and implantation with the class. Then divide the class into small groups. Have each group develop a simplified flow chart of the processes of fertilization and implantation. Each successive step should be explained. The groups must explain or define the following: fertilization, location where fertilization occurs, zygote, blastocyst, chorion, deciduas, and placenta.***
		*Class Activity **Divide the class into small groups and have the groups develop teaching plans that explain the processes of fertilization and implantation to couples considering in vitro fertilization or artificial insemination.***
Describe embryonic development.	■ Development (p. 34) ☐ Cell differentiation (p. 34) – Chorion (p. 34) – Amnion (p. 35) – Yolk sac (p. 35) – Germ layers (p. 35)	⊠▪ PPT slides 18-26 𝒆 EILR IC image 6 𝒆 EILR OBQ questions 4-6 𝒆 EILR TB questions 7, 23 𝒆 ESLR IRQ questions 4-5 SG Learning Activities, questions 7-10, 16 (pp. 16, 18) SG Review Questions, questions 2-3, 8 (pp. 18-19) **BOOK RESOURCES** Box 3-1, Body Parts that Develop from the Primary Germ Layers (p. 35) Figure 3-6, The Pregnant Uterus at 4 Weeks (p. 35) ▸ Discuss the body parts that develop from the primary germ layers (see Box 3-1, p. 35) *Class Activity **Have students make flow charts that outline and explain the process of embryonic development. The outlines should include, and explain, the terms cell differentiation, chorion, amnion, amniotic sac, yolk sac, and germ layers. Have students present their charts to the class for discussion.***

Introduction to Maternity & Pediatric Nursing, 6th ed.
Leifer

OBJECTIVES	CONTENT	TEACHING RESOURCES
Describe fetal development and maturation of body systems.	☐ Prenatal developmental milestones (p. 36)	⊠▤ PPT slides 27-29 *e* EILR TB questions 4, 9, 13-14, 17 *e* ESLR IRQ question 3 **BOOK RESOURCES** Review Questions for the NCLEX® Examination, question 1 (p. 42) Table 3-1, Embryonic and Fetal Development (pp. 36-38) ♀ GRN CTQ 1 (p. 43) ▶ Discuss reasons why it is important to include information about prenatal development milestones in patient education. What are the three basic stages that characterize prenatal development? *Class Activity **Show students a video that includes information about prenatal development, such as "From Conception to Birth" (Polymorph Films).*** *Class Activity **Review fetal development and maturation with the class. Divide the class into small groups and have each group create a teaching plan that explains fetal development in simple terms to a pregnant woman. The teaching plan should include the definitions of the terms* zygote, embryo, *and* fetus. *For each of the three stages of fetal development, the plan should include the level of development of two organ systems. Then, have each group present its teaching plan to another group for feedback and discussion.***

3.1 Homework/Assignments:

3.1 Instructor's Notes/Student Feedback:

Leifer

LESSON 3.2

CRITICAL THINKING QUESTION

A patient tells the nurse that the patient's sister had a child who had something wrong with its heart; as a result, the blood was not circulating correctly. The patient asks whether she can expect this to happen to her child as well. What should the nurse tell her?

Guidelines: The nurse should briefly explain the functions of the three fetal circulatory shunts, the ductus venosus, foramen ovale, and ductus arteriosus. Explain to the mother that it is normal for the shunts to be functionally closed within a few hours after birth. Permanent closure usually occurs by the age of 3 months in most healthy children. Because the shunts are functionally closed only within the first few months after birth, some conditions such as respiratory distress can cause increased resistance in blood flow and a reopening of one of the shunts. However, in most healthy babies the shunts will close permanently within the usual period of time.

OBJECTIVES	CONTENT	TEACHING RESOURCES
Describe the development and functions of the placenta, umbilical cord, and amniotic fluid.	■ Accessory structures of pregnancy (p. 38) ☐ Placenta (p. 38) – Placental transfer (p. 38) – Placental hormones (p. 39) – Umbilical cord (p. 39)	▣▪ PPT slides 30-39 𝒆 EILR IC images 5-6 𝒆 EILR OBQ questions 7-8 𝒆 EILR TB questions 8, 15, 22, 24, 27 𝒆 ESLR IRQ question 2 SG Learning Activities, questions 11-12 (p. 16) SG Review Questions, questions 4, 9-10 (p. 19) SG Applying Knowledge, question 1 (p. 20) **BOOK RESOURCES** Figure 3-5, Maternal-Fetal Circulation (p. 35) Figure 3-6, The Pregnant Uterus at 4 Weeks (p. 35) Nutrition Considerations, Folic Acid and Neural Tube Defects (p. 37) Review Questions for the NCLEX® Examination, questions 2, 3 (p. 42) ▸ Discuss the role of the placenta. To what extent does the placental membrane provide protection from substances ingested by the mother? Can harmful substances be transferred to the fetus? What are the potential results? *Class Activity Divide the class into small groups and give each group a list of functions of the placenta, umbilical cord, and amniotic fluid. Have students match each function with the correct structure. Then, have student pairs role-play a nurse teaching a pregnant patient about the placenta, umbilical cord, and amniotic fluid. When the teaching is completed, have the student who played the patient present to the class his or her knowledge of the development and function of the placenta, umbilical*

OBJECTIVES	CONTENT	TEACHING RESOURCES
		cord, and amniotic fluid based on the information provided in the role-plays.
Compare fetal circulation to circulation after birth.	☐ Fetal circulation (p. 39) – Circulation before birth (p. 39) – Circulation after birth (p. 39) – Closure of fetal circulatory shunts (p. 40) ■ Impaired prenatal development and subsequent illness (p. 40) ■ *Healthy People 2020* (p. 40)	▣ PPT slides 40-46 𝒆 EILR IC image 7 𝒆 EILR OBQ question 9 𝒆 EILR TB questions 5, 10-11, 16 SG Learning Activities, questions 13-15 (p. 17) SG Review Questions, questions 5-6 (p. 19) **BOOK RESOURCES** Memory Jogger (p. 39) Figure 3-7, Changes in Fetal-Newborn Circulation at Birth (p. 40) Health Promotion, *Healthy People 2020* (p. 40) Review Questions for the NCLEX® Examination, questions 3-4 (p. 42) ▸ Discuss environmental influences on fetal development at various stages including viral illness, hypoxia, drugs, and undernourishment. Invite a prenatal nurse educator to discuss prenatal education and outline problems commonly encountered in performing his or her role. *Class Activity **Have three volunteer students outline on the board the following categories: ductus venosus, foramen ovale, and ductus arteriosus. Call on students to define the functions of each while the volunteer student records the information on the board. Ask students to discuss and outline when shunt closure occurs.***
Explain the similarities and differences in the two types of twins.	■ Multifetal pregnancy (p. 41)	▣ PPT slides 47-48 𝒆 EILR IC image 8 𝒆 EILR OBQ question 10 𝒆 EILR TB questions 12, 19 SG Learning Activities, question 17 (p. 18) SG Review Questions, questions 11-12 (pp. 19-20) SG Applying Knowledge, question 2 (p. 20) **BOOK RESOURCES** Figure 3-8, Multiple Births (p. 41)

OBJECTIVES	CONTENT	TEACHING RESOURCES
		Review Questions for the NCLEX® Examination, question 5 (p. 42)
		▶ Discuss the distinction between dizygotic and monozygotic twins. What are the risks associated with multifetal pregnancies?
		Class Activity Review the similarities and differences between the two types of twins. Provide a list of all the characteristics for each type of twin, and have students match the characteristics to the appropriate twin type. Then, have students identify some important teaching points for an expectant mother who is pregnant with twins.
Performance Evaluation		PPT slides 1-50
		e EILR IC images 1-8
		e EILR OBQ questions 1-10
		e EILR TB questions 1-28
		e ESLR IRQ questions 1-5
		SG Learning Activities, questions 1-17 (pp. 15-18)
		SG Review Questions, questions 1-12 (pp. 18-20)
		SG Thinking Critically, questions 1, 2 (p. 20)
		SG Applying Knowledge, questions 1, 2 (p. 20)
		BOOK RESOURCES
		Review Questions for the NCLEX® Examination, questions 1-5 (p. 42)
		GRN CTQ 1, 2 (p. 43)

3.2 Homework/Assignments:

3.2 Instructor's Notes/Student Feedback:

Leifer

3 Lecture Outline
Fetal Development

Slide 1

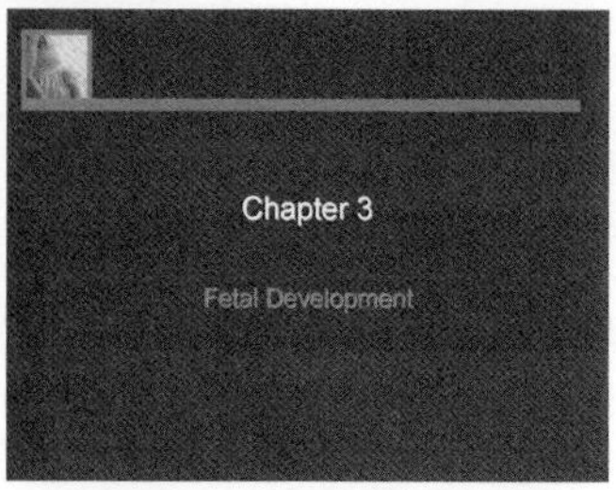

Chapter 3

Fetal Development

Slide 2

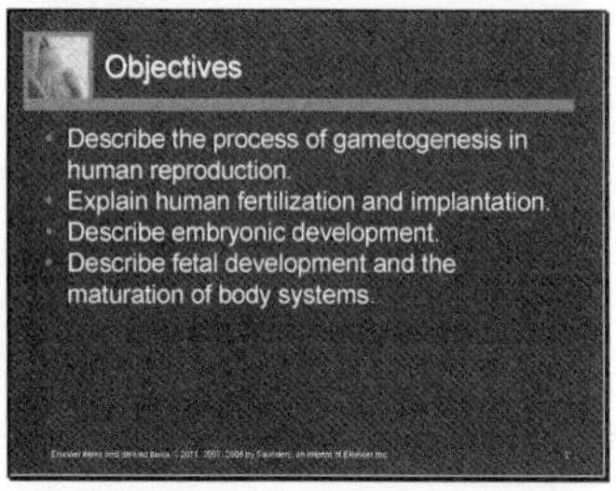

Objectives

- Describe the process of gametogenesis in human reproduction.
- Explain human fertilization and implantation.
- Describe embryonic development.
- Describe fetal development and the maturation of body systems.

Slide 3

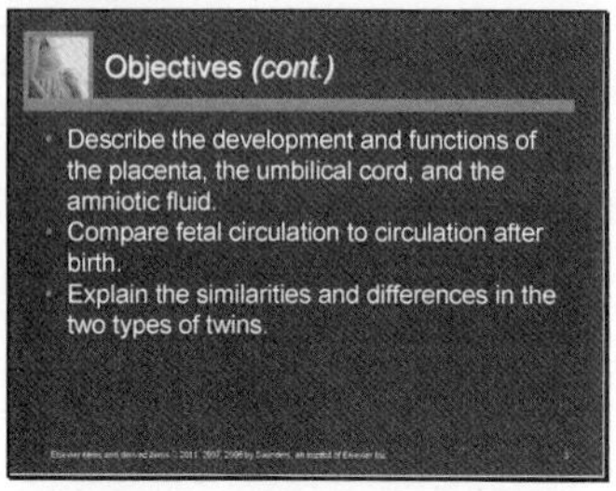

Objectives *(cont.)*

- Describe the development and functions of the placenta, the umbilical cord, and the amniotic fluid.
- Compare fetal circulation to circulation after birth.
- Explain the similarities and differences in the two types of twins.

Slide 4

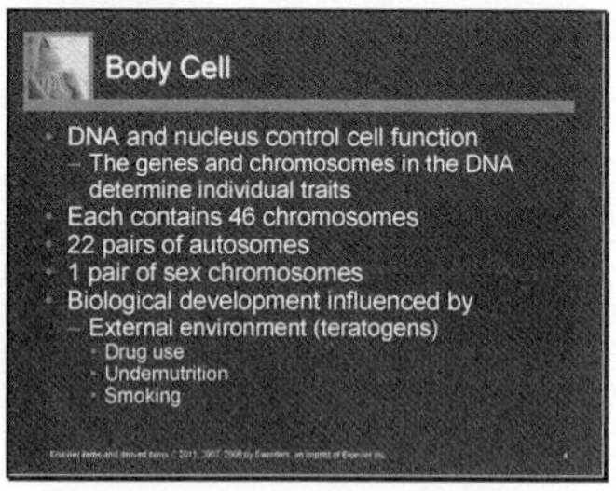

Body Cell

- DNA and nucleus control cell function
  - The genes and chromosomes in the DNA determine individual traits
- Each contains 46 chromosomes
- 22 pairs of autosomes
- 1 pair of sex chromosomes
- Biological development influenced by
  - External environment (teratogens)
    - Drug use
    - Undernutrition
    - Smoking

Slide 5

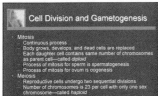

Cell Division and Gametogenesis

- Mitosis
  - Continuous process
  - Body grows, develops, and dead cells are replaced
  - Each daughter cell contains same number of chromosomes as parent cell—called *diploid*
  - Process of mitosis for sperm is spermatogenesis
  - Process of mitosis for ovum is oogenesis
- Meiosis
  - Reproductive cells undergo two sequential divisions
  - Number of chromosomes is 23 per cell with only one sex chromosome—called *haploid*
  - At fertilization, the new cell contains 23 chromosomes from the sperm and 23 chromosomes from the ova
  - Formation of gametes by this type of cell division is gametogenesis

- *Mitosis* refers to the division and multiplication of body cells.
- *Meiosis* refers to the same process when taking place in sex cells.

Audience Response Question #1

Complete the analogy. Mitosis : body cells as Meiosis : _____
  1. Gametes
  2. Sex cells
  3. Chromosomes
  4. Prokaryotic cells

Slide 6

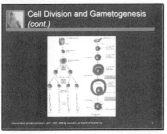

Cell Division and Gametogenesis (cont.)

Slide 7

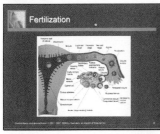

Fertilization

- Occurs when a sperm penetrates an ovum and they unite
- Takes place in the outer third of the fallopian tube, near the ovary
- As soon as it occurs, a chemical change in the membrane around the fertilized ovum prevents further sperm from penetrating the ovum

- Only a single sperm can penetrate a single egg.

Slide 8

Fertilization

- Track the process of the egg from the point of maturity until discharge from the ovary.

Slide 9

Nursing Tip

- During sexual counseling, the nurse should emphasize that the survival time of sperm ejaculated into the area of the cervix may be up to 5 days and that pregnancy can occur with intercourse as long as 5 days before ovulation

- The timing of intercourse to facilitate pregnancy can be a source of confusion to couples.
- The sperm can be present in the woman's body prior to ovulation and survive until ovulation.
- Are there any days during the woman's monthly cycle in which she cannot become pregnant?

Leifer

Slide 10

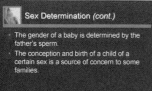

Sex Determination

- Sperm can carry either an X or Y chromosome
- Male determines the gender of the fetus
- pH of female reproductive tract influences survival rate of the X- and Y-bearing sperm, including speed of motility
- XX results in female
- XY results in male

- A number of theories exist involving interventions to increase the likelihood of a woman conceiving a child of the desired sex.
- What are the ethical implications of attempting to control the sex of the baby?

Slide 11

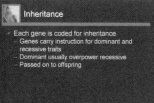

Sex Determination *(cont.)*

- The gender of a baby is determined by the father's sperm.
- The conception and birth of a child of a certain sex is a source of concern to some families.

Slide 12

Inheritance

- Each gene is coded for inheritance
  - Genes carry instruction for dominant and recessive traits
  - Dominant usually overpower recessive
  - Passed on to offspring

Slide 13

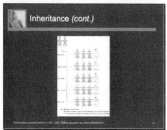

Inheritance *(cont.)*

Slide 14

Tubal Transport of the Zygote

- Zygote is formed by union of sperm and ovum
- Transported through fallopian tube into uterus
- During transport, zygote undergoes rapid mitotic division (known as *cleavage*)
- Size of zygote does not increase, individual cells become smaller as they divide, then form a solid ball (known as a *morula*)

- After fertilization, the zygote travels to the uterus for implantation.
- What action allows the zygote to travel?
- During this time, does the mother recognize she is pregnant? *No*
- What are the implications if the tubal structure is not "normal"?

Leifer

Slide 15

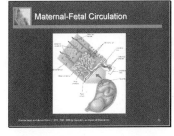

Maternal-Fetal Circulation

Slide 16

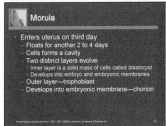

Morula

- Enters uterus on third day
  - Floats for another 2 to 4 days
  - Cells forms a cavity
  - Two distinct layers evolve
    - Inner layer is a solid mass of cells called *blastocyst*
    - Develops into embryo and embryonic membranes
  - Outer layer—trophoblast
  - Develops into embryonic membrane—chorion

Slide 17

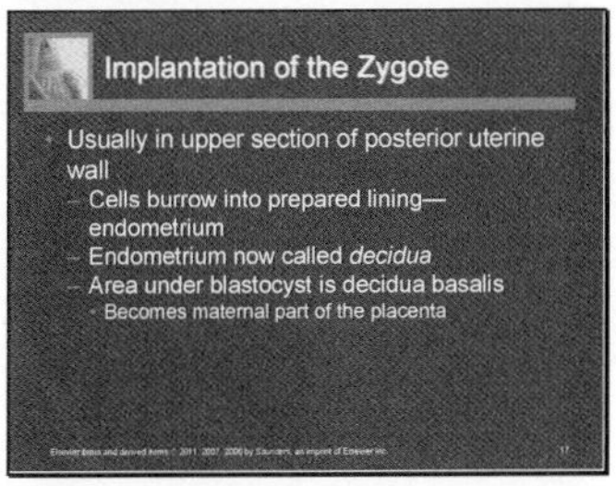

Implantation of the Zygote

- Usually in upper section of posterior uterine wall
  - Cells burrow into prepared lining—endometrium
  - Endometrium now called *decidua*
  - Area under blastocyst is decidua basalis
    - Becomes maternal part of the placenta

Slide 18

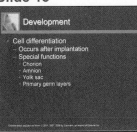

Development

- Cell differentiation
  - Occurs after implantation
  - Special functions
    - Chorion
    - Amnion
    - Yolk sac
    - Primary germ layers

- At the time of implantation, the cells are identical.
- What is the importance of differentiation?

Slide 19

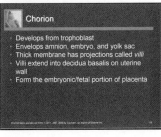

Chorion

- Develops from trophoblast
- Envelops amnion, embryo, and yolk sac
- Thick membrane has projections called *villi*
- Villi extend into decidua basalis on uterine wall
- Form the embryonic/fetal portion of placenta

Leifer

Slide 20

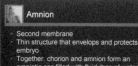

- Amnion
  - Second membrane
  - Thin structure that envelops and protects embryo
  - Together, chorion and amnion form an amniotic sac filled with fluid (bag of waters)
  - Amniotic fluid is clear, mild odor, may contain bits of vernix or lanugo
  - Volume of fluid steadily increases from ~30 mL at 10 weeks to 350 mL at 20 weeks; at 37 weeks, fluid is ~1000 mL

- To allow students to conceptualize the volumes being discussed, provide them with examples.
- 30 mL is similar in size to a small medication cup.
- 1000 mL is the amount of volume in a large IV bag.
- What terms indicate an excess or lack of adequate amniotic fluid?
- Review diagnostic mechanisms that can be used to assess amniotic fluid volume.
- Identify the source of amniotic fluid.

Audience Response Question #2

If amniotic fluid exceeds 1000 mL at term it is known as:
1. megahydramnios.
2. oligohydramnios.
3. tetramnios.
4. polyhydramnios.

Slide 21

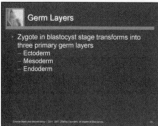

- Functions of Amniotic Fluid
  - Maintains an even temperature
  - Prevents the amniotic sac from adhering to the fetal skin
  - Allows symmetrical growth of fetus
  - Allows buoyancy and fetal movement
  - Acts as a cushion to protect the fetus and umbilical cord from injury

- What types of problems will present to the fetus with a lack of amniotic fluid?

Slide 22

- Yolk Sac
  - A cavity develops on the ninth day after fertilization
  - Functions only during embryonic life
  - Initiates production of red blood cells
  - Continues until fetal liver takes over at about 6 weeks
  - Umbilical cord encompasses yolk sac which then degenerates

Slide 23

- Germ Layers
  - Zygote in blastocyst stage transforms into three primary germ layers
    - Ectoderm
    - Mesoderm
    - Endoderm

Slide 24

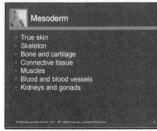

Ectoderm
- Outer layer of skin
- Oil glands and hair follicles of skin
- Nails and hair
- External sense organs
- Mucous membrane of mouth and anus

Slide 25

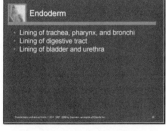

Mesoderm
- True skin
- Skeleton
- Bone and cartilage
- Connective tissue
- Muscles
- Blood and blood vessels
- Kidneys and gonads

Slide 26

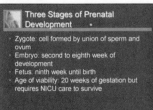

Endoderm
- Lining of trachea, pharynx, and bronchi
- Lining of digestive tract
- Lining of bladder and urethra

Slide 27

Three Stages of Prenatal Development
- Zygote: cell formed by union of sperm and ovum
- Embryo: second to eighth week of development
- Fetus: ninth week until birth
- Age of viability: 20 weeks of gestation but requires NICU care to survive

- Discuss the definition of *viability*.
- What is the size of an infant born at 20 weeks?

Slide 28

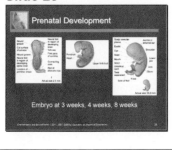

Prenatal Development

Embryo at 3 weeks, 4 weeks, 8 weeks

- Point out the changing size and shape of the embryo.
- Initially the embryo is straight, and later it appears curved.

Leifer

Slide 29

Slide 30

Accessory Structures of Pregnancy · Placenta · Umbilical cord · Fetal circulation – Supports fetus	· What is the function of each structure?

Slide 31

Placenta
 	
· Organ for fetal respiration, nutrition, and excretion
· Produces four hormones
  – Progesterone
  – Estrogen
  – Human chorionic gonadotropin (hCG)
  – Human placental lactogen (hPL)
	· The placenta produces four hormones.
	· Which, if any, of the hormones are produced by a woman's body when not pregnant? *Progesterone and estrogen*
	· Review the primary functions of each of the hormones listed.

Slide 32

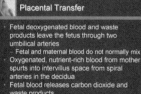

Placental Transfer

· Fetal deoxygenated blood and waste products leave the fetus through two umbilical arteries
  – Fetal and maternal blood do not normally mix
· Oxygenated, nutrient-rich blood from mother spurts into intervillus space from spiral arteries in the decidua
· Fetal blood releases carbon dioxide and waste products

Slide 33

Placental Transfer *(cont.)*
 	
· Fetal blood takes oxygen and nutrients before returning to fetus through umbilical vein
· Many harmful substances can be transferred to fetus
  – Drugs, nicotine, viral infectious agents
  – May cause fetal drug addiction, congenital anomalies, and fetal infection
	· When should patient education concerning toxic substances begin?

Slide 34

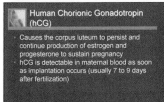

Placental Hormones

- Progesterone
- Functions during pregnancy
  - Maintains uterine lining for implantation of the zygote
  - Reduces uterine contractions to prevent spontaneous abortion
  - Prepares the glands of the breasts for lactation
  - Stimulates testes to produce testosterone, which aids the male fetus in developing the reproductive tract

Slide 35

Placental Hormones *(cont.)*

- Estrogen
- Stimulates uterine growth
  - Increases the blood flow to uterine vessels
  - Stimulates development of the breast ducts to prepare for lactation
- Effects of estrogen, not related to pregnancy
  - Increased skin pigmentation
  - Vascular changes in the skin and mucous membranes of nose and mouth
  - Increased salivation

Slide 36

Human Chorionic Gonadotropin (hCG)

- Causes the corpus luteum to persist and continue production of estrogen and progesterone to sustain pregnancy
- hCG is detectable in maternal blood as soon as implantation occurs (usually 7 to 9 days after fertilization)

- hCG is the hormone detected in early pregnancy for a positive pregnancy test.
- hCG is a test obtained by serum or urine.
- Which of the tests is most accurate? *Serum*
- Review the time of day in which a pregnant woman's hCG levels are highest.

Audience Response Question #3
A new patient has had blood drawn to determine if she is pregnant. The hormone responsible for a positive test result is:
  1. human chorionic gonadotropin (hCG).
  2. estrogen.
  3. human placental lactogen (HpL).
  4. follicle stimulating hormone (FSH).

Slide 37

Human Placental Lactogen (hPL)

- Also known as *human chorionic somatomammotropin* (hCS)
- hPL causes decreased insulin sensitivity and utilization of glucose by mother
  - Helps to make more glucose available to fetus to meet growth needs

- Review the phenomena created by the actions of hPL.

Leifer

Slide 38

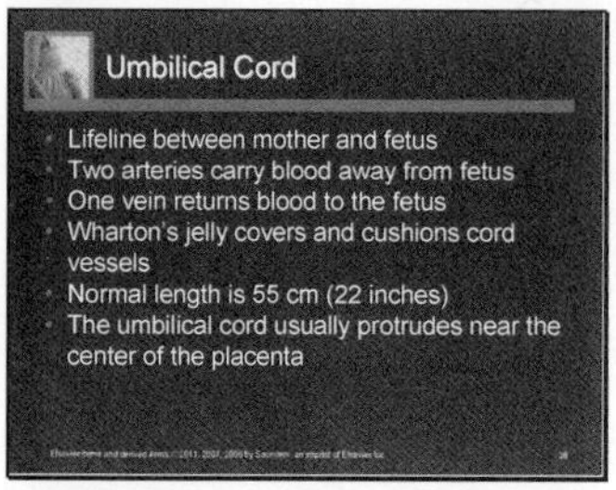

Umbilical Cord

- Lifeline between mother and fetus
- Two arteries carry blood away from fetus
- One vein returns blood to the fetus
- Wharton's jelly covers and cushions cord vessels
- Normal length is 55 cm (22 inches)
- The umbilical cord usually protrudes near the center of the placenta

- A normal placenta has three vessels.
- It is the responsibility of the nurse at the time of delivery to note the number of vessels in an umbilical cord.
- What are the implications of a two-vessel cord?

Slide 39

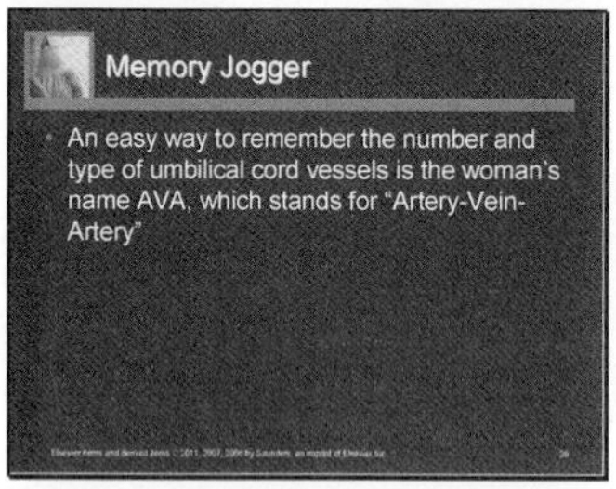

Memory Jogger

- An easy way to remember the number and type of umbilical cord vessels is the woman's name AVA, which stands for "Artery-Vein-Artery"

Slide 40

Maternal-Fetal Circulation

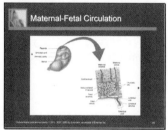

Slide 41

Fetal Circulatory Shunts

- Foramen ovale
- Ductus arteriosus
- Ductus venosus

- Outline the location and role of each of the identified structures.

Slide 42

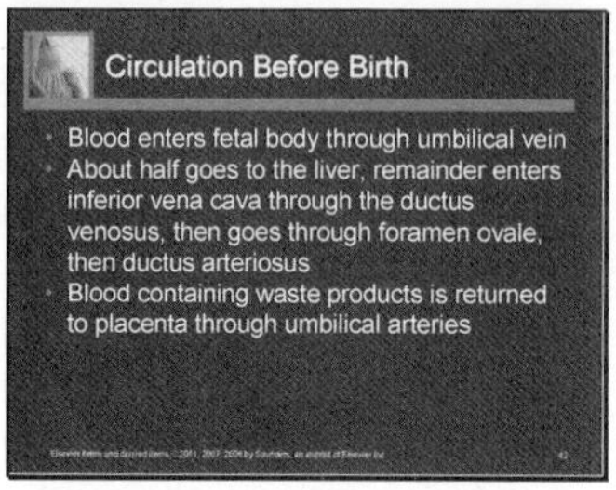

Circulation Before Birth

- Blood enters fetal body through umbilical vein
- About half goes to the liver, remainder enters inferior vena cava through the ductus venosus, then goes through foramen ovale, then ductus arteriosus
- Blood containing waste products is returned to placenta through umbilical arteries

- Fetal circulation sends a limited amount of blood through the lungs.
- Discuss the physiological reasoning for this.

Slide 43

Changes in Circulation After Birth

- Foramen ovale closes within 2 hours after birth (permanently by age 3 months)
- Ductus arteriosus closes within 15 hours (permanently in about 3 weeks)
- Ductus venosus closes functionally when cord is cut (permanently in about 1 week)
  - After permanent closure, the ductus arteriosus and ductus venosus become ligaments

Slide 44

Prenatal Development

- Undernutrition
  - Can result in permanent changes in fetal structure, physiology, and metabolism
  - Can influence development of conditions such as heart disease and stroke in adulthood
  - Exposure to toxins in utero
  - Can also influence health in later life

- Providing healthy intake during pregnancy will impact the development of the fetus.
- Which mothers are at an increased risk for undernutrition?

Slide 45

Prenatal Development *(cont.)*

- Intrauterine growth restriction may reduce number of cells in organs
  - Can predispose to the development of specific disease later in life
- Fetal growth best assessed when weight, length of gestation, placental size, and newborn head and abdominal circumference are considered
- Fetal growth limited by nutrients and oxygen received from mother
- A healthy mother can produce a healthy child who is less prone to illness

Slide 46

Multifetal Pregnancy

- Twins occur once in every 90 pregnancies
- When hormones are used to assist with ovulation, twinning and other multifetal pregnancies occur
- Monozygotic is from a single fertilized ovum (identical)
- Dizygotic is from two separate fertilized ovum (fraternal)

- Twins are increasing in numbers.
- Which mothers have an increased likelihood of becoming pregnant with twins?

Audience Response Question #4
Monozygotic twins will always be the same sex.
  1. True
  2. False

Slide 47

Multifetal Pregnancy *(cont.)*

- Identical twins might or might not share a placenta and amniotic sac.
- What factors determine this?

Slide 48

Question for Review

How long after ovulation can fertilization occur?

Slide 49

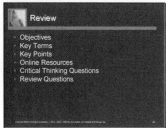

Review

- Objectives
- Key Terms
- Key Points
- Online Resources
- Critical Thinking Questions
- Review Questions

4 Prenatal Care and Adaptations to Pregnancy

TEACHING FOCUS

This chapter introduces the student to proper prenatal care and the nurse's role in helping women adapt to pregnancy. It outlines the goals of prenatal care as well as the diagnosis and signs of pregnancy. The student will have an opportunity to learn normal physiological changes and proper nutrition and exercise during pregnancy. The chapter also focuses on psychological adaptations to pregnancy and the nurse's role as educator. Finally, the chapter includes unique considerations when working with populations with special needs.

MATERIALS AND RESOURCES

☐ 3-D model of developing fetus (Lessons 4.1 and 4.2)
☐ Computer and PowerPoint projector (all lessons)
☐ Standardized prenatal teaching plan (Lesson 4.3)

LESSON CHECKLIST

Preparations for this lesson include:

- Lecture
- Guest speaker: nurse specializing in OB/GYN
- Evaluation of student comprehension and entry-level skills required for application of knowledge of prenatal care and adaptations to pregnancy, including:
  ○ Calculating the expected date of delivery and duration of pregnancy
  ○ Differentiating among the presumptive, probable, and positive signs of pregnancy
  ○ Understanding of the physiological and psychological changes during pregnancy
  ○ Developing a prenatal teaching plan

KEY TERMS

abortion (p. 47)
antepartum (p. 44)
aortocaval compression
   (p. 53)
birth plan (p. 70)
Braxton Hicks contractions
   (p. 50)
Chadwick's sign (p. 49)
chloasma (p. 49)
colostrum (p. 52)
estimated date of delivery
   (EDD) (p. 46)

gestational age (p. 47)
Goodell's sign (p. 49)
gravida (p. 47)
Hegar's sign (p. 49)
intrapartum (p. 44)
lactation (p. 52)
last normal menstrual
   period (LNMP) (p. 46)
lightening (p. 53)
McDonald's sign (p. 49)
multipara (p. 47)
Nägele's rule (p. 48)

para (p. 47)
postpartum (p. 44)
primigravida (p. 47)
primipara (p. 47)
pseudoanemia (p. 53)
quickening (p. 49)
supine hypotension
   syndrome (p. 53)
trimester (p. 48)

ADDITIONAL RESOURCES

TEACH PPT slide(s) Chapter 4, 1-69
EILR IC image(s) Chapter 4, 1-11
EILR OBQ question(s) Chapter 4, 1-10
EILR TB question(s) Chapter 4, 1-31
ESLR IRQ question(s) Chapter 4, 1-5
SG Chapter 4, pp. 21-27

ELSEVIER

Introduction to Maternity & Pediatric Nursing, 6ᵗʰ ed.

Legend

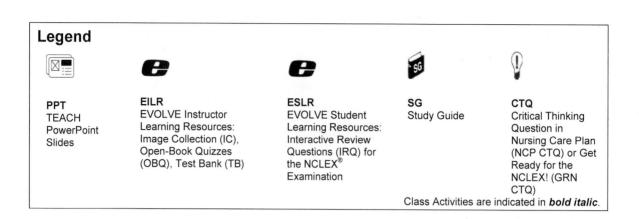

PPT
TEACH
PowerPoint
Slides

EILR
EVOLVE Instructor
Learning Resources:
Image Collection (IC),
Open-Book Quizzes
(OBQ), Test Bank (TB)

ESLR
EVOLVE Student
Learning Resources:
Interactive Review
Questions (IRQ) for
the NCLEX®
Examination

SG
Study Guide

CTQ
Critical Thinking
Question in
Nursing Care Plan
(NCP CTQ) or Get
Ready for the
NCLEX! (GRN
CTQ)

Class Activities are indicated in **bold italic**.

Leifer

LESSON 4.1

PRETEST

1. Which of the following is a common discomfort of pregnancy?
   a. hot flashes
   b. diarrhea
   c. nausea
   d. ballottement

2. Pregnant women need to consume how many additional calories per day?
   a. 100
   b. 300
   c. 500
   d. 1,000

3. When a pregnant woman stands up suddenly, she may become dizzy because of
   a. orthostatic hypotension.
   b. tachycardia.
   c. increased venous return to the heart.
   d. vasoconstriction.

4. The three phases of pregnancy are
   a. primipara, gravida, and primigravida.
   b. dilation, expulsion, and recovery.
   c. first trimester, second trimester, and third trimester.
   d. antepartum, intrapartum, and postpartum.

5. During the third trimester, the breasts secrete a thin yellow fluid called
   a. colostrum.
   b. decidua.
   c. chloasma.
   d. meconium.

6. The softening of the lower uterine segment is referred to as
   a. Goodell's sign.
   b. Hegar's sign.
   c. Chadwick's sign.
   d. McDonald's sign.

7. Nägele's rule is used to determine the
   a. sex of the fetus.
   b. fetal presentation.
   c. fundal height.
   d. estimated date of delivery.

8. When exercising, a pregnant woman's body temperature should stay below
   a. 92° F.
   b. 95° F.
   c. 100° F.
   d. 103° F.

9. The onset of quickening is an important event to record because it
   a. helps to verify gestational age.
   b. verifies that the fetus is developing properly.
   c. can be used as a tool to determine fetal position.
   d. signals the second phase of pregnancy.

10. After what age is a mother who becomes pregnant for the first time called an "elderly primip?"
    a. 25
    b. 30
    c. 35
    d. 40

Answers

1. c	3. a	5. a	7. d	9. a
2. b	4. d	6. b	8. c	10. c

BACKGROUND ASSESSMENT

Question: When and why is it important to do the following tests on a pregnant woman: a urinalysis, a complete blood count, and an Rh factor test?

Answer: A urinalysis is a routine prenatal laboratory test that is performed during the first trimester, usually as part of the first or second prenatal visit. It is used to detect the presence of infection, diabetes, and renal disease. Complete blood count and Rh factor tests are also performed during the first or second prenatal visit to check for anemia and to determine if there is a risk for maternal-fetal blood incompatibility.

ELSEVIER

Introduction to Maternity & Pediatric Nursing, 6th ed.

Elsevier items and derived items © 2011, 2007, 2006 by Saunders, an imprint of Elsevier Inc.   Leifer

Question: A woman complains of frequent urination and constipation. What are the causes of these discomforts and how could they be alleviated?

Answer: Urinary frequency and constipation are two common problems experienced during pregnancy. Urinary frequency is caused by decreased tone of the ureters and bladder and by the pressure of the growing uterus on the urinary bladder. Additionally, the pressure of the growing uterus can also cause constipation by pushing on the large intestine. Slowed peristalsis, and iron supplements also contribute to the constipation. Because there is no treatment for urinary frequency, the nurse should emphasize that the woman should not decrease her fluid intake to prevent voiding frequently. Constipation can be relieved by drinking a lot of fluids, exercising, and increasing fiber intake. Laxatives or enemas should only be taken under a physician's direction.

CRITICAL THINKING QUESTION

A woman has been compliant and has kept all of her prenatal appointments for the first six months. Now that she is in her third trimester, however, she has missed several appointments. When asked why she has missed appointments, she says that because her pregnancy has been uncomplicated to this point she doesn't think that weekly visits are necessary. What should the nurse tell her?

Guidelines: The nurse should explain that during the third trimester, the physician or nurse midwife will continually check and monitor growth and the condition of the fetus using a variety of noninvasive methods. The weekly visits also include an assessment of the fetal heart rate, fetal presentation, and position, as well as monitoring the mother for signs of late-onset complications. Even if the first six months are uneventful, problems still may occur in the third trimester. It is important to continually screen for these problems to ensure the health of both the mother and the fetus and to encourage appropriate interventions and treatments are started as soon as possible, if indicated.

OBJECTIVES	CONTENT	TEACHING RESOURCES
List the goals of prenatal care.	■ Goals of prenatal care (p. 44)	PPT slides 5-7 EILR OBQ question 1 EILR TB question 27 SG Review Questions, question 7 (p. 26) **BOOK RESOURCES** Nursing Tip (p. 45) ▸ Discuss the role of the nurse as it applies to the goals of prenatal care. *Class Activity Divide the class into small groups, and have each group outline the goals of prenatal care and develop a plan of care for each of the following patients:* *1. A 29-year-old second-time mother* *2. A 16-year-old first-time mother* *3. A 37-year-old first-time mother* *Then, have each group present its plan to the class, and ask the class to discuss how and why the goals and plans of prenatal care differ for each patient.*
Discuss prenatal care for a normal pregnancy.	☐ Prenatal visits (p. 45) ☐ Definition of terms (p. 47)	PPT slides 8-18 EILR OBQ question 2 EILR TB questions 2, 31

		SG Learning Activities, questions 1-2 (p. 21)
		SG Review Questions, question 9 (p. 26)
		BOOK RESOURCES
		Review Questions for the NCLEX® Examination, question 4 (p. 77)
		Table 4-1, Prenatal Laboratory Tests (p. 46)
		Nursing Tip (p. 47)
		Safety Alert (p. 47)
		Box 4-1, TPALM System to Describe Parity (p. 48)
		GRN CTQ 1 (p. 77)
		▸ Discuss what typically occurs during a prenatal visit during the first, second, and third trimesters.
		Class Activity **Divide the class into three groups and assign each group one of the following exercises:**
		1. Outline what is covered in the first prenatal visit.
		2. Outline what is covered in subsequent prenatal visits.
		3. Identify and list prenatal laboratory tests and the trimester in which they are performed.
		Have each group share its findings with the class, then have students discuss which tests are routine and which are not. When are nonroutine assessments performed and why?
Calculate the expected date of delivery and duration of pregnancy.	☐ Determining the estimated date of delivery (p. 48)	PPT slides 19, 20
		EILR OBQ question 3
		EILR TB questions 1-2, 6, 16-17
		SG Thinking Critically, questions 1-2 (p. 27)
		SG Applying Knowledge, questions 2-3 (p. 27)
		BOOK RESOURCES
		Box 4-2, Nägele's Rule to Determine the Estimated Date of Delivery (EDD) (p. 48)
		Review Questions for the NCLEX® Examination, question 4 (p. 77)
		▸ Discuss other tools used to calculate the estimated date of delivery.
		Class Activity **Divide the class into pairs and provide**

		students with a list of 5 to 10 dates that a woman might cite as her last known menstrual period (e.g., two weeks ago, seven weeks ago). Have each pair estimate the duration of the pregnancy and determine the expected date of delivery using Nägele's rule. Then have each pair share its results with the class. **Class Activity** *Using the calculations from the previous Class Activity, have the class discuss the answers that were found for each date. Were each group's answers the same? What is the range of answers for each date? What should the nurse do if a woman doesn't know the date of her LNMP?*
Differentiate among the presumptive, probable, and positive signs of pregnancy.	■ Diagnosis of pregnancy (p. 48) □ Presumptive signs of pregnancy (p. 48) □ Probable signs of pregnancy (p. 49) □ Positive signs of pregnancy (p. 50)	☒ PPT slides 21, 22 🅮 EILR IC images 1-4 🅮 EILR OBQ questions 4-6 🅮 EILR TB questions 3-4, 8, 23 🅮 ESLR IRQ question 4 📗 SG Learning Activities, questions 3-4 (p. 22) 📗 SG Thinking Critically, question 3 (p. 27) **BOOK RESOURCES** Box 4-3, Signs of Pregnancy (p. 48) Figure 4-1, Striae and Pigmentation of Breasts (p. 49) Figure 4-2, Abdominal Striae (p. 49) Figure 4-3, Height of Fundus During Gestation (p. 50) Figure 4-4, The Pregnant Woman's Family May Be Present During an Ultrasound (p. 51) ▸ Discuss the presumptive and probable signs of pregnancy. Which most often lead to false assumptions and why? **Class Activity** *Provide students with a list of signs and symptoms of pregnancy (it should include each type) and have students identify which are presumptive, probable, and positive signs. Then, have students explain and discuss the physiological reasons for each of the signs.*

4.1 Homework/Assignments:

4.1 Instructor's Notes/Student Feedback:

LESSON 4.2

CRITICAL THINKING QUESTION

A woman complaining of frequent urination, excessive vaginal secretions, and occasional shortness of breath asks the nurse why these changes are occurring and if they are normal. She also asks which signs might indicate an abnormality. What should the nurse tell her?

Guidelines: The nurse should reassure the woman that these are all are common discomforts of pregnancy and that they are completely normal. Frequent urination is caused by compression of the urinary bladder by the fetus and by hormones that relax the normal tone of the urinary system organs. She should be concerned if she experiences a burning sensation while urinating or if the urine has a foul odor. Vaginal secretions are caused by increased blood flow to the area. Bloody or foul-smelling secretions should be reported to her health care provider. The enlarged uterus and developing fetus can press against the diaphragm and cause shortness of breath. Although shortness of breath alone is not a cause for concern, she should be concerned if it is accompanied by a rapid heartbeat or a bluish tinge to her nailbeds. These signs should be reported to her health care provider immediately.

OBJECTIVES	CONTENT	TEACHING RESOURCES
Describe the physiological changes during pregnancy.	■ Physiological changes in pregnancy (p. 51) ☐ Endocrine system (p. 51) ☐ Reproductive system (p. 51) – Uterus (p. 51) – Cervix (p. 51) – Ovaries (p. 51) – Vagina (p. 51) – Breasts (p. 52) ☐ Respiratory system (p. 52) ☐ Cardiovascular system (p. 53) ☐ Gastrointestinal system (p. 54) ☐ Urinary system (p. 54) – Fluid and electrolyte balance (p. 55) ☐ Integumentary and skeletal systems (p. 55)	PPT slides 23-37 EILR IC images 5, 6 EILR OBQ questions 7, 8 EILR TB questions 3-5, 12, 15-16, 18, 25 ESLR IRQ questions 1, 3, 5, 7-8 SG Learning Activities, questions 5, 6 (pp. 22-23) SG Review Questions, question 4 (p. 25) **BOOK RESOURCES** Review Questions for the NCLEX® Examination, questions 2-3 (p. 77) Table 4-2, Hormones essential in pregnancy (p. 52) Figure 4-5, Supine Hypotension Syndrome (p. 53) Table 4-3, Normal Blood Values in Nonpregnant and Pregnant Women (p. 53) Figure 4-6, Compression of Abdominal Contents as Uterus Enlarges (p. 54) GRN CTQ 2 (p. 77) ▸ Discuss the physiological changes that occur during pregnancy. *Class Activity Divide the class into six groups and assign each group one of the following body systems: reproductive, respiratory, cardiovascular, gastrointestinal, urinary, integumentary, and skeletal. Have each group discuss the changes that occur in that system during pregnancy and explain the reasons for each change. Then, have groups share their findings with the class.*

OBJECTIVES	CONTENT	TEACHING RESOURCES
Identify nutritional needs for pregnancy and lactation.	■ Nutrition for pregnancy and lactation (p. 55) □ Recommended dietary allowances and recommended dietary intakes (p. 57) □ Weight gain (p. 57) □ Nutritional requirements during pregnancy (p. 59) – Protein (p. 60) – Calcium (p. 60) – Iron (p. 60) – Folic acid (p. 60) – Fluids (p. 61) – Sodium (p. 61) □ Special nutrition considerations (p. 61) – Pregnant adolescent (p. 61) – Vegetarian or vegan diet (p. 61) – Pica (p. 61) – Lactose intolerance (p. 61) – Cultural preferences (p. 62) – Gestational diabetes mellitus (p. 62) □ Nutritional requirements during lactation (p. 62)	PPT slides 38-47 *e* EILR IC images 7, 8 *e* EILR TB questions 9-10, 13-14, 21, 29, 30 SG Learning Activities, questions 7-10 (pp. 23-24) SG Review Questions, questions 5, 8, 10, 14 (pp. 25-26) SG Case Study, questions 1, 2 (p. 27) **BOOK RESOURCES** Nutrition Considerations, Maternal Diet and Fetal Health (p. 55) Safety Alert (p. 55) Figure 4-7, The 2005 Food Guide Pyramid (p. 56) Figure 4-8, The Traditional Healthy Latin American Diet Pyramid (p. 57) Safety Alert (p. 57) Nursing Care Plan 4-1, Nutrition During Pregnancy and Lactation (p. 58) Table 4-4, Distribution of Weight Gain in Pregnancy (p. 59) Table 4-5, Daily Food Pattern for Pregnancy (p. 59) Nutrition Considerations: Sample Menu for a Pregnant Woman (p. 60) GRN CTQ 1 (p. 77) ▸ Discuss the nutritional requirements for pregnancy and lactation. How do they differ and why? *Class Activity In groups, have students discuss the extra nutritional requirements of the pregnant woman. Which nutritional requirements increase, and by how much? What foods contain these nutrients? Is it possible to meet the daily requirements without taking supplements? Have students share and discuss their findings with the class.* *Class Activity Present the following scenario to the class for discussion: During the second prenatal visit a woman says that she is a vegetarian (lacto-ovo) and that she is also lactose intolerant. What nutritional recommendations are necessary for this woman?*
Discuss the importance and	■ Exercise during pregnancy (p. 62)	PPT slides 48-50

OBJECTIVES	CONTENT	TEACHING RESOURCES
limitations of exercise in pregnancy.	☐ Elevated temperature (p. 62) ☐ Hypotension (p. 64) ☐ Cardiac output (p. 64) ☐ Hormones (p. 64) ☐ Other factors (p. 64)	*e* EILR IC images 4-9 *e* EILR OBQ question 9 *e* EILR TB question 19 **BOOK RESOURCES** Figure 4-9, Exercises During Pregnancy (p. 63) Review Questions for the NCLEX® Examination, questions 1-5 (pp. 76-77) ▸ Discuss the types of exercise appropriate for both seasoned exercisers and sedentary women. *Class Activity **Divide the class into small groups and have each group develop a plan to teach a reluctant mother about the benefits of exercise during pregnancy. Each plan should include specific exercises and guidelines for exercising. Have each group share its plan with the class.***

4.2 Homework/Assignments:

4.2 Instructor's Notes/Student Feedback:

Leifer

LESSON 4.3

CRITICAL THINKING QUESTION

A woman expresses ambivalence about her pregnancy and says that she is worried about how the pregnancy will affect her relationships with her husband and two other children. What could the nurse tell her?

Guidelines: The nurse can reassure the woman that feelings of ambivalence are normal, especially in unplanned pregnancies. Feelings of ambivalence are realistic because another child can increase stress within the family as well as alter family dynamics. The nurse should encourage the woman to discuss these feelings and fears with her husband and children. The woman should also be encouraged to speak to the physician about her concerns or to seek counseling if she feels that she cannot cope with the feelings on her own. The nurse should emphasize that there are many resources available to help her and that she does not have to cope with the ambivalence on her own.

OBJECTIVES	CONTENT	TEACHING RESOURCES
Describe patient education related to travel and common discomforts of pregnancy.	■ Travel during pregnancy (p. 64) ■ Common discomforts in pregnancy (p. 65) ☐ Nausea (p. 65) ☐ Vaginal discharge (p. 65) ☐ Fatigue (p. 65) ☐ Backache (p. 65) ☐ Constipation (p. 65) ☐ Varicose veins (p. 65) ☐ Hemorrhoids (p. 66) ☐ Heartburn (p. 66) ☐ Nasal stuffiness (p. 66) ☐ Dyspnea (p. 66) ☐ Leg cramps (p. 66) ☐ Edema of lower extremities (p. 66)	▣ PPT slides 51, 52 *e* EILR OBQ question 10 *e* EILR TB questions 11, 24-25 SG Learning Activities, question 11 (p. 24) SG Review Questions, questions 6, 11-13 (pp. 25-26) **BOOK RESOURCES** ▸ Discuss methods of self-care for the common discomforts of pregnancy. ▸ Discuss travel and pregnancy and options presented on the following website: www.cdc.gov/travel. *Class Activity **Provide students with a list of common discomforts of pregnancy and have them identify appropriate interventions and/or treatments. The list of discomforts may include nausea, constipation, hemorrhoids, varicose veins, heartburn, nasal congestion, and leg cramps.***
Discuss nursing support for emotional changes that occur in a family during pregnancy.	■ Psychosocial adaptations to pregnancy (p. 66) ☐ Impact on the mother (p. 67) – First trimester (p. 67) – Second trimester (p. 67)	▣ PPT slides 53-56 *e* EILR IC images 10, 11 *e* EILR TB question 20 SG Learning Activities, question 12 (p. 25) SG Review Questions, questions 1-3 (p. 25)

OBJECTIVES	CONTENT	TEACHING RESOURCES

	– Third trimester (p. 68)
	
	☐ Impact on the father (p. 68)
		BOOK RESOURCES
		
		Figure 4-10, The Body Changes of Pregnancy (p. 68)
		
		Figure 4-11, The Father Begins to Develop a Relationship to the Fetus (p. 68)
		
		Box 4-4, Developmental Stages of Fatherhood (p. 69)
		
		Table 4-6, Physiological and psychological changes in pregnancy, Nursing interventions and teach (pp. 73-75)
		
		Review Questions for the NCLEX® Examination, question 5 (p. 77)
		
		▶ Discuss the types of emotional support a nurse can give to a first-time father.
		
		*Class Activity **Invite an OB/GYN nurse to discuss common scenarios in which nurses must provide emotional and psychological support to families during pregnancy.***
		
		*Class Activity **Divide the class into three groups. Assign each group one of the following scenarios:***
		
		   *1. **Help a spouse who feels neglected.***
		
		   *2. **Help a new grandparent adjust to his or her new role.***
		
		   *3. **Help a pregnant woman who is ambivalent about her pregnancy.***
		
		Have the groups identify methods to improve coping. Then, have each group present its plan to the class for discussion.

Identify special needs of the pregnant adolescent, the single parent, and the older couple.	☐ Impact on the pregnant adolescent (p. 69) ☐ Impact on the older couple (p. 69) ☐ Impact on the single mother (p. 69) ☐ Impact on the single father (p. 70) ☐ Impact on the grandparents (p. 70) ☐ Impact on siblings (p. 70)	⊞ PPT slides 57-62 𝒆 EILR TB questions 22, 26, 28 SG SG Applying Knowledge, question 1 (p. 27) ▶ Discuss the impact of pregnancy of adolescents, older parents, single parents, and grandparents. How does it affect these people differently? *Class Activity **In groups, have students identify the special needs of adolescents, single parents, and older parents, and discuss how these special needs should be reflected in the plan of prenatal care. Have each group share its findings with the class for discussion.***
Apply the nursing process in developing a prenatal teaching plan.	■ Prenatal education (p. 70)	⊞ PPT slide 63 𝒆 EILR IC image 12 𝒆 ESLR IRQ question 2

OBJECTIVES	CONTENT	TEACHING RESOURCES
		SG Case Study, question 1 (p. 27) **BOOK RESOURCES** Figure 4-12, Birth Plan (p. 71) *Class Activity **Provide a sample prenatal teaching plan for discussion. Divide the class into small groups and have them develop a plan devoted to a different prenatal topic using the sample as a model.***
Identify the effects of medication ingestion on pregnancy and lactation.	■ The effect of pregnancy and lactation on medication metabolism (p. 70)	PPT slides 65, 66 **BOOK RESOURCES** Box 4-5, FDA Pregnancy Risk Category for Drugs (p. 72) ▶ Discuss the changes that occur during pregnancy that affect the absorption of medications. *Class Activity **Divide the class into small groups and have each group discuss a specific FDA drug category and come up with examples of each and how they can affect the developing fetus, the mother, and the newborn.***
Review immunizations during pregnancy.	– Immunizations during pregnancy (p. 72)	PPT slide 67 ▶ Discuss the various immunizations a woman should have and which ones can be administered before pregnancy, during pregnancy, and in the postpartum period. *Class Activity **Divide the class into small groups and have each group discuss a specific vaccine. Have them list the source, contraindications, side effects to look for, and patient teaching. Have each group share its findings with the class for discussion.***
Performance Evaluation		PPT slides 1-69 *e* EILR IC images 1-11 *e* EILR OBQ questions 1-10 *e* EILR TB questions 1-31 *e* ESLR IRQ questions 1-5 SG Learning Activities, questions 1-12 (pp. 21-25) SG Review Questions, questions 1-14 (pp. 25-26) SG Case Study, questions 1-2 (p. 27) SG Thinking Critically, questions 1-3 (p. 27)

OBJECTIVES	CONTENT	TEACHING RESOURCES
		SG Applying Knowledge, questions 1-3 (p. 27)
		BOOK RESOURCES
		NCP CTQ 1, 2 (p. 58)
		Review Questions for the NCLEX® Examination, questions 1-5 (pp. 76-77)
		GRN CTQ 1, 2 (p. 77)

4.3 Homework/Assignments:

4.3 Instructor's Notes/Student Feedback:

Leifer

Lecture Outline

4

Prenatal Care and Adaptations to Pregnancy

Slide 1

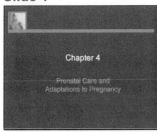

Chapter 4

Prenatal Care and
Adaptations to Pregnancy

Slide 2

Objectives

- List the goals of prenatal care.
- Discuss prenatal care for a normal pregnancy.
- Calculate the expected date of delivery and duration of pregnancy.
- Differentiate among the presumptive, probable, and positive signs of pregnancy.
- Describe the physiological changes during pregnancy.

Slide 3

Objectives *(cont.)*

- Identify nutritional needs for pregnancy and lactation.
- Discuss the importance and limitations of exercise in pregnancy.
- Describe patient education related to travel and common discomforts of pregnancy.
- Discuss nursing support of emotional changes that occur in a family during pregnancy.

Slide 4

Objectives *(cont.)*

- Identify special needs of the pregnant adolescent, the single parent, and the older couple.
- Apply the nursing process in developing a prenatal teaching plan.
- Identify the effects of medication ingestion on pregnancy and lactation.
- Review immunizations during pregnancy.

Leifer

Slide 5

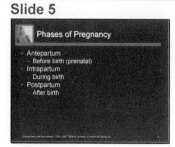

Phases of Pregnancy

- Antepartum
  - Before birth (prenatal)
- Intrapartum
  - During birth
- Postpartum
  - After birth

Slide 6

Prenatal Care Providers

- Obstetricians
- Family practice physicians
- Certified nurse midwives (CNMs)
- Nurse practitioners

- The pregnant woman can select from a variety of prenatal health care providers to manage her pregnancy.
- The individualized needs of the woman, her family, and the unborn baby will determine the best source of health care during the pregnancy.
- Geographic location might determine the availability of the various health care providers.
- Discuss the availability of the different prenatal care providers in the local community.

Slide 7

Major Goals of Prenatal Care

- Ensure a safe birth for mother and child by promoting good health habits and reducing risk factors
- Teach health habits that may be continued after pregnancy
- Educate in self-care for pregnancy
- Provide physical care
- Prepare parents for the responsibilities of parenthood

Slide 8

Prenatal Visits

- Ideally, prenatal care should begin prior to the pregnancy to assist the woman in being in optimal health prior to conception.
- The gestation of the woman at the first prenatal care visit will vary by practitioner.

Slide 9

Preconception Care

- Identifies risk factors that may be changed *before* conception
  - Reduce their negative impact on outcome of pregnancy
- Ensure good nutritional state and immunizations
- Ensure adequate intake of folic acid
  - To prevent neural tube defects in developing fetus

- What factors should be addressed prior to conception to improve the pregnancy's outcome?

Slide 10

Prenatal Care

- Complete history and physical
  - Identify problems that may affect the woman and her developing fetus
  - Ensure healthy pregnancy and delivery of healthy infant

Slide 11

Components of Prenatal Health History

- Obstetric
- Menstrual
- Contraceptive
- Medical and surgical
- Woman's family
- Partner's family
- Woman and partner's to identify risk factors
- Psychosocial

- Obstetric history includes the number and outcomes of past pregnancies.
- Menstrual history information focuses on the woman's past cycles.
- What questions will facilitate collection of data in this area?
- The information related to contraceptive history focuses on the methods which have been used. If these methods were taken prior to the pregnancy being confirmed, it will be important to determine when.
- Ensure the woman's confidentiality during the interview process.

Slide 12

Physical Examination Objectives

- Evaluate woman's general health
- Determine baseline weight and vital signs
- Evaluate nutritional status
- Identify current physical/social problems
- Determines the estimated date of delivery (EDD)

- The initial physical examination will be comprehensive. Future visits will focus on specific problems and as dictated by gestation of the pregnancy.
- Collection of baseline data provides tools to assess and pinpoint the onset of problems as they occur.

Slide 13

Pelvic Examination Objectives

- Evaluate the size, adequacy, and condition of the pelvis and reproductive organs
- Assess for signs of pregnancy

- The first examination by the physician includes a comprehensive pelvic assessment.
- What signs of pregnancy might be noted during the pelvic examination?
- Discuss the frequency and repetition of the pelvic examination.

Slide 14

Recommended Schedule of Prenatal Visits—Uncomplicated Pregnancy

- Conception to 28 weeks—every 4 weeks
- 29 to 36 weeks—every 2 to 3 weeks
- 37 weeks to birth—weekly
- Certain laboratory and/or diagnostic tests are performed at various times throughout the pregnancy
  - See Table 4-1, page 46 for listing

- Complications or concerns of the mother or health care provider necessitate a modified schedule.
- The activities of each visit will be determined by the gestation of the pregnancy and the presence of health concerns or alterations.
- Review the role of the nurse during the prenatal care visits.
- What scenarios might require more frequent prenatal visits?

Leifer

Slide 15

> **Routine Assessments at Each Prenatal Visit**
>
> · Risk factors: review known and assess for new
> · Vital signs and weight: determine if gain is normal
> · Urinalysis: protein, glucose, and ketone levels
> · Blood glucose screening
> · Fundal height: fetal growth/amniotic fluid volume
> · Leopold's maneuvers: assess presentation/position
> · Fetal heart rate
> · Nutrition intake
> · Any discomforts or problems since last visit

- Each care initiative performed must be accompanied by an explanation.
- The time spent during the physical examination and data collection provides an optimal opportunity for assessing the educational needs of the pregnant woman.
- What information should be provided to the patient concerning the urine collection completed at each visit?
- What questions will assist the nurse in obtaining the maximum amount of information during the data collection?
- What types of questions should be avoided?

Slide 16

> **Vaginal Discharge During Pregnancy**
>
> · Bacterial vaginosis is most common
>   – Caused by
>   · Decrease in lactobacilli
>   · Increase in bacteroids and other anaerobic microorganisms
>   · May be milky-white discharge
> · No other clinical symptoms may be present
> · Has been associated with preterm labor

- The hormonal changes of pregnancy promote changes in the vaginal environment.
- The hormonal changes could be associated with increased reports of discharge and the presence of vaginal infection.
- During the pregnancy, the woman must receive the needed educational tools concerning the appropriate signs and symptoms to report.

Slide 17

> **Safety Alert**
>
> Early and regular prenatal care is important for reducing the number of low birth weight infants born and for reducing morbidity and mortality for mothers and newborns

- How can nurses impact the number of low birthweight infants and the reduction of morbidity and mortality for mothers and newborns?

Slide 18

> **Terms Related to Pregnancy**
>
> · Gravida   · Multipara
> · Nulligravida   · Nullipara
> · Primigravida   · Abortion
> · Multigravida   · Gestational age
> · Para   · Fertilization age
> · Primipara   · Age of viability

- How are these terms used, and how do they need to be communicated to other members of the health care team?
- Provide a scenario to utilize these key terms.

Slide 19

Determining the Estimated Date of Delivery

- Average pregnancy is 40 weeks (280 days) after first day of LNMP, plus or minus 2 weeks
  - Nägele's rule
    - Identify first day of LNMP
    - Count backward 3 months
    - Add 7 days
    - Update year, if applicable

- See Box 4-2, page 48.
- The date of delivery will be determined by Nägele's Rule, which is calculated by subtracting 3 months and adding 7 days to the last normal menstrual period.

Audience Response Question #1

Determine EDD using Nägele's rule for a woman who's LMP began on June 7 and ended on June 12.
  1. March 14
  2. March 19
  3. March 5
  4. March 1

Slide 20

Trimesters

- Pregnancy divided into three 13-week parts
- Important to know what occurs during each trimester to both woman and fetus
- Helps provide anticipatory guidance
- Identify deviations from the expected pattern of development

- What are potential topics of interest to the pregnant woman for each trimester?

Slide 21

Presumptive Signs of Pregnancy

- Amenorrhea
- Nausea
- Breast tenderness
- Deepening pigmentation
- Urinary frequency
- Fatigue and drowsiness
- Quickening

- Presumptive signs of pregnancy are those which are frequently associated with pregnancy, but they could be attributed to many other phenomena as well.

Slide 22

Probable and Positive Signs of Pregnancy

Probable
- Goodell's sign
- Chadwick's sign
- Hegar's sign
- McDonald's sign
- Abdominal enlargement
- Braxton Hicks contractions
- Ballottement/fetal outline
- Abdominal striae
- Positive pregnancy test

Positive
- Audible fetal heartbeat
- Fetal movement felt by examiner
- Ultrasound visualization of fetus

- Probable signs are associated with pregnancy and can be evidenced by an examiner. Probable signs, like presumptive signs, can be associated with other situations.
- Positive signs can only be associated with the presence of pregnancy.

ELSEVIER

Leifer

Slide 23

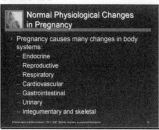

Normal Physiological Changes in Pregnancy

Pregnancy causes many changes in body systems:
- Endocrine
- Reproductive
- Respiratory
- Cardiovascular
- Gastrointestinal
- Urinary
- Integumentary and skeletal

Slide 24

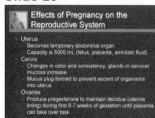

Effects of Pregnancy on the Endocrine System

- Dramatic increase in hormones affects all body systems
- Essential to maintain pregnancy
- Produced initially by the corpus luteum, later by the placenta
- Most striking change is addition of placenta as a temporary endocrine organ
- Primary role is to produce estrogen and progesterone to maintain pregnancy

Slide 25

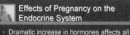

Effects of Pregnancy on the Reproductive System

- Uterus
  - Becomes temporary abdominal organ
  - Capacity is 5000 mL (fetus, placenta, amniotic fluid)
- Cervix
  - Changes in color and consistency, glands in cervical mucosa increase
  - Mucus plug formed to prevent ascent of organisms into uterus
- Ovaries
  - Produce progesterone to maintain decidua (uterine lining) during first 6-7 weeks of gestation until placenta can take over task

- The body undergoes numerous changes during pregnancy.
- These changes can be attributed to three factors: presence of estrogen, presence of progesterone, and growth of the fetus.

Slide 26

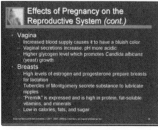

Effects of Pregnancy on the Reproductive System (cont.)

- Vagina
  - Increased blood supply causes it to have a bluish color
  - Vaginal secretions increase, pH more acidic
  - Higher glycogen level which promotes *Candida albicans* (yeast) growth
- Breasts
  - High levels of estrogen and progesterone prepare breasts for lactation
  - Tubercles of Montgomery secrete substance to lubricate nipples
  - "Premilk" is expressed and is high in protein, fat-soluble vitamins, and minerals
  - Low in calories, fats, and sugar

Slide 27

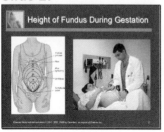

Height of Fundus During Gestation

- The height of the fundus will normally follow the milestones presented in the figure.
- What factors might be associated with a fundal height that does not match the gestational age? *Intrauterine growth restriction (IUGR), SGA, LGA, multiple gestation, and molar pregnancies*

Slide 28

Effects of Pregnancy on the Respiratory System

- Oxygen consumption increases by 15%
- Diaphragm rises ~4 cm (1.6 inches)
- Causes ribs to flare
- Dyspnea can occur until fetus descends into pelvis
- Increased estrogen causes edema or swelling of mucous membranes of nose, pharynx, mouth, and trachea
- Woman may complain of nasal stuffiness, epistaxis, and voice changes

Slide 29

Effects of Pregnancy on the Cardiovascular System

- Blood volume increases by ~45% than prepregnant state
- Increase provides for
  - Exchange of nutrients, oxygen, and waste products within the placenta
  - Needs of expanded maternal tissue
  - Reserve for blood loss at birth
- Pulse rate increases by 10 to 15 beats/min

- The increase in the circulatory volume will peak between 32 and 34 weeks gestation.
- There is a pulse rate increase during pregnancy.
- During early pregnancy, the woman frequently experiences a reduction in blood pressure. What factors can be attributed to this occurrence? *Reduced vascular resistance is responsible for the reduction in blood pressure.*

Slide 30

Supine Hypotension Syndrome

- Also called *aortocaval compression* or *vena cava syndrome*
- Occurs if woman lies flat on her back
  - Allows heavy uterus to compress inferior vena cava
  - Reduces blood returned to her heart
  - Can lead to fetal hypoxia
- Symptoms
  - Faintness
  - Lightheadedness
  - Dizziness
  - Agitation
- Turning to one side relieves pressure on inferior vena cava, preferably the left side

- The risk of supine hypotension will increase as the pregnancy advances.

Slide 31

Supine Hypotension Syndrome (cont.)

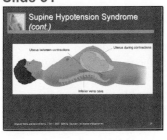

- How can positioning alleviate supine hypotension syndrome?

Slide 32

Effects of Pregnancy on the Cardiovascular System *(cont.)*

- Orthostatic hypotension
- Palpitations
- Dilutional anemia (a.k.a., pseudoanemia)
- Increased clotting factors in second and third trimesters
  - Increases risk of thrombophlebitis

- During pregnancy, the woman will normally experience orthostatic hypotension. What information should be provided to the patient concerning this condition and its management?
- Blood counts obtained in the first trimester often reflect a reduction in hemoglobin. What factors could cause this occurrence?

Audience Response Question #2
The nurse educating a pregnant woman in her last trimester, will encourage her to sleep on her side because:
  1. It will relieve bladder pressure
  2. Prevent hypotension
  3. Facilitate sleep
  4. Encourage fetal movement

Slide 33

Effects of Pregnancy on the Gastrointestinal System

- Growing uterus displaces stomach and intestines
- Increased salivary secretions
  - Oral mucosa may become tender and bleed more easily
- Appetite and thirst may increase
- Gastric acid secretions decrease
  - Delayed gastric emptying and intestinal movement
- Progesterone and estrogen relax muscle tone of gallbladder
  - Leads to retained bile salts
  - Can cause pruritus during pregnancy

- The effects of hormones of pregnancy on the gastrointestinal system can cause the expectant mother a great deal of distress.
- What types of manifestations experienced by the mother-to-be can be attributed to these factors?

Slide 34

Compression of Abdominal Contents as Uterus Enlarges

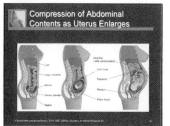

- Changes in the size of the enlarging uterus will cause the abdominal contents to shift.

Slide 35

Effects of Pregnancy on the Urinary System

- Excretes waste products of woman and fetus
  - Glomerular filtration rate of kidneys increases
  - Glycosuria and proteinuria more common
- Water retention due to increased blood volume and dissolving nutrients provided for fetus
- Progesterone causes renal pelvis and ureters to lose tone, leads to urinary stasis
- Woman more susceptible to UTIs
- 99% of sodium is reabsorbed, leads to fluid retention

- In the first and last trimester, the woman will experience frequent urination related to pressure by the uterus on the bladder.
- Additional changes in pregnancy respond to the needs of the growing fetus.
- As cardiac output and the volume of circulating blood increase, the kidneys also have an increase in workload. The kidneys work to filter this increased blood volume.
- As the body strives to keep up with the volume, the woman might "spill" glucose and protein into the urine.

ELSEVIER

Slide 36

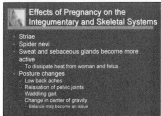

- Striae (stretch marks) will fade after the pregnancy, but they won't totally disappear.
- Safety education is vital to the pregnant woman. As balance changes and becomes affected, she might face difficulty with stairs and getting in and out of the bathtub.

Slide 37

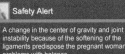

Slide 38

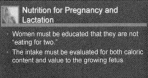

Slide 39

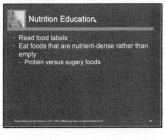

Slide 40

- Women are encouraged to increase their diet by 300 calories per day during pregnancy.
- See Figure 4-7, page 56 for explanation on how to interpret the pyramid.

Leifer

Slide 41

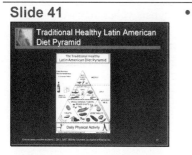

- Although the chart lists alcohol on the food pyramid, it is not recommended in pregnancy.

Slide 42

Maternal Diet and Fetal Health

- High correlation between maternal diet and fetal health
- Ensure that deficiencies do not occur during the critical first weeks of pregnancy
- The nurse explains the value of eating well-balanced meals

Slide 43

Weight Gain

- Women of normal weight: 25 to 35 pounds (11.5 to 16 kg)
- Obese women: 11 to 20 pounds (5 to 9 kg)
- Overweight women: 31 to 50 pounds (14 to 22.7 kg)
- Multifetal pregnancy: twins—woman should gain 4 to 6 pounds in first trimester, 1½ pounds per week in second and third trimesters, for a total of 37 to 54 pounds

- The weight gain of a woman during pregnancy is closely tied to her prepregnant status.
- Women who are overweight are discouraged from dieting but are encouraged to carefully monitor their diets.

Slide 44

Nutrition Requirements for Pregnant Women

- Increase kCal by 300 per day, and should include
  - Protein—60 g/day
  - Calcium—1200 mg/day
  - Iron—30 mg/day
  - Folic acid—400 mcg (0.4mg)/day

- Fluid intake should also increase by 8 to 10 ounces of fluid per day, with water being the primary source.
- Non-water sources of fluid are often sources of empty calories and warrant close evaluation.
- Low weight gain in pregnancy is associated with preterm labor.

Slide 45

RDA/RDI

- No need to provide nutrients in excess of the upper limits of the recommended dietary allowance (RDA)
  - The combination of supplements and food fortification must not exceed present upper limits of safety or adverse responses, such as toxicity, can occur
- Recommended dietary intake (RDI) is an umbrella term that includes the RDA and upper levels of intake

Slide 46

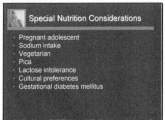

- The pregnant adolescent is often faced with concerns about body image. Education is needed to ensure she is aware of her nutritional responsibilities to the fetus. When evaluating nutritional needs of the pregnant adolescent, gynecological age must be reviewed. Gynecological age refers to the number of years between the onset of menses and the date of conception.
- Which pregnant adolescent will have the greatest nutritional needs? The shorter the gynecological age, the greater the nutritional needs.
- Although sodium intake is not totally restricted, it should be carefully considered. Identify high sodium "diet pitfalls."
- Discuss the unique concerns of vegans and methods that can be used to meet their dietary needs.
- Pica is a condition in which a woman eats nonfood substances. Potential sources of intake include dirt, mud, starch, and chalk.

Slide 47

Slide 48

- Women who have been exercising prior to the pregnancy are the best candidates for continuing in an approved exercise regimen.

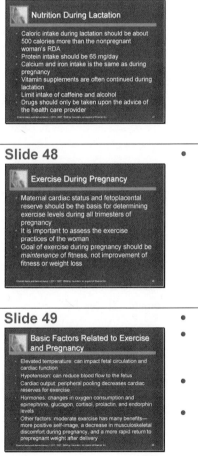

Slide 49

- The maternal temperature should not exceed 100.4° F.
- What activities are restricted in pregnancy due to their potential to elevate the mother's body temperature? *Hot tubs and saunas are to be avoided.*
- Maternal exposure to elevated temperatures during the pregnancy has been associated with miscarriage and neural tube defects.
- Safety concerns mandate the type of exercise recommended for pregnancy. Certain positions can cause supine hypotension syndrome or promote orthostatic hypotension. What activities could be associated with these concerns?
- During pregnancy, the length of continuous time spent exercising must be evaluated. Prolonged exercise sends an elevated amount of blood to the skeletal muscles. What impact does this have on the pregnancy? *This increase will reduce the amount of blood being circulated to the uterus.*

Leifer

Slide 50

Nursing Guidance for Exercise

- Start with a warm-up and end with a cool-down
- Do not exceed American College of Obstetricians and Gynecologists (ACOG) recommendations for moderate exercise
- Combined with balanced diet is beneficial
- Eating 2 to 3 hours before exercise or immediately after is recommended
- Avoid marked changes in depth of water (such as scuba diving) and/or altitude
- Avoid becoming overheated; increase fluid intake
- Intensity of exercise should be modified based on the "talk test"

Slide 51

Travel During Pregnancy

- Air travel generally safe
- Avoid sitting for extended periods of time
- Avoid locations that increase the risk of exposure to infectious diseases
- Bring a copy of obstetric records
- Obtain information about nearest health care facility
- Encourage hand hygiene and dietary precautions
- Provide the "recipe" for oral rehydration formula

- Travel is safest during the second trimester. What factors about this phase make it the better one for travel?
- What risks and discomforts are present in each trimester that will impact travel plans and safety?

Slide 52

Common Discomforts in Pregnancy

- Fatigue
- Nasal stuffiness
- Nausea
- Heartburn
- Constipation
- Hemorrhoids
- Vaginal discharge
- Backache
- Varicose veins
- Leg cramps
- Edema of the lower extremities

- What nonpharmacological methods can help manage these discomforts?

Slide 53

Psychological Adaptations to Pregnancy

- Identifying and managing psychosocial problems is essential to the positive outcome of pregnancy
- Nutritional needs and patterns relating to age, ethnicity, or financial constraints should be discussed

- Pregnancy is a time of stress and change for both the pregnant woman and her family. Close observation and early intervention are vital to the prevention of problems.
- The needs and concerns of each pregnant woman will vary by demographics.

Slide 54

Impact on Mother

- According to Reva Rubin, four maternal tasks the woman accomplishes during pregnancy include
  - Seeing safe passage for herself and her fetus
  - Securing acceptance of herself as a mother and for her fetus
  - Learning to give of self and to receive the care and concern of others
  - Committing herself to the child as she progresses through pregnancy

Slide 55

Development Stage of Fatherhood

- Announcement when pregnancy is confirmed
  - Acceptance results in strengthening of family
- Adjustment
- Focus
  - Active plans for participation in labor, birth process

Slide 56

Impact on the Father

- Cultural values influence the role of fathers because pregnancy and birth are viewed exclusively as women's work in some cultures
- The nurse should not assume that a father is uninterested if he takes a less active role in pregnancy and birth
- Acceptance of the pregnancy results in strengthening of the family support system and expansion of the social network

- How has the role of the father changed over the past few decades?
- Why has the role of the father changed in the past few decades?
- Would you share personal stories about your own delivery experiences and the role of the baby's father?

Slide 57

Impact on the Adolescent

- The nurse must assess the girl's developmental and educational level as well as her support system to best provide care for her
- Consider her developmental level and the priorities typical of her age
- Must cope with two of life's most stress-laden transitions at the same time: adolescence and parenthood

- Adolescence is a time of change and adjustment. The pregnant adolescent faces multiple hurdles as she transitions both developmentally and during pregnancy.
- What potential concerns will most likely be experienced by the pregnant adolescent?

Audience Response Question #3

What would be the first priority in working with the pregnant adolescent?
1. Obtain substance abuse history.
2. Assess her attitude toward pregnancy.
3. Determine maturational level.
4. Establish a trusting relationship.

Slide 58

Impact on the Older Couple

- Tend to adjust to the pregnancy because they are well-educated, have achieved life experiences that enable them to better cope with realities of parenthood

- The "older couple" includes a first-time mother who is 35 years of age or older.
- Despite their positive adaptation related to the realities of parenthood, older couples might have unique concerns. Frequently older parents are faced with being chronologically the oldest in their peer group. They might have additional health concerns and needs. Their established peer group might have different goals and activities that do not match well with a couple having a baby.

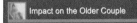

Slide 59

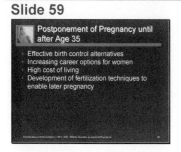

Postponement of Pregnancy until after Age 35

- Effective birth control alternatives
- Increasing career options for women
- High cost of living
- Development of fertilization techniques to enable later pregnancy

Slide 60

Impact on the Single Mother

- May be an adolescent or a mature woman
- May have unique emotional needs
- Single women who plan pregnancies often prepare for the financial and lifestyle changes

- The single mother must be approached in a nonjudgmental manner by the nurse.
- The role of the father with this baby must be considered in an individual manner, and the nurse must never make assumptions.

Slide 61

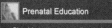

Impact on the Single Father

- May take an active interest in and financial responsibility for the child
- May want to participate in plans for the child and take part in the care of the infant after it is born
- His participation is sometimes rejected by the woman

- How should the nurse approach the single father?
- What rules will govern his involvement in the pregnancy and delivery?

Slide 62

Impact on the Grandparents

- May eagerly anticipate the woman's pregnancy
- Some will take a more active role in the care of the grandchild
- If grandparents and expectant couple have similar views of their roles, little conflict is likely
- The nurse may be able to help the new parents to understand their own parents' reactions and help them to negotiate solutions to conflicts that are satisfactory to both generations

Slide 63

Prenatal Education

- Should progress according to the nursing process:
  - *Assess* the history and cultural needs
  - *Diagnose* the knowledge deficit
  - *Plan* the goals and priorities
  - *Outcomes identification* clarifies expected outcomes
  - *Teach* (intervene) the facts and rationales
  - *Evaluate* knowledge gained and goals achieved

ELSEVIER

Introduction to Maternity & Pediatric Nursing, 6th ed.

Leifer

Slide 64

Changes in Pregnancy and Nursing Interventions

- Maternal changes
- Signs and symptoms to anticipate
- Nursing interventions that can be implemented to help the mother cope with the changes throughout her pregnancy

- See Table 4-6, pages 73-75.

Slide 65

The Effect of Pregnancy and Lactation on Medication Ingestion

- Pregnancy affects the metabolism of medications
- May have subtherapeutic levels
- Parenteral medications may be absorbed more rapidly due to increased cardiac output
- Drugs can cross the placenta, can be passed through breast milk

- The changes in drug metabolism during pregnancy require each mother to report to her health care provider all medications being taken. This accounting must include both prescription and over-the-counter medications.
- Discuss the impact of hormones on medication response.

Slide 66

FDA Pregnancy Risk Category for Drugs

- Category A: no risk demonstrated to the fetus in any trimester
- Category B: no adverse effects in animals; no human studies available
- Category C: Only prescribed after risks to the fetus are considered. Animal studies have shown adverse reaction; no human studies available
- Category D: Definite fetal risks, but may be given in spite of risks in life-threatening situations
- Category X: Absolute fetal abnormalities. Not to be used anytime during pregnancy

- When administering medications to the pregnant patient, these categories must be taken into consideration.
- What actions should be taken by the nurse when adverse reactions in pregnancy are associated with a prescribed medication?

Slide 67

Immunizations and Pregnancy

- Live virus vaccines are contraindicated during pregnancy
- Thimerosal should not be given during pregnancy due to risk of mercury poisoning
- Avoid pregnancy for at least 1 month after receiving an MMR vaccine
- Select immunizations are allowable during pregnancy, such as influenza vaccine and H1N1 vaccine

Slide 68

Question for Review

- What nutritional supplement taken early in pregnancy can reduce the incidence of neural tube defects, such as spina bifida?

- Folic acid can be taken during pregnancy to reduce the incidence of neural tube defects.
- What foods can be included in the diet to improve this nutrient's presence in the body?

Introduction to Maternity & Pediatric Nursing, 6th ed.

Leifer

Slide 69

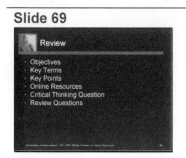

5 Nursing Care of Women with Complications During Pregnancy

TEACHING FOCUS

In this chapter, students will have the opportunity to learn about the skills required to provide care to women who have complications during pregnancy such as hyperemesis gravidarum, bleeding disorders, infection, hypertension, and blood incompatibility. Students will also have the opportunity to learn how to develop care plans and teaching plans for mothers with pregnancies complicated by medical conditions, as well as how to help women and their families cope with complications, trauma, and high-risk pregnancies.

MATERIALS AND RESOURCES

☐ Computer and PowerPoint projector (all lessons)

LESSON CHECKLIST

Preparations for this lesson include:

- Lecture
- Guest speaker: Emergency department nurse and maternity nurse
- Evaluation of student knowledge and skills needed to perform all entry-level activities related to nursing care of women with complications during pregnancy, including:
  ○ Providing care to women with complications during pregnancy such as bleeding disorders, hypertension, diabetes mellitus, and infections
  ○ Developing nursing care and teaching plans for women with complications of pregnancy
  ○ Helping women and their families cope with complications, trauma, and the potential loss of the fetus

KEY TERMS

abortion (p. 82)
cerclage (p. 82)
disseminated intravascular
   coagulation (DIC)
   (p. 90)
eclampsia (p. 91)

erythroblastosis fetalis
   (p. 96)
gestational diabetes
   mellitus (p. 97)
hydramnios (p. 97)
incompetent cervix (p. 82)
isoimmunization (p. 96)

macrosomia (p. 98)
preeclampsia (p. 91)
products of conception
   (POC) (p. 86)
teratogen (p. 107)
tonic-clonic seizure (p. 92)

ADDITIONAL RESOURCES

TEACH PPT slide(s) Chapter 5, 1-81
EILR IC image(s) Chapter 5, 1-9
EILR OBQ question(s) Chapter 5, 1-10
EILR TB question(s) Chapter 5, 1-32
ESLR IRQ question(s) Chapter 5, 1-5
SG Chapter 5, pp. 29-41

Legend

		e	SG	!
PPT TEACH PowerPoint Slides	**EILR** EVOLVE Instructor Learning Resources: Image Collection (IC), Open-Book Quizzes (OBQ), Test Bank (TB)	**ESLR** EVOLVE Student Learning Resources: Interactive Review Questions (IRQ) for the NCLEX® Examination	**SG** Study Guide	**CTQ** Critical Thinking Question in Nursing Care Plan (NCP CTQ) or Get Ready for the NCLEX! (GRN CTQ)

Class Activities are indicated in ***bold italic***.

LESSON 5.1

PRETEST

1. Which of the following is a danger sign during pregnancy and should be reported to a health care provider immediately?
   a. constipation
   b. dizziness
   c. breast changes
   d. frequent urination

2. Which of the following statements reflects effective and therapeutic communication skills for a family experiencing pregnancy loss?
   a. "I'm here if you need to talk."
   b. "You can always have more children."
   c. "I know how you feel."
   d. "It was for the best."

3. Which drug is sometimes given to women with gestational hypertension to prevent seizures?
   a. lidocaine
   b. calcium chloride
   c. Verapamil
   d. magnesium sulfate

4. Which of the following is a maternal effect of diabetes mellitus in pregnancy?
   a. dehydration
   b. anemia
   c. vaginitis
   d. preeclampsia

5. Nutritional anemias during pregnancy can be caused by a lack of
   a. zinc.
   b. folic acid.
   c. vitamin C.
   d. vitamin K.

6. Signs of hydatidiform mole can resemble those associated with
   a. hyperemesis gravidarum.
   b. nutritional anemias.
   c. blood incompatibility.
   d. diabetes mellitus.

7. Which symptom distinguishes abruptio placentae from placenta previa?
   a. urinary tract infection
   b. edema
   c. weak pulse
   d. pain

8. Development of the fetus outside the uterus occurs in
   a. multifetal pregnancy.
   b. ectopic pregnancy.
   c. hydatidiform mole.
   d. gestational diabetes.

9. TORCH is an acronym used to describe
   a. risk factors that are associated with trauma during pregnancy.
   b. treatments for hypovolemic shock.
   c. infections that can be devastating for the fetus or newborn.
   d. different types of nutritional anemias.

10. Why is the incidence of trauma during pregnancy rising?
    a. Women are increasingly employed during pregnancy.
    b. Terrorist attacks are occurring more frequently.
    c. More women are concerned with gaining weight.
    d. Numbers of single mothers are increasing.

Answers

1. b	3. d	5. b	7. d	9. c
2. a	4. c	6. a	8. b	10. a

BACKGROUND ASSESSMENT

Question: What is gestational hypertension (GH), and who is at risk for developing it?

Answer: GH occurs when a woman develops hypertension (blood pressure over 140/90 mm Hg) during pregnancy when she did not have the condition prior to pregnancy. This disorder was formerly called *toxemia*. The disorder usually develops after 20 weeks gestation, and although the cause is unknown, several risk factors are associated with GH. These factors are first pregnancy, obesity, family history of GH, women over 40 or under 19 years of age, multifetal pregnancy, chronic hypertension, chronic renal disease, and diabetes mellitus. GH resolves after delivery.

Leifer

Question: A pregnant woman is having lower abdominal pain, light vaginal bleeding, and has a history of endometriosis. What could these symptoms indicate, and how does this condition occur?

Answer: These symptoms are indicative of an ectopic pregnancy. Ectopic pregnancy occurs when a fertilized ovum is implanted outside the uterus, usually in the fallopian tube, due to an obstruction or abnormality that prevents the zygote from implanting in the uterus. This may cause the fallopian tube to rupture and bleed into the abdominal cavity. Vaginal bleeding may be minimal because most of the blood is lost in the abdomen, rather than through the vagina. Sudden severe lower abdominal pain and signs of hypovolemic shock are also indications of ectopic pregnancy. Any of these symptoms should be reported to the physician for immediate treatment.

CRITICAL THINKING QUESTION

A woman in her first trimester has been told by her physician that she should undergo amniocentesis. When the physician leaves the room, however, the woman still has questions. How could the nurse clearly explain the reason for the procedure and how it is performed?

Guidelines: The nurse should explain that amniocentesis is a prenatal test used to assess the health and status of the fetus. In early pregnancy it is used to identify chromosomal abnormalities and genetic and biochemical disorders. It is also used in late pregnancy to determine and assess maternal-fetal blood incompatibility and fetal lung maturity. Although it is not possible to test for every potential disorder, amniocentesis provides assessment of many of the most common disorders. Amniocentesis is performed by inserting a thin needle through the abdominal and uterine walls into the placental cavity in order to draw out a sample of amniotic fluid. The nurse should assure the woman that amniocentesis is a common procedure and that it is relatively painless. It is also important to mention, however, that there can be a risk of spontaneous abortion following the procedure.

OBJECTIVES	CONTENT	TEACHING RESOURCES
Explain the use of fetal diagnostic tests in women with complicated pregnancies.	■ Assessment of fetal health (p. 79)	PPT slides 4-8
		e EILR IC image 1
		e EILR OBQ question 1
		SG Learning Activities, question 10 (p. 32)
		SG Review Questions, question 2 (p. 38)
		SG Case Study, question 1 (p. 40)
		BOOK RESOURCES
		Patient Teaching, Danger Signs in-Pregnancy (p. 78)
		Figure 5-1, Amniocentesis (p. 79)
		Table 5-1, Fetal Diagnostic Tests (pp. 80-82)
		Table 5-10, Noninvasive Technologies in Prenatal Care (p. 113)
		▸ Discuss why it is important for nurses to be familiar with prenatal tests.
		▸ Discuss the various prenatal tests. Which are routine, and which are not?
		Class Activity Divide the class into four groups and assign each group one of the following fetal diagnostic tests: amniocentesis, umbilical cord blood sampling,

OBJECTIVES	CONTENT	TEACHING RESOURCES
		ultrasound, and biophysical profile (BPP). Have each group describe how and why the test is performed and what conditions it detects, and develop a plan for explaining the test to a pregnant woman. Have groups share their findings with the class.
Identify methods to reduce a woman's risk for antepartum complications.	■ Assessment of fetal health (p. 79)	*e* EILR IC image 1 **SG** SG Review Questions, question 2 (p. 38) **BOOK RESOURCES** Figure 5-1, Amniocentesis (p. 79) Table 5-1, Fetal Diagnostic Tests (pp. 80-82) ▶ Discuss factors that increase a woman's risk for antepartum complications. How can these risks be reduced? *Class Activity **In small groups, have students discuss how diet, lifestyle, and prenatal visits can reduce a woman's risk of antepartum complications. Have each group make a teaching plan for a pregnant woman to help avoid complications. Present the plans to the class.*****

Describe antepartum complications, their treatment, and their nursing care.	■ Pregnancy-related complications (p. 79)
	
	☐ Hyperemesis gravidarum (p. 79)
	
	☐ Bleeding disorders of early pregnancy (p. 82)
	
	   – Abortion (p. 82)
	
	   – Ectopic pregnancy (p. 85)
	
	   – Hydatidiform mole (p. 87)
	
	☐ Bleeding disorders of late pregnancy (p. 88)
	
	   – Placenta previa (p. 89)
	
	   – Abruptio placentae (p. 90)
		PPT slides 9-28
		
		e EILR IC images 2-5
		
		e EILR OBQ questions 2-5
		
		e EILR TB questions 1-6, 20, 23, 30, 32
		
		e ESLR IRQ question 4
		
		SG SG Learning Activities, questions 1-9 (p. 29)
		
		SG SG Review Questions, questions 6-11 (pp. 38-39)
		
		SG SG Case Study, question 1 (p. 40)
		
		SG SG Thinking Critically, question 3 (p. 40)
		
		BOOK RESOURCES
		
		Figure 5-2, Three Types of Spontaneous Abortion (p. 83)
		
		Table 5-2, Types of Abortions (p. 83)
		
		Table 5-3, Procedures Used in Pregnancy Termination (p. 84)
		
		Communication, The Family Experiencing Pregnancy Loss (p. 85)
		
		Box 5-1, Signs and Symptoms of Hypovolemic Shock (p. 85)

OBJECTIVES	CONTENT	TEACHING RESOURCES
		Nursing Care Plan 5-1, The Family Experiencing Early Pregnancy Loss (p. 86)
		Figure 5-3, The uterus and fallopian tubes, illustrating various abnormal implantation sites (p. 87)
		Figure 5-4, A Hydatidiform Mole (Gestational Trophoblastic Disease) (p. 87)
		Nursing Tip (p. 88)
		Table 5-4, Comparison of Placenta Previa and Abruptio Placentae (p. 88)
		Figure 5-5, A, Placenta Previa. B, Abruptio Placentae (p. 89)
		Nursing Tip (p. 90)
		Box 5-2, Care of the Pregnant Woman with Excessive Bleeding (p. 90)
		Review Questions for the NCLEX® Examination, questions 1-4 (p. 114)
		▶ Discuss effective communication strategies for the nurse in discussing pregnancy complications and loss with the woman and the woman's family.
		▶ Discuss ways the nurse can encourage the woman to report danger signs during pregnancy to the health care provider.
		Class Activity Divide the class into pairs and assign each pair one of the following antepartum complications: hyperemesis gravidarum, abortion, ectopic pregnancy, hydatidiform mole, placenta previa, and abruptio placentae. Have each pair role-play a nurse-patient interaction in which the woman presents with signs and symptoms of the assigned complication and the nurse outlines the treatment plan. Pairs should avoid mentioning the name of the complication during the role-play. Have the rest of the class determine which condition each pair is presenting.
		Class Activity Write two columns on the board, one for placenta previa and one for abruptio placentae. Have the class place signs and symptoms in the correct columns as they pertain to each of the conditions, in terms of bleeding, pain, clotting, fetal presentation, uterine consistency, and complications.
		Class Activity Divide the class into small groups. Have each group discuss therapeutic communication skills for

OBJECTIVES	CONTENT	TEACHING RESOURCES
		a family experiencing a pregnancy loss due to an ectopic pregnancy or molar pregnancy. Have the students consider how they would like to be treated if they had a pregnancy loss.

5.1 Homework/Assignments:

5.1 Instructor's Notes/Student Feedback:

CRITICAL THINKING QUESTION

A 33-year-old woman who was 40 lbs. overweight before pregnancy and has a grandfather with diabetes mellitus has developed gestational diabetes. She asks the nurse how she developed this condition, because she was healthy before pregnancy and has had an uneventful pregnancy thus far. How could the nurse explain this condition to the woman?

Guidelines: The nurse should explain that gestational diabetes mellitus (GDM) is common in pregnancy and usually resolves after birth. It often occurs during pregnancy in women who do not have a previous history of diabetes (DM). Because of the added stress on a woman's metabolism that occurs with pregnancy, insulin production increases in order to maintain normal metabolism in the mother and to provide adequate glucose for the fetus. Some women, however, are unable to produce the extra insulin required, which results in GDM. There are also several risk factors associated with GDM such as maternal obesity, macrosomia, mothers over 25 years old, previous unexplained stillbirth or an infant with congenital abnormalities, history of GDM, and family history of DM. The woman's weight, family history, and age all probably contributed to her condition. The nurse should explain that GDM usually resolves after the baby is born, but in some cases women with GDM may later develop overt diabetes mellitus.

OBJECTIVES	CONTENT	TEACHING RESOURCES
Describe antepartum complications, their treatment, and their nursing care.	□ Hypertension during pregnancy (p. 90) □ Manifestations of gestational hypertension (p. 91) – Hypertension (p. 91) – Edema (p. 92) – Proteinuria (p. 92) – Other manifestations of preeclampsia (p. 92) – Central nervous system (p. 92) – Eyes (p. 92) – Urinary tract (p. 92) – Respiratory system (p. 92) – Gastrointestinal system and liver (p. 92) – Blood clotting (p. 92) – Eclampsia (p. 92) – Effects on fetus (p. 92) – Treatment (p. 92)	⊠▪ PPT slides 29-39 𝓮 EILR IC image 6 𝓮 EILR OBQ question 6 𝓮 EILR TB questions 7-8, 14-19 𝓮 ESLR IRQ questions 1-3, 5 SG Learning Activities, questions 11-17 (pp. 32-34) SG Review Questions, question 12 (p. 39) SG Case Study, question 1 (p. 40) SG Thinking Critically, question 2 (p. 40) SG Applying Knowledge, questions 2, 3 (p. 41) **BOOK RESOURCES** Table 5-5, Hypertensive Disorders of Pregnancy (p. 91) Box 5-3, Risk Factors for Gestational Hypertension (p. 91) Table 5-6, Laboratory Tests for Patients with Gestational Hypertension (p. 92) Home Care Considerations, Hypertension in Pregnancy (p. 93) Nursing Care Plan 5-2, The Woman with Gestational Hypertension (p. 95) Nursing Tip (p. 96) Figure 5-6, Erythroblastosis Fetalis (p. 96)

OBJECTIVES	CONTENT	TEACHING RESOURCES
	– Drug therapy (p. 93) ☐ Promoting prenatal care (p. 94) ☐ Caring for the acutely ill women (p. 94) ☐ Blood incompatibility between the pregnant woman and the fetus (p. 94) – Rh and ABO incompatibility (p. 96)	▸ Discuss the different types of hypertension as they relate to pregnancy. What are the risks to the mother and fetus? ▸ Discuss the risks to a woman and her fetus in ABO incompatibility. *Class Activity* **Divide the class into six groups and assign each group one of the following hypertensive disorders of pregnancy: GH, preeclampsia, eclampsia, HELLP, chronic hypertension, and transient gestational hypertension. Have each group outline what causes the condition, and identify the signs and symptoms and treatments for each condition. Have groups present their findings to the class for discussion.** *Class Activity* **Present the following scenario to the class for discussion: A woman in her third trimester has just been told by the physician that her blood may be incompatible with her fetus's blood. Have students discuss simple ways for the nurse to explain Rh and ABO incompatibility to the woman so that she can understand these complex concepts. Then have students identify and discuss the assessments and treatments for this condition.**
Discuss the management of concurrent medical conditions during pregnancy.	■ Pregnancy complicated by medical conditions (p. 97) ☐ Diabetes mellitus (p. 97) – Pathophysiology (p. 97) – Effect of pregnancy on glucose metabolism (p. 97) – Preexisting diabetes mellitus (p. 97) – Gestational diabetes mellitus (p. 98) – Treatment (p. 98) – Nursing care (p. 101) ☐ Heart disease (p. 101) ☐ Anemia (p. 102) – Nutritional anemias (p. 103) – Iron deficiency anemia (p. 103)	▣ PPT slides 40-74 𝑒 EILR IC image 7 𝑒 EILR OBQ questions 7-9 𝑒 EILR TB questions 9-12, 21-22, 24-26, 29 📖 SG Learning Activities, questions 18-37 (pp. 34-36) 📖 SG Review Questions, questions 1, 3-5, 13-16 (pp. 38-40) 📖 SG Case Study, questions 1b, 1c (p. 40) 📖 SG Thinking Critically, question 4 (p. 40) 📖 SG Applying Knowledge, question 4 (p. 41) **BOOK RESOURCES** Box 5-4, Effects of Diabetes in Pregnancy (p. 97) Figure 5-7, Macrosomic Infant (p. 98) Table 5-7, Comparison of Hypoglycemia and Hyperglycemia in the Diabetic Woman (p. 98) Nursing Care Plan 5-3, The Pregnant Woman with Gestational Diabetes Mellitus (pp. 99-100)

Leifer

OBJECTIVES	CONTENT	TEACHING RESOURCES
	– Genetic anemias (p. 103)	NCP CTQ 1, 2 (p. 100)
	– Nursing care for anemias during pregnancy (p. 103)	Box 5-5, Signs of Congestive Heart Failure During Pregnancy (p. 102)
	□ Infections (p. 104)	Safety Alert (p. 102)
	– Viral infections (p. 104)	Nutritional Considerations, Foods Recommended in Pregnancy (p. 104)
	– Nonviral infections (p. 106)	Nursing Tip (p. 104)
	– Sexually transmitted diseases (p. 107)	Box 5-6, Persons at Higher Risk for Hepatitis B Infection (p. 105)
	– Urinary tract infections (p. 107)	Box 5-7, High-Risk Factors for Human Immunodeficiency Virus (HIV) (p. 105)
		Safety Alert (p. 106)
		▸ Discuss the maternal and fetal complications associated with diabetes mellitus and anemia during pregnancy.
		*Class Activity **Provide students with descriptions of interventions and treatments for preexisting DM, GDM, heart disease, anemia, viral and nonviral infections, and UTIs. Have students match each intervention with its corresponding condition, then discuss the symptoms and nursing care for each.***
		*Class Activity **Present the following scenario to the class for discussion: A woman in her first trimester says that she frequently gets cold sores around her mouth and that she is worried that they might affect her baby. Which type of infection is this? How does it affect pregnancy, and what are the treatments?***

5.2 Homework/Assignments:

5.2 Instructor's Notes/Student Feedback:

LESSON 5.3

CRITICAL THINKING QUESTION

A woman's pregnancy is considered high risk. What are some of the challenges and stressors with which she and her family must cope?

Guidelines: High-risk pregnancies have stressors beyond those of a normal pregnancy. These stressors include the potential need for bed rest, an extended period of time off from work (if she is employed), a resulting reduction in income, an increase in medical care expenditures, problems with finances, and a potential change in family dynamics. If a high-risk mother requires periods of bed rest, this may affect roles within the household as well as interfere with care for any other children. Concern and worry about the outcome of the pregnancy as well as financial issues can infiltrate and disrupt the family system. In addition, the mother may withdraw emotionally because of uncertainty about the outcome of the pregnancy.

OBJECTIVES	CONTENT	TEACHING RESOURCES
Describe environmental hazards that may adversely affect the outcome of pregnancy.	■ Environmental hazards during pregnancy (p. 107) □ Bioterrorism and the pregnant patient (p. 108) □ Substance abuse (p. 108) – Treatment and nursing care (p. 109)	▣▦ PPT slide 75 𝑒 EILR IC image 8 𝑒 EILR TB questions 13, 31 🅂🄶 SG Learning Activities, questions 38-41 (pp. 36-37) **BOOK RESOURCES** Box 5-8, Precautions Required for Common Bioterrorist Agents (p. 108) Figure 5-8, Fetal Alcohol Syndrome (p. 109) Nursing Tips (p. 109) Table 5-9, Substances Harmful to the Fetus (p. 110) ▸ Discuss the three categories of biological agents that can have an impact on pregnancy. ▸ Discuss alcohol abuse during pregnancy. What is the prognosis for infants born with fetal alcohol syndrome? *Class Activity **Present the following scenario to the class for discussion: A nurse suspects that a woman in her second trimester is abusing alcohol and possibly other drugs. The woman denies it. How should the nurse handle this situation?*** *Class Activity **Divide the class into small groups and assign each group a category of drugs or teratogens (antiinflammatory, antibiotics, anticonvulsants, etc.). Have each group list common drugs in the category, what the drugs are used to treat, their potential for abuse, and their effects on pregnancy. Have each group share its findings with the class.***
Describe how pregnancy affects care of the trauma victim.	□ Trauma during pregnancy (p. 109) – Manifestations of battering (p. 111)	▣▦ PPT slides 76, 77 𝑒 EILR OBQ question 10 🅂🄶 SG Learning Activities, question 3 (p. 37)

OBJECTIVES	CONTENT	TEACHING RESOURCES
	– Treatment and nursing care of the pregnant woman experiencing trauma (p. 111)	**SG** SG Review Questions, question 17 (p. 40) **BOOK RESOURCES** Safety Alert (p. 111) Box 5-8, Modification of Standard CPR for Pregnant Women (p. 111) Review Questions for the NCLEX® Examination, question 5 (p. 114) Appendix A (p. 771) ▸ Discuss the manifestations of battering and how a nurse could recognize signs of abuse. *Class Activity Present the following scenario to the class for discussion:* *A woman arrives at her fourth prenatal visit with visible bruising on her extremities, old and new lacerations, and a limp. She says that she slipped on the ice, but the nurse remembers that at her previous visit she claimed to be recovering from a fall down the stairs that resulted in similar injuries. The nurse is beginning to suspect abuse.* *Have students discuss how the nurse should approach this situation. How should the woman be assessed for abuse? How should the nurse approach the topic of abuse, and how could the mother be encouraged to leave the situation?*
Describe psychosocial nursing interventions for the woman who has a high-risk pregnancy and for her family.	■ Effects of a high-risk pregnancy on the family (p. 112) □ Disruption of usual roles (p. 112) □ Financial difficulties (p. 112) □ Delayed attachment to the infant (p. 112) □ Loss of expected birth experience (p. 112)	PPT slides 78, 79 *e* EILR IC image 9 *e* EILR TB questions 27, 28 **BOOK RESOURCES** Figure 5-9, Memory Kit (p. 112) Table 5-10, Noninvasive Technology in Prenatal Care (p. 113) ▸ Discuss some of the effects of a high-risk pregnancy on a family. *Class Activity Present the following scenario to the class: A mother with a high-risk pregnancy is concerned about the effect it will have on her relationships with her spouse and children as well as the financial burden. Divide the class into groups and have each make a plan to help the mother cope with these anxieties and then present its plan to the class for discussion.*

Leifer

OBJECTIVES	CONTENT	TEACHING RESOURCES
Performance Evaluation		PPT slides 1-81
		e EILR IC images 1-9
		e EILR OBQ questions 1-10
		e EILR TB questions 1-32
		e ESLR IRQ questions 1-5
		SG Learning Activities, questions 1-43 (pp. 29-37)
		SG Review Questions, questions 1-17 (pp. 38-40)
		SG Case Study, question 1 (p. 40)
		SG Thinking Critically, questions 1-3 (p. 40)
		SG Applying Knowledge, questions 1-4 (p. 41)
		BOOK RESOURCES
		NCP CTQ 1, 2 (p. 86)
		NCP CTQ 1, 2 (p. 95)
		NCP CTQ 1, 2 (p. 100)
		Review Questions for the NCLEX® Examination, questions 1-5 (p. 114)

5.3 Homework/Assignments:

5.3 Instructor's Notes/Student Feedback:

Lecture Outline

5 Nursing Care of Women with Complications During Pregnancy

Slide 1

Chapter 5

Nursing Care of Women with
Complications During Pregnancy

Slide 2

Objectives

- Explain the use of fetal diagnostic tests in women with complicated pregnancies.
- Describe antepartum complications, their treatment, and their nursing care.
- Identify methods to reduce a woman's risk for antepartum complications.
- Discuss the management of concurrent medical conditions during pregnancy.

Slide 3

Objectives *(cont.)*

- Describe environmental hazards that may adversely affect the outcome of pregnancy.
- Describe how pregnancy affects care of the trauma victim.
- Describe psychosocial nursing interventions for the women who has a high-risk pregnancy and for her family.

Slide 4

Characteristic Causes of High-Risk Pregnancies

- Can relate to the pregnancy itself
- Can occur because the woman has a medical condition or injury that complicates the pregnancy
- Can result from environmental hazards that affect the mother or her fetus
- Can arise from maternal behaviors or lifestyles that have a negative effect on the mother or fetus

Slide 5

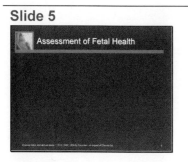

Slide 6

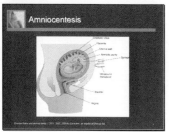

- Amniocentesis is vital in the diagnosis of fetal anomalies.

Slide 7

Nursing Responsibilities

- Preparing the patient properly
- Explaining the reason for the test
- Clarifying and interpreting results in collaboration with other health care providers

- The role of the nurse in the care of the pregnant woman experiencing potential complications of pregnancy is vital.
- What are other responsibilities of the nurse? Discuss the need to provide emotional support.

Slide 8

Danger Signs in Pregnancy

- Sudden gush of fluid from the vagina
- Vaginal bleeding
- Abdominal pain
- Persistent vomiting
- Epigastric pain
- Edema of face and hands
- Severe, persistent headache
- Blurred vision or dizziness
- Chills with fever over 38.0° C (100.4° F)
- Painful urination or reduced urine output

- During the first prenatal care visit, the patient should be advised of the danger signs in pregnancy.
- What can each of these manifestations signal?

Slide 9

Pregnancy-Related Complications

- Hyperemesis gravidarum
- Bleeding disorders
- Hypertension
- Blood incompatibility between woman and fetus

Slide 10

Hyperemesis Gravidarum

Manifestations
- Excessive nausea and vomiting
- Can impact fetal growth
- Dehydration
- Reduced delivery of blood, oxygen, and nutrients to the fetus

- Nausea and vomiting are common occurrences in early pregnancy.
- There are varied theories about why this occurs. Most relate to the elevated hormone levels experienced by the pregnant woman.
- At what point do nausea and vomiting become problematic for the mother and her unborn baby?

Slide 11

Hyperemesis Gravidarum *(cont.)*

Treatment
- Correct dehydration and electrolyte or acid-base imbalance
- Antiemetic drugs may be prescribed
- In extreme cases
  - TPN may be required
  - Hospitalization

- The medical interventions employed to manage the patient with hyperemesis gravidarum will be based on the severity of the condition.
- Identify nursing diagnoses for the patient experiencing hyperemesis gravidarum.

Slide 12

Bleeding Disorders of Early Pregnancy

Slide 13

Types of Abortions

- Spontaneous (nonintentional)
  - Threatened
  - Inevitable
  - Incomplete
  - Complete
  - Missed
  - Recurrent
- Induced
  - Therapeutic
  - Elective

- The term *abortion* is used to refer to both spontaneous and elective pregnancy terminations.
- The layperson might identify a spontaneous abortion as a miscarriage.
- Each type of abortion is named for its identifying characteristics.

Slide 14

Nursing Care of Early Pregnancy Bleeding Disorders

- Document amount and character of bleeding
- Save anything that looks like clots or tissue for evaluation by a pathologist
- Perineal pad count with estimated amount of blood per pad (i.e., 50%)
- Monitor vital signs
- If actively bleeding, woman should be kept NPO in case surgical intervention is needed

- An accurate nursing assessment is required for the patient experiencing early pregnancy bleeding disorders.
- What nursing interventions might be utilized to assist with management of the emotional concerns of these patients?

Slide 15

Post-Abortion Teaching

- Report increased bleeding
- Take temperature every 8 hours for 3 days
- Take an oral iron supplement if prescribed
- Resume sexual activity as recommended by the health care provider
- Return to health care provider at the recommended time for a checkup and contraception information
- Pregnancy can occur before the first menstrual period returns after the abortion procedure

- The nurse has the responsibility of providing comprehensive discharge education.
- What communication techniques will facilitate interaction with these patients and their families?

Slide 16

Emotional Care

- Spiritual support of the family's choice and community support groups may help the family work through the grief of any pregnancy loss

- Review effective and ineffective communication techniques found in the Communication box on page 85.

Slide 17

Ectopic Pregnancy

- 95% occur in fallopian tube
- Scarring or tubal deformity may result from
  - Hormonal abnormalities
  - Inflammation
  - Infection
  - Adhesions
  - Congenital defects
  - Endometriosis

- An ectopic pregnancy results when a pregnancy implants anywhere outside of the uterus.
- The pregnancy resulting outside of the uterus has no chance of survival. This will result in both physiological and psychological concerns for the mother. What information should be provided to her?

Slide 18

Most Common Sites for Ectopic Pregnancies

- Note the assorted areas where an implantation can occur.

Slide 19

Ectopic Pregnancy *(cont.)*

- Manifestations
  - Lower abdominal pain and may have light vaginal bleeding
  - If tube ruptures
    - May have sudden severe lower abdominal pain
    - Vaginal bleeding
    - Signs of hypovolemic shock
    - Shoulder pain may also be felt
- Treatment
  - Pregnancy test
  - Transvaginal ultrasound
  - Laparoscopic examination
  - Priority is to control bleeding
  - Three actions can be taken
    - No action
    - Treatment with methotrexate to inhibit cell division
    - Surgery to remove pregnancy from the tube

- Early recognition of an ectopic pregnancy is vital to having a positive outcome.
- What is the underlying cause of the manifestations associated with an ectopic pregnancy?
- At what point in gestation do the manifestations normally begin to present themselves?
- Discuss the pros and cons of the primary means to manage this condition.

Slide 20

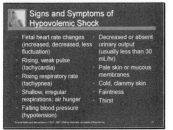

Slide 21

- A chief concern for the woman who is experiencing an ectopic pregnancy is the onset of hypovolemic shock.
- What elements should be included in the nursing assessment?

Slide 22

Slide 23

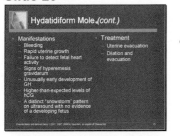

- The occurrence of a molar pregnancy is a loss to the mother. The woman might have difficulty understanding why she has experienced some of the traditional signs associated with a true pregnancy.
- Identify nursing diagnoses related to the emotional needs of this woman.

Slide 24

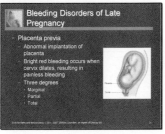

- Review Table 5-4 on page 88 and discuss the difference between the two types of bleeding.

Slide 25

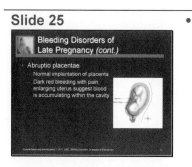

Bleeding Disorders of Late Pregnancy *(cont.)*

- Abruptio placentae
  - Normal implantation of placenta
  - Dark red bleeding with pain, enlarging uterus suggest blood is accumulating within the cavity

- Review Table 5-4 on page 88 and discuss the difference between the two types of bleeding.

Slide 26

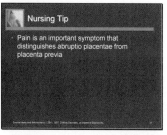

Complications or Risks

- Placenta previa
  - Infection because of vaginal organisms
  - Postpartum hemorrhage, because if lower segment of uterus was site of attachment, there are fewer muscle fibers, so weaker contractions may occur

- Abruptio placentae
  - Predisposing factors
    - Hypertension
    - Cocaine or alcohol use
    - Cigarette smoking and poor nutrition
    - Blows to the abdomen
    - Prior history of abruptio placentae
    - Folate deficiency

- Differing types and degrees of both conditions exist.
- The placenta could be low-lying, partial, or completely covering the cervical opening.
- Women pregnant with multiples have a higher incidence of placenta previa. Why? *The placenta previa could be marginal or complete.*
- Why would hypertension, cocaine, alcohol use, or cigarette smoking be a contributing factor to the development of an abruption?

Audience Response Question #1
A 33-week pregnant woman is the emergency room with painless vaginal bleeding. What nursing action is contraindicated?
1. Perform a vaginal exam.
2. Prepare for C-section.
3. Inform her that she must maintain bedrest.
4. Administer betamethasone.

Slide 27

Nursing Tip

- Pain is an important symptom that distinguishes abruptio placentae from placenta previa

Slide 28

Care of the Pregnant Woman with Excessive Bleeding

- Document blood loss
- Closely monitor vital signs, including I&O
- Observe for
  - Pain
  - Uterine rigidity or tenderness
- Verify that orders for blood typing and cross-match have been carried out
- Monitor intravenous infusion
- Prepare for surgery, if indicated
- Monitor fetal heart rate and contractions
- Monitor laboratory results, including coagulation studies
- Administer oxygen by mask
- Prepare for newborn resuscitation

- Review ways to prioritize interventions for the obstetric patient who is experiencing excessive bleeding.

Slide 29	
Hypertension During Pregnancy · Gestational hypertension (GH) 　· Preeclampsia 　· Eclampsia · Chronic hypertension · Preeclampsia with superimposed chronic hypertension · Present 20 weeks before pregnancy · New occurrence of proteinuria or thrombocytopenia	• Hypertension, which occurs in pregnancy, was formerly known as *pregnancy-induced hypertension* (PIH). • There are differing hypertensive conditions which could impact the pregnant patient. The time of onset is used as a defining criterion.

Slide 30	
Hypertension During Pregnancy (cont.) · An increase over baseline blood pressure of 30 mm Hg or more systolic · 15 mm Hg diastolic will place the woman in a high-risk category for GH	**Audience Response Question #2** A woman who is 35 weeks pregnant has been diagnosed with preeclampsia. Her blood pressure is 140/100-160/110. She reports headache, has generalized edema, and has 3+ proteinuria. What would be the most appropriate environment for this woman? 　1. Home on partial bedrest with private duty nursing care 　2. Private hospital room with bathroom privileges 　3. Labor room on strict bedrest 　4. Semiprivate hospital room on bedrest

Slide 31	
Risk Factors for GH · First pregnancy · Obesity · Family history of GH · Age over 40 years or under 19 years · Multifetal pregnancy · Chronic hypertension · Chronic renal disease · Diabetes mellitus	

Slide 32	
Manifestations of and Systems Affected by GH · Hypertension · Edema · Proteinuria · Blood clotting · Central nervous system · Eyes · Urinary tract · Respiratory system · Gastrointestinal system and liver	• The onset of GH affects multiple body systems. • Why do these manifestations occur?

Slide 33	
Management of GH · Depends on severity of the hypertension and on the maturity of the fetus · Treatment focuses on 　-- Maintaining blood flow to the woman's vital organs and to the placenta 　-- Preventing convulsions	• Prevention and early detection are vital for positive outcomes of the pregnancy affected by GH. • What education should be provided to the patient during the prenatal care visits concerning the potential for the development of GH? When should this education begin?

ELSEVIER

Introduction to Maternity & Pediatric Nursing, 6th ed.
Leifer

Slide 34

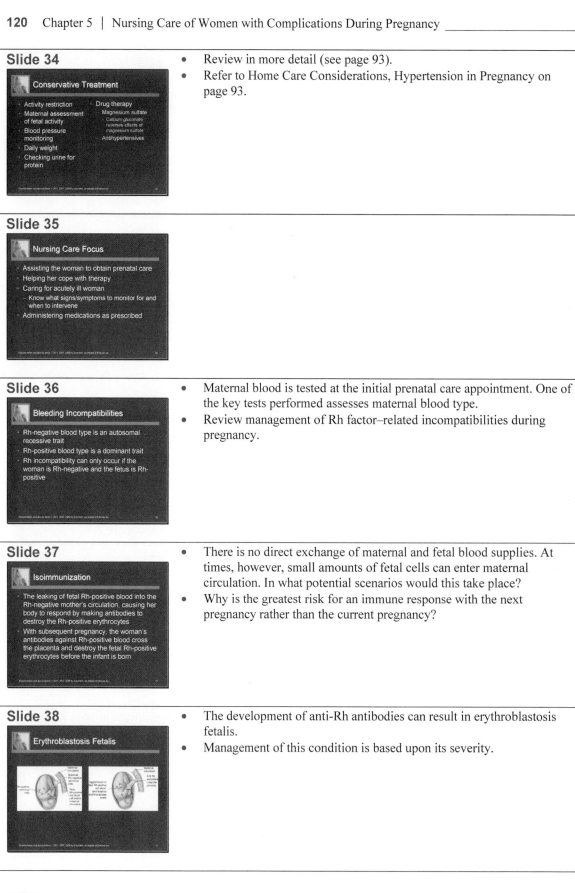

Conservative Treatment

- Activity restriction
- Maternal assessment of fetal activity
- Blood pressure monitoring
- Daily weight
- Checking urine for protein

- Drug therapy
  - Magnesium sulfate
    - Calcium gluconate reverses effects of magnesium sulfate
  - Antihypertensives

- Review in more detail (see page 93).
- Refer to Home Care Considerations, Hypertension in Pregnancy on page 93.

Slide 35

Nursing Care Focus

- Assisting the woman to obtain prenatal care
- Helping her cope with therapy
- Caring for acutely ill woman
  - Know what signs/symptoms to monitor for and when to intervene
- Administering medications as prescribed

Slide 36

Bleeding Incompatibilities

- Rh-negative blood type is an autosomal recessive trait
- Rh-positive blood type is a dominant trait
- Rh incompatibility can only occur if the woman is Rh-negative and the fetus is Rh-positive

- Maternal blood is tested at the initial prenatal care appointment. One of the key tests performed assesses maternal blood type.
- Review management of Rh factor–related incompatibilities during pregnancy.

Slide 37

Isoimmunization

- The leaking of fetal Rh-positive blood into the Rh-negative mother's circulation, causing her body to respond by making antibodies to destroy the Rh-positive erythrocytes
- With subsequent pregnancy, the woman's antibodies against Rh-positive blood cross the placenta and destroy the fetal Rh-positive erythrocytes before the infant is born

- There is no direct exchange of maternal and fetal blood supplies. At times, however, small amounts of fetal cells can enter maternal circulation. In what potential scenarios would this take place?
- Why is the greatest risk for an immune response with the next pregnancy rather than the current pregnancy?

Slide 38

Erythroblastosis Fetalis

- The development of anti-Rh antibodies can result in erythroblastosis fetalis.
- Management of this condition is based upon its severity.

Slide 39

Erythroblastosis Fetalis *(cont.)*

- Occurs when the maternal anti-Rh antibodies cross the placenta and destroy fetal erythrocytes
- Requires RhoGAM to be given at 28 weeks and within 72 hours of delivery to the mother
  - Also given after amniocentesis, woman who experiences bleeding during pregnancy
- Fetal assessment tests must be done throughout pregnancy
- An intrauterine transfusion may be done for the severely anemic fetus

- Also may need RhoGAM if version was required.

Slide 40

Pregnancy Complicated by Medical Conditions

Slide 41

Diabetes Mellitus (DM)

- Classified if preceded pregnancy
- Type 1: pathologic disorder
- Type 2: insulin resistance; genetic predisposition
- Pregestational DM: Type 1 or 2 DM
- Gestational DM (GDM)
  - Glucose intolerance with onset during pregnancy
  - In true GDM, glucose usually returns to normal by 6 weeks postpartum

- Focus on gestational DM.
- Screening for diabetes in pregnancy occurs around the 20th week of gestation. A serum test is performed.
- Discuss the criteria that must be met to confirm a diagnosis.

Slide 42

Effects of Pregnancy on Glucose Metabolism

- Hormones (estrogen and progesterone), insulinase (an enzyme), and increased prolactin levels have two effects
  - Increased resistance of cells to insulin
  - Increased speed of insulin breakdown

- Review the underlying pathophysiology for the body's cells to change resistance to insulin.
- What does this change do for the circulating blood glucose levels?

Audience Response Question #3
What would normally happen to a woman's blood glucose level during pregnancy?
1. It would elevate.
2. It would decrease.
3. It would remain stable.
4. It would fluctuate.

Slide 43

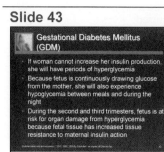

Gestational Diabetes Mellitus (GDM)

- If woman cannot increase her insulin production, she will have periods of hyperglycemia
- Because fetus is continuously drawing glucose from the mother, she will also experience hypoglycemia between meals and during the night
- During the second and third trimesters, fetus is at risk for organ damage from hyperglycemia because fetal tissue has increased tissue resistance to maternal insulin action

Slide 44

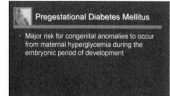

Pregestational Diabetes Mellitus

- Major risk for congenital anomalies to occur from maternal hyperglycemia during the embryonic period of development

- The *embryonic period* refers to those days and weeks prior to the 8th week of pregnancy.
- Why is the embryonic period more affected than the period of fetal development?

Slide 45

Factors Linked to GDM

- Maternal obesity (>90 kg or 198 lbs)
- Large infant (>4000 g or about 9 lbs)
- Maternal age older than 25 years
- Previous unexplained stillbirth or infant having congenital abnormalities
- History of GDM in a previous pregnancy
- Family history of DM
- Fasting glucose over 126 mg/dL or postmeal glucose over 200 mg/dL

Slide 46

Macrosomic Infant

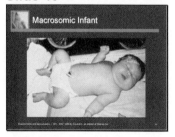

- This is the macrosomic infant.
- Why are infants born to diabetic mothers larger than other infants?

Slide 47

Treatment

- Diet
- Monitoring blood glucose levels
- Ketone monitoring
- Exercise
- Fetal assessment

- The first line of management for the diabetic mother involves diet. What are the goals of the diet?
- A home glucose monitor will assist the mother in keeping watch on blood levels at home.
- While new exercise programs are not recommended for initiation during pregnancy, exercise will impact the body's blood glucose levels.
- How does exercise impact glucose levels?

ELSEVIER

Introduction to Maternity & Pediatric Nursing, 6th ed.

Leifer

Slide 48

Care During Labor of the Woman with GDM
- Intravenous infusion of dextrose may be needed
- Regular insulin
- Assess blood glucose levels hourly and adjust insulin administration accordingly

Slide 49

Care of the Neonate Whose Mother Has GDM
- May have the following
  - Hypoglycemia
  - Respiratory distress
- Injury related to macrosomia
- Blood glucose monitored closely for at least the first 24 hours after birth
- Breastfeeding should be encouraged

- After delivery, the neonate will require close observation.
- Review the manifestations associated with hypoglycemia.
- How will hypoglycemia in the newborn be managed?
- Delivery of the macrosomic infant can be challenging. Identify related complications.

Slide 50

Heart Disease
- Manifestations
  - Increased levels of clotting factors
  - Increased risk of thrombosis
    - If woman's heart cannot handle increased workload, congestive heart failure (CHF) results
    - Fetus suffers from reduced placental blood flow

- During the course of the pregnancy, the maternal circulatory volume will increase by 40%. This increase in volume will place stress on the cardiovascular structures.

Slide 51

Signs of CHF During Pregnancy
- Persistent cough
- Moist lung sounds
- Fatigue or fainting on exertion
- Difficulty breathing on exertion
- Orthopnea
- Severe pitting edema of the lower extremities or generalized edema
- Palpitations
- Changes in fetal heart rate
  - Indicating hypoxia or growth restriction

Slide 52

Treatment
- Under care of both obstetrician and cardiologist
- Priority care is limiting physical activity
  - Drug therapy
  - May include beta-adrenergic blockers, anticoagulants, diuretics
- Vaginal birth is preferred as it carries less risk for infection or respiratory complications

- Management of cardiovascular conditions in pregnancy will require close observation by both an obstetrician and a cardiologist.
- What are the desired effects of the listed medications?

ELSEVIER

Introduction to Maternity & Pediatric Nursing, 6th ed.
Leifer

Slide 53

Anemia

- The reduced ability of the blood to carry oxygen to the cells
- Four types are significant during pregnancy
  - Two are nutritional
    - Iron deficiency
    - Folic acid deficiency
  - Two are genetic disorders
    - Sickle cell disease
    - Thalassemia

- Review normal serum hemoglobin levels for women.
- What are the levels that constitute anemia?

Slide 54

Nutritional Anemias

- Symptoms
  - Easily fatigued
  - Skin and mucous membranes are pale
  - Shortness of breath
  - Pounding heart
  - Rapid pulse (with severe anemia)

- It should be noted that not all pregnant women with anemia have signs and symptoms. Their experience may reflect vague symptoms.
- The gradual onset of anemia is usually associated with fewer symptoms.

Slide 55

Iron-Deficiency Anemia

- RBCs are small (microcytic) and pale (hypochromic)
- Prevention
  - Iron supplements
  - Vitamin C may enhance absorption
  - Do not take iron with milk or antacids
    - Calcium impairs absorption
- Treatment
  - Oral doses of elemental iron
  - Continue therapy for about 3 months after anemia has been corrected

- Review the nursing implications associated with the administration of iron supplements.
- What patient teaching should be provided?

Slide 56

Folic-Acid Deficiency Anemia

- Large, immature RBCs (megaloblastic anemia)
- Anticonvulsants, oral contraceptives, sulfa drugs, and alcohol can decrease absorption of folate from meals
- Folate essential for normal growth and development
- Prevention
  - Daily supplement of 400 mcg (0.4 mg) per day
- Treatment
  - Folate deficiency is treated with folic acid supplementation
  - 1 mg/day (over twice the amount of the preventive supplement)
    - Dose may be higher for women who have had a previous child with a neural tube defect

Slide 57

Genetic Anemias

Slide 58

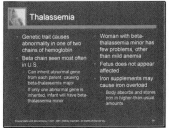

- Sickle cell disease is most prevalent in African Americans.
- What manifestations are associated with a crisis during pregnancy?

Slide 59

Thalassemia

Slide 60

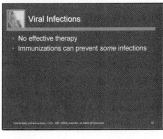

- Prevention and management of anemia must begin at the first prenatal appointment.

Slide 61

Infections

Slide 62

Viral Infections

Slide 63

Cytomegalovirus

Infected infant may have	Treatment
- Mental retardation	- No effective treatment is known
- Seizures	- Therapeutic abortion may be offered if CMV infection is discovered early in pregnancy
- Blindness	
- Deafness	
- Dental abnormalities	
- Petechiae	

- Cytomegalovirus (CMV) is the cause of congenital infections in newborns.
- The presence of CMV is widespread in the adult population.
- The adult who is affected with CMV might or might not have characteristic signs and symptoms.

Slide 64

Rubella

	Effects on embryo or fetus
- Mild viral disease	- Microcephaly (small head size)
- Low fever and rash	- Mental retardation
- Destructive to developing fetus	- Congenital cataracts
- If woman receives a rubella vaccine prior to pregnancy, she should not get pregnant for **at least 1 month**	- Deafness
	- Cardiac effects
- Not given during pregnancy because vaccine is from a live virus	- Intrauterine growth restriction (IUGR)

- During the initial prenatal care visit, the pregnant patient's rubella status is assessed.
- If the mother is not immune, what patient teaching should be provided by the nurse?

Slide 65

Herpesvirus

Two types	Neonatal herpes can be
- Type 1: likely to cause fever blisters or cold sores	- Localized
- Type 2: likely to cause genital herpes	- Disseminated (widespread) High mortality rate
- After primary infection, lies dormant in the nerves, can reactivate at any time	- Treatment and nursing care
	- Avoid contact with lesions
- Initial infection during first half of pregnancy may cause spontaneous abortion, IUGR, and preterm labor	- Mother and infant do not need to be isolated as long as direct contact with lesions is avoided
- Infant can be infected in one of two ways	- Breastfeeding is possible IF no lesions are present on the breasts

- Herpes in the newborn can result in serious complications.
- Herpesvirus is common in adults. The manifestations might be little more than an inconvenience.
- What responsibilities does the nurse have during labor if the patient has a history of genital herpes?

Slide 66

Hepatitis B

	Risk for hepatitis B
- Transmitted by blood, saliva, vaginal secretions, semen, and breast milk; can also cross the placenta	- Intravenous drug use
	- Multiple sexual partners
	- Repeated infection with STI
- Fetus may be infected transplacentally or by contact with blood or vaginal secretions during delivery	- Occupational exposure to blood products and needle sticks
	- Hemodialysis
	- Multiple blood transfusions or other blood products
- Upon delivery, the neonate should receive a single dose of hepatitis B immune globulin, followed by the hepatitis B vaccine	- Household contact with hepatitis carrier or hemodialysis patient
	- Contact with persons arriving from countries where there is a higher incidence of the disease

Slide 67

Human Immunodeficiency Virus

	Acquired in one of three ways
- Virus that causes AIDS	- Sexual contact
- Cripples immune system	- Parenteral or mucous membrane exposure to infected body fluids
- No known immunization or curative treatment	- Perinatal exposure
	- Infant may be infected
	- Transplacentally
	- Through contact with infected maternal secretions at birth
	- Through breast milk

Slide 68

Nursing Care

- Educate the HIV-positive woman on methods to reduce the risk of transmission to her developing fetus/infant
- Pregnant women with HIV/AIDS are more susceptible to infection
- Breastfeeding is absolutely contraindicated for mothers who are HIV-positive

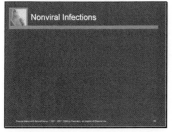

- Should HIV testing be mandated for all pregnant women?

Slide 69

Nonviral Infections

Slide 70

Toxoplasmosis

- Parasite acquired by contact with cat feces or raw meat
- Transmitted through placenta
- Congenital toxoplasmosis includes the following possible signs
  - Low birthweight
  - Enlarged liver and spleen
  - Jaundice
  - Anemia
  - Inflammation of eye structures
  - Neurological damage

- Treatment
  - Therapeutic abortion
- Preventive measures
  - Cook all meat thoroughly
  - Wash hands and all kitchen surfaces after handling raw meat
  - Avoid uncooked eggs and unpasteurized milk
  - Wash fresh fruits and vegetables well
  - Avoid materials contaminated with cat feces

Slide 71

Group B Streptococcus (GBS) Infection

- Leading cause of perinatal infection with high mortality rate
- Organism found in woman's rectum, vagina, cervix, throat, or skin
- The risk of exposure to the infant is greater if the labor is long or the woman experiences premature rupture of membranes

- GBS significant cause of maternal postpartum infection
  - Symptoms include elevated temperature within 12 hours after delivery, rapid heart rate, abdominal distention
- Can be deadly to the infant
- Treatment
  - Penicillin

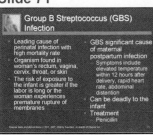

- The presence of group B streptococcus could cause the patient to believe she has a sexually transmitted infection.
- How would you respond to this concern?

Slide 72

Tuberculosis

- Increasing incidence in the U.S.
- Multidrug-resistant strains also increasing
- Mother can be tested via PPD skin test or serum Quantiferon Gold®
- If positive, chest x-ray and possibly sputum specimens will be needed
- Report to local public health department (PHD) if active pulmonary TB is suspected
- If mother active, infant *must* be kept away from mother until she has been cleared by the PHD

Slide 73

Sexually Transmitted Infections (STIs)

- Common mode of transmission is sexual intercourse
- Infections that can be transmitted
  - Syphilis, gonorrhea, Chlamydia, trichomoniasis, and Condylomata acuminata
- Vaginal changes during pregnancy increase the risk of transmission

- Education concerning the presence of sexually transmitted infections should take place in pregnancy.
- Many health care providers routinely test patients for STIs in the early prenatal period.
- Review routine STI testing.

Slide 74

Urinary Tract Infections

- Pregnancy alters self-cleaning action due to pressure on urinary structures
- Prevents bladder from emptying completely
- Retained urine becomes more alkaline

- May develop cystitis
  - Burning with urination
  - Increased frequency and urgency of urination
  - Normal or slightly elevated temperature
- Pyelonephritis
  - High fever
  - Chills
  - Flank pain or tenderness
  - Nausea and vomiting

- Pregnancy causes changes in the urinary system. What are these changes?
- Which hormones are involved in these changes?

Slide 75

Environmental Hazards During Pregnancy

- Bioterrorism and the pregnant woman
- Three basic categories
  - A—can be easily transmitted from person to person
  - B—Can be spread via food and water
  - C—Can be spread via manufactured weapons designed to spread disease

- Substance abuse
  - Questions should focus on how the information will help nurses and physicians provide the safest and most appropriate care to the pregnant woman and her infant
- Alcohol
  - A single episode of consuming two alcoholic drinks can lead to the loss of some fetal brain cells

- Define environment as inclusive of the physical environment, such as the home or place of work, as well as the condition of the pregnant woman's own body.
- How healthy are the pregnant woman's habits?

Slide 76

Trauma During Pregnancy

- Three leading causes of traumatic death
  - Automobile accidents
  - Homicide
  - Suicide
- Battering
  - Bruises in various stages of healing

- What information concerning safety should be provided to pregnant women?

Slide 77

Nursing Tip

- If a woman confides that she is being abused during pregnancy, this information must be kept absolutely confidential.
- Her life may be in danger if her abuser learns that she has told anyone.
- She should be referred to local shelters, but the decision to leave her abuser is hers alone.

- Review resources in the local community for abused women.

Slide 78

Effects of a High-Risk Pregnancy on the Family

- Disruption of usual roles
- Financial difficulties
- Delayed attachment to the infant
- Loss of expected birth experience

Slide 79

Interventions for the Grieving Process

- Allow parents to remain together in privacy
- Accept behaviors related to grieving
- Develop a plan of care to provide support to the family
- Offer a memento such as a footprint
- Offer parents an opportunity to hold the infant, if they choose
- Prepare parents for the appearance of the infant
- Provide parents with educational materials and referrals to support groups
- Discuss wishes concerning religious and cultural rituals

- It is important for care providers to treat the parents of a deceased infant as new parents.
- What statements will facilitate communication with these families?

Slide 80

Question for Review

- Compare and contrast the differences between the symptoms of placenta previa and abruptio placentae.

Slide 81

Review

- Objectives
- Key Terms
- Key Points
- Online Resources
- Critical Thinking Questions
- Review Questions

Leifer

TEACHING FOCUS

In this chapter, students will have the opportunity to learn the admitting process for patients entering the maternity unit, including data collection. Students will be introduced to the types of settings for childbirth, the components of the birth process, admission procedures during the birth process, monitoring of the patient during and after the birth, and monitoring the newborn. Students will also have the opportunity to learn the differences between true and false labor, the stages and phases of labor, and the nursing care required for vaginal births.

MATERIALS AND RESOURCES

- ☐ Anatomical models (Lesson 6.1)
- ☐ Computer and PowerPoint projector (all lessons)
- ☐ Videotapes, VCR, DVDs and projector (Lesson 6.1)

LESSON CHECKLIST

Preparations for this lesson include:

- Lecture
- Evaluation of student knowledge and skills needed to perform all entry-level activities related to nursing care during labor and birth, including:
  - ○ Different birth settings, methods of data collection, and admitting patients to the maternity unit
  - ○ Components of the birth process
  - ○ Stages and phases of labor
  - ○ Care of the mother and newborn immediately after delivery

KEY TERMS

accelerations (p. 134)
absent variability (p. 134)
acrocyanosis (p. 151)
adjustment (p. 140)
amnioinfusion (p. 137)
amniotomy (p. 137)
baseline fetal heart rate
   (p. 132)
baseline variability
   (p. 134)
bloody show (p. 126)
cold stress (p. 150)
coping (p. 140)
crowning (p. 144)
decelerations (p. 134)
dilate (p. 120)

doula (p. 143)
early decelerations
   (p. 135)
efface (p. 120)
episiotomy (p. 130)
episodic changes (p. 134)
fetal bradycardia (p. 133)
fetal tachycardia (p. 134)
fontanelle (p. 123)
late decelerations (p. 136)
Leopold's maneuver
   (p. 131)
lie (p. 123)
marked variability (p. 134)
moderate variability
   (p. 134)

molding (p. 123)
neutral thermal
   environment (p. 150)
nitrazine test (p. 138)
nuchal cord (p. 135)
ophthalmia neonatorum
   (p. 152)
periodic changes (p. 134)
prolonged decelerations
   (p. 136)
station (p. 127)
suture (p. 123)
uteroplacental insufficiency
   (p. 136)
vaginal birth after cesarean
   (VBAC) (p. 144)

ADDITIONAL RESOURCES

TEACH PPT slide(s) Chapter 6, 1-50
EILR IC image(s) Chapter 6, 1-26
EILR OBQ question(s) Chapter 6, 1-10
EILR TB question(s) Chapter 6, 1-33
ESLR IRQ question(s) Chapter 6, 1-8
SG Chapter 6, pp. 43-51

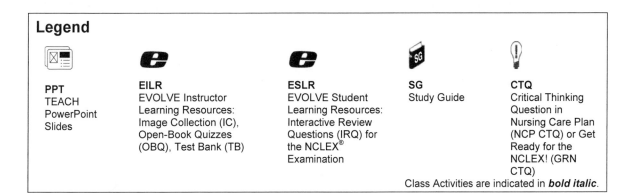

Legend

PPT
TEACH
PowerPoint
Slides

EILR
EVOLVE Instructor
Learning Resources:
Image Collection (IC),
Open-Book Quizzes
(OBQ), Test Bank (TB)

ESLR
EVOLVE Student
Learning Resources:
Interactive Review
Questions (IRQ) for
the NCLEX®
Examination

SG
Study Guide

CTQ
Critical Thinking
Question in
Nursing Care Plan
(NCP CTQ) or Get
Ready for the
NCLEX! (GRN
CTQ)

Class Activities are indicated in ***bold italic***.

LESSON 6.1

PRETEST

1. Which of the following is a reassuring pattern of contractions?
    a. frequency greater than every 1 minute and last less than 30 seconds
    b. frequency greater than every 2 minutes and last less than 90 seconds
    c. frequency greater than every 5 minutes or last longer than 30 seconds
    d. frequency greater than every hour or last longer than 90 seconds

2. Three signs of impending labor are
    a. ballottement, leg edema, and Braxton Hicks contractions.
    b. military presentation, tachycardia, and nausea.
    c. blurred vision, headache, and decreased fetal activity.
    d. bloody show, irregular contractions, and crowning.

3. The four stages of labor are
    a. quickening, labor, expulsion, and recovery.
    b. anticipation, activation, contractions, and resolution.
    c. dilation and effacement, expulsion, placental expulsion, and recovery.
    d. preparation, involvement, contractions, and recovery.

4. A pregnant woman should go to the hospital when she begins to experience
    a. frequent and intense contractions.   c. lower back pain.
    b. frequent and urgent urination.   d. effleurage accompanied by cravings.

5. The Apgar scoring system assesses
    a. fetal heart rate, respiratory effort, reflex irritability, muscle tone, and color.
    b. maternal heart rate, respiratory effort, reflex irritability, muscle tone, and color.
    c. fetal blood pressure, peripheral circulation, capillary refill, color, and alertness.
    d. maternal blood pressure, peripheral circulation, capillary refill, color, and alertness.

6. The newborn cannot be discharged until what has been passed?
    a. surfactant   c. colostrum
    b. meconium   d. placenta

7. What are the four interrelated components that make up the process of labor and birth?
    a. dilation, effacement, expulsion, and recovery
    b. membrane rupture, contractions, delivery, and recovery
    c. powers, passage, passenger, and psyche
    d. breathing, pushing, expelling, assessment

8. Spontaneous or artificial rupture of the amniotic membranes is
    a. nitrazine test.   c. Apgar.
    b. amnioinfusion.   d. amniotomy.

9. Acrocyanosis in the newborn is
    a. the bluish color of the feet and hands.   c. usually resolved after the first stool is passed.
    b. caused by a vitamin K deficiency.   d. caused by cold stress and can lead to hypothermia.

10. Which of the following is a characteristic of false labor?
    a. large amounts of bloody show   c. cervix effacement gradually increases
    b. walking relieves contractions   d. membranes must be artificially ruptured

Answers

1. b	3. c	5. a	7. c	9. a
2. d	4. a	6. b	8. d	10. b

BACKGROUND ASSESSMENT

Question: The nurse notices that the fetal heart rate is variable and that the decelerations begin after the contraction starts and continue after the contraction is over. What does this pattern indicate?

Answer: This patient is experiencing late decelerations, which are known as a *nonreassuring* pattern. Late decelerations occur when the baseline rate decreases, often indicating that the placenta is not delivering enough oxygen to the fetus (uteroplacental insufficiency).

Question: How would you describe the nursing care of the newborn immediately after birth?

Answer: The infant is dried with a towel, wrapped in warm blankets with a hat placed on the head, and placed in a radiant warmer to maintain a neutral thermal environment. Secretions are suctioned from the nose and mouth and a cord clamp is applied when the newborn is stabilized in the radiant warmer to maintain cardiorespiratory function. An Apgar score is given at 1 minute and 5 minutes after birth to evaluate the infant's condition and need for resuscitation.

CRITICAL THINKING QUESTION

A woman nearing her due date tells the nurse that she has decided to deliver at home because she doesn't want her baby to enter the world in an impersonal hospital setting. How should the nurse respond to this statement?

Guidelines: There are some advantages of a home delivery: the patient has more control over who will or will not be present for the birth, there is no risk of acquiring infections or diseases from other patients, and the comfortable and familiar environment is relaxing and peaceful for the patient. There are also decided disadvantages that should not be overlooked: most physicians and nurse-midwives will not attend home deliveries, and lay midwives have varying levels of training and experience. Emergency care and technology is also not immediately available should an emergency arise, and there can be a significant delay in receiving appropriate emergency care. If the mother's chief reason for wanting a home delivery is the atmosphere, then the nurse should explain that most hospital birthing rooms are more home-like than institutional, with furniture that hides the utilitarian purposes. These types of birthing rooms provide the comfort and atmosphere of home, but with all the necessary medical equipment and personnel. Encourage the patient to research which local hospitals offer the most ideal birthing rooms for her and to begin making her preparations.

OBJECTIVES	CONTENT	TEACHING RESOURCES
Discuss specific cultural beliefs the nurse may encounter when providing care to a woman in labor.	■ Cultural influence on birth practices (p. 116)	⊠▤ PPT slide 5 𝒆 EILR OBQ question 1 𝒆 EILR TB question 27 ▦ SG Case Study, question 1 (p. 50) **BOOK RESOURCES** Table 6-1, Birth Practices of Selected Cultural Groups (pp. 117-119) ▸ Discuss how to take cultural differences into account when providing nursing care during birth. ▸ Discuss how and why different cultures have approached the birthing process in different ways. *Class Activity **Divide the class into small groups and have each group identify and discuss four areas of the birthing process that may be different among cultures. Have students give specific examples of cultural differences,***

OBJECTIVES	CONTENT	TEACHING RESOURCES
		explain nursing care and interventions for these differences, and present their findings to the class for discussion.
Compare the advantages and disadvantages for each type of childbearing setting: hospital, freestanding birth center, and home.	■ Settings for childbirth (p. 116) ☐ Hospitals (p. 116) ☐ Freestanding birth centers (p. 116) ☐ Home (p. 116)	⊠ PPT slide 6 *e* EILR IC image 1 *e* EILR OBQ question 2 *e* EILR TB question 28 **BOOK RESOURCES** Figure 6-1, A, Typical Labor, Delivery, and Recovery Room (LDR). B, When Woman Enters Active Phase of Labor (p. 120) ▸ Discuss the different types of settings for childbirth. How do freestanding birth centers differ from hospitals? ▸ Discuss what a patient would need to successfully deliver a baby at home. *Class Activity **Divide the class into small groups and assign each group one of the childbearing settings: hospital, freestanding birth center, and home. Have each group list the advantages and disadvantages of delivering in the assigned setting and explain which type of patient or pregnancy the setting is best suited for. Have each group share its findings with the class.*** *Class Activity **Present the following scenario to the class for students to discuss: A diabetic patient insists on having a home delivery because she hates hospitals and she wants her baby to be born in its home surrounded by family. Is home delivery advisable or inadvisable for this patient? How should the nurse proceed?***
Describe the four components ("four *Ps*") of the birth process: powers, passage, passenger, and psyche.	■ Components of the birth process (p. 119) ☐ The powers (p. 120) ☐ The passage (p. 122) ☐ The passengers (p. 123) ☐ The psyche (p. 125)	⊠ PPT slides 7, 8 *e* EILR IC images 2-8 *e* EILR OBQ question 3 *e* EILR TB question 31 📙 SG Learning Activities, questions 1-3, 5-6 (p. 43) **BOOK RESOURCES** Safety Alert (p. 121) Nursing Tip (p. 121) Figure 6-2, Cervical Effacement and Dilation (p. 121) Figure 6-3, Cervical Dilation in Centimeters (p. 122) Figure 6-4, Contraction Cycle (p. 122)

OBJECTIVES	CONTENT	TEACHING RESOURCES
		Figure 6-5, Fetal Skull (p. 123)
		Figure 6-6, Lie (p. 123)
		Figure 6-7, Fetal Presentations (p. 124)
		Box 6-1, Classifications of Fetal Presentations and Positions (p. 125)
		Figure 6-8, Fetal Position (p. 126)
		Review Questions for the NCLEX® Examination, questions 1-2 (pp. 155-156)
		▸ Discuss which of the four Ps is the most crucial aspect of the birth process and why.
		▸ Discuss the role the psyche plays in the birth process.
		Class Activity Divide the class into small groups and assign each group one of the four Ps of the birth process. Have each group identify three areas about which patient teaching might be needed, make a brief teaching plan that addresses these areas, identify two specific nursing interventions, and present its plan to the class for discussion.
Describe how the four *P*s of labor interrelate to result in the birth of an infant.	■ Components of the birth process (p. 119) □ The powers (p. 120) – Uterine contractions (p. 120) □ The passage (p. 122) – Bony pelvis (p. 122) – Soft tissues (p. 122) □ The passengers (p. 123) – Fetal head (p. 123) – Lie (p. 123) – Attitude (p. 124) – Presentation (p. 124) – Position (p. 125) □ The psyche (p. 125)	PPT slides 9-18 *e* EILR IC images 2-8 *e* EILR OBQ questions 4, 7 *e* EILR TB questions 1-4, 30 *e* ESLR IRQ question 7 SG Learning Activities, questions 2-3, 6 (p. 43) SG Review Questions, questions 5-7, 9 (p. 45) SG Applying Knowledge, questions 1-2 (p. 51) **BOOK RESOURCES** Figure 6-2, Cervical Effacement and Dilation (p. 121) Nursing Tip (p. 121) Figure 6-3, Cervical Dilation in Centimeters (p. 122) Figure 6-4, Contraction Cycle (p. 122) Figure 6-5, The Fetal Skull (p. 123) Figure 6-6, Lie (p. 123) Figure 6-7, Fetal Presentations (p. 124) Box 6-1, Classifications of Fetal Presentations and

OBJECTIVES	CONTENT	TEACHING RESOURCES
		Positions (p. 125)
		Figure 6-8, Fetal Position (p. 126)
		Review Questions for the NCLEX® Examination, questions 1, 2 (pp. 155-156)
		▶ Discuss the nursing interventions and actions that can be taken to decrease the woman's fear and anxiety during labor.
		*Class Activity **Divide the class into small groups and assign each group one of the four Ps of the birth process. Have each group identify the important elements of its component and explain how it relates to the other components of the birth process. Have groups share their findings with the class.***

6.1 Homework/Assignments:

6.1 Instructor's Notes/Student Feedback:

LESSON 6.2

CRITICAL THINKING QUESTION

A woman in an outpatient clinic asks about false labor and says that she is hesitant to go to the hospital or call her physician unless she is certain that she is in labor. How should the nurse respond?
Guidelines: The nurse should explain that true labor is characterized by cervical effacement and dilation, which can only be assessed by a health care provider. The nurse should explain that false labor is very common and that it is often mistaken for true labor. Other signs of false labor are irregular, infrequent, or mild-intensity contractions that are relieved or lessened by walking; abdominal or groin discomfort; and little or no bloody show. The woman should never hesitate to go to the hospital or contact her health care provider; it is better to be mistaken and sent home than to wait too long and risk complications.

OBJECTIVES	CONTENT	TEACHING RESOURCES
Explain the normal processes of childbirth: premonitory signs, mechanisms of birth, and stages and phases of labor.	■ Normal childbirth (p. 125) ☐ Signs of impending labor (p. 126) – Braxton Hicks contractions (p. 126) – Increased vaginal discharge (p. 126) – Bloody show (p. 126) – Rupture of the membranes (p. 126) – Energy spurt (p. 127) – Weight loss (p. 127) ☐ Mechanisms of labor (p. 127) – Descent (p. 127) – Engagement (p. 127) – Flexion (p. 127) – Internal rotation (p. 127) – Extension (p. 127) – External rotation (p. 127) – Expulsion (p. 127)	☒ PPT slides 19-23 *e* EILR IC images 9, 10 *e* EILR OBQ questions 5, 6 *e* EILR TB questions 22, 32, 33 SG Learning Activities, question 11 (p. 44) SG Review Questions, questions 10, 11, 19 (pp. 46-47) **BOOK RESOURCES** Figure 6-9, Mechanisms of Labor (p. 128) Figure 6-10, Station (p. 129) Review Questions for the NCLEX® Examination, questions 3, 4 (p. 156) ▸ Discuss the various signs of impending labor and why the body reacts in such a manner shortly before delivery. ▸ Discuss what would happen if the fetus does not achieve the proper station prior to delivery. *Class Activity Divide the class into small groups and assign each group one of the following topics: normal processes of childbirth, premonitory signs, mechanisms of birth, and stages and phases of labor. Have students identify key points necessary to educate patients in their specific stages of labor and develop a teaching plan. Have each group present its plan to the class for discussion, and have the class discuss nursing interventions and possible complications or problems for each topic.*
Explain how false labor differs from true labor.	■ Admission to the hospital or birth center (p. 127) ☐ When to go to the hospital or birth center (p. 127) ☐ Admission data	☒ PPT slides 24-28 *e* EILR IC images 11, 12 *e* EILR OBQ questions 6-8 *e* EILR TB questions 2-3, 5, 7, 15-16, 19, 24-25, 29

OBJECTIVES	CONTENT	TEACHING RESOURCES
	collection (p. 129)	*e* ESLR IRQ questions 1, 3
	– Fetal condition (p. 129)	SG Learning Activities, questions 4, 7, 10-12 (p. 45)
	– Maternal condition (p. 129)	SG Review Questions, questions 1-4, 22 (p. 45)
	– Impending birth (p. 129)	SG Applying Knowledge, question 6 (p. 51)
	– Additional data collection (p. 129)	**BOOK RESOURCES**
	☐ Admission procedures (p. 130)	Nursing Tip (p. 129)
		Skill 6-1, Assisting with an Emergency Birth (p. 130)
	– Permission and Consent Forms (p. 130)	Table 6-2, Comparison of False Labor and True Labor (p. 131)
	– Laboratory tests (p. 130)	Figure 6-11, Leopold's Maneuver (p. 131)
	– Intravenous infusion (p. 130)	Safety Alert (p. 132)
		Review Questions for the NCLEX® Examination, questions 2-3, 5 (p. 156)
	– Perineal prep (p. 130)	▸ Discuss the admission process from beginning to end, as well as the role of the nurse in this process.
	– Determining fetal position and presentation (p. 131)	▸ Discuss the nursing interventions in counseling a woman who is concerned about an abnormal fetal heartbeat.
	☐ Nursing care of the woman in false labor (p. 131)	▸ Discuss the nursing interventions in counseling a woman whose labor has slowed and who is becoming increasingly anxious.
		Class Activity Have students compare and contrast the different methods for determining fetal heart rates. Then, have the students practice documenting a heart rate.
		Class Activity Present the following scenario to the class for students to discuss: A patient in her 39th week is experiencing false labor for the fourth time. When she is told to go home again and to keep waiting she gets very upset and starts to cry. How should the nurse handle this situation?

6.2 Homework/Assignments:

6.2 Instructor's Notes/Student Feedback:

ELSEVIER

Introduction to Maternity & Pediatric Nursing, 6th ed.

Leifer

LESSON 6.3

CRITICAL THINKING QUESTION

The nurse is caring for a woman who will be moving through the third and fourth stages of labor. What are the nursing responsibilities during these stages of labor to provide care for the mother and the newborn?

Guidelines: During the third and fourth stages of labor, which occur during the first few hours after birth, the biggest risks to the mother are hemorrhaging and infection. The nurse must monitor the vital signs, check the fundus, and observe for bleeding. It is essential for the nurse to minimize heat loss for the infant, ensure that the infant has a patent airway, and observe for the passage of urine or meconium.

OBJECTIVES	CONTENT	TEACHING RESOURCES
Determine appropriate nursing care for the intrapartum patient, including the woman in false labor and the woman having a vaginal birth after a cesarean birth (VBAC).	■ Nursing care before birth (p. 132) □ Monitoring the fetus (p. 132) – Fetal heart rate (p. 132) – Intermittent auscultation (p. 132) – Continuous electronic fetal monitoring (p. 132) – Inspection of amniotic fluid (p. 137) □ Monitoring the woman (p. 138) – Vital signs (p. 138) – Contractions (p. 138) – Progress of labor (p. 138) – Intake and output (p. 139) – Response to labor (p. 139) □ Helping the woman cope with labor (p. 140) □ Labor support (p. 142) – Teaching (p. 142) – Providing encouragement (p. 143)	⊠▪ PPT slides 29-38 𝒆 EILR IC images 13-19 𝒆 EILR OBQ questions 4, 6, 9 𝒆 EILR TB questions 10-12, 14 𝒆 ESLR IRQ questions 4, 5 SG Learning Activities, questions 8-9, 12 (p. 44) SG Review Questions, questions 7, 14-18, 21, 23-24 (pp. 45-46) SG Case Study, question 2 (p. 50) SG Thinking Critically, questions 1, 4 (p. 50) SG Applying Knowledge, questions 3-5 (p. 51) **BOOK RESOURCES** Skill 6-2, Determining Fetal Heart Rate (p. 133) Box 6-2, When to Auscultate and Document the Fetal Heart Rate (p. 134) Figure 6-12, Determining Placement of Fetoscope or Sensor to Assess FHR (p. 134) Skill 6-3, External Electronic Fetal Monitoring (p. 135) Figure 6-13, Recording of the FHR in the Upper Grid and the Uterine Contractions in the Lower Grid (p. 135) Figure 6-14, Variable Decelerations, Showing Their Typically Abrupt Onset and Offset (p. 136) Table 6-3, Fetal Heart Rate Categories and Nursing Care (p. 136) Safety Alert (p. 136) Figure 6-15, Late Decelerations, Showing Their Pattern of Slowing, Which Persists After Contraction Ends (p. 137)

ELSEVIER

OBJECTIVES	CONTENT	TEACHING RESOURCES
	– Supporting the partner (p. 143)	Box 6-3, Reassuring and Nonreassuring Fetal Heart Rate and Uterine Activity Patterns (p. 137)
	☐ Stages and phases of labor (p. 144)	Skill 6-4, Testing for the Presence of Amniotic Fluid (Nitrazine Paper Test) (p. 138)
	☐ Vaginal birth after cesarean birth (p. 144)	Figure 6-16, The Nurse Helps the Mother Maintain Control and Use Breathing Techniques During Active Labor (p. 138)
		Skill 6-5, Determining Contractions by Palpation (p. 139)
		Table 6-4, Describing Uterine Activity (p. 139)
		Safety Alert (p. 139)
		Table 6-5, Physiologic Changes in Labor and Nursing Interventions (pp. 140-141)
		Figure 6-17, The Nurse Explains the External Electronic Fetal Monitor to the Woman (p. 142)
		Figure 6-18, The Doula (p. 143)
		Figure 6-19, Standing and Walking During Early Labor and Leaning on Partner (p. 143)
		Nursing Tip (p. 144)
		Table 6-6, The Labor Process and the Nurse (pp. 145-146)
		▸ Discuss how the nurse could involve the woman's partner in the labor process.
		▸ Discuss how a woman having a vaginal birth after a cesarean delivery might feel.
		*Class Activity **Divide the class into small groups and assign each group one of the following scenarios:***
		1. The woman in false labor
		2. The woman in true labor
		3. The woman who is VBAC
		Have each group identify the nursing interventions that need to be performed and discuss what special needs the patient may have. Have each group share its findings with the class and discuss ways the nurse could help the patient cope with her delivery status.
Explain common nursing responsibilities during labor and birth.	■ Nursing care during birth (p. 144) ☐ Nursing responsibilities during birth (p. 144) ☐ Immediate postpartum period: the third and	⊞ PPT slides 39, 40 𝒆 EILR IC images 20-23 𝒆 EILR OBQ question 9 𝒆 EILR TB questions 12, 14 𝒆 ESLR IRQ question 8

OBJECTIVES	CONTENT	TEACHING RESOURCES
	fourth stages of labor (p. 144)	SG Learning Activities, question 9 (p. 44)
		SG Review Questions, questions 8, 12-13, 26 (p. 46)
		BOOK RESOURCES
		Figure 6-20, The Table Contains the Sterile Instruments (p. 146)
		Figure 6-21, Perineal Scrub Preparation Is Done Just Before Birth (p. 147)
		Memory Jogger (p. 147)
		Figure 6-22, The Placenta After Delivery (p. 147)
		Figure 6-23, Vaginal Birth of a Fetus in a Vertex Position (pp. 148-149)
		Review Questions for the NCLEX® Examination, questions 4-5 (p. 156)
		GRN CTQ 1 (p. 156)
		▸ Discuss how the nurse could calm the patient if problems occur during delivery.
		▸ Discuss ways the nurse could communicate with a distracted or upset patient during a difficult delivery.
		Class Activity **Write the following list of birthing responsibilities on the board and have students identify which ones the nurse is responsible for:**
		– *Preparing the multipara*
		– *Transferring the patient to a delivery room*
		– *Measuring cervix dilation and effacement*
		– *Preparing delivery instruments*
		– *Prep for perineal scrub*
		– *Performing episiotomy*
		– *Providing initial care of the newborn*
		– *Delivering the placenta*
		– *Examining the placenta*
		Have students identify and explain other nursing responsibilities during birth.
Describe the care of the newborn immediately after birth.	■ Nursing care immediately after birth (p. 147) ☐ Care of the mother (p. 147)	PPT slides 41-48 EILR IC images 24-26 EILR OBQ question 10 EILR TB questions 13, 17-18, 20-21, 23, 26

OBJECTIVES	CONTENT	TEACHING RESOURCES
	– Observing for hemorrhage (p. 147) – Promoting comfort (p. 150) ☐ Care of the newborn immediately after delivery (p. 150) – Phase I: Care of the newborn (p. 150)	**e** ESLR IRQ questions 2, 6 **sg** SG Review Questions, questions 20, 25 (p. 47) **sg** SG Thinking Critically, questions 2, 3 (p. 50) **BOOK RESOURCES** Figure 6-24, The Nurse Applies the Sensor and Assesses the Newborn in the Radiant Warmer (p. 151) Figure 6-25, The Nurse Assists the Father in Cutting the Umbilical Cord (p. 151) Table 6-7, Apgar Scoring System (p. 152) Skill 6-6, Administering Eye Ointment to the Newborn (p. 153) Figure 6-26, The Naked Infant Is Placed on the Bare Chest of the Mother (p. 153) Skill 6-7, Administering Intramuscular Injections to the Newborn (p. 154) ▸ Discuss the Apgar scoring system. What does it determine? *Class Activity **Divide the class into small groups and have each group develop a plan that outlines all of the nursing interventions related to care of the newborn immediately after birth. They should include specific assessments that are performed and their required frequency. Have each group present its plan to the class for discussion.*** *Class Activity **Divide the class into groups and have each group identify three key areas of concern for maintaining the health of the newborn. Also have groups identify one nursing intervention for those three areas.***
Performance Evaluation		PPT slides 1-50 **e** EILR IC images 1-26 **e** EILR OBQ questions 1-10 **e** EILR TB questions 1-33 **e** ESLR IRQ questions 1-8 **sg** SG Learning Activities, questions 1, 2 (pp. 43-45) **sg** SG Review Questions, questions 1, 2 (pp. 45-48) **BOOK RESOURCES** Skill 6-2, Determining Fetal Heart Rate (p. 133)

OBJECTIVES	CONTENT	TEACHING RESOURCES
		Box 6-2, When to Auscultate and Document Fetal Heart Rate (p. 134)
		Figure 6-12, Determining Placement of Fetoscope or Sensor to Assess FHR (p. 134)
		Skill 6-3, External Electronic Fetal Monitoring (p. 135)
		Figure 6-13, Recording of the FHR in the Upper Grid and the Uterine Contractions in the Lower Grid (p. 135)
		Table 6-3, Fetal Heart Rate Categories and Nursing Care (p. 136)
		Figure 6-14, Variable Decelerations, Showing Their Typically Abrupt Onset and Offset (p. 136)
		Figure 6-15, Late Decelerations, Showing Their Pattern of Slowing, Which Persists After Contraction Ends (p. 137)
		Box 6-3, Reassuring and Nonreassuring Fetal Heart Rate and Uterine Activity Patterns (p. 137)
		Figure 6-16, The Nurse Helps the Mother Maintain Control and Use Breathing Techniques During Active Labor (p. 138)
		Skill 6-4, Testing for the Presence of Amniotic Fluid (Nitrazine Paper Test) (p. 138)
		Skill 6-5, Determining Contractions by Palpation (p. 139)
		Figure 6-17, The Nurse Explains the External Electronic Fetal Monitor to the Woman (p. 142)
		Figure 6-18, The Doula (p. 143)
		Figure 6-19, Standing and Walking During Early Labor (p. 143)
		SG SG Crossword Puzzle (pp. 48-49)
		SG SG Case Study, questions 1, 2 (p. 49)
		SG SG Thinking Critically, questions 1-4 (p. 50)
		SG SG Applying Knowledge, questions 1-6 (p. 51)
		BOOK RESOURCES
		Review Questions for the NCLEX® Examination, questions 1-5 (pp. 155-156)
		GRN CTQ 1 (p. 156)

6.3 Homework/Assignments:

6.3 Instructor's Notes/Student Feedback:

Lecture Outline

6 Nursing Care of Mother and Infant During Labor and Birth

Slide 1

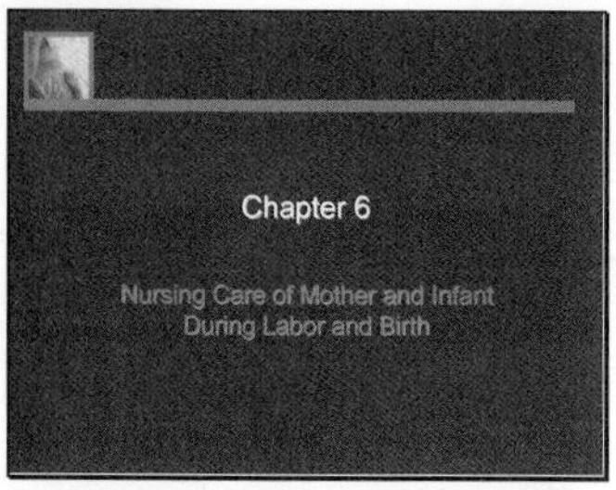

Chapter 6

Nursing Care of Mother and Infant
During Labor and Birth

Slide 2

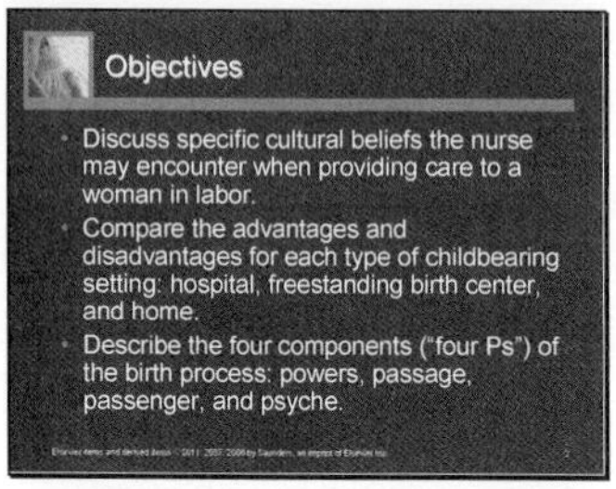

Objectives

- Discuss specific cultural beliefs the nurse may encounter when providing care to a woman in labor.
- Compare the advantages and disadvantages for each type of childbearing setting: hospital, freestanding birth center, and home.
- Describe the four components ("four Ps") of the birth process: powers, passage, passenger, and psyche.

Slide 3

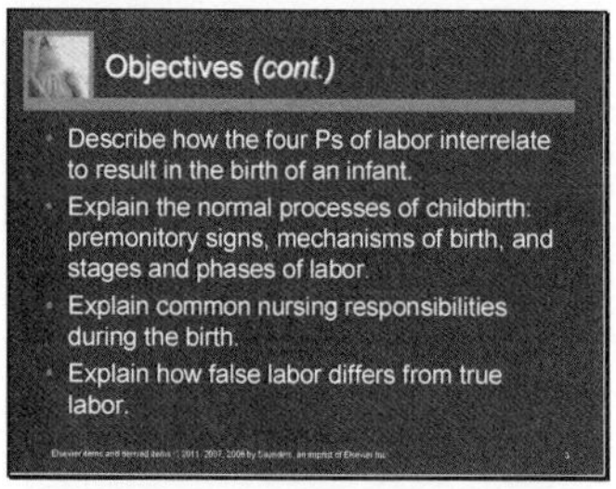

Objectives *(cont.)*

- Describe how the four Ps of labor interrelate to result in the birth of an infant.
- Explain the normal processes of childbirth: premonitory signs, mechanisms of birth, and stages and phases of labor.
- Explain common nursing responsibilities during the birth.
- Explain how false labor differs from true labor.

Slide 4

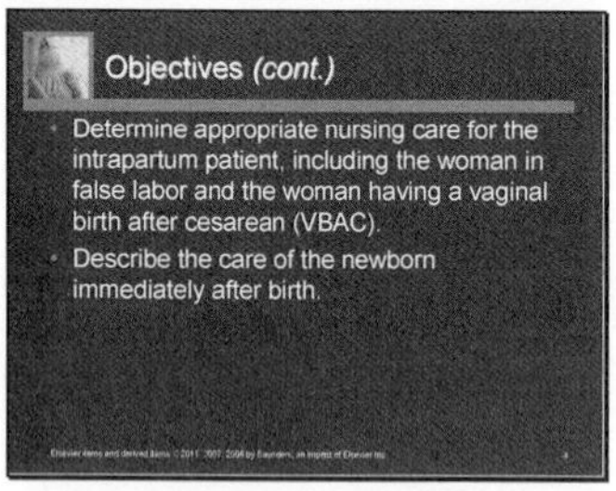

Objectives *(cont.)*

- Determine appropriate nursing care for the intrapartum patient, including the woman in false labor and the woman having a vaginal birth after cesarean (VBAC).
- Describe the care of the newborn immediately after birth.

ELSEVIER

Slide 5	• Refer to Table 6-1, pages 117-119. • Discuss the responsibilities of the nurse when interacting with families of different cultures.
Cultural Influences on Birth Practices · Role of woman in labor and delivery – Cultural preferences require flexibility · Role of father/partner in labor and delivery – May be driven by cultural practices	

Slide 6	• Review the advantages and disadvantages of each setting. • Does your community have a freestanding birth center?
Settings for Childbirth · Hospitals – Advantages – Disadvantages · Freestanding birth centers – Advantages – Disadvantages · Home – Advantages – Disadvantages	

Slide 7	• The powers that influence labor cause the cervix to dilate and move the fetus downward. Sources of power include uterine contractions and pushing efforts by the laboring woman. • The *passage* refers to the patient's pelvis. • The *passenger* is the fetus. • What impact can the patient's psyche have on the labor's progress and/or outcomes?
Components of the Birth Process · The Four "Ps" – Powers – Passage – Passenger – Psyche	

Slide 8	
Factors that Influence the Progress of Labor · Preparation · Position · Professional · Place · Procedures · People	

Slide 9	• A uterine contraction results from involuntary smooth muscle contractions. • The contractions assist in the effacement (thinning) of the cervix. • During labor, one of the nurse's roles is to monitor uterine contractions. • Define *frequency* and *duration*. • What are the differences among mild, moderate, and firm contractions?
Uterine Contractions Effect of contractions on the cervix — Efface — Dilate — Phase of contractions — Increment — Peak — Decrement — Frequency — Duration — Intensity — Mild — Moderate — Firm — Maternal pushing	

Slide 10

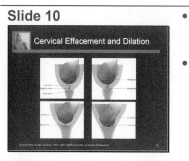

Cervical Effacement and Dilation

- Cervical effacement and dilation can be likened to sucking on a Lifesaver. As the candy becomes thinner, the center opening becomes wider.
- Describe the differences between cervical effacement and dilation for the primigravida and multigravida woman.

Slide 11

Contraction Cycle

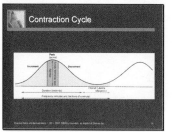

- Nurses must understand the components of the contraction cycle.
- Review the increments and peak of the contraction pattern.

Slide 12

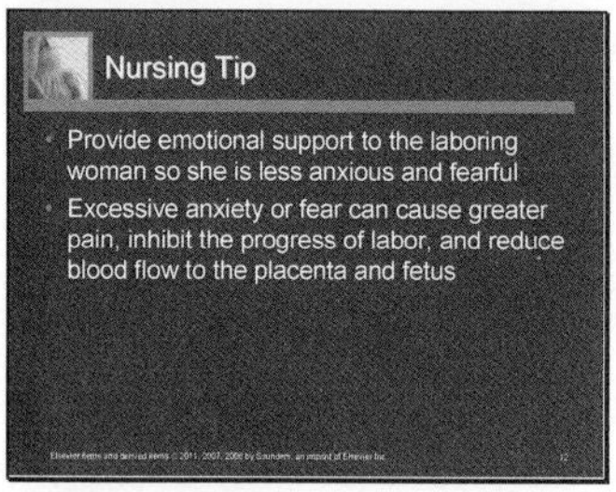

Nursing Tip
Provide emotional support to the laboring woman so she is less anxious and fearful
Excessive anxiety or fear can cause greater pain, inhibit the progress of labor, and reduce blood flow to the placenta and fetus

- What interventions can the nurse implement to reduce anxiety and fear during labor?

Slide 13

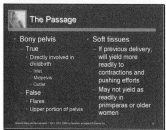

The Passage
Bony pelvis
True
Directly involved in childbirth
Inlet
Midpelvis
Outlet
False
Flares
Upper portion of pelvis
Soft tissues
If previous delivery, will yield more readily to contractions and pushing efforts
May not yield as readily in primiparas or older women

Slide 14

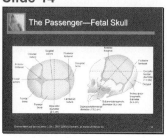

The Passenger—Fetal Skull

- The bones in the fetal head are separated by connective tissue.
- What is the importance of this tissue in relation to the birthing process?
- Compare and contrast the fontanels.

Slide 15	
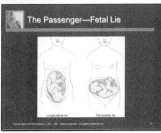	• *Fetal lie* refers to the position of the fetus in relation to the maternal spine. • Review the various fetal lie positions.

Slide 16	
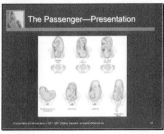	

Slide 17	
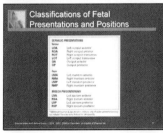	• Review the terminology used in each of the fetal presentations.

Slide 18	
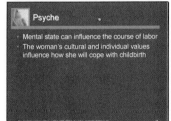	

Slide 19	

Slide 20

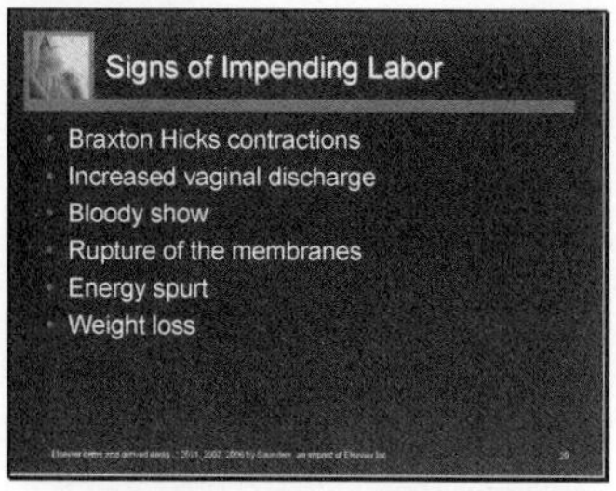

Signs of Impending Labor

- Braxton Hicks contractions
- Increased vaginal discharge
- Bloody show
- Rupture of the membranes
- Energy spurt
- Weight loss

- Compare and contrast the clinical manifestations of Braxton Hicks contractions and true labor.
- Bloody show is a normal occurrence prior to the onset of labor. Describe the manifestations associated with bloody show.
- Rupture of membranes warrants evaluation of the pregnant woman at the health care facility.

Slide 21

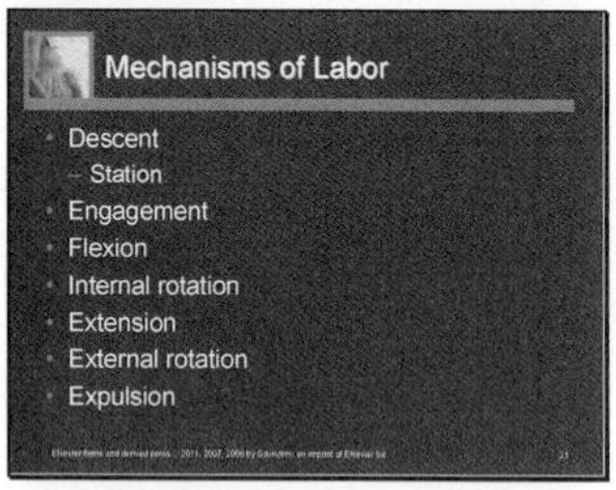

Mechanisms of Labor

- Descent
  - Station
- Engagement
- Flexion
- Internal rotation
- Extension
- External rotation
- Expulsion

- *Mechanisms of labor* refer to those physiological changes in positioning which take place during a normal vaginal delivery.
- Describe each of these positions.

Slide 22

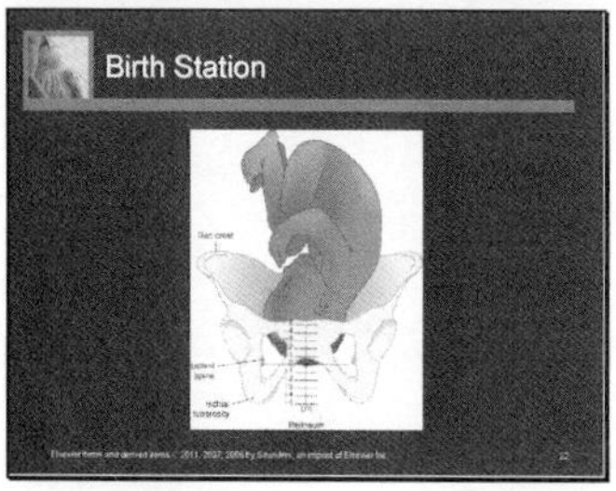

Birth Station

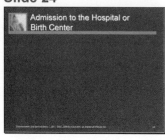

- *Station* refers to the position of the fetal head relative to the ischial spines.

Slide 23

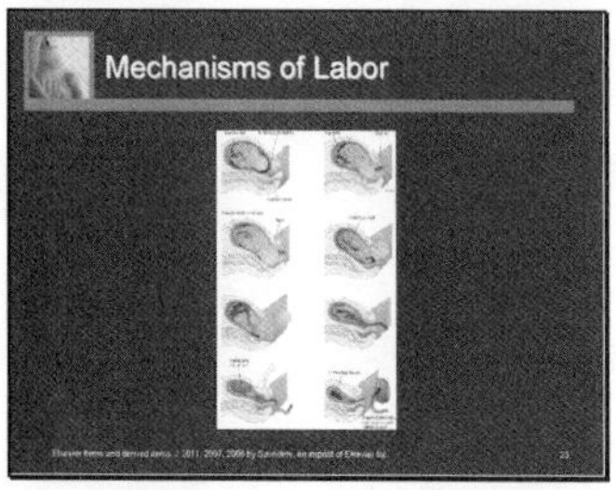

Mechanisms of Labor

- Also referred to as "cardinal movements."

Slide 24

Admission to the Hospital or Birth Center

Slide 25	
When to Go to the Hospital or Birth Center · Contractions · Ruptured membranes · Bleeding other than bloody show · Decreased fetal movement · Any other concern	• What is the timeline for patient education concerning how and when to seek care?

Slide 26	

Admission Data Collection
 	
· Three major assessments performed promptly on admission
  – Fetal condition
  – Maternal condition
  – Impending birth
	• Discuss Skill 6-1, Assisting with an Emergency Birth on page 130.

Slide 27	
Admission Procedures · Permits/consents · Laboratory tests · Intravenous infusion · Perineal prep · Determining fetal position and presentation	• Discuss the actions required for each task listed.

Slide 28	

Comparison of False and True Labor
 	
· False labor
  – Contractions irregular
  – Walking relieves contractions
  – Bloody show usually not present
  – No change in effacement/dilation of cervix
 	
· True labor
  – Contractions gradually develop a regular pattern
  – Contractions become stronger and more effective with walking
  – Discomfort in lower back/abdomen
  – Bloody show often present
  – Progressive effacement and dilation of cervix
	• Refer to Table 6-2, page 131.
	• What is the greatest difference between the types of labor? *False labor does not result in cervical changes, while true labor causes changes in cervical dilation and effacement.*
	• At what point during the pregnancy should education be provided regarding false and true labor? *Successful education should begin early in the pregnancy. This approach allows time for reinforcement throughout the pregnancy at each visit to the health care provider.*

Audience Response Question #1
Which is a characteristic of true labor?
1. Contractions are regular, and the intensity remains the same
2. Contractions are irregular, and the intensity remains the same
3. Contractions are regular and are intensified by walking
4. Contractions are regular and are not intensified by walking

Slide 29

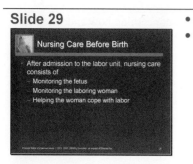

- Fetal monitoring can be intermittent or continuous.
- Review factors which can determine the type of monitoring employed.

Slide 30

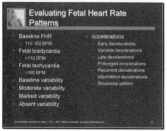

- Review Skill 6-2 on page 133, Box 6-2 on page 134, and Skill 6-3 on page 135.

Slide 31

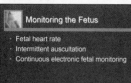

Slide 32

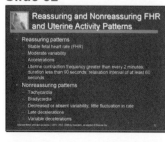

- See Box 6-3 on page 137 for more details.
- A part of the nursing assessment is the evaluation of fetal heart patterns.
- Nonreassuring patterns require reporting to the health care provider.

Slide 33

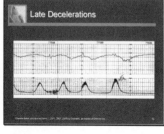

- Review Box 6-3, page 137.

Slide 34

Monitoring the Woman
- Vital signs
- Contractions
- Progress of labor
- Intake and output
- Response to labor

- Discuss the frequency of each of the items to be monitored.

Slide 35

Six Lamaze Institute Basic Practices for Maternity Care
- Labor should begin on its own
- Woman should have freedom of movement
- Woman should have a birth support person or doula
- No routine interventions should be performed
- Woman should be in non-supine positions
- Woman should not be separated from infant

Slide 36

Helping the Woman Cope with Labor
- Labor support
- Teaching
- Providing encouragement
- Supporting/teaching the partner
  - Teach how labor pains affect the woman's behavior/attitude
  - How to adapt responses to the woman's behavior
  - What to expect in his/her own emotional responses
  - Effects of epidural analgesia

- Review the components of labor support with the class.
- What are the recommended positions of comfort for the laboring women?

Slide 37

Stages and Phases of Labor
- First stage—dilation and effacement (can last 4 to 6 hours)
- Second stage—expulsion of fetus (30 minutes to 2 hours)
- Third stage—expulsion of placenta (5 to 30 minutes)
- Fourth stage—recovery

- The labor of the primigravida will last longer than that of a multigravida.
- What behaviors are associated with each of the stages of labor?

Audience Response Question #2
During which stage of labor does "crowning" occur?
  1. First
  2. Second
  3. Third
  4. Fourth

Slide 38

Vaginal Birth After Cesarean
- Main concern
- Uterine scar will rupture
- Can disrupt placental blood flow
- Lead to hemorrhage
- Woman may need more support than other laboring women
- Nurse provides empathy and support

- Discuss some of the psychological barriers that may arise for a woman with VBAC.

Leifer

Slide 39

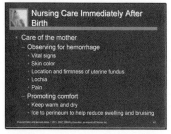

Nursing Responsibilities During Birth

- Preparing the delivery instruments and infant equipment
- Perineal scrub
- Administering medications
- Providing initial care to the infant
- Assessing Apgar score
- Assessing infant for obvious abnormalities
- Examining the placenta
- Identifying mother and infant
- Promoting parent-infant bonding

Slide 40

Immediate Postpartum Period: Third and Fourth Stages of Labor

- Third stage—expulsion of placenta
  - Schulze or Duncan's
- Fourth stage—nursing care includes
  - Identifying and preventing hemorrhage
  - Evaluating and intervening for pain
  - Observing bladder function and urine output
  - Evaluating recovery from anesthesia
  - Providing initial care to the newborn infant
  - Promoting bonding and attachment between the infant and family

- After the birth of the baby, the nurse continues to assess the mother.
- Review both normal and abnormal findings.

Slide 41

Nursing Care Immediately After Birth

- Care of the mother
  - Observing for hemorrhage
    - Vital signs
    - Skin color
    - Location and firmness of uterine fundus
    - Lochia
    - Pain
  - Promoting comfort
    - Keep warm and dry
    - Ice to perineum to help reduce swelling and bruising

Slide 42

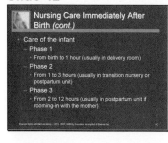

Nursing Care Immediately After Birth (cont.)

- Care of the infant
  - Phase 1
    - From birth to 1 hour (usually in delivery room)
  - Phase 2
    - From 1 to 3 hours (usually in transition nursery or postpartum unit)
  - Phase 3
    - From 2 to 12 hours (usually in postpartum unit if rooming-in with the mother)

- If the newborn does not experience any difficulty with adaptation to extrauterine life, the infant will often remain with the mother in the delivery room.

Slide 43

Phase 1: Care of the Newborn

- Initial care includes
  - Maintaining thermoregulation
  - Maintaining cardiorespiratory function
  - Observing for urination and/or passage of meconium
  - Identifying the mother, father, and newborn
  - Performing a brief assessment for major anomalies
  - Encouraging bonding/breastfeeding

Slide 44

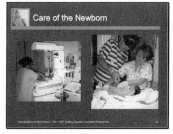

Care of the Newborn

Slide 45

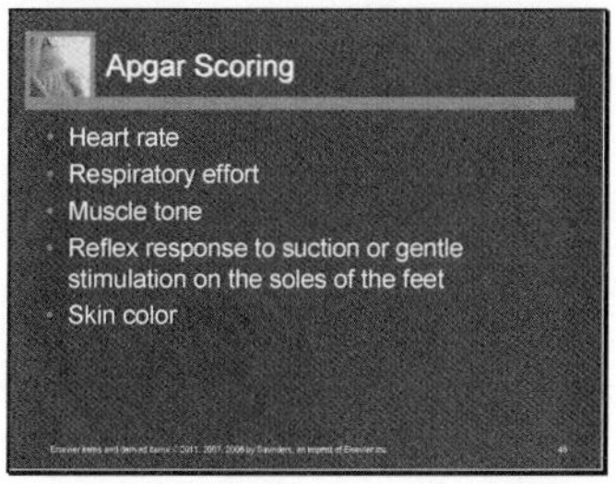

Apgar Scoring
- Heart rate
- Respiratory effort
- Muscle tone
- Reflex response to suction or gentle stimulation on the soles of the feet
- Skin color

- The Apgar is performed twice. At what times is the scoring performed?
- A point-based system is used. Each of the parameters is given a score between 0 and 2 points.
- What are the implications of the score obtained?

Audience Response Question #3
A neonate's Apgar score at 5 minutes is 9. In what category did this neonate most likely score a 1?
   1. Heart rate
   2. Respiratory effort
   3. Muscle tone
   4. Skin color
   5. Reflex response

Slide 46

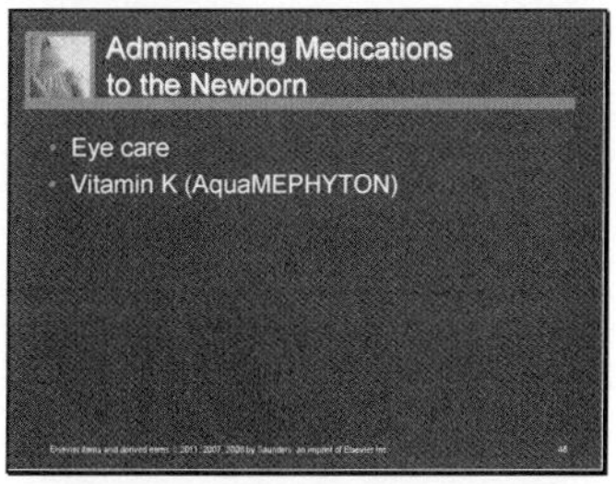

Administering Medications to the Newborn
- Eye care
- Vitamin K (AquaMEPHYTON)

- Review Skill 6-6 on page 153 and Skill 6-7 on page 154.

Audience Response Question #4
What medication is most often used for neonatal eye care?
   1. Silver nitrate 1%
   2. Triple dye
   3. Silver nitrate 2%
   4. Erythromycin ophthalmic ointment

Slide 47

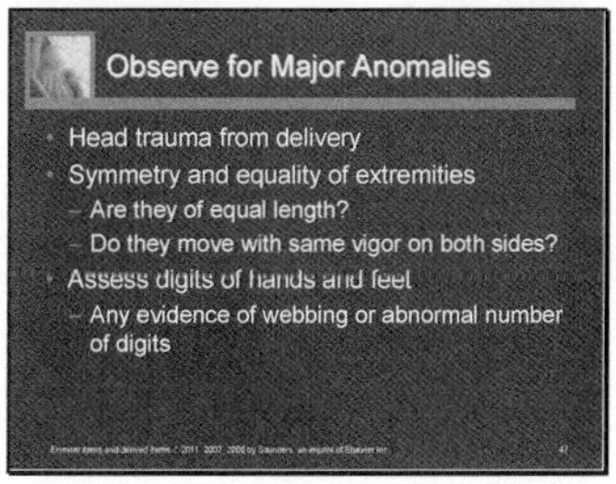

Observe for Major Anomalies
- Head trauma from delivery
- Symmetry and equality of extremities
  - Are they of equal length?
  - Do they move with same vigor on both sides?
- Assess digits of hands and feet
  - Any evidence of webbing or abnormal number of digits

- What else should be assessed in regard to major anomalies?
- Which anomalies require immediate notification to the RN or health care provider?

Introduction to Maternity & Pediatric Nursing, 6th ed.
Leifer

Slide 48

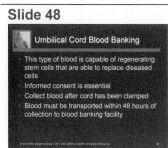

Umbilical Cord Blood Banking

- This type of blood is capable of regenerating stem cells that are able to replace diseased cells
- Informed consent is essential
- Collect blood after cord has been clamped
- Blood must be transported within 48 hours of collection to blood banking facility

Slide 49

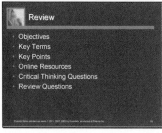

Question for Review

- State the primary fetal risk during the first and second stages of labor and the primary maternal risk during the fourth stage of labor

Slide 50

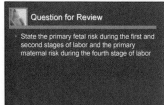

Review

- Objectives
- Key Terms
- Key Points
- Online Resources
- Critical Thinking Questions
- Review Questions

TEACHING FOCUS

In this chapter, students will have the opportunity to learn about the various ways to manage pain during labor and delivery. Students will examine methods for childbirth preparation and will be introduced to the advantages and limitations of pharmacological and nonpharmacological methods of pain management. Students also will have the opportunity to learn how pharmacological and nonpharmacological methods of pain management relate to various nursing roles.

MATERIALS AND RESOURCES

☐ Computer and PowerPoint projector (all lessons)
☐ Model of the female pelvis (all lessons)

☐ Tennis balls (Lesson 7.2)
☐ Videotape/DVD of nonpharmacological labor-management techniques (Lesson 7.2)

LESSON CHECKLIST

Preparations for this lesson include:
- Lecture
- Guest speaker: Nurse who teaches prenatal classes
- Evaluation of student knowledge and skills needed to perform all entry-level activities related to nursing management of pain during labor and birth, including:
  ○ Conducting childbearing classes to educate expectant mothers and fathers on prenatal and postnatal concerns
  ○ Assessing for pain tolerance and preference for types of pain management during labor
  ○ Implementing nonpharmacological pain management techniques as needed
  ○ Assessing pharmacological pain management options and educating patient on potential risks

KEY TERMS

blood patch (p. 169)
Bradley method (p. 160)
cleansing breath (p. 163)
effleurage (p. 162)

endorphin (p. 159)
focal point (p. 162)
Lamaze method (p. 160)
opioid (p. 165)

pain threshold (p. 159)
pain tolerance (p. 159)
vaginal birth after cesarean (VBAC) (p. 158)

ADDITIONAL RESOURCES

TEACH PPT slide(s) Chapter 7, 1-30
EILR IC image(s) Chapter 7, 1-8
EILR OBQ question(s) Chapter 7, 1-10
EILR TB question(s) Chapter 7, 1-31
ESLR IRQ question(s) Chapter 7, 1-5
SG Chapter 7, pp. 53-60

Legend

PPT
TEACH
PowerPoint
Slides

EILR
EVOLVE Instructor
Learning Resources:
Image Collection (IC),
Open-Book Quizzes
(OBQ), Test Bank (TB)

ESLR
EVOLVE Student
Learning Resources:
Interactive Review
Questions (IRQ) for
the NCLEX®
Examination

SG
Study Guide

CTQ
Critical Thinking
Question in
Nursing Care Plan
(NCP CTQ) or Get
Ready for the
NCLEX! (GRN
CTQ)

Class Activities are indicated in ***bold italic***.

Introduction to Maternity & Pediatric Nursing, 6ʰ ed.

Leifer

LESSON 7.1

PRETEST

1. Which of the following is a source of pain during labor?
   a. increased endorphin levels
   b. increased uterine blood supply during contractions
   c. stimulation of large-diameter nerve fibers
   d. dilation and effacement of the cervix

2. *Pain tolerance* refers to
   a. pain perception.
   b. the least amount of sensation perceived as painful.
   c. the amount of pain a person is willing to endure.
   d. the gate control theory of pain.

3. Effleurage is a relaxation technique that
   a. involves stroking the skin with the fingertips during contractions.
   b. uses guided imagery.
   c. must be done with a partner.
   d. includes heat therapy to reduce pain.

4. What problem is sometimes associated with modified pace breathing?
   a. accelerated labor   c. hypoventilation
   b. hyperventilation   d. slowed labor

5. Which of the following is an analgesic potentiator?
   a. naloxone (Narcan)   c. butorphanol (Stadol)
   b. promethazine (Phenergan)   d. meperidine (Demerol)

6. Which childbirth preparation method first emphasized the father's role during labor?
   a. Dick-Read method   c. Bradley method
   b. Lamaze method   d. vaginal birth after cesarean classes

7. Why is naloxone (Narcan) administered?
   a. to numb the perineum
   b. to prevent nausea and vomiting
   c. to reverse opioid-induced respiratory depression
   d. to potentiate the analgesic effect of opioids

8. What is the major advantage of regional anesthetics?
   a. They are cost-effective.
   b. They can be initiated by an LPN.
   c. They provide pain relief without unconsciousness.
   d. They are administered intravenously.

9. What is a side effect of epidural or spinal blocks?
   a. hypotension   c. drug addiction
   b. hypertension   d. diarrhea

10. What is an advantage of nonpharmacological pain management in labor?
    a. It does not harm the mother or fetus.
    b. It does not require the mother's participation.
    c. It can slow labor.
    d. It is easy to teach during late stages of labor.

Answers

1. d	3. a	5. b	7. c	9. a
2. c	4. b	6. c	8. c	10. a

Leifer

BACKGROUND ASSESSMENT

Question: What is the gate control theory, and how does it relate to the nonpharmacological management of pain during labor?

Answer: The gate control theory of pain relates to how pain impulses are transmitted to the central nervous system via small-diameter nerve fibers. According to this theory, stimulation of large-diameter nerve fibers can block the conduction of pain impulses transmitted on small-diameter nerve fibers. Stimulation of the large-diameter nerve fibers temporarily "closes a gate" to pain perception. Some of the nonpharmacological methods that stimulate the large-diameter nerve fibers and conversely block the small-diameter fibers include effleurage, massage, thermal stimulation, touch relaxation, and hydrotherapy. The gate control theory of pain is a basis for nonpharmacological nursing interventions that enhance a woman's pain tolerance during labor.

Question: What are the various types of pharmacological analgesics used during labor, and what are their functions?

Answer: An analgesic is a drug that relieves pain without loss of consciousness. Analgesics used in obstetrics include systemic narcotics such as meperidine and fentanyl; combination opioid agonists/antagonists such as butorphanol and nalbuphine; and analgesic potentiators (also called *ataractics*) such as promethazine and hydroxyzine. Narcotics are controlled substances that depress pain impulse transmission by interacting with opioid receptors. They are the most common form of labor pain relief medication in the United States. Because they can induce hypotension or respiratory depression in the mother or infant, small doses and timing of administration are important to avoid fetal respiratory depression. Naloxone is an opioid antagonist that reverses the side effects of a narcotic. It should be available to treat fetal or maternal respiratory depression. Drugs such as promethazine and hydroxyzine have a mixed agonist/antagonist effect. As a result, they may cause less respiratory depression but should not be given to a woman with drug addiction to avoid inducing withdrawal symptoms in her or her infant. Analgesic potentiators enhance the effect of narcotic analgesics, which can reduce the dose of narcotic required and provide antianxiety effects. An anesthetic is an agent that produces partial or complete loss of sensation. Examples of anesthesia used in labor and delivery are local infiltration, pudendal block, epidural block, subarachnoid block, and general anesthesia.

CRITICAL THINKING QUESTION

The nurse is admitting a 29-year-old primigravida to the labor and delivery unit. She is having contractions every 6 minutes and is 2.5 cm dilated. She is accompanied by her husband, who is holding her hand and talking gently to her. What nursing assessments and interventions should the nurse address at admission?

Guidelines: Promoting relaxation is key to enhancing the patient's labor and delivery. The nurse should begin by assessing whether the patient and her husband have attended childbirth preparation classes. The nurse can use this information to review Lamaze breathing techniques and the patient's focal point as well as explain the different procedures and equipment that may be used during labor and delivery. The nurse should ask the patient if she and her husband toured the unit beforehand and understand the setting and routine. The nurse can also determine the patient's preference regarding pain management and provide support for her decision. To promote relaxation and effective concentration, the nurse should reduce environmental distractions by ensuring low lighting; dry, clean linens; and a comfortable room temperature. The nurse can also review with the patient the pain rating scales that will help accurately assess her discomfort. Allow the patient and her husband to ask questions, and reinforce that they will have the support of labor and delivery nurses and physicians throughout their experience.

OBJECTIVES	CONTENT	TEACHING RESOURCES

List the common types of classes offered to childbearing families.	■ Education for childbearing (p. 157)
	
	□ Types of classes available (p. 157)
	
	□ Variations of basic childbirth preparation classes (p. 158)
	
	   – Refresher classes (p. 158)
	
	   – Cesarean birth classes (p. 158)
	
	   – Vaginal birth after cesarean classes (p. 158)
	
	   – Adolescent childbirth preparation classes (p. 158)
	
	□ Basic content of all childbirth preparation classes (p. 158)
	
	   – Benefits of exercise (p. 158)
	
	   – Pain control methods for labor (p. 158)
		PPT slides 4-7
		
		e EILR IC images 1, 2
		
		e EILR OBQ question 1
		
		e EILR TB questions 15, 24
		
		SG Learning Activities, question 5 (p. 54)
		
		SG Review Questions, questions 2, 10 (pp. 57-58)
		
		BOOK RESOURCES
		
		Health Promotion, Types of Prenatal Classes (p. 157)
		
		Figure 7-1, Teaching Prenatal Class (p. 158)
		
		Figure 7-2, The Partner Massages the Foot of the Pregnant Woman (p. 159)
		
		Box 7-1, Selected Nonpharmacological Pain Relief Measures (p. 161)
		
		▶ Discuss the various types of prenatal classes and the benefits associated with each.
		
		*Class Activity **If class size allows, divide the class into eight groups, and assign each group one of the prenatal classes listed in Health Promotion, Types of Prenatal Classes (p. 157). Before class, have each group research the goals, methods, and clientele for each type of class. If possible, have the groups visit one of the childbirth classes. Then have each group report its findings to the class for a discussion comparing and contrasting the various types of classes. (For students to prepare for this activity, see Homework/Assignments #1.)***

Describe factors that influence a woman's comfort during labor.	■ Childbirth and pain (p. 158)
	
	□ How childbirth pain differs from other pain (p. 159)
	
	□ Factors that influence labor pain (p. 159)
	
	   – Pain threshold and pain tolerance (p. 159)
	
	   – Sources of pain during labor (p. 159)
	
	   – Physical factors that
		PPT slides 8, 9
		
		e EILR IC image 3
		
		e EILR OBQ questions 2-4
		
		e EILR TB questions 1-2, 16, 21, 26, 30
		
		e ESLR IRQ question 5
		
		SG Learning Activities, questions 1-3 (p. 53)
		
		SG Review Questions, question 1 (p. 57)
		
		BOOK RESOURCES
		
		Nursing Tips (p. 159)
		
		Box 7-1, Selected Nonpharmacological Pain Relief

OBJECTIVES	CONTENT	TEACHING RESOURCES
	modify pain (p. 159) – Central nervous system factors (p. 159) – Maternal condition (p. 159) – Cervical readiness (p. 159) – Pelvis (p. 159) – Labor intensity (p. 160) – Fatigue (p. 160) – Fetal presentation and position (p. 160) – Interventions of caregivers (p. 160) – Psychosocial factors that modify pain (p. 160)	Measures (p. 161) Figure 7-3, Effleurage (p. 162) ▶ Discuss how pain affects a woman's ability to manage labor and what factors affect her decision to use either pharmacological or nonpharmacological methods to deal with the discomfort. *Class Activity Have each student list five factors that influence comfort during labor and provide an example of each factor. Lead a class discussion on physical and psychosocial factors that affect pain, as well as the nurse's role in modifying the patient's pain during labor.*
Discuss the advantages and limitations of nonpharmacological methods of pain management during labor.	■ Nonpharmacological childbirth preparation and pain management (p. 160) ☐ Advantages (p. 160) ☐ Limitations (p. 160)	PPT slide 10 *e* EILR IC images 3, 4 *e* EILR TB questions 3, 29 SG Learning Activities, question 1 (p. 53) SG Thinking Critically, question 3 (p. 59) **BOOK RESOURCES** Box 7-1, Selected Nonpharmacological Pain Relief Measures (p. 161) Figure 7-3, Effleurage (p. 162) Figure 7-4, Sacral Pressure (p. 162) *Class Activity Divide the class into small groups and have each group discuss how adequate physical and emotional preparation for childbirth by both mother and father can be used effectively to decrease labor discomfort and control pain through nonpharmacological means. Then, have each group share its findings with the class* *Class Activity Ask students to identify the advantages and disadvantages of nonpharmacological pain management for both the mother and the fetus. List each one on the*

OBJECTIVES	CONTENT	TEACHING RESOURCES
		board in a two-column table for comparison.
Describe the methods of childbirth preparation.	☐ Childbirth preparation methods (p. 160) – Dick-Read method (p. 160) – Bradley method (p. 160) – Lamaze method (p. 160)	🖳 PPT slide 11 𝓮 EILR TB questions 19, 20 𝓮 ESLR IRQ question 2 📘 SG Applying Knowledge, question 4 (p. 60) *Class Activity* **Lead a class discussion on the role of the husband in the preparation for childbirth. To what extent should the husband be directly involved in the preparation classes for childbirth? How would that participation be evidenced using the three methods mentioned?** *Class Activity* **Divide the class into three groups and assign each group one of the methods of childbirth preparation (Dick-Read, Bradley, and Lamaze). Prior to class, have each group research the method's theorist, philosophy, components, and practices. Then, have each group report its findings for a classroom discussion that compares and contrasts the different childbirth preparation methods. (For students to prepare for this activity, see Homework/Assignments #2.)**

7.1 Homework/Assignments:

1. Divide the class into eight groups, and assign each group one of the prenatal classes listed in Health Promotion Considerations. Before class, have each group research the goals, methods, and clientele for each type of class. If possible, have the groups visit one of the childbirth classes.

2. Divide the class into three groups and assign each group one of the methods of childbirth preparation (Dick-Read, Bradley, and Lamaze). Before class have each group research the method's theorist, philosophy, components, and practices.

7.1 Instructor's Notes/Student Feedback:

LESSON 7.2

CRITICAL THINKING QUESTION

A nurse is caring for a patient who has relied on nonpharmacological methods of pain control during her early phases of labor. Her cervix is now 5 cm dilated and her amniotic sac has ruptured. She rates her pain as a 9 on a scale of 0 to 10 (0 = no pain, 10 = maximum pain) and is requesting an epidural anesthetic. What nursing assessments and interventions should the nurse provide?

Guidelines: The nurse should have already assessed the patient during admission for any allergies (especially to dental anesthetics), as well as prior back surgery, infection, and blood pressure irregularities. The anesthesiologist or nurse anesthetist will explain the epidural procedure and its effects to the patient. It is important that the nurse reinforce this information because the patient's labor pain and anxiety make it difficult for her to concentrate and retain information. Written consent for the procedure should be documented in her chart. The patient will receive IV fluids to counteract any hypotensive effects of the anesthetic. A urinary catheter should also be inserted before the epidural to prevent urinary retention. The nurse should assist the patient in maintaining a side-lying (or sitting) position and instruct her to remain very still while the anesthesiologist or nurse anesthetist inserts a large needle and catheter into her epidural space and a test dose is administered. If she needs to remain flat to facilitate drug dispersal, put a pillow under her right hip to prevent supine hypotensive syndrome. The nurse should assess for hypotension by recording blood pressure readings and fetal heart rates every 5 minutes after the block has started and should monitor urinary output. Side rails should be kept up because the patient is at greater risk for falls due to her decreased motor response and sensation. Reinforce that the epidural may not completely alleviate labor pain but will significantly diminish her discomfort. Finally, document her tolerance of the procedure and her pain rating.

OBJECTIVES	CONTENT	TEACHING RESOURCES
Explain nonpharmacological methods of pain management for labor, including the nursing role for each.	☐ Nonpharmacological techniques (p. 161) – Relaxation techniques (p. 161) – Skin stimulation (p. 162) – Positioning (p. 162) – Diversion/ distraction (p. 162) – Breathing (p. 163) ☐ The nurse's role in nonpharmacological techniques (p. 164)	⊠▪ PPT slides 12-17 𝒆 EILR IC images 3-5 𝒆 EILR TB questions 4-6, 8, 18, 22, 25, 27-29, 31 𝒆 ESLR IRQ question 1 SG Learning Activities, questions 4, 6-8 (p. 54) SG Review Questions, questions 11, 12 (p. 58) SG Case Study, questions 1, 2 (p. 59) **BOOK RESOURCES** Figure 7-4, Sacral Pressure (p. 162) Figure 7-5, Breathing Patterns (p. 163) Box 7-2, How to Recognize and Correct Hyperventilation (p. 164) Nursing Tip (p. 164) Review Questions for the NCLEX® Examination, question 2 (p. 173) *Class Activity Lead a class discussion on the areas of the body where tension is most likely to occur and the best methods for relaxation. What is the nurse's role in providing pain relief with nonpharmacological interventions? What are the different ways a nurse can*

OBJECTIVES	CONTENT	TEACHING RESOURCES
		emotionally support a woman in significant discomfort during labor?
		Class Activity Ask students to identify signs and symptoms of hyperventilation. Then discuss proper nursing interventions to use when caring for a patient in labor who is hyperventilating.
		Class Activity Invite a nurse who teaches prenatal classes to speak to the students about nonpharmacological techniques to assist a laboring woman.
Discuss the advantages and limitations of pharmacological methods of pain management.	■ Pharmacological pain management (p. 164) ☐ Physiology of pregnancy and its relationship to analgesia and anesthesia (p. 164) ☐ Advantages (p. 164) ☐ Limitations (p. 165)	🖾 PPT slides 18-21 𝒆 EILR OBQ questions 5, 6 𝒆 ESLR IRQ question 3 📗 SG Learning Activities, questions 9, 10, 14-15 (p. 55) **BOOK RESOURCES** Table 7-1, Intrapartum Analgesics and Related Drugs (p. 165) Review Questions for the NCLEX® Examination, question 1 (p. 173) ▶ Discuss how the pain of labor may trigger a "stress response" for the patient and the appropriate procedure to follow if this occurs. ▶ Discuss the possible effects of pharmacological methods on the fetus. *Class Activity Divide the class into small groups and have each group create a table listing the advantages and disadvantages of pharmacological pain management for both the mother and the fetus. Next, have the groups share their findings with the class. List each group's suggestions on the board for comparison.* *Class Activity Lead a class discussion on the potential complications and related nursing considerations for managing labor pain in a woman who has a history of drug addiction.*
Explain each type of pharmacological pain management, including the nursing role for each.	☐ Analgesics and adjunctive drugs (p. 165) – Narcotic (opioid) analgesics (p. 165) – Narcotic antagonist (p. 165) – Adjunctive drugs (p. 166)	🖾 PPT slides 22-28 𝒆 EILR IC images 6-8 𝒆 EILR OBQ questions 7-10 𝒆 EILR TB questions 7, 9-14, 17, 23 𝒆 ESLR IRQ question 4 📗 SG Learning Activities, questions 11-13, 15-16 (p. 55)

OBJECTIVES	CONTENT	TEACHING RESOURCES
	☐ Regional analgesics and anesthetics (p. 166) – Local infiltration (p. 166) – Pudendal block (p. 166) – Epidural block (p. 167) – Subarachnoid (spinal) block (p. 169) ☐ General anesthesia (p. 169) – Adverse effects in the mother (p. 169) – Adverse effects in the neonate (p. 169) ☐ The nurse's role in pharmacological techniques (p. 169)	SG Review Questions, questions 3-9, 13-15 (pp. 57-58) SG Thinking Critically, question 2 (p. 59) SG Applying Knowledge, questions 1-3 (p. 60) **BOOK RESOURCES** Table 7-1, Intrapartum Analgesics and Related Drugs (p. 165) Figure 7-6, Pudendal Block Anesthesia (p. 166) Table 7-2, Methods of Anesthesia Administration for Childbirth (p. 167) Figure 7-7, Epidural and Spinal Anesthesia (p. 168) Figure 7-8, Epidural Blood Patch (p. 169) Safety Alert (p. 168) Nursing Care Plan 7-1, The Woman Needing Pain Management During Labor (pp. 170-172) Safety Alert (p. 172) Review Questions for the NCLEX® Examination, questions 3-5 (p. 173) ▸ Discuss the distinguishing characteristics among pudendal, epidural, and subarachnoid blocks and the appropriate use for each. ▸ Discuss the protocol a nurse should practice to ensure the patient's safety once a pharmacological method has been administered. *Class Activity **Provide students with a list of the following medications: meperidine, fentanyl, butorphanol, naloxone, promethazine, and hydroxyzine. Then, ask students to write the drug class, dosage/route, contraindications, peak onset/duration, side effects, and nursing considerations for each medication.*** *Class Activity **Divide the class into five groups and assign each group one of the types of anesthesia listed in Table 7-2 (p. 167) (local infiltration, pudendal block, epidural block, subarachnoid block, and general anesthesia). Before class, have each group research the method and nursing implications for its assigned type of anesthesia. Then, have each group share its findings with the class for comparison. (For students to prepare for this activity, see Homework/Assignments #1.)*** *Class Activity **Provide students with a photocopy of Figure 7-7 (p. 168) with the terms removed. Ask students to fill in the correct descriptions for the parts illustrating***

OBJECTIVES	CONTENT	TEACHING RESOURCES
		epidural and spinal anesthesia insertion sites and anesthesia levels during a vaginal and C-section delivery.
Performance Evaluation		☒▤ PPT slides 1-30
		e EILR IC images 1-8
		e EILR OBQ questions 1-10
		e EILR TB questions 1-31
		e ESLR IRQ questions 1-5
		📓 SG Learning Activities, questions 1-16 (pp. 53-56)
		📓 SG Review Questions, questions 1-15 (pp. 56-59)
		📓 SG Case Study, questions 1, 2 (p. 60)
		📓 SG Thinking Critically, questions 1-3 (p. 59)
		📓 SG Applying Knowledge, questions 1-4 (pp. 59-60)
		BOOK RESOURCES
		💡 NCP CTQ 1 (p. 172)
		Review Questions for the NCLEX® Examination, questions 1-5 (p. 173)

7.2 Homework/Assignments:

1. Divide the class into five groups and assign each group one of the types of anesthesia listed in Table 7-2 (p. 167) (local infiltration, pudendal block, epidural block, subarachnoid block, and general anesthesia). Before class, have each group research the method and nursing implications for its assigned type of anesthesia.

7.2 Instructor's Notes/Student Feedback:

7 Lecture Outline
Nursing Management of Pain During Labor and Birth

Slide 1

Chapter 7

Nursing Management of Pain During
Labor and Birth

Slide 2

Objectives

- List the common types of classes offered to childbearing families.
- Describe factors that influence a woman's comfort during labor.
- Describe the methods of childbirth preparation.

Slide 3

Objectives *(cont.)*

- Discuss the advantages and limitations of nonpharmacological methods of pain management during labor.
- Explain nonpharmacological methods of pain management for labor, including the nursing role for each.
- Discuss the advantages and limitations of pharmacological methods of pain management.
- Explain each type of pharmacological pain management including the nursing role for each.

Slide 4

Education for Childbearing

- Ideally, educational preparation for childbirth begins prior to conception

Slide 5

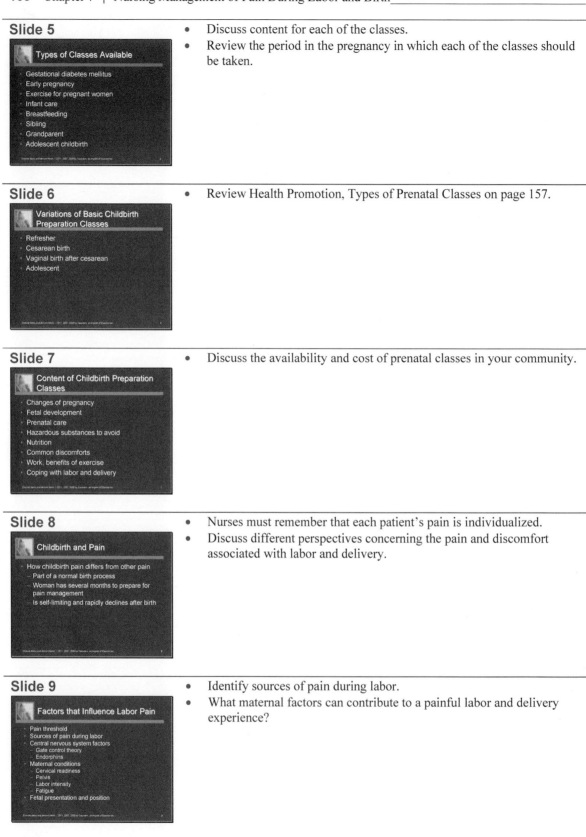

- Discuss content for each of the classes.
- Review the period in the pregnancy in which each of the classes should be taken.

Slide 6

- Review Health Promotion, Types of Prenatal Classes on page 157.

Slide 7

- Discuss the availability and cost of prenatal classes in your community.

Slide 8

- Nurses must remember that each patient's pain is individualized.
- Discuss different perspectives concerning the pain and discomfort associated with labor and delivery.

Slide 9

- Identify sources of pain during labor.
- What maternal factors can contribute to a painful labor and delivery experience?

Leifer

Slide 10	
Nonpharmacological Pain Management Advantages – Nonpharmacological methods do not harm the mother or fetus – They do not slow labor if they provide adequate pain control – They carry no risk for allergy or adverse drug effects	• Nonpharmacological methods of pain management can be used alone for a woman desiring a labor experience without medication or in conjunction with pharmacological methods. • Identify the best means to prepare the woman and her partner for the use of nonpharmacological methods of pain management.

Slide 11	
Methods of Childbirth Preparation • Dick-Read method • Bradley method • Lamaze method	• The Dick-Read method incorporates the concepts of fear, tension, and pain. • The Bradley method emphasizes slow abdominal breathing and relaxation techniques. • The Lamaze method uses mental conditioning and breathing techniques to occupy the patient's mind. • Who might be best suited for each of these methods?

Slide 12	
Selected Nonpharmacological Pain Relief Measures • Relaxation techniques • Skin stimulation • Effleurage • Sacral pressure • Thermal stimulation • Positioning • Diversion and distraction • Breathing	• A combination of nonpharmacological relief measures can be utilized by any single patient. • Discuss and demonstrate these methods. • Ask for class input concerning methods they have used or seen in the clinical setting.

Audience Response Question #1

A woman is in the first stage of labor. She reports that her she is experiencing moderate back discomfort with every contraction. The best nonpharmacological intervention you can encourage is:

    1. Diversion
    2. Sacral pressure
    3. Effleurage
    4. Thermal stimulation

Slide 13	
Skin Stimulation	• Skin stimulation evokes nerve fiber responses that are able to reduce or inhibit painful sensations. • Why should a patient be instructed to alternate methods of skin stimulation? *Skin stimulation, if repeated in the same site over time, will become less effective.*

Slide 14

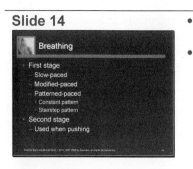

- Breathing techniques are most effective when the woman has had the techniques reviewed prior to the onset of labor.
- Review the timing of implementing breathing techniques.

Slide 15

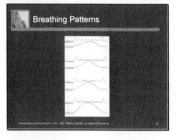

- As a class, review the patterns listed on the slide.
- Include the timing and use of each of the techniques.

Slide 16

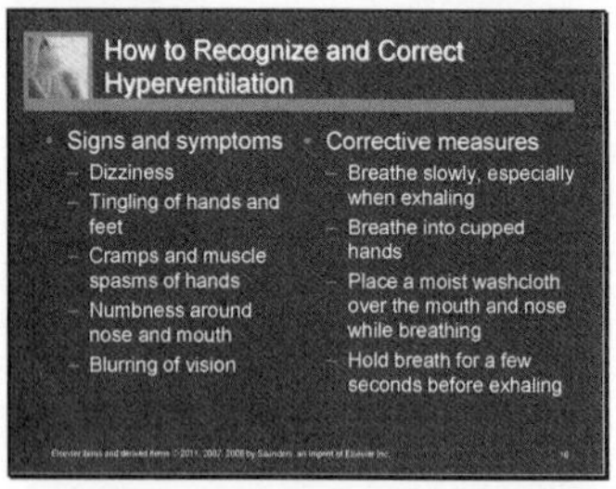

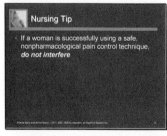

Audience Response Question #2

A laboring woman reports that she is "dizzy" and experiencing "tingling" in her hands and around her mouth and nose. You recognize that these symptoms are most likely related to:

1. hyperventilation.
2. stroke.
3. anxiety.
4. medication side effect.

Slide 17

Slide 18

Slide 19

> **Relationship of Pregnancy to Analgesia and Anesthesia**
> - Pregnant woman at higher risk for hypoxia
> - Sluggish GI tract can result in increased risk of vomiting and aspiration
> - Aortocaval compression increases risk of hypotension and shock
> - Effect on fetus must be considered

- A unique relationship exists between pregnancy and the use of pharmacological pain management techniques.
  - The pregnant woman has an increased risk for hypoxia.
  - Reduced GI activity can promote nausea and vomiting.
  - There is an increased incidence of hypotension and the onset of shock.
- Review the underlying physiological factors which are responsible for these physiological changes.

Slide 20

> **Pharmacological Methods**
> Advantages
> - Using medications during labor allows the mother to be more comfortable and relaxed.
> - Increased relaxation will aid in her ability to participate in her care.

- Review misconceptions that exist concerning the use of medications in labor.

Slide 21

> **Pharmacological Methods** *(cont.)*
> Limitations
> - Any medication used must be considered for its potential impact on the condition of the fetus.

- What is the relationship of timing of medication administration to the stage of the woman's labor?

Slide 22

> **Analgesics and Adjunctive Drugs**
> - Narcotic (opioid) analgesics
>   - Avoid if birth anticipated within 1 hour
> - Narcotic antagonist
> - Adjunctive drugs

- Narcotics are used most frequently.
- What are two commonly used narcotics?
- Narcotic antagonists are used to reverse the respiratory depression associated with opioid use.
- Name a narcotic antagonist.
- Adjunctive drugs enhance the actions of analgesics and reduce nausea.
- Name an adjunctive medication used for the laboring patient.

Slide 23

> **Regional Analgesics and Anesthetics**
> - Regional anesthesia usually involves placement of anesthetic in epidural or subarachnoid space
> - The meninges around the spinal cord
>   - Dura mater
>   - Arachnoid mater
>   - Pia mater

- Regional analgesia is the administration of an anesthetic in the epidural or subarachnoid space.
- Compare and contrast analgesics and anesthetics.

Slide 24

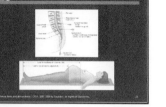

- Review nursing implications for the various types of anesthesia.

Slide 25

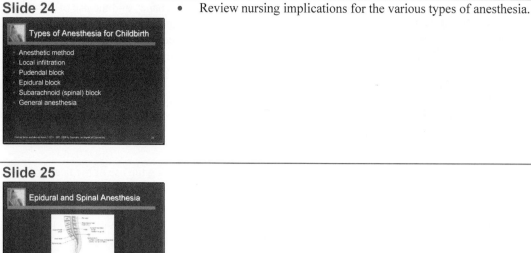

Slide 26

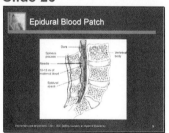

- When a spinal headache results, the anesthesiologist or CRNA can perform a blood patch.
- Review the technique used for the epidural blood patch.

Slide 27

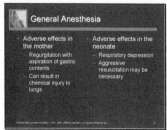

- General anesthesia is seldom used for vaginal deliveries or cesarean births.
- Discuss instances in which general anesthesia might be used.

Slide 28

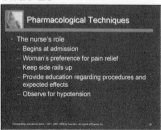

- Discuss additional interventions the nurse should undertake when a laboring woman has received anesthesia or analgesics.

Slide 29

Question for Review

- What is the most important nursing responsibility after an epidural or spinal block analgesia during labor and delivery?

Slide 30

Review

- Objectives
- Key Terms
- Key Points
- Online Resources
- Critical Thinking Questions
- Review Questions

Leifer

8 Nursing Care of Women with Complications During Labor and Birth

TEACHING FOCUS

In this chapter, students will have the opportunity to learn about the complications that can occur during labor and birth and ways to effectively manage them. Students will examine a number of obstetric procedures, including cesarean sections, used to manage the various complications that can occur during labor and delivery. Students will also have the opportunity to learn the role nurses play in dealing with each intrapartum complication.

MATERIALS AND RESOURCES

- ☐ Computer and PowerPoint projector (all lessons)
- ☐ Copies of Figure 8-8 without the figure legend (Lesson 8.3)
- ☐ Index cards (Lesson 8.1)
- ☐ Laminaria (Lesson 8.1)
- ☐ Sample IV lines and piggybacks (Lesson 8.1)
- ☐ Sample prostaglandin gels or inserts (Lesson 8.1)

LESSON CHECKLIST

Preparations for this lesson include:

- Lecture
- Demonstration
- Evaluation of student knowledge and skills needed to perform all entry-level activities related to nursing care of women with complications during labor and birth, including:
  - ○ Explaining obstetric procedures used to address intrapartum complications that may occur with mother or infant
  - ○ Assessing for abnormalities in the labor process
  - ○ Implementing appropriate interventions for complications that warrant emergency attention
  - ○ Conducting patient education with the patient and family members

KEY TERMS

artificial rupture of
  membranes (AROM)
  (p. 175)
cephalopelvic
  disproportion (p. 181)
chignon (p. 180)
chorioamnionitis (p. 192)

dysfunctional labor
  (p. 183)
dystocia (p. 183)
fibronectin test (p. 193)
hydramnios (p. 184)
laminaria (p. 176)
macrosomia (p. 186)

oligohydramnios (p. 174)
shoulder dystocia (p. 186)
spontaneous rupture of
  membranes (SROM)
  (p. 175)
tocolytic (p. 176)
version (p. 178)

ADDITIONAL RESOURCES

TEACH PPT slide(s) Chapter 8, 1-70
EILR IC image(s) Chapter 8, 1-9
EILR OBQ question(s) Chapter 8, 1-10
EILR TB question(s) Chapter 8, 1-30
ESLR IRQ question(s) Chapter 8, 1-5
SG Chapter 8, pp. 61-69

Legend

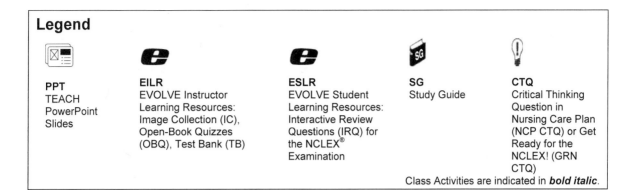

PPT
TEACH
PowerPoint
Slides

EILR
EVOLVE Instructor
Learning Resources:
Image Collection (IC),
Open-Book Quizzes
(OBQ), Test Bank (TB)

ESLR
EVOLVE Student
Learning Resources:
Interactive Review
Questions (IRQ) for
the NCLEX®
Examination

SG
Study Guide

CTQ
Critical Thinking
Question in
Nursing Care Plan
(NCP CTQ) or Get
Ready for the
NCLEX! (GRN
CTQ)

Class Activities are indicated in **bold italic**.

Leifer

LESSON 8.1

PRETEST

1. What is a potential complication related to amniotomy?
   a. prolapse of the umbilical cord
   b. hydramnios
   c. decreased uterine contractions
   d. slowed labor

2. Which of the following is an indication for labor induction?
   a. physician convenience
   b. breech fetal presentation
   c. placenta previa
   d. pregnancy-induced hypertension

3. What can be used to ripen the cervix?
   a. oxytocin
   b. tocolytics
   c. nipple stimulation
   d. prostaglandin

4. *Version* is an obstetric procedure that is performed for what purpose?
   a. changing the fetal presentation
   b. ripening the cervix
   c. stimulating contractions
   d. surgical enlargement of the vagina

5. What is the preferred type of uterine incision for cesarean delivery?
   a. classic incision
   b. low vertical incision
   c. low transverse incision
   d. Pfannenstiel incision

6. What is the most common soft tissue obstruction during labor?
   a. uterine fibroids
   b. ovarian cysts
   c. full bladder
   d. cervical scar tissue

7. Which of the following women is at risk for preterm labor?
   a. 19-year-old primigravida
   b. 38-year-old college professor
   c. 32-year-old mother of two
   d. 21-year-old woman who smokes

8. What is the drug of choice for stopping premature contractions?
   a. surfactant
   b. magnesium sulfate
   c. Pitocin
   d. antibiotics

9. How many weeks are used to define a prolonged pregnancy?
   a. 36 weeks
   b. 38 weeks
   c. 40 weeks
   d. 42 weeks

10. A prolapsed umbilical cord can cause what to occur during the labor and delivery process?
    a. fetal oxygenation
    b. maternal blood pressure
    c. strength of uterine contractions
    d. labor pain management

Answer

1. a	3. d	5. c	7. d	9. d
2. d	4. a	6. c	8. b	10. a

BACKGROUND ASSESSMENT

Question: What symptoms of preterm labor should be taught to all pregnant women, regardless of risk factors?

Answer: Preterm labor is classified as labor that occurs between 20 and 38 weeks of pregnancy. The causes of preterm labor are unknown but may be linked to infections, stress, cervical abnormalities, or other factors. The primary risk with preterm labor is fetal immaturity, especially regarding lung function. Premature labor and delivery is a leading cause of fetal morbidity and mortality. Signs of premature labor include menstrual-type cramps, persistent lower-back ache, increased vaginal discharge, bleeding or spotting, pelvic pressure, and contractions. If a pregnant woman notices any of these signs, she should contact her physician or nurse-midwife immediately.

Leifer

Question: What are the differences between hypotonic and hypertonic labor dysfunction?

Answer: Hypotonic and hypertonic labor relate to uterine contractions. In hypotonic labor, the contractions are too weak to effectively advance labor. The ineffective contractions usually begin during the active phase of labor after the cervix has dilated to 4 cm. Hypotonic labor occurs in relationship to an overdistended uterus that stretches the uterine muscle fibers, which cannot contract effectively. Causes of overdistention include multifetal pregnancy, a large fetus, and hydramnios. Amniotomy, oxytocin augmentation, and hydration are proper medical interventions. Walking, upright positions, and nipple stimulation to promote uterine contractions are common nursing interventions. Emotional support and encouragement should also be provided to the patient. Hypotonic labor is more common than hypertonic labor, which usually occurs in the latent phase of labor before 4 cm of cervical dilation. In hypertonic labor, the contractions are frequent, painful, and uncoordinated, and are not productive. Because the uterus does not relax between contractions, fetal oxygenation becomes compromised. Hypertonic labor is typically treated with tocolytic drugs and mild sedation. Nursing interventions include comfort measures and emotional support for the mother, who may be frustrated and fatigued.

CRITICAL THINKING QUESTION

A patient, gravida 2 para 1, is contemplating having a vaginal birth after a previous cesarean (VBAC). What information should she consider in making her decision?

Guidelines: One of the goals of *Healthy People 2020* is to reduce cesarean birth rates in the United States in part by recommending a trial labor before repeating cesarean-section delivery. A significant risk associated with VBAC, however, is uterine rupture. The type of uterine incision the patient had during her previous delivery helps to determine whether VBAC is an option. A low-transverse uterine incision is the least likely to cause uterine rupture, whereas a classic incision is the most likely and contraindicates a VBAC. Encourage the patient to discuss the risks and benefits of a VBAC versus a cesarean section with her obstetrician or nurse-midwife. Whatever the type of delivery, assist the patient in focusing on the birth of her baby as the most important outcome.

OBJECTIVES	CONTENT	TEACHING RESOURCES
Discuss each obstetric procedure discussed in this chapter.	■ Obstetric procedures (p. 174) □ Amnioinfusion (p. 174) □ Amniotomy (p. 175) – Technique (p. 175) – Complications (p. 175) – Nursing care (p. 175) □ Induction or augmentation of labor (p. 175) – Indications (p. 175) – Contraindications (p. 176) – Technique (p. 176) – Pharmacological methods to stimulate	⊠■ PPT slides 4-34 𝒆 EILR IC images 1-5 𝒆 EILR OBQ questions 1-4, 6-7 𝒆 EILR TB questions 8, 24, 29-30 𝒆 ESLR IRQ questions 1, 4-5 SG Learning Activities, questions 1-4, 6, 14 (pp. 61-64) SG Review Questions, questions 8, 17 (pp. 66-67) SG Case Study, question 1 (p. 68) SG Applying Knowledge, questions 3, 5 (p. 69) **BOOK RESOURCES** Review Questions for the NCLEX® Examination, question 1 (p. 198) Nursing Tip (p. 175) Table 8-1, Bishop's Scoring System (p. 176) Safety Alert (p. 177)

OBJECTIVES	CONTENT	TEACHING RESOURCES
	contractions (p. 176)	Figure 8-1, Episiotomies (p. 179)
	– Cervical ripening (p. 176)	Nutrition Considerations: Third or Fourth Degree Laceration (p. 179)
	– Oxytocin administration (p. 176)	Figure 8-2, Use of Forceps to Assist the Birth of the Fetal Head (p. 180)
	☐ Nonpharmacological methods to stimulate contractions (p. 177)	Figure 8-3, Use of the Vacuum Extractor to Rotate the Fetal Head and Assist with Delivery (p. 180)
	– Walking (p. 177)	Nursing Tip, (p. 180)
	– Nipple stimulation of labor (p. 177)	Figure 8-4, Three Types of Uterine Incisions for Cesarean Birth (p. 182)
	– Complications of augmentation of labor (p. 177)	Figure 8-5, Cesarean Section Birth (pp. 184-185)
	– Nursing care (p. 178)	▸ Discuss the specific ways amnioinfusion and amniotomy are used to prevent complications during birth and how these differ from other interventions discussed in the chapter.
	☐ Version (p. 178)	
	– Risks and contraindications (p. 178)	**Class Activity** *Divide the class into two groups: amnioinfusion and amniotomy. Ask each group to summarize its procedure. Then, have the students identify the similarities and differences between the procedures in a panel discussion.*
	– Technique (p. 178)	
	– Nursing care (p. 178)	**Class Activity** *Ask students to calculate the Bishop's score for a woman whose cervix is 1 cm dilated, firm, 1 cm cervical canal, 30% effaced, posterior position, -3 station. Is the induction prognosis favorable?*
	☐ Episiotomy and lacerations (p. 178)	
	– Indications (p. 179)	
	– Risks (p. 179)	
	– Technique (p. 179)	
	– Nursing care (p. 179)	
	☐ Forceps and vacuum extraction births (p. 179)	
	– Indications (p. 180)	
	– Contraindications (p. 180)	
	– Risks (p. 180)	
	– Technique (p. 180)	
	– Nursing care (p. 181)	

OBJECTIVES	CONTENT	TEACHING RESOURCES
	☐ Cesarean birth (p. 181)	
	– Indications (p. 181)	
	– Contraindications (p. 181)	
	– Risks (p. 181)	
	– Technique (p. 181)	
	– Sequence of events (p. 183)	
	– Nursing care (p. 183)	
Illustrate the nurse's role in each obstetric procedure.	■ Obstetric procedures (p. 174)	⊠▤ PPT slides 4-34
	☐ Amnioinfusion (p. 174)	*e* EILR IC images 1-5
	☐ Amniotomy (p. 175)	*e* EILR OBQ questions 1, 4-6
	– Nursing care (p. 175)	*e* EILR TB questions 3, 57, 21, 23, 25, 28
	☐ Induction or augmentation of labor (p. 175)	*e* ESLR IRQ questions 1, 3-4
	– Nursing care (p. 178)	▦ SG Learning Activities, questions 5, 14 (pp. 62, 64)
	☐ Version (p. 178)	
	– Nursing care (p. 178)	▦ SG Review Questions, questions 1, 4, 10-12 (pp. 65-66)
	☐ Episiotomy and lacerations (p. 178)	▦ SG Case Study, question 1 (p. 68)
	– Nursing care (p. 179)	▦ SG Applying Knowledge, question 3 (p. 69)
	☐ Forceps and vacuum extraction births (p. 179)	**BOOK RESOURCES**
		Review Questions for the NCLEX® Examination, questions 1-2 (p. 198)
	– Nursing care (p. 181)	Nutrition Considerations: Third or Fourth Degree Laceration (p. 179)
	☐ Cesarean birth (p. 181)	Nursing Care Plan 8-1, The Woman with an Unplanned Cesarean Birth (p. 187)
	– Nursing care (p. 183)	▸ Discuss the various concerns and emotions women and their families might experience when preparing for a cesarean birth. What ways might nurses effectively address these concerns and emotions and help the expectant mother as well as other family members adequately prepare for birth?
		*Class Activity **Divide the class into two groups. Have group 1 describe the pharmacological methods for stimulating uterine contractions, and have group 2 describe nonpharmacological methods. Ask each group to present its information in a discussion of pros and cons of the***

ELSEVIER

Introduction to Maternity & Pediatric Nursing, 6th ed.
Leifer

OBJECTIVES	CONTENT	TEACHING RESOURCES
		various methods.
		*Class Activity **Divide the class into two groups. Have group 1 explain the four degrees used to describe perineal lacerations and episiotomies, and have group 2 identify nursing interventions for each degree, with specific emphasis on preventing constipation.***

8.1 Homework/Assignments:

8.1 Instructor's Notes/Student Feedback:

LESSON 8.2

CRITICAL THINKING QUESTION

The nurse is caring for a patient who is in her third trimester of her second pregnancy and is anxious about the upcoming delivery. She reports that she gave birth to her first baby with less than three hours of labor. Why can a previously rapid labor and delivery intensify a woman's anxiety? What are the nursing care implications associated with precipitate birth?

Guidelines: For a woman who has given birth before, the average rate of cervical dilation is 1.5 cm/hr and fetal descent of 2.0 cm/hr. In this patient's case, this rate was greatly accelerated and did not allow for a gradual progression of contraction intensity. The abrupt and intense nature of contractions contributes to pain and anxiety. If body tissues are not able to stretch with the contractions, uterine rupture, cervical lacerations, and hematoma can result. The shortened contraction interval compromises the fetal oxygenation. Fetal injury such as intracranial hemorrhage and nerve damage can result from the rapid passage through the birth canal. The mother can also experience injury to her tissues such as lacerations and bruising to her vulva. Nursing observations and interventions address both the mother and fetus.

OBJECTIVES	CONTENT	TEACHING RESOURCES
Analyze the nurse's role in a cesarean birth.	■ Nursing care (p. 181)	⊠ PPT slides 33-34
		e EILR OBQ question 7
		e EILR TB questions 14, 16
		e ESLR IRQ question 3
		SG Learning Activities, question 7 (p. 62)
		SG Review Questions, question 13 (p. 67)
		SG Applying Knowledge, question 6 (p. 69)
		BOOK RESOURCES
		Review Questions for the NCLEX® Examination, question 3 (p. 198)
		Nursing Care Plan 8-1, The Woman with an Unplanned Cesarean Birth (p. 187)
		▸ Discuss the needs of women who have had planned and unplanned cesarean deliveries.
		▸ Discuss what nursing assessments must be done prior to and immediately after a cesarean section.
		Class Activity *Divide the class into two groups. Have one list the nursing care pre- and post-delivery for a vaginal birth and the other group list the nursing care pre- and post-delivery for a cesarean birth. Then have each group share its findings with the class.*
		Class Activity *Ask students to demonstrate the correct procedure for assessing the uterus after vaginal and cesarean-section delivery. Why is it important to assess the uterus postpartum? What is uterine inversion? Is this a medical emergency? What are nursing interventions during recovery from uterine inversion?*
Describe	■ Abnormal labor (p. 183)	⊠ PPT slides 35-36

OBJECTIVES	CONTENT	TEACHING RESOURCES
factors that contribute to an abnormal labor.		**e** EILR OBQ question 8
		e EILR TB questions 4-5, 19
		SG SG Review Questions, question 6 (p. 66)
		*Class Activity **Lead a class discussion on advanced maternal age, obesity, maternal fatigue, fear, and so on, and how they contribute to abnormal labor. Also, have students identify appropriate precautions and interventions for each.***
Explain each intrapartum complication discussed in this chapter.	■ Abnormal labor (p. 183)	PPT slides 37-63
	□ Problems with the powers of labor (p. 185)	**e** EILR IC images 6-9
		e EILR OBQ questions 9-10
	– Increased uterine muscle tone (p. 185)	**e** EILR TB question 9
		e ESLR IRQ questions 2-3
	– Decreased uterine muscle tone (p. 186)	**SG** SG Learning Activities, questions 10-13, 15-16 (pp. 64-65)
	– Ineffective maternal pushing (p. 186)	**SG** SG Review Questions, questions 3, 5-7, 16 (pp. 66-67)
	□ Problems with the fetus (p. 186)	**SG** SG Case Study, question 2 (p. 68)
	– Fetal size (p. 186)	**SG** SG Applying Knowledge, questions 1, 3 (p. 69)
		BOOK RESOURCES
	– Abnormal fetal presentation or position (p. 189)	Review Questions for the NCLEX® Examination, question 4 (p. 198)
	– Multifetal pregnancy (p. 190)	Box 8-1, Differences Between Hypertonic and Hypotonic Labor Dysfunction (p. 186)
	□ Problems with the pelvis and soft tissues (p. 190)	Nursing Care Plan 8-2, The Woman with Hypotonic Labor Dysfunction (pp. 188-189)
	– Bony pelvis (p. 190)	Figure 8-6, The Mechanism of Labor in a Breech Birth (p. 190)
	– Soft tissue obstructions (p. 191)	Figure 8-7, The Hands-And-Knees Position (p. 190)
		Box 8-2, Some Risk Factors for Preterm Labor (p. 192)
	□ Problems with the psyche (p. 191)	Figure 8-8, Prolapsed Umbilical Cord (p. 195)
	□ Abnormal duration of labor (p. 191)	Figure 8-9, Positioning of the Mother when the Umbilical Cord Prolapses (p. 196)
	– Prolonged labor (p. 191)	▶ Discuss the potential injuries that may result to both mother and infant when the woman successfully delivers a large infant. What are the appropriate interventions?
	– Precipitate birth (p. 191)	▶ Discuss the appropriate nursing interventions to take with a prolapsed umbilical cord.
		*Class Activity **Provide students with copies of Figure 8-8 without the figure legend. Ask students to identify each***

OBJECTIVES	CONTENT	TEACHING RESOURCES
	■ Premature rupture of membranes (p. 192) ■ Preterm labor (p. 192) □ Signs of impending preterm labor (p. 193) □ Tocolytic therapy (p. 193) ■ Prolonged pregnancy (p. 194) ■ Emergencies during childbirth (p. 194) □ Prolapsed umbilical cord (p. 194) □ Uterine rupture (p. 195) □ Uterine inversion (p. 196) □ Amniotic fluid embolism (p. 197)	*figure part and describe the classifications.* *Class Activity Divide the class into five groups and assign each group two of the following intrapartum complications: hypertonic labor dysfunction, hypotonic labor dysfunction, macrosomia, PROM, preterm labor, prolonged labor, precipitate birth, bony pelvis, abnormal fetal presentation/position, and multifetal pregnancy. Have each group list the description, diagnosis, assessment, and nursing interventions for both of its assigned complications. Then have each group share its findings with the class.*

8.2 Homework/Assignments:

8.2 Instructor's Notes/Student Feedback:

Leifer

LESSON 8.3

CRITICAL THINKING QUESTION

A patient in her 38th week of pregnancy calls the OB/GYN office to report clear fluid leaking from her vagina. She is not experiencing contractions. What instructions and information should the nurse provide?

Guidelines: The nurse should explain that the discharge may be amniotic fluid and should instruct the patient to come to the office as soon as possible for evaluation for premature rupture of membranes (PROM). A nitrazine test is performed on the fluid. If the test strip turns blue and shows the characteristic fern-leaf pattern under microscopy, then the PROM diagnosis is confirmed. The nurse will assess the patient's temperature, uterine tenderness, and the fetal heart rate. There is a risk of infection for both the mother and fetus, as well as a risk of cord compression related to oligohydramnios. Antibiotics and blood cultures may be ordered. Because of these risks, labor will most likely be induced within the next 24 hours if contractions do not begin before then.

OBJECTIVES	CONTENT	TEACHING RESOURCES
Discuss the nurse's role in caring for women having each intrapartum complication.	■ Abnormal labor (p. 183) ☐ Problems with the powers of labor (p. 185) – Increased uterine muscle tone (p. 185) – Decreased uterine muscle tone (p. 186) – Ineffective maternal pushing (p. 186) ☐ Problems with the fetus (p. 186) – Fetal size (p. 186) – Abnormal fetal presentation or position (p. 189) – Multifetal pregnancy (p. 190) ☐ Problems with the pelvis and soft tissues (p. 190) – Bony pelvis (p. 190) – Soft tissue obstructions (p. 191) ☐ Problems with the psyche (p. 191) ☐ Abnormal duration of labor (p. 191) – Prolonged labor	⊠ PPT slides 37-68 *e* EILR TB questions 2, 11-13, 17-18, 22, 26, 27 SG Learning Activities, questions 8-13, 15-16 (pp. 63-65) SG Review Questions, questions 2, 7, 15-16, 18 (pp. 66-68) SG Case Study, question 2 (p. 68) SG Thinking Critically, question 1 (p. 68) SG Applying Knowledge, questions 1-2, 4 (p. 69) **BOOK RESOURCES** Review Questions for the NCLEX® Examination, questions 4, 5 (p. 198) Nursing Care Plan 8-2, The Woman with Hypotonic Labor Dysfunction (pp. 188-189) ▸ Discuss some of the challenges nurses face when trying to calm women who are experiencing prolonged labor. Discuss potential nursing interventions. *Class Activity Have students list the three problems with a fetus and identify nursing measures they should take.. Also, have students define abnormal fetal presentation or position and list the problems a multifetal pregnancy has in relation to uterine rupture.*

Introduction to Maternity & Pediatric Nursing, 6th ed.

Leifer

OBJECTIVES	CONTENT	TEACHING RESOURCES
	(p. 191) – Precipitate birth (p. 191) ■ Premature rupture of membranes (p. 192) ■ Preterm labor (p. 192) ☐ Signs of impending preterm labor (p. 193) ☐ Tocolytic therapy (p. 193) ■ Prolonged pregnancy (p. 194) ■ Emergencies during childbirth (p. 194) ☐ Prolapsed umbilical cord (p. 194) ☐ Uterine rupture (p. 195) ☐ Uterine inversion (p. 196) ☐ Amniotic fluid embolism (p. 197)	
Review the nurse's role in obstetric emergencies.	■ Emergencies during childbirth (p. 194) ☐ Prolapsed umbilical cord (p. 194) ☐ Uterine rupture (p. 195) ☐ Uterine inversion (p. 196) ☐ Amniotic fluid embolism (p. 197)	⊠▪ PPT slides 64-68 𝒆 EILR IC images 8, 9 𝒆 EILR OBQ question 10 𝒆 EILR TB questions 15, 20, 26 SG Learning Activities, questions 17, 18 (p. 65) SG Review Questions, questions 9, 14, 15 (pp. 66-67) **BOOK RESOURCES** Figure 8-8, Prolapsed Umbilical Cord (p. 195) Figure 8-9, Positioning of the Mother when the Umbilical Cord Prolapses (p. 196) Review Questions for the NCLEX® Examination, question 3 (p. 198) ▶ Discuss the different nursing care required for a woman with a prolapsed umbilical cord, uterine rupture, and uterine inversion. Discuss potential nursing interventions. ▶ Discuss which emergency measures must be implemented on a woman suspected of having experienced

Leifer

OBJECTIVES	CONTENT	TEACHING RESOURCES
		an amniotic fluid embolism.
		***Class Activity** Have students list the three variations of uterine rupture and identify the cesarean-section incision with greater incidence for uterine rupture. Also, have students define **VBAC** and its relationship to uterine rupture.*
Performance Evaluation		☒■ PPT slides 1-70
		e EILR IC images 1-9
		e EILR OBQ questions 1-10
		e EILR TB questions 1-30
		e ESLR IRQ questions 1-5
		📗 SG Learning Activities, questions 1-18 (pp. 61-65)
		📗 SG Review Questions, questions 1-18 (pp. 65-68)
		📗 SG Case Study, questions 1, 2 (p. 68)
		📗 SG Thinking Critically, question 1 (p. 68)
		📗 SG Applying Knowledge, questions 1-6 (p. 68-69)
		BOOK RESOURCES
		💡 NCP CTQ 1 (p. 187)
		💡 NCP CTQ 1 (p. 189)
		Review Questions for the NCLEX® Examination, questions 1-5 (p. 198)

8.3 Homework/Assignments:

8.3 Instructor's Notes/Student Feedback:

---

8 Nursing Care of Women with Complications During Labor and Birth

Slide 1

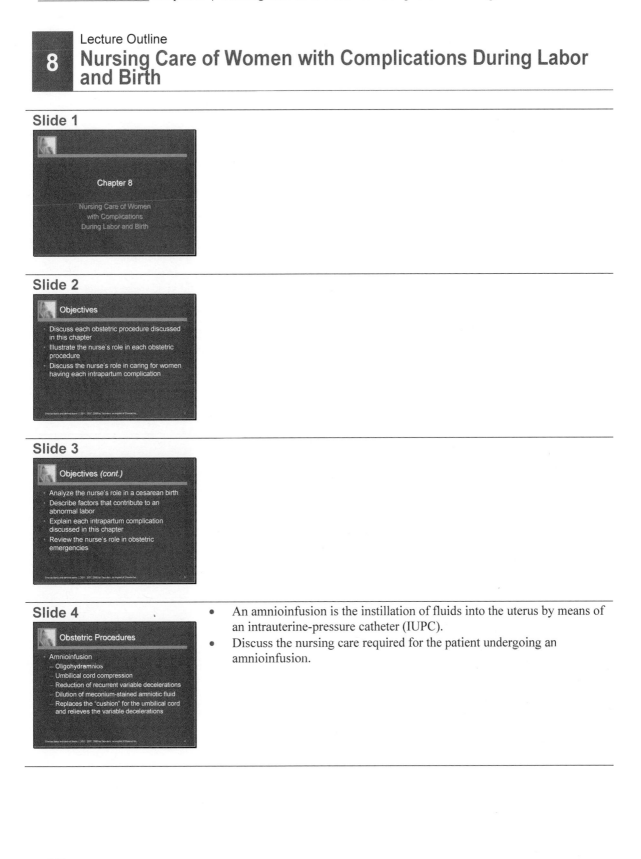

Chapter 8

Nursing Care of Women
with Complications
During Labor and Birth

Slide 2

Objectives

- Discuss each obstetric procedure discussed in this chapter
- Illustrate the nurse's role in each obstetric procedure
- Discuss the nurse's role in caring for women having each intrapartum complication

Slide 3

Objectives *(cont.)*

- Analyze the nurse's role in a cesarean birth
- Describe factors that contribute to an abnormal labor
- Explain each intrapartum complication discussed in this chapter
- Review the nurse's role in obstetric emergencies

Slide 4

Obstetric Procedures

- Amnioinfusion
  - Oligohydramnios
  - Umbilical cord compression
  - Reduction of recurrent variable decelerations
  - Dilution of meconium-stained amniotic fluid
  - Replaces the "cushion" for the umbilical cord and relieves the variable decelerations

- An amnioinfusion is the instillation of fluids into the uterus by means of an intrauterine-pressure catheter (IUPC).
- Discuss the nursing care required for the patient undergoing an amnioinfusion.

Introduction to Maternity & Pediatric Nursing, 6th ed.
Leifer

Slide 5

> **Obstetric Procedures** *(cont.)*
>
> Amniotomy
> - The artificial rupture of membranes
> - Done to stimulate or enhance contractions
> - Commits the woman to delivery
> - Stimulates prostaglandin secretion
> - Complications
>   - Prolapse of the umbilical cord
>   - Infection
>   - Abruptio placentae

- Prior to an amniotomy, a series of assessments must be completed.
- What are the needed assessments?

Slide 6

> **Obstetric Procedures** *(cont.)*
>
> - Observe for complications post-amniotomy
>   - Fetal heart rate outside normal range (110-160 beats/min) suggests umbilical cord prolapse
>   - Observe color, odor, amount, and character of amniotic fluid
>   - Woman's temperature 38° C (100.4° F) or higher is suggestive of infection
>   - Green fluid may indicate that the fetus has passed a meconium stool

- The rupture of membranes may be accompanied by complications:
  - Prolapsed umbilical cord
  - Infection
  - Abruptio placentae
- What are the signs and symptoms of each of the identified complications?
- Explain why the rupture of membranes could yield these results.

Audience Response Question #1
You are assessing characteristics of amniotic fluid post-amniotomy. You observe the color of the fluid to be green tinged. This can indicate the potential for:
1. Pre-term delivery
2. Vaginal infection
3. Cervical trauma
4. Fetal distress

Slide 7

> **Nursing Tip**
>
> - Observe for wet underpads and linens after the membranes rupture. Change them as often as needed to keep the woman relatively dry and to reduce the risk for infection or skin breakdown.

Slide 8

> **Induction or Augmentation of Labor**
>
> - *Induction* is the initiation of labor **before** it begins naturally
> - *Augmentation* is the stimulation of contractions **after** they have begun naturally

---

Slide 9

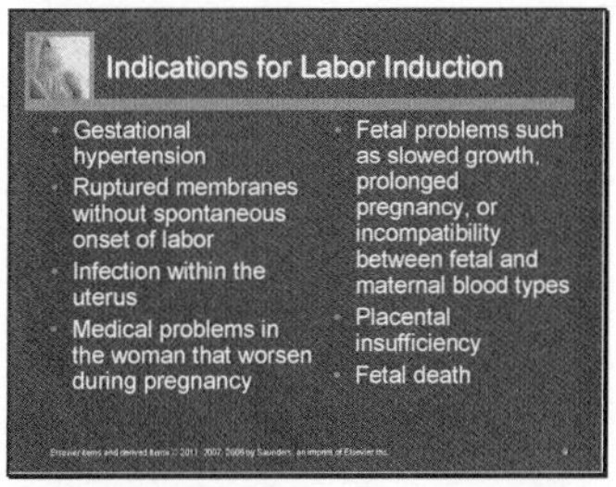

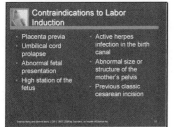

- Discuss the underlying reasons that these factors indicate labor induction.

Slide 10

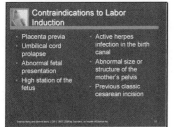

- Explain why these are contraindications for inducing labor.

Slide 11

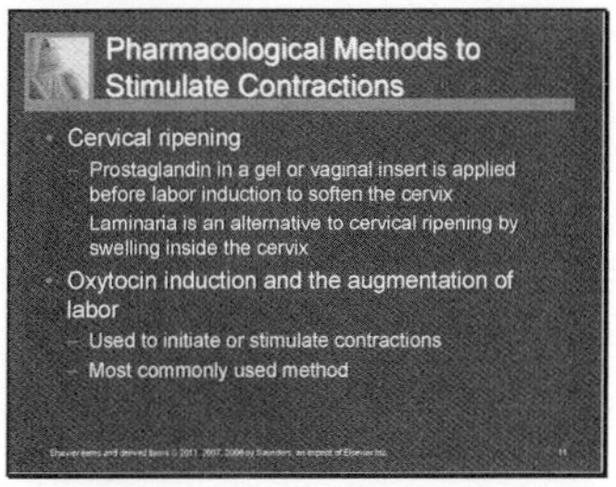

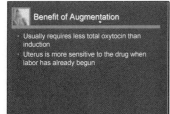

- Cervical softening assists with efforts to induce labor.
- Oxytocin does not have cervical ripening properties.
- Review the steps taken to administer prostaglandin and laminaria.

Audience Response Question #2
Cervical ripening with prostaglandin gel is considered a method of labor induction.
   1. True
   2. False

Slide 12

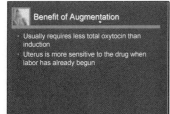

Slide 13

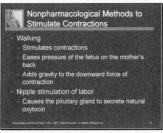

Slide 14

Complications of Oxytocin Induction and Augmentation of Labor

- Most common is related to
  - Overstimulation of contractions
    - Fetal compromise
    - Uterine rupture
- Water intoxication
  - Inhibits excretion of urine and promotes fluid retention

- Review the nursing assessments that must accompany oxytocin administration.

Slide 15

Bishop's Scoring System

- Evaluates the cervical response to induction procedures
- A high score (above 6) is predictive of successful labor induction because the cervix has ripened or softened in preparation for labor

- Health care providers can use Bishop's score to determine a patient's potential for successful induction.
- What are the parameters included in Bishop's scoring system?

Slide 16

Version

- A method used to change fetal presentation
  - Two methods
    - External
    - Internal

- The ideal position for the fetus in the period of time preceding the onset of labor is vertex.
- When the fetus is not in that position, the health care provider might be able to manually change the position of the fetus.

Slide 17

Risks and Contraindications of Version

- Disproportion between mother's pelvis and fetal size
- Abnormal uterine or pelvic size or shape
- Abnormal placental placement
- Previous cesarean birth with vertical uterine incision
- Active herpes virus infection
- Inadequate amniotic fluid
- Poor placental function
- Multifetal gestation
- Fetus can become entangled in umbilical cord

- The listed conditions are not appropriate for a version. Discuss the reasons for their being excluded.
- Review the risks which could be associated with a version.

Slide 18

Episiotomy and Lacerations

- Episiotomy—controlled surgical enlargement of the vaginal opening during birth
- Lacerations—uncontrolled tear of the tissues that results in a jagged wound

- An episiotomy can be performed at the time of delivery to assist in the birth of the baby.
- Compare and contrast episiotomies and lacerations.

Leifer

Slide 19

> **Perineal Lacerations**
>
> - First degree—
>   superficial vaginal
>   mucosa or perineal
>   skin
> - Second degree—
>   involves vaginal
>   mucosa, perineal
>   skin, and deeper
>   tissues of the
>   perineum
> - Third degree—same
>   as second degree,
>   plus involves anal
>   sphincter
> - Fourth degree—
>   extends through the
>   anal sphincter into the
>   rectal mucosa

- Episiotomies and lacerations are classified by the tissue involved.
- Discuss care of perineal lacerations.
- Women who have experienced a third- or fourth-degree lacerations are not given anything via the rectum. This includes enemas and suppositories.
- What nursing interventions might be needed for these patients to prevent constipation?

Slide 20

> **Episiotomies**

- Two commonly used types of episiotomy include the midline and mediolateral.
- Use the diagram to identify the two types. Discuss their anatomical differences.
- For which patient scenarios would each most likely be used?

Slide 21

> **Indications for an Episiotomy**
>
> - Better control over where and how much the vaginal opening is enlarged
> - An opening with a clean edge rather than the ragged opening of a tear
> - Note: Perineal massage and stretching exercises before labor may be an alternative to an episiotomy

Slide 22

> **Forceps Extraction**
>
> - Provides traction and rotation of the fetal head when the mother's pushing efforts are insufficient to accomplish a safe delivery
> - Forceps may also help the physician extract the fetal head through the incision during a cesarean birth

Slide 23

> **Forceps to Assist the Birth of the Fetal Head**

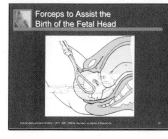

Slide 24

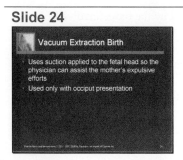

- Forceps or vacuum extraction is used at the end of the second stage of labor.
- Why would forceps or vacuum extraction be utilized?
- Discuss additional criteria that must be present for the use of forceps or vacuum extraction.

Slide 25

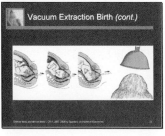

Slide 26

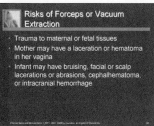

Slide 27

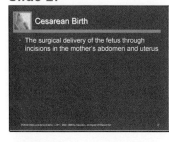

- Cesarean births account for more than 25% of all deliveries in the United States.
- Why is there a growing number of cesarean births?

Slide 28

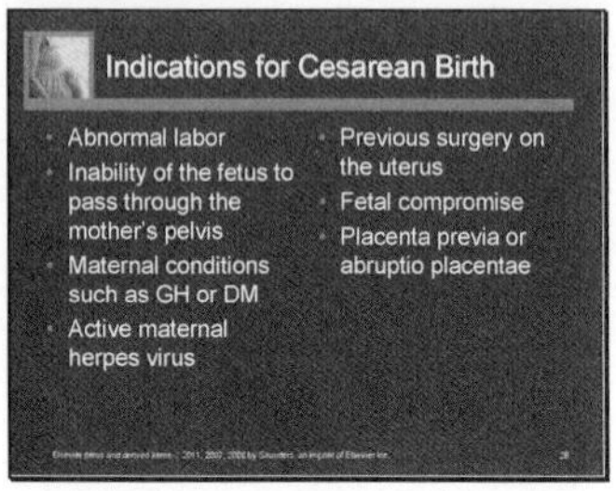

- Discuss potential contraindications to cesarean birth.

Slide 29

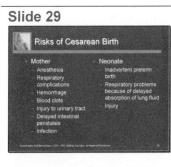

Slide 30

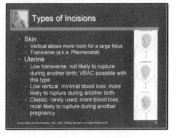

- It should be noted that the type of incision on the external abdomen is not an indicator of the type of surgical incision on the uterus.
- Which factors will be taken into consideration by the surgeon when determining what type of surgical incision to use for a cesarean section?

Slide 31

- There is a series of events which will take place during a cesarean section:
  1. Administering anesthetic
  2. Cleaning and draping the expectant mother
  3. Making skin incision
  4. Making uterine incision
  5. Rupturing membranes (if not yet completed)
  6. Removing the fetal head or buttocks
  7. Suctioning the mouth and nose
  8. Clamping the cord

Audience Response Question #3
At what point of a Cesarean section delivery would the woman's support person enter the room?
  1. With the patient
  2. During the abdominal preparation
  3. After the incision has been made
  4. After the baby has been delivered

Slide 32

- Mothers who undergo a cesarean birth might experience feelings of discontent about their inability to deliver vaginally.
- Identify behaviors which could signal this occurrence.
- What nursing interventions could assist the mother in coming to terms with these feelings?

Slide 33

> **Nursing Care in the Recovery Room**
> - Vital signs to identify hemorrhage or shock
> - IV site and rate of solution flow
> - Fundus for firmness, height, and midline position
> - Dressing for drainage
> - Lochia for quantity, color, and presence of clots
> - Urine output from the indwelling catheter

- After surgery, the patient will recover in the postanesthesia care unit (PACU).
- The nurse will be required to perform the assessments identified on the slide.
- What are assessment findings that could indicate the onset of complications?

Slide 34

> **Safety Alert**
> - Although assessing the uterus after cesarean birth causes discomfort, it is important to do so regularly
> - The woman can have a relaxed uterus that causes excessive blood loss, regardless of how she delivered her child

Slide 35

> **Abnormal Labor**
> - Called *dysfunctional labor*
>   - Does not progress
> - Dystocia
>   - Difficult labor

- The normal progression of labor involves cervical dilation, effacement, and fetal descent.
- When the 4 Ps of the labor process do not progress appropriately, the labor could be classified as abnormal.
- What are the 4 Ps of the labor process?

Slide 36

> **Risk Factors for Dysfunctional Labor**
> - Advanced maternal age
> - Obesity
> - Overdistention of uterus
>   - Hydramnios or multifetal pregnancy
> - Abnormal presentation
> - Cephalopelvic disproportion (CPD)
> - Overstimulation of the uterus
> - Maternal fatigue, dehydration, fear
> - Lack of analgesic assistance

- The conditions listed on the slide are associated with dysfunctional labor.
- Identify the elements in the "situations" that will contribute to the development of a dysfunctional labor pattern.

Slide 37

> **Problems with the Powers of Labor**
>
> **Hypertonic**
> - Increased muscle tone
> - Usually occurs during the latent phase of labor
> - Characterized by contractions that are frequent, cramplike, and poorly coordinated
> - Painful but nonproductive
>   - Uterus is tense, even between contractions, leads to reduced blood flow to the placenta
>
> **Hypotonic**
> - Decreased muscle tone
> - Labor begins normally, but diminishes during active phase
> - More likely to occur if uterus is overdistended
>   - Stretches the muscle fibers and reduces their ability to contract effectively

- Contraction patterns which are hypertonic, as well as hypotonic, could be associated with a dysfunctional labor pattern.
- Review nursing/medical interventions which might be implemented to manage these conditions.

Leifer

Slide 38

Ineffective Maternal Pushing

- Woman may not understand which technique to use or fears tearing her perineal tissues
- Epidural or subarachnoid blocks may depress or eliminate the natural urge to push
- An exhausted woman may be unable to gather enough energy to push

- When providing care to a patient who is unable to effectively push, the nurse will need to assist as needed.
- What nursing interventions could be employed?

Slide 39

Problems with the Fetus

- The passenger, or the fetus, might cause the labor's progression to be dysfunctional.
- These problems include size, presentation, or positioning.
- Other factors might include multifetal pregnancies and birth defects.

Slide 40

Fetal Size

- Macrosomia—large fetus; weighs more than 4000 g (8.8 pounds)
  - May not fit through birth canal
  - Can contribute to hypotonic labor dysfunction

- Identify populations which might be at an increased risk for a macrosomic fetus.
- Review the nursing assessments which should be implemented to monitor for potential complications in the mother and newborn after the delivery of a macrosomic infant.

Slide 41

Shoulder Dystocia

- Usually occurs when fetus is too large
- Is an emergency
- Fetal chest cannot expand and the fetus needs to be able to breathe
- After delivery, mother and infant need to be assessed for injuries
  - Mother may have torn perineal tissue
  - More at-risk for uterine atony and postpartum hemorrhage
    - Uterus does not contract well after birth
  - Infant may have fractured clavicle

Audience Response Question #4
A woman in labor is experiencing dystocia. One possible cause for this is:
  1. the cervix has reached full dilation.
  2. the umbilical cord has prolapsed.
  3. excessive size of the fetus.
  4. extreme maternal fatigue.

Slide 42

Abnormal Fetal Presentation or Position

- Prevents the smallest diameter of the fetal head to pass through the smallest diameter of the pelvis

- The most effective, efficient fetal position is flexed and cephalic.
- What fetal head presentation is best? *Occiput anterior*

Slide 43

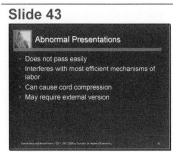

Abnormal Presentations

- Does not pass easily
- Interferes with most efficient mechanisms of labor
- Can cause cord compression
- May require external version

Slide 44

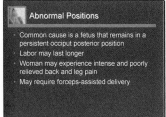

Abnormal Positions

- Common cause is a fetus that remains in a persistent occiput posterior position
- Labor may last longer
- Woman may experience intense and poorly relieved back and leg pain
- May require forceps-assisted delivery

Slide 45

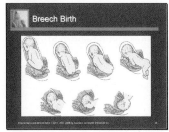

Breech Birth

Slide 46

Nursing Care for Abnormal Fetal Presentation or Positions

- Encourage woman to assume positions that favor fetal rotation and descent and reduce back pain
  - Sitting, kneeling, or standing while leaning forward
  - Rocking the pelvis back and forth while on hands and knees (encourages rotation)
  - Side-lying
  - Squatting (in second stage of labor)
  - Lunging by placing one foot in a chair with the foot and knee pointed to that side

Slide 47

Multifetal Pregnancy

- May cause dysfunctional labor
- Uterine overdistention contributes to poor contraction quality
- Abnormal presentation or position of one or more fetuses interferes with labor mechanisms
- Often one fetus is delivered as cephalic and the second as breech, unless a version is done

- The nursing care for a multifetal pregnancy during the labor process is more complex than that for a single fetus.
- What are the monitoring requirements for the fetuses?

Slide 48

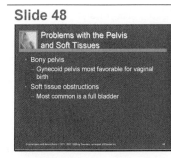

Problems with the Pelvis and Soft Tissues

- Bony pelvis
  - Gynecoid pelvis most favorable for vaginal birth
- Soft tissue obstructions
  - Most common is a full bladder

Slide 49

The Psyche

- Most common factors that can prolong labor
  - Lack of analgesic control of excessive pain
  - Absence of a support person or coach
  - Immobility and restriction to bed
  - Lack of ability to carry out cultural traditions

Slide 50

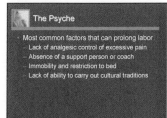

Increased Anxiety

- Causes hormones to be released
  - Epinephrine
  - Cortisol
  - Adrenocorticotropic
- Reduces contractility of the smooth muscle

Slide 51

Effects of Hormones Released

- The uterus uses more glucose for energy
- Diverts blood from the uterus
- Increases tension of pelvic muscles; can impede fetal descent
- Increases perception of pain

- Ask students to develop a nursing diagnosis that addresses the maternal psyche during the labor process.

Slide 52

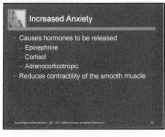

Abnormal Duration of Labor

- Friedman's curve
  - Often used to graph the progress of cervical dilation and fetal descent
  - Used as a guide to assess and manage the normal progress of labor

- Prolonged labor can cause
  - Maternal or newborn infection
  - Maternal exhaustion
  - Postpartum hemorrhage
  - Greater anxiety and fear

- When caring for a woman experiencing prolonged labor, it is vital that the nurse assist the woman to conserve her strength.
- Another key intervention involves providing encouragement to the laboring woman.

Leifer

Slide 53

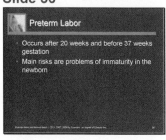

Precipitate Birth

- A birth that is completed in less than 3 hours
- Labor begins abruptly and intensifies quickly
- Contractions may be frequent and intense
- May have uterine rupture, cervical lacerations, or hematoma
- Fetal oxygenation may be compromised
- Birth injury may occur from rapid passage through the birth canal
- Injuries can include
  - Intracranial hemorrhage
  - Nerve damage

- Identify populations that could be at an increased risk for a precipitate birth.
- Review the role of the nurse when caring for the woman who experiences a precipitate delivery.

Slide 54

Premature Rupture of Membranes (PROM)

- Spontaneous rupture of membranes at term, more than 1 hour before labor contractions begin
- Vaginal or cervical infection may cause PROM
- Diagnosis confirmed by
  - Nitrazine paper test
  - Looking for a "ferning" pattern from vaginal fluid placed on a slide and viewed under the microscope

- Prompt identification of membrane rupture is needed to plan and provide adequate care to the patient.
- Women who suspect their membranes have ruptured should be advised to report to their health care facility/provider for further evaluation.
- What are the increased risks for the pregnant woman who has experienced premature membrane rupture?

Slide 55

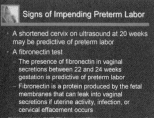

Patient Teaching for a Woman with Infection or in Preterm Labor

- Report a temperature that is above 38° C (100.4° F)
- Avoid sexual intercourse or insertion of anything into vagina
- Avoid orgasms
- Avoid breast stimulation
- Maintain any activity restrictions prescribed
- Note any uterine contractions, reduced fetal activity, and other signs of infection
- Record fetal kick counts daily and report fewer than 10 kicks in a 12-hour period

- *Premature labor* is defined as the onset of labor between 20 and 37 weeks gestation.
- Discuss the nursing assessment for the patient who has preterm labor.

Slide 56

Preterm Labor

- Occurs after 20 weeks and before 37 weeks gestation
- Main risks are problems of immaturity in the newborn

Slide 57

Signs of Impending Preterm Labor

- A shortened cervix on ultrasound at 20 weeks may be predictive of preterm labor
- A fibronectin test
  - The presence of fibronectin in vaginal secretions between 22 and 24 weeks gestation is predictive of preterm labor
  - Fibronectin is a protein produced by the fetal membranes that can leak into vaginal secretions if uterine activity, infection, or cervical effacement occurs

Slide 58

Maternal Symptoms of Preterm Labor

- Contractions that may be either uncomfortable or painless
- Feeling that the fetus is "balling up" frequently
- Menstrual-like cramps
- Constant low backache
- Pelvic pressure or a feeling that the fetus is pushing down
- A change in vaginal discharge
- Abdominal cramps with or without diarrhea
- Pain or discomfort in the vulva or thighs
- "Just feeling bad" or "coming down with something"

Slide 59

Some Risk Factors for Preterm Labor

- Exposure to DES
- Underweight
- Chronic illness
- Dehydration
- Preeclampsia
- Previous preterm labor or birth
- Previous pregnancy losses
- Substance abuse
- Chronic stress
- Infection
- Anemia
- Preterm PROM
- Inadequate prenatal care
- Poor nutrition
- Low education level
- Poverty
- Smoking
- Multifetal presentation

- Review the underlying pathology of patients at an increased risk with these particular conditions.

Slide 60

Tocolytic Therapy

- Goal is to stop uterine contractions
- Keep fetus in utero until lungs are mature enough to adapt to extrauterine life
- Magnesium sulfate IV drug of choice
- Beta-adrenergic drugs given orally
- Calcium channel blockers given orally
- Contraindications
  - Preeclampsia
  - Placenta previa
  - Abruptio placentae
  - Chorioamnionitis
  - Fetal demise

- When tocolytic therapy is utilized to manage preterm labor, nursing assessments are a key part of the plan of care.
- Discuss the nursing assessments for the patient who is undergoing tocolytic therapy.

Slide 61

Stopping Preterm Labor

- Initial measures to stop preterm labor
  - Identifying and treating infection
  - Activity restriction
  - Hydration
- If it appears preterm birth is inevitable
  - Steroids increase fetal lung maturity
    - Betamethasone
  - Thyroid-releasing hormone also enhances lung maturity in fetuses younger than 28 weeks

---

Slide 62

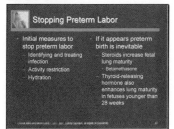

Prolonged Pregnancy

- Lasts longer than 42 weeks
- Risks
- Placenta ages
  - Delivers oxygen and nutrients to the fetus less efficiently
    - Fetus may lose weight
    - Fetal skin may peel
  - Fetus continues to grow
  - Meconium may be expelled
  - Low blood glucose levels in the fetus

- When a pregnancy continues longer than 42 weeks, it is considered postdate.
- Which patients are at greater risk for a prolonged pregnancy?

Slide 63

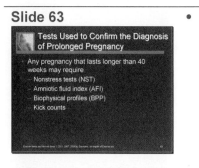

- Review the listed procedures.

Slide 64

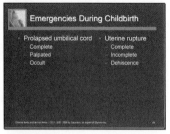

- The prolapsed cord can be classified as complete, palpated, or occult.
- Can you describe each of the types?

Slide 65

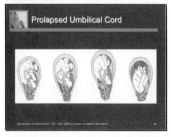

- Review the patient scenarios which are most likely to accompany a prolapsed umbilical cord.

Slide 66

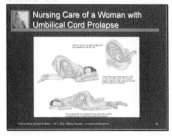

Slide 67

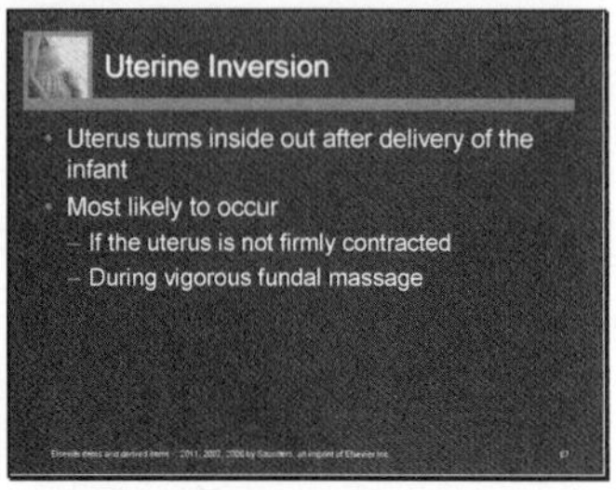

- Uterine inversion is a serious complication of labor.
- Describe the signs and symptoms that accompany uterine inversion.
- Identify nursing/medical care that must be instituted should this happen.
- What is the patient's prognosis?

Slide 68

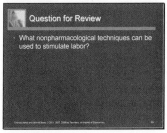

Amniotic Fluid Embolism

- Occurs when amniotic fluid, with its particles such as vernix, fetal hair, and sometimes meconium, enter the woman's circulation and typically obstructs small blood vessels in her lungs
- Characterized by abrupt onset of hypotension, respiratory distress, and coagulation abnormalities

- Another serious complication of childbirth is an amniotic fluid embolism.
- Prompt identification of the phenomenon is required to save the woman's life.
- Develop a nursing diagnosis for the woman who has experienced an amniotic fluid embolus.

Slide 69

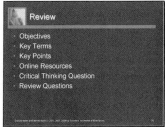

Question for Review

- What nonpharmacological techniques can be used to stimulate labor?

Slide 70

Review

- Objectives
- Key Terms
- Key Points
- Online Resources
- Critical Thinking Question
- Review Questions

ELSEVIER

Introduction to Maternity & Pediatric Nursing, 6th ed.
Leifer

TEACHING FOCUS

This chapter addresses the physiological and psychological issues for the mother, family, and newborn associated with the puerperium, or fourth trimester. Students will have the opportunity to learn about cultural differences and emotional needs, as well as ways the nurse can facilitate family adjustments. The student is introduced to nursing care of the newborn and the new mother, with particular attention to breastfeeding and nutritional issues.

MATERIALS AND RESOURCES

- ☐ Breast pumps (Lesson 9.2)
- ☐ Breastfeeding techniques video (Lesson 9.2)
- ☐ Computer and PowerPoint projector (all lessons)
- ☐ Dry infant formula samples (Lesson 9.2)
- ☐ Equipment for taking infant vital signs (temperature, blood pressure), weight, and measurement (tape) (Lesson 9.2)
- ☐ Materials for performing umbilical cord care (Lesson 9.2)
- ☐ Newborn-sized doll (Lesson 9.2)

LESSON CHECKLIST

Preparations for this lesson include:

- Lecture
- Demonstration
- Guest speakers: Nutritionist, lactation consultant
- Evaluation of student knowledge and skills needed to perform all entry-level activities related to the family after birth, including:
  - Physiology of the puerperium
  - Cultural and emotional considerations
  - Care of the newborn
  - Care of the new mother
  - Breastfeeding
  - Nutrition

KEY TERMS

afterpains (p. 201)
attachment (p. 219)
bonding (p. 219)
colostrum (p. 223)
concentrated lipid formula
    (p. 230)
diastasis recti (p. 208)
episiotomy (p. 204)

fundus (p. 200)
galactogogues (p. 223)
involution (p. 200)
let-down reflex (p. 222)
lochia (p. 201)
mature milk (p. 223)
oxytocin (p. 222)
postpartum blues (p. 211)

powdered formula (p. 230)
prolactin (p. 222)
puerperium (p. 199)
rugae (p. 203)
suckling (p. 225)
transitional milk (p. 223)

ADDITIONAL RESOURCES

TEACH PPT slide(s) Chapter 9, 1-54
EILR IC image(s) Chapter 9, 1-19
EILR OBQ question(s) Chapter 9, 1-10
EILR TB question(s) Chapter 9, 1-30
ESLR IRQ question(s) Chapter 9, 1-5
SG Chapter 9, pp. 71-80

ELSEVIER

Legend

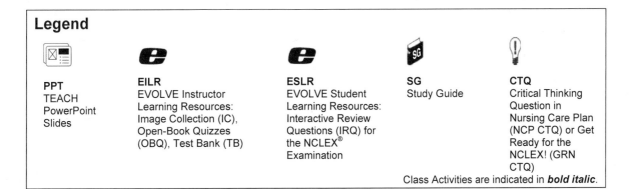

PPT
TEACH
PowerPoint
Slides

EILR
EVOLVE Instructor
Learning Resources:
Image Collection (IC),
Open-Book Quizzes
(OBQ), Test Bank (TB)

ESLR
EVOLVE Student
Learning Resources:
Interactive Review
Questions (IRQ) for
the NCLEX®
Examination

SG
Study Guide

CTQ
Critical Thinking
Question in
Nursing Care Plan
(NCP CTQ) or Get
Ready for the
NCLEX! (GRN
CTQ)

Class Activities are indicated in ***bold italic***.

ELSEVIER

Introduction to Maternity & Pediatric Nursing, 6th ed.
Leifer

LESSON 9.1

PRETEST

1. The *puerperium period* refers to the
   a. 3 weeks preceding birth.
   b. 9 weeks preceding birth.
   c. 6 weeks following birth.
   d. 12 weeks following birth.

2. The increase in blood volume in pregnancy is
   a. 25 percent.
   b. 30 percent.
   c. 50 percent.
   d. 70 percent.

3. The recommended time frame for becoming pregnant after receiving rubella vaccine is
   a. 1 month.
   b. 4 months.
   c. 6 months.
   d. 9 months.

4. Vaginal discharge that lasts about three days after giving birth is called
   a. lochia serosa.
   b. lochia alba.
   c. lochia rubra.
   d. lochia sanguineous.

5. After birth, the mother's gastrointestinal system resumes normal activity due to
   a. increased progesterone levels.
   b. decreased progesterone levels.
   c. increased estrogen levels.
   d. decreased estrogen levels.

6. Hypoglycemia and respiratory distress can occur in the newborn as a result of
   a. hyperthermia.
   b. dehydration.
   c. normothermia.
   d. hypothermia.

7. An umbilical cord with two vessels is associated with
   a. internal anomalies.
   b. external anomalies.
   c. skin disorders.
   d. endocrine disorders.

8. The screening test that is mandatory for all newborns in the United States is
   a. phenylketonuria.
   b. thyroid-stimulating hormone.
   c. complete blood count.
   d. sickle cell screen.

9. Breast fluid immediately after birth containing protective antibodies is called
   a. mature milk.
   b. transitional milk.
   c. hind milk.
   d. colostrum.

10. The breastfeeding woman needs more calories than the woman who is not breastfeeding.
    a. 500.
    b. 800.
    c. 1000.
    d. 1200.

Answers

1. c	3. a	5. b	7. a	9. d
2. c	4. c	6. d	8. a	10. a

BACKGROUND ASSESSMENT

Question: What needs to be done if an Rh-negative mother gives birth to an Rh-positive infant? Why?
Answer: The mother (not the infant) must receive $Rh_o(D)$ immune globulin (RhoGAM) within 72 hours after birth. RhoGAM is given IM in the deltoid muscle. The mother is given an identification card that indicates the date RhoGAM was given and her Rh status. Giving the mother RhoGAM prevents her from being sensitized to Rh-positive red cells that may have entered her bloodstream during the birth process.

Question: What changes occur in the mother's reproductive and cardiovascular systems after birth?
Answer: The changes that occur in the reproductive system after birth include a decrease in blood levels of placental hormones, human placental lactogen, HCG, estrogen, and progesterone. These changes help her body return to its prepregnant state. The uterus undergoes a rapid reduction in size and by five to six weeks postpartum, it is back to its prepregnant size. The fundus descends about 1 cm daily. The uterine lining sheds after the placenta is expelled. The placental site heals in six to seven weeks and new endometrium is generated. Changes in the cardiovascular system include an increase in cardiac output and blood volume despite blood loss. This occurs because blood that was previously shunted toward the uterus and placenta returns to normal circulation. The mother may have bradycardia (low heart rate) for about 48 hours after delivery. The body reestablishes normal fluid balance by diuresis and by diaphoresis. White blood cell count may be elevated after delivery and returns to normal about 12 days postpartum. This is a protective mechanism in response to inflammation, pain, and stress and helps to prevent infection.

CRITICAL THINKING QUESTION

A 36-year-old first-time mother develops complications during labor and requires an emergency cesarean section. How does postpartum nursing care differ for this mother? What assessment and monitoring should the nurse perform?
Guidelines: The mother is likely to have questions and may be anxious about the surgical procedure and why it was necessary. The nurse should spend extra time answering questions and providing support. The incision should be assessed along with fundal height, and the nurse should be careful not to increase pain in the area during assessment. The nurse should monitor lochia, which may be less than with a vaginal delivery because surgical sponges are used to remove uterine contents. Surgical dressings should be assessed for infection using the REEDA (redness, edema, ecchymosis, drainage, approximation) method. Urine output is measured using an indwelling catheter, which is removed within 24 hours of delivery. Monitoring fluid intake and output is done until the intravenous fluids and catheters are discontinued. The nurse should instruct the mother about signs and symptoms of urinary tract infections because an indwelling catheter increases the risk of infection. Pulmonary assessment is necessary to check for any abnormal lung sounds and to make sure respiratory secretions are expelled. The nurse should instruct the mother about coughing and deep-breathing exercises and use of the incentive spirometer. Early ambulation aids in mobilization of lung secretions. The nurse should assess pain levels for severity, character, and location and show the mother how to support her abdomen to reduce discomfort when moving, coughing, or breathing. Epidural and patient-controlled anesthesias are typically used to control postoperative pain. The nurse should also instruct the patient about leg exercises to prevent thrombophlebitis.

OBJECTIVES	CONTENT	TEACHING RESOURCES
Describe how to individualize postpartum and newborn nursing care for different patients.	■ Adapting nursing care for specific groups and cultures (p. 199)	⊠ PPT slides 7-9 𝓮 EILR OBQ question 1 ▸ Discuss the unique considerations the nurse must be aware of when caring for specific groups or patients from cultures he or she is not familiar with. *Class Activity Divide the class into small groups, and assign each group one of the patient groups listed below. Have the groups describe special patient education challenges the nurse may encounter. Then, have groups share their ideas with the class.* *– Adolescent mother* *– Single, working mother with other children* *– Low-income family* *– Family with multiple births*

OBJECTIVES	CONTENT	TEACHING RESOURCES
Describe specific cultural beliefs that the nurse may encounter when providing postpartum and newborn care.	☐ Cultural influences on postpartum care (p. 200) – Using translators (p. 200) – Dietary practices (p. 200)	⊞ PPT slides 8-10 𝒆 EILR IC image 1 𝒆 ESLR IRQ question 1 **BOOK RESOURCES** Figure 9-1, Mother, Husband, and Grandmother (p. 200) ▸ Discuss how the nurse can identify when cultural beliefs and practices about infant care, postpartum care, and family roles, as well as language barriers, must be addressed in order to facilitate nursing care. *Class Activity Facilitate a class discussion in which students describe the nurse's role in solving patient care problems that could arise due to cultural differences and language issues. Students should consider:* – *The role of each family member (father, siblings, grandparents)* – *Variations in dietary beliefs and practices* – *Beliefs about health care and health care practitioners* – *Verbal and nonverbal communication behaviors* – *When and how to use a translator* *How should the nurse determine if information is understood? What should the nurse do if the patient refuses necessary care because she believes it is harmful? What opportunities or limitations does the nurse have for meeting patients' expressed wishes?*
Describe postpartum changes in maternal systems and the nursing care associated with those changes.	■ Postpartum changes in the mother (p. 200) ☐ Reproductive system (p. 200) – Uterus (p. 200) – Cervix (p. 203) – Vagina (p. 203) – Perineum (p. 204) – Return of ovulation and menstruation (p. 206) – Breasts (p. 206) ☐ Cardiovascular system (p. 206)	⊞ PPT slides 11-19 𝒆 EILR IC image 2 𝒆 EILR OBQ questions 3-5 𝒆 EILR TB questions 2, 4-8, 11-12, 25, 27 🕮 SG Learning Activities, questions 1-7, 9-14 (pp. 71-72) 🕮 SG Review Questions, questions 1-5, 7, 12-13, 16 (p. 76) **BOOK RESOURCES** Table 9-1, Summary of Nursing Assessment Postpartum (p. 201) Nursing Tips, (p. 201)

OBJECTIVES	CONTENT	TEACHING RESOURCES
	– Cardiac output and blood volume (p. 206) – Coagulation (p. 206) – Blood values (p. 206) – Chills (p. 207) – Orthostatic hypotension (p. 207) ☐ Urinary system (p. 207) ☐ Gastrointestinal system (p. 207) ☐ Integumentary system (p. 208) ☐ Musculoskeletal system (p. 208) ☐ Immune system (p. 208) – Rh$_o$(D) immune globulin (p. 208) – Rubella (German measles) immunization (p. 208)	Figure 9-2, The Height of the Uterine Fundus Changes (p. 201) Skill 9-1, Estimating the Volume of Lochia (p. 202) Skill 9-2, Observing and Massaging the Uterine Fundus (p. 203) Nursing Tip (p. 203) Skill 9-3, Assessment of the Perineum (p. 204) Memory Jogger (p. 204) Skill 9-4, Assisting with a Sitz Bath (p. 205) Skill 9-5, How to Perform Perineal Care (p. 205) Nursing Tip (p. 207) Review Questions for the NCLEX® Examination, question 2 (p. 234) ▸ Discuss how hormones affect changes in the mother's body after birth as it returns to its prepregnant state. ▸ Discuss postpartum procedures for Rh-negative mothers. ▸ Discuss the procedure to follow if the mother has not been immunized against rubella. *Class Activity Divide the class into small groups, and assign each group a body system that undergoes changes after birth. Discuss nursing assessments, monitoring, interventions, nursing care, and patient education for each system, as appropriate. What are normal signs and symptoms, and which indicate possible complications? What are the nurse's responsibilities? Have each group present a brief report to the class. Invite questions and discussion.*
Modify nursing assessments and interventions for the woman who has a cesarean birth.	☐ Adaptation of nursing care following cesarean birth (p. 209) – Uterus (p. 210) – Lochia (p. 210) – Dressing (p. 210) – Urinary catheter (p. 210) – Respiratory care (p. 210) – Preventing thrombophlebitis	PPT slide 20 𝒆 EILR OBQ questions 2, 6 𝒆 EILR TB questions 5, 19, 24 𝒆 ESLR IRQ question 5 SG Learning Activities, questions 8, 15 (pp. 72-73) SG Thinking Critically, question 1 (p. 80) SG Applying Knowledge, question 1 (p. 80) **BOOK RESOURCES**

OBJECTIVES	CONTENT	TEACHING RESOURCES
	(p. 210) – Pain management (p. 210)	Nursing Care Plan 9-1, The Woman Having a Cesarean Birth (p. 209) Review Questions for the NCLEX® Examination, question 1 (p. 234) ▶ Discuss the variations in postpartum care required for the mother who has had a cesarean birth. ▶ Discuss the alternatives available for post-cesarean pain management. What special considerations must be made when epidural narcotics are used? *Class Activity Lead students in a discussion about similarities and differences between vaginal and cesarean births, including potential complications of each.* *Class Activity Based on the previous class activity, make two columns on the board. Label one Cesarean Delivery and the other Vaginal Delivery. Have students list key nursing assessments and monitoring requirements under the appropriate column for postpartum care associated with the reproductive, cardiovascular, urinary, respiratory, and gastrointestinal systems. Have students also list options for pain management and patient education that should be provided upon discharge.*
Explain the emotional needs of postpartum women and their families.	■ Emotional care (p. 211) ☐ Mothers (p. 211) ☐ Fathers (p. 211) ☐ Siblings (p. 212) ☐ Grandparents (p. 212) ☐ Grieving parents (p. 212) ■ Parenthood (p. 213) ■ The family care plan (p. 213)	PPT slides 21-28 EILR IC images 3, 4 EILR TB question 16 SG Learning Activities, questions 16, 17, 19, 24 (p. 73) SG Applying Knowledge, question 2 (p. 80) **BOOK RESOURCES** Box 9-1, Rubin's Psychological Changes of the Puerperium (p. 211) Figure 9-3, The father shows intense interest in his new infant (p. 212) Figure 9-4, Daughter's Arm Around Mother (p. 212) Nursing Care Plan 9-2, The Family Care Plan (p. 214) Review Questions for the NCLEX® Examination, question 4 (p. 234) ▶ Discuss the emotional changes the mother typically experiences after the birth of a baby, using Box 9-1, Rubin's Psychological Changes of the Puerperium

Leifer

OBJECTIVES	CONTENT	TEACHING RESOURCES
		(p. 211).
		▶ Discuss the various types of grieving processes that may be encountered in the postpartum setting. How can the nurse assist the family?
		*Class Activity **Divide the class into small groups, and assign each group a different family member: postpartum mother, father, sibling, and grandparents. Ask students to discuss how the arrival of the newborn into the family can change family dynamics. What emotional reaction is each family member likely to have? What adjustments might each member need to make? Have groups share their conclusions. Lead a class discussion about how the nurse can assess if each member is adapting appropriately and what the nurse's role should be.***
Recognize the needs of a grieving parent.	☐ Grieving parents (p. 212)	⊞ PPT slide 25
		▶ Discuss therapeutic communication techniques the nurse can use in caring for the mother after a neonatal demise.
		▶ Discuss the five stages of grief the woman and her family are likely to display after a neonatal demise.
		*Class Activity **Arrange for a grief counselor to come to class and discuss appropriate and inappropriate techniques in providing care to a grieving family.***

9.1 Homework/Assignments:

9.1 Instructor's Notes/Student Feedback:

Leifer

LESSON 9.2

CRITICAL THINKING QUESTION

A newborn male weighs 10 pounds when born close to his expected delivery date. He has hypoglycemia, with a glucose level of 34 mg/dl. His mother had gestational diabetes during the pregnancy. What can be done to prevent the newborn's glucose level from dropping lower? What signs and symptoms should the nurse watch for? Why is this infant at risk for hypoglycemia? What other risk factors are associated with hypoglycemia?

Guidelines: Feeding the newborn will prevent decrease in blood glucose levels. The nurse should watch for jitteriness, poor muscle tone, sweating, respiratory difficulty, hypothermia, poor sucking, high-pitched cry, lethargy, and seizures. The infant is at risk for hypoglycemia because he is large for gestational age and because his mother has diabetes with limited glucose control. Other risk factors for hypoglycemia are preterm or postterm infants, infants small for gestational age, those with intrauterine growth retardation, asphyxiated infants, cold-stressed infants, and infants whose mother took ritodrine or terbutaline to stop preterm labor.

OBJECTIVES	CONTENT	TEACHING RESOURCES
Describe nursing care of the normal newborn.	■ Phase 2: Care of the newborn: (p. 214) □ Admission to the postpartum or nursery unit (p. 214) – Supporting thermoregulation (p. 215) – Observing bowel and urinary function (p. 215) – Providing for security (p. 215)	▣ PPT slides 29, 30 𝒆 EILR IC image 5 𝒆 EILR OBQ questions 7, 8 𝒆 EILR TB questions 13, 21 SG Learning Activities, questions 19-23 (pp. 73-74) SG Review Questions, question 15 (p. 78) **BOOK RESOURCES** Review Questions for the NCLEX® Examination, question 3 (p. 234) Table 9-2, Nursing Interventions to Prevent Heat Loss in Newborns (p. 215) Figure 9-5a, Umbilical Clamp (p. 216) Figure 9-5b, Identification Bracelets (p. 216) Safety Alert (p. 216) ▸ Discuss the three phases of the newborn's transition to extrauterine life. ▸ Discuss how to correctly identify the infant after birth and how security is maintained in the hospital. *Class Activity Divide the class into groups, and assign each group one of the following topics related to nursing care of the newborn: thermoregulation or bowel and urinary functions. Ask each group to describe the nursing assessments, monitoring, and patient care that must take place. What are the nurse's responsibilities in meeting nursing goals? Have each group share its findings with the class. Invite feedback and questions.*

OBJECTIVES	CONTENT	TEACHING RESOURCES

Identify signs and symptoms that may indicate a complication in the postpartum mother or newborn.	– Evaluating gestational age (p. 216)
	
	– Observing for injuries or anomalies (p. 217)
	
	– Obtaining vital signs (p. 217)
	
	– Obtaining weights and other measurements (p. 217)
	
	– Providing umbilical cord care (p. 218)
	
	– Hypoglycemia (p. 218)
	
	– Screening tests (p. 218)
	
	– Skin care (p. 219)
	
	– Promoting bonding and attachment (p. 219)
	
	– Providing and teaching routine care (p. 221)
		PPT slides 30-33
		
		e EILR IC images 5-7
		
		e EILR TB questions 1, 14, 22-23
		
		e ESLR IRQ question 4
		
		SG Review Questions, question 6 (p. 77)
		
		SG Applying Knowledge, question 4 (p. 80)
		
		BOOK RESOURCES
		
		Nursing Tip, (p. 217)
		
		Skill 9-6, Providing Umbilical Cord Care (p. 219)
		
		Figure 9-6, Heel Stick (p. 220)
		
		Figure 9-7a, Mother and Infant Bonding (p. 220)
		
		Figure 9-7b, Uncle and Infant Bonding (p. 220)
		
		Figure 9-7c, Siblings and Infant Bonding (p. 220)
		
		▸ Discuss how to obtain vital signs in a newborn. How often are they taken?
		
		Class Activity Lead a discussion in which students describe nursing assessments that indicate a potential complication, including injuries or anomalies, in the newborn. What vital sign ranges may indicate problems? Students should consider infant movements, facial expressions, crying, trauma or puncture, bruising, appearance of feet and toes, length of arms and legs, and urine and meconium.
		
		Class Activity Make a grid on the board as follows:
		
		  – *Two columns, headed Preterm and Postterm*
		
		  – *Seven rows, labeled Skin, Vernix, Hair, Ears, Breast Tissue, Genitalia, and Sole Creases*
		
		Ask students to differentiate the signs and symptoms that indicate gestational age—pre- or postterm. Describe a sign or symptom (refer to pp. 216-217), and have students place the sign or symptom in the appropriate grid location.

Describe nursing interventions to promote optimal infant nutrition.	■ Breastfeeding (p. 221) ☐ Advantages and disadvantages (p. 221)	PPT slides 35-37 SG Case Study, question 1 (p. 80) SG Applying Knowledge, question 5 (p. 80) ▸ Discuss ways to promote maternal nutrition and what

OBJECTIVES	CONTENT	TEACHING RESOURCES
		effects certain foods may have on the infant.
		▶ Discuss the various types of infant formula available and how to safely prepare it and feed it to the infant.
		*Class Activity **Invite a nutritionist to speak to the class about maternal and newborn nutritional needs. Ask the speaker to address breastfeeding versus bottle-feeding. What patient education should the nurse provide while mother and infant are in the hospital and upon discharge? Ask students to prepare questions in advance.***
Explain the physiological characteristics of lactation.	☐ Physiology of lactation (p. 222) – Infectious diseases and breastfeeding (p. 222) – Hormonal stimulation (p. 222) – Phases of milk production (p. 223)	PPT slide 36 *e* EILR IC image 8 *e* EILR OBQ question 9 *e* EILR TB questions 17, 28-30 *e* ESLR IRQ questions 2, 3 SG Learning Activities, question 25 (p. 74) SG Review Questions, questions 8, 9 (p. 77) **BOOK RESOURCES** Figure 9-8, Lactation Reflex Arc (p. 222) Nursing Tip (p. 223) ▶ Discuss how lactation occurs, the types of milk produced, and the phases of milk production.
Compare various maternal and newborn positions used during breastfeeding.	☐ Assisting the mother to breastfeed (p. 223) – Positions for breastfeeding (p. 223) – Breastfeeding techniques (p. 225)	PPT slides 37-41 *e* EILR IC images 9, 10 SG Applying Knowledge, question 3 (p. 80) **BOOK RESOURCES** Communication, Cross-Cultural Communication (p. 223) Cultural Considerations, Galactagogues (p. 223) Table 9-3, Teaching the New Mother How to Breastfeed (p. 224) Figure 9-9, Positions for Nursing (p. 224) Box 9-2, Essential Techniques in Breastfeeding (p. 225) Figure 9-10, Infant Latching on to Breast (p. 226)
Discuss the influences related to the	■ Breastfeeding (p. 221) ☐ Evaluating intake of	PPT slides 42-44 *e* EILR IC images 11-13

Leifer

OBJECTIVES	CONTENT	TEACHING RESOURCES
choice of breastfeeding or bottle-feeding the newborn.	infant (p. 225) ☐ Preventing problems (p. 225) – Frequency and duration of feedings (p. 225) – The sleepy infant (p. 227) – The fussy infant (p. 227) – Flat or inverted nipples (p. 227) – Supplemental feedings and nipple confusion (p. 227) – Breast engorgement (p. 227) – Nipple trauma (p. 228) – Hygiene (p. 228) ☐ Special breastfeeding situations (p. 228) – Multiple births (p. 228) – Premature birth (p. 228) – Delayed feedings (p. 228)	𝒆 EILR OBQ question 10 𝒆 EILR TB questions 3, 9 SG Learning Activities, questions 26-28 (p. 75) SG Review Questions, questions 10, 17 (pp. 77-78) **BOOK RESOURCES** Box 9-3, Recognizing Hunger in Newborns (p. 226) Figure 9-11, Breaking Suction (p. 227) Safety Alert (p. 227) Figure 9-12, Burping the Infant (p. 227) Figure 9-13, Breast Pumps (p. 228) Review Questions for the NCLEX® Examination, question 5 (p. 234) ▸ Discuss the various issues women face when determining whether to breastfeed or bottle-feed their infant. *Class Activity **Divide classes into groups. Have one group discuss pros and cons of breastfeeding and the other the pros and cons of formula feeding. Have them present the results to the entire class.***
Identify principles of breast pumping and milk storage.	☐ Storing and freezing breast milk (p. 228)	🖳 PPT slide 45 𝒆 EILR TB question 20 SG Review Questions, question 18 (p. 78)
Discuss the dietary needs of the lactating mother.	– Maternal nutrition (p. 229)	🖳 PPT slide 46 𝒆 EILR IC image 14 𝒆 EILR TB question 10 SG Learning Activities, question 27 (p. 75) ▸ Discuss the nutritional needs of the lactating woman. Include caloric needs and fluids.

OBJECTIVES	CONTENT	TEACHING RESOURCES
		▶ Discuss what foods should be avoided to prevent stomach upset for her breastfeeding infant.
		Class Activity Invite a lactation consultant to speak about and demonstrate proper breastfeeding and bottle-feeding techniques. Ask the speaker to discuss ways the nurse can support the new mother and what types of nursing challenges may be encountered. Also, ask the speaker to discuss special feeding situations, such as multiple births and premature birth. Ask students to prepare questions in advance.
Discuss the principles of weaning the infant from the breast.	☐ Weaning (p. 229)	🖳 PPT slide 47 𝒆 EILR TB question 15 ▶ Discuss the four tips found on p. 229 that the nurse can give to the mother to help wean her infant from the breast. *Class Activity Present and discuss the following clinical scenario:* 　*A 6-month old infant has been breastfed since birth. The mother is preparing to return to work and wants to start weaning her infant.* *What should the nurse tell the mother? Is there a "good time" to wean? If done abruptly, what are some of the side effects that can be experienced by both the mother and her infant?*
Illustrate techniques of formula feeding.	■ Formula feeding (p. 229) ☐ Types of infant formula (p. 229) ☐ Preparation (p. 230) ☐ Feeding the infant (p. 230)	🖳 PPT slides 48-50 𝒆 EILR TB questions 18, 26 📕 SG Learning Activities, questions 30, 31 (p. 75) **BOOK RESOURCES** Safety Alert (p. 230) Skill 9-7, Bottle Feeding the Infant (p. 231) ▶ Discuss with the class the advantages and disadvantages to formula feeding. *Class Activity Provide different bottles and nipples for the class to inspect. What type would be best for a premature infant? What type is best for a term infant? What type is best for an infant with a cleft palate?* *Class Activity Divide the class into small groups. Have them review the different formulas and their ingredients. Then have each group discuss which formulas are best for infants with PKU, maple syrup urine disease, and other metabolic disorders.*

OBJECTIVES	CONTENT	TEACHING RESOURCES
Plan appropriate discharge teaching for the postpartum woman and her infant.	■ Discharge planning (p. 230) ☐ Postpartum self-care (p. 230) – Follow-up appointments (p. 231) – Hygiene (p. 232) – Sexual intercourse (p. 232) – Diet and exercise (p. 232) – Danger signs (p. 232) ☐ Newborn discharge care (p. 232)	▣▤ PPT slides 51, 52 𝒆 EILR IC image 14 SG Learning Activities, questions 32-34 (p. 75) SG Review Questions, questions 11, 14, 19 (p. 78) **BOOK RESOURCES** Nursing Tip, (p. 232) Figure 9-14, A new mother prepares to leave the birth facility (p. 233) ▸ Discuss the various aspects of discharge planning. List possible danger signs that the mother must be aware of. *Class Activity **Divide the class into small groups. Ask half of the groups to discuss and prepare a brief presentation on key patient education points the nurse should share with the new mother upon discharge. Ask the other half to discuss key patient education points specifically addressing care of the newborn at home. Each group should include signs and symptoms of potential problems and resources the family can call on for help.***
Performance Evaluation		▣▤ PPT slides 1-54 𝒆 EILR IC images 1-14 𝒆 EILR OBQ questions 1-10 𝒆 EILR TB questions 1-30 𝒆 ESLR IRQ questions 1-5 SG Learning Activities, questions 1-34 (pp. 71-76) SG Review Questions, questions 1-19 (pp. 76-78) SG Crossword puzzle (pp. 79-80) SG Case Study, question 1 (p. 80) SG Thinking Critically, question 1 (p. 80) SG Applying Knowledge, questions 1-5 (p. 80) **BOOK RESOURCES** NCP CTQ 1 (p. 209) NCP CTQ 1 (p. 214)

OBJECTIVES	CONTENT	TEACHING RESOURCES
		Review Questions for the NCLEX® Examination, questions 1-5 (p. 234)

9.2 Homework/Assignments:

9.2 Instructor's Notes/Student Feedback:

9 Lecture Outline
The Family After Birth

Slide 1

Chapter 9

The Family After Birth

Slide 2

Objectives

- Describe how to individualize postpartum and newborn nursing care for different patients.
- Describe specific cultural beliefs that the nurse may encounter when providing postpartum and newborn care.
- Describe postpartum changes in maternal systems and the nursing care associated with those changes.

Slide 3

Objectives *(cont.)*

- Identify signs and symptoms that may indicate a complication in the postpartum mother or newborn.
- Describe the nursing care of the normal newborn.
- Describe nursing interventions to promote optimal infant nutrition.
- Modify nursing assessments and interventions for the woman who has a cesarean birth.

Slide 4

Objectives *(cont.)*

- Explain the emotional needs of postpartum women and their families.
- Recognize the needs of a grieving parent.
- Discuss the influences related to the choice of breastfeeding or bottle feeding the newborn.
- Explain the physiological characteristics of lactation.

Slide 5

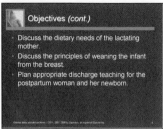

Objectives *(cont.)*

- Compare various maternal and newborn positions used during breastfeeding.
- Identify principles of breast pumping and milk storage.
- Illustrate techniques of formula feeding.
- Compare nutrients of human milk with those of cow's milk.

Slide 6

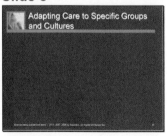

Objectives *(cont.)*

- Discuss the dietary needs of the lactating mother.
- Discuss the principles of weaning the infant from the breast.
- Plan appropriate discharge teaching for the postpartum woman and her newborn.

Slide 7

Puerperium

- Known as *postpartum period*
- Six weeks following childbirth
  - Sometimes referred to as the *fourth trimester of pregnancy*

- The puerperium is a time of transition for both the new mother and her family.

Audience Response Question #1
Pregnancy: 40 weeks as Puerperium:_____
   1. 5 weeks
   2. 6 weeks
   3. 2 months
   4. 1 year

Slide 8

Adapting Care to Specific Groups and Cultures

Slide 9

Nursing Considerations for Specific Groups of Patients

- Adolescents
- Single women
- Families at or below the poverty level
- Families who have twins (or more)

- The nurse caring for the childbearing family has a responsibility to provide culturally sensitive care. The special needs of each patient group must be incorporated into the care provided.
- Identify the unique concerns for adolescents, single women, families at or below the poverty level, and families who are expecting multiples.
- What is the best manner in which to approach each of the groups identified?

Slide 10

- Nurses must use caution not to stereotype clients based upon outward appearances.
- The nurse must remain flexible when planning the care to be provided.
- Review the resources that might be available on the nursing unit to meet unique patient concerns relating to language barriers.
- What resources are available for nurses to review cultural practices?

Slide 11

Postpartum Changes in the Mother

Slide 12

Reproductive System

- Immediately after delivery, the mother begins to experience changes in her reproductive system.
- The nurse must provide a comprehensive assessment of the patient's reproductive system.
- What are normal and abnormal findings from the nursing assessment of the reproductive system?

Audience Response Question #2
During post-partum discharge teaching a woman expresses that "since she is breastfeeding her newborn" she will not require birth control. The nurse will:
1. Inform the physician
2. Tell the woman she will require birth control when she is weaning the baby.
3. Inform her that breastfeeding is not a form a birth control.
4. Inform her that she must use oral contraceptives in supplement to breastfeeding.

Slide 13

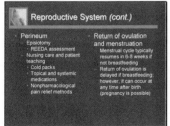

Reproductive System *(cont.)*

Slide 14

Cardiovascular System

- Cardiac output and blood volume
- Coagulation
- Blood values
- Chills
- Orthostatic hypotension
- Nursing care

- During pregnancy, the woman experiences a 50% increase in circulating blood volume.
- Physiological changes during labor and delivery cause further cardiac changes.
- Review the pathophysiology that is responsible for the changes in blood coagulation and laboratory values.

Audience Response Question #3
It is considered normal for a woman's blood pressure to increase during pregnancy.
1. True
2. False

Slide 15

Urinary System

- A full bladder can displace the uterus and lead to postpartum hemorrhage
- The woman who voids frequent, small amounts of urine may have increased residual urine because her bladder does not fully empty
- Residual urine in the bladder may promote the growth of microorganisms

- During pregnancy, the bladder experiences a reduction in tone.
- During labor, administering intravenous fluids and anesthesia could impact urinary elimination.
- Review the assessment of the urinary bladder during the postpartum period.
- For what signs and symptoms should the nurse assess?
- What should be reported?

Slide 16

Gastrointestinal System

- Constipation
  - To help alleviate this problem, encourage woman to
    - Increase fluid and fiber intake
    - Increase activity, such as walking

- After delivery, gastrointestinal function returns to normal rapidly.
- The patient might have concerns regarding the first bowel movement.
- What information concerning bowel health should be provided to the patient?
- When will pharmacological interventions be employed?

Slide 17

Integumentary System

- Hyperpigmentation of the skin changes as hormone levels decrease
  - Linea nigra disappears
  - Striae fade to silver

Leifer

Slide 18

Musculoskeletal System

- Diastasis recti
- Hypermobility of the joints
- Exercises
  - Abdominal muscle tightening
  - Head lift
  - Pelvic tilt
  - Kegel exercises

- Many women might not be realistic concerning their appearance in the immediate postpartum period.
- What information should be given to the woman during the prenatal period concerning her physical appearance after delivery?
- At what point in the pregnancy should this information be provided?

Slide 19

Immune System

- Prevent blood incompatibilities and infection
  - RhoGAM if woman is Rh negative and baby is Rh positive
  - Give mother immunization for rubella if she is not immune
    - Titer < 1:8 requires immunization

- Assessment of the woman's blood type and immune status is completed during the pregnancy. If concerns are identified, they are monitored closely during the pregnancy.
- Review the Rh status of the father in the identified scenario.
- RhoGAM is a product obtained from the hospital's blood bank. Discuss precautions that are indicated when administering this agent.
- Discuss the administration of the rubella vaccine.

Slide 20

Changes After Cesarean Birth and Adaptation of Nursing Care

- Same as with normal vaginal delivery except
  - Monitoring of abdominal dressing
  - Lochia generally less
  - Urinary catheter
  - Respiratory care
  - Prevention of thrombophlebitis
  - Interventions for pain

- The mother who delivers via cesarean section may experience feelings of failure because of her inability to deliver vaginally.
- How should the nurse address these concerns?

Slide 21

Emotional Care

- The birth of an infant brings about physical changes in the mother but also causes many emotional and relationship changes in all family members

Slide 22

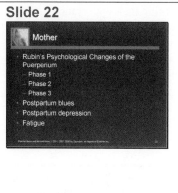

- Review each of Rubin's phases.
- What is the primary focus and task for each of the phases?
- What are signs and symptoms the patient is not progressing normally through each of the phases?

Audience Response Question #4
Which of the following groups of signs and symptom are the most representative of postpartum "blues"?
1. Crying, loss of appetite, constipation, abdominal pain, and anxiety.
2. Crying, loss of appetite, difficulty sleeping, and anxiety.
3. Crying, increased appetite, urinary retention, anxiety, and fear of the unknown.
4. Crying, despondency, poor concentration, diarrhea, and anxiety.

Slide 23

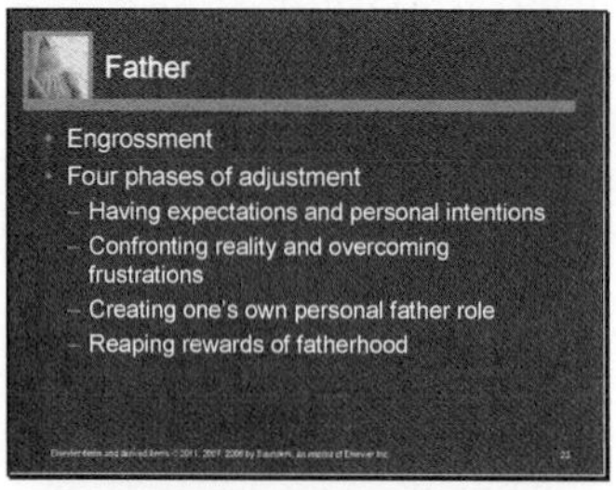

- The relationship between the father and mother will have the greatest impact on the father's responses to the infant.
- What additional factors will influence the father's actions/reactions?

Slide 24

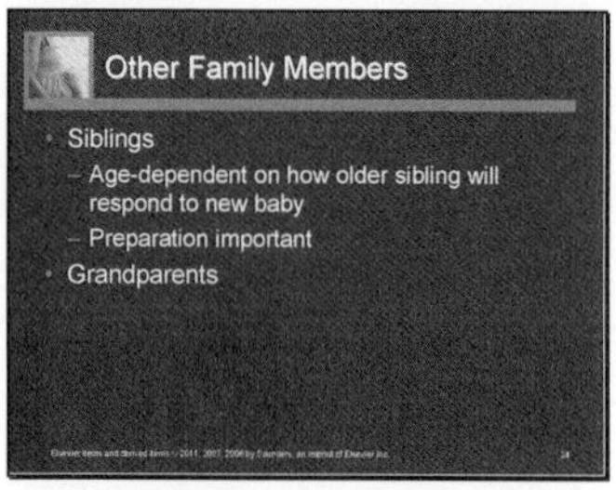

- Today's method of obstetrical care incorporates the needs and desires of the entire family into the birthing experience.
- What interventions can the nurse perform to promote inclusion of the siblings and grandparents into the plan of care?

Slide 25

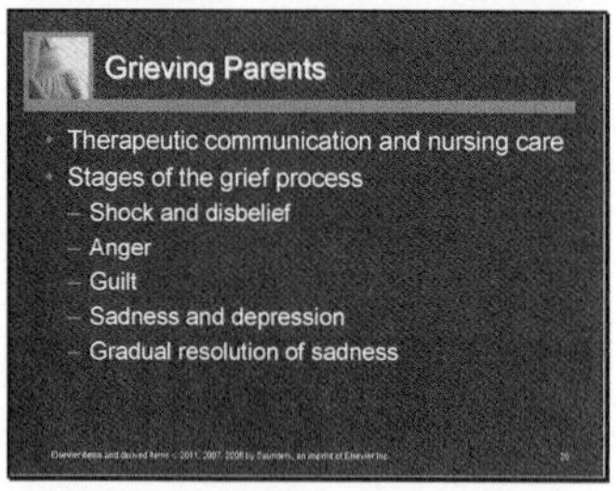

- The support of the nurses is vital to the family during the grief process.
- What can the nurse do to offer emotional support?
- Discuss the types of questions and responses that should be avoided.

Slide 26

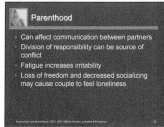

Slide 27

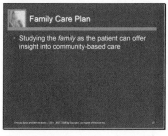

Slide 28

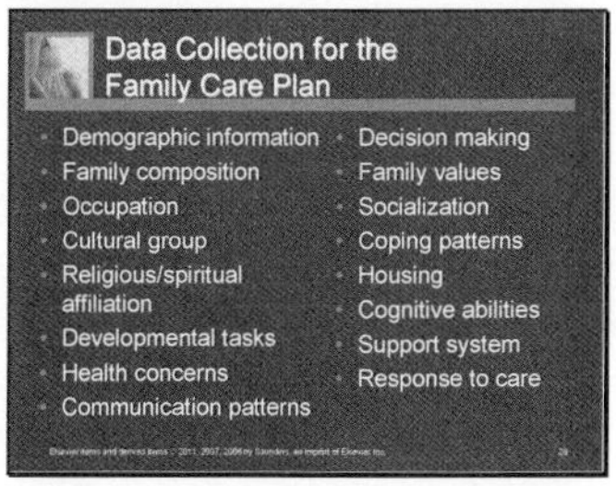

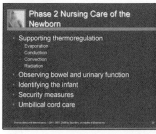

- The development of a successful plan of care requires the nurse to be comprehensive in scope.
- In addition to the patient interview, what are other sources of data?

Slide 29

Slide 30

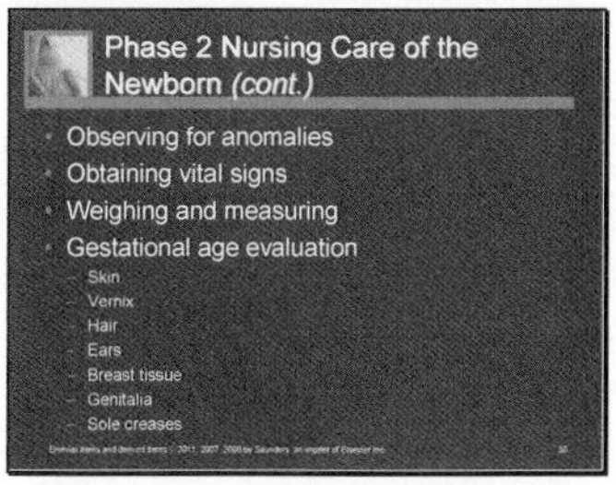

- After delivery, the infant must have a complete assessment.
- Abnormal findings must be reported.
- Discuss normal findings for each category.
- What other security measures may need to be implemented?

Slide 31

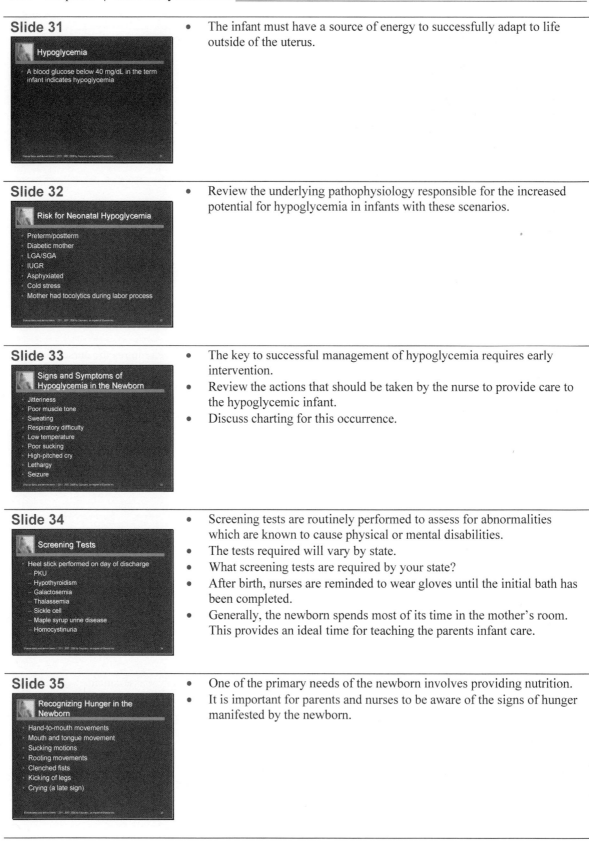

- The infant must have a source of energy to successfully adapt to life outside of the uterus.

Slide 32

- Review the underlying pathophysiology responsible for the increased potential for hypoglycemia in infants with these scenarios.

Slide 33

- The key to successful management of hypoglycemia requires early intervention.
- Review the actions that should be taken by the nurse to provide care to the hypoglycemic infant.
- Discuss charting for this occurrence.

Slide 34

- Screening tests are routinely performed to assess for abnormalities which are known to cause physical or mental disabilities.
- The tests required will vary by state.
- What screening tests are required by your state?
- After birth, nurses are reminded to wear gloves until the initial bath has been completed.
- Generally, the newborn spends most of its time in the mother's room. This provides an ideal time for teaching the parents infant care.

Slide 35

- One of the primary needs of the newborn involves providing nutrition.
- It is important for parents and nurses to be aware of the signs of hunger manifested by the newborn.

Introduction to Maternity & Pediatric Nursing, 6th ed.

Leifer

Slide 36
 	
Breastfeeding
 	
· Choosing whether to breastfeed
· Physiology of lactation
    - Hormonal stimulation
      · Prolactin
      · Oxytocin
· Composition of milk
    - Foremilk
    - Hindmilk
· Phases of milk production
    - Colostrum
    - Transitional
    - Mature
	• Selection of a method of feeding is often an area of concern for new mothers.
	• It is helpful to provide as much information as possible to assist in the decision-making process.

Slide 37
 	
Assisting the Mother to Breastfeed
 	
· Advantages of breastfeeding are
    - Promotes mother-infant bonding
    - Maintains infant temperature
    - Suckling stimulates oxytocin release to
      contract mother's uterus
    - Cultural use of galactogogues
	• As a point of class discussion, inquire about why some women might choose not to breastfeed.
	• The cultural use of galactogogues refers to the use of "breast milk stimulators." These are interventions taken by the mother to facilitate lactation. Nurses must be culturally respectful of these practices.
	• What are commonly used breast milk stimulators?

Slide 38
 	
Positions for Breastfeeding
	• Positions for nursing.
	   – Cradle hold.
	   – Football hold.
	   – Side-lying position.
	• Which of the positions would be most comfortable for a mother after a cesarean section?

Slide 39
 	
Breastfeeding Techniques
 	
· Positions of the mother's hands
· Latch-on
· Suckling patterns
· Removing the infant from the breast
	• Essential factors in breastfeeding involve:
	   – Proper body alignment
	   – Correct grasp of the areola
	   – Proper hand positions of the mother on the breast
	• The mother should wash her hands before breastfeeding.
	• Attempting to express some colostrum on the nipple prior to breastfeeding will increase the erectness of the nipples.
	• Which breast should the mother use to initiate breastfeeding?

Slide 40 Latch-on	• What actions can the mother take to cause the infant to open the mouth and turn toward the breast?

Leifer

Slide 41

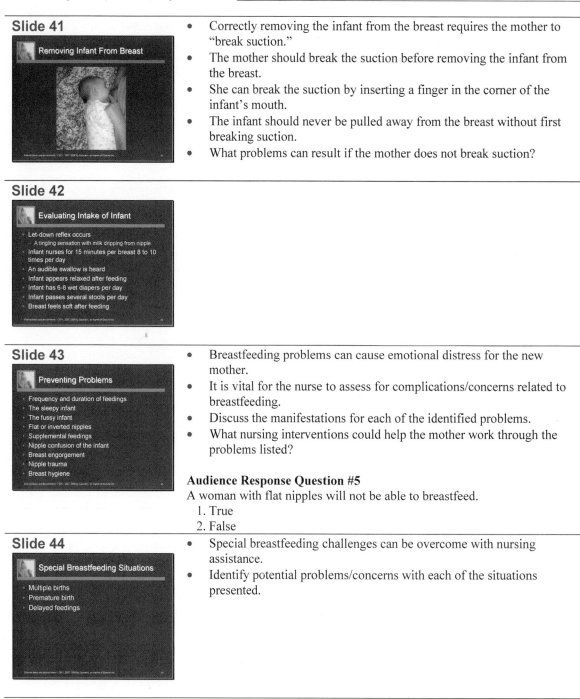

- Correctly removing the infant from the breast requires the mother to "break suction."
- The mother should break the suction before removing the infant from the breast.
- She can break the suction by inserting a finger in the corner of the infant's mouth.
- The infant should never be pulled away from the breast without first breaking suction.
- What problems can result if the mother does not break suction?

Slide 42

Evaluating Intake of Infant

- Let-down reflex occurs
  - A tingling sensation with milk dripping from nipple
- Infant nurses for 15 minutes per breast 8 to 10 times per day
- An audible swallow is heard
- Infant appears relaxed after feeding
- Infant has 6-8 wet diapers per day
- Infant passes several stools per day
- Breast feels soft after feeding

Slide 43

Preventing Problems

- Frequency and duration of feedings
- The sleepy infant
- The fussy infant
- Flat or inverted nipples
- Supplemental feedings
- Nipple confusion of the infant
- Breast engorgement
- Nipple trauma
- Breast hygiene

- Breastfeeding problems can cause emotional distress for the new mother.
- It is vital for the nurse to assess for complications/concerns related to breastfeeding.
- Discuss the manifestations for each of the identified problems.
- What nursing interventions could help the mother work through the problems listed?

Audience Response Question #5
A woman with flat nipples will not be able to breastfeed.
   1. True
   2. False

Slide 44

Special Breastfeeding Situations

- Multiple births
- Premature birth
- Delayed feedings

- Special breastfeeding challenges can be overcome with nursing assistance.
- Identify potential problems/concerns with each of the situations presented.

Slide 45

Storing and Freezing Breast Milk
• Milk at room temperature for more than 4 hours increases potential for bacterial contamination
• Container size should hold no more than one feeding
• Safely stored or frozen in glass or hard plastic containers
• Milk can be stored in refrigerator at 4° C (39°F) for 24 hours or in the freezer at –4° C (-20°F) for up to 3 months (although freezing breast milk can destroy some antimicrobial factors)
• Can be thawed in refrigerator for 24 hours prior to using
• Microwaving of breast milk is not advised because it destroys immune factors in the milk

- Important points to stress with class and when teaching mother/caregiver.
  - Milk stored in the refrigerator compartment should be stored toward the back of the refrigerator.
  - Milk stored in the freezer should also be stored toward the back as the temperature is more constant in this area.

Slide 46

Maternal Nutrition
• Mother needs an additional 500 calories over the nonpregnant diet
• 8-10 glasses of fluids per day
• Some foods eaten by mother may cause a change in the taste of the milk or cause the infant to develop gas (flatus)
• Medications taken by the mother may be secreted in the breast milk

- Dietary changes might be required if certain substances are found to cause distress in the infant.
- Discuss common foods that can be a source of problems when eaten by the breastfeeding mother.

Slide 47

Weaning
• Gradual weaning is preferred
• There is no "best time" to wean
• Technique of weaning
– Eliminate one feeding at a time
– Omit daytime feedings first
– Eliminate the favorite feeding last
• Infant will need "comfort nursing" if tired or ill
• Breast pumping not advised in order to decrease the milk supply cycle

- Abrupt weaning can cause engorgement, mastitis, and discomfort in the mother, and the infant could become distressed.
- As solid foods are gradually introduced into the diet, the infant will gradually lose interest in breastfeeding.

Slide 48

Formula Feeding
• Types of formulas — Ready to feed — Concentrated liquid — Powdered	• Regardless of type, it is important to follow manufacturer's instruction on preparation and storage of formula products

- The mother who decides to formula feed her infant will require education from the nurse concerning this method.
- Formulas are available in a variety of stages of preparation.
- What are the necessary steps to prepare each type of commercial formula?

Slide 49

Safety Alert
• Overdilution or underdilution of concentrated liquid or powdered formulas can result in serious illness

Slide 50

Feeding the Infant with Formula

- Feed every 3 to 4 hours because formula is digested more slowly than breast milk
- Do not microwave formula
- Do not prop bottle
- Involve partner and family in bottle feeding of infant

- Many women desire to warm their infant's formula. This is not necessary.
- Why should the use of the microwave be avoided?
- Although bottle propping may seem like a timesaver for the mother, it must be avoided. Why?

Slide 51

Discharge Planning

Slide 52

Postpartum Self-Care Teaching

- Ample written materials regarding mother and newborn care should be provided and reviewed
  - Follow-up appointments
  - Hygiene
  - Sexual intercourse
  - Diet and exercise
  - Danger signs to watch for and report
  - Newborn follow-up care
  - Infant safety seats
  - Reassure mother that hospital staff is available by telephone should any questions arise

- Childbirth and the addition of a new family member will require education for both the mother and father.
- What is the best time to begin discharge teaching?
- Discuss ideal times for providing discharge education.

Slide 53

Question for Review

- What are the essential nursing assessments of the new postpartum mother?

Slide 54

Review

- Objectives
- Key Terms
- Key Points
- Online Resources
- Critical Thinking Question
- Review Questions

Leifer

10 Lesson Plan
Nursing Care of Women with Complications After Birth

TEACHING FOCUS

This chapter will introduce students to the various complications that can occur postpartum, such as shock, hemorrhage, thrombosis, infection, uterine abnormalities, and mood disorders. Students will have the opportunity to learn how to recognize the signs and symptoms associated with these complications and to learn appropriate nursing interventions for each. Medical management of complications will also be discussed.

MATERIALS AND RESOURCES

☐ Computer and PowerPoint projector (all lessons)

LESSON CHECKLIST

Preparations for this lesson include:

- Lecture
- Demonstration
- Evaluation of student knowledge and skills needed to perform all entry-level activities related to nursing care of women with postpartum complications, including:
  ○ Assessing for signs and symptoms of postpartum complications
  ○ Nursing interventions for postpartum complications
  ○ Common medical therapies employed for complications
  ○ Recognizing the signs of postpartum mood disorders and providing appropriate support measures

KEY TERMS

atony (p. 238)
curettage (p. 240)
endometritis (p. 241)
hematoma (p. 239)

hypovolemic shock
 (p. 236)
involution (p. 244)
mania (p. 246)
mastitis (p. 243)

mood (p. 245)
psychosis (p. 245)
puerperal sepsis (p. 241)
subinvolution (p. 244)

ADDITIONAL RESOURCES

TEACH PPT slide(s) Chapter 10, 1-32
EILR IC image(s) Chapter 10, 1-3
EILR OBQ question(s) Chapter 10, 1-10
EILR TB question(s) Chapter 10, 1-29
ESLR IRQ question(s) Chapter 10, 1-5
SG Chapter 10, pp. 81-88

Legend

	e EILR	*e* ESLR	SG	CTQ
PPT TEACH PowerPoint Slides	**EILR** EVOLVE Instructor Learning Resources: Image Collection (IC), Open-Book Quizzes (OBQ), Test Bank (TB)	**ESLR** EVOLVE Student Learning Resources: Interactive Review Questions (IRQ) for the NCLEX® Examination	**SG** Study Guide	**CTQ** Critical Thinking Question in Nursing Care Plan (NCP CTQ) or Get Ready for the NCLEX! (GRN CTQ)

Class Activities are indicated in ***bold italic***.

LESSON 10.1

PRETEST

1. Which type of shock occurs when blood volume is depleted and cannot fill the circulatory system?
   a. cardiogenic shock
   b. anaphylactic shock
   c. hypovolemic shock
   d. septic shock

2. Late postpartum hemorrhage occurs how long after birth?
   a. before 12 hours
   b. 24 hours to 6 weeks
   c. 6 weeks to 12 weeks
   d. 12 weeks to 3 months

3. One of the first signs of hypovolemia is
   a. bradycardia.
   b. elevated hematocrit.
   c. tachycardia.
   d. elevated blood pressure.

4. Uterine atony, reproductive tract lacerations, and reproductive tract hematomas are all causes of
   a. early postpartum hemorrhage.
   b. late postpartum hemorrhage.
   c. distended bladder.
   d. bladder infections.

5. A 38-year-old woman who is 24 hours postpartum is complaining of swelling in her right leg and calf. The nurse should assess this patient for which sign?
   a. Goodell's sign
   b. Chadwick's sign
   c. Homans' sign
   d. Chvostek's sign

6. When the uterus returns to its nonpregnant state more slowly than normal, it is referred to as
   a. involution.
   b. subinvolution.
   c. hematoma.
   d. gravid uterus.

7. Lack of interest in life, intense feelings of inadequacy, and loss of mental concentration are all signs of
   a. postpartum psychosis.
   b. postpartum depression.
   c. mood disorder.
   d. chronic fatigue.

8. What can increase a woman's risk of developing postpartum endometritis?
   a. lochial flow
   b. retained placenta
   c. passing of blood clots
   d. elevated fundus

9. Which of the following can help prevent thromboses from forming?
   a. breastfeeding
   b. uterine massage
   c. early ambulation
   d. bedrest

10. Treatment of mastitis includes
    a. antibiotics.
    b. bedrest.
    c. ice packs.
    d. cessation of breastfeeding.

Answers

1. c	3. c	5. c	7. b	9. c
2. b	4. a	6. b	8. b	10. a

BACKGROUND ASSESSMENT

Question: What are the signs of puerperal sepsis, and what nursing interventions would be appropriate?
Answer: Puerperal sepsis occurs after childbirth and results from septicemia. Infections, if left untreated, can lead to septicemia. Causes of infections include trauma to vaginal tissue during labor, an open wound at the placental site, surgical incisions (episiotomy or cesarean section), cracks in the nipples, and increased vaginal pH. Puerperal fever is indicated by a temperature over 100.4° F, after the first 24 hours postpartum and on at least 2 days during the first 10 days after birth. An elevated pulse rate is also a sign of infection, as well as localized erythema, warmth, and swelling. The nurse should instruct the woman on proper hand hygiene techniques, the importance of rest and nutrition, and the correct application of perineal pads.

Question: How would you differentiate between postpartum depression and postpartum psychosis?
Answer: Postpartum depression affects approximately 15% of women during the postpartum period. It is a depressive illness with nonpsychotic manifestations and usually occurs within 2 weeks of delivery. Signs of postpartum depression include a lack of enjoyment in life, lack of interest in others, intense feelings of inadequacy and inability to cope, loss of mental concentration, disturbed sleep, fatigue, and feelings of ill health. Women with postpartum psychosis have an impaired sense of reality. Postpartum psychosis is much less common than postpartum depression; bipolar disorder and major depression are the most common postpartum psychotic disorders. Women who suffer from postpartum depression or psychosis may be a danger to themselves and their infants; they require counseling and should be referred to a psychiatrist. If psychotropic medications are prescribed, then the mother should be instructed not to breastfeed.

CRITICAL THINKING QUESTION

Three weeks postpartum, a woman reports that her period has returned and that it is very heavy; each time she changes her pad it is soaked through. What postpartum complication might this woman be experiencing, and what instructions or information should the nurse provide?

Guidelines: This patient may be experiencing late postpartum hemorrhage, which occurs after 24 hours and up to six weeks postpartum. It is typically caused by retained placental fragments or subinvolution of the uterus. Placental fragments are retained if the placenta does not cleanly separate from its implantation site. This causes clots to start sloughing off, which can result in hemorrhage. The nurse should instruct the woman to report any bright-red bleeding, or a return of any bleeding after vaginal discharge is pink, white, or has ceased. Late postpartum hemorrhage is treated with drugs such as oxytocin, methylergonovine, or prostaglandins. Ultrasound is also used to detect retained placental fragments. If fragments are noted and bleeding continues, then curettage is performed to remove blot clots and placental fragments. Antimicrobials will be given if the woman has an infection.

OBJECTIVES	CONTENT	TEACHING RESOURCES
Describe signs and symptoms for each postpartum complication.	■ Shock (p. 235) ■ Hemorrhage (p. 235) ☐ Hypovolemic shock (p. 236) ☐ Anemia (p. 236) ☐ Early postpartum hemorrhage (p. 236) – Uterine atony (p. 238) – Lacerations of the reproductive tract (p. 239) – Hematomas of the reproductive tract (p. 239) ☐ Late postpartum hemorrhage (p. 240) ■ Thromboembolic disorders (p. 240) ■ Infection (p. 241) ☐ Mastitis and breastfeeding (p. 243)	PPT slides 4-30 EILR IC images 1-3 EILR OBQ questions 1, 3, 4, 8-10 EILR TB questions 1-2, 9, 14, 19-22, 25 ESLR IRQ questions 1, 3 SG Learning Activities, questions 1-15 (pp. 81-83) SG Review Questions, questions 1, 7, 9, 12, 16 (p. 85) **BOOK RESOURCES** Safety Alert, (p. 236) Table 10-1, Types of Early Postpartum Hemorrhage (p. 238) Nursing Tips (p. 238) Figure 10-1, A Distended Bladder (p. 239) Safety Alert (p. 239) Figure 10-2, Homan's Sign (p. 241) Table 10-2, Observation of Venous Thrombosis (p. 241) Nursing Tip (p. 241)

Leifer

OBJECTIVES	CONTENT	TEACHING RESOURCES
	■ Subinvolution of the uterus (p. 244) ■ Mood disorders (p. 245) □ Postpartum depression (p. 245) □ Postpartum psychosis (p. 246) ■ The homeless mother and newborn (p. 246)	Table 10-3, Postpartum Infections (p. 242) Safety Alert (p. 242) Figure 10-3, Mastitis (p. 244) Patient Teaching, Mastitis (p. 244) Nursing Tip (p. 245) Review Questions for the NCLEX® Examination, questions 1, 3 (p. 247) ▸ Discuss the significance of uterine atony. ▸ Discuss how a nurse might recognize that a woman is homeless. *Class Activity Write the following headings on the board, and have students identify the characteristics, signs, symptoms, and causes of each, as well as the nursing interventions that should be implemented to prevent further complications:* – *Cardiogenic shock* – *Hypovolemic shock* – *Anaphylactic shock*
Identify factors that increase a woman's risk for developing each complication.	■ Shock (p. 235) ■ Hemorrhage (p. 235) □ Hypovolemic shock (p. 236) □ Anemia (p. 236) □ Early postpartum hemorrhage (p. 236) – Uterine atony (p. 238) – Lacerations of the reproductive tract (p. 239) – Hematomas of the reproductive tract (p. 239) □ Late postpartum hemorrhage (p. 240) ■ Thromboembolic disorders (p. 240) ■ Infection (p. 241) □ Mastitis and	⊠▪ PPT slides 4-30 🄴 EILR IC images 1-3 🄴 EILR OBQ question 8 🄴 EILR TB questions 13, 17 🄴 ESLR IRQ question 4 📓 SG Learning Activities, questions 16, 17, 19 (p. 83) 📓 SG Review Questions, question 17 (p. 87) **BOOK RESOURCES** Nursing Care Plan 10-1, The Woman with Postpartum Hemorrhage (p. 237) Table 10-1, Types of Early Postpartum Hemorrhage (p. 238) Review Questions for the NCLEX® Examination, question 2 (p. 247) ▸ Discuss factors that increases a woman's risk for genital trauma during delivery. ▸ Discuss the risk factors and contributing factors for development of hematomas in the reproductive tract

Leifer

OBJECTIVES	CONTENT	TEACHING RESOURCES
	breastfeeding (p. 243)	during delivery.
	■ Subinvolution of the uterus (p. 244)	▶ Discuss why the pregnant woman and the woman who has recently delivered a baby are at increased risk for thrombus formation.
	■ Mood disorders (p. 245)	*Class Activity Divide the class into groups. Have each group identify and discuss the factors that increase a woman's risk for developing complications. Which factors can be controlled, and which cannot? How can a woman decrease her risk of developing complications? Have each group share its findings with the class for discussion.*
	□ Postpartum depression (p. 245)	
	□ Postpartum psychosis (p. 246)	
	■ The homeless mother and newborn (p. 246)	*Class Activity Divide the class into groups, and have them compare and contrast the signs and symptoms of each of the following disorders:*
		– *Postpartum blues*
		– *Postpartum depression*
		– *Postpartum psychosis (bipolar disorder)*
		– *Major depression*
Explain nursing measures that reduce a woman's risk for developing specific postpartum complications.	■ Shock (p. 235)	⊠■ PPT slides 4-30
	■ Hemorrhage (p. 235)	*e* EILR TB questions 4, 8, 13, 24, 26-27, 29
	□ Hypovolemic shock (p. 236)	SG Learning Activities, questions 18, 20 (p. 84)
	□ Anemia (p. 236)	SG Review Questions, questions 2-5 (p. 85)
	□ Early postpartum hemorrhage (p. 236)	**BOOK RESOURCES**
	– Uterine atony (p. 238)	Nursing Care Plan 10-1, The Woman with Postpartum Hemorrhage (p. 237)
	– Lacerations of the reproductive tract (p. 239)	Nursing Care Plan 10-2, The Woman with Postpartum Infection (p. 243)
	– Hematomas of the reproductive tract (p. 239)	Patient Teaching, Mastitis, (p. 244)
		▶ Discuss nursing measures that can help prevent urinary tract infections.
	□ Late postpartum hemorrhage (p. 240)	▶ Discuss what the nurse can do to reduce a new mother's risk of postpartum depression.
	■ Thromboembolic disorders (p. 240)	*Class Activity Divide the class into five groups, and assign each group one of the following complications:*
	■ Infection (p. 241)	– *Cardiogenic, hypovolemic, anaphylactic, and septic shock*
	□ Mastitis and breastfeeding (p. 243)	– *Thromboembolic disorders*
	■ Subinvolution of the	– *Postpartum hemorrhage*
		– *Puerperal infection*

Introduction to Maternity & Pediatric Nursing, 6th ed.

Elsevier items and derived items © 2011, 2007, 2006 by Saunders, an imprint of Elsevier Inc.

Leifer

OBJECTIVES	CONTENT	TEACHING RESOURCES
	uterus (p. 244) ■ Mood disorders (p. 245) □ Postpartum depression (p. 245) □ Postpartum psychosis (p. 246) ■ The homeless mother and newborn (p. 246)	– *Mastitis* *Have each group identify the risk factors for developing its assigned complication and discuss the nursing measures that can help reduce those risks. Have each group present its findings to the class for discussion.*

10.1 Homework/Assignments:

10.1 Instructor's Notes/Student Feedback:

LESSON 10.2

CRITICAL THINKING QUESTION

You record a blood loss of 550 mL from a woman who had a cesarean delivery less than 24 hours ago and note she appears to be developing hypovolemic shock. What signs and symptoms of hypovolemic shock should the nurse recognize? What medical management is indicated?

Guidelines: Signs and symptoms of hypovolemic shock include tachycardia, narrow pulse pressure, and hypotension. In an effort to increase blood flow to vital organs, the body decreases blood to nonessential organs. If blood loss continues and hypovolemia is not corrected, then blood flow decreases to vital organs such as the brain and kidneys. Anxiety, restlessness, and lethargy are symptoms of decreased blood flow to the brain. Cessation of urine occurs as blood flow to the kidneys decreases and the kidneys attempt to conserve fluid. Medical management of hypovolemic shock includes stabilization to decrease harmful consequences. Blood loss must be controlled, so blood and intravenous fluids are issued to maintain circulating volume and replace fluids and erythrocytes. Oxygenation is monitored by the use of a pulse oximeter and supplemental oxygen is given. An indwelling Foley catheter is inserted for accurate measurement of urine output.

OBJECTIVES	CONTENT	TEACHING RESOURCES
Compare and contrast mood disorders in the postpartum period.	■ Mood disorders (p. 245) ☐ Postpartum depression (p. 245) ☐ Postpartum psychosis (p. 246) ■ The homeless mother and newborn (p. 246)	⊠ PPT slides 22-30 𝒆 EILR TB questions 12, 15-16 𝒆 ESLR IRQ question 5 SG Learning Activities, question 22 (p. 84) SG Review Questions, questions 19, 20 (p. 87) **BOOK RESOURCES** Review Questions for the NCLEX® Examination, question 5 (p. 247) ▸ Discuss the effects of postpartum mood disorders on the infant and other family members. What are the dangers of postpartum psychosis? ▸ Discuss signs and symptoms of postpartum depression and treatment options available within the community. *Class Activity Divide the class into three groups, and assign each group one of the following topics:* *– Postpartum depression* *– Postpartum psychosis* *– Community resources for homeless women* *Have each group identify the immediate problems that its complication presents. Then discuss additional problems that can result and identify ways to prevent those problems from developing. Have each group present its findings to the class for discussion.*
Describe the medical and nursing	■ Shock (p. 235) ■ Hemorrhage (p. 235)	⊠ PPT slides 4-30 𝒆 EILR IC images 1-3

OBJECTIVES	CONTENT	TEACHING RESOURCES
management of postpartum complications.	□ Hypovolemic shock (p. 236) □ Anemia (p. 236) □ Early postpartum hemorrhage (p. 236) – Uterine atony (p. 238) – Lacerations of the reproductive tract (p. 239) – Hematomas of the reproductive tract (p. 239) □ Late postpartum hemorrhage (p. 240) ■ Thromboembolic disorders (p. 240) ■ Infection (p. 241) □ Mastitis and breastfeeding (p. 243) ■ Subinvolution of the uterus (p. 244) ■ Mood disorders (p. 245) □ Postpartum depression (p. 245) □ Postpartum psychosis (p. 246) ■ The homeless mother and newborn (p. 246)	*e* EILR OBQ question 26 *e* EILR TB questions 5-6, 10 18-20, 23 *e* ESLR IRQ question 2 SG Review Questions, questions 6, 8, 13-14, 16 (pp. 85-87) **BOOK RESOURCES** Table 10-3, Postpartum Infections (p. 242) Review Questions for the NCLEX® Examination, question 1 (p. 247) ▶ Discuss the management of hematomas that occur in the reproductive tract, and compare how treatments differ for small and large hematomas. ▶ Discuss treatment modalities for superficial and deep vein thrombosis. What measures are usually employed for pulmonary embolism? *Class Activity Divide the class into groups, and assign each group two or three postpartum complications. Have each group discuss the signs and symptoms for its assigned complications and outline their treatments and management. Have each group present its findings to the class for discussion.* *Class Activity Present the following scenario to the class for discussion:* *A postpartum woman has developed mastitis. At a previous physician appointment, it was noted that she was experiencing postpartum blues, but she assured the nurse that she would "snap out of it." However, at the follow-up appointment, the nurse notices that her symptoms of depression have progressed.* *Have students identify how the nurse should proceed and discuss the medical management of this patient. What can be done if the woman refuses to seek treatment or help?*
Explain general and specific nursing care for each complication.	■ Shock (p. 235) ■ Hemorrhage (p. 235) □ Hypovolemic shock (p. 236) □ Anemia (p. 236) □ Early postpartum hemorrhage (p. 236)	PPT slides 4-30 *e* EILR IC images 1-3 *e* EILR TB questions 2-4, 11, 20, 22-23, 28 SG Learning Activities, question 18 (p. 84) SG Review Questions, questions 9-11, 15, 18 (p. 86) **BOOK RESOURCES**

OBJECTIVES	CONTENT	TEACHING RESOURCES
	– Uterine atony (p. 238) – Lacerations of the reproductive tract (p. 239) – Hematomas of the reproductive tract (p. 239) ☐ Late postpartum hemorrhage (p. 240) ■ Thromboembolic disorders (p. 240) ■ Infection (p. 241) ☐ Mastitis and breastfeeding (p. 243) ■ Subinvolution of the uterus (p. 244) ■ Mood disorders (p. 245) ☐ Postpartum depression (p. 245) ☐ Postpartum psychosis (p. 246) ■ The homeless mother and newborn (p. 246)	Nursing Care Plan 10-1, The Woman with Postpartum Hemorrhage (p. 237) Table 10-3, Postpartum Infections (p. 242) Nursing Care Plan 10-2, The Woman with Postpartum Infection (p. 243) ▸ Discuss the nursing care measures that are employed to monitor for hypovolemic shock and list the early signs of shock. ▸ Discuss general methods the nurse can use to promote adjustment during puerperium. ▸ Discuss the measures that the nurse can take to help the homeless mother find suitable resources for herself and her infant. *Class Activity **Divide the class into five groups, and assign each group one of the following complications:*** *– **Shock*** *– **Postpartum hemorrhage*** *– **Infection*** *– **Thrombosis*** *– **Subinvolution of the uterus*** ***Have each group discuss the management of its assigned complication, describe nursing interventions and care, and discuss patient teaching. Have each group present its findings to the class for discussion.*** *Class Activity **As a class, have students discuss the development of thromboembolic disorders in the pregnant and postpartum woman. Why are these women especially prone to thrombosis? How does it develop, and how is it treated? What are the different types of thrombosis, and what are the risks?***
Performance Evaluation		⊠■ PPT slides 1-32 𝒆 EILR IC images 1-3 𝒆 EILR OBQ questions 1-10 𝒆 EILR TB questions 1-29 𝒆 ESLR IRQ questions 1-5 SG Learning Activities, questions 1-22 (pp. 81-84) SG Review Questions, questions 1-20 (pp. 85-87) SG Case Study, question 1 (p. 87)

ELSEVIER

Introduction to Maternity & Pediatric Nursing, 6th ed.

Leifer

OBJECTIVES	CONTENT	TEACHING RESOURCES
		SG Thinking Critically, questions 1, 2 (p. 88)
		SG Applying Knowledge, questions 1-4 (p. 88)
		BOOK RESOURCES
		NCP CTQ 1 (p. 237)
		NCP CTQ 1 (p. 243)
		Review Questions for the NCLEX® Examination, questions 1-5 (p. 247)

10.2 Homework/Assignments:

10.2 Instructor's Notes/Student Feedback:

10 Lecture Outline
Nursing Care of Women with Complications After Birth

Slide 1

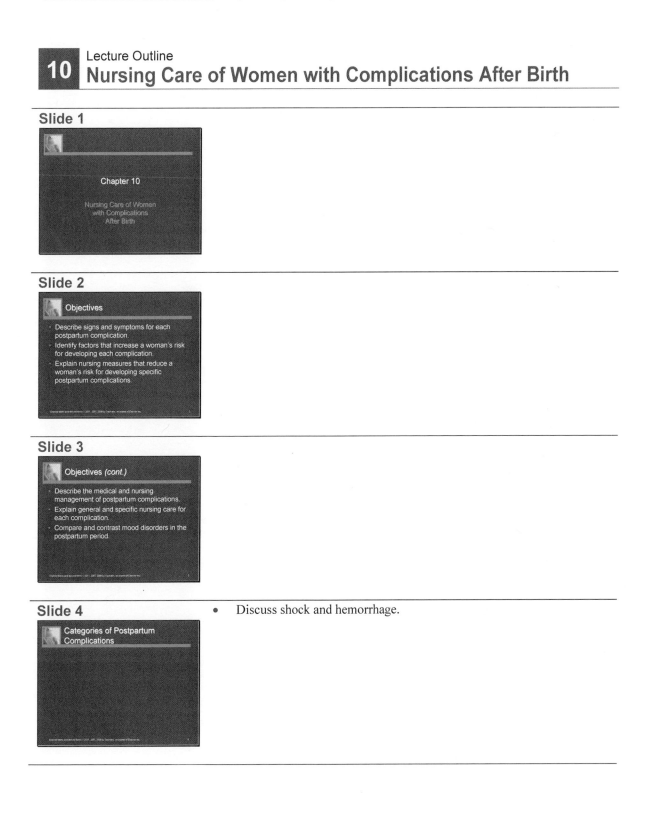

Chapter 10

Nursing Care of Women
with Complications
After Birth

Slide 2

Objectives

- Describe signs and symptoms for each postpartum complication.
- Identify factors that increase a woman's risk for developing each complication.
- Explain nursing measures that reduce a woman's risk for developing specific postpartum complications.

Slide 3

Objectives *(cont.)*

- Describe the medical and nursing management of postpartum complications.
- Explain general and specific nursing care for each complication.
- Compare and contrast mood disorders in the postpartum period.

Slide 4

Categories of Postpartum Complications

- Discuss shock and hemorrhage.

ELSEVIER

Introduction to Maternity & Pediatric Nursing, 6th ed.
Leifer

Slide 5

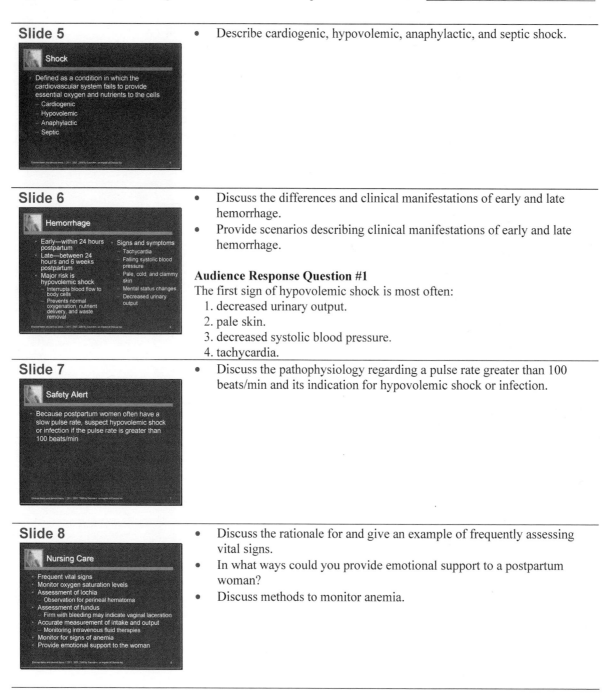

- Describe cardiogenic, hypovolemic, anaphylactic, and septic shock.

Slide 6

- Discuss the differences and clinical manifestations of early and late hemorrhage.
- Provide scenarios describing clinical manifestations of early and late hemorrhage.

Audience Response Question #1

The first sign of hypovolemic shock is most often:
1. decreased urinary output.
2. pale skin.
3. decreased systolic blood pressure.
4. tachycardia.

Slide 7

- Discuss the pathophysiology regarding a pulse rate greater than 100 beats/min and its indication for hypovolemic shock or infection.

Slide 8

- Discuss the rationale for and give an example of frequently assessing vital signs.
- In what ways could you provide emotional support to a postpartum woman?
- Discuss methods to monitor anemia.

Slide 9

Early Postpartum Hemorrhage

- Causes
  - Uterine atony
  - Lacerations or tears of the reproductive tract
  - Hematomas in the reproductive tract

- Describe the pathophysiology for each cause listed.

Slide 10

Late Postpartum Hemorrhage

- Causes
  - Retention of placental fragments
  - Subinvolution
- Nursing care
  - Teach the woman to report persistent bright red bleeding
  - Return of red bleeding after it has changed to pink or white
- Prepare for intravenous medication
- Prepare for possible surgical intervention

- What is the medical treatment for postpartum hemorrhage?

Slide 11

Thromboembolic Disorders

- A venous thrombosis is a blood clot within a vein
- Causes or risks
  - Venous stasis during pregnancy
  - Pressure behind knees if legs are in stirrups
  - Fibrinogen levels increase during pregnancy, whereas clot-dissolving factors in the blood are normally decreased during pregnancy
  - Varicose veins
- Types of thromboembolic disorders
  - Superficial vein thrombosis (SVT)
  - Deep vein thrombosis (DVT)
  - Pulmonary embolism (PE)

- Discuss the pathophysiology regarding the causes or risks of thromboembolic disorders.
- Describe each type of thromboembolic disorder.

Audience Response Question #2
Classic symptoms of DVT include muscle pain, positive Homans' sign, and swelling of the affected limb.
  1. True
  2. False

Slide 12

Nursing Care to Prevent a Thromboembolism

- Watch for signs or symptoms of PE
  - Dyspnea
  - Coughing
  - Chest pain
- Teach woman not to cross legs, as it impedes blood flow
- Avoid pressure in the popliteal space behind the knee
- Early ambulation and range of motion exercises
- If antiembolic stockings are prescribed, the nurse should teach the woman the correct method of putting on the stockings

- Describe the correct method to put on antiembolic stockings.

Slide 13

Anticoagulant Therapy

- Teach the woman taking this type of medication
  - Danger signs
    - Prolonged bleeding from minor injuries
    - Nosebleeds
    - Unexplained bruising
  - Use a soft-bristled toothbrush
- Stress the importance of completing follow-up blood tests
- Help the woman cope with this form of medical therapy

- What is the nurse's role regarding anticoagulant therapy and patient education?

Leifer

Slide 14

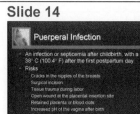

Puerperal Infection

- An infection or septicemia after childbirth, with a fever of 38° C (100.4° F) after the first postpartum day
- Risks
  - Cracks in the nipples of the breasts
  - Surgical incision
  - Tissue trauma during labor
  - Open wound at the placental insertion site
  - Retained placenta or blood clots
  - Increased pH of the vagina after birth
  - Endometritis (inflammation of the lining of the uterus)

Slide 15

The Dangers of Puerperal Infection

- A localized infection of the perineum, vagina, or cervix can ascend the reproductive tract and spread to the uterus, fallopian tubes, and peritoneum, causing peritonitis, a life-threatening condition

- Discuss the pathophysiology of peritonitis and the necessity for rapid assessment and treatment of the disorder.

Slide 16

Safety Alert

- Proper hand hygiene is the primary method to avoid the spread of infectious organisms
- Gloves should be worn when in contact with any blood, body fluids, or any other potentially infectious materials

Slide 17

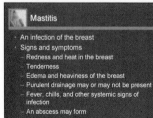

Nursing Care

- The objective is to prevent the infection from occurring
  - Use and teach hygienic measures
  - Promote adequate rest and nutrition for healing
  - Teach and observe for signs of infection
  - Teach the woman how to correctly apply perineal pads (front to back)
  - Teach the woman to take all antimicrobial medications as prescribed

- What hygienic measures would you teach the patient?
- What should the nurse teach the patient about signs and symptoms of infection?
- Discuss the rationale for correct application of perineal pads.

Slide 18

Mastitis

- An infection of the breast
- Signs and symptoms
  - Redness and heat in the breast
  - Tenderness
  - Edema and heaviness of the breast
  - Purulent drainage may or may not be present
  - Fever, chills, and other systemic signs of infection
  - An abscess may form

ELSEVIER

Slide 19

Treatment of Mastitis

- Prescribed antibiotics, mild analgesics
- Continue to breastfeed with unaffected breast
- Pump and discard the milk from affected breast (weaning can lead to engorgement and stasis of milk, which can worsen the infection)
- Heat promotes blood flow to the area
- Massage the area of inflammation to improve milk flow and reduce stasis
- Encourage fluid intake
- Wear a supportive bra
- Provide emotional support to the woman

- What is the nurse's role in providing emotional support to the patient with mastitis?

Audience Response Question #3

A woman develops mastitis in the postpartum period. She states "I am so sad I have to stop breastfeeding my baby." The nurse responds:
1. "I will provide with the information regarding formula feeding."
2. "You can always breastfeed if you have another child."
3. "I will inform your physician that you are feeling sad."
4. "It is not necessary that you discontinue breastfeeding."

Slide 20

Subinvolution of the Uterus

- The slower-than-expected or failure of the uterus to return to its normal prepregnant condition
- Normally the uterus descends at the rate of 1 cm per day

Signs and symptoms
- Fundal height greater than expected
- Persistence of lochia rubra
- Pelvic pain and heaviness
- Fatigue

- Discuss the location of a prepregnant uterus.
- How does the nurse assess the fundus?

Slide 21

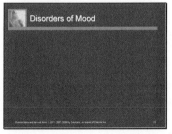

Nursing Care of the Woman with Subinvolution

- Teach the normal changes to expect
- Report abnormal pattern
  - Fever, pain, persistent red lochia
  - Foul-smelling vaginal discharge
- Comfort measures
- Prepare for possible surgical intervention
- Explain medications prescribed

- What are some comfort measures for subinvolution?
- Discuss nursing interventions to prepare the patient for surgery.
- Discuss typical medications ordered for a patient with subinvolution.

Slide 22

Disorders of Mood

Slide 23

What Is a Mood Disorder?

- Pervasive and sustained emotion that can color one's view of life

- Give examples of mood disorders.

Leifer

Slide 24

> **Postpartum Blues ("Baby Blues")**
> - Common after birth
> - Has periods where she feels let down
> - Finds pleasure in her new role
> - Usually self-limiting as woman adjusts to her new role

- In what ways would a new mother feel depressed?

Slide 25

> **Postpartum Depression or Psychosis**
> - Serious impairment of one's perception of reality
> - More serious than postpartum blues
> - Usually manifests within 4 weeks after delivery
> - May interfere with mother's ability to respond to her infant's cues
> - Maternal-infant bonding may also be affected

- Give an example of a patient's impaired sense of reality when severely depressed.
- How are postpartum blues different from postpartum depression?

Slide 26

> **Postpartum Depression**
> - Risk factors
>   - Inadequate social support
>   - Poor relationship with partner
>   - Life and childcare stress
>   - Low self-esteem
>   - Unplanned pregnancy

- How does inadequate social support affect the mother?
- Discuss how a poor relationship with a partner can contribute to postpartum depression.
- What other stressors can contribute to postpartum depression?

Audience Response Question #4
Postpartum depression is an expected reaction following childbirth.
  1. True
  2. False

Slide 27

> **Signs and Symptoms of Postpartum Depression**
> - Lack of enjoyment in life
> - Lack of interest in others
> - Intense feeling of inadequacy
> - Inability to cope
> - Loss of mental concentration
> - Disturbed sleep
> - Constant fatigue and feeling of ill health

- What are manifestations of a mother who lacks enjoyment in life?
- Describe situations in which a mother might lose mental concentration.

Slide 28

> **Nursing Care**
> - Refer to a multidisciplinary team
> - Be a sympathetic listener for the woman
> - Elicit feelings
> - Observe for complaints of sleeplessness or chronic fatigue
> - Provide support
> - Help woman identify her support system
> - Determine if the mother is getting enough exercise, sleep, and nutrition
> - Help the woman identify ways to meet her own needs
> - Refer to support groups

- Who would be appropriate on a multidisciplinary team?
- What methods are used to elicit feelings?
- Give examples of support systems for a postpartum patient.

Leifer

Slide 29

- What is the difference between postpartum depression and psychosis?
- Give an example of a possible fatal situation for a mother with postpartum psychosis.
- What medications treat postpartum psychosis?

Slide 30

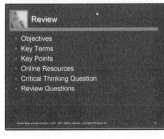

Slide 31

Slide 32

Leifer

Lesson Plan
11 The Nurse's Role in Women's Health Care

TEACHING FOCUS

Students will be introduced to women's preventive health care, particularly the care of menstrual disorders and gynecological infections. Students will have the opportunity to learn about the various methods of birth control and the use of natural family planning methods. Students will have the opportunity to examine the possible causes and treatment of infertility, the changes and care of women during menopause, and the care of women with pelvic floor dysfunction or benign growths in the reproductive tract.

MATERIALS AND RESOURCES

☐ Computer and PowerPoint projector (all lessons)

LESSON CHECKLIST

Preparations for this lesson include:

- Lecture
- Demonstration
- Evaluation of student knowledge and skills needed to perform all entry-level activities related to the nurse's role in women's health care, including:
  ○ Explaining preventive health care to women, such as monthly breast self-examination care, mammograms, and routine gynecological examinations
  ○ Explaining gynecological infections
  ○ Describing various birth control methods
  ○ Understanding the causes and treatment options for infertility
  ○ Explaining physical changes associated with perimenopause and menopause

KEY TERMS

amenorrhea (p. 251)
climacteric (p. 272)
coitus interruptus (p. 266)
dysmenorrhea (p. 251)
dyspareunia (p. 252)
endometriosis (p. 252)
leiomyoma (p. 276)

menopause (p. 272)
menorrhagia (p. 251)
metrorrhagia (p. 251)
mittelschmerz (p. 251)
myomas (p. 269)
osteoporosis (p. 272)

retrograde ejaculation (p. 268)
spermicide (p. 262)
spinnbarkeit (p. 259)
stress incontinence (p. 276)

ADDITIONAL RESOURCES

TEACH PPT slide(s) Chapter 11, 1-52
EILR IC image(s) Chapter 11, 1-5
EILR OBQ question(s) Chapter 11, 1-10
EILR TB question(s) Chapter 11, 1-30
ESLR IRQ question(s) Chapter 11, 1-5
SG Chapter 11, pp. 89-99

Legend

				!
PPT TEACH PowerPoint Slides	**EILR** EVOLVE Instructor Learning Resources: Image Collection (IC), Open-Book Quizzes (OBQ), Test Bank (TB)	**ESLR** EVOLVE Student Learning Resources: Interactive Review Questions (IRQ) for the NCLEX® Examination	**SG** Study Guide	**CTQ** Critical Thinking Question in Nursing Care Plan (NCP CTQ) or Get Ready for the NCLEX! (GRN CTQ)

Class Activities are indicated in **bold italic**.

LESSON 11.1

PRETEST

1. A mammogram is recommended by the American Cancer Society for women over the age of 40 every
   a. 1-2 years.
   b. 3 years.
   c. 5 years.
   d. 10 years.

2. The pain experienced by women around ovulation is
   a. dysmenorrhea.
   b. amenorrhea.
   c. mittelschmerz.
   d. endometriosis.

3. *Staphylococcus aureus* produces toxins that cause
   a. hypertension.
   b. yeast infections.
   c. endometriosis.
   d. toxic shock syndrome.

4. One of the goals for family planning as outlined by *Healthy People 2020* is to reduce the number of unintended pregnancies by
   a. 18%.
   b. 25%.
   c. 30%.
   d. 50%.

5. A 40-year-old patient inquires about birth control pills. She reports that last year she was in the hospital because of a clot in her right leg. Which of the following statements would be an appropriate response for the nurse to provide?
   a. "It does not matter that you had a blood clot."
   b. "Women who have a history of blood clots should not take oral contraceptives."
   c. "Because it has been over a year since the hospitalization, you can take the pill."
   d. "You can take the pill, but only for 21 days, not 28 days."

6. When is the best time for a woman to measure her basal body temperature?
   a. any time
   b. right before bed
   c. midday
   d. first thing in the morning

7. Risks associated with surgical sterilization, such as infection and injury, are
   a. the same as for any surgical procedure.
   b. less than the risks for other surgical procedures.
   c. greater than the risks for other surgical procedures.
   d. only increased for male sterilization.

8. The process of strengthening the pubococcygeal muscle can be achieved by
   a. performing Kegel exercises.
   b. toning the abdomen.
   c. deep-breathing exercises.
   d. avoiding exercise.

9. Elevated scrotal temperature
   a. improves sperm production.
   b. has no effect on sperm.
   c. increases sperm motility.
   d. impairs sperm production.

10. Women treated for osteoporosis with alendronate (Fosamax) should
    a. also take part in high-impact exercises.
    b. take the drug with 8 oz of plain water.
    c. avoid dark green, leafy vegetables.
    d. remain supine for 30 minutes following drug administration.

Answers

1. a	3. d	5. b	7. a	9. d
2. c	4. c	6. d	8. a	10. b

ELSEVIER

BACKGROUND ASSESSMENT

Question: What is the role of the nurse in family planning?

Answer: The role of the nurse in family planning is to discuss with the patient the options that are available for contraception. This discussion should include both temporary and permanent methods. The advantages and disadvantages of each option should be discussed so that the patient can make an informed decision. Patient education regarding proper usage of temporary measures must be discussed to improve the effectiveness of the selected method, thereby decreasing the incidence of unwanted pregnancies. Success or failure of temporary contraception to prevent pregnancy depends in part on patient compliance.

Question: A 28-year-old woman has a transvaginal ultrasound, and is diagnosed with uterine fibroids (leiomyomas). What information about uterine fibroids should the nurse provide the patient?

Answer: The nurse should provide the patient with information regarding uterine fibroids—the signs and symptoms and treatment options. Uterine fibroids are benign tumors dependent on estrogen for growth. Fibroids are more common during childbearing years and reduce in size as estrogen levels decrease due to the onset of menopause. Fibroids may develop within the uterine muscle, inside or outside the uterine surface, or on a pedicle. Fibroids may be either asymptomatic or cause problems such as irregular bleeding, pelvic pressure, pressure on the bladder, or dysmenorrhea. Surgical treatments include hysterectomy (if past childbearing age) or laparoscopic myomectomy, myolysis, or electrosurgical destruction of the fibroids. Nonsurgical treatments include medication therapy and uterine fibroid embolization.

CRITICAL THINKING QUESTION

A 22-year-old woman arrives at the clinic complaining of a 2-day history of worsening abdominal pain, fever, nausea, and vaginal discharge. The health care provider determines that she has pelvic inflammatory disease (PID). What other findings might accompany PID? What treatment is available for PID? What information should the nurse give to the patient regarding PID prevention?

Guidelines: Laboratory findings indicative of PID include an elevation in white blood cell count or an elevated sedimentation rate. These findings indicate an inflammatory process. Vaginal cultures will be obtained to determine the causative agent of PID, although treatment with antimicrobials is usually started before the results of the vaginal cultures are known. If needed, the antimicrobial may be changed if the organism is resistant to the current antimicrobials. Treatment of PID can be done on an inpatient or outpatient basis, depending on the severity of the symptoms. Because multiple cases of PID can cause infertility, the patient should be instructed on safe-sex practices such as avoiding multiple sexual partners, using protection during intercourse (latex condoms), avoiding douching (this may destroy vaginal flora), and seeking early treatment for any abnormal vaginal discharge.

OBJECTIVES	CONTENT	TEACHING RESOURCES
Explain aspects of preventive health care for women.	■ Goals of *Healthy People 2020* (p. 248) ■ Preventive health care for women (p. 248) □ Breast care (p. 249) – Breast self-examination (p. 249) – Professional breast examination (p. 249) – Mammography (p. 249) □ Vulvar self-	PPT slides 5, 6 EILR OBQ questions 1, 2 EILR TB questions 1, 2 SG Learning Activities, questions 2-4 (p. 89) SG Review Questions, questions 1-2 (p. 97) SG Applying Knowledge, questions 2, 3 (p. 99) **BOOK RESOURCES** Nursing Tips (p. 249) Skill 11-1, How to Perform Breast Self-Examination (p. 250)

Introduction to Maternity & Pediatric Nursing, 6th ed.
Leifer

OBJECTIVES	CONTENT	TEACHING RESOURCES
	examination (p. 249) ☐ Pelvic examination (p. 249)	Review Questions for the NCLEX® Examination, question 1 (p. 278) ▸ Discuss the kinds of teaching methods nurses can use to teach women how to perform BSE while demonstrating cultural competence. *Class Activity* **Divide the class into pairs and assign each pair two of the components of Healthy People 2020 (e.g., breast and cervical cancer; osteoporosis and STIs, etc.) to discuss and present to the class. Students must include in their presentation a description of what must be done to achieve the goals set forth by this initiative.**
Describe each menstrual disorder and its care.	■ Menstrual disorders (p. 251) ☐ Amenorrhea (p. 251) ☐ Abnormal uterine bleeding (p. 251) ☐ Menstrual cycle pain (p. 251) – Mittelschmerz (p. 251) – Dysmenorrhea (p. 251) ☐ Endometriosis (p. 252) ☐ Premenstrual dysphoric disorder (p. 252)	☒▪ PPT slides 7-13 𝒆 EILR OBQ question 3 𝒆 EILR TB question 10 SG Learning Activities, questions 1, 5-8 (p. 89) SG Review Questions, question 3 (p. 97) **BOOK RESOURCES** Review Questions for the NCLEX® Examination, questions 2, 4 (p. 278) ▸ Discuss how nurses can provide emotional support to patients who are experiencing menstrual disorders. *Class Activity* **Divide the class into small groups. Assign each group a menstrual disorder topic to research and present in class. Students must include causes and treatment options for each. Alternative therapies should also be included.** *(For students to prepare for this activity, see Homework/Assignments #1.)*
Explain each gynecological infection in terms of cause, transmission, treatment, and care.	■ The normal vagina (p. 252) ☐ Gynecological infections (p. 253) ☐ Toxic shock syndrome (p. 253) ☐ Sexually transmitted infections (p. 253) ☐ Pelvic inflammatory disease (p. 254)	☒▪ PPT slides 14-20 𝒆 EILR OBQ questions 4, 5, 21 𝒆 EILR TB question 17 𝒆 ESLR IRQ question 2 SG Learning Activities, questions 9-15 (pp. 91-93) SG Review Questions, questions 4-7 (p. 97) SG Case Study, question 1 (p. 99) SG Applying Knowledge, questions 1, 4 (p. 99)

OBJECTIVES	CONTENT	TEACHING RESOURCES

		BOOK RESOURCES
		
		Health Promotion, Preventing Vaginal Infections (p. 253)
		
		Safety Alert (p. 253)
		
		Table 11-1, Sexually Transmitted Infections (pp. 255-257)
		
		▸ Discuss how nurses can identify high-risk behavior and provide nonjudgmental counseling to patients.
		
		▸ Discuss signs and symptoms of toxic shock syndrome and nursing interventions or teaching the nurse can provide to prevent this complication from recurring.
		
		*Class Activity **Divide the class into four groups. Assign each group one of the following case studies. Ask the student to identify probable causes, modes of transmission, treatment, and nursing interventions for each.***
		
		    – *A 17-year-old woman presenting with symptoms of gonorrhea*
		
		    – *A 53-year-old woman with a confirmed diagnosis of HIV*
		
		    – *A 23-year-old woman with symptoms of herpes simplex virus II*
		
		    – *A 33-year-old woman with human papillomavirus*

11.1 Homework/Assignments:

1. Divide the class into small groups. Assign each group a menstrual disorder topic to research and present in class. Students must include causes and treatment options for each topic. Alternative therapies should also be included.

11.1 Instructor's Notes/Student Feedback:

LESSON 11.2

CRITICAL THINKING QUESTION

What are the social and psychological implications of infertility for a couple? How can the nurse assist a couple with infertility problems?

Guidelines: Infertility can be devastating to a couple. Cultural influences and expectations have an impact on how a couple deals with infertility issues. Infertility may result in rejection of the spouse or divorce. The psychological effects of infertility include feelings of guilt. The individual who has the problem may feel that he or she is depriving the other person of the opportunity to have children. He or she may also feel guilty because of past sexual practices that have affected the reproductive system, such as contracting sexually transmitted infections that cause fallopian tube scarring. Isolation is common, as infertile couples may avoid communication with each other. Depression may also develop as the couple tries to cope with infertility. The relationship may become strained as sexual intimacy becomes a task and loses its spontaneity and pleasure. The role of the nurse is to be supportive to the couple as decisions are made regarding infertility treatments. The nurse should use therapeutic communication with the couple to facilitate open discussion about feelings. The couple should be referred to a support group to help them during this difficult time.

OBJECTIVES	CONTENT	TEACHING RESOURCES

Describe the various methods of birth control, including side effects and contraindications of each method.	■ Family planning (p. 258)
	
	  – Contraception (p. 258)
	
	  – Natural family planning (p. 258)
	
	  – Basal body temperature (p. 258)
	
	  – Cervical mucus (p. 259)
	
	  – Calendar, or rhythm, method (p. 259)
	
	  – Marquette method (p. 259)
	
	☐ Temporary contraception (p. 259)
	
	  – Abstinence (p. 259)
	
	  – Hormonal contraceptives (p. 259)
	
	  – Oral contraceptives ("the pill") (p. 260)
	
	  – Hormone implants (p. 261)
	
	  – Medroxyprogesterone acetate (Depo-
		🖥 PPT slides 21-32
		
		𝒆 EILR IC images 1-5
		
		𝒆 EILR OBQ questions 6-8, 22
		
		𝒆 EILR TB questions 3-9, 18, 19, 23-24
		
		𝒆 ESLR IRQ questions 1, 3
		
		📓 SG Learning Activities, questions, 16-22 (pp. 89-93)
		
		📓 SG Review Questions, questions 8-14 (pp. 97-98)
		
		BOOK RESOURCES
		
		Figure 11-1, Basal Body Temperature Chart (p. 259)
		
		Figure 11-2, Spinnbarkeit (p. 259)
		
		Figure 11-3, Contraceptives (p. 260)
		
		Safety Alert (p. 260)
		
		Memory Jogger (p. 261)
		
		Nursing Tip (p. 261)
		
		Safety Alert (p. 262)
		
		Skill 11-2, How to Use a Diaphragm (p. 263)
		
		Figure 11-4, Female Condom (p. 264)
		
		Skill 11-3, How to Use the Male Condom (p. 265)
		
		Figure 11-5, Surgical Methods of Birth Control (p. 266)
		
		Nursing Tip (p. 267)
		
		Review Questions for the NCLEX® Examination, question 3 (p. 278)

Introduction to Maternity & Pediatric Nursing, 6th ed.

OBJECTIVES	CONTENT	TEACHING RESOURCES
	SubQProvera-104) (p. 261)	▸ Discuss the important factors that patients should consider when choosing contraception.
	– Intrauterine devices (p. 262)	*Class Activity* **Divide students into two groups. Assign one group permanent methods of birth control, and the other group temporary methods of birth control. Have students identify the least effective methods and the most effective methods within each category. Students should discuss advantages and disadvantages of each method, including side effects and contraindications. Have students also identify patient education information for each. Have each group present its findings to the class.**
	– Transdermal patch (p. 262)	
	– Vaginal ring (p. 262)	
	– Barrier methods (p. 262)	
	– Sponge (p. 262)	
	– Diaphragm and cervical cap (p. 262)	
	– Male condom (p. 264)	
	– Female condom (p. 264)	
	– Spermicides (p. 265)	
	☐ Emergency contraception (p. 266)	
	☐ Unreliable contraceptive methods (p. 266)	
	– Withdrawal (p. 266)	
	– Douching (p. 266)	
	– Breastfeeding (p. 266)	
	☐ Permanent contraception (p. 266)	
	– Sterilization (p. 266)	
	– Male sterilization (p. 266)	
	– Female sterilization (p. 267)	

Leifer

OBJECTIVES	CONTENT	TEACHING RESOURCES
Describe how to use natural family planning methods for contraception or infertility management.	– Natural family planning (p. 258) – Basal body temperature (p. 258) – Cervical mucus (p. 259) – Calendar, or rhythm, method (p. 259) – Marquette method (p. 259) □ Emergency contraception (p. 266) □ Unreliable contraceptive methods (p. 266) – Withdrawal (p. 266) – Douching (p. 266) – Breastfeeding (p. 266) □ Permanent contraception (p. 266) – Sterilization (p. 266) – Male sterilization (p. 266) – Female sterilization (p. 267)	PPT slides 24, 25, 30-32 *e* EILR IC images 1, 2, 5 *e* EILR TB questions 7-9, 18, 23 *e* ESLR IRQ question 4 SG Learning Activities, questions 1, 23-25 (pp. 89, 94) SG Review Questions, question 14 (p. 98) **BOOK RESOURCES** Figure 11-1, Basal Body Temperature Chart (p. 259) Figure 11-2, Spinnbarkeit (p. 259) Figure 11-5, Surgical methods of birth control (p. 266) ▸ Discuss religious and cultural considerations in family planning. *Class Activity Lead a class discussion in which students discuss natural family planning techniques and the advantages and disadvantages of each. Have students discuss cultural aspects of infertility and how to support a family with infertility issues. Finally, have students identify relevant patient education information.*
Describe possible causes and treatment of infertility.	■ Infertility (p. 267) □ Social and psychological implications (p. 267) – Assumption of fertility (p. 267) – Psychological reactions (p. 267) – Cultural and religious considerations (p. 268) □ Factors affecting infertility (p. 268)	PPT slides 33-39 *e* EILR OBQ questions 9, 25 *e* EILR TB questions 11, 29 *e* ESLR IRQ question 5 SG Learning Activities, questions 1, 26-29 (pp. 89, 94-95) **BOOK RESOURCES** Nursing Tip (p. 268) Table 11-2, Summary of Assisted Reproductive Therapies (ARTs) (p. 271) ▸ Discuss how nurses can provide support to infertile

Leifer

OBJECTIVES	CONTENT	TEACHING RESOURCES
	– Male factors (p. 268)	couples who are struggling with stress and blame.
	– Female factors (p. 268)	*Class Activity* **Divide the class into two groups and assign one group female causes of infertility and the other group male causes of infertility. Discuss the evaluation and treatment options for each.**
	☐ Other factors that may influence fertility (p. 269)	
	☐ Evaluation of infertility (p. 269)	
	– Male testing (p. 269)	
	– Female testing (p. 269)	
	☐ Therapy for infertility (p. 270)	
	– Medications (p. 270)	
	– Surgical procedures (p. 270)	
	– Therapeutic insemination (p. 270)	
	– Surrogate parenting (p. 270)	
	– Advanced reproductive techniques (p. 270)	
	– Bypassing obstacles to contraception (p. 270)	
	– Microsurgical techniques (p. 271)	
	☐ Outcomes of infertility therapy (p. 271)	
	☐ Legal and ethical factors in assisted reproduction (p. 271)	
	☐ Nursing care related to infertility treatment (p. 272)	

11.2 Homework/Assignments:

11.2 Instructor's Notes/Student Feedback:

LESSON 11.3

CRITICAL THINKING QUESTION

A 49-year-old woman complains of decreased interest in sexual activity due to pain and vaginal dryness. She also reports a new onset of hot flashes and intermittent menstruation. Based on the above symptoms, the nurse suspects that the woman is perimenopausal. What information should the nurse provide regarding menopause? What medical and alternative treatments are available for menopause?

Guidelines: The nurse should inform the woman about the signs, symptoms, and treatments for menopause. Menopause is the cessation of menstruation for a period of 12 months. During the perimenopausal phase, the menstrual cycles are anovulatory and irregular. The production of estrogen decreases during perimenopause; however, a woman can still become pregnant during this time, so birth control methods should be continued. Once menopause ensues, women are at increased risk for developing osteoporosis, elevated cholesterol, and arteriosclerosis due to the decrease in estrogen. Symptoms of menopause may include dyspareunia, irritability, mood swings, and a hot or burning sensation of the skin followed by perspiration. Some women may experience chills, palpitations, and dizziness. The woman should be instructed about health maintenance such as regular exercise, increasing dietary calcium and magnesium, and following a low-fat and high-fiber diet. Hormonal replacement therapy (HRT) may be considered to counteract the effects of decreased estrogen. HRT is beneficial for preventing osteoporosis, but recent studies have suggested that other significant health risks may be associated with HRT. Some alternative over-the-counter therapies include yam root, which contains progesterone; soy products, which reduce hot flashes; and vitamin E, which helps to stabilize estrogen levels.

OBJECTIVES	CONTENT	TEACHING RESOURCES
Explain the changes that occur during the perimenopausal period and after menopause.	■ Menopause (p. 272) ☐ Physical changes (p. 272) ☐ Psychological and cultural variations (p. 272) ☐ Treatment options (p. 273) ☐ Complementary and alternative therapies (p. 273) ☐ Therapy for osteoporosis (p. 273)	⊠ PPT slides 40-44 𝓮 EILR TB questions 12-16, 26 SG Learning Activities, questions 1, 30-33 (pp. 89, 95) SG Review Questions, questions 15-18 (pp. 98-99) SG Thinking Critically, question 1 (p. 99) **BOOK RESOURCES** Review Questions for the NCLEX® Examination, question 5 (p. 278) ▸ Discuss the ways nurses can facilitate "partnership-building communication" with the health care team to help a woman cope with these lifestyle changes. *Class Activity **Have students discuss the differences and similarities between perimenopause and postmenopause. Have students discuss the advantages and disadvantages of traditional medication therapy versus alternative treatment for menopause.***
Explain the medical and nursing care of women who are nearing or have completed menopause.	☐ Nursing care of the menopausal woman (p. 273)	⊠ PPT slide 44 SG Learning Activities, question 1 (p. 89) **BOOK RESOURCES** Nursing Care Plan 11-1, The Woman Experiencing

OBJECTIVES	CONTENT	TEACHING RESOURCES
		Perimenopausal Symptoms (p. 274) ▶ Discuss ways to assess a patient's understanding of verbal teaching and follow-up strategies to ensure compliance. *Class Activity **Have students identify patient education information for women that a nurse should provide to women experiencing the phases of perimenopause and postmenopause. This should include the risks and benefits associated with vitamins and hormone replacement therapy. Social and psychological influences should also be addressed.***
Discuss the medical and nursing care of women with pelvic floor dysfunction or problems related to benign growths in the reproductive tract.	■ Pelvic floor dysfunction (p. 275) ☐ Vaginal wall prolapse (p. 275) – Cystocele (p. 275) – Rectocele (p. 275) ☐ Uterine prolapse (p. 275) ☐ Management of pelvic floor dysfunction (p. 275) ☐ Nursing care of the woman with pelvic floor dysfunction (p. 275) ☐ Urinary incontinence (p. 276) – Treatment and nursing care (p. 276) ■ Other female reproductive tract disorders (p. 276) ☐ Uterine fibroids (p. 276) – Treatment (p. 276) ☐ Ovarian cysts (p. 276) ■ Cultural aspects of pain control (p. 277)	PPT slides 45-50 EILR OBQ question 10 EILR TB questions 20, 27-28, 30 SG Learning Activities, questions 1, 34, 35 (pp. 89, 96) SG Review Questions, questions 19, 20 (p. 99) ▶ Discuss the psychological implications of pelvic floor dysfunction and the nurse's role in addressing them. *Class Activity **Divide the class into small groups. Assign each group one of the disorders related to pelvic floor dysfunction or benign reproductive tract growths. Ask students to identify causes, treatment options, and nursing interventions. Have each group present its information to the class.***
Describe the nursing care and treatment	■ Other female reproductive tract disorders (p. 276)	PPT slides 47-50 EILR TB question 20

OBJECTIVES	CONTENT	TEACHING RESOURCES
of a woman with leiomyomas.	☐ Uterine fibroids (p. 276) – Treatment (p. 276) ☐ Ovarian cysts (p. 276) ■ Cultural aspects of pain control (p. 277)	🔖 SG Learning Activities, question 1 (p. 89) 🔖 SG Review Questions, questions 19, 20 (p. 99) **BOOK RESOURCES** Review Questions for the NCLEX® Examination, questions 1-5 (p. 278) ▸ Discuss how leiomyomas can grow and symptoms and treatment options. *Class Activity **Divide the class into small groups. Assign each group one of the disorders related to pelvic floor dysfunction or benign reproductive tract growths. Ask students to identify causes, treatment options, and nursing interventions. Have each group present its information to the class.***
Performance Evaluation		🖾 PPT slides 1-52 𝒆 EILR IC images 1-5 𝒆 EILR OBQ questions 1-10 𝒆 EILR TB questions 1-30 𝒆 ESLR IRQ questions 1-5 🔖 SG Learning Activities, questions 1-35 (pp. 89-96) 🔖 SG Review Questions, questions 1-20 (pp. 97-99) 🔖 SG Case Study, question 1 (p. 99) 🔖 SG Thinking Critically, question 1 (p. 99) 🔖 SG Applying Knowledge, questions 1-4 (p. 99) **BOOK RESOURCES** 💡 NCP CTQ 1 (p. 274) Review Questions for the NCLEX® Examination, questions 1-5 (p. 278)

Elsevier items and derived items © 2011, 2007, 2006 by Saunders, an imprint of Elsevier Inc.
Leifer

11.3 Homework/Assignments:

11.3 Instructor's Notes/Student Feedback:

11 Lecture Outline
The Nurse's Role in Women's Health Care

Slide 1

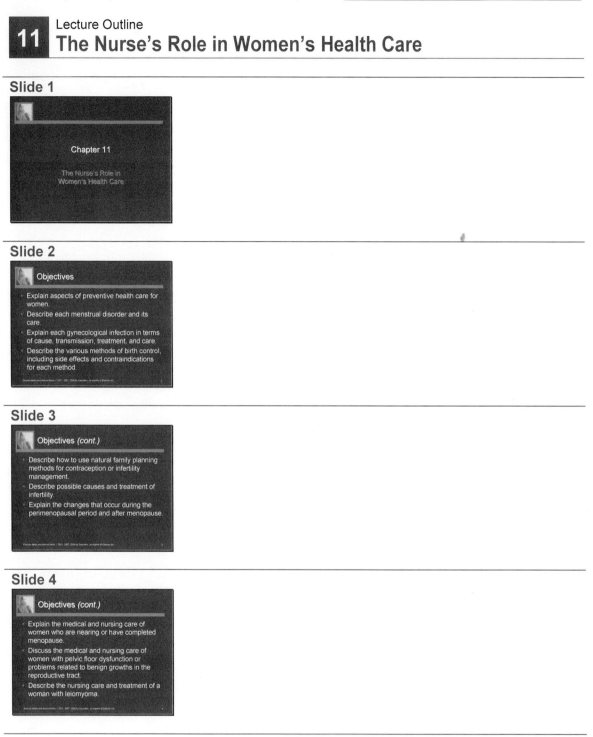

Chapter 11

The Nurse's Role in
Women's Health Care

Slide 2

Objectives

- Explain aspects of preventive health care for women.
- Describe each menstrual disorder and its care.
- Explain each gynecological infection in terms of cause, transmission, treatment, and care.
- Describe the various methods of birth control, including side effects and contraindications for each method.

Slide 3

Objectives *(cont.)*

- Describe how to use natural family planning methods for contraception or infertility management.
- Describe possible causes and treatment of infertility.
- Explain the changes that occur during the perimenopausal period and after menopause.

Slide 4

Objectives *(cont.)*

- Explain the medical and nursing care of women who are nearing or have completed menopause.
- Discuss the medical and nursing care of women with pelvic floor dysfunction or problems related to benign growths in the reproductive tract.
- Describe the nursing care and treatment of a woman with leiomyoma.

Slide 5	• How can the health care system assist patients in meeting these goals?
Goals of *Healthy People 2020* · Culturally competent communication key to empowering women to feel confident abut her ability to care for herself and her family · Increasing the number of women who engage in preventive health care, thereby reducing breast and cervical cancer, vertebral fractures, sexually transmitted infections · Achieving these goals requires preventive care, screening, and increased accessibility to health care	

Slide 6	• Discuss the nurse's role in teaching breast self-examination and vulvar self-examination. • What is the importance of Pap tests? NOTE: Toward the end of 2009, National Health Recommendations came out stating a woman does not need to start having Pap tests until age 21 and may not need to have them yearly. This is highly controversial and remains an unresolved issue at the time of publication.
Preventive Health Care for Women · Teaching how to perform breast self-examination (BSE) · Mammography · Vulvar self-examination (VSE) · Pap test for all women 18 years or older (or whenever they become sexually active [whichever comes first]) – Includes pelvic examination	

Slide 7	
Menstrual Disorders · Common nursing roles include – Explaining any recommended treatments – Caring for the woman before and after procedures – Provide emotional support	

Slide 8	• What are the differences between primary and secondary amenorrhea?
Amenorrhea · The absence of menstruation · Normal before menarche, during pregnancy, and after menopause – Primary – Secondary · Treatment depends on cause identified	

Slide 9	• Describe the three types of uterine bleeding. • What are typical endocrine disorders that could cause abnormal uterine bleeding?
Abnormal Uterine Bleeding · Three types – Too frequent – Too long in duration – Excessive in amount · Common causes – Pregnancy complications – Lesions of the vagina, cervix, or uterus – Breakthrough bleeding when on contraceptives – Endocrine disorders – Failure to ovulate	

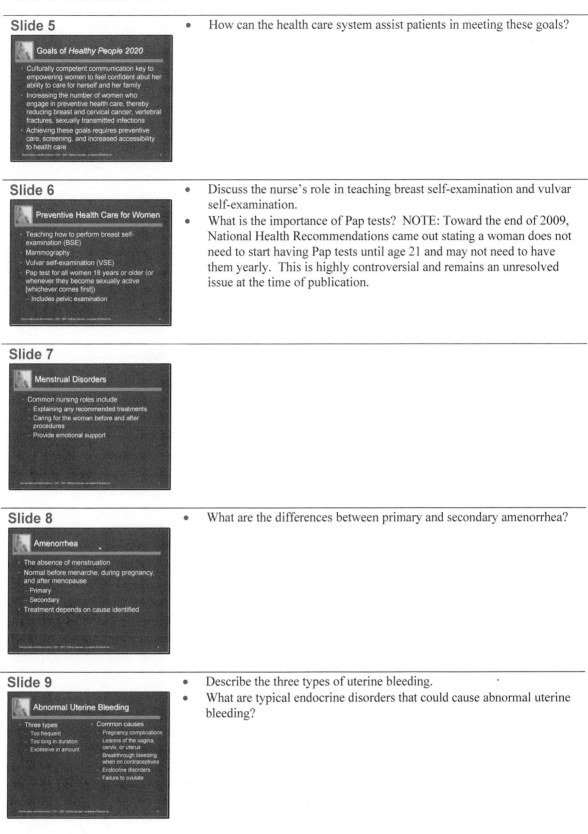

Slide 10

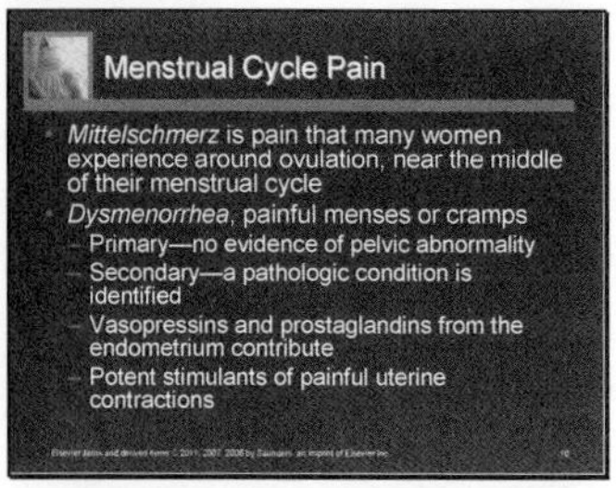

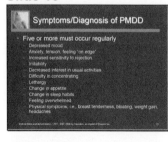

- What are some methods to ease these menstrual cycle pains?

Slide 11

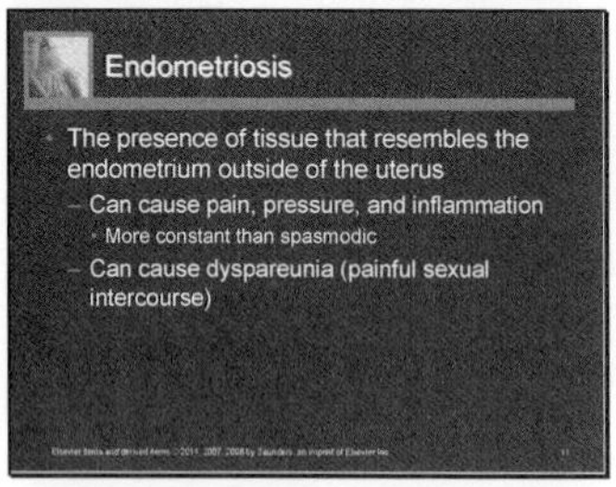

Endometriosis

- Discuss treatment for endometriosis.

Slide 12

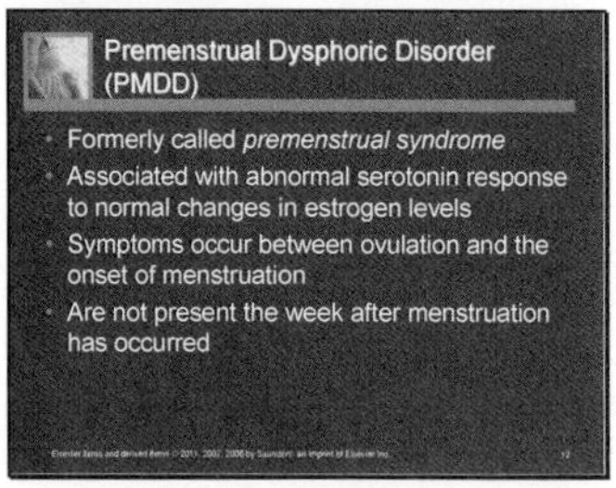

Premenstrual Dysphoric Disorder (PMDD)

- What are typical signs and symptoms of PMDD?
- Discuss patient education to minimize the effects of PMDD.

Slide 13

Symptoms/Diagnosis of PMDD

Slide 14

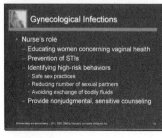

Gynecological Infections

Leifer

Slide 15

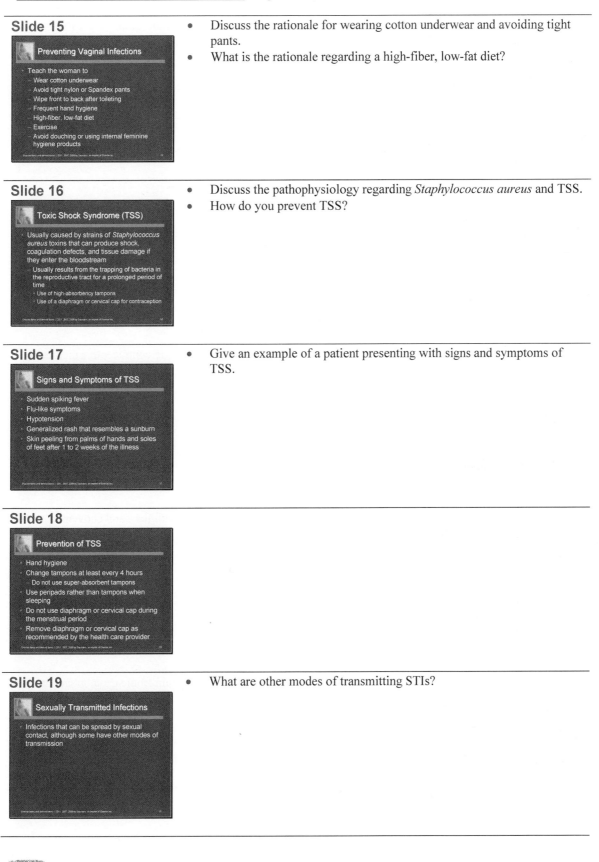

Preventing Vaginal Infections
· Teach the woman to
– Wear cotton underwear
– Avoid tight nylon or Spandex pants
– Wipe front to back after toileting
– Frequent hand hygiene
– High-fiber, low-fat diet
– Exercise
– Avoid douching or using internal feminine hygiene products

- Discuss the rationale for wearing cotton underwear and avoiding tight pants.
- What is the rationale regarding a high-fiber, low-fat diet?

Slide 16

Toxic Shock Syndrome (TSS)
· Usually caused by strains of *Staphylococcus aureus* toxins that can produce shock, coagulation defects, and tissue damage if they enter the bloodstream
– Usually results from the trapping of bacteria in the reproductive tract for a prolonged period of time
· Use of high-absorbency tampons
· Use of a diaphragm or cervical cap for contraception

- Discuss the pathophysiology regarding *Staphylococcus aureus* and TSS.
- How do you prevent TSS?

Slide 17

Signs and Symptoms of TSS
· Sudden spiking fever
· Flu-like symptoms
· Hypotension
· Generalized rash that resembles a sunburn
· Skin peeling from palms of hands and soles of feet after 1 to 2 weeks of the illness

- Give an example of a patient presenting with signs and symptoms of TSS.

Slide 18

Prevention of TSS
· Hand hygiene
· Change tampons at least every 4 hours
– Do not use super-absorbent tampons
· Use peripads rather than tampons when sleeping
· Do not use diaphragm or cervical cap during the menstrual period
· Remove diaphragm or cervical cap as recommended by the health care provider

Slide 19

Sexually Transmitted Infections
· Infections that can be spread by sexual contact, although some have other modes of transmission

- What are other modes of transmitting STIs?

ELSEVIER

Introduction to Maternity & Pediatric Nursing, 6th ed.

Leifer

Slide 20

- Discuss each STI listed and its mode of transmission.
- How can the transmission of STIs be avoided?
-

Audience Response Question #1
What puts the patient at greatest risk for developing cervical cancer?
  1. History of fibroid tumors
  2. Repeated gonorrheal infections
  3. History of endometriosis
  4. History of human papillomavirus

Slide 21

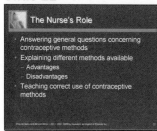

Slide 22

- What questions might a woman ask regarding contraceptive methods?
- Give examples of proper and improper education regarding contraceptive methods.

Slide 23

- Give examples of situations in which age, religion, and convenience affect a woman's contraceptive choices.

Slide 24

- How can a woman determine when to abstain from sexual intercourse to prevent pregnancy?

Leifer

Slide 25

Types of Natural Family Planning
Basal body temperature
Cervical mucus
Calendar or rhythm method
Marquette method

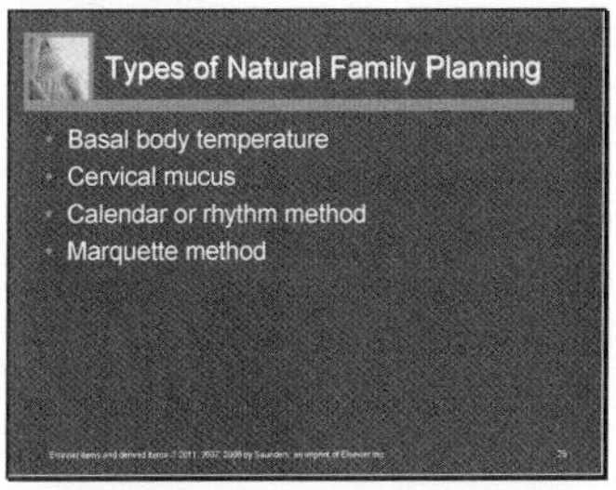

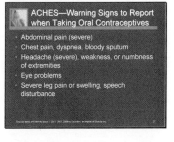

- Discuss each method and how it is utilized.

Slide 26

Hormonal Contraception
Is another form of *temporary* birth control
Types
Monthly
Extended
Delayed menstruation
Implants
Injections
Transdermal patch
Vaginal ring
IUD
Prevents ovulation
Makes cervical mucus thick and resistant to sperm penetration
Makes uterine endometrium less hospitable if fertilized ovum arrives
Does not protect either partner from STIs, including HIV

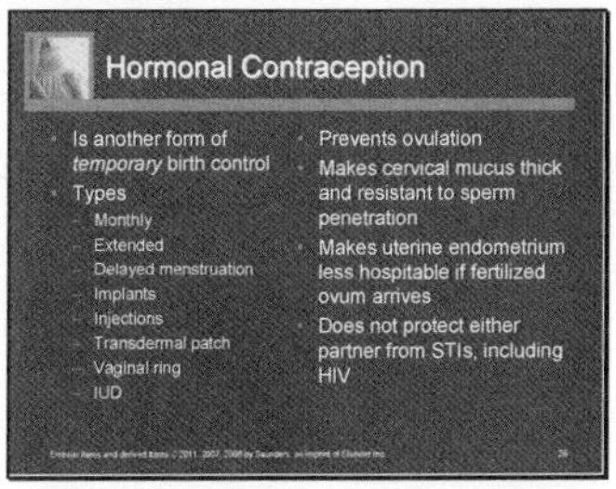

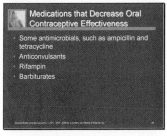

- Describe each type of temporary birth control method.
- What safety measures need to be taken (e.g., blood tests)?

Slide 27

ACHES—Warning Signs to Report when Taking Oral Contraceptives
Abdominal pain (severe)
Chest pain, dyspnea, bloody sputum
Headache (severe), weakness, or numbness of extremities
Eye problems
Severe leg pain or swelling, speech disturbance

Slide 28

Medications that Decrease Oral Contraceptive Effectiveness
Some antimicrobials, such as ampicillin and tetracycline
Anticonvulsants
Rifampin
Barbiturates

Slide 29

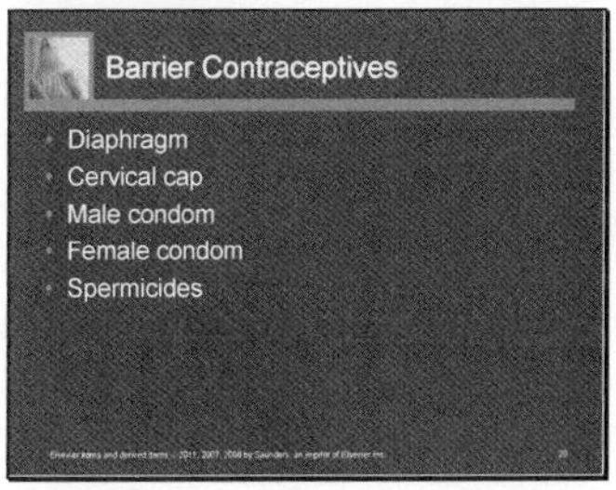

Barrier Contraceptives
Diaphragm
Cervical cap
Male condom
Female condom
Spermicides

- Discuss and describe each barrier device.
- What are the two types of female condoms?

Audience Response Question #2

A 16-year-old female comes to the family planning clinic for contraceptive advice. She says she wants to take "the pill." Her vital signs are within normal limits. What assessment information is priority?

1. Exercise history
2. Nutritional information
3. Smoking history
4. Stress assessment

Slide 30 Emergency Contraception · The "morning after pill" is a method of preventing pregnancy · Must be taken no later than 72 hours after unprotected sexual intercourse and may need to be repeated 12 hours after the first pill – Depends on the type of pill purchased	• In what situations would this type of contraception be used? • Discuss potential complications with this method.
Slide 31 Unreliable Contraceptive Methods · Withdrawal · Douching · Breastfeeding – Providing 10 breast feedings in a 24-hour period can inhibit ovulation due to increased prolactin secretion	• Why are these methods unreliable?

Slide 32
 	
Permanent Contraception
 	
· Male sterilization
  – Vasectomy
· Female sterilization
  – Tubal ligation
  – Hysteroscopic sterilization
	• Discuss Figure 11-5 on page 266.

Slide 33 Infertility Care · Infertility occurs when a couple who has regular unprotected sexual intercourse for 1 year cannot conceive	

Slide 34
 	
Social and Psychological Implications Related to Infertility
 	
· Assumption of fertility
· Psychological reactions
  – Guilt
  – Isolation
  – Depression
  – Stress on the relationship
· Cultural and religious considerations
	• Discuss the psychological reactions to infertility and how a nurse can provide emotional support to the patient.
	• What are some cultural and religious implications for couples who are experiencing infertility?

Leifer

Slide 35

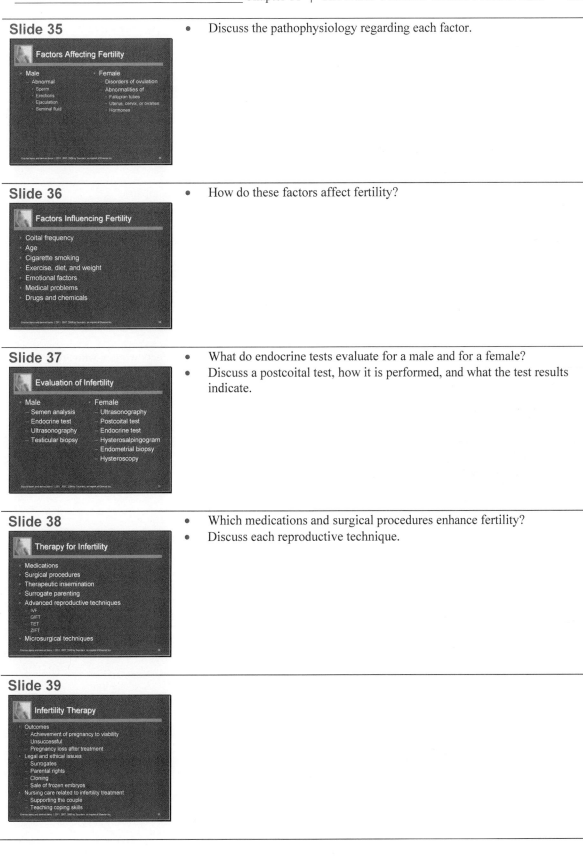

- Discuss the pathophysiology regarding each factor.

Slide 36

- How do these factors affect fertility?

Slide 37

- What do endocrine tests evaluate for a male and for a female?
- Discuss a postcoital test, how it is performed, and what the test results indicate.

Slide 38

- Which medications and surgical procedures enhance fertility?
- Discuss each reproductive technique.

Slide 39

Slide 40

> **Menopause**
> - Cessation of menstrual periods for a 12-month period because of decreased estrogen production
> - *Climacteric*—change of life—is also known as the *perimenopausal period* (which is 2 to 8 years before menstruation ceases)
> - Pregnancy can still occur during the climacteric

- How can a woman become pregnant during the climacteric?

Slide 41

> **Physical Changes in Menopause**
> - Usually caused by a decrease in estrogen
> - Changes in the menstrual cycle
> - Vasomotor instability, known as *hot flashes*
> - Decreased elasticity and moisture of the vagina
> - Dyspareunia
> - Some may notice change in libido (sexual desire)
> - Breast atrophy
> - Loss of protective effect of estrogen on the cardiovascular and skeletal systems

- How does the menstrual cycle change in menopause?
- Discuss the pathophysiology of hot flashes.
- What is dyspareunia?

Slide 42

> **Psychological and Cultural Variations**
> - Can threaten the woman's feelings of health and self-worth
> - Liberation from monthly periods
> - Ends fear of unwanted pregnancy

- Discuss the American culture and how it affects women who are experiencing menopause.

Slide 43

> **Treatment Options**
> - Exercise
> - Increase in calcium, magnesium, and high-fiber diet
> - Hormone replacement therapy (HRT), which may increase risk of heart attack and stroke, is based on the individual patient and discussions with her health care provider
> - Complementary and alternative therapies
> - Prevention of osteoporosis

- Discuss the pros and cons of HRT.
- What are examples of complementary and alternative therapies? Discuss side effects for each.
- How can you prevent osteoporosis?

Audience Response Question #3
Hormone replacement therapy increases a woman's risk of breast cancer.
1. True
2. False

Slide 44

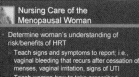

> **Nursing Care of the Menopausal Woman**
> - Determine woman's understanding of risk/benefits of HRT
>   - Teach signs and symptoms to report; i.e., vaginal bleeding that recurs after cessation of menses, vaginal irritation, signs of UTI
>   - Teach woman how to take prescribed medications correctly and side effects to report
>   - Teach value of weight-bearing exercises

Slide 45

Pelvic Floor Dysfunction

- Occurs when the muscles, ligaments, and fascia that support the pelvic organs are damaged or weakened
- Can result in
  - Vaginal wall prolapse
    - Cystocele
    - Rectocele
  - Uterine prolapse
    - Kegel exercises
    - Treated with surgery or pessary
  - Urinary incontinence

- How is a cystocele different from a rectocele?
- Discuss urinary incontinence and how it is affected by the pelvic floor muscles.

Slide 46

Nursing Care for Pelvic Floor Dysfunction

- Instructing the woman on
  - The use of exercises
  - Diet
  - Prevention of constipation
  - Adequate fluid intake

- What are pelvic floor exercises?
- Give examples of natural methods to prevent constipation.
- What types of fluids should a woman take and avoid?

Slide 47

Other Female Reproductive Tract Disorders

- Uterine fibroids, also known as *leiomyomas*
  - Benign growth of uterine muscle cells
  - Grow under influence of estrogen
  - Result in irregular bleeding, pelvic pressure, dysmenorrhea, menorrhagia

- How do uterine fibroids affect the uterus?
- Discuss the pathophysiology of irregular bleeding, pelvic pressure, dysmenorrhea, and menorrhagia.

Slide 48

Treatment of Fibroids

- If asymptomatic, observed and periodically reevaluated by health care provider
- Hormones
- Surgical interventions
  - Myomectomy
  - Myolysis
  - Embolization
  - Hysterectomy

- Discuss how fibroids are monitored by the health care provider.
- How are hormones used in treating fibroids?
- Describe each surgical intervention.

Slide 49

Ovarian Cysts

- Follicular ovarian cysts develop if follicle fails to rupture and release its ovum during the menstrual cycle
- Lutein cyst occurs after ovulation, the corpus luteum fails to regress
- Ovarian cyst that ruptures or becomes twisted, cutting off blood supply, causes pelvic pain and tenderness
- Diagnosed by transvaginal ultrasound
- Laparotomy is the treatment of choice

- What is a laparotomy procedure?

Slide 50

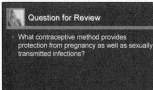

Cultural Aspects of Pain Control
- Pain is the fifth vital sign
- Culture can influence the expression of pain
- Ethnicity can affect drug metabolism
- Diet can affect drug absorption
- CAM can affect action of prescribed drugs
- Pain clinics are available
- Some cultural groups will not report embarrassing side effects of drugs
- Nurses must understand the cultural influences on pain expression

- Why is pain considered the fifth vital sign?
- Give an example of how one's culture influences the expression of pain.
- Why would a woman's culture make her hesitate to report a drug's side effects?

Slide 51

Question for Review
- What contraceptive method provides protection from pregnancy as well as sexually transmitted infections?

Slide 52

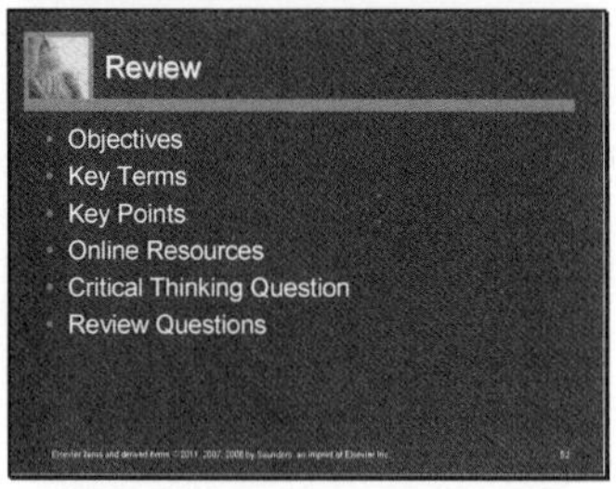

Review
- Objectives
- Key Terms
- Key Points
- Online Resources
- Critical Thinking Question
- Review Questions

12 Lesson Plan
The Term Newborn

TEACHING FOCUS

This chapter will introduce students to the neonate's physiological and psychological adjustments to extrauterine life. Normal reflexes of the neonate, ways to maintain body temperature, and the methods for preventing infection in a newborn will be discussed. Students will also have the opportunity to learn about skin manifestations in the newborn, including the cause and appearance of physiological jaundice.

MATERIALS AND RESOURCES

☐ Computer and PowerPoint projector (all lessons)

LESSON CHECKLIST

Preparations for this lesson include:

- Lecture
- Evaluation of student knowledge and skills needed to perform all entry-level activities related to the care of the term newborn, including:
  - ○ Normal reflexes in the neonate and the time of their disappearance
  - ○ Physical characteristics and nursing care of the neonate
  - ○ Ways to maintain body temperature and methods for preventing infection
  - ○ Cause and appearance of physiological jaundice and other skin manifestations

KEY TERMS

acrocyanosis (p. 292)
caput succedaneum (p. 281)
cephalhematoma (p. 281)
circumcision (p. 290)
dancing reflex (p. 290)
Epstein's pearls (p. 292)
fontanelles (p. 281)

head lag (p. 280)
icterus neonatorum (p. 293)
lanugo (p. 292)
meconium (p. 297)
milia (p. 292)
molding (p. 280)
Mongolian spots (p. 292)

Moro reflex (p. 280)
rooting reflex (p. 280)
scarf sign (p. 290)
tissue turgor (p. 280)
tonic neck reflex (p. 292)
vernix caseosa (p. 292)

ADDITIONAL RESOURCES

TEACH PPT slide(s) Chapter 12, 1-42
EILR IC image(s) Chapter 12, 1-17
EILR OBQ question(s) Chapter 12, 1-10
EILR TB question(s) Chapter 12, 1-30
ESLR IRQ question(s) Chapter 12, 1-5
SG Chapter 12, pp. 101-109

Legend

PPT TEACH PowerPoint Slides	**EILR** EVOLVE Instructor Learning Resources: Image Collection (IC), Open-Book Quizzes (OBQ), Test Bank (TB)	**ESLR** EVOLVE Student Learning Resources: Interactive Review Questions (IRQ) for the NCLEX® Examination	**SG** Study Guide	**CTQ** Critical Thinking Question in Nursing Care Plan (NCP CTQ) or Get Ready for the NCLEX! (GRN CTQ)

Class Activities are indicated in ***bold italic***.

LESSON 12.1

PRETEST

1. The *neonatal mortality rate* refers to any deaths that occur during the
   a. first week of life.
   c. first three months of life.
   b. first month of life.
   d. first year of life.

2. When an infant turns the head in the direction of anything that touches the cheek, the infant is exhibiting the
   a. rooting reflex.
   c. tonic neck reflex.
   b. Moro reflex.
   d. Babinski reflex.

3. An infant is born with low-set ears. This may indicate
   a. a congenital anomaly.
   c. a hearing deficit.
   b. normal ear development.
   d. visual problems.

4. When determining pain in the neonate, the nurse should note
   a. responses to stimuli.
   c. elevation in body temperature.
   b. changes in heart rate.
   d. Moro reflex.

5. Swelling of the soft tissues of the scalp is called
   a. macrocephaly.
   c. microcephaly.
   b. cephalohematoma.
   d. caput succedaneum.

6. What is the approximate volume of circulating blood in a newborn?
   a. 150 ml
   c. 300 ml
   b. 250 ml
   d. 500 ml

7. The newborn should have about
   a. two wet diapers per day.
   c. six wet diapers per day.
   b. four wet diapers per day.
   d. ten wet diapers per day.

8. Failure of the testes to descend into the scrotum is called
   a. hydrocele.
   c. varicocele.
   b. cryptorchidism.
   d. inguinal hernia.

9. Infants need extra vitamin
   a. A.
   c. E.
   b. B$_{12}$.
   d. D.

10. Conjugation of bilirubin, glucose regulation, and blood coagulation are all functions of the
    a. liver.
    c. spleen.
    b. heart.
    d. pancreas.

Answers

1. b	3. a	5. d	7. c	9. d
2. a	4. b	6. c	8. b	10. a

BACKGROUND ASSESSMENT

Question: How are the physiological changes that occur as the neonate adjusts to extrauterine life described?

Answer: The adaptation from fetal to extrauterine life involves changes in all the body systems. The first breath the infant takes opens the alveoli, which allows the infant to sustain respiratory and cardiac functioning. The circulatory changes include the closing of the foramen ovale, which enables the infant's blood to flow through the lungs. Other changes include the development of enzymes to help the digestive system, the primitive neurological system, and limited kidney function due to decreased glomerular filtration rate and the ability to concentrate urine. The newborn also passes through several phases of sleep-and-wake states as part of the extrauterine adjustment.

Question: How would you describe the neonate's phases of sleep immediately after birth?

Answer: At birth, the newborn passes through several phases of sleep-wake states and sleeps approximately 15 to 20 hours a day. The first phase is the first reactive phase. This occurs during the first 30 minutes of the newborn's life and is the best time for parental bonding because the newborn is alert. The infant then moves into the sleep phase, which lasts for several hours. The infant gradually becomes less responsive and sleepier during this time. After a deep sleep, the infant enters the second reactive phase and again becomes alert and responsive. The stability phase occurs after the first 24 hours of the neonate's life. The sleep-wake pattern becomes more stabilized at this time, and the newborn gradually adjusts to sleeping at night and being awake during the day.

CRITICAL THINKING QUESTION

It is July, and the mother of a 2-day-old infant asks the nurse why her newborn always has to have so many blankets whenever he leaves the nursery. She also mentions that her husband overheats easily and that he likes to keep the air conditioning set at 65° F. How should the nurse respond?
Guidelines: Because newborns are unable to regulate their body temperature, their environment influences their body temperature. Immediately after birth, their body temperature falls to about 96° F. Within a few hours the temperature slowly increases to around 98° or 99° F. The newborn's room should be kept between 69° and 75° F, with humidity between 45% and 55%. The room should also be free from drafts. Whenever the newborn leaves this regulated environment, he must be wrapped in blankets because he is unable to adapt to changes in temperature. When the newborn is discharged, it is extremely important that the parents maintain an environment similar to that of the hospital nursery. If the patient's husband refuses to keep the house above 65°, perhaps it would be possible to heat only the newborn's room to the appropriate temperature. The mother should be taught to assess the infant for signs of overheating or cold stress. The mother should also be aware that infants overheat easily because they have underdeveloped sweat glands.

OBJECTIVES	CONTENT	TEACHING RESOURCES
Briefly describe three normal reflexes of the neonate, including the approximate age of their disappearance.	■ Adjustment to extrauterine life (p. 280) ■ Phase 3: Care of the newborn (p. 280) □ Nervous system: reflexes (p. 280) □ Head (p. 280) Eyes (p. 281) Ears (p. 281) □ Sensory overload (p. 284) □ Sleep (p. 284) □ Pain (p. 285) □ Conditioned responses (p. 286) □ Neonatal behavioral assessment scale (p. 286) □ Respiratory system (p. 286)	PPT slides 4-21 *e* EILR IC images 1-4 *e* EILR OBQ questions 4, 5, 23, 26 *e* EILR TB question 5 *e* ESLR IRQ question 5 SG Learning Activities, questions 1, 2 (p. 101) SG Review Questions, questions 1, 2, 16 (pp. 105, 107) **BOOK RESOURCES** Figure 12-1, Head Lag (p. 280) Figure 12-2, Grasp Reflex (p. 280) Figure 12-3, Moro Reflex and Abnormal Moro Reflex (p. 281) Figure 12-4, Spontaneous Tonic Neck Reflex (p. 281) Table 12-1, Ages of Appearance and Disappearance of Neurological Signs Unique to Infancy (p. 282) Skill 12-1, Taking Head and Chest Measurements (p. 283) Figure 12-5, A, Molding of the Head. B, Cephalhematoma (p. 284) Figure 12-6, Ear Position (p. 284) Figure 12-7, Algo Hearing Screener Shows How the Test Is Accomplished (p. 285)

OBJECTIVES	CONTENT	TEACHING RESOURCES
		Figure 12-8, Pain in the Newborn (p. 286)
		Skill 12-2, Bulb Suctioning (p. 287)
		Review Questions for the NCLEX® Examination, question 2 (p. 304)
		▸ Discuss the nurse's role in educating parents about normal newborn reflexes.
		▸ Discuss how to assess pain in the newborn.
		*Class Activity **Divide the class into groups and have them create time lines that identify, describe, and illustrate normal newborn reflexes and the usual age of their disappearance. Have each group present its time line to the class for discussion.***
State four methods of maintaining the body temperature of a newborn.	☐ Providing warmth (p. 288) ☐ Obtaining temperature, pulse rate, and respirations (p. 288)	⊠▤ PPT slides 22-24 *e* EILR IC image 9 *e* EILR TB question 24 *e* ESLR IRQ question 2 SG Learning Activities, question 9 (p. 102) SG Review Questions, question 6 (p. 106) SG Case Study, question 1 (p. 109) **BOOK RESOURCES** Skill 12-3, Swaddling the Newborn (p. 288) Figure 12-9, Maintaining Body Temperature of the Newborn (p. 289) ▸ Discuss the various methods that can be implemented to prevent heat loss in the newborn. *Class Activity **Divide the class into groups and have them discuss the importance of maintaining and regulating the newborn's body temperature. What happens with the respiratory and cardiac systems if the infant's body temperature is not maintained? What are the signs that the newborn is overheated or is experiencing cold stress, and what are safe interventions to take?***
Demonstrate the steps in the physical assessment of the newborn.	☐ Apgar score (p. 287) ☐ Circulatory system (p. 287) ☐ Musculoskeletal system (p. 289) ☐ Length and weight	⊠▤ PPT slides 20-29 *e* EILR IC images 5-8, 10-12 *e* EILR OBQ questions 2-7 *e* EILR TB questions 1-3, 6, 11, 12, 15, 16, 18, 21, 25, 28

OBJECTIVES	CONTENT	TEACHING RESOURCES
	(p. 290) ☐ Genitourinary system (p. 290) – Male genitalia (p. 290) – Circumcision (p. 290) – Female genitalia (p. 292)	*e* ESLR IRQ questions 1, 3 SG Learning Activities, questions 3-8, 13-15 (pp. 102-104) SG Review Questions, questions 3-5, 7, 9, 18-20 (pp. 105-107) SG Applying Knowledge, questions 1, 3, 4 (p. 109) **BOOK RESOURCES** Safety Alert (p. 285) Figure 12-10, Assessing an Apical Pulse (p. 289) Figure 12-11, Weighing the Infant (p. 290) Figure 12-12, Circumcision Board (p. 291) Patient Teaching, Home care of the penis (p. 292) Review Questions for the NCLEX® Examination, question 5 (p. 304) ▸ Discuss the pros and cons of circumcision. ▸ Discuss the nurse's role in circumcision. *Class Activity **Divide the class into groups and have them practice how to perform a physical assessment on a male and female newborn. Then have them demonstrate this to the class. Have them point out what is similar and what is unique to each.***

12.1 Homework/Assignments:

12.1 Instructor's Notes/Student Feedback:

LESSON 12.2

CRITICAL THINKING QUESTION

What is the nurse's responsibility in preventing infections in the newborn?

Guidelines: In order to prevent infections, hand hygiene must be performed before and after caring for the newborn. The nurse must also perform hand hygiene between handling different babies. Medical equipment should be cleaned and properly stored, and soiled diapers and linens should be disposed of properly. The infection preventionist is also responsible for monitoring the nursery and providing education on infection prevention and control. Separate supplies are provided for each infant, including bath equipment and linens, and should never be shared among infants. Organizations such as the American Academy of Pediatrics and hospital accreditation boards set forth the guidelines for nursery standards. The nurse also educates the parents on hand hygiene techniques and the importance of proper umbilical cord care to prevent infections. Because infections can be fatal to a newborn, any person who has signs of a cold, earache, skin infection, intestinal upset, or is just not feeling well should not come into the hospital nursery or visit in the home.

OBJECTIVES	CONTENT	TEACHING RESOURCES
Define the following skin manifestations in the newborn: lanugo, vernix caseosa, Mongolian spots, milia, acrocyanosis, desquamation.	☐ Integumentary system (p. 292) – Skin (p. 292)	⊠ PPT slide 30, 31 *e* EILR IC images 13, 14 *e* EILR TB questions 17, 19, 22 ▪ SG Review Questions, questions 10, 11 (p. 106) **BOOK RESOURCES** Review Questions for the NCLEX® Examination, question 4 (p. 304) Figure 12-13, Testing Tissue Turgor (p. 292) Figure 12-14, Vernix (p. 292) Table 12-2, Changing Laboratory Values (p. 293) Safety Alert (p. 293) Table 12-3, Common Skin Manifestations in the Newborn (pp. 294-295) ▶ Discuss the signs and symptoms of the various skin manifestations common to newborns. *Class Activity **Choose student volunteers to describe each of the skin manifestations listed below to the class. Have the rest of the class identify the appropriate treatment and nursing interventions, if indicated.*** – *lanugo* – *vernix caseosa* – *milia* – *Epstein's pearls* – *Mongolian spots* – *acrocyanosis* – *cutis marmorata*

OBJECTIVES	CONTENT	TEACHING RESOURCES
		– *desquamation*
		– *erythema toxicum*
		– *harlequin color change*
		– *port-wine stain*
State the cause and appearance of physiological jaundice in the newborn.	☐ Integumentary system (p. 292) – Skin (p. 292) – The interactive bath (p. 293) ☐ Gastrointestinal system (p. 297) – Stools (p. 297) – Constipation (p. 297) – Hiccoughs (p. 297) – Digestion (p. 297) – Vitamins (p. 298)	PPT slides 31-34 *e* EILR IC image 15 *e* EILR OBQ questions 8, 9 *e* EILR TB questions 9, 10, 27, 29, 30 SG Learning Activities, questions 16-20 (pp. 104-105) SG Review Questions, questions 8, 13-15, 17 (pp. 106-107) SG Applying Knowledge, questions 2, 6 (p. 109) **BOOK RESOURCES** Skill 12-4, Assessing for jaundice (p. 293) Skill 12-5, Bathing the newborn (p. 296) Nursing Tip (p. 297) Figure 12-15, The Normal Infant Stool Cycle (p. 298) Review Questions for the NCLEX® Examination, question 1 (p. 304) ▸ Discuss the genetic and cultural factors that can affect the severity of physiological jaundice. *Class Activity* **Present the following scenario to the class for students to discuss:** **The mother of a 2-day-old infant is alarmed because she notices that her baby's skin has developed a yellow tinge. She is worried that it is caused by something she did or ate during pregnancy.** **What is this condition, and how should the nurse explain its causes and treatment to the mother?**
State the methods of preventing infection in newborns.	■ Preventing infection (p. 299)	PPT slides 35-38 *e* EILR TB question 20 SG Learning Activities, question 21 (p. 105) SG Review Questions, question 12 (p. 106) **BOOK RESOURCES**

ELSEVIER

OBJECTIVES	CONTENT	TEACHING RESOURCES
		Review Questions for the NCLEX® Examination, question 3 (p. 304) Safety Alert (p. 299) ▸ Discuss the most common causes of infection in newborns. *Class Activity As a class, have students identify potential causes of infection in newborns. Have the class determine appropriate nursing interventions to prevent these infections. Is it possible to prevent all infections? What are the most common causes?*
Interpret discharge teaching for the mother and her newborn.	■ Discharge planning and parent teaching (p. 299) ■ Home care (p. 299) □ Furnishings (p. 299) □ Clothing (p. 303)	PPT slides 39, 40 EILR IC images 16, 17 EILR OBQ question 10 EILR TB questions 7, 13, 14 ESLR IRQ question 4 SG Case Study, question 1 (p. 109) SG Applying Knowledge, questions 1, 5 (p. 109) **BOOK RESOURCES** Safety Alert (p. 299) Clinical Pathway 12-1 (pp. 300-302) Figure 12-16, Note that the diaper is folded so that it does not touch the umbilical cord stump (p. 303) Figure 12-17, Dressing the Newborn (p. 303) ▸ Discuss the discharge process for the mother and her newborn. *Class Activity As a class, have students identify teaching topics that should be included in the discharge process, such as bathing, diapering, cord and skin care, selection of clothing, furniture, safety in the home and in the car, feeding the infant and follow-up appointments with the pediatrician.*
Performance Evaluation		PPT slides 1-42 EILR IC images 1-17 EILR OBQ questions 1-10 EILR TB questions 1-30 ESLR IRQ questions 1-5

OBJECTIVES	CONTENT	TEACHING RESOURCES
		SG Learning Activities, questions 1-21 (pp. 101-105)
		SG Review Questions, questions 1-20 (pp. 105-107)
		SG Crossword Puzzle (p. 108)
		SG Case Study, question 1 (p. 109)
		SG Applying Knowledge, questions 1-6 (p. 109)
		BOOK RESOURCES
		Review Questions for the NCLEX® Examination, questions 1-5 (p. 304)
		GRN CTQ 1 (p. 304)

12.2 Homework/Assignments:

12.2 Instructor's Notes/Student Feedback:

---

12 Lecture Outline
The Term Newborn

Slide 1

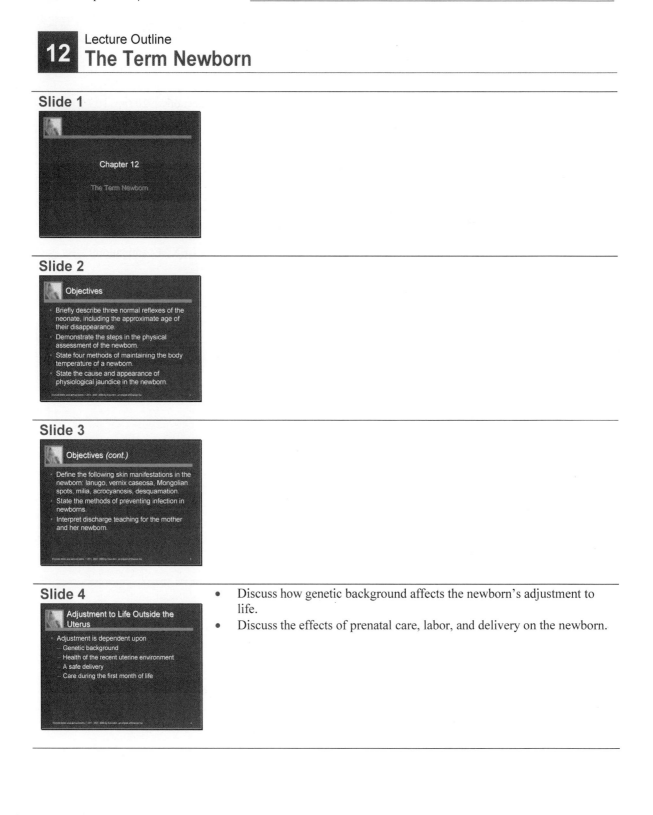

Chapter 12

The Term Newborn

Slide 2

Objectives

- Briefly describe three normal reflexes of the neonate, including the approximate age of their disappearance.
- Demonstrate the steps in the physical assessment of the newborn.
- State four methods of maintaining the body temperature of a newborn.
- State the cause and appearance of physiological jaundice in the newborn.

Slide 3

Objectives *(cont.)*

- Define the following skin manifestations in the newborn: lanugo, vernix caseosa, Mongolian spots, milia, acrocyanosis, desquamation.
- State the methods of preventing infection in newborns.
- Interpret discharge teaching for the mother and her newborn.

Slide 4

Adjustment to Life Outside the Uterus

- Adjustment is dependent upon
  - Genetic background
  - Health of the recent uterine environment
  - A safe delivery
  - Care during the first month of life

- Discuss how genetic background affects the newborn's adjustment to life.
- Discuss the effects of prenatal care, labor, and delivery on the newborn.

Leifer

Slide 5

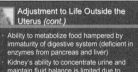

Adjustment to Life Outside the Uterus *(cont.)*

- Respirations stimulated due to chilling and chemical changes in the blood
  - Sensory and physical stimuli
  - First breath opens alveoli
  - Independent air exchange begins
- Initiates cardiopulmonary interdependence

- What is the nurse's role in providing sensory and physical stimuli to assist the newborn in breathing?

Slide 6

Adjustment to Life Outside the Uterus *(cont.)*

- Ability to metabolize food hampered by immaturity of digestive system (deficient in enzymes from pancreas and liver)
- Kidney's ability to concentrate urine and maintain fluid balance is limited due to decreased rate of glomerular flow and limited renal tubular reabsorption
- Neurological functions are primitive

Slide 7

Physical Characteristics

Slide 8

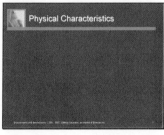

Nervous System: Reflexes

- Moves arms and legs vigorously but cannot control them
- Full-term infants are born with the following reflexes (which help keep them alive)
  - Blinking
  - Sneezing
  - Gagging
  - Sucking
  - Grasping
- They can also cry, swallow, and lift their head (slightly) when lying on their abdomen

- Describe each of the reflexes listed.

Slide 9

Reflexes

- Moro
- Rooting
- Tonic neck
- Dancing

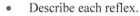

- Describe each reflex.
- What is the nurse's role in assessing the newborn's reflexes?

Leifer

Slide 10

Head

- Molding from delivery process
  - May have swelling of the soft tissues of the scalp, called *caput succedaneum*
  - May see a cephalhematoma—a collection of blood beneath the periosteum of the cranial bone
    - Does not cross the suture line
- Fontanels (soft spots) protect the head during delivery and allow further brain growth

- Refer to Figure 12-5 on page 284 and discuss caput succedaneum and cephalhematoma.
- Why is the newborn's head circumference measured?

Slide 11

Visual Stimuli and Sensory Overload

- Can see and fixate on points of contrast
  - Toys with contrasting colors or those that make noise attract the newborn's attention
- Tears are absent until 1 to 3 months of age
- Sensory overload can occur if there is too much detrimental stimulation
- Important for the nurse to keep surrounding environment as calm and quiet as possible, no bright lighting or loud alarms

Slide 12

Hearing

- Ears well-developed, but small
- Hearing ability present at birth (sick or premature newborn may not respond to sounds)
- Normal drainage and sneezing occurs after birth to rid ear canals of amniotic fluid
- May react to sudden sounds by increased pulse or respiratory rate or startle reflex
- Responds to voices by decreasing motor activity, sucking activity, and turning head toward the sound
- Hearing screening performed before discharge

Slide 13

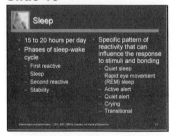

Sleep

- 15 to 20 hours per day
- Phases of sleep-wake cycle
  - First reactive
  - Sleep
  - Second reactive
  - Stability
- Specific pattern of reactivity that can influence the response to stimuli and bonding
  - Quiet sleep
  - Rapid eye movement (REM) sleep
  - Active alert
  - Quiet alert
  - Crying
  - Transitional

- Describe each phase of the sleep-wake cycle.
- Discuss each of the patterns of reactivity listed.

Slide 14

Pain

- Produces catecholamines and cortisol
  - Heart and respiratory rates change
  - Blood pressure increases as does blood glucose levels
- Untreated pain can have long-term effects
  - Pain pathways and structures required for long-term memory are well developed by 24 weeks gestation
- Unrelieved pain can cause exhaustion, irritability, and delay the healing process

- What is the nurse's role in assessing pain in the newborn?

ELSEVIER

Slide 15

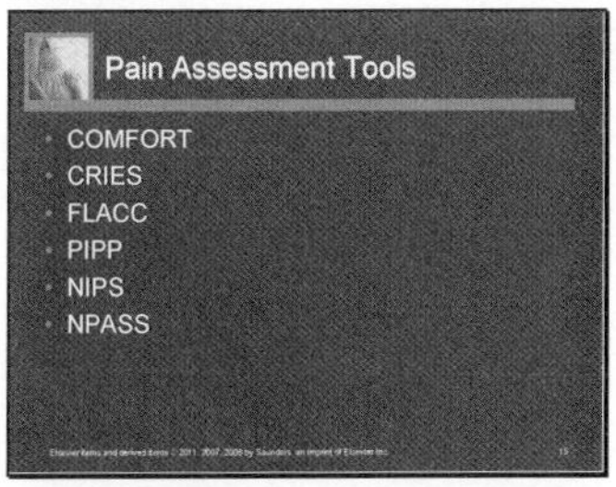

Pain Assessment Tools

- COMFORT
- CRIES
- FLACC
- PIPP
- NIPS
- NPASS

- Discuss the CRIES 10-point scale, the PIPP profile, the NIPS scale, and the NPASS scale.

Slide 16

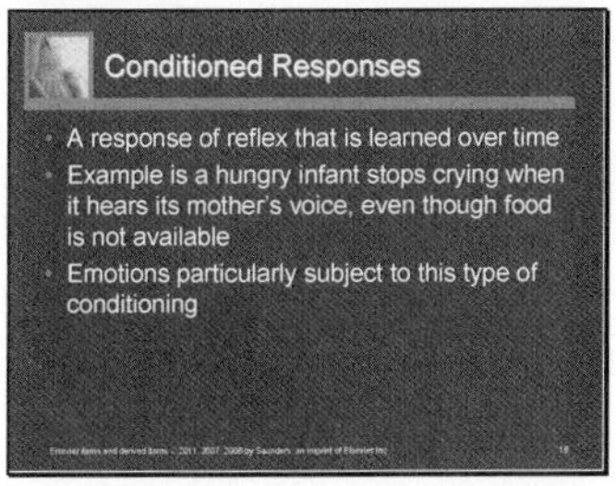

Conditioned Responses

- A response of reflex that is learned over time
- Example is a hungry infant stops crying when it hears its mother's voice, even though food is not available
- Emotions particularly subject to this type of conditioning

- What are some examples of conditioned responses?

Slide 17

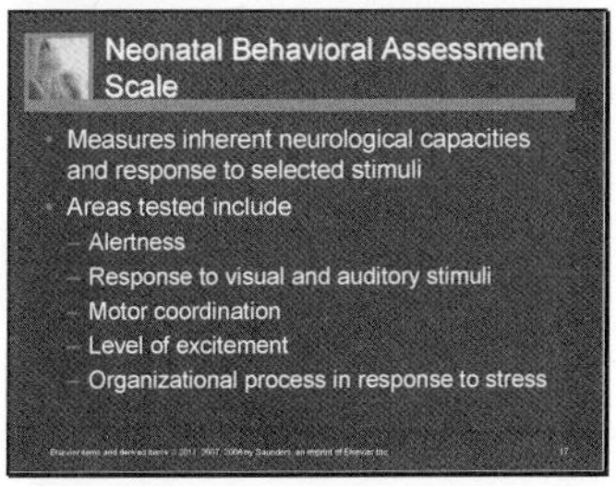

Neonatal Behavioral Assessment Scale

- Measures inherent neurological capacities and response to selected stimuli
- Areas tested include
  - Alertness
  - Response to visual and auditory stimuli
  - Motor coordination
  - Level of excitement
  - Organizational process in response to stress

- How can this scale help new parents?

Slide 18

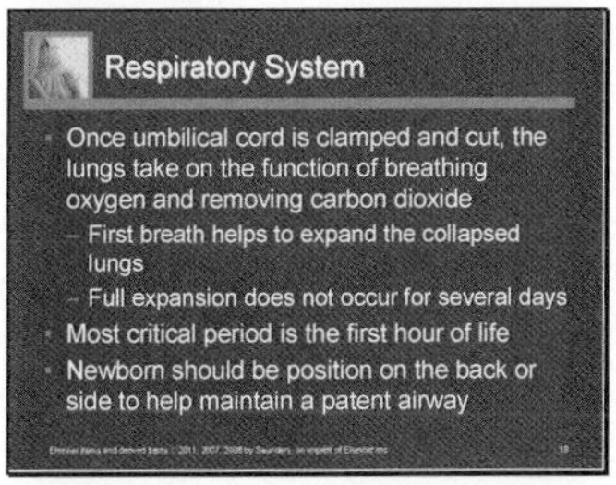

Respiratory System

- Once umbilical cord is clamped and cut, the lungs take on the function of breathing oxygen and removing carbon dioxide
  - First breath helps to expand the collapsed lungs
  - Full expansion does not occur for several days
- Most critical period is the first hour of life
- Newborn should be position on the back or side to help maintain a patent airway

- What is the nurse's role in maintaining a patent airway in the newborn?

Slide 19

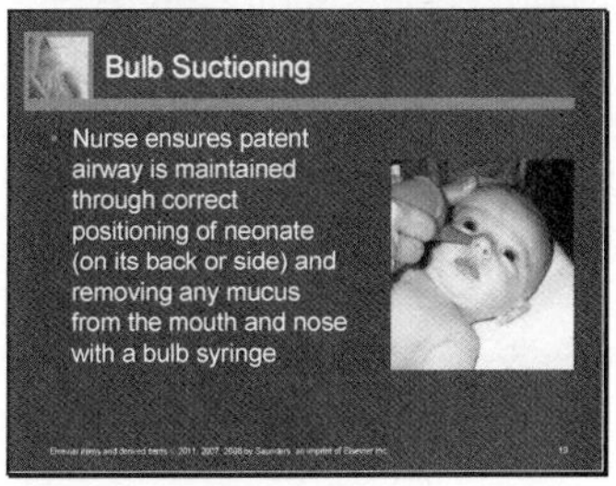

Bulb Suctioning

- Nurse ensures patent airway is maintained through correct positioning of neonate (on its back or side) and removing any mucus from the mouth and nose with a bulb syringe

- Describe proper suctioning with a bulb syringe.

Slide 20

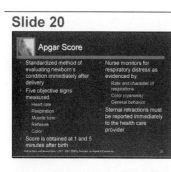

Apgar Score

- Standardized method of evaluating newborn's condition immediately after delivery
- Five objective signs measured
  - Heart rate
  - Respiration
  - Muscle tone
  - Reflexes
  - Color
- Score is obtained at 1 and 5 minutes after birth

- Nurse monitors for respiratory distress as evidenced by
  - Rate and character of respirations
  - Color (cyanosis)
  - General behavior
- Sternal retractions must be reported immediately to the health care provider

- Give an example of how to measure the Apgar score.
- What are the implications of sternal retractions and the nurse's role in managing this urgent situation?

Audience Response Question #1
An Apgar score of 5 at 5 minutes indicates the neonate is in:
1. Good condition
2. Fair condition
3. Poor condition
4. Critical condition

Slide 21

Circulatory System

- Has approximately 300 mL of circulating blood volume
- Neonatal circulation differs from fetal circulation
- Dependent upon ducts within the heart to close at certain points in time, such as
  - Foramen ovale
  - Ductus arteriosus

- If the ducts fail to close when they are supposed to, the neonate may become cyanotic because the blood bypasses the lungs and does not pick up any oxygen

- Discuss the difference between neonatal circulation from that of a fetus.
- Describe the location and pathophysiology of the foramen ovale and ductus arteriosus.

Slide 22

Providing Warmth

- Unstable heat-regulating system
- Acrocyanosis is evident because of sluggish peripheral circulation
- Cannot adapt to change in temperatures easily
- Sweat glands do not function during neonatal period, so infant is at risk for developing elevated temperature if overdressed or placed in overheated environment

- How can you ensure the newborn is kept warm?
- Hands and feet are not used as a guide to determine warmth because the extremities tend to be cooler than the rest of the body.

Slide 23

Obtaining Temperature, Pulse Rate, and Respirations

- Temperature: can be taken rectally or in the axilla
- Pulse and respiratory rates: count before taking temperature as infant may cry when disturbed

- The nurse should report
  - Temperature elevations >99.8° F or <97.1° F
  - Pulse rates >160 or <110 beats/min
  - Respirations >60 or <30 breaths/min
  - Noisy respirations
  - Nasal flaring or chest retraction

- Discuss proper methods to count respiratory and pulse rates.
- How would you describe noisy respirations, nasal flaring, and chest retractions?

Audience Response Question #2
A neonate's vital signs are assessed as follows: axillary temperature 96.5° F, pulse 125 bpm, respirations 44. The nurse is aware that:
1. these are within normal limits.
2. pulse is elevated.
3. respirations and temperature are normal.
4. temperature is decreased.

Slide 24

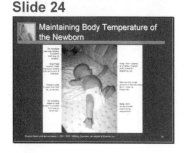

Maintaining Body Temperature of the Newborn

- What is another reason for swaddling a newborn besides temperature control?

Slide 25

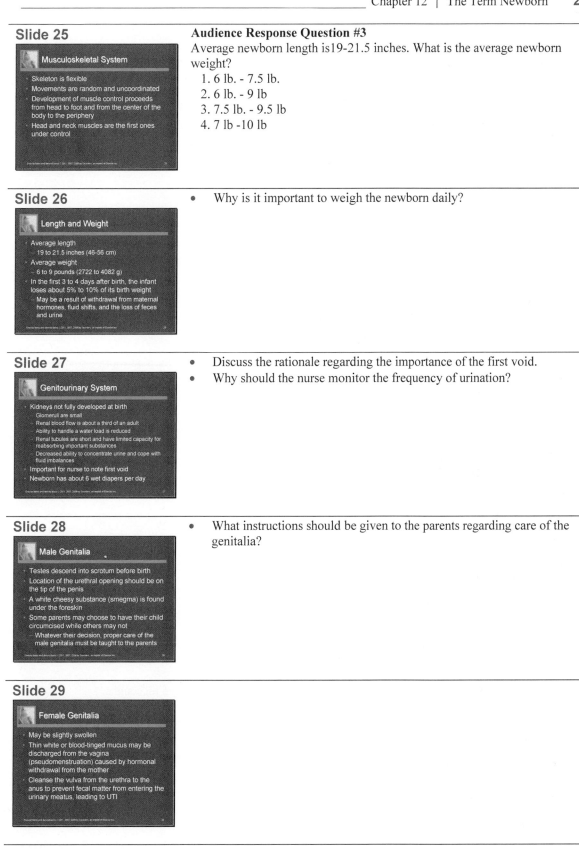

Musculoskeletal System

- Skeleton is flexible
- Movements are random and uncoordinated
- Development of muscle control proceeds from head to foot and from the center of the body to the periphery
- Head and neck muscles are the first ones under control

Audience Response Question #3
Average newborn length is19-21.5 inches. What is the average newborn weight?
1. 6 lb. - 7.5 lb.
2. 6 lb. - 9 lb
3. 7.5 lb. - 9.5 lb
4. 7 lb -10 lb

Slide 26

Length and Weight

- Average length
  - 19 to 21.5 inches (46-56 cm)
- Average weight
  - 6 to 9 pounds (2722 to 4082 g)
- In the first 3 to 4 days after birth, the infant loses about 5% to 10% of its birth weight
  - May be a result of withdrawal from maternal hormones, fluid shifts, and the loss of feces and urine

- Why is it important to weigh the newborn daily?

Slide 27

Genitourinary System

- Kidneys not fully developed at birth
  - Glomeruli are small
  - Renal blood flow is about a third of an adult
  - Ability to handle a water load is reduced
  - Renal tubules are short and have limited capacity for reabsorbing important substances
  - Decreased ability to concentrate urine and cope with fluid imbalances
- Important for nurse to note first void
- Newborn has about 6 wet diapers per day

- Discuss the rationale regarding the importance of the first void.
- Why should the nurse monitor the frequency of urination?

Slide 28

Male Genitalia

- Testes descend into scrotum before birth
- Location of the urethral opening should be on the tip of the penis
- A white cheesy substance (smegma) is found under the foreskin
- Some parents may choose to have their child circumcised while others may not
  - Whatever their decision, proper care of the male genitalia must be taught to the parents

- What instructions should be given to the parents regarding care of the genitalia?

Slide 29

Female Genitalia

- May be slightly swollen
- Thin white or blood-tinged mucus may be discharged from the vagina (pseudomenstruation) caused by hormonal withdrawal from the mother
- Cleanse the vulva from the urethra to the anus to prevent fecal matter from entering the urinary meatus, leading to UTI

Leifer

Slide 30

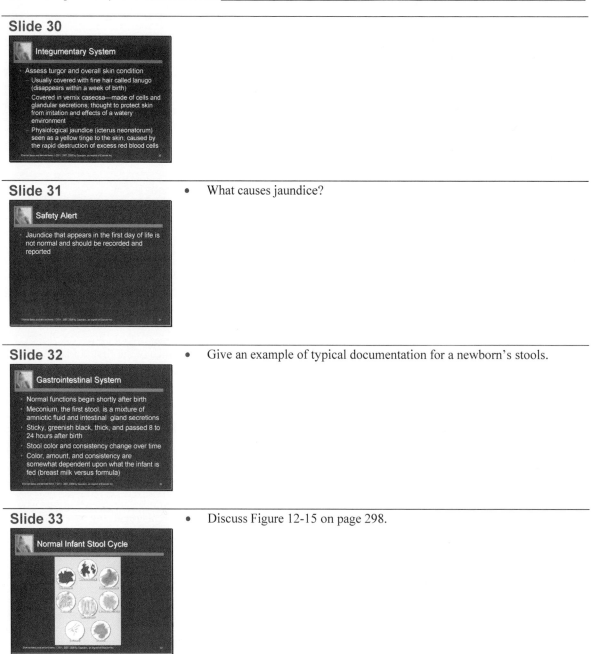

Integumentary System

- Assess turgor and overall skin condition
  - Usually covered with fine hair called lanugo (disappears within a week of birth)
  - Covered in vernix caseosa—made of cells and glandular secretions; thought to protect skin from irritation and effects of a watery environment
  - Physiological jaundice (icterus neonatorum) seen as a yellow tinge to the skin; caused by the rapid destruction of excess red blood cells

Slide 31

Safety Alert

- Jaundice that appears in the first day of life is not normal and should be recorded and reported

- What causes jaundice?

Slide 32

Gastrointestinal System

- Normal functions begin shortly after birth
- Meconium, the first stool, is a mixture of amniotic fluid and intestinal gland secretions
- Sticky, greenish black, thick, and passed 8 to 24 hours after birth
- Stool color and consistency change over time
- Color, amount, and consistency are somewhat dependent upon what the infant is fed (breast milk versus formula)

- Give an example of typical documentation for a newborn's stools.

Slide 33

Normal Infant Stool Cycle

- Discuss Figure 12-15 on page 298.

Slide 34

Gastrointestinal System Upsets

- Constipation
- Hiccoughs
- Digestion

- Discuss methods to manage constipation and hiccoughs.
- What is the gastrocolic reflex?
- What vitamins are necessary for the newborn?

Slide 35

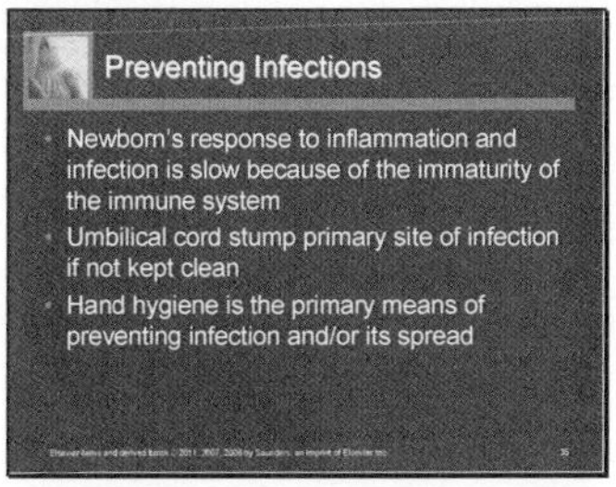

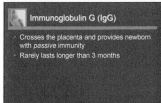

- What is considered proper umbilical cord care?
- Discuss the importance of hand hygiene.

Slide 36

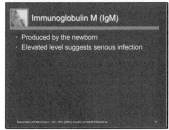

Slide 37

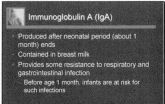

Slide 38

Slide 39

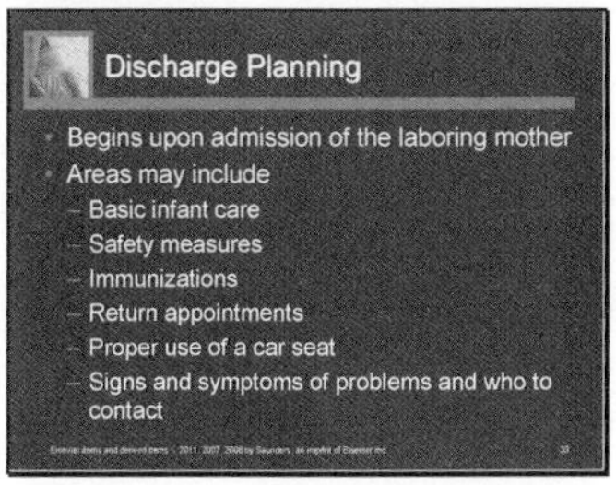

- What information should be provided to parents in each of the areas listed?

Leifer

Slide 40

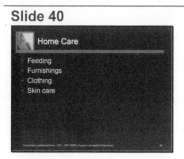

Home Care

- Feeding
- Furnishings
- Clothing
- Skin care

Slide 41

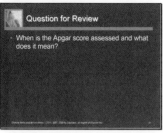

Question for Review

- When is the Apgar score assessed and what does it mean?

Slide 42

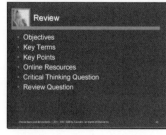

Review

- Objectives
- Key Terms
- Key Points
- Online Resources
- Critical Thinking Question
- Review Question

13 Lesson Plan
Preterm and Postterm Newborns

TEACHING FOCUS

This chapter focuses on the assessment, common physiological problems, and common family reactions to the preterm infant. Along with the importance of assessment and observation, the chapter demonstrates to the student appropriate nursing interventions in a variety of situations. The chapter stresses nursing goals for both preterm and postterm infants and the importance of organization to minimize handling and stimulation. Students will have the opportunity to learn about the most common nursing goals—improving respiration, maintaining body heat, conserving the infant's energy, preventing infection, providing nutrition and hydration, providing good skin care, and supporting and encouraging the parents. The chapter also discusses physical characteristics of and nursing needs for postterm infants.

MATERIALS AND RESOURCES

- ☐ Ballard score forms (Lesson 13.1)
- ☐ Computer and PowerPoint projector (all lessons)
- ☐ Doll or preterm model (all lessons)
- ☐ Gavage feeding equipment (Lesson 13.2)
- ☐ Incubator or radiant heat crib (Lesson 13.1)
- ☐ Index cards (Lesson 13.1)
- ☐ Infant dolls (all lessons)
- ☐ Oxygen hood (Lesson 13.1)
- ☐ Pulse oximeter (Lesson 13.1)
- ☐ Thermometer (Lesson 13.1)

LESSON CHECKLIST

Preparations for this lesson include:

- Lecture
- Demonstration
- Guest speaker: NICU nurse
- Evaluation of student knowledge and skills needed to perform all entry-level activities related to preterm and postterm newborns, including:
  - ○ The ability to differentiate between preterm, low-birthweight, and postterm infants
  - ○ Demonstrating knowledge of common preterm problems and nursing goals
  - ○ Understanding of the key role of nursing observations in dealing with preterm infants
  - ○ Familiarity with psychological issues surrounding the families of preterm newborns and appropriate nursing interventions

KEY TERMS

apnea (p. 309)
Ballard scoring system (p. 306)
bradycardia (p. 309)
bronchopulmonary dysplasia (p. 309)
cold stress (p. 310)
gestational age (p. 306)
hyperbilirubinemia (p. 312)
hypocalcemia (p. 310)
hypoglycemia (p. 310)
hypoxia (p. 309)

icterus (p. 312)
kangaroo care (p. 314)
lanugo (p. 318)
late preterm (p. 306)
necrotizing enterocolitis (NEC) (p. 311)
neutral thermal environment (p. 313)
postterm (p. 306)
preterm (p. 306)
previability (p. 306)
pulse oximeter (p. 309)

respiratory distress syndrome (RDS) (p. 307)
retinopathy of prematurity (ROP) (p. 311)
sepsis (p. 310)
surfactant (p. 307)
thermoregulation (p. 313)
total parenteral nutrition (TPN) (p. 316)

ADDITIONAL RESOURCES

TEACH PPT slide(s) Chapter 13, 1-55
EILR IC image(s) Chapter 13, 1-8
EILR OBQ question(s) Chapter 13, 1-10
EILR TB question(s) Chapter 13, 1-31
ESLR IRQ question(s) Chapter 13, 1-6
SG Chapter 13, pp. 111-117

ELSEVIER

Introduction to Maternity & Pediatric Nursing, 6th ed.
Leifer

Legend

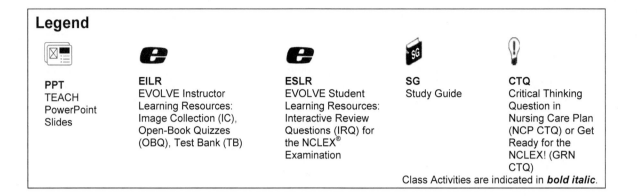

PPT
TEACH
PowerPoint
Slides

EILR
EVOLVE Instructor
Learning Resources:
Image Collection (IC),
Open-Book Quizzes
(OBQ), Test Bank (TB)

ESLR
EVOLVE Student
Learning Resources:
Interactive Review
Questions (IRQ) for
the NCLEX®
Examination

SG
Study Guide

CTQ
Critical Thinking
Question in
Nursing Care Plan
(NCP CTQ) or Get
Ready for the
NCLEX! (GRN
CTQ)

Class Activities are indicated in ***bold italic***.

LESSON 13.1

PRETEST

1. When is surfactant sufficiently produced to support respiration at birth?
   - a. 24 weeks of gestation
   - b. 30 weeks of gestation
   - c. 34 weeks of gestation
   - d. 36 weeks of gestation

2. Heat loss in the preterm infant is related to
   - a. hyperactivity.
   - b. excess brown fat.
   - c. leg contraction.
   - d. surface area that is large in proportion to body weight.

3. Jaundice can lead to what serious complication?
   - a. kernicterus
   - b. hypoglycemia
   - c. sepsis
   - d. dehydration

4. *Total parenteral nutrition* (TPN) refers to
   - a. supplemental vitamins.
   - b. intravenous infusion of lipids and nutrients.
   - c. gavage feedings.
   - d. preterm infant formula.

5. What is the developmental age of a 3-month-old preterm infant born at 36 weeks' gestation?
   - a. newborn
   - b. 1 month old
   - c. 2 months old
   - d. 3 months old

6. Respiratory distress in the postterm infant is usually related to
   - a. meconium aspiration.
   - b. limited surfactant.
   - c. polycythemia.
   - d. seizures.

7. Which thermoregulation method uses skin-to-skin contact?
   - a. incubator
   - b. radiant heat crib
   - c. ultraviolet lamp
   - d. kangaroo care

8. Hypoglycemia in the infant begins when the blood glucose level reaches
   - a. 40 mg/dl.
   - b. 50 mg/dl.
   - c. 65 mg/dl.
   - d. 70 mg/dl.

9. A sign of cold stress in the infant is
   - a. bradycardia.
   - b. tachycardia.
   - c. fever.
   - d. flushed skin.

10. The ideal nutrition for a preterm infant is
    - a. TPN.
    - b. breast milk.
    - c. soy milk formula.
    - d. cow's milk formula.

Answers

1. c	3. a	5. c	7. d	9. a
2. d	4. b	6. a	8. a	10. b

BACKGROUND ASSESSMENT

Question: What are the physical characteristics of the postterm infant as compared with those of the preterm infant?

Answer: The postterm infant appears long and thin with loose skin around the buttocks and thighs, which is due to in utero depletion of fat stores. There is minimal lanugo or vernix caseosa present, causing the skin to be dry, cracked, and peeling. The hair and fingernails are longer than usual. Fingernails may be stained with meconium. In contrast, the preterm infant has abundant lanugo and vernix caseosa, and extremities and fingernails are short. Genitalia are small, and in female infants the labia majora may be open. The soles of the preterm infant's feet have few creases. Like postterm infants, the skin of preterm neonates is loose but for a different reason: They have not developed adequate subcutaneous fat stores.

Introduction to Maternity & Pediatric Nursing, 6th ed.

Elsevier items and derived items © 2011, 2007, 2006 by Saunders, an imprint of Elsevier Inc.   Leifer

Question: What factors contribute to poor control of body temperature in the preterm infant, and how can a nurse promote a neutral thermal environment?

Answer: The preterm newborn is vulnerable to cold stress for a variety of reasons. Subcutaneous fat stores are undeveloped. Radiant heat loss can be excessive because of the ratio of large surface area to body weight. The preterm infant's immature central nervous system and sweat glands are not able to regulate internal body temperature. Compensatory mechanisms such as shivering are less effective because the preterm infant is hypoactive and has weak muscle tone. The extended posture of the legs exacerbates the problem by increasing body surface area and the potential for radiant heat loss. Metabolic needs are high, yet the preterm infant has depleted fuel sources and is prone to hypoglycemia. Nursing interventions include monitoring the body temperature of the preterm infant using abdominal temperature probes. Thermoregulation measures such as kangaroo care (skin-to-skin care) and placing the infant in a radiant warmer or incubator to maintain body temperatures within the optimal range of 36° to 37° C (97° to 98° F) are indicated. The nurse must continually assess for signs of cold stress, which include lethargy, skin mottling, decreased skin temperature, bradycardia, and tachypnea with periods of apnea.

CRITICAL THINKING QUESTION

A nurse is assessing a preterm infant of 38 weeks gestation who was born 72 hours ago and notes a yellow tinge to the infant's sclera and skin. What condition does this finding indicate, and how should the nurse respond?

Guidelines: A yellowish-orange tinge to the sclera, mucous membranes, and skin of a newborn indicates jaundice (also called *icterus*). Newborns have immature livers that cannot adequately process the bilirubin that results from the normal destruction of red blood cells that occurs after birth. Thus, bile pigments build up in the blood and cause a discoloration noticed in the newborn's sclera and skin. In full-term infants the peak in bilirubin levels tends to occur 2 to 3 days postpartum, but in preterm infants the peak occurrence is typically delayed (3 to 4 days postpartum) and can be prolonged, which predisposes the preterm infant to a buildup of bilirubin (hyperbilirubinemia). Serum blood levels must be monitored to assess for hyperbilirubinemia, a condition that can lead to serious but preventable neurological complications (kernicterus). A rise of more than 5 mg/dl of bilirubin in a 24-hour period is significant and must be reported to the physician immediately. Promoting adequate feedings for the infant is important in encouraging excretion of the bile pigments. The nurse should also monitor the infant's lab results and notify the physician of any increase in bilirubin levels. If necessary, phototherapy may be initiated to reduce the bilirubin buildup.

OBJECTIVES	CONTENT	TEACHING RESOURCES
Differentiate between the preterm and the low-birthweight newborn.	■ The preterm newborn (p. 305)	⊠ PPT slides 4-6
		e EILR IC images 1-3
		e EILR OBQ question 7
		e EILR TB questions 1, 22
		SG Learning Activities, questions 1, 4 (p. 111)
		SG Review Questions, question 2 (p. 114)
		BOOK RESOURCES
		Figure 13-1, Two Term Infants of the Same Gestational Age (p. 306)
		Figure 13-2, The New Ballard Scale Estimates Gestational Age (p. 307)
		Figure 13-3, The Preterm Newborn (p. 308)
		Review Questions for the NCLEX® Examination, question

OBJECTIVES	CONTENT	TEACHING RESOURCES
		4 (p. 320)
		Class Activity Ask students to define the following phrases: small-for-gestational age, large-for-gestational age, intrauterine growth restriction, gestational age, and preterm and postterm infants. Using these definitions, ask students to explain how preterm infants are classified.
		Class Activity Using an infant doll, demonstrate how to assess neuromuscular maturity. Then, provide students with a blank Ballard score form and ask them to correctly document the positions and assessments you perform with the infant doll. Call out sample characteristics for the physical maturity section and again have students document the correct score. Have students tally the score and discuss the results. Provide comparisons of a midterm and full-term infant.
List three causes of preterm birth.	☐ Causes (p. 306) ☐ Physical characteristics (p. 306)	⊠ PPT slides 7, 8 *e* EILR IC image 3 *e* EILR OBQ questions 1, 2 *e* EILR TB questions 17, 28, 31 *e* ESLR IRQ question 1 SG Learning Activities, questions 1, 2 (p. 111) SG Review Questions, question 1 (p. 114) SG Applying Knowledge, question 1 (p. 116) **BOOK RESOURCES** Figure 13-3, The Preterm Newborn (p. 308) Review Questions for the NCLEX® Examination, question 1 (p. 319) *Class Activity Have student pairs take turns role-playing a pregnant woman and a nurse during a prenatal visit in which the nurse must educate the mother about risks for preterm deliveries. Have each student identify three risks associated with preterm birth. Then, have each pair summarize why prenatal teaching and nursing care is an important prevention tool for preterm birth. Have a volunteer pair provide their findings to the class.*
Describe selected problems of preterm birth and the nursing goals	☐ Related problems (p. 306) – Inadequate respiratory function (p. 306)	⊠ PPT slides 9-35 *e* EILR IC images 4, 5 *e* EILR OBQ questions 3-7

OBJECTIVES	CONTENT	TEACHING RESOURCES
associated with each problem.	– Respiratory distress syndrome (p. 307) – Apnea (p. 309) – Neonatal hypoxia (p. 309) – Sepsis (p. 310) – Poor control of body temperature (p. 310) – Hypoglycemia and hypocalcemia (p. 310) – Increased tendency to bleed (p. 311) – Retinopathy of prematurity (p. 311) – Poor nutrition (p. 311) – Necrotizing enterocolitis (p. 311) – Immature kidneys (p. 311) – Jaundice (p. 312)	*e* EILR TB questions 2, 4, 2-8, 10-12, 14, 16, 18, 20, 26, 30 *e* ESLR IRQ questions 2, 5, 6 SG Learning Activities, questions 1, 3, 5-11 (p. 111) SG Review Questions, questions 3-5, 10-12, 14 (p. 114) SG Case Study, question 1 (p. 116) SG Applying Knowledge, question 5 (p. 117) **BOOK RESOURCES** Figure 13-4, Oxygen Administration Via an Oxygen Hood (p. 309) Figure 13-5, Signs of Respiratory Distress in a Preterm Infant (p. 309) Nursing Tip (p. 310) Nursing Tip (p. 311) Safety Alert (p. 311) Skill 13-1, Applying a Pulse Oximeter (p. 312) Box 13-1, Nursing Goals for the Preterm Newborn (p. 313) Nursing Care Plan 13-1, The Preterm Newborn (p. 314) Review Questions for the NCLEX® Examination, questions 2, 3, 5 (pp. 319-320) *Class Activity List the following complications associated with preterm birth on the board: inadequate respiratory function, respiratory distress syndrome, sepsis, poor control of body temperature, hypoglycemia, hypocalcemia, clotting problems, retinopathy, poor nutrition, and necrotizing enterocolitis. Under each category, have students provide a brief description of each problem, as well as the nursing goals and nursing interventions associated with it. List the correct answers on the board under the corresponding complication.* *Class Activity Demonstrate how to use an oxygen hood and pulse oximeter. Allow students to practice placing a pulse oximeter probe on an infant doll. Next, have students define normal values for heart rate, respiratory rate, oxygenation saturation, and temperature in infants. Also, have students list complications involved in oxygen therapy.*

13.1 Homework/Assignments:

13.1 Instructor's Notes/Student Feedback:

LESSON 13.2

CRITICAL THINKING QUESTION

A newborn of 29 weeks gestation is admitted to the neonatal intensive care unit (NICU). Her mother is a 17-year-old single mother who lives with her parents. The mother did not attend prenatal classes and has limited experience caring for infants or children. How can the nurse facilitate bonding between the mother and infant?

Guidelines: The infant's prematurity presents special challenges compounded by the mother's age and family situation. The nursing team should provide teaching and encouragement to help the mother gain confidence in her ability to take care of the infant. Encouraging the mother to touch her infant and participate in daily activities promotes bonding and parental attachment, and it is important for the infant's growth and development. The mother should be encouraged to talk about her feelings and should be assured that it is not unusual to be afraid or worried about taking care of the baby. The nurse should explain the different procedures or equipment used in the NICU and should assure the mother that a team of health care professionals will support her during her stay in the hospital and after discharge. Also, the mother's parents should be involved in the nurse's teaching sessions because they are part of her support system. The nurse should describe special considerations in caring for a premature infant, such as energy conservation and maintaining a neutral thermal environment. The nurse should observe the mother and her parents as they participate in the infant's care to verify understanding of the patient/family teaching. The nurse should also arrange for follow-up care after discharge.

OBJECTIVES	CONTENT	TEACHING RESOURCES
Describe the symptoms of cold stress and methods of maintaining thermoregulation.	☐ Special needs (p. 313) – Thermoregulation (warmth) (p. 313) – Incubator (p. 313) – Radiant heat (p. 314) – Kangaroo care (p. 314)	⊞ PPT slides 36-40 𝑒 EILR IC image 6 𝑒 EILR OBQ questions 8, 9 𝑒 EILR TB questions 9, 23, 24, 29 𝑒 ESLR IRQ question 3 SG Learning Activities, question 1 (p. 111) SG Review Questions, question 6 (p. 115) **BOOK RESOURCES** Figure 13-6, The Incubator (p. 313) Nursing Care Plan 13-1, The Preterm Newborn (p. 314) Skill 13-2, Kangaroo Care (p. 315) *Class Activity Divide the class into two groups. Have Group 1 list the symptoms of cold stress and the physiological causes of these symptoms in the preterm infant. Have Group 2 list the nursing assessments and care for promoting a neutral thermal environment. Then bring the two groups together to discuss how both lists are interrelated.* *Class Activity Demonstrate how to use an incubator, radiant crib warmer, and kangaroo care using an infant doll. Ask students to identify the advantages and disadvantages of each technique.*

OBJECTIVES	CONTENT	TEACHING RESOURCES
Contrast the techniques for feeding preterm and full-term newborns.	– Nutrition (p. 315) – Close observation (p. 316) – Positioning and nursing care (p. 316) ☐ Prognosis (p. 317)	⊠ PPT slides 41-44 *e* EILR IC image 7 *e* EILR TB questions 3, 5, 27 SG Learning Activities, questions 12-14 (p. 113) SG Review Questions, question 7 (p. 115) **BOOK RESOURCES** Table 13-1, Nursing Observations in Care of the Preterm Infant (p. 316) Figure 13-7, Infant Nesting (p. 316) *Class Activity Ask students to identify and list the physiological reasons why preterm infants face nutritional challenges, as well as the nurse's role in providing proper nutrition to the preterm infant.* *Class Activity Demonstrate how gavage feedings are performed, including the purpose of aspirating stomach contents prior to feeding. Ask students to explain when the nurse should withhold a feeding.*
Discuss two ways to help facilitate maternal-infant bonding for a preterm newborn.	☐ Family reaction (p. 317)	⊠ PPT slides 45, 46 *e* EILR IC image 8 SG Review Questions, question 9 (p. 115) SG Applying Knowledge, question 4 (p. 117) **BOOK RESOURCES** Figure 13-8, This Father Holds His Preterm Infant in a Moment of Bonding (p. 317) *Class Activity Have students identify ways to facilitate maternal and family bonding with a preterm infant immediately after birth, 48 hours postpartum in the NICU, and in the home setting after discharge.*
Describe the family reaction to preterm infants and nursing interventions.	☐ Family reaction (p. 317)	⊠ PPT slide 45 *e* EILR TB questions 13, 15 **BOOK RESOURCES** Figure 13-8, This Father Holds His Preterm Infant in a Moment of Bonding (p. 317) Nursing Tip (p. 318) *Class Activity Invite an NICU nurse to discuss common family reactions and challenges in caring for a preterm*

OBJECTIVES	CONTENT	TEACHING RESOURCES
		infant. How does the nurse facilitate family adjustment and bonding? How does the environment of the NICU affect the family and neonate? What are the advantages and disadvantages of technology in caring for infants? How is continuity of care provided once the infant is at home?
List three characteristics of the postterm infant.	■ The postterm newborn (p. 318) □ Physical characteristics (p. 318) □ Nursing care (p. 318) ■ Transporting the high-risk newborn (p. 318) ■ Discharge of the high-risk (preterm birth) newborn (p. 318)	⊞ PPT slides 47-53 *e* EILR OBQ question 1 *e* EILR TB questions 19, 21, 25 *e* ESLR IRQ question 4 SG Learning Activities, questions 1, 15, 16 (pp. 111, 114) SG Review Questions, questions 8, 13 (p. 115) SG Applying Knowledge, question 3 (p. 117) **BOOK RESOURCES** Class Activity *Have students compare and contrast the physical characteristics of the preterm and postterm infant. Also, have students discuss the reasons for the differences between the two and how they affect an infants' care.* Class Activity *Divide the class into small groups and have each group explain how placental deterioration contributes to postterm complications. Also, have the groups identify the proper nursing interventions for postterm newborns.*
Performance Evaluation		⊞ PPT slides 1-55 *e* EILR IC images 1-8 *e* EILR OBQ questions 1-10 *e* EILR TB questions 1-31 *e* ESLR IRQ questions 1-6 SG Learning Activities, questions 1-6 (pp. 111-114) SG Review Questions, questions 1-14 (pp. 114-116) SG Case Study, question 1 (p. 116) SG Thinking Critically, question 1 (p. 116) SG Applying Knowledge, questions 1-5 (pp. 116-117)

OBJECTIVES	CONTENT	TEACHING RESOURCES
		BOOK RESOURCES
		NCP CTQ 1 (p. 314)
		Review Questions for the NCLEX® Examination, questions 1-5 (pp. 319-320)

13.2 Homework/Assignments:

13.2 Instructor's Notes/Student Feedback:

13 | Lecture Outline
Preterm and Postterm Newborns

Slide 1

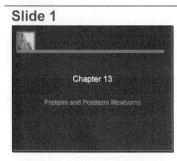

Chapter 13

Preterm and Postterm Newborns

Slide 2

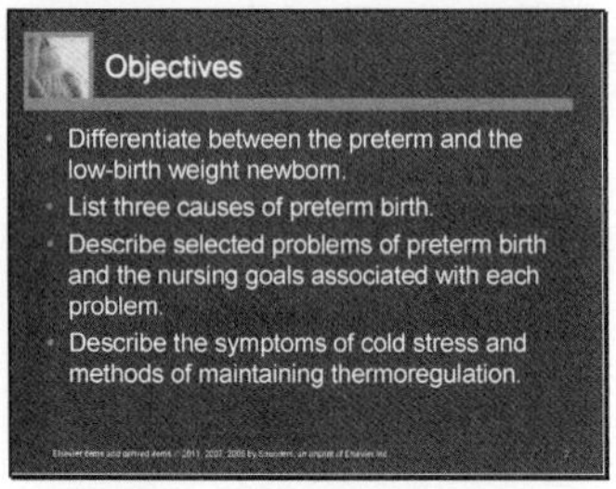

Objectives

- Differentiate between the preterm and the low-birth weight newborn.
- List three causes of preterm birth.
- Describe selected problems of preterm birth and the nursing goals associated with each problem.
- Describe the symptoms of cold stress and methods of maintaining thermoregulation.

Slide 3

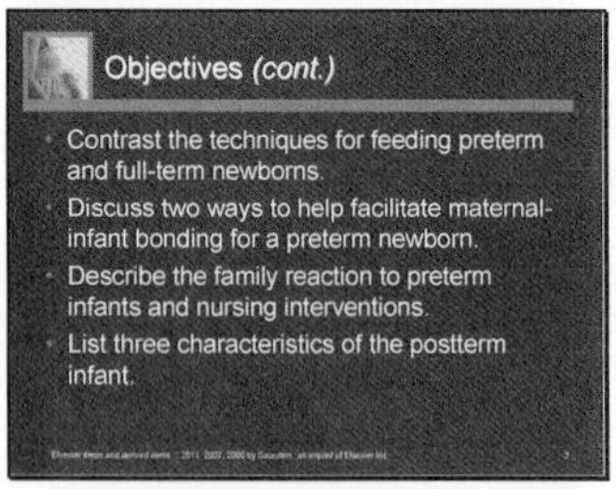

Objectives *(cont.)*

- Contrast the techniques for feeding preterm and full-term newborns.
- Discuss two ways to help facilitate maternal-infant bonding for a preterm newborn.
- Describe the family reaction to preterm infants and nursing interventions.
- List three characteristics of the postterm infant.

Slide 4

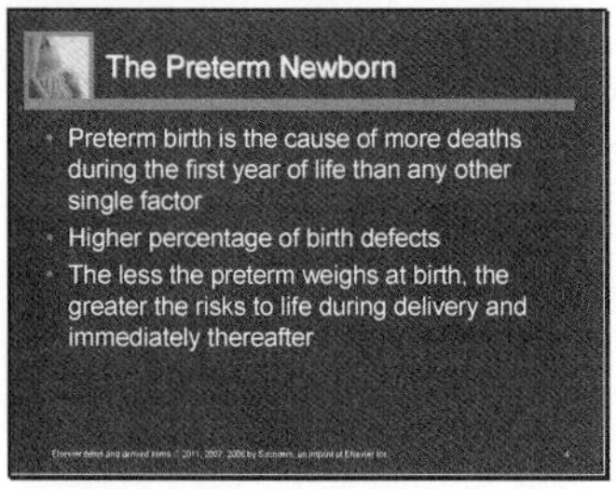

The Preterm Newborn

- Preterm birth is the cause of more deaths during the first year of life than any other single factor
- Higher percentage of birth defects
- The less the preterm weighs at birth, the greater the risks to life during delivery and immediately thereafter

---

Slide 5

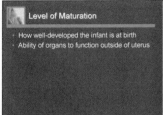

Gestational Age

- Actual time from conception to birth that the fetus remains in the uterus
- Preterm is less than 38 weeks
- Term is 38 to 42 weeks
- Postterm is greater than 42 weeks
  - Standardized method used to determine gestational age is Ballard score
    - Uses external characteristics and neurological development

Slide 6

Level of Maturation

- How well-developed the infant is at birth
- Ability of organs to function outside of uterus

- Discuss physical examination, observation of behavior, and family history as they apply to levels of maturation.

Slide 7

Causes of Preterm Birth

- Multiple births
- Maternal illness
- Hazards of actual pregnancy (e.g., GH)
- Placental abnormalities
  - Placenta previa
  - Premature separation of the placenta from uterine wall

- What maternal illnesses and hazards could cause preterm birth?

Slide 8

Possible Physical Characteristics of a Preterm Infant

- Skin transparent or loose
- Superficial veins visible on abdomen and scalp
- Lack of subcutaneous fat
- Lanugo covering forehead, shoulders, and arms
- Vernix caseosa abundant
- Extremities appear short
- Soles of feet have few creases
- Abdomen protrudes
- Nails are short
- Genitalia are small
- In the female, the labia majora may be open

- Discuss Figure 13-3 on page 308 and the physical characteristics listed.

Slide 9

Related Problems of Preterm Births

Leifer

Slide 10

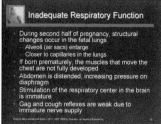

Inadequate Respiratory Function

- During second half of pregnancy, structural changes occur in the fetal lungs
  - Alveoli (air sacs) enlarge
  - Closer to capillaries in the lungs
- If born prematurely, the muscles that move the chest are not fully developed
- Abdomen is distended, increasing pressure on diaphragm
- Stimulation of the respiratory center in the brain is immature
- Gag and cough reflexes are weak due to immature nerve supply

Slide 11

Respiratory Distress Syndrome (RDS) Type 1

- Also called *hyaline membrane disease*
- Result of immature lungs, leads to decreased gas exchange
- Surfactant is a fatty protein that is high in lecithin, its presence is necessary for the lungs to absorb oxygen
  - Begins to form at 24 weeks gestation and by 34 weeks, if fetus is delivered, should be able to breathe adequately
  - If infant is premature, the surfactant level is insufficient

- How would you describe hyaline membrane disease?

Slide 12

Manifestations of RDS

- Can take up to several hours after birth to be manifested
- Respirations increase to 60 breaths/min or higher (tachypnea)
- The tachypnea may be accompanied by gruntlike sounds, nasal flaring, cyanosis, as well as intercostal and sternal retractions
- Edema, lassitude, and apnea occur as the condition worsens
- Mechanical ventilation may be necessary

- Describe intercostal and sternal retractions and the pathophysiology regarding the use of these accessory muscles.

Slide 13

Treatment for RDS

- If amniocentesis of mother while fetus is still in utero shows a low L/S ratio, the mother may be given corticosteroids to stimulate lung maturity 1 to 2 days before delivery
- In preterm infants, surfactant can be administered via ET tube at birth or when symptoms of RDS occur
- Improvement in the neonate's lung function is generally seen within 72 hours after administration

- What is the nurse's role in monitoring the neonate during the management of RDS?

Slide 14

Surfactant Production

- Can be altered
  - During cold stress
  - Hypoxia
  - Poor tissue perfusion

- Discuss the pathophysiology regarding these effects of surfactant production.

Slide 15

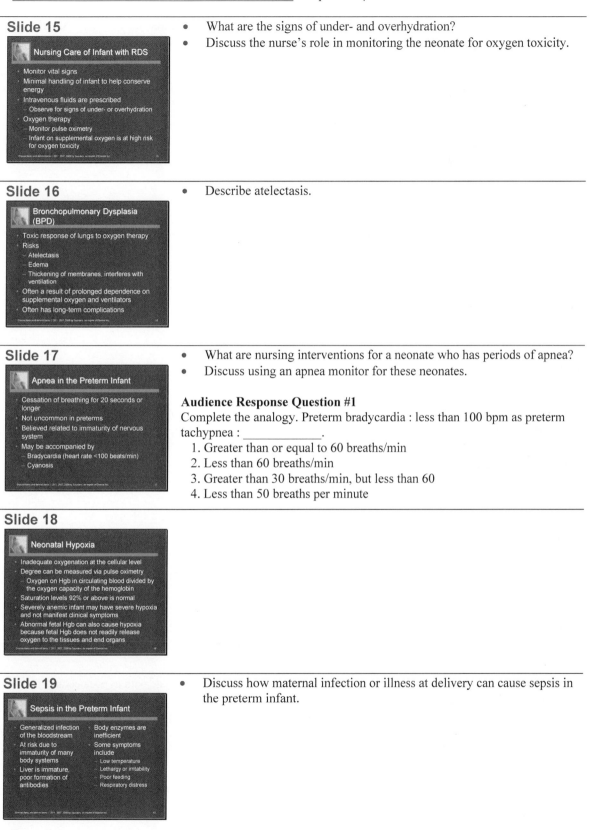

- What are the signs of under- and overhydration?
- Discuss the nurse's role in monitoring the neonate for oxygen toxicity.

Slide 16

- Describe atelectasis.

Slide 17

- What are nursing interventions for a neonate who has periods of apnea?
- Discuss using an apnea monitor for these neonates.

Audience Response Question #1
Complete the analogy. Preterm bradycardia : less than 100 bpm as preterm tachypnea : _____.
  1. Greater than or equal to 60 breaths/min
  2. Less than 60 breaths/min
  3. Greater than 30 breaths/min, but less than 60
  4. Less than 50 breaths per minute

Slide 18

Slide 19

- Discuss how maternal infection or illness at delivery can cause sepsis in the preterm infant.

Leifer

Slide 20

Treatment of Sepsis

- Administration of intravenous antimicrobials
- Maintenance of warmth and nutrition
- Close monitoring of vital signs
- Care should be organized to help infant conserve as much energy as possible
- Following Standard Precautions, including strict hand hygiene, is essential

- Which methods provide warmth and nutrition?
- Give an example of organized care to minimize energy expenditure.
- Discuss how standard precautions may protect the preterm neonate.

Slide 21

Poor Control of Body Temperature

- Lack of brown fat (body's own "insulation")
- Radiation from a surface area that is large in proportion to body weight
- Heat-regulating center of brain is immature
- Sweat glands are not functioning to capacity
- Preterm is inactive, has muscles that are weak/less resistant to cold; unable to shiver
- Preterm body position is one of leg extension
- High metabolism, prone to low blood glucose levels
- Can result in cold stress

Slide 22

Safety Alert

- Signs and symptoms of cold stress
  - Decreased skin temperature
  - Increased respiratory rate with periods of apnea
  - Bradycardia
  - Mottling of skin
  - Lethargy

Slide 23

Hypoglycemia

- Plasma glucose levels <40 mg/dL in a term infant and <30 mg/dl in preterm infant
- Preterm infants have not remained in utero long enough to build up stores of glycogen and fat
  - Aggravated by increased need for glycogen in the brain, heart, and other tissues
- Any condition that increases metabolism increases glucose needs
- Energy requirements place more stress on the already deficient stores

Slide 24

Hypocalcemia

- Calcium transported across placenta in higher quantities in third trimester
- *Early* hypocalcemia occurs when the parathyroid fails to respond to the preterm infant's low calcium levels
- *Late* hypocalcemia occurs about 1 week in infants who are fed cow's milk, as it increases serum phosphate levels causing serum calcium levels to fall

- Discuss the treatment for the preterm neonate with hypocalcemia.

Leifer

Slide 25

Increased Tendency to Bleed

- Blood is deficient in prothrombin
- Fragile capillaries of the head are susceptible to injury during birth, which can lead to intracranial hemorrhage
- Nursing care includes
  - Monitoring neurological status
  - Report bulging fontanels, lethargy, poor feeding, seizures
  - Slight Fowler's position
  - Unnecessary stimulation can increase intracerebral pressure

- Describe assessment of the preterm neonate's neurological status.
- Discuss the pathophysiology regarding bulging fontanels and the rationale for a slight Fowler's position.

Slide 26

Retinopathy of Prematurity (ROP)

- Separation and fibrosis of the retina, can lead to blindness
- Damage to immature retinal blood vessels thought to be caused by high oxygen levels in arterial blood
- Leading cause of blindness in infants weighing <1500 grams
- Has several stages
- Maintaining sufficient levels of vitamin E and avoiding excessively high concentrations of oxygen may help prevent ROP from occurring
- Cryosurgery may reduce long-term complications

Slide 27

Poor Nutrition

- Stomach capacity is small
- Sphincters at either end of stomach are immature
- Increased risk of regurgitation and vomiting
- Sucking and swallowing reflexes are immature
- Ability to absorb fat is poor
- Increased need for glucose and other nutrients to promote growth and prevent brain damage are contributing factors
- Parenteral or gavage feedings may be needed until infant's systems are more mature

- What is the nurse's role in providing parenteral and/or gavage feedings?

Slide 28

Necrotizing Enterocolitis (NEC)

- Acute inflammation of the bowel that leads to bowel necrosis
- Factors include
  - Diminished blood supply to bowel lining
    - Leads to hypoxia or sepsis
    - Causes a decrease in protective mucus
  - Results in bacterial invasion
  - Source of bacterial growth if receiving milk formula or hypertonic gavage feedings

Slide 29

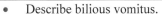

Signs of NEC

- Abdominal distention
- Bloody stools
- Diarrhea
- Bilious vomitus

- Describe bilious vomitus.

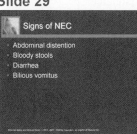

Leifer

Slide 30

> **Nursing Care of Infant with NEC**
> - Observing vital signs
>   - Measuring abdomen
>   - Auscultating for bowel sounds
> - Carefully resuming fluids as ordered
> - Maintaining infection prevention and control techniques
> - Surgical removal of the necrosed bowel may be indicated

- What infection control techniques should be used for an infant with NEC?

Slide 31

> **Immature Kidneys**
> - Cannot eliminate body wastes effectively
> - Contributes to electrolyte imbalance and disturbed acid-base relationships
> - Dehydration occurs easily
> - Tolerance to salt is limited
> - Susceptibility to edema is increased

Slide 32

> **Nursing Care of Infant with Immature Kidneys**
> - Accurate measurement of intake and output
> - Weigh diapers per hospital procedures
> - Urine output should be between 1 and 3 mL/kg/hr
> - Observe for signs of dehydration or overhydration
> - Document status of fontanels, tissue turgor, weight, and urinary output

- Give an example of a situation in which the nurse must determine whether the infant's output is adequate.

Slide 33

> **Jaundice**
> - Immature liver, contributes to condition called *icterus*
> - Causes skin and whites of eyes to assume a yellow-orange cast
> - Liver unable to clear blood of bile pigments which result from the normal postnatal destruction of RBCs
> - The higher the serum bilirubin level, the higher the jaundice and the greater the risk for neurological damage

- Describe icterus.

Slide 34

> **Jaundice *(cont.)***
> - An increase of >5 mg/dl in 24 hours or a bilirubin level above 12.9 mg/dl requires careful investigation
> - Pathological jaundice
>   - If occurs within 24 hours of birth, may be related to an abnormal condition such as ABO incompatibility
> - Breastfed infants can show signs of jaundice about 4 days after birth
> - Total serum bilirubin levels typically peak about 3 to 5 days after birth

- Should breastfeeding continue for infants with jaundice?
- Discuss the pathophysiology regarding peaked levels 3 to 5 days postbirth.

Audience Response Question #2
Physiologic jaundice occurs within 48 hours after birth.
1. True
2. False

Slide 35

Goals of Treating Jaundice

- Prevent kernicterus by preventing the rising bilirubin levels from staining the basal nuclei of the brain
- Nursing care goals should be to
  - Observe skin, sclera, and mucous membranes for signs of jaundice
  - Report the progression of jaundice from the face to the abdomen and feet
  - Monitor and report any abnormal lab results
  - Response to phototherapy

- Discuss the pathophysiology of phototherapy and the treatment of jaundice.

Slide 36

Special Needs of the Preterm Infant

Slide 37

Nursing Goals for the Preterm Newborn

- Improve respiration
- Maintain body heat
- Conserve energy
- Prevent infection
- Provide proper nutrition and hydration
- Give good skin care
- Observe infant carefully and record observations
- Support and encourage the parents

- In what ways can the nurse support and encourage the parents?

Slide 38

Incubators

- It is important for the nurse to know how to use the various types of incubators available in their health care facility in order to provide safe and effective care to the infant who is in one

- Discuss Figure 13-6 on page 313.

Slide 39

Radiant Heat Warmers

- Supplies overhead heat
- Allows easier access to infant

Slide 40

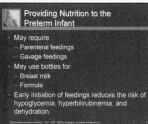

Kangaroo Care
- Uses skin-to-skin contact
- Infant wears only a diaper (and sometimes a cap) and is placed on the parent's naked chest
- The skin warms and calms the child
- Promotes bonding

• Discuss Skill 13-2 on page 315.

Slide 41

Providing Nutrition to the Preterm Infant
- May require
  - Parenteral feedings
  - Gavage feedings
- May use bottles for
  - Breast milk
  - Formula
- Early initiation of feedings reduces the risk of hypoglycemia, hyperbilirubinemia, and dehydration

Slide 42

Nursing Care Related to Nutrition
- Observe and record bowel sounds and passage of meconium stools
- For gavage feeding, aspiration of gastric contents prior to feeding is important
- If no residual received, it's safe to start the feeding
- If a higher-than-ordered limit of gastric contents is received, feeding may need to be held and the health care provider notified

• Why must gastric contents be aspirated prior to gavage feedings?

Slide 43

Positioning and Nursing Care
- Preterm is placed on the side or prone with head of mattress slightly elevated
  - Decreases respiratory effort, improves oxygenation
  - Promotes more organized sleep pattern and lessens physical activity that burns up energy needed for growth and development
- Should be compatible with drainage of secretions and prevention of aspiration
- Do not leave infant in one position for a long period of time, as it increases the risk of skin breakdown

Slide 44

Prognosis for Preterm Infant
- Growth rate nears the term infant's about the second year of life, but very-low-birth weight infants may not catch up, especially if chronic illness, insufficient nutritional intake, or inadequate caregiving has occurred
- Growth and development of the preterm infant are based on
  - Current age minus the number of weeks before term the infant was born
  - This calculation helps prevent unrealistic expectations for the infant

Slide 45

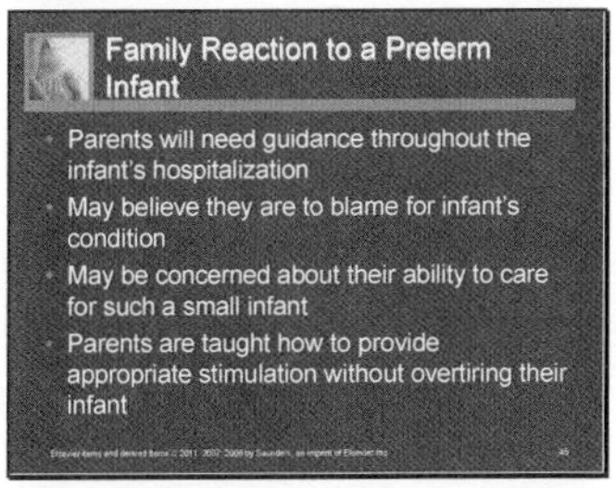

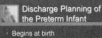

Family Reaction to a Preterm Infant

- Parents will need guidance throughout the infant's hospitalization
- May believe they are to blame for infant's condition
- May be concerned about their ability to care for such a small infant
- Parents are taught how to provide appropriate stimulation without overtiring their infant

- In what ways could a parent overtire an infant?
- What nursing interventions would assist the family in managing a preterm infant?

Slide 46

Discharge Planning of the Preterm Infant

- Begins at birth
- Parents will need to demonstrate and practice routine and/or specialized care
- Home nursing visits may be required to assess home, infant, and family

Slide 47

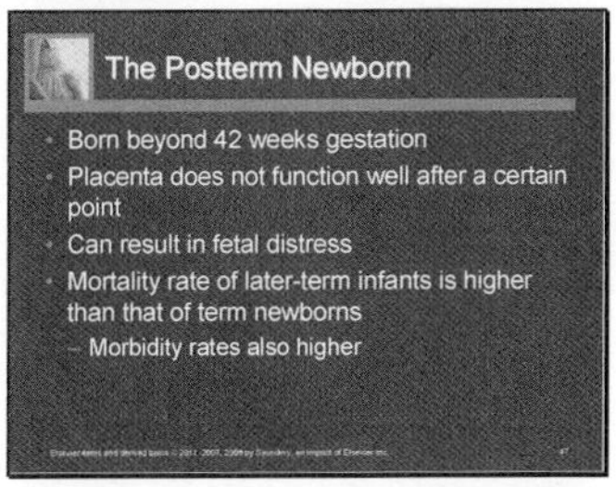

The Postterm Newborn

- Born beyond 42 weeks gestation
- Placenta does not function well after a certain point
- Can result in fetal distress
- Mortality rate of later-term infants is higher than that of term newborns
  - Morbidity rates also higher

Slide 48

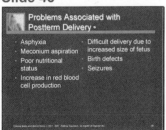

Problems Associated with Postterm Delivery

- Asphyxia
- Meconium aspiration
- Poor nutritional status
- Increase in red blood cell production
- Difficult delivery due to increased size of fetus
- Birth defects
- Seizures

- Discuss the pathophysiology of each complication listed.

Slide 49

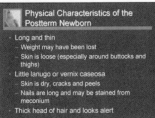

Physical Characteristics of the Postterm Newborn

- Long and thin
  - Weight may have been lost
  - Skin is loose (especially around buttocks and thighs)
- Little lanugo or vernix caseosa
  - Skin is dry, cracks and peels
  - Nails are long and may be stained from meconium
- Thick head of hair and looks alert

Slide 50

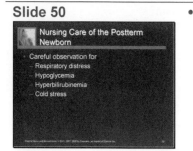

Nursing Care of the Postterm Newborn

- Careful observation for
  - Respiratory distress
  - Hypoglycemia
  - Hyperbilirubinemia
  - Cold stress

- How does the nurse assess each of these conditions?

Slide 51

Transporting the High-Risk Newborn

- Stabilization of the newborn prior to transport is essential
- Baseline data such as vital signs and blood work should also be obtained and provided to the transport team members
- Copies of all medical records are made, including the mother's prenatal history and how the delivery progressed

Slide 52

Transporting the High-Risk Newborn *(cont.)*

- Ensure infant is properly identified and that the mother has the same identification number band
- Provide parents with name and location of the NICU the infant is being transported to, including telephone numbers
- If possible, allow parents a few moments with their infant prior to transporting
- If possible, take a picture of the baby and give to parents

Slide 53

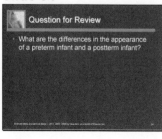

Discharge of the High-Risk Newborn

- Parents must be familiar with infant's care
- The newborn's behavioral patterns are discussed and realistic expectations are reviewed
- Communication can be maintained with the hospital through "warm lines"
- Social services may be of help in ensuring the home environment is satisfactory and special needs of the infant can be met
- Support group referrals are given
- Newborn CPR techniques are reviewed

- What is the nurse's role in the discharge process of a high-risk newborn?

Slide 54

Question for Review

- What are the differences in the appearance of a preterm infant and a postterm infant?

Slide 55

Review

- Objectives
- Key Terms
- Key Points
- Online Resources
- Question for Review
- Review Questions

14 The Newborn with a Perinatal Injury or Congenital Malformation

TEACHING FOCUS

This chapter provides an overview of congenital birth defects—abnormalities of structure, function, and metabolism that may result in a physical or mental disability, shortened lifespan, or fatality. Students will be introduced to the five major classifications of defects, including a detailed description of the most common. Students will have the opportunity to learn the characteristics of each defect, prevention techniques (where applicable), key elements of assessment and symptoms, appropriate treatments, and nursing care. Abnormalities affecting newborns, as well as those occurring in older children, affect whole families emotionally, physically, and financially. Students will have the opportunity to understand the nurse's role as a frontline health care provider in helping families cope with the news of a birth defect by providing education and supportive care.

MATERIALS AND RESOURCES

☐ Biliblanket or other warming device (Lesson 14.2)
☐ Computer and PowerPoint projector (all lessons)
☐ Infant-sized doll (Lesson 14.2)
☐ Internet access (Lesson 14.1)
☐ List of online resources for more information on specific defects (Lesson 14.1)

☐ Photocopy of Figure 14-3, Shunting Procedure for Hydrocephalus (Lesson 14.1)
☐ Phototherapy Bilibed or facsimile (Lesson 14.2)
☐ Sample body cast or Pavlik harness (Lesson 14.2)
☐ Samples of Lofenalac, Phenyl-free, and Phenex-2 (Lesson 14.2)

LESSON CHECKLIST

Preparations for this lesson include:

- Lecture
- Guest speaker: Hospital social worker
- Evaluation of student knowledge and skills needed to perform all entry-level activities related to newborns with a congenital malformation, including:
  ○ Knowledge of the key terms related to common birth defects
  ○ Assessing early symptoms of a wide range of birth defects
  ○ Developing an appropriate nursing care plan for patients with diagnosed birth defects
  ○ Understanding effective nursing interventions for birth defects affecting various body systems

KEY TERMS

birth defect (p. 321)
cheiloplasty (p. 328)
cleft lip (p. 327)
cleft palate (p. 328)
clubfoot (p. 329)
congenital malformation (p. 322)
erythroblastosis fetalis (p. 337)
habilitation (p. 326)
hydrocephalus (p. 322)

hyperbilirubinemia (p. 339)
kernicterus (p. 339)
macrosomia (p. 344)
meconium aspiration syndrome (MAS) (p. 344)
meningocele (p. 325)
meningomyelocele (p. 326)
myelodysplasia (p. 325)
neonatal abstinence syndrome (NAS) (p. 344)

Ortolani's sign (p. 330)
Pavlik harness (p. 331)
phototherapy (p. 339)
RhoGAM (p. 339)
shunt (p. 323)
spica cast (p. 331)
spina bifida (p. 325)
transient tachypnea of the newborn (TTN) (p. 343)
transillumination (p. 322)

ADDITIONAL RESOURCES
TEACH PPT slide(s) Chapter 14, 1-102
EILR IC image(s) Chapter 14, 1-17
EILR OBQ question(s) Chapter 14, 1-10
EILR TB question(s) Chapter 14, 1-31
ESLR IRQ question(s) Chapter 14, 1-7
SG Chapter 14, pp. 119-128

Legend

PPT
TEACH
PowerPoint
Slides

EILR
EVOLVE Instructor
Learning Resources:
Image Collection (IC),
Open-Book Quizzes
(OBQ), Test Bank (TB)

ESLR
EVOLVE Student
Learning Resources:
Interactive Review
Questions (IRQ) for
the NCLEX®
Examination

SG
Study Guide

CTQ
Critical Thinking
Question in
Nursing Care Plan
(NCP CTQ) or Get
Ready for the
NCLEX! (GRN
CTQ)

Class Activities are indicated in ***bold italic***.

Introduction to Maternity & Pediatric Nursing, 6th ed.

LESSON 14.1

PRETEST

1. An example of an inborn error of metabolism is
   a. congenital hip dysplasia.
   c. maple syrup urine disease.
   b. hydramnios.
   d. fetal alcohol syndrome.

2. The classic sign of hydrocephalus is
   a. seizures.
   c. Dandy-Walker syndrome.
   b. sunken fontanels.
   d. increase in head size.

3. What prenatal intervention can reduce the incidence of neural tube defects?
   a. folic acid supplements before conception and during pregnancy
   b. adequate sleep during pregnancy
   c. elimination of caffeine
   d. prophylactic antibiotics during labor

4. Which type of spina bifida is the most serious?
   a. spina bifida occulta
   c. spina bifida cystica meningomyelocele
   b. spina bifida cystica meningocele
   d. myelodysplasia

5. Postoperative care following a cheiloplasty includes
   a. positioning the infant in a prone position.
   b. preventing the infant from sucking and crying.
   c. avoiding use of restraints.
   d. using a bottle for feedings.

6. What assessment finding indicates hip dysplasia?
   a. skin fold symmetry
   c. limited abduction on affected side
   b. lengthening of femur on affected side
   d. knee is higher on affected side

7. What dietary substance(s) should be restricted for a child with phenylketonuria (PKU)?
   a. breast milk
   c. chocolate flavoring
   b. Lofenalac
   d. most meat, dairy products, and diet drinks

8. Down syndrome results from
   a. a chromosomal abnormality.
   c. a blood disorder.
   b. a metabolic defect.
   d. perinatal damage.

9. Jaundice occurring during the first 24 hours postpartum
   a. is called *physiological jaundice*.
   c. is a normal finding.
   b. is called *pathological jaundice*.
   d. causes a sweet odor of the urine and sweat.

10. *Macrosomia* refers to
    a. anemia caused by Rh-incompatibility.
    c. an infant large for gestational age.
    b. intracranial hemorrhage.
    d. cushingoid appearance.

Answers
| 1. c | 3. a | 5. b | 7. d | 9. b |
| 2. d | 4. c | 6. c | 8. a | 10. c |

BACKGROUND ASSESSMENT

Question: Why is prenatal care important in the prevention of birth defects such as spina bifida?
Answer: The cause of many birth defects is unknown but often relates to the interplay of factors such as genetics, uterine environment, and exposure to teratogens. Spina bifida is a congenital neural tube malformation that has a significantly reduced incidence when taking 0.4 mg of folic acid before conception and through the first 12 weeks of pregnancy when the neural tube is developing.

Question: How have early detection methods and administration of RhoGAM significantly reduced erythroblastosis fetalis?

Answer: Erythroblastosis fetalis (EF) is a hemolytic disease of the newborn caused when maternal antibodies destroy the fetus's red blood cells, which can lead to anemia and heart failure in the infant. Sensitization (or isoimmunization) happens when an Rh-negative mother develops antibodies against her Rh-positive fetus. Although the maternal/fetal blood system is separate during pregnancy, small leaks can cause sensitization, as can an ectopic pregnancy, an abortion, or a blood transfusion. The risk of EF is lower during a mother's first pregnancy, but subsequent pregnancies with an Rh-positive fetus increase the maternal antibodies produced and therefore increase complications. Maternal health histories and blood typing during prenatal care identify women at risk. Administering an intramuscular injection of RhoGAM, an immune globulin that prevents further development of Rh-positive antibodies, can prevent EF. The injection is given after a normal delivery, an ectopic pregnancy, an abortion, amniocentesis, or other circumstances when bleeding during pregnancy occurs. RhoGAM also may be given at 28 weeks of gestation.

CRITICAL THINKING QUESTION

Why is the nursing role of managing communication among parents and health care professionals essential in caring for an infant with a congenital malformation? What nursing interventions are generally appropriate for newborns with birth defects?

Guidelines: Caring for a newborn can be stressful for any parent, but the stress is compounded when the infant is born with a congenital malformation. To meet the frequently complex health care needs of the infant with a birth defect, a multidisciplinary team of physicians, nurses, nutritionists, physical therapists, social workers, and home care professionals must work together to provide care to the entire family. A primary nursing role is facilitating communication among the various disciplines to ensure continuity of care as well as to educate and emotionally support the family. Newborns with birth defects often require admission to the neonatal intensive care unit (NICU), which has a high-tech environment that may intimidate parents. The nurse can alleviate anxiety by giving simple explanations and by encouraging parents to participate in their infant's care as much as possible. Often the mother is discharged before the newborn, which can affect family bonding with the newborn. By providing sensitive encouragement and practical advice, a nurse can increase the parents' sense of control and connection with their infant. Facilitating referrals to support groups dedicated to the specific congenital malformation is another important nursing role.

OBJECTIVES	CONTENT	TEACHING RESOURCES
List and define the more common disorders of the newborn.	■ Birth defects (p. 321)	⊠▤ PPT slides 5-7 𝒆 EILR OBQ question 1 **BOOK RESOURCES** Box 14-1, Classification of Birth Defects (p. 322) ▸ Discuss ways in which a nurse can be an important frontline resource for families of a newborn with a congenital malformation. *Class Activity **Compile and distribute a list of websites for organizations providing information and support for those affected by some of the more common birth defects (see Online Resources, p. 345). Use a computer with an Internet connection to access some of these websites during class.*** *Class Activity **Invite a hospital social worker to class to discuss the emotional, physical, and financial toll that birth defects can take on a family.***

OBJECTIVES	CONTENT	TEACHING RESOURCES
		Class Activity Assign each student one congenital malformation and ask them to research a support group or foundation dedicated to that disorder. What services can the organization provide to families that have a newborn with the disorder? Is there any information included of benefit to nurses caring for affected families? (For students to prepare for this activity, see Homework/Assignments #1.)
Describe the classifications of birth defects.	■ Malformations present at birth (p. 322)	⊠▤ PPT slides 6, 7 📖SG SG Learning Activities, question 2 (p. 119) **BOOK RESOURCES** Box 14-1, Classification of Birth Defects (p. 322) *Class Activity Ask students to identify five classifications of birth defects, then compare and contrast them.* *Class Activity Name a particular birth defect and ask students to respond with the correct classification of each disorder.*
Outline the nursing care for the newborn with hydrocephalus.	☐ Nervous system (p. 322) – Neural tube defects (p. 322) – Hydrocephalus (p. 322)	⊠▤ PPT slides 8-17 𝒆 EILR IC images 1-3 𝒆 EILR OBQ question 2 𝒆 EILR TB questions 1-4, 6, 28, 29, 31 𝒆 ESLR IRQ questions 1, 7 📖SG SG Learning Activities, questions 1-6 (p. 119) 📖SG SG Case Study, question 2 (p. 127) **BOOK RESOURCES** Figure 14-1, Cerebrospinal Fluid Circulation (p. 323) Figure 14-2, Marked Hydrocephalus with "Setting Sun" Sign of the Eyes (p. 323) Figure 14-3, Shunting Procedure for Hydrocephalus (p. 324) Review Questions for the NCLEX® Examination, question 2 (p. 345) *Class Activity Divide the class into pairs and provide each pair with a photocopy of Figure 14-3, Shunting Procedure for Hydrocephalus. Then, have the pairs take turns role-playing a nurse explaining to a parent the pathophysiology and treatment for his or her infant with hydrocephalus. Next, have students discuss what they learned from the role-play.*

OBJECTIVES	CONTENT	TEACHING RESOURCES
		Class Activity Divide the class into three groups. Have Group 1 discuss preoperative nursing care for hydrocephalus, Group 2 discuss postoperative nursing care, and Group 3 discuss home care visits and the parent teaching and assessment that occurs after discharge. Then, have each group present its findings to the class.
Discuss the prevention of neural tube anomalies.	– Spina bifida (p. 325)	⊠ PPT slides 18-31
		e EILR IC images 4-6
		e EILR OBQ question 3
		e EILR TB question 30
		e ESLR IRQ question 2
		SG Learning Activities, questions 1, 7, 9 (p. 119)
		SG Case Study, question 1 (p. 127)
		BOOK RESOURCES
		Figure 14-4, Types of Spina Bifida (p. 325)
		Figure 14-5, A Child with a Hairy Patch in the Lumbosacral Region Indicating the Site of a Spina Bifida Occulta (p. 325)
		Nursing Tip (p. 326)
		Figure 14-6, Incontinence in the Newborn (p. 327)
		Review Questions for the NCLEX® Examination, question 3 (p. 345)
		Class Activity Using the library or the Internet, have students find one research article discussing the benefits of folic acid. They should summarize the information from the article in easy-to-understand language to use as a teaching tool for an education session with a pregnant woman. (For students to prepare for this activity, see Homework/Assignments #2.)
		Class Activity Students should identify foods high in folic acid and the recommended dosage of folic acid to be taken prior to conception and during pregnancy.

Leifer

OBJECTIVES	CONTENT	TEACHING RESOURCES
Outline the preoperative and postoperative nursing care of a newborn with spina bifida cystica.	– Spina bifida (p. 325)	⊠▪ PPT slides 25-31 *e* EILR IC image 6 *e* EILR TB question 5 🔖 SG Learning Activities, question 9 (p. 119) **BOOK RESOURCES** Figure 14-5, A Child with a Hairy Patch in the Lumbosacral Region Indicating the Site of a Spina Bifida Occulta (p. 325) Figure 14-6, Incontinence in the Newborn (p. 327) *Class Activity Divide the class into two groups. Have Group 1 describe the preoperative care for a newborn with spina bifida cystica and Group 2 do the same for postoperative care. Have the two groups present their information in a class discussion.* *Class Activity Have students list at least five nursing objectives related to the care of a newborn with spina bifida cystica. Discuss the specific preoperative and postoperative nursing interventions.*

14.1 Homework/Assignments:

1. Assign each student one congenital malformation and ask them to research a support group or foundation dedicated to that disorder. What services can the organization provide to families that have a newborn with the malformation?

2. Using the library or the Internet, have students find one research article discussing the benefits of folic acid. They should summarize the information from the article in easy-to-understand language to use as a teaching tool for an education session with a pregnant woman.

14.1 Instructor's Notes/Student Feedback:

LESSON 14.2

CRITICAL THINKING QUESTION

A 7-pound newborn who was born breech has limited abduction of the left leg and a positive Barlow's test. What other physical findings would one expect and what teaching should the nurse provide to the newborn's parents?

Guidelines: The limited abduction of the leg is a classic sign of developmental hip dysplasia. Other signs include asymmetrical skinfolds and a shortened femur on the affected side. Ortolani's sign is a diagnostic indicator present when the thigh is abducted and a "click" is heard, and the physician detects the instability of the newborn's hip. Ultrasound or x-rays confirm the diagnosis. The nurse can review with the newborn's parents the common occurrence of developmental hip dysplasia, especially among girls and with breech deliveries. Explain that the hip joint is a ball and socket joint. Bailey's acetabulum (the "socket") is shallow and allows the head of her femur (the "ball") to dislocate. Treatment is aimed at keeping the hips flexed and abducted so that the socket deepens to keep the femur in place. A Pavlik harness worn for 4 to 8 weeks can often correct the dislocation. In some cases, traction with a body spica cast or surgery may be required. The nurse should review with the parents what the Pavlik harness looks like, how to maintain the harness, and how to keep it clean. The nurse should also explain that the newborn will be checked frequently during follow-up visits to verify the correct fit of the harness and that ultrasound or x-rays will be used to confirm proper hip placement.

OBJECTIVES	CONTENT	TEACHING RESOURCES
Differentiate between cleft lip and cleft palate.	☐ Gastrointestinal system (p. 327) – Cleft lip (p. 327) – Cleft palate (p. 328)	🖼 PPT slides 32-41 𝒆 EILR IC image 7 𝒆 EILR OBQ question 4 𝒆 EILR TB questions 7-10, 19 📖 SG Learning Activities, questions 1, 10 (pp. 119, 121) 📖 SG Applying Knowledge, question 3 (p. 128) **BOOK RESOURCES** Figure 14-7, An Infant with a Unilateral Cleft Lip and Palate (p. 327) Safety Alert (p. 329) *Class Activity Have students create a table that lists the characteristics, nursing goals, and interventions for a newborn with a cleft lip and cleft palate. Ask volunteers to present their tables to the class.* *Class Activity Have students list the complications associated with a cleft palate. Lead a class discussion to identify the ancillary health professionals who can assist in caring for problems associated with a cleft palate.*

OBJECTIVES	CONTENT	TEACHING RESOURCES
Discuss the early signs of developmental hip dysplasia.	☐ Musculoskeletal system (p. 329) – Clubfoot (p. 329) – Developmental hip dysplasia (p. 330)	⊠ PPT slides 42-54 𝑒 EILR IC images 8-11 𝑒 EILR OBQ questions 5, 6 𝑒 EILR TB questions 11, 12, 16, 22, 26 𝑒 ESLR IRQ question 3 SG Learning Activities, questions 11-14 (pp. 119, 121) **BOOK RESOURCES** Figure 14-8, Clubfoot (p. 329) Nursing Tip (p. 330) Figure 14-9, Early Signs of Dislocation of the Right Hip (p. 331) Figure 14-10, The Pavlik Harness (p. 331) Figure 14-11, A, Infant in a Spica Body Cast. B, Traction Is Sometimes Necessary Before Surgery or Casting (p. 332) Nursing Care Plan 14-1, The Infant or Child with a Spica Cast (p. 333) Skill 14-1, Technique for Turning the Child in a Body Cast (p. 334) Review Questions for the NCLEX® Examination, questions 4, 5 (p. 345) *Class Activity **Demonstrate the use of casts and harnesses. Discuss the purpose of the casts and harnesses, and then allow students to practice applying them.*** *Class Activity **Using an infant-sized doll (or infant simulator that allows for Barlow's test), demonstrate how to assess for hip dislocation. Allow students to practice the assessment techniques.*** *Class Activity **Have students call out the early signs of hip dislocation and differentiate between Barlow's test and Ortolani's sign.***
Discuss the dietary needs of a newborn with phenylketonuria.	■ Metabolic defects (p. 332) ☐ Phenylketonuria (p. 332) ☐ Maple syrup urine disease (p. 335) ☐ Galactosemia (p. 335)	⊠ PPT slides 55-68 𝑒 EILR OBQ question 7 𝑒 EILR TB questions 13, 14 𝑒 ESLR IRQ question 4 SG Learning Activities, questions 15, 16 (p. 122) **BOOK RESOURCES**

OBJECTIVES	CONTENT	TEACHING RESOURCES
		Safety Alert (p. 334) ▸ Discuss why aspartame is contraindicated in PKU and what products contain aspartame. *Class Activity Ask students to define the following terms: phenylalanine, phenylalanine hydroxylase, tyrosine, phenylpyruvic acid, and Guthrie blood test. Students should then explain the significance of these terms in the context of PKU.* *Class Activity Ask students to list the maintenance range for serum phenylalanine and the implications of values above or below the normal range. Discuss the Guthrie blood test and the importance of early detection and treatment of PKU. Discuss the methods and recommended frequency for monitoring levels of phenylalanine in an infant with PKU.* *Class Activity Bring in samples of Lofenalac, Phenyl-free, and Phenex-2 to demonstrate protein substitutes for the different stages of child development. Discuss the dietary needs of infants with PKU. Which foods should be favored, and which foods should be avoided?*

14.2 Homework/Assignments:

14.2 Instructor's Notes/Student Feedback:

ELSEVIER

LESSON 14.3

CRITICAL THINKING QUESTION

A newborn was delivered by cesarean section 12 hours ago. The nurse blanches the newborn's skin over his clavicle and notes a yellow-orange tinge. The nurse also notes scleral yellowing. What is the appropriate nursing action in response to these signs and what treatment might the physician order?
Guidelines: The nurse should promptly notify the physician of her findings, which suggest pathological jaundice. Laboratory tests to evaluate bilirubin levels will be ordered, and phototherapy and exchange transfusion might be ordered, depending on the serum bilirubin levels. If phototherapy is ordered, the nurse should place the newborn in an incubator with phototherapy lights. His eyes will be covered with patches to protect them from the high-intensity light. He will wear a diaper to protect his gonads. The newborn will be repositioned frequently to protect his skin integrity and to provide adequate exposure of his entire body to the phototherapy. He will be at risk for impaired skin integrity because frequent loose stools result from his body's increased excretion of bilirubin. The nurse will assess hydration status and will monitor frequent feedings that will support his nutritional status and promote excretion of the bilirubin. The nurse will also monitor the newborn's body temperature in order to provide a neutral thermal environment. The nurse will check laboratory values and report any abnormal levels or spread of jaundice discoloration. The nurse will also provide information to the newborn's parents about his condition and the treatment interventions.

OBJECTIVES	CONTENT	TEACHING RESOURCES
Discuss the care of the newborn with Down syndrome.	■ Chromosomal abnormalities (p. 335) ☐ Down syndrome (p. 335)	▣ PPT slides 69-76 𝒆 EILR IC image 12 𝒆 EILR TB questions 15, 23, 24 𝒆 ESLR IRQ question 6 📖 SG Learning Activities, questions 1, 17, 18 (pp. 119, 122-123) 📖 SG Applying Knowledge, questions 1, 2 (p. 128) **BOOK RESOURCES** Figure 14-12, Down syndrome (p. 336) Table 14-1, Time of Occurrence of Development Milestones in Normal Children and Those with Down Syndrome (p. 337) Table 14-2, Time of Occurrence of Self-Help Skills in Normal Children and Those with Down Syndrome (p. 337) *Class Activity **Lead a class discussion of the risk factors and physical characteristics associated with Down syndrome.*** *Class Activity **Divide the class into five groups to devise a nursing care plan for a Down syndrome newborn. Assign each group one of the following areas: thermoregulation, cardiorespiratory system, gastrointestinal system, infection, and psychosocial adjustment of the family. Discuss appropriate nursing interventions for each area.*** *Class Activity **Ask students to describe other health problems that are likely to occur during the lifespan of a***

OBJECTIVES	CONTENT	TEACHING RESOURCES
		person with Down syndrome. What is the expected longevity of a person with Down syndrome?
Outline the causes and treatment of hemolytic disease of the newborn (erythroblastosis fetalis).	■ Perinatal injuries (p. 337) □ Hemolytic disease of the newborn: erythroblastosis fetalis (p. 337)	⊠ PPT slides 77-85 *e* EILR IC image 13 *e* EILR TB question 17 SG Learning Activities, questions 1, 19, 20 (p. 119) SG Applying Knowledge, question 5 (p. 128) **BOOK RESOURCES** Box 14-2, Terms Helpful in Understanding Rh Sensitization (p. 338) Box 14-3, ABO Incompatibility (p. 338) Figure 14-13, Maternal Sensitization Producing Erythroblastosis in the Newborn (p. 338) Nursing Tip (p. 339) Safety Alert (p. 339) *Class Activity Provide students with a list of the following terms: antigen, antibody, Coombs' test, sensitization, RhoGAM, erythroblastosis fetalis, anemia, hydrops fetalis, anasarca, and pathological jaundice. Ask students to define the terms and identify the birth defect(s) with which they are associated.* *Class Activity Ask students to describe the process of sensitization depicted in Figure 14-13 (p. 338).* *Class Activity Ask students to describe when RhoGAM should be administered. What are the indications for RhoGAM administration? What route is used to administer RhoGAM to Rh-negative mothers?*
Devise a plan of care for a newborn receiving phototherapy.	□ Hemolytic disease of the newborn: erythroblastosis fetalis (p. 337)	⊠ PPT slides 86-89 *e* EILR IC images 14, 15 *e* EILR OBQ questions 8, 9 *e* EILR TB questions 18, 20 SG Applying Knowledge, question 4 (p. 128) **BOOK RESOURCES** Figure 14-14, Phototherapy (p. 340) Nursing Tips (p. 340) Nursing Care Plan 14-2, The Infant Receiving Phototherapy (pp. 341-342)

OBJECTIVES	CONTENT	TEACHING RESOURCES
		Figure 14-15, Phototherapy Bilibed (p. 343)
		Box 14-4, Phototherapy Tips (p. 343)
		Figure 14-16, Biliblanket plus High Output Phototherapy System (p. 343)
		Class Activity Divide the class into seven groups and assign each group one of the nursing diagnoses in Nursing Care Plan 14-2 (pp. 341-342). Using an infant model and a phototherapy Bilibed (or something similar), have students demonstrate how phototherapy is provided to a neonate in relationship to the group's nursing diagnosis.
Describe home phototherapy.	☐ Hemolytic disease of the newborn: erythroblastosis fetalis (p. 337)	⊠ PPT slide 89 *e* EILR IC image 16 SG Learning Activities, question 21 (p. 124) **BOOK RESOURCES** Figure 14-16, Biliblanket Plus High Output Phototherapy System (p. 343) Box 14-4, Phototherapy Tips (p. 343) *Class Activity Divide the class into small groups and have each group develop discharge instructions for parents taking home an infant requiring home phototherapy.*
Describe the symptoms of increased intracranial pressure.	☐ Intracranial hemorrhage (p. 340) ☐ Transient tachypnea of the newborn (p. 343) ☐ Meconium aspiration syndrome (p. 344) ☐ Neonatal abstinence syndrome (p. 344)	⊠ PPT slides 90-97 *e* EILR OBQ question 10 *e* EILR TB questions 25, 27 *e* ESLR IRQ question 5 SG Learning Activities, questions 1, 22-24 (pp. 119, 124) **BOOK RESOURCES** Review Questions for the NCLEX® Examination, question 1 (p. 345) *Class Activity Ask students to identify the signs and symptoms of increasing intracranial pressure.* *Class Activity Lead a class discussion on the pathophysiology of intracranial hemorrhage and obstetric complications that can lead to it.*
Discuss the assessment and nursing care of a newborn with	■ Infant of a diabetic mother (p. 344)	⊠ PPT slides 98-100 *e* EILR IC image 17

OBJECTIVES	CONTENT	TEACHING RESOURCES
macrosomia.		**e** EILR TB question 21
		SG SG Learning Activities, questions 1, 25 (p. 119, 124)
		BOOK RESOURCES
		Figure 14-17, Macrosomia (p. 344)
		▶ Discuss the nursing assessments required and interventions needed to help the newborn of a diabetic mother.
		Class Activity Ask students to list the areas of assessment that would be observed in a newborn with and without macrosomia. What nursing interventions are needed? What parent teaching is required?
Performance Evaluation		PPT slides 1-102
		e EILR IC images 1-17
		e EILR OBQ questions 1-10
		e EILR TB questions 1-31
		e ESLR IRQ questions 1-7
		SG SG Learning Activities, questions 1-25 (pp. 119-124)
		SG SG Review Questions, questions 1-21 (pp. 125-127)
		SG SG Case Study, questions 1-2 (p. 27)
		SG SG Applying Knowledge, questions 1-5 (p. 128)
		BOOK RESOURCES
		NCP CTQ 1 (p. 333)
		NCP CTQ 1 (p. 342)
		Review Questions for the NCLEX® Examination, questions 1-5 (p. 345)

14.3 Homework/Assignments:

14.3 Instructor's Notes/Student Feedback:

Lecture Outline

14 The Newborn with a Perinatal Injury or Congenital Malformation

Slide 1

Chapter 14

The Newborn with a Perinatal Injury
or Congenital Malformation

Slide 2

Objectives

- List and define the more common disorders of the newborn.
- Describe the classifications of birth defects.
- Outline the nursing care for the infant with hydrocephalus.
- Describe the symptoms of increased intracranial pressure.
- Discuss the prevention of neural tube anomalies.

Slide 3

Objectives *(cont.)*

- Outline the preoperative and postoperative nursing care of a newborn with spina bifida cystica.
- Differentiate between cleft lip and cleft palate.
- Discuss the dietary needs of an infant with phenylketonuria.
- Discuss the early signs of developmental hip dysplasia.

Slide 4

Objectives *(cont.)*

- Discuss the care of the newborn with Down syndrome.
- Outline the causes and treatment of hemolytic disease of the newborn (erythroblastosis fetalis).
- Devise a plan of care for an infant receiving phototherapy.
- Describe home phototherapy.
- Discuss the assessment and nursing care of a newborn with macrosomia.

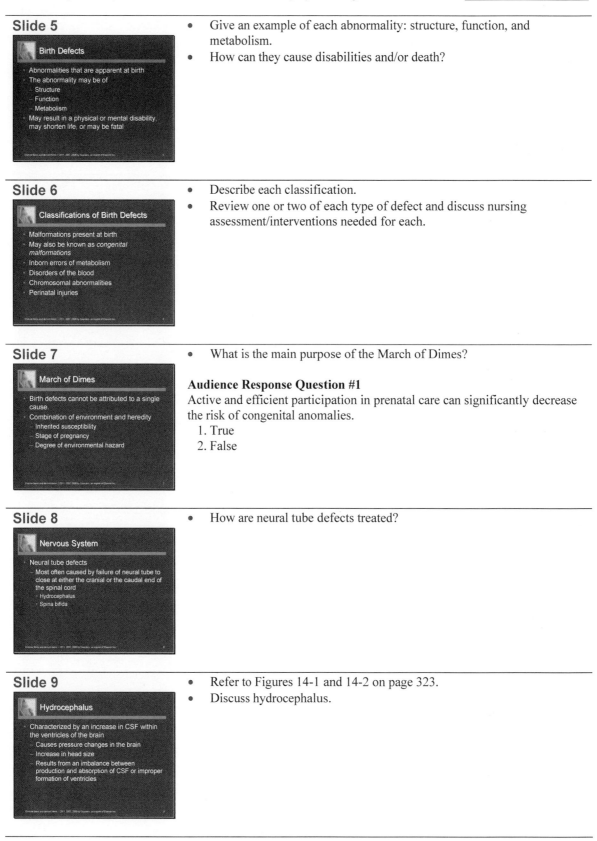

Slide 5

Birth Defects

- Abnormalities that are apparent at birth
- The abnormality may be of
  - Structure
  - Function
  - Metabolism
- May result in a physical or mental disability, may shorten life, or may be fatal

- Give an example of each abnormality: structure, function, and metabolism.
- How can they cause disabilities and/or death?

Slide 6

Classifications of Birth Defects

- Malformations present at birth
- May also be known as *congenital malformations*
- Inborn errors of metabolism
- Disorders of the blood
- Chromosomal abnormalities
- Perinatal injuries

- Describe each classification.
- Review one or two of each type of defect and discuss nursing assessment/interventions needed for each.

Slide 7

March of Dimes

- Birth defects cannot be attributed to a single cause.
- Combination of environment and heredity
  - Inherited susceptibility
  - Stage of pregnancy
  - Degree of environmental hazard

- What is the main purpose of the March of Dimes?

Audience Response Question #1
Active and efficient participation in prenatal care can significantly decrease the risk of congenital anomalies.
  1. True
  2. False

Slide 8

Nervous System

- Neural tube defects
  - Most often caused by failure of neural tube to close at either the cranial or the caudal end of the spinal cord
    - Hydrocephalus
    - Spina bifida

- How are neural tube defects treated?

Slide 9

Hydrocephalus

- Characterized by an increase in CSF within the ventricles of the brain
  - Causes pressure changes in the brain
  - Increase in head size
  - Results from an imbalance between production and absorption of CSF or improper formation of ventricles

- Refer to Figures 14-1 and 14-2 on page 323.
- Discuss hydrocephalus.

Slide 10

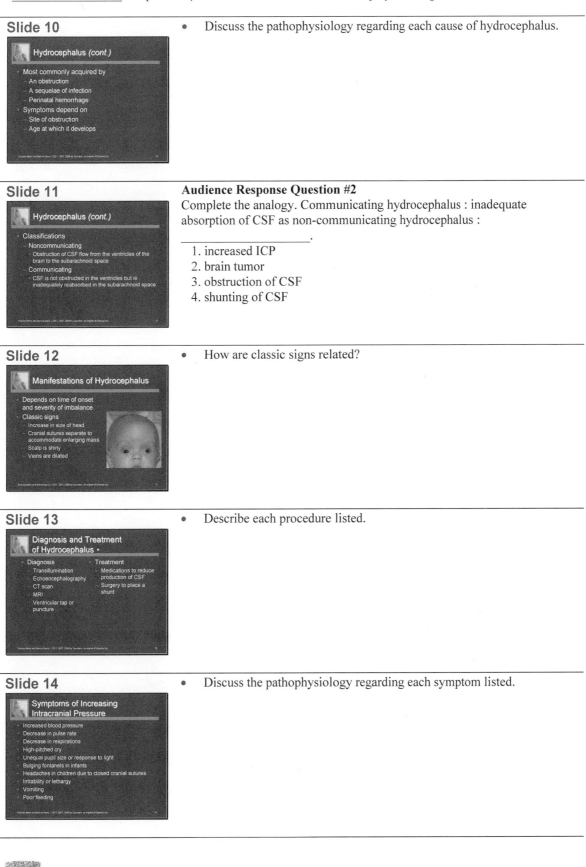

> Hydrocephalus *(cont.)*
>
> · Most commonly acquired by
>   - An obstruction
>   - A sequelae of infection
>   - Perinatal hemorrhage
> · Symptoms depend on
>   - Site of obstruction
>   - Age at which it develops

- Discuss the pathophysiology regarding each cause of hydrocephalus.

Slide 11

> Hydrocephalus *(cont.)*
>
> · Classifications
>   - Noncommunicating
>   · Obstruction of CSF flow from the ventricles of the brain to the subarachnoid space
>   - Communicating
>   · CSF is not obstructed in the ventricles but is inadequately reabsorbed in the subarachnoid space

Audience Response Question #2

Complete the analogy. Communicating hydrocephalus : inadequate absorption of CSF as non-communicating hydrocephalus :

_____.

1. increased ICP
2. brain tumor
3. obstruction of CSF
4. shunting of CSF

Slide 12

> Manifestations of Hydrocephalus
>
> · Depends on time of onset and severity of imbalance
> · Classic signs
>   - Increase in size of head
>   - Cranial sutures separate to accommodate enlarging mass
>   - Scalp is shiny
>   - Veins are dilated

- How are classic signs related?

Slide 13

> Diagnosis and Treatment of Hydrocephalus ·
>
> · Diagnosis
>   - Transillumination
>   - Echoencephalography
>   - CT scan
>   - MRI
>   - Ventricular tap or puncture
>
> · Treatment
>   - Medications to reduce production of CSF
>   - Surgery to place a shunt

- Describe each procedure listed.

Slide 14

> Symptoms of Increasing Intracranial Pressure
>
> · Increased blood pressure
> · Decrease in pulse rate
> · Decrease in respirations
> · High-pitched cry
> · Unequal pupil size or response to light
> · Bulging fontanels in infants
> · Headaches in children due to closed cranial sutures
> · Irritability or lethargy
> · Vomiting
> · Poor feeding

- Discuss the pathophysiology regarding each symptom listed.

Slide 15

Ventriculoperitoneal Shunt
Treatment
Medications to reduce CSF production
Surgery
Shunt acts as a focal spot for infection and may need to be removed if infections persist

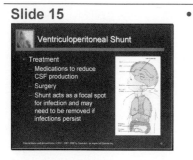

- Discuss Figure 14-3 on page 324.

Slide 16

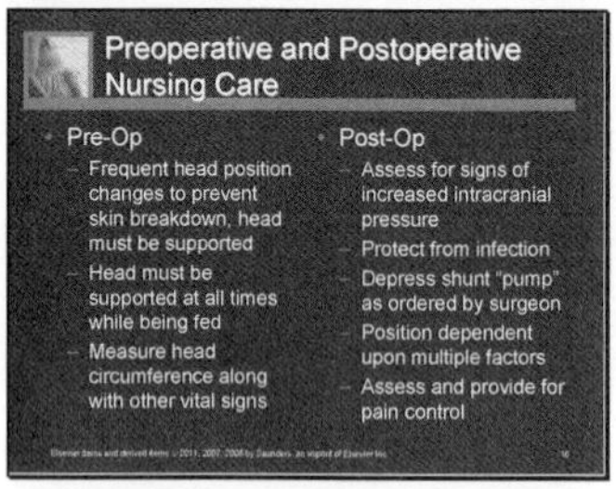

Preoperative and Postoperative Nursing Care
Pre-Op
Frequent head position changes to prevent skin breakdown, head must be supported
Head must be supported at all times while being fed
Measure head circumference along with other vital signs
Post-Op
Assess for signs of increased intracranial pressure
Protect from infection
Depress shunt "pump" as ordered by surgeon
Position dependent upon multiple factors
Assess and provide for pain control

- Discuss the proper procedure to measure head circumference.
- What methods protect the infant from infection?
- How is pain measured in an infant?

Slide 17

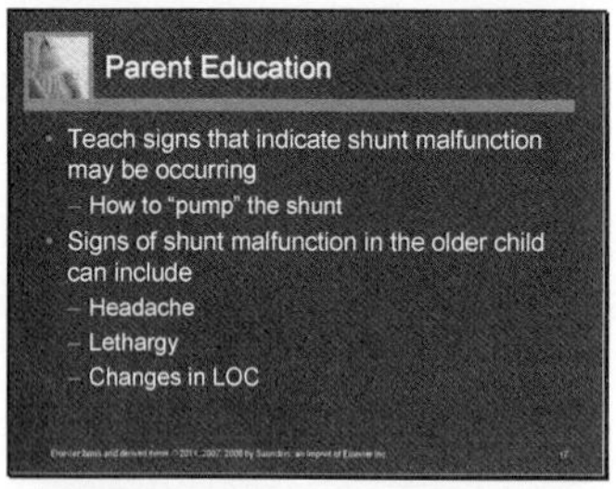

Parent Education
Teach signs that indicate shunt malfunction may be occurring
How to "pump" the shunt
Signs of shunt malfunction in the older child can include
Headache
Lethargy
Changes in LOC

Slide 18

Spina Bifida (Myelodysplasia)

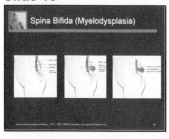

- Discuss Figure 14-4 on page 325.

Slide 19

Spina Bifida (Myelodysplasia) (cont.)
Group of CNS disorders characterized by malformation of the spinal cord
A congenital embryonic neural tube defect with an imperfect closure of the spinal vertebrae
Two types
Occulta (hidden)
Cystica (sac or cyst)

- How are the two types of spina bifida different?

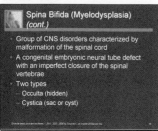

Slide 20

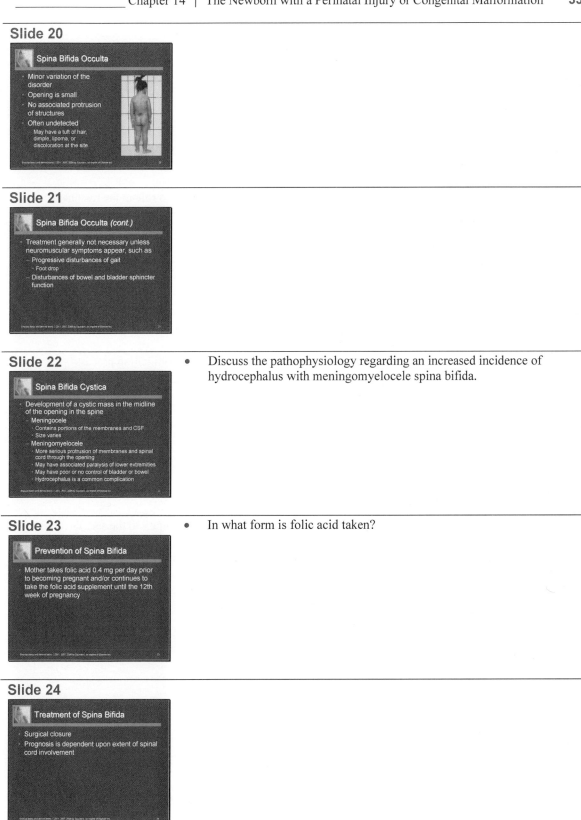

Spina Bifida Occulta

- Minor variation of the disorder
- Opening is small
- No associated protrusion of structures
- Often undetected
  - May have a tuft of hair, dimple, lipoma, or discoloration at the site

Slide 21

Spina Bifida Occulta *(cont.)*

- Treatment generally not necessary unless neuromuscular symptoms appear, such as
  - Progressive disturbances of gait
    - Foot drop
  - Disturbances of bowel and bladder sphincter function

Slide 22

Spina Bifida Cystica

- Development of a cystic mass in the midline of the opening in the spine
  - Meningocele
    - Contains portions of the membranes and CSF
    - Size varies
  - Meningomyelocele
    - More serious protrusion of membranes and spinal cord through the opening
    - May have associated paralysis of lower extremities
    - May have poor or no control of bladder or bowel
    - Hydrocephalus is a common complication

- Discuss the pathophysiology regarding an increased incidence of hydrocephalus with meningomyelocele spina bifida.

Slide 23

Prevention of Spina Bifida

- Mother takes folic acid 0.4 mg per day prior to becoming pregnant and/or continues to take the folic acid supplement until the 12th week of pregnancy

- In what form is folic acid taken?

Slide 24

Treatment of Spina Bifida

- Surgical closure
- Prognosis is dependent upon extent of spinal cord involvement

Slide 25

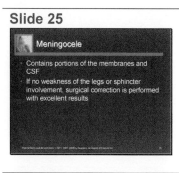

Meningocele

- Contains portions of the membranes and CSF
- If no weakness of the legs or sphincter involvement, surgical correction is performed with excellent results

---

Slide 26

Meningomyelocele

- Protrusion of the membranes and spinal cord through the opening
- Surgical intervention is done for cosmetic reasons and to help prevent infection
- *Habilitation* is usually necessary post-op because the legs remain paralyzed and the patient is incontinent of urine and feces

- Discuss the term *habilitation* and the nurse's role in the treatment process.

Slide 27

Habilitation

- Patient is disabled from birth
- Aim is to minimize the child's disability
- Constructively use all unaffected parts of the body
- Every effort is made to help the child develop a healthy personality so that he or she may experience a happy and productive life

- What methods assist the child during the habilitation process?
- Discuss methods to assist the parents and child in developing a healthy personality.

Slide 28

Nursing Care of Spina Bifida

- Prevent infection of, or injury to, the sac
- Correct positioning to prevent pressure on sac
- Prevent development of contractures
- Good skin care
- Adequate nutrition
- Accurate observations and charting
- Education of the parents
- Continued medical supervision and habilitation

- Discuss methods to prevent infection and injury to the sac.
- Which nursing interventions prevent contractures?
- What is the nurse's role in providing education for the parents of a child with spina bifida?

Slide 29

Nursing Care of Spina Bifida (cont.)

- Upon delivery, the newborn is placed in an incubator
- Moist, sterile dressing of saline or an antibiotic solution may be ordered to prevent drying of the sac
- Protection from injury and maintenance of a sterile environment for the open lesion are essential

---

Slide 30

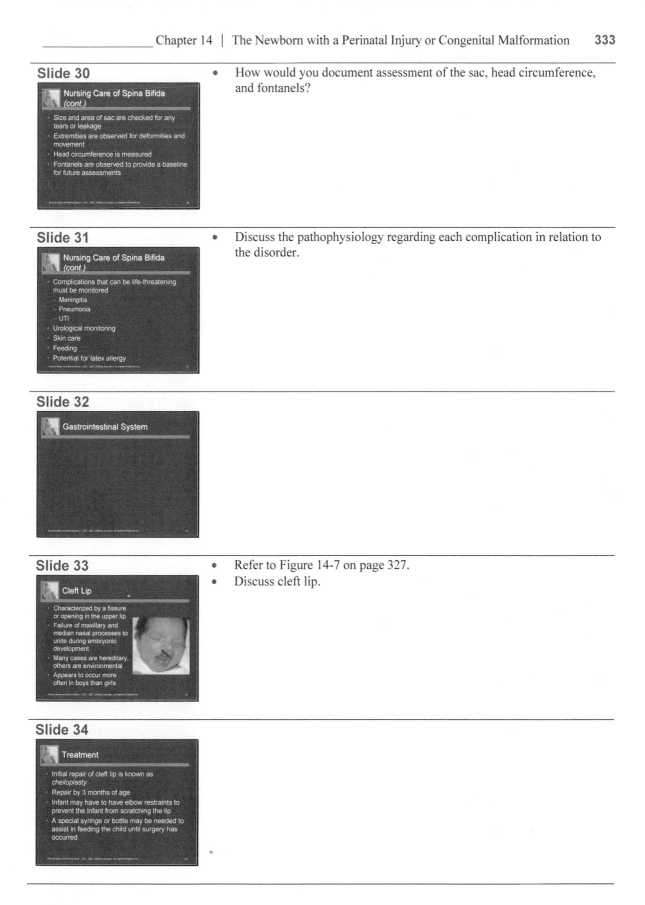

Nursing Care of Spina Bifida *(cont.)*

- Size and area of sac are checked for any tears or leakage
- Extremities are observed for deformities and movement
- Head circumference is measured
- Fontanels are observed to provide a baseline for future assessments

- How would you document assessment of the sac, head circumference, and fontanels?

Slide 31

Nursing Care of Spina Bifida *(cont.)*

- Complications that can be life-threatening must be monitored
  - Meningitis
  - Pneumonia
  - UTI
- Urological monitoring
- Skin care
- Feeding
- Potential for latex allergy

- Discuss the pathophysiology regarding each complication in relation to the disorder.

Slide 32

Gastrointestinal System

Slide 33

Cleft Lip

- Characterized by a fissure or opening in the upper lip
- Failure of maxillary and median nasal processes to unite during embryonic development
- Many cases are hereditary, others are environmental
- Appears to occur more often in boys than girls

- Refer to Figure 14-7 on page 327.
- Discuss cleft lip.

Slide 34

Treatment

- Initial repair of cleft lip is known as *cheiloplasty*
- Repair by 3 months of age
- Infant may have to have elbow restraints to prevent the infant from scratching the lip
- A special syringe or bottle may be needed to assist in feeding the child until surgery has occurred

Slide 35

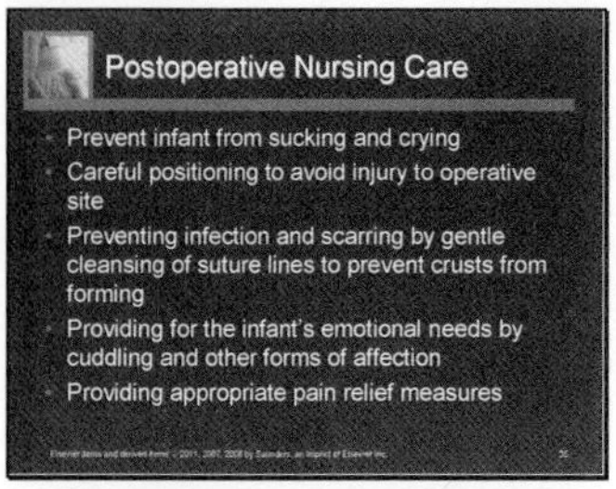

Postoperative Nursing Care

- Prevent infant from sucking and crying
- Careful positioning to avoid injury to operative site
- Preventing infection and scarring by gentle cleansing of suture lines to prevent crusts from forming
- Providing for the infant's emotional needs by cuddling and other forms of affection
- Providing appropriate pain relief measures

- Discuss the rationale for preventing sucking and crying.
- Describe a Logan's bow.

Slide 36

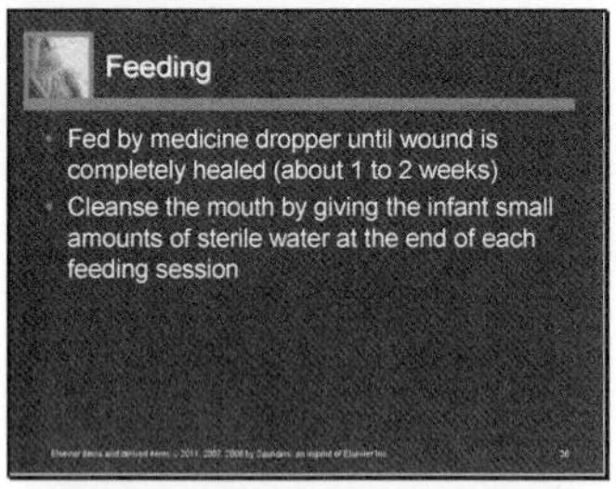

Feeding

- Fed by medicine dropper until wound is completely healed (about 1 to 2 weeks)
- Cleanse the mouth by giving the infant small amounts of sterile water at the end of each feeding session

Slide 37

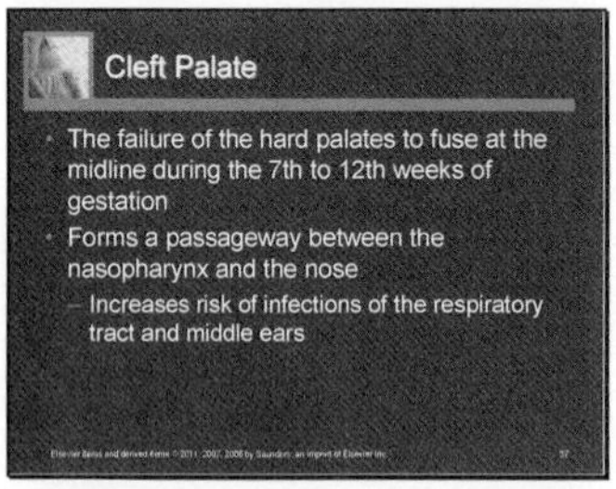

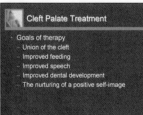

Cleft Palate

- The failure of the hard palates to fuse at the midline during the 7th to 12th weeks of gestation
- Forms a passageway between the nasopharynx and the nose
  - Increases risk of infections of the respiratory tract and middle ears

- What is the difference between a cleft lip and a cleft palate?
- Discuss potential life-threatening complications associated with cleft palate.

Slide 38

Cleft Palate Treatment

- Goals of therapy
  - Union of the cleft
  - Improved feeding
  - Improved speech
  - Improved dental development
  - The nurturing of a positive self-image

Slide 39

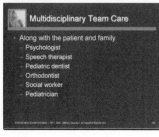

Multidisciplinary Team Care

- Along with the patient and family
  - Psychologist
  - Speech therapist
  - Pediatric dentist
  - Orthodontist
  - Social worker
  - Pediatrician

- What can each member of the team contribute to the therapy of a child with cleft palate?

Leifer

Slide 40

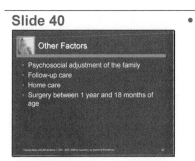

Other Factors

- Psychosocial adjustment of the family
- Follow-up care
- Home care
- Surgery between 1 year and 18 months of age

- Discuss the nurse's role in assisting the family and child with each factor listed.

Slide 41

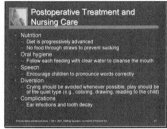

Postoperative Treatment and Nursing Care

- Nutrition
  - Diet is progressively advanced
  - No food through straws to prevent sucking
- Oral hygiene
  - Follow each feeding with clear water to cleanse the mouth
- Speech
  - Encourage children to pronounce words correctly
- Diversion
  - Crying should be avoided whenever possible; play should be of the quiet type (e.g., coloring, drawing, reading to the child)
- Complications
  - Ear infections and tooth decay

Slide 42

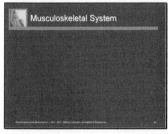

Musculoskeletal System

Slide 43

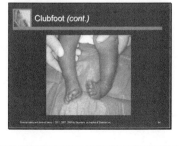

Clubfoot

- Most common deformities
- Congenital anomaly
  - Foot twists inward or outward
- *Talipes equinovarus* is the most common type
  - Feet turned inward
  - Child walks on toes and outer borders of feet
  - Generally involves both feet

- Describe talipes equinovarus.

Slide 44

Clubfoot *(cont.)*

- Refer to Figure 14-8 on page 329.
- Discuss clubfoot.

Leifer

Slide 45

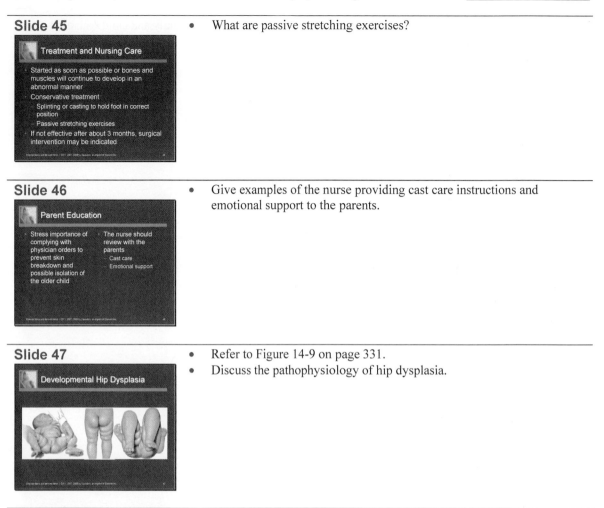

- What are passive stretching exercises?

Slide 46

- Give examples of the nurse providing cast care instructions and emotional support to the parents.

Slide 47

- Refer to Figure 14-9 on page 331.
- Discuss the pathophysiology of hip dysplasia.

Slide 48

- Describe the gait of a child in which hip dysplasia is suspected.

Slide 49

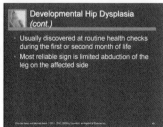

Slide 50

> **Diagnostics for Hip Dysplasia**
>
> · *Barlow's test*: upon adduction and extension of the hips (with health care provider providing stabilization to the pelvis), may "feel" the dislocation actually occur
> · *Ortolani's sign* (or click): health care provider can actually feel and hear the femoral head slip back into the acetabulum under gentle pressure

Audience Response Question #3
Complete the analogy. Barlow's test : feeling as Ortolani's sign : _____.
1. seeing
2. hearing
3. auscultating
4. palpating

Slide 51

> **Treatment of Hip Dysplasia**
>
> · Hips are maintained in constant flexion and abduction for 4 to 8 weeks
>   - Keeps head of femur within the hip socket
> · Constant pressure enlarges and deepens acetabulum
> · Can use a *Pavlik harness* to provide the necessary positioning
> · Surgical intervention may be necessary

- Refer to Figure 14-10 on page 331.
- Discuss the Pavlik harness.

Slide 52

> **Pavlik Harness, Body Cast, and Traction**

- See Figure 14-10 on page 331 and Figure 14-11 on page 332.

Slide 53

> **Nursing Care of Infant/ Child in a Spica Cast**
>
> · Neurovascular assessment of affected extremities
> · Place firm, plastic-covered pillows beneath the curves of the cast for support
> · In the older child, a "fracture" bedpan should be readily available for toileting
> · Head of bed slightly elevated to help drain any body fluids away from cast
> · Frequent changes of position are needed to prevent skin breakdown

- Describe neurovascular assessment of the affected extremity.

Slide 54

> **Nursing Care of Infant/Child in a Spica Cast** *(cont.)*
>
> · Toys that are small enough to "hide" in the cast should not be given to the child
> · Important to meet everyday needs
> · A special wagon with pillows inside it for support is one of the safest ways to transport a child in a spica cast

- Give an example of a toy that might fit inside the cast.

Slide 55

- Give an example of an assessment of an infant with a suspected metabolic defect.

Metabolic Defects

Inborn errors of metabolism involve a genetic defect that may not be apparent until after birth

Symptoms to report would include
- Lethargy
- Poor feeding
- Hypotonia
- Unique odor to body or urine
- Tachypnea
- Vomiting

Slide 56

Phenylketonuria (PKU)

- Faulty metabolism of phenylalanine, an amino acid essential to life and found in all protein foods
- Infant unable to digest this essential acid and phenylalanine accumulates in blood and is found in the urine within the first week of life
- Results in severe mental retardation if not caught early

Slide 57

- Discuss the pathophysiology regarding the manifestations listed.

Phenylketonuria (PKU) *(cont.)*

- Appears normal at birth
- By the time urine test is positive, brain damage has already occurred
- Delayed development apparent at 4-6 months
- May have failure to thrive, eczema, or other skin conditions
- Child has a musty odor
- Personality disorder
- Occurs mainly in blonde, blue-eyed children
- Results from a lack of tyrosine (needed for melanin formation)

Slide 58

- Does your state require early screening for PKU?

PKU Diagnostics

- *Guthrie* test
- Blood for this test should be obtained 48 to 72 hours after birth
- Preferably after the infant has ingested proteins
- Many states require this test to be performed prior to discharge from hospital

---

Slide 59

- What are some dietary restrictions for the infant or child with PKU?

PKU Treatment

- Close dietary management
- Frequent evaluation of blood phenylalanine level
- Synthetic food that provides enough protein for growth and tissue repair
  - Special formulas are available
    - Infants: Lofenalac or Phenex-1
    - Children: Phenyl-free
    - Adolescents: Phenex-2

Slide 60

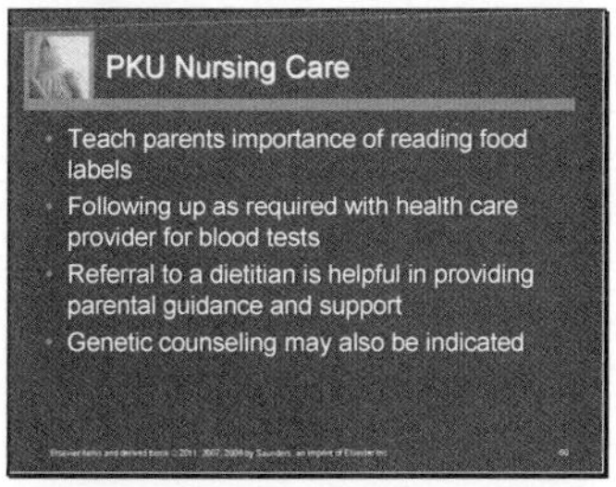

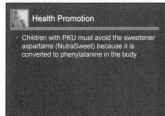

PKU Nursing Care

- Teach parents importance of reading food labels
- Following up as required with health care provider for blood tests
- Referral to a dietitian is helpful in providing parental guidance and support
- Genetic counseling may also be indicated

- What foods need to be restricted in the infant's or child's diet? *Most meats, dairy products, and diet drinks.*

Slide 61

Health Promotion

- Children with PKU must avoid the sweetener aspartame (NutraSweet) because it is converted to phenylalanine in the body

---

Slide 62

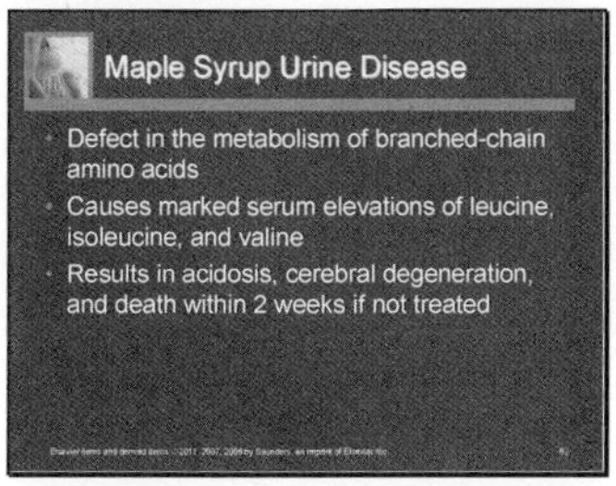

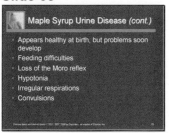

Maple Syrup Urine Disease

- Defect in the metabolism of branched-chain amino acids
- Causes marked serum elevations of leucine, isoleucine, and valine
- Results in acidosis, cerebral degeneration, and death within 2 weeks if not treated

- What is acidosis?

Slide 63

Maple Syrup Urine Disease *(cont.)*

- Appears healthy at birth, but problems soon develop
- Feeding difficulties
- Loss of the Moro reflex
- Hypotonia
- Irregular respirations
- Convulsions

Slide 64

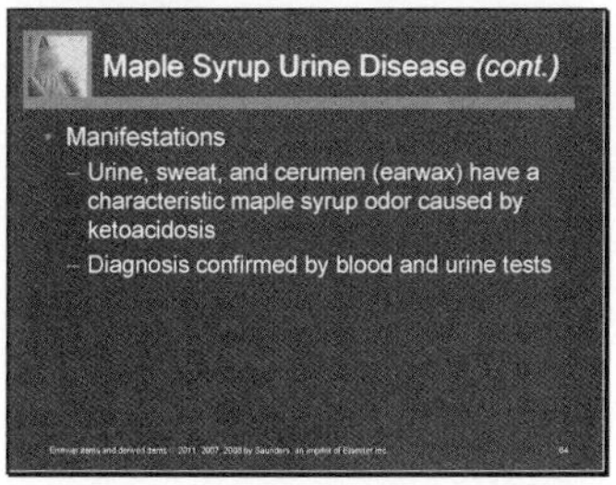

Maple Syrup Urine Disease *(cont.)*

- Manifestations
  – Urine, sweat, and cerumen (earwax) have a characteristic maple syrup odor caused by ketoacidosis
  – Diagnosis confirmed by blood and urine tests

- Discuss the pathophysiology of the sweat characteristics and ketoacidosis.

Slide 65

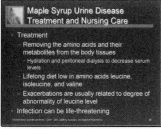

Maple Syrup Urine Disease
Treatment and Nursing Care

- Treatment
  - Removing the amino acids and their metabolites from the body tissues
    - Hydration and peritoneal dialysis to decrease serum levels
  - Lifelong diet low in amino acids leucine, isoleucine, and valine
  - Exacerbations are usually related to degree of abnormality of leucine level
- Infection can be life-threatening

Slide 66

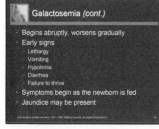

Galactosemia

- Unable to use galactose and lactose
  - Enzyme needed to help the liver convert galactose to glucose is defective or missing
  - Results in an increased serum galactose level (galactosemia) and in the urine (galactosuria)
- If untreated can cause
  - Cirrhosis of the liver
  - Cataracts
  - Mental retardation
- Galactose is present in milk in the form of sugar; therefore, early diagnosis is essential

Slide 67

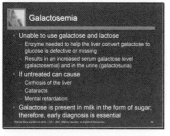

Galactosemia *(cont.)*

- Begins abruptly, worsens gradually
- Early signs
  - Lethargy
  - Vomiting
  - Hypotonia
  - Diarrhea
  - Failure to thrive
- Symptoms begin as the newborn is fed
- Jaundice may be present

- If this defect is left untreated, what can occur? *Cirrhosis of the liver, cataracts, and mental retardation.*

Slide 68

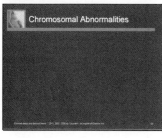

Galactosemia Treatment
and Nursing Care

- Milk and lactose-containing products are eliminated from the diet
- Breastfeeding *must* be stopped
- Lactose-free formulas or soy protein–based formulas are often used instead
- Parental support and education is essential

- In what ways can you provide parental support and education?

Slide 69

Chromosomal Abnormalities

Slide 70	• Discuss the pathophysiology regarding the parent's age and this disorder.

Down Syndrome
· Most common chromosomal abnormality
· Risk increases with
  Mothers 35 years and older
  Fathers 55 years and older
· Infant has mild to severe mental retardation
· Some physical abnormalities are also seen
	• Occurs in 9 of 10,000 live births and may increase to 1 in 365 live births in mothers older than 35.
	• Paternal age is also a factor, especially if he is older than 55.

Slide 71	• What is nondisjunction? *The failure of a chromosome to follow the normal separation process into daughter cells.*

Down Syndrome *(cont.)*
· Three phenotypes
  Trisomy 21
   · Most common
   · There are three number 21 chromosomes instead of the usual two
   · Results from nondisjunction (failure to separate)
  Mosaicism
   · Occurs when both normal and abnormal cells are present
   · Tend to be less severely affected in appearance and intelligence
  Translocation of a chromosome
   · A piece of chromosome in pair 21 breaks away and attaches itself to another chromosome	

Slide 72	• Discuss AFP, HCG, inhibin-A, and unconjugated estriol levels and confirmation of Down syndrome by amniocentesis.
Down Syndrome *(cont.)* · Screening for this is offered during prenatal care starting around week 15 of gestation – Allows parents the opportunity to decide on whether to continue or terminate the pregnancy · "Quad Test": Alpha-fetoprotein (AFP), hCG, unconjugated estriol, inhibin-A levels are used for diagnosis · Amniocentesis is most accurate	

Slide 73	• Refer to Figure 14-12 on page 336. • Discuss the manifestations of Down syndrome.
Down Syndrome Manifestations	

Slide 74	• In what ways can the nurse assist the parents of a child with Down syndrome?

Down Syndrome Manifestations *(cont.)*
· Limp, flaccid posture caused by hypotonicity of muscles
  – More difficult to position and hold
  – Contributes to heat loss
· Prone to respiratory illnesses and constipation due to the hypotonicity
· Incidence of acute leukemia is higher
· Alzheimer's disease more common to those who reach middle adult life
· Encourage parents to express their feelings and concerns
· Provide parents with support and community referrals	

Leifer

Slide 75

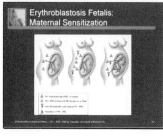

Developmental Milestones

- Sitting
- Rolling over
- Sitting alone
- Crawling
- Creeping
- Standing
- Walking
- Talking

- Compare a normal child's development to the development of a child with Down syndrome.
- Refer to Table 14-1 on page 337.

Slide 76

Self-Help Skills

- Eating
- Toilet training
- Dressing

- Compare the normal child to the child with Down syndrome regarding feeding, toileting, and dressing.
- Refer to Table 14-2 on page 337.

Slide 77

Perinatal Injuries

Slide 78

Hemolytic Disease of the Newborn (Erythroblastosis Fetalis)

- Becomes apparent in utero or soon after birth
- Rh-negative mother and Rh-positive father produce Rh-positive fetus
- Even though maternal and fetal blood do not mix during pregnancy, small leaks may allow fetal blood to enter the maternal circulation causing the mother's body to start producing antibodies that cross the placenta and destroy the blood cells of the fetus, which can cause anemia and heart failure in the developing/growing fetus

- Review terms related to this condition in Box 14-2 on page 338.

Slide 79

Erythroblastosis Fetalis: Maternal Sensitization

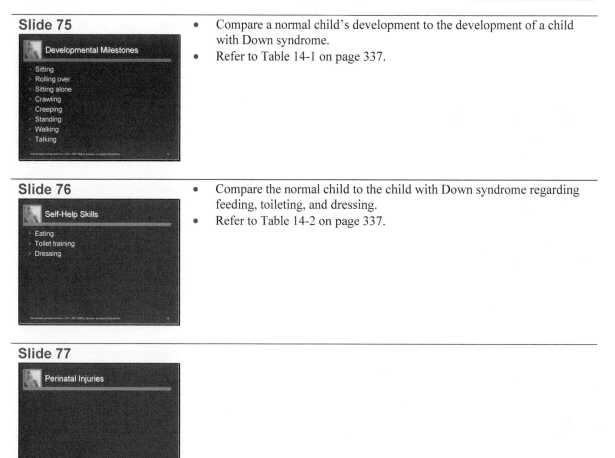

Slide 80

> **Erythroblastosis Fetalis:**
> **Maternal Sensitization** *(cont.)*
>
> · Mother accumulates antibodies with each pregnancy
> · Chance of complications occurs with each subsequent pregnancy
> · Severe form, *hydrops fetalis*, progressive hemolysis causes anemia, heart failure, fetal hypoxia, and anasarca

- Discuss the maternal sensitization process in the newborn.
- Refer to Figure 14-13 on page 338.
- What is anasarca?

Slide 81

> **Erythroblastosis Fetalis**
> **Diagnosis and Prevention**
>
> · Maternal health history that includes
>   – Previous Rh sensitizations
>   – Ectopic pregnancy
>   – Abortion
>   – Blood transfusions
>   – Child who developed jaundice or anemia during a neonatal period
> · Indirect Coombs' test will indicate previous exposure to Rh-positive antigens

- Discuss the maternal health history and erythroblastosis fetalis.
- Describe the indirect Coombs' test.

Slide 82

> **Erythroblastosis Fetalis**
> **Diagnosis and Prevention** *(cont.)*
>
> · Confirmed by amniocentesis and monitoring of bilirubin levels in the amniotic fluid
> · Fetal Rh status can be determined non-invasively via free DNA in maternal plasma
> · Diagnostic studies will help the physician to determine if early interventions, such as induction of labor or intrauterine fetal transfusions, are needed

- Discuss the pathophysiology of early induction of labor and/or intrauterine fetal transfusions.

Slide 83

> **Erythroblastosis Fetalis**
> **Diagnosis and Prevention** *(cont.)*
>
> · Use of Rh(D) immune globulin (RhoGAM)
> · Administered within 72 hours of delivery with an infant who is Rh-positive, an ectopic pregnancy, or after an abortion
> · May also be given to the pregnant woman at 28 weeks gestation

- Why is RhoGAM used in treatment?

Slide 84

> **Erythroblastosis Fetalis**
> **Manifestations**
>
> · Direct Coombs' test on umbilical cord blood
> · Symptoms vary
>   – Anemia caused by hemolysis of large numbers of erythrocytes
>   – *Pathological jaundice* occurs within 24 hours of delivery; liver cannot handle the amount of hemolysis, bilirubin levels rise rapidly
>   – Enlargement and edema of liver and spleen
>   – Oxygen-carrying capacity of the blood is diminished, including blood volume
>   – Infant at major risk of shock or heart failure

ELSEVIER

Introduction to Maternity & Pediatric Nursing, 6th ed.

Leifer

Slide 85

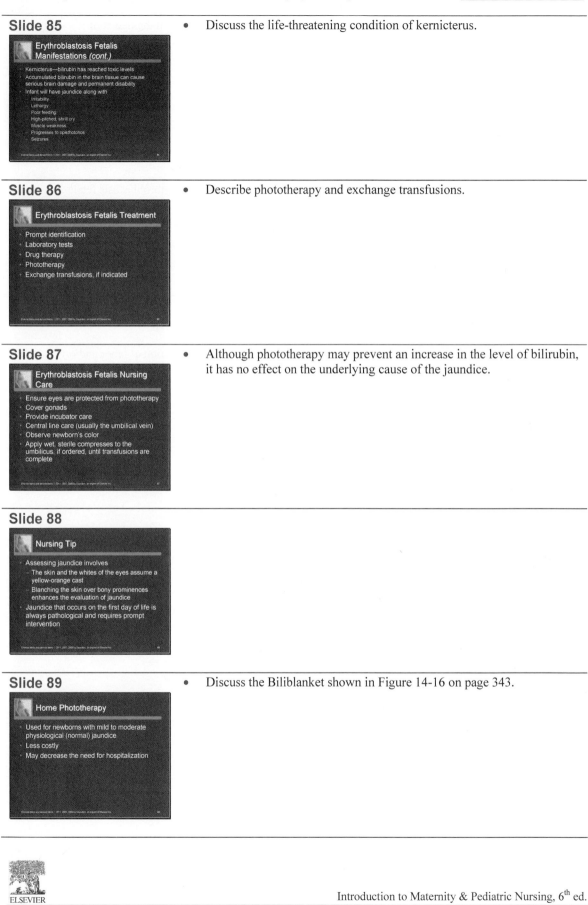

Erythroblastosis Fetalis Manifestations *(cont.)*
- Kernicterus—bilirubin has reached toxic levels
- Accumulated bilirubin in the brain tissue can cause serious brain damage and permanent disability
- Infant will have jaundice along with
  - Irritability
  - Lethargy
  - Poor feeding
  - High-pitched, shrill cry
  - Muscle weakness
  - Progresses to opisthotonos
  - Seizures

• Discuss the life-threatening condition of kernicterus.

Slide 86

Erythroblastosis Fetalis Treatment
- Prompt identification
- Laboratory tests
- Drug therapy
- Phototherapy
- Exchange transfusions, if indicated

• Describe phototherapy and exchange transfusions.

Slide 87

Erythroblastosis Fetalis Nursing Care
- Ensure eyes are protected from phototherapy
- Cover gonads
- Provide incubator care
- Central line care (usually the umbilical vein)
- Observe newborn's color
- Apply wet, sterile compresses to the umbilicus, if ordered, until transfusions are complete

• Although phototherapy may prevent an increase in the level of bilirubin, it has no effect on the underlying cause of the jaundice.

Slide 88

Nursing Tip
- Assessing jaundice involves
  - The skin and the whites of the eyes assume a yellow-orange cast
  - Blanching the skin over bony prominences enhances the evaluation of jaundice
- Jaundice that occurs on the first day of life is always pathological and requires prompt intervention

Slide 89

Home Phototherapy
- Used for newborns with mild to moderate physiological (normal) jaundice
- Less costly
- May decrease the need for hospitalization

• Discuss the Biliblanket shown in Figure 14-16 on page 343.

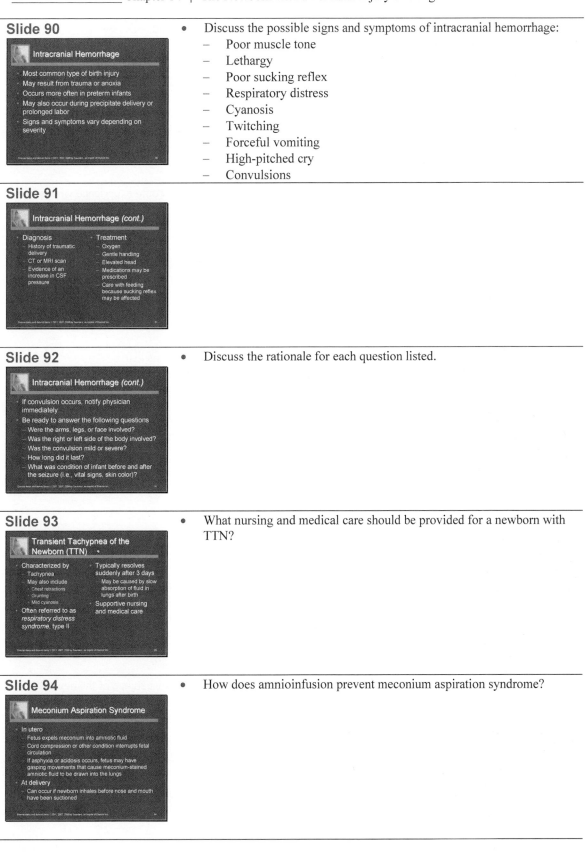

Slide 90

> **Intracranial Hemorrhage**
> - Most common type of birth injury
> - May result from trauma or anoxia
> - Occurs more often in preterm infants
> - May also occur during precipitate delivery or prolonged labor
> - Signs and symptoms vary depending on severity

- Discuss the possible signs and symptoms of intracranial hemorrhage:
  - Poor muscle tone
  - Lethargy
  - Poor sucking reflex
  - Respiratory distress
  - Cyanosis
  - Twitching
  - Forceful vomiting
  - High-pitched cry
  - Convulsions

Slide 91

> **Intracranial Hemorrhage** *(cont.)*
>
> **Diagnosis**
> - History of traumatic delivery
> - CT or MRI scan
> - Evidence of an increase in CSF pressure
>
> **Treatment**
> - Oxygen
> - Gentle handling
> - Elevated head
> - Medications may be prescribed
> - Care with feeding because sucking reflex may be affected

Slide 92

> **Intracranial Hemorrhage** *(cont.)*
> - If convulsion occurs, notify physician immediately
> - Be ready to answer the following questions
>   - Were the arms, legs, or face involved?
>   - Was the right or left side of the body involved?
>   - Was the convulsion mild or severe?
>   - How long did it last?
>   - What was condition of infant before and after the seizure (i.e., vital signs, skin color)?

- Discuss the rationale for each question listed.

Slide 93

> **Transient Tachypnea of the Newborn (TTN)**
> - Characterized by
>   - Tachypnea
> - May also include
>   - Chest retractions
>   - Grunting
>   - Mild cyanosis
> - Often referred to as *respiratory distress syndrome*, type II
> - Typically resolves suddenly after 3 days
> - May be caused by slow absorption of fluid in lungs after birth
> - Supportive nursing and medical care

- What nursing and medical care should be provided for a newborn with TTN?

Slide 94

> **Meconium Aspiration Syndrome**
> - In utero
>   - Fetus expels meconium into amniotic fluid
>   - Cord compression or other condition interrupts fetal circulation
>   - If asphyxia or acidosis occurs, fetus may have gasping movements that cause meconium-stained amniotic fluid to be drawn into the lungs
> - At delivery
>   - Can occur if newborn inhales before nose and mouth have been suctioned

- How does amnioinfusion prevent meconium aspiration syndrome?

Leifer

Slide 95

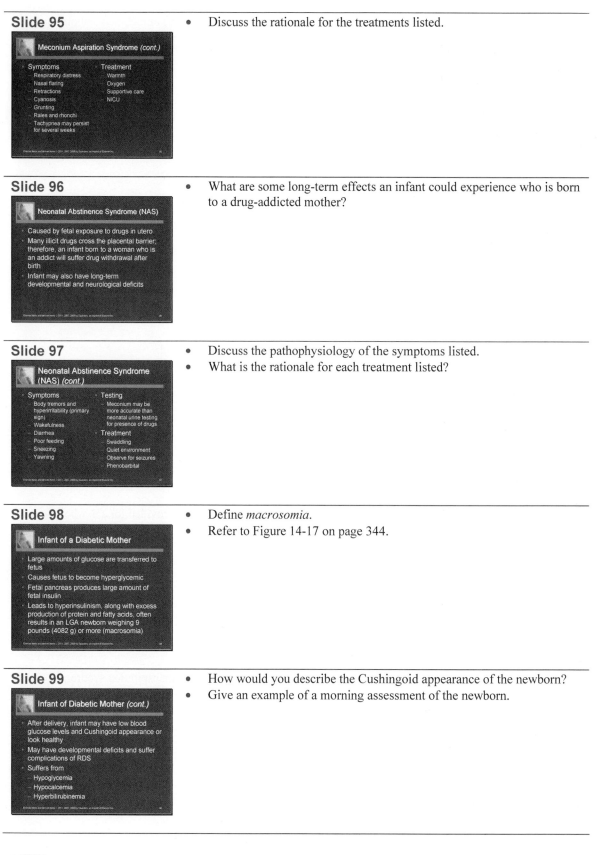

- Discuss the rationale for the treatments listed.

Slide 96

- What are some long-term effects an infant could experience who is born to a drug-addicted mother?

Slide 97

- Discuss the pathophysiology of the symptoms listed.
- What is the rationale for each treatment listed?

Slide 98

- Define *macrosomia*.
- Refer to Figure 14-17 on page 344.

Slide 99

- How would you describe the Cushingoid appearance of the newborn?
- Give an example of a morning assessment of the newborn.

Slide 100

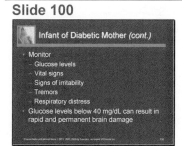

Infant of Diabetic Mother *(cont.)*

- Monitor
  - Glucose levels
  - Vital signs
  - Signs of irritability
  - Tremors
  - Respiratory distress
- Glucose levels below 40 mg/dL can result in rapid and permanent brain damage

Slide 101

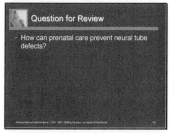

Question for Review

- How can prenatal care prevent neural tube defects?

Slide 102

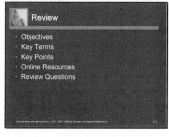

Review

- Objectives
- Key Terms
- Key Points
- Online Resources
- Review Questions

Leifer

15 Lesson Plan
An Overview of Growth, Development, and Nutrition

TEACHING FOCUS

In this chapter, students learn about topics related to growth, development, and nutrition for the growing child, including growth charts and developmental patterns, personality development, dental care, and therapeutic play. Proper nutrition for the sick and well child, cognitive and moral development, and various developmental theories will also be covered. Finally, students will have the opportunity to learn how to develop care plans and assessment for the child and the family relating to growth, development, and nutrition.

MATERIALS AND RESOURCES

- ☐ Computer and PowerPoint projector (all lessons)
- ☐ Dolls (Lesson 15.3)
- ☐ Food pyramid (Lesson 15.2)
- ☐ Growth chart (Lesson 15.1)
- ☐ Measuring tape (Lesson 15.1)
- ☐ Toothbrush, small (Lesson 15.3)

LESSON CHECKLIST

Preparations for this lesson include:

- Lecture
- Demonstration
- Guest speaker: Dentist or registered dental hygienist
- Evaluation of student knowledge and skills needed to perform all entry-level activities related to growth, development, and nutrition in pediatric patients, including:
  - ○ Assessing length, height, and weight of infants
  - ○ Nutritional needs of infants, toddlers, children, and adolescents
  - ○ Nutritional requirements based on the Food Guide Pyramid
  - ○ Using and interpreting growth charts
  - ○ Dental care for children

KEY TERMS

adolescent (p. 350)
cephalocaudal (p. 350)
cognition (p. 364)
community (p. 357)
competitive play (p. 383)
cooperative play (p. 383)
deciduous (p. 380)
dysfunctional family (p. 357)
Erikson (p. 366)

extended family (p. 356)
fluorosis (p. 381)
growth (p. 350)
height (p. 350)
infant (p. 350)
Kohlberg (p. 366)
length (p. 350)
Maslow (p. 364)
maturation (p. 350)
metabolic rate (p. 352)

neonate (p. 349)
nuclear family (p. 356)
nursing caries (p. 381)
parallel play (p. 383)
personality (p. 364)
Piaget (p. 364)
proximodistal (p. 350)
therapeutic play (p. 383)
toddler (p. 350)

ADDITIONAL RESOURCES

TEACH PPT slide(s) Chapter 15, 1-69
EILR IC image(s) Chapter 15, 1-4
EILR OBQ question(s) Chapter 15, 1-10
EILR TB question(s) Chapter 15, 1-32
ESLR IRQ question(s) Chapter 15, 1-5
SG Chapter 15, pp. 129-136

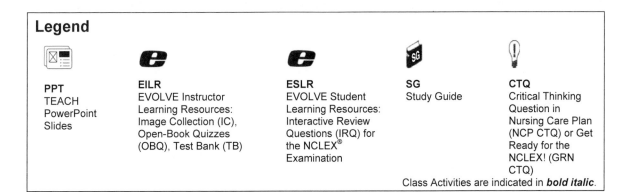

Legend

PPT
TEACH
PowerPoint
Slides

EILR
EVOLVE Instructor
Learning Resources:
Image Collection (IC),
Open-Book Quizzes
(OBQ), Test Bank (TB)

ESLR
EVOLVE Student
Learning Resources:
Interactive Review
Questions (IRQ) for
the NCLEX®
Examination

SG
Study Guide

CTQ
Critical Thinking
Question in
Nursing Care Plan
(NCP CTQ) or Get
Ready for the
NCLEX! (GRN
CTQ)

Class Activities are indicated in **bold italic**.

LESSON 15.1

PRETEST

1. Which developmental pattern proceeds from head to toe?
   a. cephalocaudal development
   b. cephalic development
   c. proximodistal development
   d. cognitive development

2. Which developmental pattern proceeds from the center of the body outward to the extremities?
   a. cephalocaudal development
   b. cephalic development
   c. cognitive development
   d. proximodistal development

3. Newborns increase cardiac output by
   a. decreasing heart rate.
   b. increasing heart rate.
   c. increasing body temperature.
   d. increasing blood pressure.

4. Physiologic anemia can occur in infants due to
   a. blood loss during labor.
   b. hereditary factors.
   c. loss of maternal iron stores.
   d. multiple blood transfusions.

5. The developmental screening test used for children during the first 6 years of life is the
   a. Maslow test.
   b. Erikson development test.
   c. Piaget cognitive assessment.
   d. Denver II.

6. In infants, fat and cholesterol aid in the development of the
   a. skeletal system.
   b. muscular system.
   c. central nervous system.
   d. cardiovascular system.

7. At what age should solid food be introduced to infants?
   a. 4 months
   b. 6 months
   c. 9 months
   d. 12 months

8. An antibiotic that stains developing teeth is
   a. penicillin.
   b. erythromycin.
   c. tetracycline.
   d. cephalosporin.

9. Dental caries can be prevented by initiating the use of fluoride after age
   a. 2 months.
   b. 6 months.
   c. 1 year.
   d. 2 years.

10. The hierarchy of basic needs was developed by
    a. Maslow.
    b. Piaget.
    c. Kohlberg.
    d. Erickson.

Answers

1. a	3. b	5. d	7. b	9. b
2. d	4. c	6. c	8. c	10. a

BACKGROUND ASSESSMENT

Question: How are growth and development assessed?
Answer: In infants and children, growth is measured in terms of height (length) and weight. Growth charts are used to interpret the measurements; they make it possible to compare the measurement of a child to others of the same age and sex and to compare the child's measurements with a former pattern of growth. Development is assessed by using a screening test called the Denver II. This test assesses the developmental status of children during the first 6 years of life in four different categories. Developmental milestones and social interactions are also assessed to determine the level of growth and development.

Question: A 3-year-old boy is experiencing decreased appetite, diarrhea, cough, fever, and earache. His mother states that he has not been playing with his toys for the past 2 days. Using Maslow's hierarchy of needs, how would you determine the order in which the patient's signs and symptoms should be addressed?
Answer: Because of his illness, the patient's basic physiologic needs are not being met at this time. His illness has also interrupted his interactions with his family and environment. According to Maslow's hierarchy of needs, the basic physiologic needs must first be met before any other need can be fulfilled.

These physiologic needs include air, food, water, elimination, and rest. Once the physiologic needs have been met and the child is better, the need for activity can be addressed. This includes the child's need for stimulation, novelty, and change; after his physical symptoms have been resolved he should begin to play with his toys again.

CRITICAL THINKING QUESTION

A 6-year-old patient has come to the clinic for her annual school physical. Her mother states that the child does not like to eat and that she believes the child is underweight; she is concerned the child will become ill if she does not eat. What assessments need to be done in order to determine the best course of action for the child?

Guidelines: The nurse should first obtain measurements of the child's height and weight to determine where she falls among children of her same age group and sex. This is done by plotting the child's measurements onto a growth chart. If the child does appear to be underweight, then further investigation needs to be done to determine the reason and appropriate interventions. The determination of any potential physiologic problems must also be addressed. A nutritional assessment should be performed to determine what foods the child likes and dislikes and the types of food eaten at home. This will provide the nurse with information that will identify if the child is receiving adequate nutrients and provide opportunity for family teaching about diet modification and proper nutrition.

OBJECTIVES	CONTENT	TEACHING RESOURCES

Discuss the nursing implications of growth and development.	■ Growth and development (p. 347)
	
	□ The impact of growth and development on nursing care (p. 348)
		▣ PPT slides 6-10
		
		e EILR OBQ questions 1, 2
		
		sG SG Learning Activities, question 2 (p. 129)
		
		BOOK RESOURCES
		
		Box 15-1, Emerging Patterns of Behavior from Age 1 to 5 Years (p. 348)
		
		Box 15-2, The Nursing Process Applied to Growth and Development (p. 349)
		
		Nursing Tips (p. 349)
		
		Class Activity **Divide the class into small groups, and have each group discuss how illness influences growth and development in the following scenarios:**
		
		   1. A 3-year-old girl with asthma requires intermittent oral steroids.
		
		   2. A 7-year-old boy has type 1 diabetes and must administer daily insulin injections.
		
		   3. A 5-year-old boy is admitted to the hospital with viral pneumonia.
		
		Have each group share its findings with the class, then lead a class discussion about the nursing implications for each of these children. How does their handling differ from that of adults?

Explain the differences between growth, development,	□ Terminology (p. 349) □ Directional patterns (p. 350)	▣ PPT slides 11-13 *e* EILR IC images 1, 2 *e* EILR TB questions 1, 23, 25, 32

OBJECTIVES	CONTENT	TEACHING RESOURCES
and maturation.	☐ Some developmental differences between children and adults (p. 350) – Height (p. 350) – Weight (p. 350) – Body proportions (p. 350) – Metabolic rate (p. 352) – Respirations (p. 352) – Cardiovascular system (p. 352) – Immunity (p. 352) – Kidney function (p. 352) – Nervous system (p. 352) – Sleep patterns (p. 353) – Bone growth (p. 353) – Critical periods (p. 353) – Integration of skills (p. 353)	*e* ESLR IRQ question 5 SG Learning Activities, questions 1, 3-11 (p. 129) SG Review Questions, questions 1, 2, 9, 15 (pp. 133-134) **BOOK RESOURCES** Box 15-3, Key Terms in Child Development (p. 350) Figure 15-1, The Development of Muscular Control Proceeds from Head to Foot and from the Center of the Body to its Periphery (p. 350) Skill 15-1, Assessing the Length and Height of Infants and Children (p. 351) Figure 15-2, Changes in Body Proportions (p. 352) ▸ Discuss the developmental differences between children and adults. *Class Activity* **Present the following scenario to students for a class discussion:** *The father of a 14-month-old child is worried that his son is not maturing properly because he has not yet begun to speak, seems small for his age, and cannot walk independently.* *Have students explain where this child should be in terms of growth, development, and maturation, and discuss the differences among the terms.*
Recognize and read a growth chart for children.	☐ Growth standards (p. 353) ☐ Developmental screening (p. 353)	PPT slides 14-16 *e* EILR IC image 3 *e* EILR TB question 4 SG Learning Activities, questions 12, 13 (p. 130) SG Applying Knowledge, questions 1, 3 (p. 135) **BOOK RESOURCES** Nursing Tip, (p. 354) Figure 15-3, Sample of a Complete Growth Chart (pp. 354-355) ▸ Discuss how the nurse can determine if conditions such as neuromuscular development have affected an infant's

Leifer

OBJECTIVES	CONTENT	TEACHING RESOURCES
		growth and development.
		Class Activity **Provide students with copies of growth charts and various child profiles (e.g., 6-year-old female weighs 55 lbs.; 4-year-old boy weighs 38 lbs.). In groups, have students use the growth charts to determine which children are growing normally and which are growing abnormally (i.e., underweight or overweight). What recommendations and nursing interventions should be done? What additional information, if any, is needed? Have each group share its findings with the class for discussion.**

15.1 Homework/Assignments:

15.1 Instructor's Notes/Student Feedback:

Leifer

LESSON 15.2

CRITICAL THINKING QUESTION

A 9-year-old boy is the second of three children. His parents are divorced and he sees his father once a month. He is often in trouble with his teachers, he does not get along with his classmates, and his grades are below average. How would you apply the theories of Erikson, Freud, and Piaget to the child?

Guidelines: Erikson's theory of child development places the child in the industry/inferiority stage. The child most likely has problems functioning in school because of the divorce of his parents; because he only sees his father once a month, he is not properly learning to relate to his own sex. His lack of coping skills in school is also a direct result of his home and social environment; because he is not being productive (getting good grades) he is not receiving recognition, which creates his feelings of inferiority. Freud places the child in the latency period, a period that is marked by achieving and learning to live in groups. The child's poor peer relations and bad grades are evidence that he is having trouble mastering this phase. Piaget places this child in the concrete operations period. This period involves the development of logical and systematic reasoning that is limited to one's own experience. The child's behavior appears to be illogical and he is not capable of functioning independently; his poor peer and adult relations also suggest that his egocentrism is not decreasing as it should.

OBJECTIVES	CONTENT	TEACHING RESOURCES
List five factors that influence growth and development.	☐ Influencing factors (p. 354) – Hereditary traits (p. 354) – Nationality and race (p. 355) – Ordinal position in the family (p. 355) – Gender (p. 356) – Environment (p. 356)	🖳 PPT slide 17 𝒆 EILR OBQ questions 3, 4 𝒆 EILR TB questions 3, 5, 20, 22 **BOOK RESOURCES** Table 15-1, Variations of Family Living (p. 356) Nursing Tips (p. 356) ▸ Discuss the impact of cultural influences on the growth and development of infants and children. What approaches can be taken to deter negative influences? *Class Activity **Divide the class into five groups, and assign each group one of the following topics: hereditary traits, nationality and race, ordinal position in the family, gender, and environment. Have each group explain how its assigned factor impacts the growth and development of a child.***
Recognize the influence of the family and cultural practices on growth, development, nutrition, and health care.	– The family (p. 356) – The family as part of a community (p. 357) – The homeless family (p. 357)	🖳 PPT slides 18-21 𝒆 EILR OBQ question 6 𝒆 EILR TB questions 19, 29 📖 SG Learning Activities, question 15 (p. 130) 📖 SG Review Questions, question 6 (p. 133) **BOOK RESOURCES** Nursing Tip (p. 357) Table 15-2, Cultural Influences on the Family (pp. 358-

OBJECTIVES	CONTENT	TEACHING RESOURCES
		364)
		▶ Discuss the influence of family and culture on nutrition, growth, and development. How can negative influences be overcome?
		Class Activity Using Table 15-2 (pp. 358-364), have students discuss each of the cultures represented in relation to family, nutrition, and health care. How would the nursing care and patient teaching differ for each culture, and how do the practices affect child development and nutrition? What other cultures might nurses encounter that are not identified in the table?
Discuss the importance of family-centered care in pediatrics.	– The family (p. 356)	⊠ PPT slides 18-21 ▶ Discuss the roles of various family members in family-centered care, including parents, siblings, grandparents, aunts and uncles, and so on. *Class Activity In groups, have students form their own definition of the term "family-centered care" in relation to pediatrics. Then have each group share and discuss its definition with the class. Have students choose their favorite definition or components of several definitions to develop a comprehensive definition for the class. Why is family-centered care important, and how can a nurse encourage this type of care?*
Describe three developmental theories and their impact on planning the nursing care of children.	☐ Personality development (p. 357) – Cognitive development (p. 364) – Moral development (p. 366) ☐ The growth and development of a parent (p. 366)	⊠ PPT slides 22-38 𝒆 EILR IC images 4, 5 𝒆 EILR OBQ question 7 𝒆 EILR TB questions 2, 3, 14, 21, 30 SG Learning Activities, questions 17, 20 (p. 131) SG Review Questions, question 5 (p. 133) SG Thinking Critically, question 1 (p. 135) **BOOK RESOURCES** Table 15-3, Comparison of the Developmental Theories of Erikson, Freud, Kohlberg, Sullivan, and Piaget (p. 365) Figure 15-4, Maslow's Hierarchy of Basic Needs (p. 366) Table 15-4, Piaget's Theory of Cognitive Development in Relation to Feeding and Nutrition (p. 366) Table 15-5, The Growth and Development of a Parent (pp. 367-368) Figure 15-5, Infant Carriers (p. 368)

OBJECTIVES	CONTENT	TEACHING RESOURCES
		Review Questions for the NCLEX® Examination, question 4 (p. 385)
		▶ Discuss each of the developmental theories presented in the text. Where do the theorists agree, and where do they differ?
		Class Activity **Divide the class into groups, and present the following scenario to the class:**
		An 11-year-old girl is quiet and withdrawn with parents and peers, receives bad grades in school, and displays sudden bursts of temper or sadness.
		Have each group discuss this child's development according to each of the theorists presented in the text, and explain what problems this child is exhibiting and why. Then have each group present its findings to the class for discussion.
Discuss the nutritional needs of growing children.	■ Nutrition (p. 367) ☐ Family nutrition (p. 368) ☐ Nutritional care plan (p. 372) ☐ Nutrition and health (p. 372) ☐ Nutrition and health promotion (p. 372) ☐ Feeding the healthy child (p. 373) – The infant (p. 373) – The toddler (p. 374) – The preschool child (p. 376) – The school-age child (p. 376) – The adolescent (p. 376) ☐ Childhood obesity (p. 378) ☐ Feeding the ill child (p. 378) ☐ Food-drug interactions (p. 379)	▣ PPT slides 39-60 *e* EILR IC images 6-12 *e* EILR OBQ questions 8-10 *e* EILR TB questions 9-12, 15, 17, 26-28 *e* ESLR IRQ questions 2, 4 SG Learning Activities, questions 21-27 (p. 132) SG Review Questions, questions 4, 7, 10, 12-14, 17 (pp. 133-135) SG Case Study, question 1b (p. 135) SG Thinking Critically, question 2 (p. 135) SG Applying Knowledge, question 2 (p. 135) **BOOK RESOURCES** Table 15-6, Culturally Diverse Food Patterns of Americans (p. 369) Figure 15-6, The Children's Food Pyramid (p. 370) Figure 15-7, The Vegetarian Diet Pyramid (p. 371) Nutrition Considerations (p. 371) Table 15-7, High-Fiber Foods for Relief of Mild Constipation in Children Over 12 Months of Age (p. 372) Safety Alert, (p. 372) Figure 15-8, Nutrient Digestion (p. 373)

Leifer

OBJECTIVES	CONTENT	TEACHING RESOURCES
		Health Promotion: Methods to Reduce Cholesterol in School-Age Children (p. 372)
		Box 15-4, National Cholesterol Evaluation Program Recommendations for Detecting and Managing Hypercholesterolemia in Children and Adolescents (p. 374)
		Nursing Tip (p. 374)
		Table 15-8, Nursing Interventions for Meeting the Nutritional Needs of Children (pp. 375-376)
		Figure 15-9, Spoon Feeding (p. 376)
		Figure 15-10, The Self feeding toddler (p. 376)
		Health Promotion: nutrition resources within the community (p. 377)
		Skill 15-2, Calculating the Body Mass Index (BMI) (p. 378)
		Figure 15-11, The Portion Plate for Kids (p. 379)
		Figure 15-12, Non-Nutritive Sucking (p. 379)
		Review Questions for the NCLEX® Examination, question 2 (p. 385)
		▸ Discuss the various cultural food influences and how these influences impact an infant or child's nutritional intake. What are the steps to educate the parents to incorporate appropriate nutritional components in the child's diet?
		Class Activity Divide the class into five groups, and assign each group one of the following age groups: infant, toddler, preschooler, school-age child, and adolescent. Have each group discuss the special nutritional requirements for its age group, then develop a sample menu for one day that includes meals, snacks, beverages, and mealtimes. Have each group present its menu to the class for discussion.
		Class Activity Present the following scenario to students for a class discussion:
		A father brings his 15-year-old daughter to the doctor's office because he is concerned about her weight. She has been steadily and rapidly losing weight, looks too thin, has an unhealthy pallor to her skin, and does not eat well. She says that she is "just not hungry."
		Have students identify what nursing interventions should be done for this patient, what patient teaching should be provided and how it should be delivered, and what kinds of education and support should be provided to the father.

15.2 Homework/Assignments:

15.2 Instructor's Notes/Student Feedback:

LESSON 15.3

CRITICAL THINKING QUESTION

When performing assessments on a 2-year-old girl, you observe numerous nursing caries in the child's mouth. What kinds of recommendations and teaching should the nurse provide for the parents, and what are the dangers of this problem if healthier habits are not adopted?

Guidelines: Nursing caries, also known as *bottle-mouth caries*, occur when a child falls asleep while breastfeeding or with a bottle of milk or juice. This causes sugar to pool in the mouth, which results in severe tooth decay. The nurse should refer the parents to a dentist to have the existing caries treated and recommend that the parents either eliminate the bedtime bottle or substitute the juice with water. If left untreated, the caries could lead to periodontal disease later in life. The nurse should also provide the parents with information about oral care in toddlers and children. It is important that the parents begin to practice and teach proper dental hygiene at a young age in order to reinforce healthy habits that will last a lifetime. They should begin by brushing the child's teeth each day with a small, soft brush and a pea-sized amount of toothpaste. In the next year or so, a bedtime brushing routine should be established, and flossing should be introduced by the parents.

OBJECTIVES	CONTENT	TEACHING RESOURCES
Differentiate between permanent and deciduous teeth and list the times of their eruption.	☐ The teeth (p. 380) – Deciduous teeth (p. 380) – Permanent teeth (p. 380) – Oral care in health and illness (p. 381)	🖾 PPT slides 61-67 𝒆 EILR IC images 13, 14 𝒆 EILR TB questions 6-8, 16, 31 📕 SG Learning Activities, questions 28-33 (p. 132) 📕 SG Review Questions, questions 3, 8, 16, 18 (pp. 133-135) **BOOK RESOURCES** Figure 15-13, Permanent and Deciduous Teeth and Age of Eruption (p. 380) Nursing Tip (p. 381) Health Promotion, Developmental Dental Hygiene (p. 381) Figure 15-14, Nursing Caries (p. 382) Table 15-9, Medical Problems and Dental Health (p. 383) Nursing Tip (p. 383) Review Questions for the NCLEX® Examination, questions 1, 3 (pp. 384-385) ▸ Discuss how and when oral care should be initiated in children. *Class Activity **In groups, have students create a timeline that illustrates proper oral care from the eruption of deciduous teeth through adolescence. Have each group share its timeline with the class for discussion.*** *Class Activity **Using a toothbrush and dolls, choose several student volunteers to demonstrate for the class***

Introduction to Maternity & Pediatric Nursing, 6th ed.

OBJECTIVES	CONTENT	TEACHING RESOURCES
		the proper way to care for the teeth in an infant, toddler, preschooler, and school-age child. Have the rest of the class offer suggestions.
Understand the characteristics of play at various age levels.	■ Play (p. 383)	▣▤ PPT slide 66 *e* EILR TB questions 18, 24 *e* ESLR IRQ question 3 [SG] SG Learning Activities, question 1a (p. 135) **BOOK RESOURCES** Table 15-10, Development of Play (p. 383) Review Questions for the NCLEX® Examination, question 5 (p. 385) ▸ Discuss what differentiates the play of each age level. *Class Activity Divide the class into small groups and assign each group one of the following age groups: infant, 1 to 2 years, 3 to 5 years, 5 to 8 years, 8 to 10 years, 13 to19 years. Have groups discuss the characteristics of their assigned age group's play. Lead a class discussion about what differentiates or characterizes each age group's play.* *Class Activity Divide the class into five groups and assign each group one of the following developmental theories: Erikson, Freud, Kohlberg, Sullivan, or Piaget. Have each group discuss how the characteristics of play at various age levels either support or reject its assigned theory and present its findings to the class for discussion.*
Describe the relationship of play to physical, cognitive, and emotional development.	■ Play (p. 383)	▣▤ PPT slide 66 [SG] SG Learning Activities, question 34 (p. 133) [SG] SG Review Questions, question 11 (p. 134) **BOOK RESOURCES** ▸ Discuss what signs might indicate that a child is developmentally lagging, either physically, cognitively, or emotionally. *Class Activity Divide the class into five groups, and assign each group one of the following age groups: infant, 1 to 2 years, 3 to 5 years, 5 to 8 years, or 8 to 10 years. Have each group develop three to five play activities that will promote physical, cognitive, and emotional development for a child in its assigned age group. Have each group present its activities to the class for discussion.*

Leifer

OBJECTIVES	CONTENT	TEACHING RESOURCES
Understand the role of computers and computer games in play at various ages.	■ Play (p. 383)	▸ Discuss the role of computers and computer games in play. How do video games differ from computer games? Is one more beneficial than the other? *Class Activity **Divide the class into three groups and assign each group one of the following age groups: 5 to 7 years, 8 to 11 years, or 12 to 18 years. Have each student research two computer or video games for its assigned age group: one that is beneficial and facilitates learning and development, and one that does not. Have each group discuss the games that were found, choose two beneficial and two harmful games, and explain in detail how each game either promotes or hinders learning. Have each group present its findings to the class for discussion. (For students to prepare for this activity, see Homework/Assignments #1.)***
Define *therapeutic play*.	■ Play (p. 383)	⊞ PPT slide 66 ▸ Discuss the role of play in a hospital setting. ▸ Discuss how play differs for sick and well children. *Class Activity **Present the following scenarios to students for a class discussion:*** *1. **A 9-year-old boy has cancer and is hospitalized in the pediatric oncology unit.*** *2. **A 7-year-old girl is in the pediatric unit because of complications arising from juvenile diabetes.*** *3. **A 4-year-old girl has contracted the measles and is hospitalized.*** ***Have students discuss what types of play are appropriate for each patient, and identify how therapeutic play might be useful.*** *Class Activity **In small groups, have students design a playroom for a hospital's pediatric unit. They should include floorplans, toys and games, and color schemes. Have each group present its design to the class for feedback and discussion.***
Understand the use of play as an assessment tool.	■ Play (p. 383) – Ongoing health supervision (p. 384)	⊞ PPT slide 67 ▸ Discuss how play can be used as an assessment tool. What is it used to assess? *Class Activity **Have students identify the age group that most likely will engage in the following types of play:*** – *Exploration and imitation* – *Parallel play* – *Creative and cooperative play*

OBJECTIVES	CONTENT	TEACHING RESOURCES
		– *Group play, secret clubs*
		' – *Competitive play*
		– *Fantasy play, cliques*
		What suggested play activities would be appropriate for each type of play? How can a nurse identify delays in development through observing the stages of play?
Performance Evaluation		⊠▤ PPT slides 1-69
		e EILR IC images 1-14
		e EILR OBQ questions 1-10
		e EILR TB questions 1-32
		e ESLR IRQ questions 1-5
		[SG] SG Learning Activities, questions 1-34 (pp. 129-133)
		[SG] SG Review Questions, questions 1-18 (pp. 133-135)
		[SG] SG Case Study, question 1 (p. 135)
		[SG] SG Thinking Critically, questions 1, 2 (p. 135)
		[SG] SG Applying Knowledge, questions 1-3 (pp. 135-136)
		BOOK RESOURCES
		Review Questions for the NCLEX® Examination, questions 1-5 (pp. 384-385)

15.3 Homework/Assignments:

1. Divide the class into three groups and assign each group one of the following age groups: 5 to 7 years, 8 to 11 years, or 12 to 18 years. Have each student research two computer or video games for its assigned age group: one that is beneficial and facilitates learning and development, and one that does not.

15.3 Instructor's Notes/Student Feedback:

Introduction to Maternity & Pediatric Nursing, 6th ed.

Leifer

15 Lecture Outline
An Overview of Growth, Development, and Nutrition

Slide 1

Slide 2

Slide 3

Slide 4

Slide 5

> Objectives *(cont.)*
>
> · Understand the role of computers and
>   computer games in play at various ages.
> · Define *therapeutic play.*
> · Understand the use of play as an
>   assessment tool.

Slide 6

> Growth and Development
>
> · Differences between adult and child
>   - The child is in a continuous process of growth
>   and development
>   - Growth spurts followed by plateaus
>   - The growth is measurable, can be observed
>   and studied
>   - Not all parts mature at the same time

- Review Box 15-1 on page 348 and discuss the emerging behavior patterns that can be anticipated based on age.
- Growth, such as height and weight, is measurable.
- The process of development is the mastery of a skill that allows the infant or child to progress to the next skill.
- Give examples of growth and developmental skills for each of these categories: physical, social, emotional, and intellectual skills.

Slide 7

> The Impact of Growth and
> Development on Nursing Care
>
> · Developmental needs will have an impact on
>   a child's response to illness
> · The nurse must know what is normal in order
>   to recognize any deviations within a given
>   age group and plan care accordingly
>   - A child differs in anatomy and physiology as
>   compared to the adult; therefore, illnesses and
>   their responses to them, including treatments,
>   may be different

- Children are not miniature adults. For this reason, their plan of care is different than the plan of care for an adult.
- Recognizing developmental and growth delays will assist the nurse in formulating his/her plan of care but may also provide an opportunity for early intervention by the health care team to prevent further developmental delays.
- How are infants and children different from adults?

Slide 8

> The Nursing Process Applied to
> Growth and Development
>
> · Data collection
>   - Height and weight, plot standard growth chart
>   - Record developmental milestones achieved
>   related to age of child
>   - Observe infant; interview parents
> · Analysis/nursing diagnosis
>   - Determine appropriate nursing diagnoses
>   related to parenting, coping skills, and unmet
>   developmental needs

- Give examples of different methods to obtain height and weight on a neonate, infant, and child.
- What is the purpose of a growth chart?
- What are some developmental milestones for an infant?
- How will the nurse obtain the information to assess developmental milestones?

Slide 9

> The Nursing Process Applied to
> Growth and Development *(cont.)*
>
> · Planning
>   - Offer guidance and teaching to family, school
>   personnel, and child to meet developmental
>   needs
> · Implementation
>   - Interventions that foster growth and
>   development in the hospital setting can include
>   encouraging age-appropriate self-care
>   - Anticipatory guidance may be given to parents
>   so they understand changes in behavior, eating
>   habits, and play for the growing child

- Review Box 15-2 on page 349, The Nursing Process Applied to Growth and Development.
- Examples of appropriate nursing diagnoses:
- Breastfeeding, ineffective, related to inability of infant to nurse properly
- Caregiver role strain, related to inexperience
- Family coping, compromised, related to infant's medical diagnosis

---

Elsevier items and derived items © 2011, 2007, 2006 by Saunders, an imprint of Elsevier Inc.   Leifer

Slide 10

The Nursing Process Applied to Growth and Development *(cont.)*

- Evaluation
  - Ongoing evaluation of growth and development of the child and follow-up of teaching and guidance offered at prior clinic/home visits are essential

- Give an example of how a nurse might evaluate effective communication between a parent and a toddler.
- Why is evaluation an ongoing process for growth and development?

Slide 11

Key Terms in Child Development

- Development
  - A progressive increase in the function of the body
- Growth
  - An increase in physical size, measured in feet or meters and pounds or kilograms
- Maturation
  - The total way in which a person grows and develops, as dictated by inheritance

- How can these terms related to age benefit health care professionals?
- Give an example of a toddler and maturation.
- Give an example of progressing development of a preschool child.
- Stages of growth and development
  - Fetus: 9th gestational week to birth
  - Neonate: birth to 4 weeks
  - Infant: 4 weeks to 1 year
  - Toddler: 1-3 years
  - Preschool: 3-6 years
  - School-age: 6-12 years
  - Adolescent: 12-18 years

Slide 12

Directional Patterns

- Fundamental to all humans
  - Cephalocaudal
    - Proceeds from head to toe
  - Proximodistal
    - From midline to periphery

- What are examples of cephalocaudal development? *Raising head and chest precedes sitting; sitting precedes standing.*
- Proximodistal begins at the central portion of the body and extends outward to the extremities (i.e., the infant grasps with the hands before developing the pincer grasp or the infant bats at an object before being able to grasp the object).

Audience Response Question #1
Cephalocaudal : head to toe as proximodistal : _____.
   1. midline to periphery
   2. crown to rump
   3. neck to waist
   4. weight to length

Slide 13

Some Developmental Differences Between Children and Adults

Height	Kidney function
Weight	Nervous system
Body proportions	Sleep patterns
Metabolic rates	Bone growth
Respirations	Critical periods
Cardiovascular system	Integration of skills
Immunity	

- Why is it important for the nurse to recognize the differences between children and adults?
- How is an infant's metabolic rate different from an adult's?
- How are the following body systems of a child different from an adult's: renal, nervous, musculoskeletal, respiratory, immune, and cardiovascular?

Slide 14

Growth Standards

Measured in dimensions
- Height
- Weight
- Volume
- Tissue thickness

Standardized
- Compare the measurement of a child to others of the same age and sex
- Compare the child's present measurements with the former rate of growth and pattern of progress

- Why do we have growth standards?
- How does this benefit the nurse, pediatric patient, and/or parent?
- Why does the nurse compare a child's former growth rate to the current growth rate?

Slide 15

Growth Charts

- Children who are in good health tend to follow a consistent pattern of growth
- At any age, there are wide individual differences in measured values
- There are separate charts for boys and girls

- Give an example of when this tool might be utilized.
- Why are there separate growth charts for boys and girls?

Audience Response Question #2
Childhood obesity is decreasing in the United States.
1. True
2. False

Slide 16

Developmental Screening

Denver Developmental Screening Test
- Assesses the developmental status of children during the first 6 years of life in four categories
  - Personal-social
  - Fine motor-adaptive
  - Language
  - Gross motor
- Purpose is to identify children unable to perform at an age-appropriate level
- Not an intelligence test

- In what instances would the Denver Developmental Screening Test be utilized?
- Why would a nurse want this information?

Slide 17

Influencing Factors

All of the following factors are closely related and dependent on one another in their effect on the growth and development of the child
- Heredity
- Nationality and race
- Ordinal position within the family
- Gender
- Environment

- How do these factors affect growth and development of a child?

Audience Response Question #3
Environment plays a minimal role in childhood development.
1. Strongly agree
2. Agree
3. Disagree
4. Strongly disagree
5. Unsure

Slide 18

Types of Families

- Nuclear
- Extended
- Single parent
- Foster parent
- Alternative
- Dual career
- Blended
- Polygamous
- Homosexual
- Cohabitation

- Give an example of each of the types of families listed.
- How do these different types affect children of school age?

Slide 19 **Family Apgar** · Used to assess family function – Adaptation – Partnership – Growth – Affection – Resolve · Enables the nurse to develop interventions that aid the family to achieve a healthier adaptation to the child's health needs	• Adaptation: How the family helps and shares resources. Give examples of types of resources. • Partnership: Lines of communication and partnership in the family. Give an example of a familial partnership. • Growth: How responsibilities for growth and development of child are shared. Give an example of shared responsibilities. • Affection: Overt and covert emotional interactions among family members. Give an example of overt and covert emotions. • Resolve: How time, money, and space are allocated to prevent and solve problems. Give an example of how time, money, and space can be manipulated to solve a familial problem.
Slide 20 **Family as Part of a Community** · Factors to consider – Housing – Access to public transportation – City services – Safety – Health care delivery system – Assessment of community is important in creating discharge plans for family	• How do these factors affect the family? • What can nurses do within their community to cause effective change in the community?
Slide 21 **Homeless Family** · Has an impact on the growth and development of a child · Support system and financial resources often lacking · School or emergency department nurse may be the only contact with health care or may be the first to identify the status of the family · Community referrals for food, housing, education, and financial assistance are essential	• How does homelessness affect growth and development of a child? • How can the nurse assist these families to receive adequate health care? • How can the nurse become informed regarding available resources within his/her community?
Slide 22 **Personality Development** · Personality is the result of interaction between biological and environmental heritages · Unique organization of characteristics that determine the individual's typical or recurrent pattern of behavior	• Give an example of how one's environment can affect one's personality. • Why is nursing concerned about a child's personality?

Introduction to Maternity & Pediatric Nursing, 6th ed.

Leifer

Slide 23

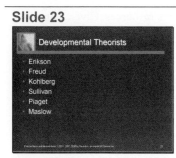

- Why does nursing focus on these developmental theorists?
- How do they affect the nursing plan of care?

Audience Response Question #4
The theorist that has most influenced knowledge on childhood development is:
1. Freud.
2. Erikson.
3. Piaget.
4. Kohlberg.

Slide 24

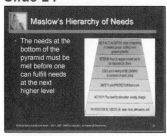

- Describe how Maslow's Hierarchy of Basic Needs affects nursing care.
- How would you utilize this pyramid in your nursing plan of care?

Slide 25

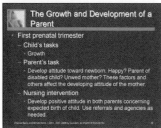

Slide 26

Slide 27

Slide 28

The Growth and Development of a Parent *(cont.)*

- Birth
  - Child's task
    - Adjust to external environment
  - Parent's task
    - Elicit positive responses from child and respond by meeting child's need for food and closeness. If parents receive only negative responses (e.g., sleepy infant, crying infant, difficult feeder, congenital anomaly), parental development will be inhibited.
  - Nursing intervention
    - Encourage early touch, feeding, and other practices. Explain behavior and appearance of newborn to allay fears. Help parents to identify positive responses. (Use infant's reflexes, such as grasp reflex, to identify a positive response by placing mother's finger into infant's hand.)

- Give an example of how the child must adjust to his/her environment.
- Give an example of how the nurse might instruct a parent on caring for the infant.

Slide 29

The Growth and Development of a Parent *(cont.)*

- Infant
  - Child's task
    - Develop trust.
  - Parent's task
    - Learn "cues" presented by infant to determine individual needs.
  - Nursing intervention
    - Help parents assess and interpret needs of infant (avoid feelings of helplessness or incompetence). Do not let grandparents take over parental tasks. Help parents cope with problems such as colic.

- Give an example of how a child might interact with his/her parent if trust hasn't been developed.
- What cues might the parents assess regarding their infant?

Slide 30

The Growth and Development of a Parent *(cont.)*

- Toddler
  - Child's task
    - Autonomy
  - Parent's task
    - Try to accept the pattern of growth and development. Accept some loss of control but maintain some limits for safety.
  - Nursing intervention
    - Help parents cope with transient independence of child (e.g., allow child to go on tricycle but don't yell "Don't fall" or anxiety will be radiated).

- Give an example of a toddler who is striving to attain autonomy.
- How might the nurse educate the parents during this frustrating developmental stage?

Slide 31

The Growth and Development of a Parent *(cont.)*

- Preschool
  - Child's task
    - Initiative
  - Parent's task
    - Learn to separate from child.
  - Nursing intervention
    - Help parents show standards but "let go" so child can develop some independence. A preschool experience may be helpful.

- Give an example of a child asserting initiative.
- Why must the parent learn to separate from the child?
- Why are these children striving for independence? How does this help them in the future?

Slide 32

The Growth and Development of a Parent *(cont.)*

- School-age
  - Child's task
    - Industry
  - Parent's task
    - Accept importance of child's peers and learn to accept some rejection from child at times.
    - Patience is needed to allow children to do for themselves, even if it takes longer. Do not do the school project for the child. Provide chores for child appropriate to his age level.
  - Nursing intervention
    - Help parents understand that child is developing his or her own limits and self-discipline. Be there to guide child, but do not constantly intrude. Help child get results from his or her own efforts at performance.

- Give an example of industry.
- Why must parents practice patience at this stage?
- How does patience on the parent's part assist the child's development?

Slide 33

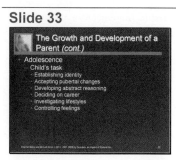

The Growth and Development of a Parent *(cont.)*

- Adolescence
  - Child's task
    - Establishing identity
    - Accepting pubertal changes
    - Developing abstract reasoning
    - Deciding on career
    - Investigating lifestyles
    - Controlling feelings

Slide 34

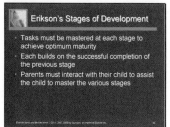

The Growth and Development of a Parent *(cont.)*

- Parent's task
  - Parents must learn to let child live his or her own life and not expect total control over the child.
  - Expect, at times, to be discredited by teenager.
  - Expect differences in opinion and respect them. Guide but do not push.
- Nursing intervention
  - Help parents adjust to changing role and relationship with adolescent.
  - Expose child to varied career fields and life experiences. Help child to understand emerging emotions and feelings brought about by puberty.

Slide 35

Erikson's Stages of Development

- Tasks must be mastered at each stage to achieve optimum maturity
- Each builds on the successful completion of the previous stage
- Parents must interact with their child to assist the child to master the various stages

Slide 36

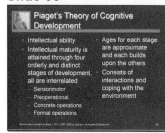

Piaget's Theory of Cognitive Development

- Intellectual ability
- Intellectual maturity is attained through four orderly and distinct stages of development, all are interrelated
  - Sensorimotor
  - Preoperational
  - Concrete operations
  - Formal operations
- Ages for each stage are approximate and each builds upon the others
- Consists of interactions and coping with the environment

- Give an example of a cognitive skill for each of Piaget's stages.
- Why would nurses want to assess cognitive ability?
- Give an example of a child who has not progressed to the cognitive level of a peer.

Slide 37

Kohlberg's Theory of Moral Development

- Sequential
- Theory is based upon Piaget's
- Three levels
  - Preconventional
  - Conventional
  - Postconventional
- Each level contains two stages
- Emphasis on the conscience of the individual within society

- Why would a nurse want to assess moral development?
- Give an example of moral development for each of the three levels.

Leifer

Slide 38

Parent Teaching

- Experiences in dealing with challenges and disappointments prepare the child to function independently in adulthood
- Encourage child to deal with successes and failures, provide socially acceptable outlets, and intervene only if the frustrations become overwhelming
- Parent's task is to provide the child with skills and tools appropriate for each age level to deal with current events

Slide 39

Nutrition

Slide 40

Nutritional Heritage

- Some families do not consider food a priority
- A lack of adequate nutrition can lead to mental retardation
- The obese child may be subject to decreased motor skills and peer rejection
- The nurse identifies children at risk and assists the family in modifying eating habits to ensure adequate nutrition is provided for growth and development

- Refer to Table 15-6, page 369, for culturally diverse food patterns.
- Why should the nurse be informed regarding food and one's culture?
- Give examples of how a nurse might apply this information in his/her plan of care.

Slide 41

Family Nutrition

- USDA dietary guidelines
  - Intended to help families make informed decisions about what they eat
- A well-balanced diet supplies all essential nutrients in the necessary amounts

- Give an example of a well-balanced diet for a school-age child.
- What can result if a child has a poor diet?

Slide 42

Food

- Provides heat and energy
- Builds and repairs tissues
- Regulates body processes
- Is given in a mixture of elements
  - Minerals
  - Compounds
  - Water

- Give an example of how a good versus a poor diet might affect a child's body when recovering from an illness.

Slide 43

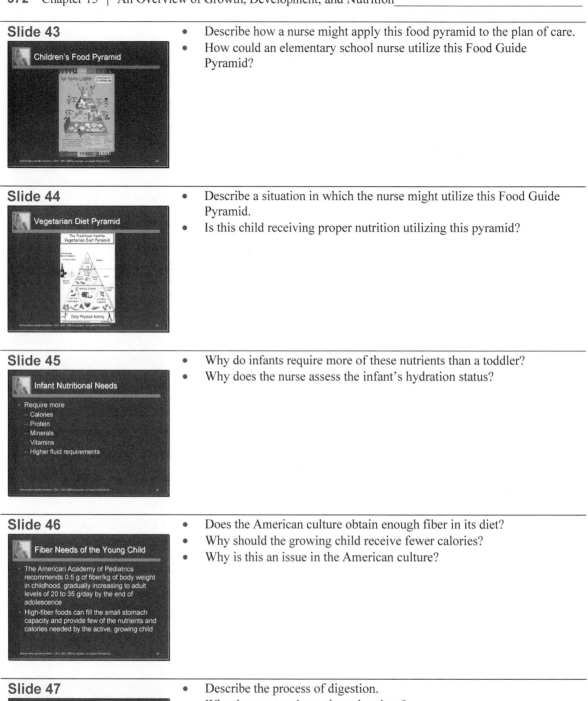

- Describe how a nurse might apply this food pyramid to the plan of care.
- How could an elementary school nurse utilize this Food Guide Pyramid?

Slide 44

Vegetarian Diet Pyramid

- Describe a situation in which the nurse might utilize this Food Guide Pyramid.
- Is this child receiving proper nutrition utilizing this pyramid?

Slide 45

Infant Nutritional Needs

- Require more
  - Calories
  - Protein
  - Minerals
  - Vitamins
  - Higher fluid requirements

- Why do infants require more of these nutrients than a toddler?
- Why does the nurse assess the infant's hydration status?

Slide 46

Fiber Needs of the Young Child

- The American Academy of Pediatrics recommends 0.5 g of fiber/kg of body weight in childhood, gradually increasing to adult levels of 20 to 35 g/day by the end of adolescence
- High-fiber foods can fill the small stomach capacity and provide few of the nutrients and calories needed by the active, growing child

- Does the American culture obtain enough fiber in its diet?
- Why should the growing child receive fewer calories?
- Why is this an issue in the American culture?

Slide 47

Nutrient Digestion

- Describe the process of digestion.
- Why does water absorption take place?
- In what area does the body absorb most of the nutrients from food?

Slide 48

Nutritional Care Plan

- Can be used in
  - Hospital
  - Home
  - Outpatient departments
- Provides information and stores it in one place

- Give an example of a nutritional care plan for each: hospital, home, and outpatient departments.
- Why should the information be kept in one place?

Slide 49

Nutrition and Health

- Digestive system of the newborn
  - Immature and functions minimally for the first 3 months of life
  - Saliva is minimal
  - Hydrochloric acid and rennin in the stomach and trypsin found in the intestines aid in the digestion of milk
  - The physiology of the digestive tract is the basis for introduction of various foods in the first year of life

- Why must foods be introduced slowly during the first year of life?
- At what age are complex carbohydrates digested efficiently?
- How does the liver function during the first year of life?

Slide 50

Nutrition and Health Promotion

- To help prevent some illnesses, it is not recommended to significantly restrict fat and cholesterol as they are needed for calories and the development of the central nervous system
- Nutritional needs may be changed due to the severity of illness
  - Total parenteral nutrition and enteral feedings allow children who need nutritional support to be cared for at home

- Why is the development of the central nervous system crucial during the first year of life?
- Give an example of parenteral and enteral nutrition.
- When might these types of feeding be implemented?

Slide 51

Feeding the Healthy Child: Infant

- Symptoms of underfeeding
  - Restlessness
  - Crying
  - Failure to gain weight
- Symptoms of overfeeding
  - Regurgitation
  - Mild diarrhea
  - Too rapid weight gain
- High-fat diets cause
  - Delayed gastric emptying
  - Abdominal distention
- High carbohydrates
  - Abdominal distention
  - Flatus
  - Excessive weight gain
- Constipation
  - Too much fat or protein
  - Deficiency in "bulk"

- Provide a nursing intervention for the infant who is failing to gain weight.
- Provide a nursing intervention to address overfeeding an infant.

Slide 52

Nursing Tip

- Whole milk should not be introduced before 1 year of age
- Low-fat milk should not be introduced before 2 years of age

- Why should whole milk not be introduced during the first year of life?
- Why does a child require whole milk during the second year of his/her life?

Leifer

Slide 53

Feeding the Healthy Child: Toddler

- Can feed themselves by end of second year
  - Important in order to develop a sense of independence
- Parent should be present at mealtimes
- Difficulties may arise from parental anxiety and/or a lack of time during meals

- Why is it important for a toddler to develop a sense of independence?
- Why should a parent be present at mealtimes?
- Why might the parent be anxious?

Slide 54

Feeding the Healthy Child: Preschool

- Likes finger-foods
- Dawdling and regression common in this age group
- More vulnerable to protein-calorie deficiencies

- Give examples of finger-foods.
- What is dawdling?
- Why is this population more vulnerable to protein deficiencies?

Slide 55

Feeding the Healthy Child: School-age

- Attitude toward food unpredictable
- Intake of protein, calcium, vitamin A, and ascorbic acid tends to be low
- Intake of sweets decreases appetite and provides "empty" calories

- How does an increase in sweets affect the child's appetite?
- How might the parent impact this population's diet?

Slide 56

Feeding the Healthy Child: Adolescent

- Grow rapidly and expend large amounts of energy
- Important to involve adolescent in food selections that are nutritious and appetizing
- Fad food drives a lot of food selections
- Fatigue is common in this age group

- Give an example of types of foods adolescents typically consume.
- How could parents impact their adolescent's diet?
- Why is fatigue common at this age?

Slide 57

Childhood Obesity

- One-third of all children in the U.S. are overweight
  - 30% to 40% of those are considered obese
- Related to obesity in adulthood
- Most often related to diet and inactivity
- Basal metabolic index (BMI) percentile
  Weight in pounds
  Height in inches² × 705

- Why does the U.S. struggle with an obesity problem?
- What types of foods do Americans typically consume?
- How can nursing affect this cultural problem?

Slide 58

Feeding the Ill Child

- Many hospitalized children have poor appetites
- Causes vary depending on illness/disease
- May also refuse food as a means of manipulating parents
- Nurse should assess
  - Does child have any teeth?
  - Are there any lesions in the mouth?
  - Can child eat independently or is assistance needed?

- How might the nurse manage feeding a child with lesions in his/her mouth?
- How would the nurse assess the hydration status of a child?

Slide 59

Feeding the Ill Child (cont.)

- A tablespoonful of food for each year of age is a good guide to follow when feeding a child
- Sweet drinks and snacks should not be served just before meals
- Infants who are placed on NPO status should be provided with a pacifier to meet their sucking needs

- Give an example of educating a parent about feeding an infant, toddler, and preschool child.

Slide 60

Food-Drug Interactions

- Drug-drug: nurse needs to know the side effects of each drug prescribed and administered
- Drug-environment: involves interaction of the effects of a drug on the response of the patient to the environment (i.e., certain antibiotics cause pronounced photosensitivity)
- Drug-food: nurse needs to know if any foods are contraindicated when child is receiving certain drugs (i.e., Coumadin and foods containing high levels of vitamin K)

- Give an example of a food-drug interaction.
- How should the nurse plan care of an infant who is receiving medications and formula?
- Give an example of drug-environment interactions.

Slide 61

The Teeth

Permanent and deciduous teeth and age of eruption

- What are deciduous teeth?
- How do teeth affect digestion?
- When does the first tooth typically appear in an infant?

Slide 62

The Teeth (cont.)

- Important not to neglect baby teeth
- Deciduous teeth serve not only in the digestive process but also in the development of the jaw
- If these teeth are lost too early, the permanent teeth can come in poorly aligned
- Delayed or early eruption can be indicative of certain endocrine disorders or other pathologic conditions

- What is bottle mouth?
- Why is it important for the permanent teeth to develop in alignment?
- How would the nurse instruct a parent to care for his/her infant's teeth?

Leifer

Slide 63

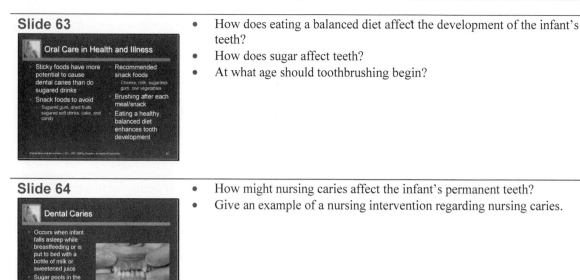

- How does eating a balanced diet affect the development of the infant's teeth?
- How does sugar affect teeth?
- At what age should toothbrushing begin?

Slide 64

Dental Caries

- How might nursing caries affect the infant's permanent teeth?
- Give an example of a nursing intervention regarding nursing caries.

Slide 65

Education on Tooth Hygiene

- Why should a toothbrush be replaced every 3 months?
- Why should closed toothbrush containers be avoided?
- Why should parents avoid tasting their baby's food?

Slide 66

Play

- Describe how play is a child's work.
- How do children benefit from play?
- Why should stuffed animals be avoided in the asthmatic child?
- Give an age-appropriate activity for each of the following: infant, toddler, preschooler, school-age child, and adolescent.

Slide 67

Medical Problems and Dental Health

Slide 68

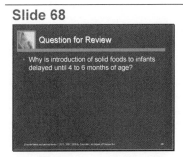

Slide 69

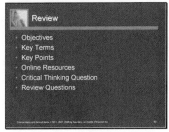

TEACHING FOCUS

In this chapter, students will have the opportunity to learn about the skills required to provide care to growing and developing infants. Students will also have the opportunity to learn about the physical and emotional development of the infant, health maintenance and illness prevention, feeding and nutrition, and safety. Toys, play, and the emergence of sleep patterns will also be discussed.

MATERIALS AND RESOURCES

- ☐ Computer and PowerPoint projector (all lessons)
- ☐ Infant-sized dolls (Lesson 16.2)

LESSON CHECKLIST

Preparations for this lesson include:

- Lecture
- Demonstration
- Evaluation of student knowledge and skills needed to perform all entry-level activities related to the care of the growing infant, including:
  - ○ Milestones of infant growth and development
  - ○ Physical, cognitive, emotional, and psychosocial development
  - ○ Infant nutritional needs, food preparation, and the development of feeding skills
  - ○ Safety issues related to toys, cars, and falls
  - ○ Caring for an infant with colic

KEY TERMS

colic (p. 395)	object permanence (p. 404)	satiety (p. 398)
extrusion reflex (p. 397)	oral stage (p. 387)	separation anxiety (p. 387)
grasp reflex (p. 387)	parachute reflex (p. 387)	weaning (p. 403)
milestones (p. 386)	pincer grasp (p. 387)	
norms (p. 386)	prehension (p. 387)	

ADDITIONAL RESOURCES

TEACH PPT slide(s) Chapter 16, 1-38
EILR IC image(s) Chapter 16, 1-4
EILR OBQ question(s) Chapter 16, 1-10
EILR TB question(s) Chapter 16, 1-30
ESLR IRQ question(s) Chapter 16, 1-6
SG Chapter 16, pp. 137-143

Legend

PPT
TEACH
PowerPoint
Slides

EILR
EVOLVE Instructor
Learning Resources:
Image Collection (IC),
Open-Book Quizzes
(OBQ), Test Bank (TB)

ESLR
EVOLVE Student
Learning Resources:
Interactive Review
Questions (IRQ) for
the NCLEX®
Examination

SG
Study Guide

CTQ
Critical Thinking
Question in
Nursing Care Plan
(NCP CTQ) or Get
Ready for the
NCLEX! (GRN
CTQ)

Class Activities are indicated in ***bold italic***.

Leifer

LESSON 16.1

PRETEST

1. Around what age do infants normally begin to experience separation anxiety?
   - a. 6 months
   - b. 9 months
   - c. 12 months
   - d. 15 months

2. The coordination of index finger and thumb is called the
   - a. pincer grasp.
   - b. grasp reflex.
   - c. parachute reflex.
   - d. plantar reflex.

3. An 8-month-old infant should be able to
   - a. stand alone.
   - b. pull to a standing position.
   - c. creep.
   - d. walk when led.

4. An infant's birthweight is expected to double around what age?
   - a. 4 months
   - b. 6 months
   - c. 9 months
   - d. 10 months

5. Placing infants in the supine position helps to prevent
   - a. asthma.
   - b. GERD.
   - c. colic.
   - d. SIDS.

6. A technique to soothe an irritable or colicky infant is to
   - a. increase environmental stimulation.
   - b. remove blankets and bulky clothing.
   - c. slowly rock the infant.
   - d. walk or pace while holding the infant.

7. A rear-facing car seat is needed for infants
   - a. younger than 1 year.
   - b. older than 1 year.
   - c. younger than 2 years.
   - d. 3 years and older.

8. At what age does the posterior fontanel close?
   - a. 2 months
   - b. 4 months
   - c. 10 months
   - d. 18 months

9. Breastfed babies require feeding more often because
   - a. formula contains fewer calories than breast milk.
   - b. formula is more easily digested than breast milk.
   - c. breast milk contains more calories than formula.
   - d. breast milk is more easily digested than formula.

10. The average pulse rate of infants under 1 year of age is
    - a. 78-100 beats per minute.
    - b. 80-110 beats per minute.
    - c. 100-118 beats per minute.
    - d. 120-140 beats per minute.

Answers

1. b	3. b	5. d	7. a	9. d
2. a	4. b	6. c	8. a	10. c

BACKGROUND ASSESSMENT

Question: How would you explain the development of locomotion, prehension, and perception in a 4-month-old infant?
Answer: At 4 months old, the infant should reach the following developmental milestones: locomotion, prehension, and perception. Locomotion is noted by the infant's ability to roll over without assistance. Prehension is noted by the infant's attempt to reach overhead in order to grasp objects with fingers, with or without success. The infant perceives differences in the facial expressions of others.

Question: When does an infant's birth weight triple? What is the average head circumference of a 1-year-old infant? When does the anterior fontanel close, and why?
Answer: Infants should triple their birth weights around 1 year of age; the normal head circumference of an infant that age is around 18 inches. The head and chest circumference are also equal at 1 year of age. The anterior fontanel does not close until 18 months, allowing space for the continued growth of the brain. Early closure of the anterior fontanel can result in neurological deficits if left untreated.

ELSEVIER

CRITICAL THINKING QUESTION

A 26-year-old woman brings her 3-week-old son to the clinic for a follow-up visit. She expresses concern about holding the baby too much when he cries because she is afraid of spoiling him. What should the nurse tell the mother about the infant's emotional development?

Guidelines: The nurse should explain that picking up the baby when he is crying will not spoil him. In attending to the baby's needs, the mother is actually building trust and creating a strong bond between herself and her child. By consistently showing the baby love and affection and attending to his needs, she is establishing a strong foundation of love and trust, which is essential for healthy emotional and personality development. Children who are consistently picked up when they cry have fewer crying episodes and show less aggressive behavior during the toddler years. It is helpful to communicate with the baby through talking, singing, and touch.

OBJECTIVES	CONTENT	TEACHING RESOURCES
Describe normal vital signs for a 1-year-old infant.	■ Introduction (p. 386)	⊠ PPT slide 6 *e* EILR IC image 1 *e* EILR OBQ question 1 *e* ESLR IRQ question 1 **BOOK RESOURCES** Figure 16-1, Average Vital Signs of the Infant (p. 387) *Class Activity* ***In groups, have students discuss how the vital signs of a 1-year-old infant compare to those of adults. What physiologic and environmental factors account for the differences? Have each group share its findings with the class for discussion.***
Describe the physical and psychosocial development of infants from age 1 to 12 months, listing age-specific events and guidance when appropriate.	■ General characteristics (p. 387) ☐ Oral stage (p. 387) ☐ Motor development (p. 387) ☐ Emotional development (p. 387)	⊠ PPT slides 7-14 *e* EILR IC images 2, 3 *e* EILR OBQ question 5 *e* EILR TB questions 7, 8, 11-12, 16, 21, 28, 30 *e* ESLR IRQ questions 2, 4 [SG] SG Learning Activities, questions 1-3 (p. 137) [SG] SG Review Questions, questions 2, 4, 11, 17 (pp. 140-142) [SG] SG Thinking Critically, question 1 (p. 143) [SG] SG Applying Knowledge, question 3 (p. 143) **BOOK RESOURCES** Figure 16-2, Pacifier (p. 387) Figure 16-3, The Development of Locomotion, Prehension, and Perception (pp. 388-389) Review Questions for the NCLEX® Examination, question

Leifer

OBJECTIVES	CONTENT	TEACHING RESOURCES
		1 (p. 405) ▸ Discuss the characteristics and the importance of the oral stage. When does the oral stage begin, and when does it end? *Class Activity **In groups, have students create a time line that illustrates the physical and psychosocial milestones that should be reached during the first 18 months of life. Have each group share its time line with the class for discussion.***
Discuss the major aspects of cognitive development in the first year of life.	☐ Emotional development (p. 387) ☐ Need for constant care and guidance (p. 388)	⊠ PPT slides 12, 13 *e* EILR TB question 24 SG Learning Activities, questions 4, 5 (p. 138) SG Review Questions, question 1 (p. 140) **BOOK RESOURCES** Nursing Tip (p. 388) ▸ Discuss the signs of delayed emotional or cognitive development. How could the nurse help the family cope with the delays? *Class Activity **As a class, have students discuss cognitive development. How is cognitive development defined? How does it differ from physical and emotional development? What are the developmental milestones from infancy to adulthood?***
Identify the approximate age for each of the following: posterior fontanel has closed, central incisors appear, birthweight has tripled, child can sit steadily alone, child shows fear of strangers.	▪ Development and care (p. 389) ▪ Community-based care: A multidisciplinary team (p. 389)	⊠ PPT slides 13-16 *e* EILR TB questions 2-5, 9 *e* ESLR IRQ question 6 SG Learning Activities, question 6 (p. 138) SG Review Questions, question 3 (p. 140) **BOOK RESOURCES** Box 16-1, Physical Development, Social Behavior, and Care and Guidance of Infants (pp. 390-394) ▸ Discuss the milestones of infant growth. *Class Activity **Divide the class into four groups and assign each group one of the following topics: physical development, social behavior, and care and guidance. Assign two groups to discuss care and guidance; have one group discuss 1 month to 6 months, and the other 7 months to 12 months. Have the other groups outline how its assigned topic progresses and changes in infants from***

OBJECTIVES	CONTENT	TEACHING RESOURCES
		the age of 1 month to 12 months. Then, have each group share its findings with the class for discussion.
Relate the nursing responsibilities in health promotion and illness prevention in infants in the first year of life.	■ Health promotion: role of the nurse (p. 394) ☐ Infants with special needs (p. 396) ☐ Illness prevention (p. 396) ☐ Immunizations (p. 397)	⊠▦ PPT slides 16-22 *e* EILR TB questions 17, 27 *e* ESLR IRQ question 3 SG Learning Activities, question 8 (p. 138) SG Review Questions, question 7 (p. 141) SG Case Study, question 1 (p. 143) **BOOK RESOURCES** Nursing Tip (p. 395)

16.1 Homework/Assignments:

16.1 Instructor's Notes/Student Feedback:

LESSON 16.2

CRITICAL THINKING QUESTION

A 3-month-old infant has been extremely irritable and restless for the past few days. Her parents are getting frustrated because nothing they do seems to calm the crying infant. What recommendations could the nurse give to help the parents cope with this situation?

Guidelines: The nurse should first ask the parents questions to determine why the infant might be so irritable. For instance, when does the infant seem most irritable? Is there a pattern or consistency to the irritability? If no explanation is found, the infant may have colic; a physician should be consulted to rule out any physiologic problems. Intestinal obstruction and infection may mimic symptoms of colic. To calm the irritable infant, the goal is to provide a calm environment in which the infant feels safe. This can be achieved by reducing environmental stimuli such as bright light, loud noises, and sudden movement. Parents should sit quietly with the infant, without talking or singing. When changing positions, the infant should be moved slowly, without sudden or jerky movements, and parents should swaddle the infant in a light blanket with extremities flexed and hands near the face. Other measures to help relieve symptoms of colic are the colic carry, abdominal massage, wind-up swings, and car rides. It is also important that parents provide each other with periods of rest or breaks in order to minimize stress and frustration.

OBJECTIVES	CONTENT	TEACHING RESOURCES
Discuss the approach and care of an infant with colic.	☐ Health promotion: role of the nurse (p. 394) ☐ Coping with an irritable infant (p. 394) – Coping with colic (p. 395) ☐ Coping with the lethargic infant (p. 396)	▣ PPT slides 15-18 *e* EILR OBQ questions 2-4 *e* EILR TB questions 1, 14, 18 SG Learning Activities, question 1 (p. 137) SG Review Questions, question 19 (p. 142) SG Case Study, question 1 (p. 143) SG Applying Knowledge, question 5 (p. 143) **BOOK RESOURCES** Nursing Care Plan 16-1, The Family Care Plan When the Infant has Colic (p. 395) GRN CTQ 1 (p. 405) See Figure 22-4, D, The Colic Carry (p. 490) ▸ Discuss how an irritable or colicky infant can lead to parental fatigue and distress. What are some ways to minimize the stress? *Class Activity **Using infant-sized dolls, have student volunteers demonstrate for the class methods of calming a colicky infant. Have the rest of the class offer comments and suggestions.*** *Class Activity **Present the following to the class for students to discuss:*** *A single mother has a 3-month-old infant with colic. The mother works during the day and places her infant with a babysitter during that time. The babysitter has*

OBJECTIVES	CONTENT	TEACHING RESOURCES
		said that she will not care for the baby until the colic is resolved. ***What are possible solutions to this problem?***
Discuss the development of favorable sleep patterns.	☐ Developing positive sleep patterns (p. 396) – Infants with special needs (p. 396)	⊠ PPT slide 19 *e* EILR OBQ question 5 *e* EILR TB questions 20, 29 📖 SG Learning Activities, question 7 (p. 138) 📖 SG Review Questions, question 5 (p. 140) 📖 SG Case Study, question 1 (p. 143) **BOOK RESOURCES** Safety Alert (p. 396) ▶ Discuss how to develop positive sleep habits of the infant and toddler. *Class Activity* **Present the following scenario to the class for students to discuss:** ***The mother of a newborn works in an office during the day while her husband cares for the child. The husband works at night. The mother complains that the baby keeps her up all night, and that not only is her work suffering, but she is becoming ill from the stress and fatigue.*** ***What could a nurse suggest to make this situation more bearable?***
List four common concerns of parents about the feeding of infants.	– Nutrition counseling (p. 397) – Parental concerns (p. 397) – Breastfeeding and bottle feeding (p. 398)	⊠ PPT slide 23-34 *e* EILR OBQ questions 6, 7 *e* EILR TB question 22 📖 SG Review Questions, questions 6, 18 (pp. 141-142) 📖 SG Learning Activities, questions 1, 9, 11 (p. 143) 📖 SG Applying Knowledge, question 2 (p. 143) **BOOK RESOURCES** Nursing Tip (p. 397) Review Questions for the NCLEX® Examination, question 3 (p. 405) ▶ Discuss cultural and ethnic issues that can affect infant feeding and nutrition.

OBJECTIVES	CONTENT	TEACHING RESOURCES
		‣ Discuss how the adequacy or inadequacy of an infant's diet is determined.
		Class Activity **In groups, have students identify common parental concerns about feeding infants and discuss the guidelines, patient teaching, and nursing interventions that nurses could use to address each concern. What changes in feeding patterns suggest potential problems? What are the signs of infant satiety and hunger? Have each group share its findings with the class for discussion.**
Compare breastfeeding, bottle feeding, and the various infant formulas available.	■ Breastfeeding and bottle feeding (p. 398) □ Safe bottle feeding (p. 399)	☒ PPT slides 23-28 𝒆 EILR TB question 23 📖 SG Review Questions, question 9 (p. 141) **BOOK RESOURCES** Table 16-1, Common Milk Preparation for the First Year (p. 398) Table 16-2, Development of Mealtime Behavior and Implications for Caregivers (p. 399) Table16-3, Commercially Prepared Infant Formulas (p. 400) Nursing Tip (p. 401) ‣ Discuss the different formulas available and the pros and cons of using those versus breast milk. *Class Activity* **Divide the class into two groups. One group is to list the different formulas available and what they can be used for, i.e., allergy to milk, PKU, etc. The other is to list the advantages and disadvantages of breastfeeding. The information can then be presented to the entire class.**
Describe how to select and prepare solid foods for the infant.	□ Adding solid foods (p. 401) □ Recommended fat intake during infancy (p. 402) – Buying, storing, and serving foods (p. 403)	☒ PPT slides 29-34 𝒆 EILR IC image 4 𝒆 EILR OBQ questions 8, 9 𝒆 EILR TB questions 6, 10, 13, 26 𝒆 ESLR IRQ question 5 📖 SG Learning Activities, questions 12-17 (p. 139) 📖 SG Review Questions, questions 8, 12, 14, 15, 20 (pp. 141-142) 📖 SG Case Study, question 2 (p. 143)

Introduction to Maternity & Pediatric Nursing, 6th ed.
Leifer

OBJECTIVES	CONTENT	TEACHING RESOURCES
		SG SG Applying Knowledge, question 1 (p. 143)
		BOOK RESOURCES
		Table 16-1, Common Milk Preparation for the First Year (p. 398)
		Table 16-3 Commercially Prepared Infant Formulas (p. 400)
		Health Promotion, Directions for Home Preparation of Infant Foods (p. 401)
		Nursing Tips (p. 401)
		Nursing Tip (p. 402)
		Safety Alert (p. 402)
		▸ Discuss how to prepare and store foods for infants. What problems occur if foods are poorly stored or prepared?
		Class Activity In groups, have students develop a plan that explains when and how solid food should be introduced into an infant's diet. Each group should develop a patient teaching handout for parents to take home as a supplement to verbal instructions. Plans should include preparation instructions and a list of foods that should and should not be given to infants. Have each group share its plan with the class for discussion.
Compare and contrast natural, organic, and processed foods.	– Organic and natural foods (p. 403)	**PPT** PPT slides 27, 34 **BOOK RESOURCES** Nursing Tip (p. 403) *Class Activity Choose two student volunteers to role-play a nurse explaining when and how solid food should be introduced into an infant's diet to an uncertain mother who asks many questions about the benefits of natural, organic, and processed foods. Have the rest of the class discuss the interaction and offer suggestions for improvement.*
Examine nutrition counseling for the infant.	– Nutrition counseling (p. 397)	**PPT** PPT slides 29-31 **SG** SG Learning Activities, question 10 (p. 139)

Leifer

16.2 Homework/Assignments:

16.2 Instructor's Notes/Student Feedback:

Leifer

LESSON 16.3

CRITICAL THINKING QUESTION

When a 1-year-old boy is brought to the physician's office for his immunizations, the child cries, kicks, and screams. His father responds by saying that he will not subject his son to any more shots because he does not want him to be traumatized. How should the nurse respond?

Guidelines: First, the nurse should address the father's reaction to seeing his son upset. Then the nurse should explain that the child's discomfort is temporary and that the immunizations will prevent him from acquiring serious, possibly life-threatening, diseases. It is essential that the child be immunized regularly, as a delay or lack of immunizations can lead to serious illness, developmental delays, and potentially fatal complications. Development of these illnesses or complications will also result in a loss of valuable working hours, which could cause significant financial strain. Immunizations are required for admittance into school. If the child does not have an accurate immunization record, he will either be required to receive the immunizations prior to entering school, or he will not be allowed to register. Because it is likely that the child throws similar tantrums at home, the nurse should show the father ways to calm the child, create a safe home environment, and prevent falls or other injuries.

OBJECTIVES	CONTENT	TEACHING RESOURCES
Discuss the nutritional needs of growing infants.	– Recommended fat intake during infancy (p. 402)	☒▪ PPT slide 31 *e* EILR IC image 4 SG Review Questions, question 12 (p. 141) **BOOK RESOURCES** Figure 16-4, Development of Feeding Skills in Infants and Toddlers (p. 402) Review Questions for the NCLEX® Examination, question 5 (p. 405) ▸ Discuss how the nutritional needs of infants and toddlers differ from those of adults. *Class Activity **In groups, have students discuss the nutritional needs of infants, from newborns to 18 months of age. They should include caloric and nutritional requirements, and explain how and why the requirements change as the infant grows.***
Discuss the development of feeding skills in the infant.	– Adding solid foods (p. 401) – Weaning (p. 403)	☒▪ PPT slides 29-33 *e* EILR IC image 4 *e* EILR OBQ question 10 **BOOK RESOURCES** Figure 16-4, Development of Feeding Skills in Infants and Toddlers (p. 402) ▸ Discuss the growth and development of mealtime behavior. *Class Activity **In groups, have students outline the development of feeding skills in infants and toddlers. What other physical, emotional, and psychosocial***

OBJECTIVES	CONTENT	TEACHING RESOURCES
		developmental milestones accompany each feeding skill? How are each of these developmental areas interrelated? Are there differences in the development of feeding skills depending on whether the infant is breastfeeding or bottle feeding? Have each group share its findings with the class for discussion.
Discuss safety issues in the care of infants.	■ Infant safety (p. 403) ☐ Car safety (p. 403) ☐ Fall prevention (p. 403) ☐ Toy safety (p. 403)	▣▦ PPT slide 35 *e* EILR TB questions 15, 25 ▣sg SG Review Questions, questions 13, 21 (pp. 141-142) **BOOK RESOURCES** Table 16-4, Toys for the First Year (p. 404) Review Questions for the NCLEX® Examination, question 2 (p. 405) ▸ Discuss ways to make the home environment safe for infants and toddlers. *Class Activity In groups, have students identify five risk areas or safety issues regarding infant care that are not listed in the text and explain what precautions or safety measures can be adopted to minimize risks. Have each group share its list with the class for discussion.*
Discuss principles of safety during infancy.	■ Infant safety (p. 403) ☐ Car safety (p. 403) ☐ Fall prevention (p. 403)	▣▦ PPT slide 35 **BOOK RESOURCES** Review Questions for the NCLEX® Examination, questions 2, 4 (p. 405) ▸ Discuss the guidelines and laws pertaining to child safety seats. What are the risks of improper use? *Class Activity Present the following scenario to the class for discussion: The mother of a 5-month-old infant states that she and her husband are planning a family vacation to Europe. What recommendations should the nurse make regarding safety and travel? Can infants ride in airplanes?*
Identify age-appropriate toys and their developmental or therapeutic value.	☐ Toy safety (p. 403) ■ Summary of major developmental changes in the first year (p. 404)	▣▦ PPT slides 35, 36 *e* EILR TB questions 5, 19 ▣sg SG Learning Activities, question 1 (p. 137) ▣sg SG Review Questions, question 16 (p. 142) **BOOK RESOURCES** Table 16-4, Toys for the First Year (p. 404) ▸ Discuss the guidelines for toy safety.

OBJECTIVES	CONTENT	TEACHING RESOURCES
		Class Activity **Divide the class into four groups and assign each group one of the following age groups: birth to 2 months, 3-5 months, 6-9 months, 10-12 months. Have students discuss appropriate methods of visual, auditory, and sensorimotor stimulation and research which toys on the market are best for their assigned age level. Have each group choose three to five toys to present to the class for discussion.** *(For students to prepare for this activity, see Homework/Assignments #1.)*
Performance Evaluation		⊠ PPT slides 1-38
		e EILR IC images 1-4
		e EILR OBQ questions 1-10
		e EILR TB questions 1-30
		e ESLR IRQ questions 1-6
		SG Learning Activities, questions 1-17 (pp. 137-140)
		SG Review Questions, questions 1-21 (pp. 140-142)
		SG Case Study, questions 1, 2 (p. 143)
		SG Thinking Critically, question 1 (p. 143)
		SG Applying Knowledge, questions 1-4 (p. 143)
		BOOK RESOURCES
		Review Questions for the NCLEX® Examination, questions 1-5 (p. 405)
		GRN CTQ 1 (p. 405)

16.3 Homework/Assignments:

1. Divide the class into four groups and assign each group one of the following age groups: 0-2 months, 3-5 months, 6-9 months, 10-12 months. Have students discuss appropriate methods of visual, auditory, and sensorimotor stimulation and research which toys on the market are best for their assigned age level.

16.3 Instructor's Notes/Student Feedback:

Introduction to Maternity & Pediatric Nursing, 6th ed.

Leifer

16 Lecture Outline
The Infant

Slide 1

Chapter 16

The Infant

Slide 2

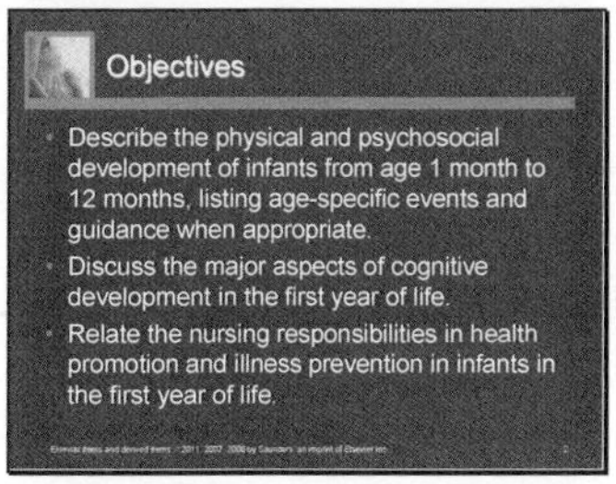

Objectives

- Describe the physical and psychosocial development of infants from age 1 month to 12 months, listing age-specific events and guidance when appropriate.
- Discuss the major aspects of cognitive development in the first year of life.
- Relate the nursing responsibilities in health promotion and illness prevention in infants in the first year of life.

Slide 3

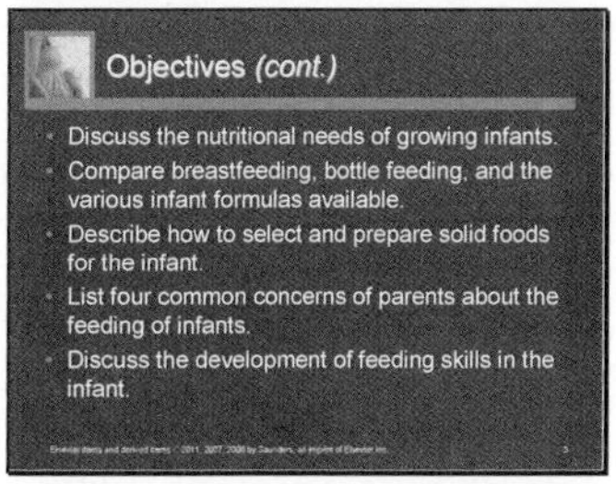

Objectives *(cont.)*

- Discuss the nutritional needs of growing infants.
- Compare breastfeeding, bottle feeding, and the various infant formulas available.
- Describe how to select and prepare solid foods for the infant.
- List four common concerns of parents about the feeding of infants.
- Discuss the development of feeding skills in the infant.

Slide 4

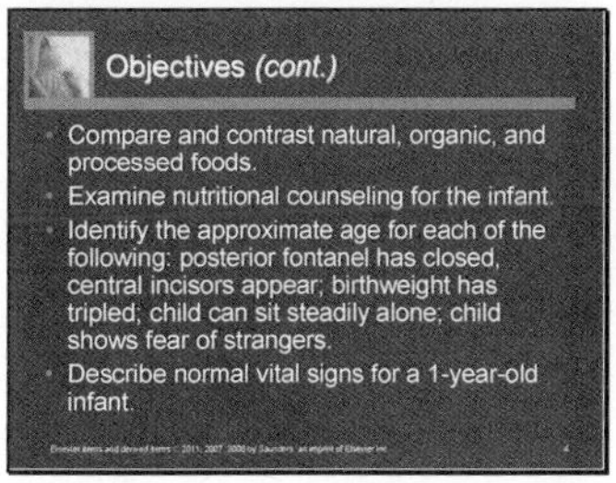

Objectives *(cont.)*

- Compare and contrast natural, organic, and processed foods.
- Examine nutritional counseling for the infant.
- Identify the approximate age for each of the following: posterior fontanel has closed, central incisors appear; birthweight has tripled; child can sit steadily alone; child shows fear of strangers.
- Describe normal vital signs for a 1-year-old infant.

Slide 5

Objectives (cont.)

- Discuss safety issues in the care of infants.
- Discuss the approach and care of an infant with colic.
- Identify age-appropriate toys and their developmental or therapeutic value.
- Discuss principles of safety during infancy.
- Discuss the development of positive sleep patterns.

Slide 6

Milestones

- Describes general patterns of achievement at various stages
  - Often referred to as *norms*
  - Nurse must understand normal range for milestone achievement
    - Establishment of sleep-wake cycle
    - Social smile
    - Drinking from cup
    - Separation anxiety

- Give an example of a normal sleep-wake cycle for an infant.
- When does an infant begin to smile?
- When does the infant begin to drink from a cup?
- Describe separation anxiety. When does it begin?

Slide 7

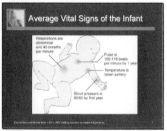

Average Vital Signs of the Infant

Respirations are abdominal and 40 breaths per minute

Pulse is 100-118 beats per minute by 1 year

Temperature is taken axillary

Blood pressure is 90/60 by first year

- Why should the nurse obtain an apical pulse for 1 minute on the infant?
- Describe abdominal respirations.

Slide 8

Oral Stage

- Sucking brings comfort and relief from tension
- Important to hold infant during feedings
- Allow sufficient time for infant to suck
- Infants on IV fluid/nutrition need additional attention and a pacifier to ensure the need for sucking is satisfied
- When infants are able to use their hands more skillfully, they will gradually derive pleasure and comfort from other sources

- How does an infant relieve tension?
- Why do infants need to suck?
- Describe non-nutritive sucking.

Slide 9

Motor Development

- Grasp reflex disappears around 3 months of age
- Prehension occurs around 5 to 6 months of age and follows an orderly sequence of development
- Parachute reflex appears around 7 to 9 months as a protective mechanism
- Pincer grasp well-established by 1 year of age

- Describe the grasp reflex.
- What is prehension?
- Describe the parachute reflex.
- What is the pincer grasp?

Leifer

Slide 10

The Development of Locomotion, Prehension, and Perception

- Describe the progression of the different developmental milestones of locomotion, prehension, and perception of the infant from 1 to 8 months.

Slide 11

The Development of Locomotion, Prehension, and Perception *(cont.)*

- Describe the progression of the different developmental milestones of locomotion, prehension, and perception of the infant from 9 to 15 months.

Slide 12

Emotional Development

- Consistency must be established to develop trust, which is vital to the development of a healthy personality
- Infants who are consistently picked up when they cry tend to have fewer crying episodes and less aggressive behavior as toddlers
- Infants will easily accomplish various activities if they are not forced before they reach readiness
- When infant shows readiness to learn a task, parents should provide encouragement

- Give an example of when a parent must allow for an infant to be ready for a task.
- How does a sense of trust promote emotional development?

Slide 13

Need for Constant Care and Guidance

- Sensory stimulation is essential for the development of the infant's thought processes and perceptual abilities
- A crying child should be soothed
- If the infant appears hungry, do not delay the feeding in order to adhere to a specific routine
- An infant can recognize warmth and affection or the lack thereof

- Describe how sensory stimulation is important to the development of an infant's cognition.
- Give an example of an infant's actions which convey a recognition of warmth and affection.

Slide 14

Development and Care

- Important to note that no two infants are the same
- Physical patterns cannot be separated from social patterns
- Abrupt changes do not take place with each new month of life

- Describe a situation in which a nurse must utilize her critical thinking skills when determining if a child is or is not developmentally delayed, if the infant does not fit into the norm.

Leifer

Slide 15

Community-Based Care:
A Multidisciplinary Team

Slide 16

Health Promotion

- Nurse's responsibilities
  - Guide parents and assist in the acquisition of necessary skills to ensure the healthy growth and development of their infant
  - Provide appropriate community referrals as indicated

- Give an example of how a nurse can assist parents in providing proper care for their infant.
- How does the nurse influence the community regarding the infant's health?
- Why is it beneficial to the community for the nurse to educate and intervene regarding the health of infants in the community?

Slide 17

Coping with an Irritable or Lethargic Infant

- Whether irritable or lethargic, many of the same interventions can be used
- An irritable baby cries and may be difficult to soothe
- A lethargic baby may "shut down" and sleep in order to avoid an excessively stimulating (loud or noisy) environment

- Shield infant's eyes from bright light
- Sit quietly with infant; don't talk or sing
- Eliminate as much noise as possible
- Talk in a soft voice
- Swaddle snugly
- Change infant's position slowly
- Provide nonnutritive sucking

- Give an example of when an infant might become lethargic and shut down from a situation.
- How does the environment affect the irritable or lethargic infant?

Slide 18

Colic

- Periods of unexplained irritability and crying in an otherwise healthy and well-fed infant

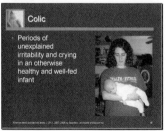

- How does the manner in which the woman is holding the infant in Figure 22-4, D, on page 490, assist the colicky infant?
- What other measures can soothe a colicky infant?

Slide 19

Developing Positive Sleep Patterns

- Newborns sleep in 4-hour intervals
  - By 4 to 6 months, can be up to 8 hours
- Synchronizing circadian rhythm of infant to family routine is a learned behavior
- Position infants on their backs on a firm mattress
- Infants rely on parent to soothe them back to sleep if awakened during the night
  - Assist infant to learn self-soothing behaviors

- Discuss what the parent can do to teach the infant to self-soothe.

ELSEVIER

Slide 20 ![Illness Prevention: Parent Education] **Illness Prevention: Parent Education** · Stress importance of periodic health checks · Ensure infant receives recommended vaccinations at appropriate times · Provide education and anticipatory guidance for the developmental changes that occur · Stress importance of changing diaper when it becomes wet or soiled · Monitor growth of infant by documenting measurements on a growth chart · Ensure adequate fluid and nutrition are provided	• What are the guidelines for well-baby checks in the United States? • Why are vaccinations encouraged in the United States? • Give an example of anticipatory guidance. • Why is skin care such an issue for infants? • How might the nurse educate parents regarding skin care for the infant who has a diaper rash?

Slide 21
 	
Illness Prevention: Physical Examination
 	
· Physical examination in the clinic setting at least five times in the first year
  – Hearing and vision assessments as indicated
  – Screening tests administered as required
  – Growth grids and developmental screening
  – Immunizations
  – Nutritional counseling
  – Provide appropriate education and/or explanations to the parents
	• Describe a method in which the nurse can assess whether the infant is receiving adequate nutrition.
	• How does the nurse determine whether the infant is receiving adequate nutrition with a mother who is breastfeeding and a mother who is bottle feeding?
	• Describe how growth and developmental screenings assist in illness prevention.
	• Describe an incident in which nutritional counseling would be appropriate from the nurse.
	• Bottle versus breastfeeding was discussed in earlier chapters. It may be helpful to review specific points in this area, including how to heat formula, how to determine if infant is getting enough to eat based on number of wet diapers, ability of infant to sleep, etc.

Slide 22 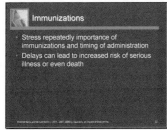 **Immunizations** · Stress repeatedly importance of immunizations and timing of administration · Delays can lead to increased risk of serious illness or even death

Slide 23
 	
Nutrition Counseling
 	
· Solid food can slowly be added beginning around 6 months of age
  – The tongue extrusion reflex has completely disappeared
  – GI tract is mature enough to digest food
· Between 4 and 6 months, sucking is more mature, and munching or an up-and-down chewing/chomping motion ensues
	Audience Response Question #1
	The reason solids foods are introduced slowly in the infant is to:
	  1. prevent choking.
	  2. assess ability to swallow solids.
	  3. allow the infant to get used to each food.
	  4. assess for reactions to different foods.

ELSEVIER

Introduction to Maternity & Pediatric Nursing, 6th ed.
Leifer

Slide 24

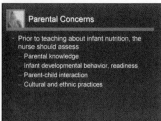

Slide 25

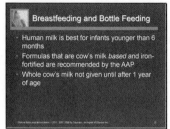

- Refer to Table 16-3 on page 400 for more detailed information on the various formulas and their nutritional components.

Slide 26

Audience Response Question #2
A breastfeeding mother is running a fever of $102°$ F. She reports "nasal congestion and sore throat." Should she be instructed to delay breastfeeding her infant?
  1. Yes
  2. No
  3. Not sure

Slide 27

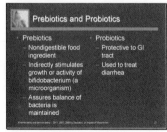

Slide 28

Slide 29

> **Adding Solid Foods**
>
> - Do not introduce new food if infant is ill, as adverse effects such as allergic reactions may not be appropriately identified
> - Rice cereal is recommended as first food
> - Do not mix cereal or baby food with formula
> - Introduce one food at a time in small amounts
> - Delay introduction of foods known to cause allergic responses, such as orange juice, fish, nuts, strawberries, chocolate, and egg whites

- Why should new foods not be introduced when an infant is ill?
- Why is rice cereal preferred over other cereals?
- Why should baby formula not be mixed with cereal or foods?
- Why are orange juice, fish, strawberries, chocolate, and egg whites more likely to cause food allergies?

Slide 30

> **Nursing Tip**
>
> - New solid foods should be introduced before the milk feeding to encourage the infant to try the new experience
> - As solid food intake increases, the amount of formula or milk should decrease to avoid overfeeding

- Provide a rationale for providing solid foods before milk feedings in the infant.
- If milk or formula feedings decrease as solid foods increase, how does the nurse determine hydration status?

Slide 31

> **Recommended Fat Intake During Infancy**
>
> - Infants require almost three times more calories per kilogram of weight than adults
> - Easily digestible fats are needed for growth and development, including brain development
> - By age 6 months, the digestive tract has the ability to digest fats present in food
> - A well-balanced diet provides appropriate fat and cholesterol intake
> - A low-fat diet should not be given to infants under 2 years of age

- Why do infants require more calories than toddlers, preschoolers, school-age children, and adults? *To maintain their rapid growth and development in the first year of life.*
- Why are fats essential for infants?

Slide 32

> **Health Promotion**
>
> - Encourage breastfeeding
> - Discourage overfeeding
> - Teach recognition of signs of satiety
> - Prevent early introduction of solid foods

Slide 33

> **Weaning**
>
> - Signs of readiness include
>   - Infant eagerly looks forward to new tastes and textures found on the spoon
>   - May not want to be held close during feedings
>   - May start to "bite" the nipple as teeth erupt
>   - Imitates parents/siblings
> - Should be gradual; start with daytime then progress to nighttime

Slide 34

Slide 35

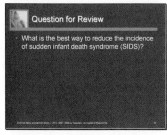

- Why should an infant be placed in a rear-facing car seat?
- What measures can be taken to prevent infant injury from a swimming pool, electrical outlets, stairs, and pets?
- Describe toys that are not appropriate for an infant.

Slide 36

Audience Response Question #3
A newborn's birth weight was 6 pounds. What would you expect this child's weight to be at 6 months?
1. 10 pounds
2. 12 pounds
3. 18 pounds
4. 20 pounds

Slide 37

Question for Review

What is the best way to reduce the incidence of sudden infant death syndrome (SIDS)?

Slide 38

Review

- Objectives
- Key Terms
- Key Points
- Online Resources
- Review Questions

Leifer

Lesson Plan

17 The Toddler

TEACHING FOCUS

This chapter gives students the opportunity to learn about the physical, psychosocial, and cognitive development of toddlers (ages 1 to 3 years), along with guidelines for discipline, nutrition, and injury prevention. The chapter also covers toilet training and behavior problems such as temper tantrums during this developmental stage and practical ways to manage these behaviors effectively. Students also have the opportunity to consider the role nurses can play in educating parents about development, play, and safety issues.

MATERIALS AND RESOURCES

☐ Computer and PowerPoint projector (all lessons)

LESSON CHECKLIST

Preparations for this lesson include:

- Lecture
- Guest speaker: Child psychologist
- Evaluation of student knowledge and skills required for entry-level activities related to care of a toddler between 1 and 3 years of age, including:
  ○ Parent education on injury prevention and appropriate toddler discipline
  ○ Potential abnormalities in physical, cognitive, or speech development
  ○ Appropriate interventions for behavioral problems such as temper tantrums and excessive fears
  ○ Appropriate nutrition and feeding guidelines for toddlers

KEY TERMS

autonomy (p. 406)

cooperative play (p. 418)

egocentric thinking
   (p. 418)

negativism (p. 406)

object permanence (p. 408)

parallel play (p. 418)

ritualism (p. 406)

separation anxiety (p. 408)

temper tantrum (p. 410)

time-out (p. 410)

toddler (p. 406)

ADDITIONAL RESOURCES

TEACH PPT slide(s) Chapter 17, 1-31

EILR IC image(s) Chapter 17, 1-7

EILR OBQ question(s) Chapter 17, 1-10

EILR TB question(s) Chapter 17, 1-28

ESLR IRQ question(s) Chapter 17, 1-6

SG Chapter 17, pp. 145-149

Legend

	e	**e**	**SG**	🔔
PPT TEACH PowerPoint Slides	**EILR** EVOLVE Instructor Learning Resources: Image Collection (IC), Open-Book Quizzes (OBQ), Test Bank (TB)	**ESLR** EVOLVE Student Learning Resources: Interactive Review Questions (IRQ) for the NCLEX® Examination	**SG** Study Guide	**CTQ** Critical Thinking Question in Nursing Care Plan (NCP CTQ) or Get Ready for the NCLEX! (GRN CTQ)

Class Activities are indicated in ***bold italic***.

Leifer

LESSON 17.1

PRETEST

1. A common characteristic of toddlers is
   a. saying "yes" frequently.
   b. changing their routine.
   c. performing rituals.
   d. taking five naps a day.

2. An example of a gross motor skill is
   a. holding a spoon.
   b. saying "bye-bye."
   c. copying a circle.
   d. hopping on one foot.

3. The average age that toilet training is complete is
   a. 1-2 years.
   b. 2-3 years.
   c. 3-4 years.
   d. 4-5 years.

4. Which of the following indicates that a communication disorder may be present?
   a. A 14-month-old does not babble and make sounds.
   b. An 18-month-old does not say "thank you."
   c. A 20-month-old is startled by a loud sound.
   d. A 30-month-old is using short sentences.

5. Which of the following is an effective guideline for managing toddler behavior issues?
   a. Withhold naps if child doesn't want it.
   b. Reward good behavior.
   c. Provide fluid for hydration before bedtime.
   d. Provide time-out when a toileting accident occurs.

6. Because caloric requirements are decreased in the toddler, the suggested amount of daily milk intake is
   a. 6 ounces.
   b. 12 ounces.
   c. 18 ounces.
   d. 24 ounces.

7. Parallel play differs from group play because it
   a. involves no other playmates.
   b. involves one other playmate.
   c. involves several playmates.
   d. only occurs in day care facilities.

8. The leading cause of death in childhood is
   a. accidents.
   b. SIDS.
   c. poison.
   d. disease.

9. A guideline for amount of solid food per meal for toddlers is
   a. two cups of liquid.
   b. one-half percent of the child's weight.
   c. one tablespoon of solid food per year of age.
   d. one-quarter pound of solid food per year of age.

10. In order for toddlers to learn how to play safely, allow them to play with
    a. pots and pans.
    b. high-priced toys.
    c. boxes with lids.
    d. marbles.

Answers

1. c	3. b	5. b	7. b	9. c
2. d	4. a	6. d	8. a	10. a

BACKGROUND ASSESSMENT

Question: It is important that staff in a health care provider's office interact with the children during the exam process in order to assess their developmental capabilities. What type of physical attributes and social behaviors should the nurse assess?

Answer: The nurse should measure the child's height and weight and compare them to previous measurements and to national standards. Unusual measurements should be further investigated. The nurse should evaluate social development, such as imitating adult activities and engaging in parallel play, stating words such as "mine" and "no" often, and playing with an imaginary friend. Typically, toddlers are toilet-independent by age 3, can hold a cup and spoon, and can feed and undress themselves. The nurse should notice language skills, such as starting with "bye-bye" and progressing to saying full name and asking "Why?" often. The nurse should observe cognition skills such as imitation by memory, exploring, and recognizing colors.

Leifer

Question: What important areas of parenting should the nurse focus on to educate parents about toddlers? What types of support are available in the community?

Answer: Parents need to be most aware of safety issues associated with toddlers. The nurse can advise parents that because toddlers are exploring new physical and mental capabilities and testing their independence, they can easily get into harmful situations. Supervision is recommended, even when playing with other children. Most toddlers respond positively to approvals from parents and other family members and also need clear boundary guidelines. Parents should understand that they are not alone in feeling frustrated by the "terrible twos." The toddler often says "no," and in trying out new physical and mental skills may spill and break things, eat unhealthy foods, have accidents, and engage in embarrassing behaviors. Inform parents that these behaviors will change, and emphasize that it is an exciting time of growth and learning for the child. If boundary-making begins in the toddler years, then discipline in later years will be easier. Toddlers feel comfortable with routine, and deviation may cause them concern. Toilet training can be challenging, but books on the subject can provide information and support. Encourage parents to contact the nurse or physician with any questions or concerns. Many communities have support groups, recreational centers, counseling agencies, and informal parent-toddler play groups where children are supervised as parents socialize and share information.

CRITICAL THINKING QUESTION

At a routine well-child health care provider's visit, the mother of a 2-year-old boy tells the nurse that a friend's daughter of the same age recognizes several colors and all the numbers on a deck of cards. The mother is worried that her son does not demonstrate the same abilities. How should the nurse respond?

Guidelines: The nurse can explain that each child develops at a different rate. One factor is the amount of time the parent spends working on certain tasks with the child. The nurse can suggest that parents spend extra time with the child reading books or working on learning skills. The learning experience should be fun and enjoyable for the child so he will want to continue. The parent should avoid showing frustration if progress is not as expected. If the child eagerly investigates and explores his environment and expresses likes and dislikes toward activities and foods, reassure the mother that this is normal development and learning specific skills will occur in reasonable time. If the mother is still concerned that her child is not making age-appropriate progress, suggest that she ask the physician about cognitive tests that can be performed.

OBJECTIVES	CONTENT	TEACHING RESOURCES
Describe the physical, psychosocial, and cognitive development of children from 1 to 3 years of age, listing age-specific events and guidance when appropriate.	■ General characteristics (p. 406) ☐ Physical development (p. 406) ☐ Sensorimotor and cognitive development (p. 408)	⊠▤ PPT slides 5-12 𝒆 EILR OBQ question 1 𝒆 EILR TB questions 1, 2, 10, 13, 18, 19, 24, 25 𝒆 ESLR IRQ questions 1-4 SG Learning Activities, questions 1, 2 (p. 145) SG Review Questions, questions 1, 2, 9, 12 (pp. 147-148) SG Applying Knowledge, questions 2, 3, 5 (p. 149) **BOOK RESOURCES** Table 17-1, Physical Development, Social Behavior, and Abilities of Toddlers (p. 407) Figure 17-1, Change in Body Contour (p. 407) Review Questions for the NCLEX® Examination, question

Leifer

OBJECTIVES	CONTENT	TEACHING RESOURCES
		2 (p. 419)
		▶ Discuss the normal physiologic changes that occur as an infant grows into a toddler. What are normal vital signs for a 2-year-old? What are normal height, weight, and head circumference measurements?
		Class Activity Divide students into groups and assign each group one of these important developmental tasks for the toddler: – *toilet training* – *self-feeding* – *self-dressing* – *developing speech* – *satisfying curiosity* *Ask the groups to discuss how the specific examples of the developmental attributes (social, fine motor, gross motor, language, and cognition) listed in Table 17-1 (pp. 407) apply to each of the above tasks. Have groups report their findings to the class.*
Describe the task to be mastered by the toddler according to Erikson's stages of growth and development.	■ General characteristics (p. 406)	☒ PPT slides 10-13 𝒆 ESLR IRQ question 4 SG Learning Activities, question 3 (p. 145) **BOOK RESOURCES** Review Questions for the NCLEX® Examination, question 1 (p. 419) ▶ Discuss the major developmental tasks facing the toddler as he or she becomes more independent. What are a parent's main roles and responsibilities at this age? *Class Activity Invite a child psychologist to speak to the class about the challenges for the toddler relative to Erikson's stages of growth and development. How does autonomy versus shame and doubt apply practically as the child seeks to master his or her environment? What is the parent's related developmental task during this period? Have students refer to Chapter 15, Tables 15-3 (p. 365) and 15-5 (p. 367). Ask students to prepare questions in advance.* *Class Activity Divide the class into groups and assign each group one of the categories of toddler development: social, fine motor, gross motor, language, and cognition. Have each group discuss behaviors the child exhibits as he or she develops. What appropriate guidance and training should the parent provide for each toddler age? Have groups make a presentation to the class. Invite*

OBJECTIVES	CONTENT	TEACHING RESOURCES
		questions and discussion.
List two developmental tasks of the toddler period.	■ Sensorimotor and cognitive development (p. 408)	⊠▪ PPT slides 10-12
		e EILR OBQ questions 1, 2
		e ESLR IRQ questions 4, 5
		BOOK RESOURCES
		Table 17-1, Physical Development, Social Behavior, and Abilities of Toddlers (p. 407)
		Review Questions for the NCLEX® Examination, question 2 (p. 419)
		▶ Discuss the common symptoms of separation anxiety and the developmental reasons most toddlers experience it. How does the concept of object permanence allow the toddler to overcome separation anxiety eventually?
		*Class Activity **Lead a discussion in which students describe two important developmental tasks for the toddler: sensorimotor and cognition. In what ways are these inseparable for a child of this age? What aspects of physical development and memory are important?***

17.1 Homework/Assignments:

17.1 Instructor's Notes/Student Feedback:

Introduction to Maternity & Pediatric Nursing, 6th ed.

Leifer

LESSON 17.2

CRITICAL THINKING QUESTION

A 21-month-old child's grandmother says that the child should be punished for not using the toilet because soiling his pants at that age is unacceptable. The mother is upset and asks the nurse what is "normal." What information should the nurse provide?

Guidelines: The nurse can inform the mother that a child's physical readiness is an important factor in developing toilet independence. Voluntary control of anal and urethral sphincters occurs between 18 and 24 months of age. Waking up dry in the morning or after a nap, being aware of the physical sensation of needing to void or have a bowel movement, being able to communicate, and willingness to sit on the potty for several minutes are signs of readiness. Toddlers respond well to approval, praise, and rewards. Demands, threats, and punishment create stress and slow the process, whereas patience and praise make a challenging task more pleasant.

OBJECTIVES	CONTENT	TEACHING RESOURCES
Discuss speech development in the toddler.	☐ Speech development (p. 408)	⊠ PPT slides 13, 14
		e EILR OBQ question 3
		e EILR TB questions 14, 20
		SG Learning Activities, question 8 (p. 146)
		SG Review Questions, questions 3, 8, 11 (pp. 147-148)
		BOOK RESOURCES
		Table 17-2, Language Milestones (p. 409)
		Table 17-3, When a Child with a Communication Disorder Needs Help (p. 409)
		Box 17-1, Screening for Signs of Autism (p. 410)
		▸ Discuss how a parent can facilitate language skill acquisition in a child without pushing the process too quickly or shaming the child for slower than normal development.
		▸ Discuss behavioral signs and symptoms that may indicate a child has a communication disorder.
		Class Activity Divide the class into groups to discuss language milestones. Assign each group one of the following age ranges: 2-6 months, 7-16 months, and 17-36 months. Ask groups to discuss what is meant by the terms expressive language *and* receptive language. *Then have them list examples of expressive language and receptive language in their assigned age range. Students also should discuss how parents can guide and encourage each type of language development. Students may refer to Table 17-2 (p. 409). Have groups present to the class for feedback and discussion.*
		Class Activity Based on group presentations in the previous activity, lead a class discussion in which students describe how cognitive development is crucial

OBJECTIVES	CONTENT	TEACHING RESOURCES
		for expressive language, such as repeating sounds, identifying names, and stringing words together.
Discuss how adults can assist small children in combating their fears.	■ Guidance and discipline (p. 408)	⊞ PPT slides 15-17 *e* EILR TB questions 3, 5 📖 SG Learning Activities, question 5 (p. 145) 📖 SG Applying Knowledge, question 1 (p. 149) **BOOK RESOURCES** Nursing Tip (p. 410) Table 17-4, Behavior Problems During Early Childhood (p. 411) ▸ Discuss ways parents can encourage their child to explore the environment safely and develop self-control in a positive manner. *Class Activity Lead a discussion in which students identify fears or insecurities toddlers typically have and behavioral signals that may be present. What role do a parent's own fears play in the potential development of their child's fears? How can a parent teach a toddler to have a healthy fear of something dangerous, such as a hot stovetop, while not inhibiting the desire to try something new?*
Discuss the principles of guidance and discipline for a toddler.	■ Guidance and discipline (p. 408)	⊞ PPT slides 15-17 *e* EILR TB questions 3, 15 📖 SG Learning Activities, questions 6, 7 (p. 146) 📖 SG Review Questions, question 15 (p. 148) 📖 SG Case Study, question 1 (p. 149) **BOOK RESOURCES** Table 17-4, Behavior Problems During Early Childhood (p. 411) Review Questions for the NCLEX® Examination, question 4 (p. 419) ▸ Discuss various ways to deal with the strong-willed toddler who doesn't respond appropriately to conventional limit-setting and timing approaches. *Class Activity Divide the class into small groups and assign each a toddler behavior listed in Table 17-4 (pp. 411). Ask each group to discuss typical toddler actions and reactions and how parents can provide*

OBJECTIVES	CONTENT	TEACHING RESOURCES
		appropriate guidance and discipline. Then, ask each group to identify at what point normal expectations are not being met, what the contributing factors could be, and how parents might solve the problem. Have each group make a brief presentation to the class for feedback and discussion.
		Class Activity Ask students to research books on child discipline and guidance that have been published in the past 50 years. How have parental attitudes been shaped by child development experts? In what ways has expectations changed, both for child behavior and parental guidance? What books could the nurse recommend to parents? (For students to prepare for this activity, see Homework/Assignments #1.)
Identify the principles of toilet training (bowel and bladder) that will assist in guiding parents' efforts to provide toilet independence.	■ Daily care (p. 410) ■ Toilet independence (p. 412)	▣▆ PPT slides 18-21 *e* EILR IC image 2 *e* EILR TB questions 8, 17, 22, 26, 28 ▩ SG Learning Activities, questions 9-11 (p. 146) ▩ SG Review Questions, questions 2, 5 (p. 147) ▩ SG Applying Knowledge, question 4 (p. 149) **BOOK RESOURCES** Figure 17-2, Toilet Training (p. 412) Nursing Tip (p. 413) ▸ Discuss positive ways in which a parent can encourage toilet independence. In contrast, how can negative demands or threats delay toilet training? *Class Activity Divide the class into small groups and have them design a plan to help parents guide their toddler toward toilet independence. The plan should cover topics such as physical readiness, temperament, various techniques, and parental attitude. Have the groups present their plans to the class for evaluation and feedback.* *Class Activity Provide the class the following toilet training situations and ask students how a parent should respond:* *1. The child stays dry at home and asks to go to the potty when he needs to, but soils training pants at play group.* *2. The child refuses to go to the toilet unless she can bring her dolly.*

OBJECTIVES	CONTENT	TEACHING RESOURCES
		3. The child has started to wake up dry from naps and in the morning and follows an older sibling into the bathroom to watch.

17.2 Homework/Assignments:

1. Ask students to research books on child discipline and guidance that have been published in the past 50 years. How have parental attitudes been shaped by child development experts? In what ways have expectations changed, both for child behavior and parental guidance? What books could the nurse recommend to parents?

17.2 Instructor's Notes/Student Feedback:

LESSON 17.3

CRITICAL THINKING QUESTION

The mother of a 30-month-old boy tells the nurse that reminding him not to touch or play with fragile and cherished decorative items in the home is exhausting her. She has provided ample age-appropriate educational toys. The mother wants to know how she can get the child to play with his own toys and leave her fragile items alone. How should the nurse respond?

Guidelines: The nurse can explain that the child is displaying normal behavior for his age. Toddlers are curious and need and want to explore their world. They may actually feel frustrated by being prevented from exploring their environment and can become even more assertive. Whereas an adult may enjoy simply looking at objects, a toddler needs to explore them with all the senses. Suggest that, although a child does need to learn that some things are out of bounds, removing fragile items or those that could be dangerous to the child will increase everyone's comfort level. The decorative items can be displayed when the child is older. Explain that sturdier household items, such as pots and pans, unbreakable containers and dishes, building blocks, and riding toys placed where the child can easily access them typically keep toddlers engaged and also build important skills. Emphasize that safety is always a concern, so the child should be supervised to prevent injury.

OBJECTIVES	CONTENT	TEACHING RESOURCES
Describe the nutritional needs and self-feeding abilities of a toddler.	■ Nutritional counseling (p. 413)	▣ PPT slide 22 🄴 EILR TB questions 6, 7, 16, 23 📖 SG Learning Activities, questions 12-14 (p. 146) 📖 SG Review Questions, question 4 (p. 147) **BOOK RESOURCES** Table 17-5, Approximate Serving Sizes per Meal (p. 413) Nursing Tip (p. 413) ▶ Discuss techniques that can be used to make meals for toddlers an enjoyable experience for both parent and child. ▶ Discuss potential consequences of forcing a toddler to eat when the child isn't hungry. *Class Activity* **Divide the class into groups and have them design teaching posters suitable for display in a health care provider's office or clinic about the nutritional needs of toddlers at different ages. The posters should include caloric requirements and serving sizes of each type of food as well as the type of nutrition provided. Students may refer to Figure 15-6, The Children's Food Pyramid (p. 370).** *Class Activity* **Using information from the previous activity, have groups of students plan a 3-day menu suitable for the self-feeding skills of an 18-month-old child and for a 3-year-old child. What forms of foods are best for each group (mashed, small pieces, finger food, spoonable)? What foods can parents assist with? What are some alternatives if the toddler is having a picky day?**

OBJECTIVES	CONTENT	TEACHING RESOURCES

List two methods of preventing the following: automobile accidents, burns, falls, suffocation and choking, poisoning, drowning, electric shock, and animal bites.	■ Day care (p. 413)
	
	■ Injury prevention (p. 414)
	
	  □ Consumer education (p. 414)
		⊠■ PPT slides 23-27
		
		e EILR IC images 3, 4
		
		e EILR TB questions 4, 11-12, 21
		
		e ESLR IRQ question 3
		
		SG Learning Activities, questions 16, 17 (p. 147)
		
		SG Review Questions, questions 6, 10, 13, 14 (pp. 147-148)
		
		SG Thinking Critically, question 1 (p. 149)
		
		SG Applying Knowledge, questions 3, 6 (p. 149)
		
		BOOK RESOURCES
		
		Figure 17-3, Beginning Social Skills (p. 414)
		
		Nursing Tip (p. 414)
		
		Health Promotion, How to Prevent Hazards Caused by the Behavioral Characteristics of Toddlers (pp. 415-416)
		
		Figure 17-4, The playful toddler needs close supervision during water play (p. 417)
		
		Figure 17-5, Car Seats (p. 417)
		
		Figure 17-6, Close supervision is necessary when a child plays in any home where there is a pet, whether large or small (p. 418)
		
		Figure 17-7, Childproofing the Home (p. 418)
		
		Review Questions for the NCLEX® Examination, question 5 (p. 419)
		
		GRN CTQ 1 (p. 419)
		
		▸ Discuss ways nurses can teach parents about preventing injury to toddlers. Which issues are of most concern and must be communicated if teaching time is limited during a clinic visit?
		
		*Class Activity **Have pairs of students take turns role-playing a nurse instructing parents about toddler behaviors that increase risk for injury. The nurse should teach parents appropriate hazard and injury prevention strategies. Assign groups one of the following categories:***
		
		  – *automobile*
		
		  – *burns*
		
		  – *falls*

Leifer

OBJECTIVES	CONTENT	TEACHING RESOURCES
		– suffocation and choking
		– poisoning
		– drowning, electric shock, animal bites
		– general safety
		– toys and household objects
Describe the characteristic play and appropriate toys for a toddler.	■ Toys and play (p. 417)	PPT slides 28-29
		EILR IC images 4, 6-7
		EILR OBQ questions 8-10
		EILR TB questions 9, 27
		ESLR IRQ question 6
		SG Learning Activities, question 1 (p. 145)
		SG Review Questions, question 7 (p. 148)
		BOOK RESOURCES
		Figure 17-4, The playful toddler needs close supervision during water play (p. 417)
		Figure 17-6, Close supervision is necessary when a child plays in any home where there is a pet, whether large or small (p. 418)
		Figure 17-7, Childproofing the Home (p. 418)
		▶ Discuss the levels of supervision the toddler requires during different types of play (alone, during water play, with pets, parallel play, cooperative play, with toys).
		*Class Activity **Lead a discussion in which students describe the play characteristics of toddlers at different ages. Compare and contrast parallel versus cooperative play. What does "Play is the work of the toddler" mean? What types of toys are suitable for the toddler who is driven to master skills and explore his or her world?***
Performance Evaluation		PPT slides 1-31
		EILR IC images 1-7
		EILR OBQ questions 1-10
		EILR TB questions 1-28
		ESLR IRQ questions 1-6
		SG Learning Activities, questions 1-17 (pp. 145-147)
		SG Review Questions, questions 1-15 (pp. 147-149)

Leifer

OBJECTIVES	CONTENT	TEACHING RESOURCES
		SG Case Study, question 1 (p. 149)
		SG Thinking Critically, questions 1a-c (p. 149)
		SG Applying Knowledge, questions 1-6 (p. 149)
		BOOK RESOURCES
		Review Questions for the NCLEX® Examination, questions 1-5 (p. 419)
		GRN CTQ 1 (p. 419)

17.3 Homework/Assignments:

17.3 Instructor's Notes/Student Feedback:

17 | Lecture Outline
The Toddler

Slide 1

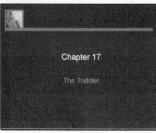

Chapter 17

The Toddler

Slide 2

Objectives

- Describe the physical, psychosocial, and cognitive development of children from 1 to 3 years of age, listing age-specific events and guidance when appropriate.
- Discuss speech development in the toddler.
- Describe the task to be mastered by the toddler according to Erikson's stages of growth and development.

Slide 3

Objectives *(cont.)*

- List two developmental tasks of the toddler period.
- Discuss the principles of guidance and discipline for a toddler.
- Discuss how adults can assist small children in combating their fears.
- Identify the principles of toilet training (bowel and bladder) that will assist in guiding parents' effort to provide toilet independence.

Slide 4

Objectives *(cont.)*

- Describe the nutritional needs and self-feeding abilities of a toddler.
- List two methods of preventing the following: automobile accidents, burns, falls, suffocation and choking, poisoning, drowning, electric shock, and animal bites.
- Describe the characteristic play and appropriate toys for a toddler.

Leifer

Slide 5

General Characteristics

- A toddler is between 1 to 3 years of age
- No longer completely dependent on others
- Rapid growth and development during infancy slows down
- Erikson's stage of autonomy versus shame and doubt

- Discuss Erikson's stage of autonomy versus shame and doubt as based on a continuum of trust established during infancy.
- Ask students to give examples of autonomy, shame, and doubt in the toddler.
- Ask students how lack of trust can likely affect the toddler's growth and development.

Slide 6

General Characteristics (cont.)

- Major parental responsibility
  - Maintaining safety for the toddler while allowing the opportunity for social and physical independence
  - Maintain positive self-image and body image in child
- Negativism can be countered by offering limited choices and the use of distraction in handling toddlers whose favorite word is "no"

- Discuss a situation or method in which a parent can provide the opportunity for socialization while providing a safe environment.
- What situations and choices might a parent offer to distract the toddler?

Slide 7

General Characteristics (cont.)

- Developing self-control and socially acceptable outlets for aggression and anger are important in the formation of personality and behavior
- Rituals increase the toddler's sense of security by making compulsive routines of simple tasks

- Have students offer examples of how a parent can assist the toddler in expressing anger.
- What rituals could instill a sense of security in the toddler?

Audience Response Question #1
The first thing a toddler does when visiting his grandmother is to ask for a drink in his favorite cup. The nurse tells the parents he does this because:
1. it increases his sense of security.
2. it is a form of obsessive compulsive disorder.
3. he is thirsty.
4. toddlers require increased fluids.

Slide 8

Physical Development

- Birthweight quadruples by 2.5 years of age
- Rate of brain growth slows
- Body proportions change
  - Head and trunk grow more slowly
- Musculoskeletal system grows and bones begin to ossify
- Protuberant abdomen flattens when muscle fibers increase in size and strength
- Myelination of spinal cord nearly complete by 2 years
- Bowel and bladder control usually complete by 2.5 to 3 years of age

- Discuss why a toddler might not be ready for toilet training based upon age and development.

Audience Response Question #2
A parent should be concerned if his or her child is not bowel and bladder trained by age 3.
1. True
2. False

Slide 9

Physical Development (cont.)

- Respirations still mainly abdominal but shift to thoracic as child reaches school-age
- Capable of maintaining stable body temperature
- Eruption of deciduous teeth complete by 2.5 years
- Defense mechanisms of the skin and blood are more effective
- Digestive processes and stomach capacity increase to allow three-meal-a-day schedule

- Describe abdominal respirations versus thoracic respirations.
- Discuss the eruption of teeth and proper oral hygiene.

Slide 10

Sensorimotor and Cognitive Development

- Sensory and motor abilities do not function independently
- Memory strengthens
- Is able to assimilate information through trial, error, and repetition
- Piaget's sensorimotor and preconceptual phase of development emerges rapidly in this age group

- Discuss how sensory and motor functions are synchronized.
- Review Table 17-1 on page 407 with the class.
- Give an example of how a toddler learns from trial and error.
- What are examples of Piaget's sensorimotor and preconceptual phases of development?

Slide 11

Sensorimotor and Cognitive Development (cont.)

- Able to tolerate longer periods of separation from parents to explore environment
- Aware of cause and effect
- Concept of spatial relationships develops
- Begins to internalize standards of behavior
- Copies words and roles of the models seen in the home

- Discuss how the toddler has progressed to manage longer periods of time away from his or her parents.
- What is an example of cause and effect?
- Give examples of how toddlers model behavior.

Slide 12

Sensorimotor and Cognitive Development (cont.)

- May confuse essential with nonessential body parts/functions
- Expelling feces and urine and then flushing it down the toilet may be upsetting as the toddler may see it as flushing a part of themselves away
- Nurse should teach parents skills that will enable the toddler to feel loved even if behavior is not acceptable

- What are essential and nonessential body parts?
- Give an example of a situation in which a parent might provide love when a toddler has exhibited improper behavior.

Slide 13

Speech Development

- Parallels cognitive growth
- Expressive and receptive language continue to develop
- Respond to tone of voice and facial expressions of those around them
- Showing empathy toward the toddler who is trying to communicate verbally will help minimize frustrations

- Give an example of parallel cognitive growth.
- What is receptive language?
- Make facial expressions and ask students to identify the emotions behind them.

Slide 14

Screening for Signs of Autism

- Preliminary symptoms may include
  - No pointing, gesturing (e.g., bye-bye) by 12 months
  - No single words by 16 months
  - No spontaneous two-word phrases by 24 months
  - Loss of achieved language or social skills
- Important to rule out lead poisoning, hearing deficit, neurological disorders, musculoskeletal diseases and inborn errors of metabolism.

- Discuss the nurse's role when assessing a toddler who might have autism.
- How can the nurse communicate with a toddler who has autism?
- Discuss the term pervasive developmental disorder (PDD).

Leifer

Slide 15

Guidance and Discipline

- Goal is to teach, *not* punish
- Discipline involves guidance
- Parent responses to temper tantrums can either reinforce the desirability of or the risks involved in such behavior
- Expectations must be in line with the child's physical and cognitive abilities
  – Limit-setting
  – Time-outs

- Give an example of how parents' reactions to the toddler's temper tantrum can affect the toddler's behavior in the future.
- What is an example of a limit and time-out for a toddler?

Slide 16

Guidance and Discipline *(cont.)*

- Child seeks approval
  – Use positive approach whenever possible
  – Approval increases self-confidence
- Use of fear or physical aggression with a toddler does not foster self-control
  – Can lead to physical and emotional abuse

- Give examples of positive reactions to a toddler's behavior by the parents.
- Discuss how the parents' reaction to a toddler's behavior affects the toddler's self-confidence.
- How can physical aggression and fear tactics affect the toddler negatively?

Slide 17

Guidance and Discipline *(cont.)*

- Fear-provoking event affects extent of toddler's reaction
  – If alone, fear may be greater
  – Once fear has been learned, it is more difficult to eliminate
- Stress increases fear of separation
  – Self-consoling behaviors include favorite possession or repetitive rituals

- Give an example of a fear-evoking event.
- What self-consoling behavior might a toddler implement when dealing with fear and separation?

Slide 18

Daily Care

- Adults should be at eye level when talking to toddler
  – Seems less overwhelming
- Flexible schedule organized around needs of entire household is best
- Clothing should be easily put on and removed
- Sunburn protection

- Give an example of a household item which needs to be adjusted to meet the needs of the entire household.
- Describe how flexibility with a household schedule assists the family (household) during the day.
- Which clothing could interfere with toilet training?
- What methods can be used to protect the toddler from sunburn?

Slide 19

Daily Care *(cont.)*

- Shoes should fit shape of foot and be ½ inch longer and ¼ inch wider than the foot
- Important for toddler to wear their regular shoes to the clinic as it shows the health care provider how the body is being used
- Posture is greatly influenced by that of other family members

- What are examples of proper and improper footwear for the toddler?

Slide 20

Toilet Independence

- Much depends on temperament of the toddler and the person guiding toilet training
- Voluntary control of anal and urethral sphincters begins around 18 to 24 months of age

- Discuss methods that assist the toddler in toilet training.
- What methods are detrimental to toilet training?
- Give an example of a situation in which a parent is trying to force the toddler toward toilet independence.

Slide 21

Toilet Independence *(cont.)*

- Use potty chair or place the child on the toilet facing the tank
- Bowel training usually attempted first
- Do not leave toddler on toilet for more than a few minutes at a time
- Bladder training can begin when toddler stays dry for about 2 hours
- If toddler has special words for defecation or urination, be sure to tell other health care providers and document in care plan for toddler

- Discuss why it is necessary to place the toddler on the toilet for just a few minutes.
- What words might a toddler use to indicate defecation and/or urination?

Slide 22

Nutrition Counseling

- Caloric needs decline to about 100 calories/kg/day
- Limit milk intake to no more than 24 ounces (720 mL) per day
- Serving size is 1 tablespoon of solid food per year of age
- Food is chopped into fine pieces
- Various foods are offered
- A 2-year-old likes finger foods

- Why is it important to limit milk intake?
- Give an example of various foods to offer during a meal.
- What are examples of finger-foods?
- If well-nourished, the toddler shows steady and proportional gain in height and weight.

Slide 23

Day Care

- Must meet families'
  - Personal preferences
  - Cultural perspectives
  - Financial and special needs
- Should be state-approved

- Give an example of a personal preference a family might have and how it affects their choice of day care.
- Which cultural issue could affect a toddler in the day care setting?
- Discuss special needs a toddler might have and how this could affect the care provided in the day care setting.

Slide 24

Day Care *(cont.)*

- Differs for toddlers because
  - Shorter attention span
  - Tendency to engage in parallel play rather than group play
  - Need closer supervision to maintain safety

- Give an example of a toddler's attention span.
- What is parallel play?

Slide 25

> **Nursing Tip**
>
> A major task for parents is to "let go" and allow the toddler to interact with influences outside the family in day care centers or preschools

- Give an example of how parents might have to release their inhibitions and allow others to influence their toddler.
- Discuss the facility's responsibility to provide an environment which does not influence the toddler negatively.

Slide 26

> **Injury Prevention**
>
> - Best prevention is knowledge of age-appropriate risk and anticipatory guidelines
> - Parents need to understand their child's activities at certain ages in order to prevent injuries by taking appropriate precautions
> - Toddlers are curious and mobile

- Give an example of age-appropriate risks for the toddler.
- Provide an age-appropriate initiative by a parent to enhance safety in the home.
- What is a curious activity a toddler might engage in within the home?

Audience Response Question #3
When a toddler is leaving the hospital, it is the nurse's responsibility to ensure the child is appropriately buckled in his or her car seat.
   1. True
   2. False

Slide 27

> **Injury Prevention** *(cont.)*

- Discuss proper guidelines for car seats.

Slide 28

> **Toys and Play**
>
> - Parents must be taught to inspect toys and to buy toys suitable to the age, skills, and abilities of their child
> - Play is the work of toddlers
>
> - Through play they learn how to
>   - Manipulate and understand their environment
>   - Socialize
>   - Explore their world

- Give an example of a toy parents might decide not to purchase for their toddler because of safety issues.
- How is play toddler's work?

Slide 29

> **Toys and Play** *(cont.)*
>
> - Social development takes form
> - Egocentric thinking
> - Parallel play gradually leads to cooperative play
> - Protect the child from sunburn, mosquitoes, and other vectors
> - Childproofing the home is also important

- Discuss egocentric thinking.
- Discuss other vectors within your community from which the toddler must be protected.
- What methods would you use to childproof a home?
- Discuss childproofing the grandparent's and/or sitter's home.

Slide 30

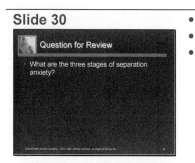

- Protest
- Despair
- Detachment

Slide 31

Leifer

TEACHING FOCUS

In this chapter, students have the opportunity to learn about the physical, psychosocial, and cognitive development of preschoolers (3 to 5 years of age) along with guidelines for discipline and injury prevention. The chapter covers behavior issues such as speech acquisition, enuresis, thumb-sucking, and sexual curiosity during this developmental stage, as well as practical ways to manage these behaviors effectively. Students also will have the opportunity to consider ways nurses can educate parents about appropriate types of play and choosing a school that meets the child's needs.

MATERIALS AND RESOURCES

- ☐ Computer and PowerPoint projector (all lessons)
- ☐ Chart summarizing Piaget's and Erikson's stages of development (Lesson 18.2)
- ☐ Videotape of play therapy (Lesson 18.2)

LESSON CHECKLIST

Preparations for this lesson include:

- Lecture
- Demonstration
- Guest speakers: Child psychologist, speech therapist, preschool teacher
- Evaluation of student knowledge and skills required for entry-level activities related to care of a preschooler between 3 and 5 years of age, including:
  - ○ Parent education on types of play, injury prevention, and appropriate discipline
  - ○ Potential abnormalities in physical, cognitive, or speech development
  - ○ Appropriate interventions for problematic behaviors such as enuresis, thumb-sucking, and sexual curiosity
  - ○ Cognitive capabilities and how they affect reasoning and conceptualization

KEY TERMS

animism (p. 421)
art therapy (p. 432)
artificialism (p. 421)
associative play (p. 425)
centering (p. 421)
echolalia (p. 422)
egocentrism (p. 421)

enuresis (p. 428)
modeling (p. 427)
parallel play (p. 425)
play therapy (p. 432)
preconceptual stage (p. 421)

preoperational phase (p. 421)
separation anxiety (p. 433)
symbolic functioning (p. 421)
therapeutic play (p. 432)
time-out (p. 427)

ADDITIONAL RESOURCES

TEACH PPT slide(s) Chapter 18, 1-47
EILR IC image(s) Chapter 18, 1-5
EILR OBQ question(s) Chapter 18, 1-10
EILR TB question(s) Chapter 18, 1-30
ESLR IRQ question(s) Chapter 18, 1-5
SG Chapter 18, pp. 151-155

Legend

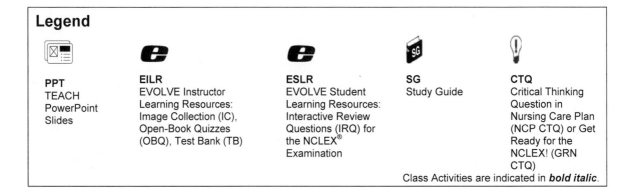

PPT
TEACH
PowerPoint
Slides

EILR
EVOLVE Instructor
Learning Resources:
Image Collection (IC),
Open-Book Quizzes
(OBQ), Test Bank (TB)

ESLR
EVOLVE Student
Learning Resources:
Interactive Review
Questions (IRQ) for
the NCLEX®
Examination

SG
Study Guide

CTQ
Critical Thinking
Question in
Nursing Care Plan
(NCP CTQ) or Get
Ready for the
NCLEX! (GRN
CTQ)

Class Activities are indicated in ***bold italic***.

Leifer

LESSON 18.1

PRETEST

1. An abnormal physical development in a child between 3 and 5 years of age would be
   a. the loss of chubbiness since toddlerhood.
   b. pulse rate of 50 beats per minute.
   c. visual acuity of 20/30.
   d. 20 primary teeth have erupted.

2. One of the best ways to promote the mastery of language in the preschool child is to
   a. engage in interactive reading.
   b. limit the number of books in the child's room.
   c. provide crayons and coloring books.
   d. allow them to talk with other 3-year-olds.

3. What would be the signal that a problem is occurring due to the perceptual process?
   a. delayed mastery of the alphabet   c. difficulty telling time
   b. difficulty following directions   d. letter confusion

4. Bedtime habits should include
   a. playful activities.   c. vigorous exercise.
   b. specific rituals.   d. allowing attention-getting behavior.

5. At what age do children begin to have refined motor skills, such as cutting with scissors?
   a. 3 years   c. 5 years
   b. 4 years   d. 6 years

6. An effective method of encouraging positive behavior involves
   a. strict discipline.   c. modeling.
   b. calling time-outs.   d. offering a reward.

7. The term that describes daytime wetting is
   a. diurnal.   c. enuresis.
   b. echolalia.   d. nocturnal.

8. Which toy would be appropriate for a 4-year-old diagnosed with pneumonia to bring to the hospital?
   a. stuffed bear   c. beach ball
   b. remote-controlled car   d. crayons and coloring book

9. A type of play that helps children communicate their feelings by drawings is called
   a. animism.   c. art.
   b. play.   d. therapeutic.

10. A nurse would be concerned about parenting patterns when she hears a parent state
   a. they use time-outs.   c. they "child-proofed" their home.
   b. they have problems with day care.   d. negative comments only.

Answers

1. b	3. d	5. b	7. a	9. c
2. a	4. b	6. d	8. d	10. d

BACKGROUND ASSESSMENT

Question: What are the major tasks of the preschooler that parents need to be aware of? In what developmental areas can the parent provide guidance and support to help the child master these tasks?
Answer: The major tasks include learning how to play cooperatively, controlling body functions, accepting separation, and preparing to enter school. The preschooler also increases communication skills, memory, and attention span. The parent can provide opportunities for physical development to occur and can support cognitive and speech development. The parent can provide opportunities for the child to discover new skills and thinking processes through play and can guide the child in developing habits of self-control. Safety should always be a primary concern in this age group.

Introduction to Maternity & Pediatric Nursing, 6th ed.

Elsevier items and derived items © 2010, 2007, 2006 by Saunders, an imprint of Elsevier Inc.   Leifer

Question: Preschoolers, even though they are more aware of dangers and have better self-control than toddlers, are still prone to accidents. What major threats are present and what preventions should parents implement?

Answer: Head injuries from falls are a common occurrence, so 3- to 5-year-olds should be supervised when on play equipment and around stairs and should always wear sturdy, properly fitted shoes. Automobiles are also a threat, so parents should tell children where they can ride tricycles and play ball safely, with supervision. Children should not be left alone in or around cars and should always be belted in car seats. Burns can result from playing with lighters or hot liquids so parents should explain the risks and keep dangerous items out of reach. Poisoning can occur if dangerous chemicals such as cleaning solvents are easily accessible, so parents should keep these locked and out of children's reach. Toys should be sturdy and age-appropriate, reducing the risk of breaking and causing injury. Preschoolers should not be asked to do anything potentially dangerous, such as carrying glass containers, hot foods, or sharp implements. Because preschoolers like to mimic adults, pills and other medicines should be locked up to avoid temptation. Children should be told about the dangers of going with strangers and instructed not to play in lonely places or accept tempting gifts from people they do not know. Close supervision of preschoolers is necessary at all times.

CRITICAL THINKING QUESTION

At a physician visit to treat a cut knee, the mother of a strong-willed 4-year-old says her daughter's defiance and insistence on getting her own way are wearing her down. In addition, the need for constant watchfulness to prevent the high-energy child from injuring herself, other children, or household objects adds to the parenting challenge. She says she envies a neighbor who boasts that her child is cooperative, plays quietly with friends, and cleans up toys. The mother asks what she is doing wrong and how she can get her daughter to be more like the neighbor child. How should the nurse respond?

Guidelines: The nurse can explain that each child's temperament and energy level differ. Some are tractable, whereas others are more willful and stay focused on a particular course of action. Four-year-olds like to show off developing skills and may assert dominance. They can get frustrated easily and may demonstrate mood swings. A preschooler is absorbing tremendous amounts of new information, and physical capabilities are developing, so play is more imaginative and often active, increasing the risk of injury. Parents should provide toys that help to direct energy safely and that stimulate the imagination. Using time-outs judiciously, rewarding desired behaviors, striving for consistency, and using brief, direct explanations can help influence behaviors in a positive way. Advise the mother to continue raising her child in a loving manner that sets appropriate behavioral boundaries.

OBJECTIVES	CONTENT	TEACHING RESOURCES

List the major developmental tasks of the preschool-age child.	■ General characteristics (p. 420)	PPT slides 6, 7
		
		SG Learning Activities, question 2 (p. 151)
		
		▶ Discuss the various ways that parents can effectively prepare their child to enter school and engage in cooperative play with peers.
		
		Class Activity Lead a class discussion in which students describe and provide examples of the following developmental tasks of a preschooler:
		
		  — *Preparing to enter school*
		
		  — *Developing cooperative play*
		
		  — *Controlling body functions*
		
		  — *Accepting separation*
		
		  — *Increasing communication skills*
		
		  — *Increasing in memory and attention span*

OBJECTIVES	CONTENT	TEACHING RESOURCES
Describe the physical, psychosocial, and spiritual development of children from age 3 to 5 years, listing age-specific events and guidance when appropriate.	■ General characteristics (p. 420) ☐ Physical development (p. 420) ☐ Cognitive development (p. 421) ☐ Effects of cultural practices (p. 421) ☐ Language development (p. 421) ☐ Development of play (p. 421) ☐ Spiritual development (p. 421) ☐ Sexual curiosity (p. 424) ☐ Bedtime habits (p. 424) ■ Physical, mental, emotional, and social development (p. 424) ☐ The 3-year-old (p. 424) ☐ The 4-year-old (p. 425) – The concept of death (p. 425) ☐ The 5-year-old (p. 426)	PPT slides 8-28 *e* EILR IC images 1, 2 *e* EILR TB questions 1, 4, 5, 9, 12, 15, 17, 18, 23, 27, 30 *e* ESLR IRQ questions 1-5 SG Learning Activities, questions 1, 4-10 (pp. 151-152) SG Review Questions, questions 1-4, 6, 12, 13 (pp. 153-154) SG Applying Knowledge, question 1 (p. 155) **BOOK RESOURCES** Table 18-1, Preschool Growth and Development (p. 422) Figure 18-1, The Family Meal (p. 423) Figure 18-2, Grandpa Reads to the Children (p. 423) Table 18-2, Selected Perceptual, Cognitive, and Language Processes Required for Elementary School Success (p. 423) Table 18-3, Not Talking: A Clinical Classification (p. 424) Review Questions for the NCLEX® Examination, question 5 (p. 434) ▸ Discuss ways that spiritual ideals can be communicated to preschool children who cannot yet understand abstract concepts. *Class Activity Divide the class into groups and assign each group one of the developmental tasks listed in the previous Class Activity. Have the groups describe the preschooler's physical, cognitive, and language skills that contribute to mastering each task. What is the role of play? Have groups make a brief presentation to the class for discussion.* *Class Activity Invite a child psychologist to discuss the development of 3-, 4-, and 5-year-olds. Ask the speaker to compare and contrast behaviors relative to physical, mental, emotional, and social development. What guidance can the nurse provide to parents relative to aiding development and teaching behavioral controls at each age? Ask students to prepare questions in advance.*

18.1 Homework/Assignments:

18.1 Instructor's Notes/Student Feedback:

LESSON 18.2

CRITICAL THINKING QUESTION

A father wants to send his son to a morning playgroup twice a week. The parent is concerned that the child will not get enough attention because he is quiet and reserved. What suggestions can the nurse provide for the parent to stimulate the boy's confidence and language skills?

Guidelines: Encourage the father and other family members to read to the child often. Ask the child questions about the books, encourage him to answer, and have conversations about the stories. Prompt him if he has difficulty expressing himself and encourage him to make up his own stories. Limit passive television and DVD watching, and use interactive educational computer programs that involve age-appropriate language and skill building. Also, play CDs with sing-alongs and story telling.

OBJECTIVES	CONTENT	TEACHING RESOURCES
Describe the development of the preschool child in relation to Piaget's, Erikson's, and Kohlberg's theories of development.	■ General characteristics (p. 420) □ Physical development (p. 420) □ Cognitive development (p. 421) □ Effects of cultural practices (p. 421) □ Language development (p. 421)	▣▤ PPT slides 8-13 𝒆 EILR OBQ questions 1, 2 𝒆 EILR TB questions 3, 9, 18, 19, 23, 27 𝒆 ESLR IRQ questions 2, 3 **SG** SG Learning Activities, questions 3-5 (p. 151) **SG** SG Review Questions, questions 3, 11, 13 (pp. 153-154) **BOOK RESOURCES** Table 18-1, Preschool Growth and Development (p. 422) Table 18-2, Selected Perceptual, Cognitive, and Language Processes Required for Elementary School Success (p. 423) Table 18-3, Not Talking: A Clinical Classification (p. 424) ▸ Discuss how the concept of egocentrism interferes with a preschool child's ability to see another person's perspective. What are the missing elements of the child's cognitive and emotional development that inhibit ability to consider an alternate viewpoint? *Class Activity **Divide the class into groups and assign each group one of the following topics:*** – *Physical development* – *Cognitive development* – *Cultural practices* – *Language development* *Ask each group to make a presentation on its assigned topic according to Piaget's, Erikson's, and Kohlberg's theories of development as it pertains to the preschool child. What is the parent's role and what are appropriate nursing interventions in furthering the developmental*

Leifer

OBJECTIVES	CONTENT	TEACHING RESOURCES
		process? Students may refer to Chapter 15, Tables 15-3, 15-4, and 15-5 (pp. 365-367).
Describe the speech development of the preschool child.	■ General characteristics (p. 420) □ Physical development (p. 420) □ Cognitive development (p. 421) □ Effects of cultural practices (p. 421) □ Language development (p. 421)	PPT slides 8-13 *e* EILR IC images 1, 2 *e* EILR TB questions 9, 15, 20 SG Learning Activities, question 5 (p. 151) SG Thinking Critically, question 2 (p. 155) **BOOK RESOURCES** Table 18-1, Preschool Growth and Development (p. 422) Figure 18-1, The Family Meal (p. 423) Figure 18-2, Grandpa Reads to the Children (p. 423) Table 18-2, Selected Perceptual, Cognitive, and Language Processes Required for Elementary School Success (p. 423) Table 18-3, Not Talking: A Clinical Classification (p. 424) ▶ Discuss ways to manage preschool children who are frustrated by their inability to express themselves verbally. How can nurses educate parents to practice these management techniques at home? *Class Activity **Invite a speech therapist to discuss normal speech development and signs of potential problems in a preschool child. Ask the therapist to explain ways a parent can encourage speech development and counter difficulties. What are appropriate nursing interventions if a child demonstrates problems or parents have questions? (For students to prepare for this activity, see Homework/Assignments #1.)***
Discuss the development of positive bedtime habits.	□ Sexual curiosity (p. 424) □ Bedtime habits (p. 424)	PPT slides 16-18 *e* EILR OBQ questions 2, 3 *e* EILR TB questions 8, 10, 13, 14, 16, 24 SG Learning Activities, questions 6, 16-18, 24 (pp. 151-152) SG Review Questions, questions 6, 9, 10, 14 (pp. 151-152, 154) **BOOK RESOURCES** Review Questions for the NCLEX® Examination, question 3 (p. 434)

OBJECTIVES	CONTENT	TEACHING RESOURCES
		▸ Discuss how the nurse can best counsel parents who inquire about their children's sexual curiosity.
		*Class Activity **Divide the class into groups and have each group outline how it would address a preschooler's questions about sex. Have each group present its outline to the class to evaluate for content, effectiveness, and appropriateness.***
		▸ Discuss the value of bedtime rituals and why preschoolers find these comforting.
		*Class Activity **Present the following bedtime scenarios to the class:***
		The father of a 3-year-old roughhouses with him just before bed.
		A 4-year-old girl insists she cannot sleep, so her mother takes her into her own bed.
		A 5-year-old boy wants his favorite teddy bear to sleep with him every night.
		Ask students why each practice is appropriate or inappropriate and why. What role might cultural practices play in developing children's bedtime habits?
Discuss one method of introducing the concept of death to a preschool child.	■ Physical, mental, emotional, and social development (p. 424) ☐ The 3-year-old (p. 424) ☐ The 4-year-old (p. 425) – The concept of death (p. 425)	🖥 PPT slides 19-24 𝒆 EILR OBQ question 4 𝒆 EILR TB question 6 📕 SG Review Questions, question 5 (p. 153) ▸ Discuss approaches of how to explain the death of a real person to a preschool child. *Class Activity **Lead a discussion in which students describe the concept of death, as 3-, 4-, and 5-year-olds understand it. What are some concrete terms a parent can use to answer a child's question at each age?***

18.2 Homework/Assignments:

1. Invite a preschool teacher to share how enuresis, thumb-sucking, and sexual curiosity are handled in the classroom. Ask students to prepare questions in advance.

18.2 Instructor's/Student Feedback:

Introduction to Maternity & Pediatric Nursing, 6th ed.

Elsevier items and derived items © 2010, 2007, 2006 by Saunders, an imprint of Elsevier Inc.

Leifer

LESSON 18.3

CRITICAL THINKING QUESTION

A foster parent takes care of a 5-year-old who is required to visit her biological mother every weekend. The child wets the bed for 1 or 2 nights when she returns to the foster home, then stays dry until after the next weekend. The foster mother calls the clinic and asks the nurse how she should handle the bedwetting. What counseling can the nurse provide?

Guidelines: The nurse can clarify that the bedwetting is likely due to stress from visiting the biological mother, and is not an unusual response in an emotionally trying circumstance. The foster mother should inform the child's social worker and possibly the child's physician about the bedwetting issue. The nurse should encourage the foster mother to be supportive and not punish the child for the event. Inform the foster mother that there are new products, such as absorbent pull-on underpants, for larger-sized children that could be worn for a night or two after the child returns. This would prevent wetting the entire bed and keep the child more comfortable. The nurse can suggest that the child and the biological mother may require some special counseling or supervised visitations to reduce the child's stress from the weekend visits.

OBJECTIVES	CONTENT	TEACHING RESOURCES
Discuss the value of the following: time-out periods, consistency, role modeling, and rewards.	■ Guidance (p. 426) □ Discipline and limit setting (p. 426) – Timing the time-out (p. 426) – Reward (p. 427) – Consistency and modeling (p. 427) □ Jealousy (p. 427)	PPT slides 29-31 EILR IC image 3 EILR OBQ questions 5, 6 EILR TB questions 7, 29 SG Learning Activities, questions 11-15 (p. 152) SG Review Questions, questions 7, 8 (p. 154) SG Thinking Critically, questions 2, 3 (p. 155) SG Case Study, question 1 (p. 155) SG Applying Knowledge, questions 2, 4 (p. 155) **BOOK RESOURCES** Figure 18-3, Child and New Sibling (p. 427) Review Questions for the NCLEX® Examination, question 4 (p. 434) ▸ Discuss the positive and negative aspects of rewards. Which rewards are effective in setting limits, building self-confidence, and increasing task mastery? *Class Activity Lead a discussion about how parents can use time-outs, rewards, consistency, and modeling to set limits and help preschoolers develop self-control. Ask students which of the following examples are appropriate or not and why.* *1. A father says he will get his 5-year-old son his favorite candy bar if he behaves at the grocery store.*

OBJECTIVES	CONTENT	TEACHING RESOURCES
		2. *A mother places her 3-year-old girl on a small chair facing the corner and sets a timer for 3 minutes when she misbehaves.*
		3. *The parents of a strong-willed 4-year-old boy sometimes use time-outs, but sometimes ignore inappropriate behavior. They are frustrated when he does not listen.*
Discuss the approach to problems such as enuresis, thumb-sucking, and sexual curiosity in the preschool child.	☐ Thumb-sucking (p. 428) ☐ Enuresis (p. 428) – Pathophysiology (p. 428) – Treatment and nursing care (p. 428)	⊠▤ PPT slides 32-35 𝒆 EILR OBQ question 7 𝒆 EILR TB questions 8, 10, 13, 14 SG Learning Activities, questions 15, 16, 22 (pp. 152-153) SG Review Questions, questions 9, 10 (p. 154) **BOOK RESOURCES** Review Questions for the NCLEX® Examination, question 3 (p. 434) ▸ Discuss ways that nurses could help families cope with the emotional and social challenges of a preschool child with enuresis. Provide practical interventions that might help prevent secondary emotional problems from developing in the child. Class Activity *Divide the class into groups and assign each group the topic of enuresis or thumb sucking in the preschool child. Ask each group to discuss what is considered normal behavior and, in the case of enuresis, how to recognize signs of possible pathophysiology. How can a nurse advise a parent about appropriate behavior goals? How can secondary emotional problems be avoided? How can consistency and rewards contribute to positive outcomes?*
Designate two toys suitable for the preschool child, and provide the rationale for each choice.	■ Play in health and illness (p. 430) ☐ Value of play (p. 430) ☐ The nurse's role (p. 431)	⊠▤ PPT slides 39, 40 𝒆 EILR OBQ questions 8, 21, 22 SG Applying Knowledge, question 5 (p. 155) ▸ Discuss the use of toys such as crayons, blocks, books, and large puzzles versus toys such as jacks, marbles, scissors, and dice. What are the potential hazards associated with the latter group? Class Activity *Ask students to bring to class examples of toys that are appropriate and inappropriate for preschoolers of different ages. What makes a toy suitable or unsuitable for the child's age? What features make*

Leifer

OBJECTIVES	CONTENT	TEACHING RESOURCES
		the toy dangerous? What kinds of toys or other objects can advance the child's mastery of various developmental tasks? (For students to prepare for this activity, see Homework/Assignments #1.)

18.3 Homework/Assignments:

1. Ask students to bring to class examples of toys that are appropriate and inappropriate for preschoolers of different ages. What makes a toy suitable or unsuitable for the child's age? What features make the toy dangerous? What kinds of toys or other objects can advance the child's mastery of various developmental tasks?

18.3 Instructor's Notes/Student Feedback:

LESSON 18.4

CRITICAL THINKING QUESTION

One parent wants to send her child to a preschool program for three mornings a week. Another parent who has a mentally handicapped child also wants to have her child experience the benefits of a group care setting for part of the week. How should each parent evaluate potential programs to determine suitability for the child? What special features should the parent of the handicapped child look for?

Guidelines: Both parents should contact a state licensing facility for a list of local centers and should obtain state accreditation criteria. Parents should inquire about the teachers' training and experience in early childhood education, as well as the child-to-staff ratio. The philosophies of the school regarding discipline, safety, sanitation, and approach to teaching and play should be considered. Schedules and facilities for active and passive play indoors and outdoors should be reviewed, and the parent should be encouraged to visit the facility and observe the environment. Parents should receive clear, complete information about fees, schedules, hours of operation, snacks, meals, and rest time. The center should routinely require a personal and health history of the child before admission. Schools that focus on handicapped children should be brighter and more colorful, with large rooms for running and playing. The ratio of teachers to children should be lower than regular day care centers, and staff should be specially trained to work with handicapped children. Some may require more stimulation to interact with other children, whereas others may need to have aggressive behavior limited. Teachers in these special settings should provide more stimulation and supervision, teach children how to play, introduce group play gradually, and present materials and toys one at a time, depending on mental and emotional levels. Objects and toys should have a variety of textures and sizes and should be provided according to the child's capabilities. The lesson plans should vary for each child, with improvised games and songs tailored for individual needs.

OBJECTIVES	CONTENT	TEACHING RESOURCES
Describe the developmental characteristics that predispose the preschool child to certain accidents, and suggest methods of prevention for each type of accident.	■ Daily care (p. 429) □ Clothing (p. 429) □ Accident prevention (p. 430)	PPT slides 37, 38 *e* EILR IC image 4 *e* EILR TB question 25 SG Review Questions, question 15 (p. 155) **BOOK RESOURCES** Figure 18-4, Unsupervised Water Play Can Quickly Lead to Unexpected Injuries (p. 430) ▶ Discuss the types of clothing children should wear and ways parents can prevent accidents. Discuss what level of supervision is needed for preschoolers in light of their cognitive and physical development. *Class Activity **Invite a day care supervisor to discuss behaviors and developmental characteristics that make preschoolers vulnerable to harm and certain kinds of injuries. What types of supervision are needed? How do schools counter a preschooler's accident-prone traits? What methods can families use to reduce the risk of various kinds of accidents? Ask students to prepare questions in advance. (For students to prepare for this activity, see Homework/Assignments #1.)***
Discuss the characteristics of a good	■ Preschool (p. 429)	PPT slide 36 *e* EILR TB question 26

Leifer

OBJECTIVES	CONTENT	TEACHING RESOURCES
preschool.		**SG** SG Applying Knowledge, question 3 (p. 155) ▸ Discuss ways nurses can help families choose an appropriate school to meet their child's needs. What criteria are considered most important when selecting a nursery or preschool? *Class Activity **Divide the class into small groups and ask them to design an informative booklet for parents titled "Choosing a Nursery School." What key points should the booklet include? What criteria should parents consider when evaluating if a preschool is right for their child? Have students present their booklets, and have the class evaluate.***
Discuss the value of play in the life of a preschool child.	■ Play in health and illness (p. 430) ☐ The value of play (p. 430) ☐ The nurse's role (p. 431) ☐ Types of play (p. 431) – Play and the handicapped child (p. 432) – Therapeutic play (p. 432) – Play therapy (p. 432) – Art therapy (p. 432) ■ Nursing implications of preschool growth and development (p. 432)	PPT slides 39-45 *e* EILR IC images 4, 5 *e* EILR OBQ questions 8-10 *e* EILR TB questions 5, 9, 11-13, 28 **SG** SG Learning Activities, questions 18-25 (pp. 152-153) **SG** SG Applying Knowledge, question 5 (p. 155) **BOOK RESOURCES** Figure 18-4, Unsupervised Water Play Can Quickly Lead to Unexpected Injuries (p. 430) Figure 18-5, A self-image begins to develop during the preschool years with imaginative play (p. 430) Nursing Tip (p. 431) Review Questions for the NCLEX® Examination, questions 1-2 (p. 433) ▸ Discuss the types of play that a nurse could facilitate with a preschool child that may help alleviate stress or fear. What is meant by *therapeutic play*? *Play therapy*? *Art therapy*? *Class Activity **Lead a discussion in which students relate preschool play activities, such as climbing a jungle gym, sorting blocks, learning rhymes, or playing house, to mastering developmental tasks. What physical, cognitive, cultural, spiritual, and psychosocial factors are important? If a child is hospitalized, what is the nurse's role in enabling the child to continue development through play?***
Explain the use of therapeutic play with a handicapped child.	☐ Play and the handicapped child (p. 432)	PPT slide 42 ▸ Discuss factors that need to be considered in selecting toys and games for a handicapped child.
Performance Evaluation		PPT slides 1-47 *e* EILR IC images 1-5

OBJECTIVES	CONTENT	TEACHING RESOURCES
		e EILR OBQ questions 1-10
		e EILR TB questions 1-30
		e ESLR IRQ questions 1-5
		SG Learning Activities, questions 1-22 (pp. 151-153)
		SG Review Questions, questions 1-15 (pp. 153-155)
		SG Case Study, question 1 (p. 155)
		SG Thinking Critically, questions 1-2 (p. 155)
		SG Applying Knowledge, questions 1-5 (p. 155)
		BOOK RESOURCES
		Review Questions for the NCLEX® Examination, questions 1-5 (pp. 433-434)

18.4 Homework/Assignments:

1. Invite a day care supervisor to discuss behaviors and developmental characteristics that make preschoolers vulnerable to harm and certain kinds of injuries. Ask students to prepare questions in advance.

18.4 Instructor's Notes/Student Feedback:

ELSEVIER

Introduction to Maternity & Pediatric Nursing, 6th ed.
Leifer

18 Lecture Outline
The Preschool Child

Slide 1

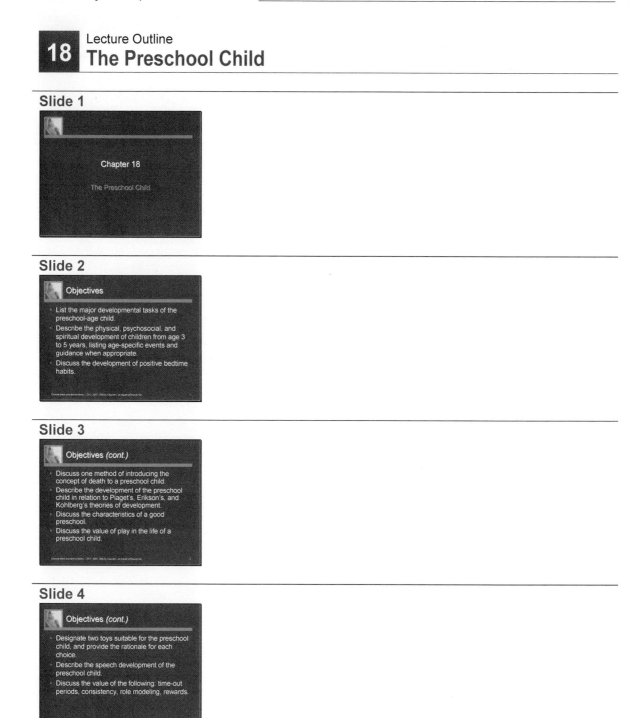

Chapter 18

The Preschool Child

Slide 2

Objectives

- List the major developmental tasks of the preschool-age child.
- Describe the physical, psychosocial, and spiritual development of children from age 3 to 5 years, listing age-specific events and guidance when appropriate.
- Discuss the development of positive bedtime habits.

Slide 3

Objectives *(cont.)*

- Discuss one method of introducing the concept of death to a preschool child.
- Describe the development of the preschool child in relation to Piaget's, Erikson's, and Kohlberg's theories of development.
- Discuss the characteristics of a good preschool.
- Discuss the value of play in the life of a preschool child.

Slide 4

Objectives *(cont.)*

- Designate two toys suitable for the preschool child, and provide the rationale for each choice.
- Describe the speech development of the preschool child.
- Discuss the value of the following: time-out periods, consistency, role modeling, rewards.

Leifer

Slide 5

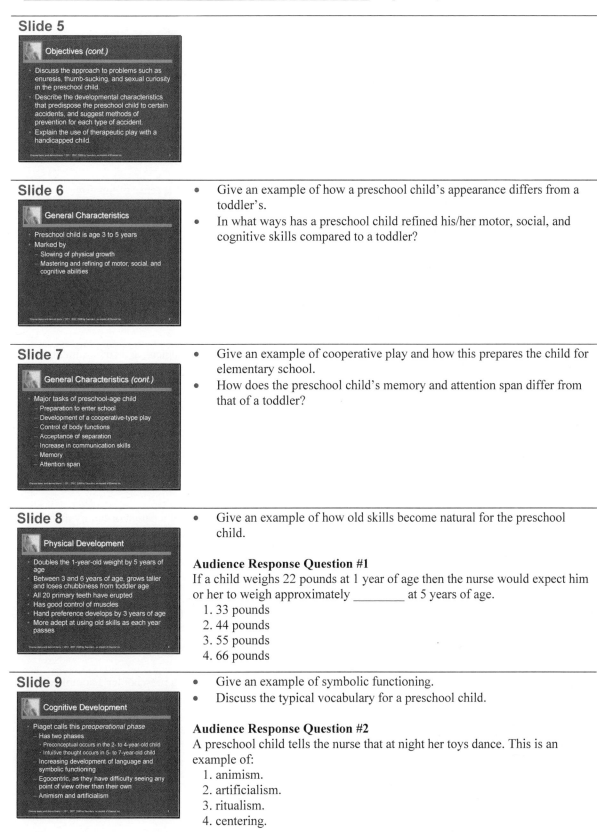

Slide 6

- Give an example of how a preschool child's appearance differs from a toddler's.
- In what ways has a preschool child refined his/her motor, social, and cognitive skills compared to a toddler?

Slide 7

- Give an example of cooperative play and how this prepares the child for elementary school.
- How does the preschool child's memory and attention span differ from that of a toddler?

Slide 8

- Give an example of how old skills become natural for the preschool child.

Audience Response Question #1

If a child weighs 22 pounds at 1 year of age then the nurse would expect him or her to weigh approximately _____ at 5 years of age.
1. 33 pounds
2. 44 pounds
3. 55 pounds
4. 66 pounds

Slide 9

- Give an example of symbolic functioning.
- Discuss the typical vocabulary for a preschool child.

Audience Response Question #2

A preschool child tells the nurse that at night her toys dance. This is an example of:
1. animism.
2. artificialism.
3. ritualism.
4. centering.

Slide 10	• Discuss prelogical thinking.

Cognitive Development *(cont.)*

- Piaget's *intuitive thought stage*
  - Occurs in the 4- to 7-year-old child
  - Prelogical thinking
  - Experience and logic are based on outside appearance
  - Distinct characteristic is *centering*
  - Tendency to concentrate on a single outstanding characteristic of an object and exclude other features

• Discuss prelogical thinking.
• What is centering?
• Give an example of how the preschool child will exclude other features of an object while focusing on one outstanding aspect of that object.

Slide 11

Effects of Cultural Practices

- Can influence the development of a sense of initiative
- Parents and older siblings model language development

• Give an example of how culture affects one's sense of initiative.
• How is a preschool child's language development affected by those in the family?

Slide 12

Language Development

- Delays or problems can be caused by
  - Physiological
  - Psychological
  - Environmental stressors
- Includes both the understanding of language and the expressing of oneself in language

• Give an example of physiological, psychological, and environmental factors that can cause developmental delays.

Slide 13

Not Talking: A Clinical Classification

WHEN PARENTS SAY	CLASSIFY THE SYMPTOMS AS
"I'm the only one who understands what she says."	Articulation disorder
"She'll do what I say, but when she wants something, she just points."	Expressive language delay
"He can't play 'show me your nose,' and the only word he says is 'mama'."	Global language delay
"He never made those funny baby sounds or said 'mama' and 'dada,' and now he just repeats everything I say."	Language disorder
"He used to say things like 'Joey go bye-bye,' but now he doesn't talk at all."	Language loss

• Ask students to give other examples of what a parent or family member might say for each of the following classifications:
  – Articulation
  – Expressive language delay
  – Global language delay
  – Language disorder
  – Language loss

Slide 14

Development of Play

- Play activities increase in complexity
- Enables child to experience multiple roles and emotional outlets
- Appealing to child's magical thinking is best approach to communicating with a preschooler

• Give an example of how play can increase a preschooler's complexities.
• Discuss a scenario in which a child might mimic a role to display emotions.
• How might a nurse provide a magical concept to assist in communicating with a preschooler?

Introduction to Maternity & Pediatric Nursing, 6th ed.

Leifer

Slide 15

Spiritual Development

- Learn religious beliefs and practices at home
- Cannot understand abstract concepts
- In the hospitalized preschooler, observing religious traditions practiced in the home may be calming for the child

- Give examples of religious practices a preschool child might participate in at home.
- What is an example of an abstract concept a preschool child would not comprehend?
- Discuss how routine, which could include religious traditions, would assist the hospitalized child.

Slide 16

Sexual Curiosity

- Nurses should use the following principles of teaching and learning common to other patients

- Give an example of how the nurse could assist the parents in discussing sexual education for their child.

Slide 17

Sexual Curiosity *(cont.)*

- Assess knowledge base of child
- Assess what specific information the child is seeking
- Be honest and accurate
- Use correct terminology

- Provide sex education at the time the child asks the questions
- Parents must understand that sexual curiosity starts as an inquiry into anatomical differences

- Give an example of an honest and accurate conversation between a nurse and preschool child that is appropriate for the child's level.
- Provide an example of terminology a nurse might use when discussing sexual curiosity with the preschool child.
- In what situation might a preschool child ask questions regarding his or her anatomical differences?

Slide 18

Sexual Curiosity *(cont.)*

- Preschool children are as matter-of-fact about sexual investigation as they are about any other leaning experience and are easily distracted by other activities

- May be displayed in the form of masturbation
  - Considered harmless if the child is outgoing, sociable, and not preoccupied with the activity
  - Assure parents that this behavior is normal

- Give an example of how a nurse or parent might distract a preschool child who is constantly touching his or her private parts.
- How can the nurse help parents understand and deal with this milestone in their child's development?

Slide 19

Physical, Mental, Emotional, and Social Development

- What is an example of a social developmental lag in the preschool child?

Leifer

Slide 20

The 3-Year-Old

- Helpful and can assist in household chores
- Temper tantrums less frequent
- Better able to direct primitive instincts
- Can help dress themselves, use the toilet, wash their hands, and eat independently
- Talk in longer sentences
- Able to express thoughts and ask questions

- Give examples of how the preschool child can assist the parent in the household.
- How can this age group function independently or assist in daily activities?

Slide 21

The 3-Year-Old *(cont.)*

- Play in loosely associated groups
- Highly imaginative play
- Begin to lose interest in mother and prestige of the father begins
- Develop romantic attachment to parent of opposite gender
- Identify themselves with parent of same gender

- Give examples of a 3-year-old's vocabulary.
- Discuss how the 3-year-old's imagination is different from the school-age child's.
- How might a 3-year-old display an identification with a parent of the same sex?

Slide 22

The 3-Year-Old *(cont.)*

- Become angry when someone tries to take their possessions
- Resent being disturbed during play
- Are sensitive and feelings are easily hurt
- Has fear of bodily harm

- Describe a situation in which the nurse might have to manage the hurt feelings of a 3-year-old.
- Discuss how the nurse could help decrease the 3-year-old child's fear of bodily harm while hospitalized.

Slide 23

The 4-Year-Old

- More aggressive
- Eager to let others know they are superior
- Pick on playmates
- Boisterous, tattle on others
- Can use scissors with success
- Can tie their shoes

- Give an example of how a 4-year-old child might be more aggressive than a 3-year-old.
- What education could the nurse provide to parents in dealing with an aggressive 4-year-old who picks on other children?
- Give an example of how a 4-year-old might display superiority over peers.

Slide 24

The 4-Year-Old *(cont.)*

- Vocabulary has increased to about 1500 words
- Many feats done for a purpose
- Begin to prefer playing with friends of same gender

- Give examples of the typical vocabulary of a 4-year-old.
- Discuss types of achievements a 4-year-old might accomplish.

Leifer

Slide 25

The 4-Year-Old *(cont.)*

- Concept of death
  - Begin to wonder about death and dying
  - Realize others die, but do not relate death to themselves
  - Parents should reassure child that people do not generally die until they have lived a really long time
  - Parents should encourage questions as they appear and help the child accept the truth about death without fear

- Discuss how 4-year-old children play scenarios in which death is a concept.
- Discuss how a parent might encourage or stimulate discussion so this child can discuss death or the fear of it.

Slide 26

The 5-Year-Old

- More responsible
- Enjoys doing what is expected of them
- Have more patience
- Tend to want to finish what they have started
- Talk constantly
- Inquisitive

- What actions would indicate how a 5-year-old child is more responsible than a 4-year-old?
- Discuss how the 5-year-old is very talkative and how parents can deal with the constant chatter.

Slide 27

The 5-Year-Old *(cont.)*

- Play games governed by rules
- Less fearful of environment
- Worries less profound
- May begin losing deciduous teeth

- Give an example of how a 5-year-old might react to rules of a game versus a 4-year-old child.
- In what ways is this age group less fearful of the environment?

Slide 28

The 5-Year-Old *(cont.)*

- Should be encouraged to develop motor skills, such as hammering a nail
- Should not be scorned for failure to meet adult standards
- Must learn to do tasks themselves for the experience to be satisfying

- Give examples of other skills a 5-year-old might be encouraged to accomplish.
- How might a parent discuss the failure of a desired skill attempted by a 5-year-old?

Slide 29

Guidance

Leifer

Slide 30

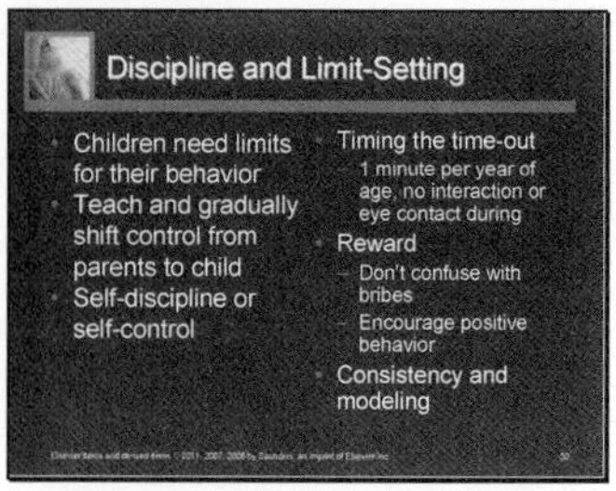

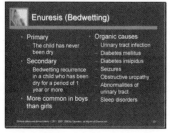

- Limits make children feel secure, protect them from danger, and relieve them from decisions that they are too young to make.
- How do limits make children feel secure?
- Discuss how limits and self-discipline differ from each other and the parent's role in each.
- How do rewards differ from bribes?
- Discuss how modeling by the parent affects the child.
- Parents should establish a general style for discipline.

Audience Response Question #3
The best time to offer a reward for good behavior is:
  1. during poor behavior.
  2. following an episode of poor behavior.
  3. when the child finishes a time-out episode.
  4. before the poor behavior occurs.

Slide 31

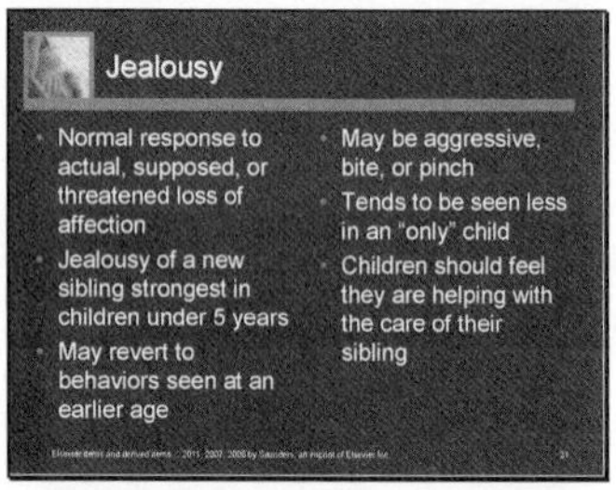

- How would a child display jealousy?
- Discuss how a parent might address a preschool child who is displaying jealousy.

Audience Response Question #4
Encouraging a 4-year-old child to assist with the care of his newborn brother will assist in his adjustment to having a sibling.
  1. True
  2. False

Slide 32

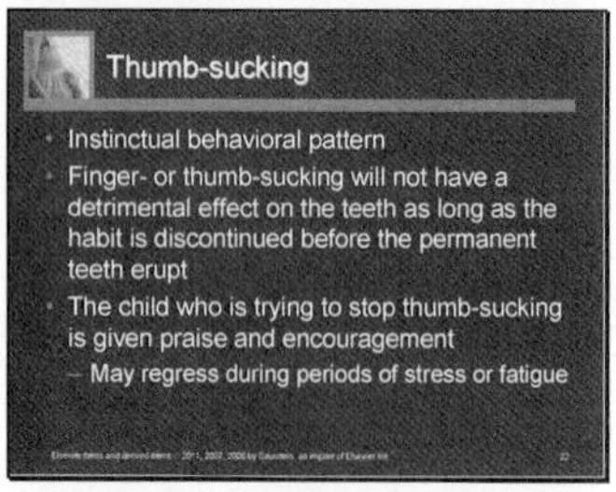

- Discuss regression.
- How can a parent effectively discourage thumb-sucking?

Slide 33

- What organic causes can bring about enuresis?

Leifer

Slide 34

Enuresis (Bedwetting) *(cont.)*

- Treatment and nursing care
- Data collection
- Pattern of wetting
- Number of times per night or week
- Number of daytime voidings
- Type of stream
- Dysuria
- Amount of fluid taken between dinner and bedtime
- Family history
- Stress
- Medications
- Developmental landmarks, including toilet training

- Discuss information the nurse would collect regarding family history, stress, medications, and developmental milestones.

Slide 35

Enuresis (Bedwetting) *(cont.)*

- Child needs to be center of management program
- Liquids should be limited after dinner
- Child should void before going to bed

- Treatment options
  - Counseling
  - Hypnosis
  - Behavior modification
  - Pharmacotherapy
  - Bladder training exercises to stretch and increase the bladder size

- What might the child contribute to manage his or her enuresis?
- Discuss behavior modification and bladder training exercises.
- Discuss medications that can help with enuresis.

Slide 36

Nursery School

- Preschool programs
  - Structured activities
  - Foster group cooperation
  - The development of coping skills
- Child gains
  - Self-confidence
  - Positive self-esteem if in a good program

- Discuss types of group activities that would promote cooperation among preschool children.
- What are examples of a positive or negative program and how it can affect a child's self-esteem?

Slide 37

Daily Care

- Does not require extensive physical care but still needs to bathe each day and shampoo hair at least twice a week
- Clothing should be loose enough to prevent restriction of movement, washable; sturdy and supportive shoes

- Discuss how a nurse or parent can provide education at a preschool child's level so the child understands the importance of hygiene on a daily basis.
- Provide examples of restrictive versus nonrestrictive clothing.

Slide 38

Accident Prevention

- Accidents are a major threat for 3- to 5-year-olds
- Car safety is essential
- Burns occur due to child's experimentation
- Poisoning can occur due to increased freedom and access to items within the environment
- Child should be taught about the dangers of talking to or getting in the car with strangers, as well as the dangers of playing in secluded areas
- Indirect supervision necessary due to poor judgment

- Discuss methods parents or caregivers could institute to minimize accidents for this population.
- In what situations could children become victims of predators?
- Give an example of indirect supervision.

Slide 39

Play in Health and Illness

Value of Play
- Important to physical, mental, emotional, and social development
- Increases communication with other children

The Nurse's Role
- Important to include in the child's plan of care
- Factors to consider
  - State of health
  - Overstimulation and fatigue
  - Diagnosis should be considered when choosing toys for the child

- Give examples of situations in which the child might not visit the playroom or interact with others while in the hospital environment.
- What are appropriate toys for the preschool-age child?

Slide 40

Value of Play

- Should be noncompetitive
- Helps the child adjust to an expanding world and increased independence

- Discuss education for parents or methods the nurse can institute so play is not competitive between children.
- In what ways is play important to the physical, psychosocial, and emotional development of the preschool child?

Slide 41

Nursing Tip

- Imaginary playmates are common and normal during the preschool period and serve many purposes, such as relief from loneliness, mastery of feats, and a "scapegoat"

- Give examples of how the nurse might interact with a preschool child who is interacting with his or her playmate.

Slide 42

Play and the Handicapped Child

- Mentally disabled child needs more stimulation through play than the child who is not impaired
- Consider mental and not chronological age
- Play needs to be supervised due to poorer judgment and potential for aggressive behavior
- Repetition of play experiences is necessary

- Discuss why the handicapped child requires more stimulation through play versus a nonimpaired child.
- Give examples of situations in which mental age differs from chronological age and how the nurse can manage these children.
- How does repetitive play affect the handicapped child?

Slide 43

Play

Therapeutic play
- Retrain muscles
- Improve eye-hand coordination
- Help children to crawl and walk

Other types of play
- Play therapy
  - Used when child is under stress
- Art therapy
  - Child can express feelings and communicate with others through drawings

- Give situations and examples of how therapeutic play can help rehabilitate or enhance development in the child.
- How can the nurse incorporate play therapy into the plan of care?

Introduction to Maternity & Pediatric Nursing, 6th ed.

Leifer

Slide 44

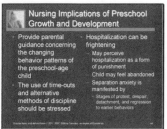

Nursing Implications of Preschool Growth and Development

- Provide parental guidance concerning the changing behavior patterns of the preschool-age child
- The use of time-outs and alternative methods of discipline should be stressed
- Hospitalization can be frightening
  - May perceive hospitalization as a form of punishment
  - Child may feel abandoned
  - Separation anxiety is manifested by
    - Stages of protest, despair, detachment, and regression to earlier behaviors

- Discuss the stages of separation anxiety and how the nurse can assist the child to transition through anxiety.
- How can the nurse address and inform the child's parents about management of separation anxiety?

Slide 45

Nursing Implications of Preschool Growth and Development *(cont.)*

- Important nursing assessment includes observing the child
  - What is the child's approach to play?
  - Does the child join in freely or linger outside the group?
  - Does the child prefer active or quiet activities?
  - Can the child talk with his or her playmates and convey ideas?
  - What type of attention span does the child have?

- Discuss the nurse's rationale for obtaining information about how the preschool child interacts socially.

Slide 46

Question for Review

- What kind of therapeutic play would be appropriate for a postoperative preschool child?

Slide 47

Review

- Objectives
- Key Terms
- Key Points
- Online Resources
- Critical Thinking Question
- Review Questions

Leifer

19 Lesson Plan
The School-Age Child

TEACHING FOCUS

This chapter presents both the physical and psychological development of the school-age child. Several theories of development are discussed and the student will have the opportunity to learn the major characteristics of the child during each year of life from ages 6 to 12. Special issues that are addressed are safety precautions and health examinations for this age group, latchkey children, and pet ownership.

MATERIALS AND RESOURCES

- ☐ Childhood development videos (all lessons)
- ☐ Computer and PowerPoint projector (all lessons)

LESSON CHECKLIST

Preparations for this lesson include:

- Lecture
- Demonstration
- Guest speakers: School or community health nurse, school health teacher, or guidance counselor
- Evaluation of student knowledge and skills needed to perform all entry-level activities related to the school-age child, including an understanding of:
  - ○ Theories of development
  - ○ Preparing the child and parent for dealing with school responsibilities
  - ○ Safety issues during childhood
  - ○ Health issues and examinations for school-age children
  - ○ Latchkey children
  - ○ Pet ownership

KEY TERMS

androgynous (p. 437)
concrete operations (p. 435)
latchkey children (p. 440)
preadolescent (p. 443)

Sex Information and Education Council of the United States (SIECUS) (p. 437)

sexual latency (p. 435)
stage of industry (p. 435)

ADDITIONAL RESOURCES

TEACH PPT slide(s) Chapter 19, 1-45
EILR IC image(s) Chapter 19, 1-7
EILR OBQ question(s) Chapter 19, 1-10
EILR TB question(s) Chapter 19, 1-28
ESLR IRQ question(s) Chapter 19, 1-5
SG Chapter 19, pp. 157-161

Legend

PPT
TEACH
PowerPoint
Slides

EILR
EVOLVE Instructor
Learning Resources:
Image Collection (IC),
Open-Book Quizzes
(OBQ), Test Bank (TB)

ESLR
EVOLVE Student
Learning Resources:
Interactive Review
Questions (IRQ) for
the NCLEX®
Examination

SG
Study Guide

CTQ
Critical Thinking
Question in
Nursing Care Plan
(NCP CTQ) or Get
Ready for the
NCLEX! (GRN
CTQ)

Class Activities are indicated in ***bold italic***.

LESSON 19.1

PRETEST

1. Which thought process involves logical thinking for the school-age child and an understanding of cause and effect?
   - a. stage of industry
   - b. sexual latency
   - c. concrete operations
   - d. androgynous

2. In terms of gender identity, some adults develop a concept of gender identity that includes both masculine and feminine qualities. This is known as
   - a. neutrality.
   - b. ambivalence.
   - c. assertive sensitivity.
   - d. androgynous.

3. Nurses can assist parents and children with sex education through careful listening and
   - a. anticipatory guidance.
   - b. constructive criticism.
   - c. fostering interdependence.
   - d. strong discipline.

4. Latchkey children are those left unsupervised after school because parents or extended family members work outside the home. They are at a higher risk of feeling isolated and subject to a higher rate of
   - a. study hours.
   - b. after-school activities.
   - c. accidents.
   - d. parental supervision.

5. At what age do the child's arms and hands seem to grow faster than the rest of their body?
   - a. 6 years old
   - b. 7 years old
   - c. 8 years old
   - d. 9 years old

6. Which age category is characterized by disorganization and children who are intense, observant, all-knowing, energetic, meddlesome, and argumentative?
   - a. 5-7 years
   - b. 8-10 years
   - c. 11-12 years
   - d. 16-18 years

7. At what age are hand-eye coordination and fine motor skills well-established and movements graceful and coordinated?
   - a. 4-6 years
   - b. 6-8 years
   - c. 8-10 years
   - d. 10-12 years

8. Studies have documented that after the age 7, children can be responsible for care of a family pet and that pets
   - a. are time-consuming.
   - b. cause disease.
   - c. prevent disease.
   - d. improve medical outcomes after surgery.

9. Immunocompromised children are at risk of contracting illnesses spread by some types of animals because the animals cannot be screened for potential pathogens, have few vaccines, and are most likely to transmit disease. For these reasons, which animal below is the best choice of a companion for an immunocompromised child?
   - a. bird
   - b. dog
   - c. turtle
   - d. iguana

10. Although pet ownership may nurture a sense of responsibility and encourage socialization with shy children, which of the following is essential?
    - a. choosing a shy domestic animal for the family
    - b. selecting an appropriate pet for the family
    - c. providing exposure to farm animals
    - d. choosing a puppy less than 1 year old

Answers

1. c	3. a	5. c	7. d	9. b
2. d	4. c	6. c	8. d	10. b

BACKGROUND ASSESSMENT

Question: What are some nursing interventions the nurse may find useful in the growth and development of the school-age child in school-related tasks?

Answer: Nursing interventions include contacting and facilitating parent-teacher-child interaction, evaluating and providing guidance and positive support, providing guidance on dealing with behavior problems and signs of prejudice, providing referrals to community agencies and organizations when needed, and encouraging child independence.

Question: How would you compare nutritional development of a child at 6 to 7 years of age to that of an 11- to 12-year-old?

Answer: A 6- to 7-year-old tends to dislike many foods and have deficiencies in iron, vitamin A, and riboflavin. A child in this age bracket needs 100 ml/kg of water per day and 3 g/kg of protein. Boys age 11- to 12 years old need 2500 calories/day while girls need 2250 calories/day. Both boys and girls need 75 ml/kg of water/day and 2 g/kg of protein daily.

CRITICAL THINKING QUESTION

A shy, reserved 8-year-old child tends to isolate himself from other children and doesn't want to be part of the group. What type of interventions and guidance can the school nurse provide?

Guidelines: The school nurse can observe teacher-parent-child interaction, evaluate and provide guidance, and encourage socialization in community groups, such as church and club environments. Additionally, the nurse can encourage positive feedback from parents and set realistic goals for the child. The child should be screened for any possible health issues, such as hearing deficits and learning disabilities, and an assessment of physical activity and school performance should be taken. The child may benefit from an increase in structure, while decreasing potential distractions. The nurse should encourage consistent parent-teacher interaction, including participation in the parent-teacher association. The nurse could suggest that the child be given the responsibility of caring for a family pet. This could initiate the socialization process and lead to more contact with others.

OBJECTIVES	CONTENT	TEACHING RESOURCES
Contrast two major theoretical viewpoints of personality development during the school years.	■ General characteristics (p. 435)	⊞ PPT slides 4-7 𝒆 EILR OBQ questions 1-4 𝒆 EILR TB questions 2, 28 𝒆 ESLR IRQ question 2 SG Learning Activities, questions 1-6 (p. 157) SG Review Questions, questions 1-3 (p. 159) SG Case Study, question 1 (p. 160) SG Applying Knowledge, question 1 (p. 161) **BOOK RESOURCES** Box 19-1, Features of Major Theories of Development During Later Childhood (p. 436) ▸ Discuss the major points of the theories of Sigmund Freud, Erik Erikson, and Jean Piaget with regard to personality development. With which do you agree most? Why?

OBJECTIVES	CONTENT	TEACHING RESOURCES
		Class Activity Divide the class into three groups and assign each group one of the three major theories of development during later childhood: Freud, Erikson, or Piaget. The groups should discuss their theory and briefly present it to the class, comparing and contrasting their assigned theory to the other two. How might their selected theory affect the nursing process for children with developmental problems?
Describe the physical and psychosocial development of children from 6 to 12 years of age, listing age-specific events and type of guidance where appropriate.	■ General characteristics (p. 435) □ Physical growth (p. 436) □ Sexual development (p. 437) □ Gender identity (p. 437) □ Sex education (p. 437)	PPT slides 8-15 *e* EILR IC image 1 *e* EILR OBQ question 5 *e* EILR TB questions 1-6, 8, 9, 12, 14-16, 21, 27, 28 SG Learning Activities, questions 1, 6-8 (p. 157) SG Review Questions, questions 4, 9 (p. 159) SG Thinking Critically, question 1 (p. 161) **BOOK RESOURCES** Figure 19-1, School aged children are often evaluated by their peers (p. 436) Nursing Tip (p. 437) Table 19-1, Using the Nursing Process in Sex Education of the School-Age Child (p. 438) Review Questions for the NCLEX® Examination, question 1 (p. 449) ▸ Discuss the average weight gain and increase in height to be expected in a school-age child prior to the puberty growth spurt. ▸ Discuss the vital signs of the child and identify their normal values. ▸ Discuss how sex roles are fostered in the family, school, and society. ▸ Discuss when sex education should begin. How is a child's readiness to learn about sex evaluated? *Class Activity Divide the class into three groups, assigning each group one of the following: physical growth, gender identity, or sex education. Have each group present its topic as it pertains to children 6-12 years old. Have each group present information to the class.* *Class Activity Lead a class discussion about the nursing*

OBJECTIVES	CONTENT	TEACHING RESOURCES
		process and sex education of the school-age child. Discuss each intervention and observation as it applies. (See Table 19-1, p. 438.)
Discuss how to assist parents in preparing a child for school.	■ Influences from the wider world (p. 438) □ School-related tasks (p. 438)	▣ PPT slides 16-19 *e* EILR TB questions 7, 13, 16 📖 SG Case Study, question 1 (p. 160) 📖 SG Applying Knowledge, question 2 (p. 161) **BOOK RESOURCES** Table 19-2, Growth and Development of the School-Age Child in School-Related Tasks (p. 438) Patient Teaching, Parental Guidance for Children Starting School (p. 439) ▶ Discuss the various ways in which the parent can prepare the child for school by fostering communication (between parent and child, parent and school, and parent and teacher). ▶ Discuss how parents can encourage and support good study habits. ▶ Discuss the role of "anticipatory guidance" in the switch from elementary school to middle school. *Class Activity Have students write a small essay on their early childhood years at school and how their experiences with teachers, community activities, and pet ownership compare to the experiences of the school-age child today. Ask students to share their experiences with the class.* *Class Activity Divide the class into small groups and have each group complete an outline for parents on fostering good study habits in their school-age children.* *Class Activity Have students work in small groups and discuss ways that parents can provide guidance to children who are starting school. Have groups present their findings to the class.*
List two ways in which school life influences the growing child.	□ School-related tasks (p. 438)	▣ PPT slides 17-19 📖 SG Learning Activities, question 4 (p. 158) **BOOK RESOURCES** Table 19-2, Growth and Development of the School-Age Child in School-Related Tasks (p. 438) Review Questions for the NCLEX® Examination, question 2 (p. 449)

Leifer

OBJECTIVES	CONTENT	TEACHING RESOURCES
		▸ Discuss the effects of peers on the development of the school-age child.
		▸ Discuss what effects school has on the socialization of children.
		*Class Activity **Divide the class into small groups. Provide groups with a list of school-related tasks of the child, and ask the groups to identify corresponding tasks of the parents that support the growth and development of the school-age child. Each group should share its list with the class.***
		*Class Activity **Lead a class discussion about school-related tasks for the child and the parent. Ask students to identify specific nursing interventions associated with each task.***
Discuss accident prevention in this age group.	☐ Play (p. 439) ☐ Observing play (p. 440) ☐ Latchkey children (p. 440)	⊠ PPT slides 20-22 *e* EILR IC image 2 *e* EILR OBQ questions 6, 7 *e* EILR TB questions 10, 13 *e* ESLR IRQ question 5 SG Learning Activities, questions 1, 9 (p. 157) SG Case Study, question 2 (p. 160) SG Applying Knowledge, question 2 (p. 161) **BOOK RESOURCES** Nursing Tip (p. 440) Figure 19-2, Developing the skills of a team sport is important to the school-age child (p. 440) Safety Alert (p. 440) Health Promotion, Guidance for Latchkey Families (p. 440) ▸ Discuss specific safety guidelines for latchkey children. ▸ Discuss safety precautions with which every child and parent should be familiar (e.g., not talking to strangers, Internet safety, gun safety, use of seatbelts, bike and traffic safety, etc.) *Class Activity **Divide the class into three groups. Have one group identify reasons why children may be "latchkey children" and common accidents that involve children at home. Have the second group list guidelines that could be used to teach a child about safety. Have the third***

OBJECTIVES	CONTENT	TEACHING RESOURCES
		group list guidance points to teach parents how to ensure the safety of their child. Then have groups present their findings to the class.
Describe the physical and psychosocial development of children from 6 to 12 years of age, listing age-specific events and type of guidance where appropriate.		**BOOK RESOURCES** Review Questions for the NCLEX® Examination, questions 1-5 (pp. 449-450)

19.1 Homework/Assignments:

19.1 Instructor's Notes/Student Feedback:

LESSON 19.2

CRITICAL THINKING QUESTION

The parents of a 7-year-old immunocompromised boy state they want to get a dog for their son. The parents tell the nurse that they have read some studies about the positive influence and benefits of pet ownership, but they want to know what risks may be involved. What information can the nurse provide the parents about some of the diseases transmitted by dogs to humans and how the parents might protect their child from these risks?

Guidelines: The nurse can inform the parents that dogs can transmit diseases such as cellulitis, septicemia, *Campylobacter pylori,* rabies, parasites, pneumonia, hypereosinophilia, toxocariasis, and leptospirosis. Protection measures include selecting healthy animals, neutering the animal, feeding the animal commercial dog food or cooked meat, keeping the animal indoors, treating the animal for fleas, and keeping immunizations current with regular veterinarian visits. Encourage handwashing after handling the pet, do not allow the child to sleep with the pet or kiss the animal. Most importantly, children should avoid all contact with saliva, and animal feces and urine.

OBJECTIVES	CONTENT	TEACHING RESOURCES
Describe the physical and psychosocial development of children from 6 to 12 years of age, listing age-specific events and type of guidance where appropriate.	■ Physical, mental, emotional, and social development (p. 441) □ The six-year-old (p. 441) □ The seven-year-old (p. 441) □ The eight-year-old (p. 442) □ The nine-year-old (p. 442) □ Preadolescence (p. 443) 　– The ten-year-old (p. 443) 　– Eleven- and twelve-year-olds (p. 443) □ Chores as a teaching tool (p. 444)	PPT slides 23-37 *e* EILR OBQ questions 5-10 *e* EILR TB questions 1-6, 8-9, 12, 14-17, 20, 23, 26 *e* ESLR IRQ question 1 SG Learning Activities, questions 1, 10-16 (pp. 157-159) SG Review Questions, questions 3, 5-13 (pp. 159-160) SG Case Study, question 2 (p. 161) **BOOK RESOURCES** Figure 19-3, Loss of Primary Teeth (p. 441) Figure 19-4, Competitive Sports (p. 442) Figure 19-5, Healthy Outlet for Feelings (p. 442) Figure 19-6, Protective Clothing (p. 443) Figure 19-7, Household Chores (p. 443) Table 19-3, Summary of Growth and Development and Health Maintenance of School-Age Children (pp. 445-446) Review Questions for the NCLEX® Examination, questions 3, 5 (pp. 449-450) ▶ Discuss the major growth and development characteristics of 6-, 7-, 8-, and 9-year-olds. ▶ Discuss the major growth and development characteristics of 10-, 11-, and 12-year-olds. *Class Activity **Divide the class into three groups and***

Leifer

OBJECTIVES	CONTENT	TEACHING RESOURCES
		assign each group one of the following age categories: 6 years, 7 years, and 8 years. Ask each group to make a presentation about the physical, psychological, emotional, and social development of children in their assigned age category. Have each group present its information to the class.
		Class Activity Lead a class discussion about the value of play and the different forms of play for children who are 6, 7, and 8 years old.
		Class Activity Divide the class into small groups and have each group create a poster display of the physical and psychosocial development of the 10-year-old child and the 11- to 12-year-old child. Have each group present its poster to the class for discussion.
Discuss the role of the school nurse in providing guidance and health supervision for the school-age child.	■ Guidance and health supervision (p. 444) ☐ Health examinations (p. 444)	⊠▤ PPT slides 38-40 𝒆 EILR OBQ questions 5, 7-9 𝒆 EILR TB questions 19, 22 𝒆 ESLR IRQ question 4 🕮 SG Learning Activities, question 16 (p. 159) 🕮 SG Review Questions, questions 3, 8, 9 (pp. 159-160) 🕮 SG Case Study, question 2 (p. 161) 🕮 SG Applying Knowledge, question 1 (p. 161) **BOOK RESOURCES** Table 19-3, Summary of Growth and Development and Health Maintenance of School-Age children (pp. 445-446) Nursing Tip (p. 447) Review Questions for the NCLEX® Examination, question 4 (p. 449) *Class Activity Divide the class into small groups and have each group create a parent education brochure that provides a recommended schedule of health exams for school-age children. Groups should then present their brochures to the class for feedback on completeness and accuracy.* *Class Activity One week prior to class, have students collect data from their local elementary school about the meals they will be providing to students. In small groups, have students compare the meal plans and discuss whether they meet the suggested nutritional guidelines for children who attend the school. Then have each*

OBJECTIVES	CONTENT	TEACHING RESOURCES
		group present its findings to the class. (For students to prepare for this activity, see Homework/Assignment #1.)
Discuss the value of pet ownership for the healthy school-age child and the family education necessary for the allergic or immuno-compromised child.	☐ Pet ownership (p. 447)	▣ PPT slides 41-43
		e EILR OBQ questions 9, 10
		e EILR TB questions 11, 24, 25
		e ESLR IRQ question 3
		SG Learning Activities, question 17 (p. 159)
		SG Applying Knowledge, question 3 (p. 161)
		BOOK RESOURCES
		Health Promotion, Ways to Protect Immunocompromised Children from Pet-Transmitted Disease (p. 447)
		Table 19-4, Diseases that Can Be Transmitted by Pets to Humans (p. 448)
		▸ Discuss the value of pet ownership and what it can teach a child and add to his or her life.
		▸ Discuss the pros and cons of having a pet when the child has an allergy. What can be done?
		*Class Activity **Lead a class discussion about the ways to protect an immunocompromised child from pet-transmitted diseases. Ask students to identify the risks of pet ownership to an immunocompromised child and how these risks can be reduced.***
Performance Evaluation		▣ PPT slides 1-45
		e EILR IC images 1-7
		e EILR OBQ questions 1-10
		e EILR TB questions 1-28
		e ESLR IRQ questions 1-5
		SG Learning Activities, questions 1-17 (pp. 157-159)
		SG Review Questions, questions 1-13 (pp. 159-160)
		SG Case Study, questions 1-2 (p. 160)
		SG Thinking Critically, question 1 (p. 161)
		SG Applying Knowledge, questions 1-3 (p. 161)
		BOOK RESOURCES

ELSEVIER

Leifer

OBJECTIVES	CONTENT	TEACHING RESOURCES
		Review Questions for the NCLEX® Examination, questions 1-5 (pp. 449-450)
		GRN CTQ 1 (p. 450)

19.2 Homework/Assignments:

1. One week prior to class, have students collect data from their local elementary school about the meals they will be providing to children. In small groups, have students compare the meal plans and discuss whether they meet the suggested nutritional guidelines for children who attend the school.

19.2 Instructor's Notes/Student Feedback:

19 Lecture Outline
The School-Age Child

Slide 1

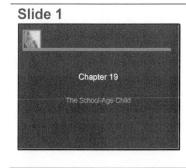

Chapter 19

The School-Age Child

Slide 2

Objectives

- Describe the physical and psychosocial development of children from 6 to 12 years of age, listing age-specific events and type of guidance where appropriate.
- Discuss how to assist parents in preparing a child for school.
- List two ways in which school life influences the growing child.
- Discuss accident prevention in this age group.

Slide 3

Objectives *(cont.)*

- Contrast two major theoretical viewpoints of personality development during the school years.
- Discuss the role of the school nurse in providing guidance and health supervision for the school-age child.
- Discuss the value of pet ownership for the healthy school-age child and the family education necessary for the allergic or immunocompromised child.

Slide 4

General Characteristics

- Ages 6-12 years
- More engrossed in fact than fantasy
- Develop first close peer relationships outside the family group
- Often judged by their performance
- Sense of industry and development of positive self-esteem directly influenced by peer group

- Give an example of how the school-age child relates to facts instead of fantasy.
- Discuss situations in which school-age children might be judged by their peers based on their performance.
- In what way would a school-age child exhibit Erikson's stage of industry?

Leifer

Slide 5

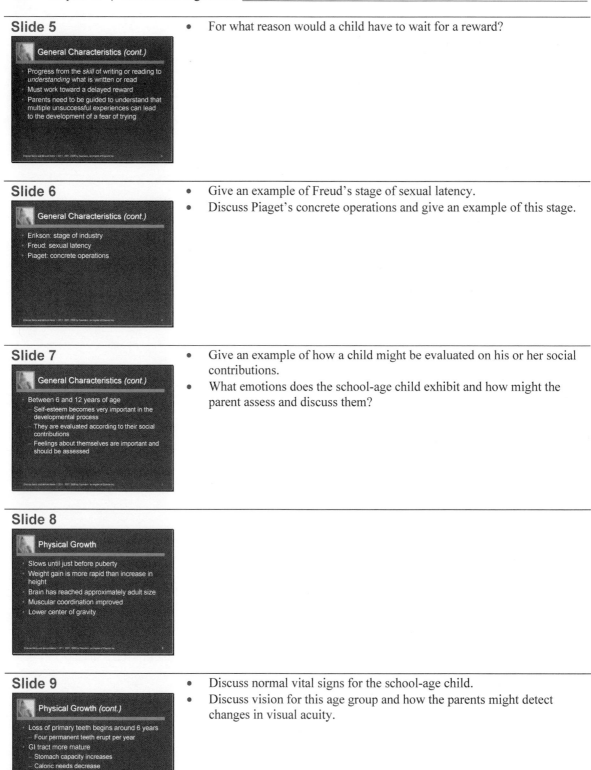

General Characteristics *(cont.)*

- Progress from the *skill* of writing or reading to *understanding* what is written or read
- Must work toward a delayed reward
- Parents need to be guided to understand that multiple unsuccessful experiences can lead to the development of a fear of trying

- For what reason would a child have to wait for a reward?

Slide 6

General Characteristics *(cont.)*

- Erikson: stage of industry
- Freud: sexual latency
- Piaget: concrete operations

- Give an example of Freud's stage of sexual latency.
- Discuss Piaget's concrete operations and give an example of this stage.

Slide 7

General Characteristics *(cont.)*

- Between 6 and 12 years of age
  - Self-esteem becomes very important in the developmental process
  - They are evaluated according to their social contributions
  - Feelings about themselves are important and should be assessed

- Give an example of how a child might be evaluated on his or her social contributions.
- What emotions does the school-age child exhibit and how might the parent assess and discuss them?

Slide 8

Physical Growth

- Slows until just before puberty
- Weight gain is more rapid than increase in height
- Brain has reached approximately adult size
- Muscular coordination improved
- Lower center of gravity

Slide 9

Physical Growth *(cont.)*

- Loss of primary teeth begins around 6 years
  - Four permanent teeth erupt per year
- GI tract more mature
  - Stomach capacity increases
  - Caloric needs decrease
- Heart grows slowly
  - Smaller in proportion to body size

- Discuss normal vital signs for the school-age child.
- Discuss vision for this age group and how the parents might detect changes in visual acuity.

Introduction to Maternity & Pediatric Nursing, 6th ed.

Elsevier items and derived items © 2011, 2007, 2006 by Saunders, an imprint of Elsevier Inc.

Leifer

Slide 10

Physical Growth *(cont.)*

- Important to note
  - Size is not correlated with emotional maturity
  - Problems can occur when a child faces higher expectations because he or she is taller and heavier than peers

- Discuss the paradigm between physical size and maturity.

Slide 11

Gender Identity

- Sex role development influenced by parents
- Differential treatment and identification
  - In the family
  - In society
- Influence of school environment
  - Aggressive behavior more accepted in boys than girls
- Incorporation of traditionally masculine and feminine positive attributes may lead to fuller human functioning

- How is the school-age child's role different within the family versus the school?
- Give an example of a boy displaying timid behavior and a girl displaying aggressive behavior in the school environment and how the educator might react.

Slide 12

Sex Education

- Lifelong process
- Accomplished less by talking or formal instruction than by the whole climate of the home
- Questions should be answered simply
- Correct names for genitalia should also be used
- Private masturbation is normal

- What education is needed for this age group regarding sex?
- Give an example of how a school-age child might learn more about sex in the social environment versus what is taught at school.
- Compare and contrast a simple versus a complex sexual question for this age group.

Slide 13

Sex Education *(cont.)*

- Boys should be prepared for erections and nocturnal emissions
- Girls should be prepared for menarche and taught how to use the supplies
- Can be taught in the context of the normal process and function of the human body
- Facts must be provided

- Give examples of terminology that might mislead the school-age child.

Slide 14

Sexually Transmitted Infections (STIs)

- Education on how to prevent STIs and HIV/AIDS should be presented in simple terms
- Factual and concrete information is an essential component
- Facts concerning harmful effects of drugs and unprotected sex should be communicated to the child without scare tactics

- How would you explain prevention of STIs?
- Give an example of concrete information regarding STIs and HIV.
- How are scare tactics used versus factual comments regarding drugs and STIs?

ELSEVIER

Introduction to Maternity & Pediatric Nursing, 6th ed.
Leifer

Slide 15

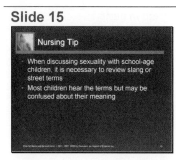

Nursing Tip

- When discussing sexuality with school-age children, it is necessary to review slang or street terms
- Most children hear the terms but may be confused about their meaning

- What slang terms are used to discuss sex?
- Give an example of how a child might misinterpret a slang term when discussing sexuality.

Slide 16

Influences from the Wider World

Slide 17

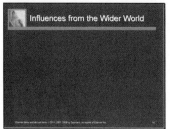

School-Related Tasks

- Children bring what they have learned and experienced at home to school
- May be unable to verbalize needs
- Success requires an integration of cognitive, receptive, and expressive skills

- Give an example of what a child has learned at home and brought to school.
- Discuss how the use of slang words at home could cause difficulty for the child to communicate his or her understanding or needs.
- What are examples of cognitive, receptive, and expressive skills?

Slide 18

School-Related Tasks *(cont.)*

- Holistic attitude must also focus on qualities such as
  - Artistic expression
  - Creativity
  - Joy
  - Cooperation
  - Responsibility
  - Industry
  - Love
- Anticipatory guidance includes
  - Review of normal physiology
  - How it changes with puberty
  - Child is encouraged to ask questions at the time they arise

- Discuss how parents can help their child in developing a holistic attitude.
- In what ways can parents guide a school-age child who is near puberty?

Slide 19

School-Related Tasks *(cont.)*

- Parents and children should set realistic goals
- Develop heightened awareness for things such as attendance problems, tardiness, and signs of loneliness or depression
  - Should continue to encourage children to discuss school problems, feelings, and worries
- Homework is the responsibility of the child

- Give an example of an unrealistic versus a realistic goal for the school-age child.
- What signs of depression might a school-age child exhibit?
- How could a parent promote accountability for the child's completion of homework?

Leifer

Slide 20

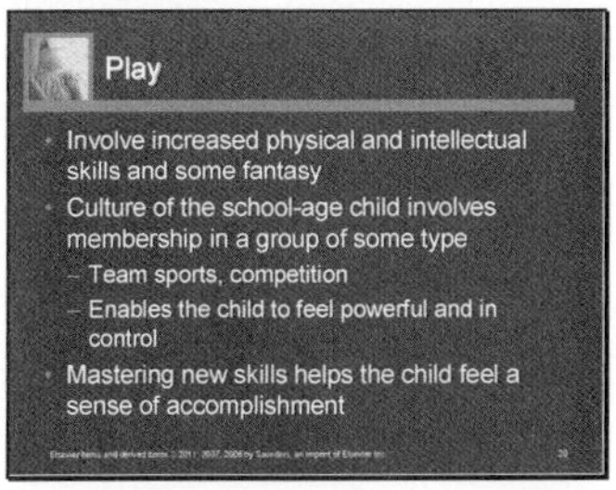

Play

- Involve increased physical and intellectual skills and some fantasy
- Culture of the school-age child involves membership in a group of some type
  - Team sports, competition
  - Enables the child to feel powerful and in control
- Mastering new skills helps the child feel a sense of accomplishment

- In what situation can a school-age child feel powerful within his or her environment?
- Give a similar example of a situation in which a school-age child would feel out of control in his or her environment.

Slide 21

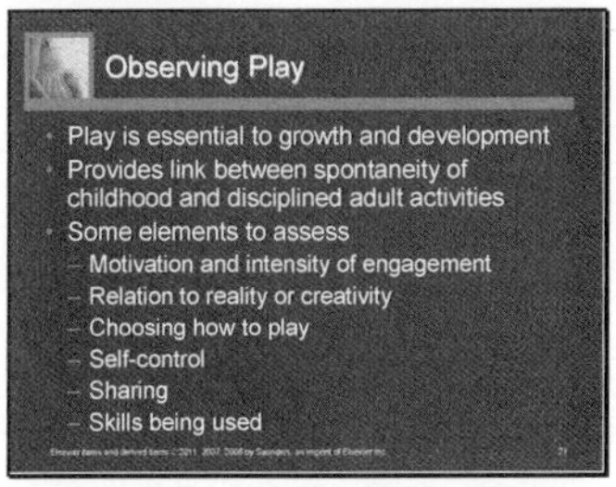

Observing Play

- Play is essential to growth and development
- Provides link between spontaneity of childhood and disciplined adult activities
- Some elements to assess
  - Motivation and intensity of engagement
  - Relation to reality or creativity
  - Choosing how to play
  - Self-control
  - Sharing
  - Skills being used

Slide 22

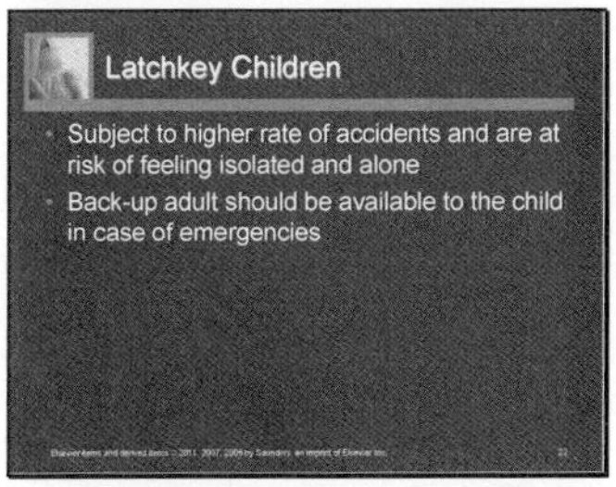

Latchkey Children

- Subject to higher rate of accidents and are at risk of feeling isolated and alone
- Back-up adult should be available to the child in case of emergencies

- Discuss potential accidents this population might encounter.
- Discuss how these children might feel isolated.
- Who is an example of a back-up adult?

Slide 23

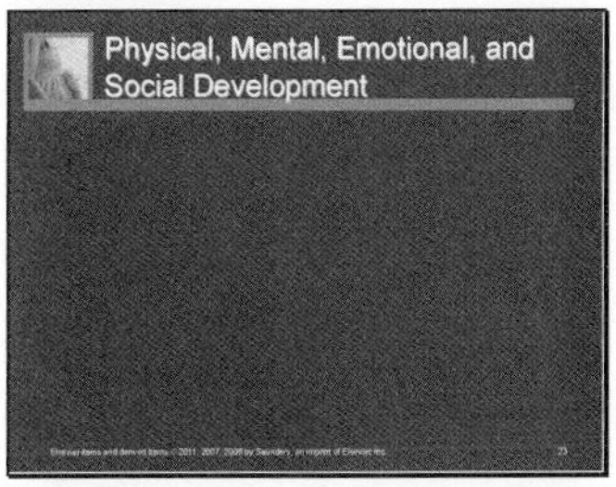

Physical, Mental, Emotional, and Social Development

Slide 24

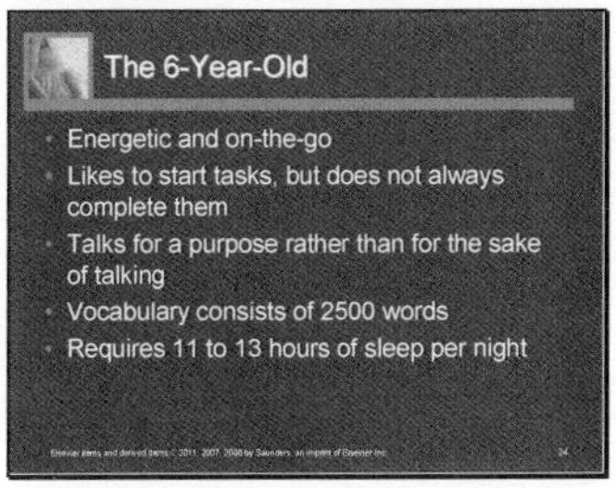

The 6-Year-Old

- Energetic and on-the-go
- Likes to start tasks, but does not always complete them
- Talks for a purpose rather than for the sake of talking
- Vocabulary consists of 2500 words
- Requires 11 to 13 hours of sleep per night

- What is a task a 6-year-old might begin but not complete?

Slide 25

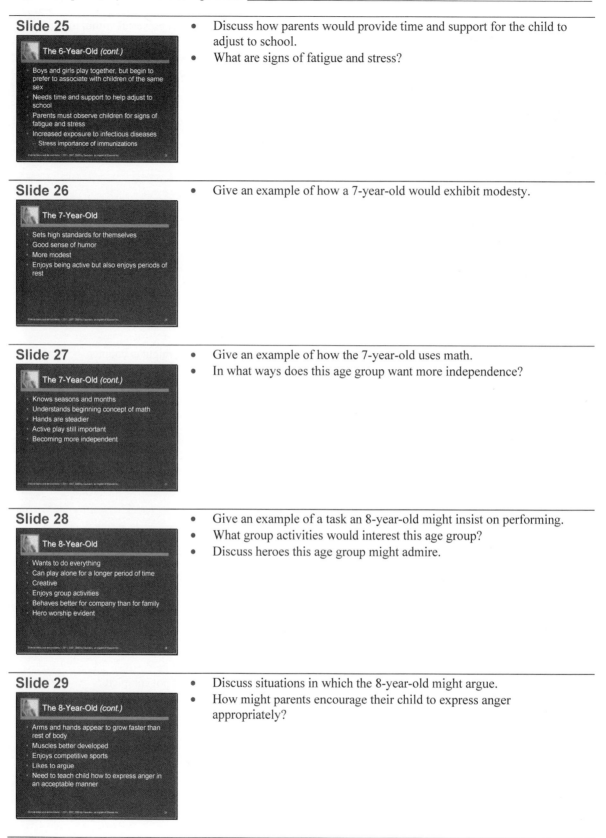

The 6-Year-Old *(cont.)*

- Boys and girls play together, but begin to prefer to associate with children of the same sex
- Needs time and support to help adjust to school
- Parents must observe children for signs of fatigue and stress
- Increased exposure to infectious diseases
  – Stress importance of immunizations

- Discuss how parents would provide time and support for the child to adjust to school.
- What are signs of fatigue and stress?

Slide 26

The 7-Year-Old

- Sets high standards for themselves
- Good sense of humor
- More modest
- Enjoys being active but also enjoys periods of rest

- Give an example of how a 7-year-old would exhibit modesty.

Slide 27

The 7-Year-Old *(cont.)*

- Knows seasons and months
- Understands beginning concept of math
- Hands are steadier
- Active play still important
- Becoming more independent

- Give an example of how the 7-year-old uses math.
- In what ways does this age group want more independence?

Slide 28

The 8-Year-Old

- Wants to do everything
- Can play alone for a longer period of time
- Creative
- Enjoys group activities
- Behaves better for company than for family
- Hero worship evident

- Give an example of a task an 8-year-old might insist on performing.
- What group activities would interest this age group?
- Discuss heroes this age group might admire.

Slide 29

The 8-Year-Old *(cont.)*

- Arms and hands appear to grow faster than rest of body
- Muscles better developed
- Enjoys competitive sports
- Likes to argue
- Need to teach child how to express anger in an acceptable manner

- Discuss situations in which the 8-year-old might argue.
- How might parents encourage their child to express anger appropriately?

Introduction to Maternity & Pediatric Nursing, 6th ed.

Leifer

Slide 30

> **The 9-Year-Old**
> - Dependable
> - Shows more interest in family activities
> - Assumes more responsibility
> - More likely to complete tasks
> - More able to accept criticism for their actions
> - Worries and mild compulsions are common

- Discuss appropriate responsibilities for a 9-year-old.
- What compulsions would this age group exhibit?

Slide 31

> **The 9-Year-Old** *(cont.)*
> - Hand and eye coordination well-developed
> - Manual activities are managed with skill
> - About 10 hours of sleep are needed each night
> - Permanent teeth still erupting
> - More active in competitive sports
> - Important to teach proper technique and the use of adequate safety devices

- Give examples of safety devices this age group should use.

Slide 32

> **Preadolescence**

Slide 33

> **The 10-Year-Old**
> - Marks beginning of preadolescence
> - Girls more physically mature than boys
> - Begins to show self-direction
> - Wants to be independent
> - Group ideas more important than individual ones
> - Sexual curiosity continues

- Give an example of a boy and a girl exhibiting self-direction.
- Discuss situations in which the 10-year-old might request more independence.
- How does this age group exhibit sexual curiosity?

Slide 34

> **The 10-Year-Old** *(cont.)*
> - Girls more poised than boys
> - Slang terms used
> - Begins to identify himself or herself with skills that pertain to the sex role
> - Takes more interest in personal appearance
> - Knows abstract numbers

- Give examples of slang terms.
- What skills pertain to their sexual identity?

Slide 35

11- and 12-Year-Olds

- Intense, observant, energetic
- May be argumentative and meddlesome
- Hormone influence on physical growth more apparent
- Need freedom within limits and recognition they are no longer infants

- Give examples of hormonal influence on physical growth, for each sex, that a parent might detect.

Slide 36

11- and 12-Year-Olds *(cont.)*

- Less concerned with appearance
- Seem preoccupied
- Ability to concentrate decreases
- Group participation still important
- Interested in their bodies and watch for signs of growing up

- Discuss how this age group might appear when they are not concerned about their appearance.
- How are their bodies changing?

Slide 37

11- and 12-Year-Olds *(cont.)*

- Need freedom within limits and recognition that they are no longer infants
- Should know why parents make a decision
- Conscience enables them to understand and accept reasonable discipline
- Will ignore constant verbal nagging
- Chores are good teaching tool for this age

- Give an example of how a parent might provide freedom within a limit that is age-appropriate.
- Discuss a situation in which this child experiences verbal nagging and how he or she reacts to it.

Slide 38

Guidance and Health Supervision

Slide 39

Health Examinations

- Usually given in spring preceding school admission
- If inattentive at school, should be screened for vision or hearing deficits and language or learning disabilities
- Assessment of physical activity and school performance is important

- Give examples of food preferences for this age group.
- If a child has a deficit, how might he or she act in the classroom?

Leifer

Slide 40

Health Examinations *(cont.)*

- If ill, the school-age child can understand simple explanations of the illness
- Need time and a place to study
- Must learn to take responsibility for their assignments and school supplies
- An allowance or at least a means of earning money provides children with opportunities to learn its value

- Give examples of acquiring and using an allowance.

Slide 41

Pet Ownership

- Pets that have close contact with children have the potential of transmitting disease
- Handicapped children especially benefit from interacting with pets
- Allows the ill child who feels separated from other people to feel companionship and positive attitude

- Discuss diseases that can be transmitted from a pet to the child.
- How might a handicapped child benefit from having a pet?

Slide 42

Pet Ownership *(cont.)*

- Age of child, allergies, immune issues are major deciding factors
- Infections can occur via contact with the pet's saliva, feces, or urine, or by inhalation or skin contact with organisms
- Risk factors can be further reduced if children are cautioned not to kiss pets, do not allow animals to sleep in bed with them, and are encouraged to perform hand hygiene

- Discuss a good age for a child to participate in pet care.
- How can a child protect himself or herself from disease transmission from a pet?

Slide 43

Pet Ownership *(cont.)*

- Having an allergy to animal dander does not always rule out having a pet
- Cats are most often the allergen offender because the allergens are secreted in the saliva and by sebaceous glands
- If an allergenic pet is in the home, more frequent bathing of the animal can reduce some of the allergens

- Discuss how pet dander affects a person who is allergic.

Slide 44

Question for Review

- Why is teaching fitness and exercises in school important to growth and development?

Slide 45

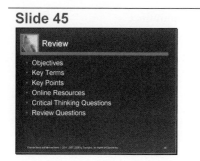

Lesson Plan
20 | The Adolescent

TEACHING FOCUS

This chapter focuses on the physical and psychological development of the adolescent. Particular attention is given to the physical stages of development and the psychological and social problems that arise during this time. The role of peer groups, cliques, and friends is presented, and ways of dealing with peer pressure are discussed. The guiding role of parents and nurses is also stressed, as well as nutrition, safety, substance abuse, and depression among adolescents.

MATERIALS AND RESOURCES

☐ Computer and PowerPoint projector (all lessons)

LESSON CHECKLIST

Preparations for this lesson include:

- Lecture
- Demonstration
- Guest speaker: Child psychologist or social worker
- Evaluation of student knowledge and skills needed to perform all entry-level activities related to the physical and psychological development of adolescents, including:
  - ○ Physical development, puberty, and sex education for adolescent girls and boys
  - ○ Three major theories of personality development
  - ○ Common psychosocial problems encountered during adolescence
  - ○ The search for identity
  - ○ Safety and health practices

KEY TERMS

abstract thinking (p. 452)
adolescence (p. 451)
asynchrony (p. 452)
cliques (p. 458)
epiphyseal closure (p. 456)
formal operations (p. 460)

gay (p. 462)
gender roles (p. 452)
growth spurt (p. 452)
homosexual (p. 462)
intimacy (p. 452)
lesbian (p. 462)

menarche (p. 455)
puberty (p. 452)
self-concept (p. 456)
sexual maturity ratings
  (SMR) (p. 456)

ADDITIONAL RESOURCES

TEACH PPT slide(s) Chapter 20, 1-47
EILR IC image(s) Chapter 20, 1-14
EILR OBQ question(s) Chapter 20, 1-10
EILR TB question(s) Chapter 20, 1-28
ESLR IRQ question(s) Chapter 20, 1-5
SG Chapter 20, pp. 163-167

Legend

PPT
TEACH
PowerPoint
Slides

EILR
EVOLVE Instructor
Learning Resources:
Image Collection (IC),
Open-Book Quizzes
(OBQ), Test Bank (TB)

ESLR
EVOLVE Student
Learning Resources:
Interactive Review
Questions (IRQ) for
the NCLEX®
Examination

SG
Study Guide

CTQ
Critical Thinking
Question in
Nursing Care Plan
(NCP CTQ) or Get
Ready for the
NCLEX! (GRN
CTQ)

Class Activities are indicated in ***bold italic***.

Leifer

LESSON 20.1

PRETEST

1. Developing intimacy in adolescence is tied to resolving one's
   a. social development.
   b. identity.
   c. sexual orientation.
   d. body image.

2. One characteristic of cognitive development during adolescence is the emergence of
   a. egocentrism.
   b. peer relationships.
   c. a sense of identity.
   d. abstract thinking.

3. Emancipation is critical to the establishment of
   a. identity.
   b. intimacy.
   c. menarche.
   d. adolescence.

4. Which of the following statements, if made by an adolescent, might be cause for concern?
   a. "I don't know what major to choose in college."
   b. "My best friend is moving 3000 miles away."
   c. "I babysit every weekend."
   d. "I have a crush on a girl at church."

5. Which of the following statements indicates that more sex education is needed?
   a. "HIV can lead to AIDS."
   b. "It's okay to say 'no' to sex."
   c. "I found a chat room that explains sex."
   d. "My parents read a book with me about sexual changes."

6. One of the five I's of psychosocial development during adolescence is
   a. Interaction.
   b. Involvement.
   c. Immersion.
   d. Independence.

7. Which of the following nutrients is an adolescent most likely to receive inadequate amounts of?
   a. calcium
   b. protein
   c. sodium
   d. folic acid

8. Which of the following foods inhibits iron absorption in adolescents?
   a. nuts
   b. bran
   c. eggs
   d. tofu

9. For hygienic reasons, adolescents should not share
   a. jewelry.
   b. clothing.
   c. razors.
   d. lotion.

10. A PACE interview can assist in determining if an adolescent is
    a. anorectic or bulimic.
    b. sexually active.
    c. using drugs or alcohol.
    d. depressed or suicidal.

Answers

1. b	3. a	5. c	7. a	9. c
2. d	4. b	6. d	8. b	10. c

BACKGROUND ASSESSMENT

Question: What are the pubertal changes in boys and girls?

Answer: In boys, puberty begins between 10 and 13 years of age. It is marked by an enlargement of testicles and internal reproductive structures, pigmentation of the scrotum, and enlargement of the penis. Boys also begin to experience erections and nocturnal emissions at this time, and between the ages of 13 and 14 sperm production take place. Other physical changes include a widening of the shoulders; enlarged pectoral muscles; a deepening voice; and hair growth on the face, chest, axillae, and pubic areas. In girls, pubertal changes occur 6 months to 2 years before boys; the most recognizable change is the onset of menstruation, which commonly occurs between 12 and 13 years of age. Other physical changes take place before menarche, such as fat deposits on the hips and thighs; breast enlargement; enlargement of the external genitalia; and hair growth in the pubic and axillary areas.

ELSEVIER

Question: What are the theories of Freud, Erikson, and Piaget regarding development during adolescence?
Answer: Freud's theory of development states that adolescence is in the genital stage, the final stage of psychosexual development. The genital stage involves the disappearance of self-love, the appearance of love for others, and a decrease in peer and parental influence. Erikson's theory of development states that during adolescence, individuals focus on self-definition and self-esteem and experience an identity crisis due to numerous physical and sexual changes. The adolescent adapts to these changes by developing a new self-concept and learning to understand the self in relation to others' perceptions and expectations. According to Piaget, adolescence occurs during the stage of formal operations, which involves the development of logical and abstract thinking. The adolescent also becomes more adept at problem-solving at this time.

CRITICAL THINKING QUESTION

A patient's mother complains to the nurse that her 14-year-old son has become increasingly lazy in the last couple of years. He lies around the house and sleeps all day on Saturdays, and also complains about being tired a lot. How could the nurse explain this behavior?

Guidelines: Adolescents commonly experience increased tiredness and fatigue. This is caused by the numerous physical and chemical changes that take place during this time. The nurse should suggest that the mother encourage her son to get plenty of sleep, while still maintaining his regular chores and responsibilities. It is also essential that he receive adequate nutrition during this time to promote proper growth and development. The nurse should suggest that the mother encourage her son to eat a balanced, healthy diet and to avoid fast-food and other unhealthy foods. It is also important that the mother keep all lines of communication with her son open to assure this difficult transition goes as smoothly as possible.

OBJECTIVES	CONTENT	TEACHING RESOURCES
Discuss three major theoretical viewpoints on the personality development of adolescents.	■ General characteristics (p. 451)	⊠▤ PPT slides 6-9
		𝒆 EILR IC images 1, 2
		𝒆 EILR OBQ questions 1, 2
		𝒆 EILR TB questions 6, 17
		SG Learning Activities, questions 1, 2-4, 10, 11 (p. 163)
		SG Review Questions, question 2 (p. 165)
		BOOK RESOURCES
		Box 20-1, Features of Major Theories of Development During Adolescence (p. 452)
		Figure 20-1, Adolescents Need Privacy (p. 452)
		Figure 20-2, Roadmap of Social Interaction (p. 453)
		Review Questions for the NCLEX® Examination, question 1 (p. 469)
		▸ Discuss the theories of Freud, Erikson, and Piaget.
		*Class Activity **In small groups, have students discuss the theories of Freud, Erikson, and Piaget, and create a Venn diagram that compares and contrasts the three theories. Have each group then present its diagram to the class for discussion.***
		*Class Activity **Divide the class into three groups and***

OBJECTIVES	CONTENT	TEACHING RESOURCES
		assign each group the theory of one of the following theorists: Freud, Erikson, or Piaget. Have each group outline the changes and developmental processes of adolescence according to its theory and identify specific examples of adolescence that either support or conflict with their theory. Then have groups present their outlines to the class for discussion.
Discuss two main challenges during the adolescent years to which the adolescent must adjust.	■ General characteristics (p. 451) ■ Growth and development (p. 452) ☐ Physical development (p. 452)	PPT slide 10-14 *e* EILR IC image 3 *e* EILR OBQ question 2 *e* EILR TB questions 1, 8, 14, 26 SG Learning Activities, questions 1, 4, 5 (p. 163) SG Review Questions, questions 1, 2-4 (p. 165) **BOOK RESOURCES** Figure 20-3, Developmental Changes Between Infancy and Adolescence (p. 453) Table 20-1, Growth and Development of the Adolescent (p. 454) Review Questions for the NCLEX® Examination, question 4 (p. 469) ▶ Discuss how physical development during this time contributes to the challenges of adolescence. ▶ Discuss the relationship between hormones and epiphyseal closure. *Class Activity As a class, have students identify the challenges faced by adolescents during the teen years and keep a running list on the board. When the list is complete, have the class identify the three most difficult or important challenges, as well as the appropriate nursing interventions to assist parents and teens with each.* *Class Activity In groups, have students identify the cognitive, social, and emotional developmental challenges of adolescence, then discuss how each of those challenges relates to or is affected by the physical developments. Have each group share its conclusions with the class and identify the nursing interventions to assist parents and teens coping with the challenges.*
List major physical changes that occur during adolescence.	■ Growth and Development (p. 452) ☐ Physical development (p. 452)	PPT slides 10-14 *e* EILR IC image 3

Leifer

OBJECTIVES	CONTENT	TEACHING RESOURCES
		SG Learning Activities, question 6 (p. 163)
		BOOK RESOURCES
		Figure 20-3, Developmental Changes Between Infancy and Adolescence (p. 453)
		Table 20-1, Growth and Development of the Adolescent (p. 454)
		Nursing Tip (p. 454)
		Review Questions for the NCLEX® Examination, question 3 (p. 469)
Identify two major developmental tasks of adolescence.	■ Growth and development (p. 452) ☐ Physical development (p. 452) – Boys (p. 454) – Girls (p. 455) ☐ Psychosocial development (p. 456)	PPT slides 15-18 EILR IC images 3, 4 EILR OBQ questions 1, 3 EILR TB questions 2, 7, 11 ESLR IRQ question 4 SG Learning Activities, questions 1, 6-9 (p. 163) SG Review Questions, questions 3, 4, 9, 10 (pp. 165-166) SG Thinking Critically, question 2 (p. 167) SG Applying Knowledge, question 1 (p. 167) **BOOK RESOURCES** Figure 20-3, Developmental Changes Between Infancy and Adolescence (p. 453) Table 20-1, Growth and Development of the Adolescent (p. 454) Figure 20-4, Sexual Maturity Ratings (p. 455) Box 20-2, Tanner's Stages of Sexual Maturity (p. 456) Nursing Tip (p. 456) ▶ Discuss problems that adolescents have in establishing their own identities. ▶ Discuss in detail two major developmental tasks faced during adolescence. *Class Activity **Divide the class into small groups and assign each group either boys' or girls' development. Have each group create a time line that outlines the physical and emotional development of its assigned***

Leifer

OBJECTIVES	CONTENT	TEACHING RESOURCES
		gender during adolescence, and present its findings to the class.
Describe menstruation to a 13-year-old girl.	– Girls (p. 455)	⊞ PPT slides 16, 17 *e* EILR IC image 5 *e* EILR OBQ question 4 *e* EILR TB questions 8-28 SG Learning Activities, questions 1, 10 (p. 163) **BOOK RESOURCES** Figure 20-5, Menstruation (p. 457) ▸ Discuss the stages of pubertal development in the female, including the reproductive organs. *Class Activity Choose two student volunteers to role-play a nurse explaining menstruation to a confused 13-year-old girl, and then have the class discuss the interaction. How might the explanation differ for a 10-year-old girl?*
Describe Tanner's stages of breast development.	– Girls (p. 455)	⊞ PPT slide 16 *e* EILR OBQ question 5 **BOOK RESOURCES** Box 20-2, Tanner's Stages of Sexual Maturity (p. 456) ▸ Discuss the stages of breast development. *Class Activity Present the following scenario to the class for students to discuss:* *During a routine physical exam, a 13-year-old girl tells the nurse that she is worried because her breasts have not yet begun to develop. All her other friends are already wearing bras.*
List five life events that contribute to stress during adolescence.	☐ Psychosocial development (p. 456) – Sense of identity (p. 456) – Sense of intimacy (p. 456)	⊞ PPT slide 18 *e* EILR IC image 6 *e* EILR TB question 21 *e* ESLR IRQ question 3 SG Learning Activities, questions 1, 11-14 (p. 164) SG Review Question, question 11 (p. 166) SG Case Study, question 1 (p. 167)

Introduction to Maternity & Pediatric Nursing, 6th ed.

OBJECTIVES	CONTENT	TEACHING RESOURCES
		SG Thinking Critically, question 1 (p. 167)
		SG Applying Knowledge, question 1 (p. 167)
		BOOK RESOURCES
		Nursing Tip (p. 456)
		Nursing Tip (p. 458)
		Figure 20-6, Adolescent Moving Toward Adulthood (p. 458)
		Review Questions for the NCLEX® Examination, question 4 (p. 469)
		▸ Discuss the quest for a sense of identity during adolescence and identify ways parents can assist in achieving it.
		▸ Discuss how much privacy an adolescent really needs. How do parents achieve a balance between the adolescent's privacy and safety?
		*Class Activity **Invite a child psychologist or a social worker to speak to the class about the stresses and challenges of adolescence. Have students prepare questions and discussion points.***
		*Class Activity **In groups, have students identify five events that cause stress during adolescence and discuss the nursing interventions to assist parents and teens coping with the challenges. Have each group share its findings with the class for discussion.***

20.1 Homework/Assignments:

20.1 Instructor's Notes/Student Feedback:

LESSON 20.2

CRITICAL THINKING QUESTION

A parent states that his 15-year-old daughter has suddenly entered a period of rebellion and is breaking all the household rules. Last night she came home an hour after curfew with no explanation, and she often becomes angry and sullen when disciplined. The parent asks the nurse why his daughter's behavior has suddenly changed and what he can do to stop it. What advice should the nurse give?

Guidelines: The nurse should explain to the father that during middle adolescence children experience several physical and emotional changes. For instance, the child is probably experiencing identity confusion as she attempts to establish her own identity. This conflict causes her self-concept to fluctuate, which can lead to impulsive, angry, and impatient behavior. At this time she is also struggling for autonomy from her family. She does this by rebelling, withdrawing, and demanding privacy. The nurse should assure the parent that things will get better as the adolescent's personality, identity, and independence emerge. Then her family relationships will be reestablished. In the meantime, the nurse should suggest that the father sit down with his daughter and, in a calm manner, assure the child of his love for her and explain that in disciplining her he wants only to look out for her and ensure her safety. He should also explain that he is aware of the many changes she is undergoing and that while he respects her desire and need for freedom, there are dangers and responsibilities that go along with independence. Until the child becomes more fully developed, a balance between the parent and child will need to be found to maintain communication, independence, and privacy. If needed, there are many family and community counselors that can provide additional help.

OBJECTIVES	CONTENT	TEACHING RESOURCES
Identify two ways in which a person's cultural background might contribute to behavior.	– Cultural and spiritual considerations (p. 457) – Body image (p. 458)	⊠▪ PPT slides 19, 20 𝒆 EILR IC image 7 𝒆 EILR OBQ questions 6, 7 𝒆 EILR TB question 23 SG Learning Activities, question 15 (p. 164) SG Review Questions, question 5 (p. 165) SG Thinking Critically, question 1 (p. 167) **BOOK RESOURCES** Figure 20-7, Adolescents can understand abstract concepts and symbols, and religious traditions can help to stabilize identity (p. 458) Nursing Tip (p. 458) ▸ Discuss the role that culture and religion play in the development of the adolescent. *Class Activity Divide the class into small groups and assign each group a different ethnic or cultural group. Have students research how their assigned cultural group views adolescence, then discuss appropriate nursing interventions to help parents and teens cope with the challenges of the period. Have each group present its*

OBJECTIVES	CONTENT	TEACHING RESOURCES
		findings to the class. (For students to prepare for this activity, see Homework/Assignments #1.)
Discuss the importance of peer groups, cliques, and best friends in the developmental process of an adolescent.	☐ Peer relationships (p. 458) ☐ Career plans (p. 459) ☐ Responsibility (p. 460) ☐ Cognitive development (p. 460) ☐ Daydreams (p. 460)	PPT slides 19-24 EILR IC images 8-10 EILR OBQ questions 7, 8 EILR TB questions 3, 5, 9, 13, 15, 16, 25, 26 SG Learning Activities, questions 14, 16-19 (p. 164) SG Review Questions, questions 6, 11 (p. 166) SG Thinking Critically, question 2 (p. 167) **BOOK RESOURCES** Figure 20-8, Immersion into a Peer Group (p. 459) Figure 20-9, Adolescent Practices Facial Expressions (p. 459) Figure 20-10, Parent Should Encourage Adolescent to Take Advantage of their Talents (p. 459) ▶ Discuss typical sexual behavior of the adolescent. What factors make these early experiences stressful? What can parents and nurses do to make this a less stressful time? ▶ Discuss how the nurse can address the adolescent's concerns about being "different." Class Activity *In groups, have students discuss the importance of peer groups and best friends during adolescence. Why is it more important for adolescents to have best friends and peer groups than adults or children of other ages? Have students share their findings with the class.* Class Activity *Present the following scenario to the class for students to discuss:* *The mother of a 15-year-old boy is worried because her son does not have any close friends and just sits at home on the computer. He has an older brother with whom he is close, but she is worried that when the brother graduates from high school, her younger son will no longer have any friends at school.* *What suggestions could a nurse make to this mother?*
List a source for planning sex education programs for	☐ Sexual behavior (p. 460) – Sex education	PPT slides 25-30 EILR IC image 11

ELSEVIER

Leifer

OBJECTIVES	CONTENT	TEACHING RESOURCES
adolescents.	(p. 461) – Concerns about being "different" (p. 461) – Homosexuality (p. 462) ☐ Parenting the adolescent (p. 462)	*e* EILR OBQ questions 8, 9 *e* EILR TB questions 20, 24 [SG] SG Learning Activities, questions 1, 15, 20, 21 (p. 163) [SG] SG Case Study, question 2 (p. 167) **BOOK RESOURCES** Table 20-2, Using the Nursing Process in Planning Sex Education for the Adolescent (p. 462) Nursing Tip (p. 463) Health Promotion: Effective approaches to problems (p. 463) Figure 20-11, Listening Is an Important Tool (p. 463) Nursing Tip (p. 464) Table 20-3, Developmental and Physiological Impact of Pregnancy on the Adolescent (p. 467) Table 20-4, Nursing Care and the Effect of Adolescence on the Tasks of an Unplanned Pregnancy (p. 467) ▸ Discuss various sources of sex education programs for adolescents. What factors need to be considered when planning a sex education program? *Class Activity As a class, have students discuss sexual behavior, consequences, and safety concerns of adolescents. What type of behavior is healthy, and what is unhealthy? What are some indications that more (or different) sex education is needed? How should homosexuality be addressed?* *Class Activity Divide the class into four groups and assign each group one of the phases of the nursing process: data collection, analysis, planning/implementation, and evaluation. Have each group discuss how its assigned phase is used to plan sex education for the adolescent, and then share and discuss with the class.*
Summarize the nutritional requirements of the adolescent.	■ Health promotion and guidance (p. 464) ☐ Nutrition (p. 464) – Vegetarian diets (p. 464) – Sports and nutrition (p. 464)	PPT slides 31-33 *e* EILR TB questions 10, 12, 22 [SG] SG Learning Activities, questions 16-18, 22-27 (pp. 164-165) [SG] SG Review Questions, questions 7, 12, 13 (p. 166)

ELSEVIER

OBJECTIVES	CONTENT	TEACHING RESOURCES
	– Nutrition and school examinations (p. 465)	SG Thinking Critically, question 1 (p. 167) **BOOK RESOURCES** Review Questions for the NCLEX® Examination, question 5 (p. 469) GRN CTQ 1 (p. 469) ▸ Discuss factors that negatively influence good nutrition habits in adolescents. ▸ Discuss whether a teenager can safely pursue a vegetarian diet. *Class Activity **Divide the class into small groups and assign each group one of the following topics: hygiene, dental health, or sunbathing. Have each group discuss why its assigned topic is important, how it contributes to the pressure felt during adolescence, and why teens neglect the area. Have each group present its findings to the class for discussion.*** *Class Activity **As a class, have students discuss the nutritional needs of adolescents and identify factors that hinder proper nutrition. Do the nutritional requirements differ for each stage of adolescence? Why do teens always seem to be hungry? What are some ways to promote healthful habits and encourage patient compliance?***

List three guidelines of importance for the adolescent participating in sports.	☐ Personal care (p. 465)
	
	  – Hygiene (p. 465)
	
	  – Dental health (p. 465)
	
	  – Sunbathing (p. 465)
	
	☐ Safety (p. 465)
	
	  – Sports injuries (p. 465)
		PPT slide 34-36
		
		EILR IC images 12-14
		
		EILR OBQ question 10
		
		EILR TB questions 4, 19, 27
		
		SG Review Questions, question 8 (p. 166)
		
		SG Applying Knowledge, questions 2- 4 (p. 167)
		
		BOOK RESOURCES
		
		Health Promotion, Effective Approaches to Problems (p. 463)
		
		Nursing Tip (p. 466)
		
		Figure 20-12, Adolescents Look Forward to Getting Their Driver's License (p. 466)
		
		Table 20-3, Developmental and Physiological Impact of Pregnancy on the Adolescent (p. 467)
		
		Table 20-4, Nursing Care and the Effect of Adolescence

OBJECTIVES	CONTENT	TEACHING RESOURCES
		on the Tasks of an Unplanned Pregnancy (p. 467)
		Figure 20-13, Graduation from High School (p. 468)
		Figure 20-14, Moving Away from Home (p. 468)
		Review Questions for the NCLEX® Examination, question 2 (p. 469)
		▶ Discuss what to eat and when to eat to achieve maximum athletic performance. Explain the biochemical principles on which this is based.
		Class Activity In groups, have students discuss the guidelines to follow regarding participation in sports and identify potential problems that can occur. What are the considerations for boys and girls, and how do the considerations differ for early, middle, and late adolescence? What factors contribute to the development of problems? Have each group share its findings with the class for discussion.
Discuss the common problems of adolescence and the nursing approach.	■ Common problems of adolescence (p. 466) ☐ Substance abuse (p. 466) ☐ Depression (p. 466) ☐ Adolescent pregnancy (p. 467) ■ The nursing approach to adolescents (p. 468)	▥ PPT slides 37-45 𝒆 EILR OBQ question 10 𝒆 EILR TB question 18 𝒆 ESLR IRQ question 5 ▤ SG Learning Activities, question 21 (p. 164) ▤ SG Applying Knowledge, questions 3-4 (p. 167) **BOOK RESOURCES** Memory Jogger (p. 466) ▶ Discuss the use of the PACE interview in evaluating the adolescent's risk for substance abuse. ▶ Discuss early signs of depression in the adolescent.
Performance Evaluation		▥ PPT slides 1-47 𝒆 EILR IC images 1-14 𝒆 EILR OBQ questions 1-10 𝒆 EILR TB questions 1-28 𝒆 ESLR IRQ questions 1-5 ▤ SG Learning Activities, questions 1-21 (pp. 163-165) ▤ SG Review Questions, questions 1-13 (pp. 165-166)

OBJECTIVES	CONTENT	TEACHING RESOURCES
		![SG] SG Case Study, questions 1, 2 (p. 167)
		![SG] SG Thinking Critically, questions 1, 2 (p. 167)
		![SG] SG Applying Knowledge, questions 1-4 (p. 167)
		BOOK RESOURCES
		Review Questions for the NCLEX® Examination, questions 1-5 (p. 469)
		GRN CTQ 1 (p. 469)

20.2 Homework/Assignments:

1. Divide the class into small groups and assign each group a different ethnic or cultural group. Have students research how their assigned cultural group views adolescence, then discuss appropriate nursing interventions to help parents and teens cope with the challenges of the period.

20.2 Instructor's Notes/Student Feedback:

20 Lecture Outline
The Adolescent

Slide 1

Chapter 20

The Adolescent

Slide 2

Objectives

- List major physical changes that occur during adolescence.
- Identify two major developmental tasks of adolescence.
- Discuss three major theoretical viewpoints on the personality development of adolescents.
- List five life events that contribute to stress during adolescence.

Slide 3

Objectives *(cont.)*

- Describe Tanner's stages of breast development.
- Describe menstruation to a 13-year-old girl.
- Identify two ways in which a person's cultural background might contribute to behavior.

Slide 4

Objectives *(cont.)*

- Discuss the importance of peer groups, cliques, and best friends in the developmental process of an adolescent.
- List three guidelines of importance for the adolescent participating in sports.
- Summarize the nutritional requirements of the adolescent.

Leifer

Slide 5

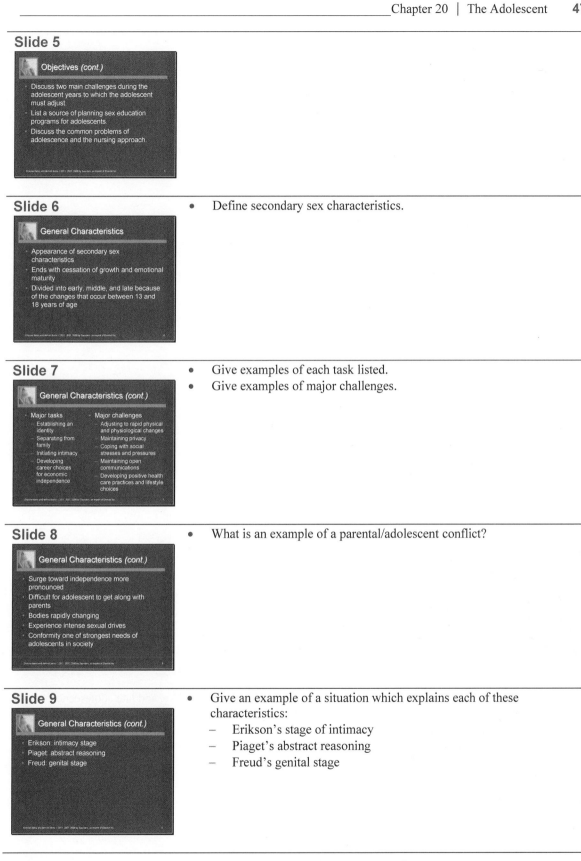

Slide 6

- Define secondary sex characteristics.

Slide 7

- Give examples of each task listed.
- Give examples of major challenges.

Slide 8

- What is an example of a parental/adolescent conflict?

Slide 9

- Give an example of a situation which explains each of these characteristics:
  - Erikson's stage of intimacy
  - Piaget's abstract reasoning
  - Freud's genital stage

Leifer

Slide 10

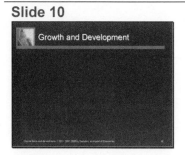

Slide 11

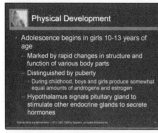

- Define puberty.

Slide 12

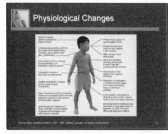

Slide 13

Slide 14

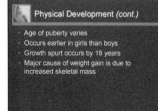

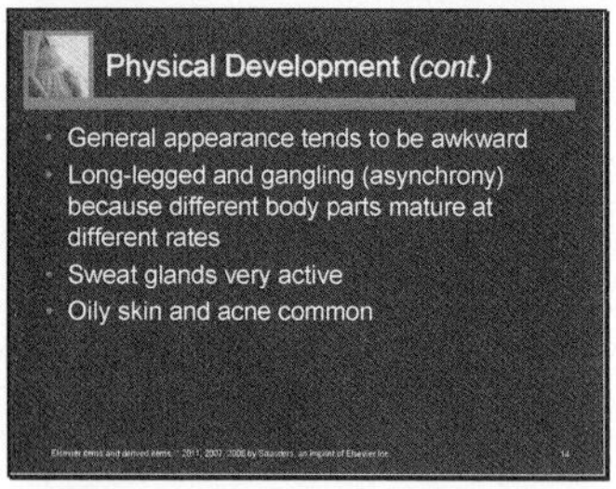

- Discuss the differences among early, middle, and late adolescence regarding growth, behavior, peers, family, and cognitive development.

Leifer

Slide 15

Boys

- Puberty begins with hormonal changes between 10 and 13 years of age
- Hair begins to grow on face, chest, axillae, and pubic areas
- Shoulders widen, pectoral muscles enlarge, voice deepens
- Genitals increase in size, pigment changes occur, erection and nocturnal emissions
- Important to teach testicular self-examination

- When should testicular self-examination begin?
- What is the nurse's role regarding this education?

Slide 16

Tanner's Stages of Sexual Maturity

- Compare and contrast the changes for both boys and girls.

Slide 17

Girls

- Pubertal changes occur 6 months to 2 years before they occur in boys
- Easily recognized in girls by onset of menstruation, called menarche
- Commonly occurs around 12 to 13 years
- Fat is deposited in hips, thighs, and breasts
- Energy balance, activity, and nutrition are important factors to evaluate when menstruation is delayed

- Discuss the importance of wearing a properly fitting bra.
- Discuss the importance of breast self-examination.

Slide 18

Psychosocial Development

- Sense of identity
  - Fluctuates during adolescence
  - Molded by demands from a variety of people
- Sense of intimacy
  - Closely entwined with resolving of a person's sense of identity
  - Period of trying and testing
  - Need practice in making decisions
- Cultural and spiritual considerations
  - Good of family takes precedence over personal goals
  - Focus on values and ideals of family
  - Decide to either embrace or separate from family values and ideals
- Realistic body image
  - Believe everyone is looking at them
  - Take pride in their abilities
  - Every effort is made to be like peers

- How does an adolescent's identity fluctuate at this stage in life?
- Give an example of a situation in which an adolescent learns by trial and error.
- In what cultural and spiritual situations might an adolescent distance himself or herself from the family?

Slide 19

Cognitive Development

- Piaget
  - Development is systematic, sequential, and orderly
  - Still in concrete phase of thinking
  - By middle adolescence, ability to think abstractly has increased
  - Stage of formal operations

- Give an example of how an adolescent develops cognitively from early, middle, and late development.

Leifer

Slide 20

Cognitive Development *(cont.)*

- Older adolescents can see situations from many viewpoints
- Abstract thinking emerges
- Nurse must focus on concrete issues and concerns when teaching early adolescents
- Able to sympathize and empathize
- Can understand their own values and actions
- Can understand and accept differing values and actions from others

- What is abstract thinking?
- How would an adolescent exhibit acceptance of differing values and actions?

Slide 21

Peer Relationships

- Help adolescents feel like they belong
- School assumes important role
- Belonging to a group is extremely important
- Cliques form
- Develops close personal relationship with one peer of the same sex
  - Vitally important in helping adolescents define themselves
  - Social norms and pressures exerted by peers may cause problems

- Discuss how peer relationships change from childhood to adolescence.
- Give an example of a situation in which an adolescent might learn from a personal, intimate relationship.

Slide 22

Career Plans

- To choose a career that is best-suited for them, they must first know themselves
- Parents should observe interests of their children and encourage them to take advantage of their talents
- School guidance counselor administers aptitude tests
- To be happy in career choice, adolescent must choose it of their own free will

- Which traits could assist an individual toward a career?
- Give an example of a parent/adolescent situation in which the parent encourages a talent.

Slide 23

Responsibility

- Parents must encourage their children to take on new challenges
  - Working
  - Driving
- Must be taught value of money
  - Teach adolescent how to use and balance a checkbook

- Discuss the parent's role in assisting the adolescent to become responsible.

Slide 24

Daydreams

- Most of this behavior is normal and natural for this age group
- Usually considered harmless
- Also a valuable safety valve for the expression of strong feelings

- Discuss how daydreaming helps the adolescent anticipate and cope with real situations.

Audience Response Question #1
Daydreams assist the adolescent to:
1. improve school performance.
2. try on different roles.
3. communicate effectively.
4. All of the above
5. None of the above

Slide 25

Sexual Behavior

- Must meet and become acquainted with members of opposite sex
- Dating
  - Groups
  - Couples
  - Single-couple

- Give an example of group dates.
- How does dating provide psychosocial development?

Slide 26

Sexual Behavior *(cont.)*

- Sexual experimentation often occurs as a response to peer pressure
- Can affect growth and development
- Unplanned pregnancy and STIs are two major complications of adolescent sexual interaction, because few use protection

- Discuss how sexual behavior can affect growth and development.

Slide 27

Sex Education

- Challenging for the adolescent
- Should be presented as age-appropriate
- Coping skills for dating and sexuality, pregnancy, and birth can be reviewed
- Abstinence and contraception are also discussed
- Decision-making is emphasized

- How can the nurse's biases hinder sex education?
- Give an example of coping skills appropriate for this age group.

Slide 28

Sex Education *(cont.)*

- Studies have shown that adolescents who obtain early sex education information from caring parents or well-informed adults do not have a higher rate of sexual activity
- Concerns about being different
  - Sexual maturity not same as peers
- Homosexuality
  - Behavior not uncommon in adolescence

Slide 29

Parenting

- Can be difficult for parents to cope with adolescents
- Some parents are unsure of their own opinions and may hesitate to exert authority
- Adolescents need to talk about their fears
- Need assistance in sorting out confused feelings
- Important to keep lines of communication open

- In what ways can parents enhance an open dialogue with an adolescent?
- Give an example of how parents can hinder open communication with an adolescent.

Slide 30

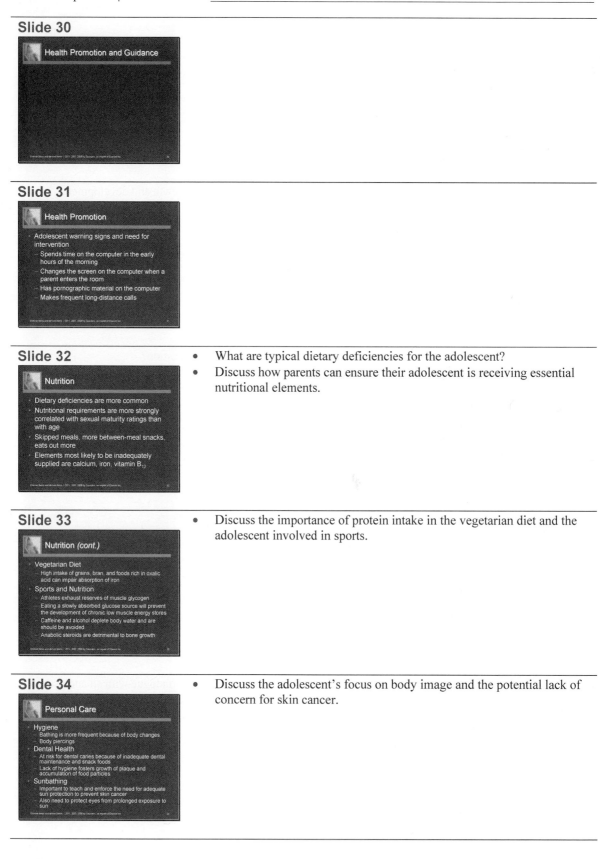

Health Promotion and Guidance

Slide 31

Health Promotion

- Adolescent warning signs and need for intervention
  - Spends time on the computer in the early hours of the morning
  - Changes the screen on the computer when a parent enters the room
  - Has pornographic material on the computer
  - Makes frequent long-distance calls

Slide 32

Nutrition

- Dietary deficiencies are more common
- Nutritional requirements are more strongly correlated with sexual maturity ratings than with age
- Skipped meals, more between-meal snacks, eats out more
- Elements most likely to be inadequately supplied are calcium, iron, vitamin B_{12}

- What are typical dietary deficiencies for the adolescent?
- Discuss how parents can ensure their adolescent is receiving essential nutritional elements.

Slide 33

Nutrition (cont.)

- Vegetarian Diet
  - High intake of grains, bran, and foods rich in oxalic acid can impair absorption of iron
- Sports and Nutrition
  - Athletes exhaust reserves of muscle glycogen
  - Eating a slowly absorbed glucose source will prevent the development of chronic low muscle energy stores
  - Caffeine and alcohol deplete body water and are should be avoided
  - Anabolic steroids are detrimental to bone growth

- Discuss the importance of protein intake in the vegetarian diet and the adolescent involved in sports.

Slide 34

Personal Care

- Hygiene
  - Bathing is more frequent because of body changes
  - Body piercings
- Dental Health
  - At risk for dental caries because of inadequate dental maintenance and snack foods
  - Lack of hygiene fosters growth of plaque and accumulation of food particles
- Sunbathing
  - Important to teach and enforce the need for adequate sun protection to prevent skin cancer
  - Also need to protect eyes from prolonged exposure to sun

- Discuss the adolescent's focus on body image and the potential lack of concern for skin cancer.

Leifer

Slide 35

Safety
Road and off-road motor vehicle accidents (MVAs) kill and cripple adolescents at an alarming rate
Preventing MVAs is of utmost importance
Learning how to swim and practice water safety are important
Body contact sports can be hazardous
Encourage the adolescent to wear appropriate protective gear

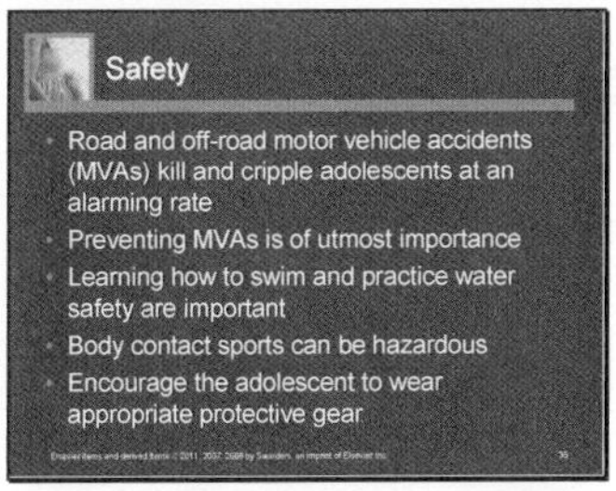

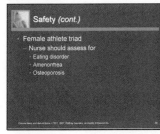

- In what ways can adolescents drive more safely?
- Discuss the importance of routine sports examinations.

Slide 36

Safety (cont.)
Female athlete triad
Nurse should assess for
Eating disorder
Amenorrhea
Osteoporosis

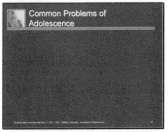

- What are signs and symptoms of eating disorders?

Slide 37

Common Problems of Adolescence

Slide 38

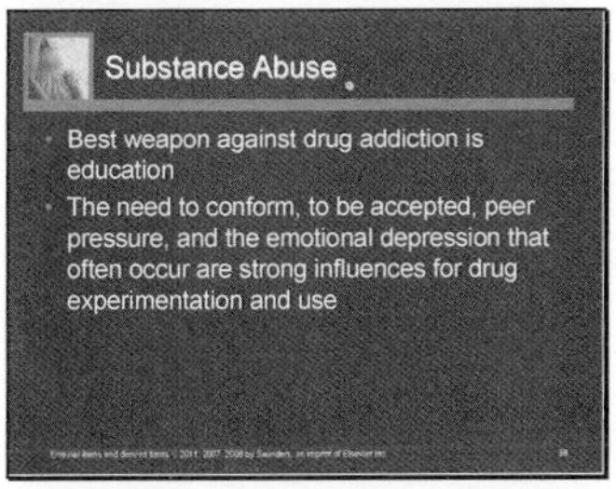

Substance Abuse
Best weapon against drug addiction is education
The need to conform, to be accepted, peer pressure, and the emotional depression that often occur are strong influences for drug experimentation and use

- Give an example of a situation in which the school nurse provides substance abuse information to the adolescent and the parent.

Slide 39

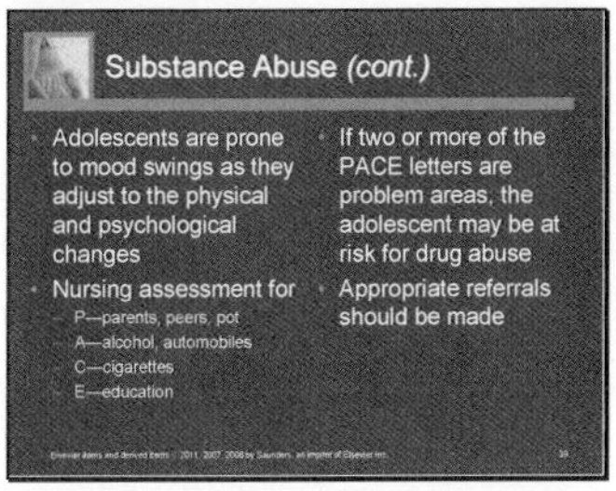

Substance Abuse (cont.)
Adolescents are prone to mood swings as they adjust to the physical and psychological changes
Nursing assessment for
P—parents, peers, pot
A—alcohol, automobiles
C—cigarettes
E—education
If two or more of the PACE letters are problem areas, the adolescent may be at risk for drug abuse
Appropriate referrals should be made

- Discuss the assessment of the acronym PACE.
- Give an example of a situation which corresponds to each letter.

Slide 40

- Give an example of a situation in which there has been a change in the adolescent's behavior which could be a warning sign of depression.
- What could be warning signs regarding the threat of suicide?

Slide 41

- Give an example of a situation in which the school nurse must assess and intervene with a depressed adolescent.

Slide 42

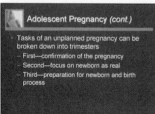

- Discuss the risk factors associated with age and the pregnant adolescent.

Slide 43

Slide 44

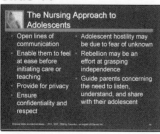

Slide 45

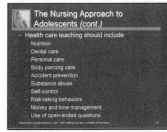

The Nursing Approach to
Adolescents *(cont.)*

- Health care teaching should include
  - Nutrition
  - Dental care
  - Personal care
  - Body piercing care
  - Accident prevention
  - Substance abuse
  - Self-control
  - Risk-taking behaviors
  - Money and time management
  - Use of open-ended questions

Slide 46

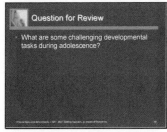

Question for Review

- What are some challenging developmental tasks during adolescence?

Slide 47

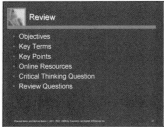

Review

- Objectives
- Key Terms
- Key Points
- Online Resources
- Critical Thinking Question
- Review Questions

Lesson Plan
21 The Child's Experience of Hospitalization

TEACHING FOCUS

This chapter will introduce students to the implications of hospitalization on a child and his or her siblings and parents. Students will review the management of pain in infants and children, explore the differences in the ways that preschool and school-age children deal with hospitalization, and learn about the phases of separation anxiety. Students will also examine various health care delivery settings, clinical pathways, and nursing plans for hospitalized children, and the strengths of adolescents that can contribute to nursing care plans.

MATERIALS AND RESOURCES

☐ Blank Kardex cards (Lesson 21.2)
☐ Computer and PowerPoint projector (all lessons)

LESSON CHECKLIST

Preparations for this lesson include:

- Lecture
- Evaluation of student knowledge and skills needed to perform all entry-level activities related to the child's experience of hospitalization, including:
  ○ Stages of separation anxiety
  ○ Pain management in infants and children
  ○ Clinical pathways and nursing plans for hospitalized children
  ○ Child and parent reactions to hospitalization

KEY TERMS

clinical pathway (p. 480)
conscious sedation (p. 475)
emancipated minor (p. 484)
narcissistic (p. 484)

personal space (p. 477)
pictorial pathway (p. 480)
regression (p. 475)
respite care (p. 485)

separation anxiety (p. 472)
transitional object (p. 481)

ADDITIONAL RESOURCES

TEACH PPT slide(s) Chapter 21, 1-58
EILR IC image(s) Chapter 21, 1-7
EILR OBQ question(s) Chapter 21, 1-10
EILR TB question(s) Chapter 21, 1-28
ESLR IRQ question(s) Chapter 21, 1-7
SG Chapter 21, pp. 169-175

Legend

	𝑒	**𝑒**	SG	💡
PPT TEACH PowerPoint Slides	**EILR** EVOLVE Instructor Learning Resources: Image Collection (IC), Open-Book Quizzes (OBQ), Test Bank (TB)	**ESLR** EVOLVE Student Learning Resources: Interactive Review Questions (IRQ) for the NCLEX® Examination	**SG** Study Guide	**CTQ** Critical Thinking Question in Nursing Care Plan (NCP CTQ) or Get Ready for the NCLEX! (GRN CTQ)

Class Activities are indicated in ***bold italic***.

Leifer

LESSON 21.1

PRETEST

1. Separation anxiety occurs usually around which age?
   a. 3 months
   b. 6 months
   c. 12 months
   d. 18 months

2. Excessive amounts of acetaminophen in children can cause what type of complication?
   a. respiratory depression
   b. nausea and vomiting
   c. liver failure
   d. constipation

3. Preventive pain control involves
   a. administering analgesics on a regular schedule.
   b. administering analgesic medications and local anesthetics as needed.
   c. conscious sedation.
   d. the patient pressing a button to administer a bolus of medication.

4. A 5-year-old child is hospitalized and wants to drink from a bottle. This is an example of
   a. regression.
   b. separation anxiety.
   c. detachment.
   d. temper tantrum.

5. When children are hospitalized,
   a. the parents should provide all care.
   b. the entire family is affected.
   c. siblings should be shielded from any information.
   d. try to find out if the parents are to blame.

6. How does a pediatric nursing care plan differ from an adult care plan?
   a. It is based on the nursing process.
   b. It does not use established nursing diagnoses.
   c. It focuses on the therapy rather than the patient.
   d. It includes growth and developmental processes.

7. Separation anxiety is most pronounced among
   a. infants.
   b. toddlers.
   c. preschoolers.
   d. preteens.

8. Which of the following is an example of an emancipated minor?
   a. an infant who is adopted from a foreign country
   b. a 5-year-old child who is cared for by his grandparents
   c. a 15-year-old who is home-schooled
   d. a 17-year-old female who is married

9. When a child points to where her pain falls on a scale, she is using which pain-rating scale?
   a. poker chip
   b. descriptive word
   c. visual analog
   d. oucher

10. An example of a transitional object is a
    a. favorite toy.
    b. PCA pump.
    c. hospital wagon.
    d. favorite food.

Answers

1. b	3. a	5. b	7. b	9. c
2. c	4. a	6. d	8. d	10. a

BACKGROUND ASSESSMENT

Question: What is respite care?

Answer: Respite care is the care of acute or chronically ill children that takes place in the home. The purpose of respite care is to relieve the family from the responsibilities and worries involved in caring for an ill child. Trained health care workers go to the child's home for scheduled periods, during which the caregiver is able to do errands or take personal time away from caring for the child. During visits, the health care worker assesses how well a family is adjusting and coping with the child's illness and care plan, the effects of the child's illness on siblings and other family members, and other individual factors.

Question: What are the stages of separation anxiety commonly experienced by hospitalized children?
Answer: The three stages of separation anxiety are protest, despair, and detachment or denial. The first stage, protest, is expressed by loud or continuous crying or other protests against the parent leaving. This stage then progresses to despair. The crying gradually stops and the child becomes sad, depressed, and withdrawn, and does not actively play with toys. The third stage is denial or detachment. The child appears to deny his or her need for the parent, becomes detached or uninterested during their visits, and takes greater interest in toys and surroundings. This stage is a superficial adjustment to lessen the pain of separation. It does not indicate that the child has adjusted to the separation and no longer misses the parent. A prolonged detachment phase can affect parent-child bonding and should be addressed by the nurse. Understanding the various phases of separation anxiety and their implications helps the nurse establish trust and promote family relationships throughout the hospitalization.

CRITICAL THINKING QUESTION

The mother of a 2-year-old patient says that she has decided not to visit for the next couple of days because it upsets her daughter too much when she has to leave. She says that it will "be easier on everyone" if she stays away until it is time for her daughter to be discharged. How should the nurse respond?
Guidelines: The nurse should explain to the mother that the child is experiencing separation anxiety. By crying and clinging to the mother, she is demonstrating the protest stage of separation anxiety. By ceasing her hospital visits, the mother will actually make her daughter's separation anxiety worse. Her child will feel abandoned, and consequently the parent-child relationship will be damaged. The mother should continue her regular hospital visits, no matter how painful it is when she leaves. It is also important that she not sneak out while her daughter is sleeping; this can damage trust.

OBJECTIVES	CONTENT	TEACHING RESOURCES
Identify various health care delivery settings.	■ Health care delivery settings (p. 470) ☐ Outpatient clinic (p. 470) – Types of outpatient clinics (p. 470) – Promoting a positive experience (p. 471) ☐ Home (p. 471) ☐ Children's hospital unit (p. 472)	⊠ PPT slides 5-13 *e* EILR OBQ question 1 *e* EILR TB questions 1, 2, 24 SG Learning Activities, question 2 (p. 169) **BOOK RESOURCES** Box 21-1, Preparing a Child for Treatments or Procedures (p. 471) ▶ Discuss the nurse's role in educating patients about the various health care settings. ▶ Discuss the admission procedures for adults and children. *Class Activity* **Divide the class into groups, and then compare and contrast the different health care delivery settings (such as inpatient and outpatient) and discuss the level of pediatric care offered in each. Which type of patient benefits most from each setting? Have each group share its findings with the class for discussion.**
Describe three phases of separation anxiety.	■ The child's reaction to hospitalization (p. 472) ☐ Separation anxiety (p. 472)	⊠ PPT slides 14-17 *e* EILR IC image 1 *e* EILR OBQ questions 3, 4 *e* EILR TB questions 1, 2, 4, 13

OBJECTIVES	CONTENT	TEACHING RESOURCES
		SG Learning Activities, questions 4, 5, 7, 8 (pp. 169-170)
		SG Review Questions, question 3 (p. 173)
		SG Case Study, question 1 (pp. 174-175)
		BOOK RESOURCES
		Figure 21-1, The Nurse Greets the Child at Eye Level in a Non-Threatening Manner (p. 472)
		Nursing Tip (p. 472)
		Nursing Tip (p. 473)
		Review Questions for the NCLEX® Examination, questions 1, 3 (p. 486)
		▸ Discuss aspects of hospitalization that can cause stress in children.
		▸ Discuss the factors that affect a child's level of stress.
		Class Activity *Present the following scenarios for students to discuss:*
		1. A 2-year-old boy has lost interest in his favorite toys, appears sad and depressed, and shies away from unfamiliar health care staff.
		2. A 2-year-old girl is occupied with her toys, activities, and surroundings and is uninterested in her parents' visits.
		3. A 2-year-old boy cries hysterically when his parents leave his room. He does not stop until he cries himself to sleep.
		4. A 2-year-old girl is interested in her toys and surroundings, but cries when her parents appear for visits.
		Have students identify the stage of separation anxiety described in each scenario and discuss appropriate nursing interventions.
Discuss the management of pain in infants and children.	☐ Pain (p. 473) ☐ Response to drugs (p. 474) – Drugs used for pain relief in infants and children (p. 474) – Conscious sedation (p. 475)	PPT slides 18-29 *e* EILR IC images 2, 3 *e* EILR OBQ questions 5, 6 *e* EILR TB questions 7, 20, 22 *e* ESLR IRQ questions 1, 2, 5, 6 SG Learning Activities, questions 1, 9-14 (pp. 169-

OBJECTIVES	CONTENT	TEACHING RESOURCES

	☐ Fear (p. 475)
	
	 ☐ Regression (p. 475)
		170)
		
		 SG Review Questions, questions 7, 14 (p. 173)
		
		 BOOK RESOURCES
		
		 Figure 21-2, Pain Assessment Tools for Children (p. 474)
		
		 Figure 21-3, EMLA Cream, a Topical Anesthetic (p. 475)
		
		 Nursing Care Plan 21-1, The Hospitalized Child and Family (p. 476)
		
		 Review Questions for the NCLEX® Examination, question 2 (p. 486)
		
		 GRN CTQ 1 (p. 486)
		
		 ▸ Discuss nonpharmacological methods of pain management that are appropriate for infants and children.
		
		 ▸ Discuss the drugs used for pain relief in infants and children, and compare and contrast the uses of each.
		
		 *Class Activity **Have the students consider assessing pain in the following children:***
		
		   – 2-year-old child
		
		   – 4-year-old child
		
		   – 6-year-old child
		
		   – 9-year-old child
		
		 Ask the class to discuss which assessment tool is most appropriate for each child.
		
		 *Class Activity **Divide the class into groups and provide students with various height and weight measurements for an infant, toddler, preschooler, school-aged child, and adolescent. Have the groups calculate appropriate dosages of acetaminophen, NSAIDs, and opioid analgesics for each. Use a drug reference book for determining dosage ranges. Have each group share its findings with the class for discussion.***

21.1 Homework/Assignments:

21.1 Instructor's Notes/Student Feedback:

LESSON 21.2

CRITICAL THINKING QUESTION

An 8-year-old boy is admitted to the pediatric oncology unit for his first round of chemotherapy. While the family is visiting, the nurse observes the patient's 4-year-old sister crying and repeatedly asking her parents to give her a bandage for her "owie." The mother tells the child that she is fine and to stop crying so as not to disturb the other patients. What does the child's behavior suggest, and how does it affect the patient's nursing care plan?

Guidelines: A sibling's hospitalization is very stressful for children. The girl is crying and requests for a bandage suggest that she resents the attention her brother is getting, feels left out, or is frightened that she will become sick as well. A holistic nursing care plan for the patient involves the entire family, and might include allowing both children to play with hospital equipment (such as a stethoscope) and tending to the child's imaginary injury. Special attention should be paid to the girl by engaging her in play, discussing how she feels about her brother's hospitalization, and describing the hospital environment and treatment interventions that will occur. Assistance should also be given to the parents to help them provide extra care and support for their daughter, which will ease the adjustment for all of them. Integrating support services, such as the pediatric social worker, is also indicated to assist the parents in dealing with the stress of caring for a sick child and their younger daughter at the same time.

OBJECTIVES	CONTENT	TEACHING RESOURCES
List two ways in which the nurse can lessen the stress of hospitalization for the child's parents.	☐ Cultural Response (p. 476) ☐ Intercultural communication: responses to hospitalization (p. 477) – Personal space (p. 477) – Smiling (p. 477) – Eye contact (p. 477) – Touch (p. 477) – Focus (p. 477)	⊠▤ PPT slides 30-37 *e* EILR OBQ question 7 *e* EILR TB questions 14, 15 *e* ESLR IRQ question 3 SG Learning Activities, question 6 (p. 170) **BOOK RESOURCES** Review Questions for the NCLEX® Examination, question 4 (p. 486) Nursing Tips (p. 478) ▸ Discuss common reactions of parents to a child's hospitalization. *Class Activity **Divide the class into groups and have students discuss cultural, religious, socioeconomic, and other factors that might influence parents' behavior and expectations in the hospital. Ask them to also discuss how the nurse should respond. Have each group share its findings with the class for discussion.***
Identify two problems confronting the siblings of the hospitalized child.	■ The parents' reactions to the child's hospitalization (p. 477)	⊠▤ PPT slides 33, 34 *e* EILR TB questions 6, 12 SG Learning Activities, questions 15, 16, 29 (pp. 171-172) SG Case Study, question 1 (p. 174-175)

OBJECTIVES	CONTENT	TEACHING RESOURCES
		SG Applying Knowledge, question 4 (p. 172)
		BOOK RESOURCES
		Nursing Tips (p. 478)
		▸ Discuss common reactions of siblings to a child's hospitalization.
		*Class Activity **Divide the class into groups and have students discuss how siblings are affected by a child's hospitalization. How do older and younger siblings react? How can they be included in plans of care? What other special considerations should be made for siblings? Have each group share its findings with the class for discussion.***
Organize a nursing care plan for a hospitalized child.	■ The nurse's role in the child's hospitalization (p. 478) □ Admissions (p. 478) ■ Developing a pediatric nursing care plan (p. 479)	PPT slides 35-37 *e* EILR IC image 4 *e* EILR OBQ questions 8, 9 *e* EILR TB questions 9, 15, 26 SG Learning Activities, question 17 (p. 171) SG Case Study, question 1 (pp. 174-175) SG Thinking Critically, question 1 (p. 175) SG Applying Knowledge, questions 1, 3 (p. 175) **BOOK RESOURCES** Nursing Tips (p. 479) Figure 21-4, The Nurse Enters Data and Retrieves Information (p. 479) ▸ Discuss how nursing care plans for children differ from those for adults. *Class Activity **Divide the class into groups and assign each group one of the following age groups: infant, toddler, preschool, and school-age. Have each group outline the preparations that should be made before a child is hospitalized and present its findings to the class. What preparations or comfort measures can be taken in emergencies?*** *Class Activity **Divide the class into four groups and have each group complete a blank Kardex card for one of the following scenarios:*** *– An 8-year-old girl undergoing chemotherapy*

OBJECTIVES	CONTENT	TEACHING RESOURCES
		– A 9-year-old boy who had heart surgery
		– A 5-year-old girl with severe pneumonia
		– A 3-year-old boy having a sickle cell crisis
		Have each group present its findings to the class for discussion.
Interpret a clinical pathway for a hospitalized child.	■ Clinical pathways (p. 480)	PPT slides 38, 39
		e EILR IC image 5
		e EILR TB question 21
		SG Learning Activities, question 1 (p. 169)
		BOOK RESOURCES
		Figure 21-5, Pictorial Clinical Pathway (p. 480)
		▶ Discuss how pictorial clinical pathways differ from clinical pathways, and how they are helpful with hospitalized children.
		Class Activity ***Using the scenarios from the previous class activity, have students identify and differentiate between elements of a nursing care plan and a clinical pathway. Then have them explain the roles of other health care providers in the care of each patient.***

21.2 Homework/Assignments:

21.2 Instructor's Notes/Student Feedback:

ELSEVIER

Leifer

CRITICAL THINKING QUESTION

A 16-year-old high school junior and varsity athlete is admitted to the pediatric unit following a car accident. She has head and facial lacerations and a fractured femur. During the initial nursing assessment, she avoids eye contact during the conversation and is withdrawn. She also says that her junior year has been ruined and that she cannot possibly go to the prom looking like this. What developmental concerns influence her recovery, and how can she be included in the nursing care plan and goals?

Guidelines: The developmental tasks of middle adolescence focus on attracting the opposite sex, peer groups, and emancipation and independence. Because she has received facial lacerations and will likely have scarring, her mood and self-esteem are damaged. Physical appearance and the ability to attract the opposite sex are very important during adolescence. She is also nearing late adolescence, which means that she is beginning to be concerned about her education, career, and life goals. Her hospitalization and fractured leg mean that she may not be able to play sports for a while, if ever. Allowing her to talk about her fears and providing reassurance regarding the healing process and the temporary nature of her injuries can help her to adjust. Allowing her to participate in her wound care fosters independence. She should also be encouraged to accept visits from her teammates, coach, and friends. This will provide her with extra support, as well as a connection to her school and social environments.

OBJECTIVES	CONTENT	TEACHING RESOURCES
Describe two milestones in the psychosocial development of the preschool child that contribute either positively or negatively to the adjustment to hospitalization.	■ Meeting the needs of the hospitalized child (p. 480) □ The hospitalized infant (p. 480) □ The hospitalized toddler (p. 481) □ The hospitalized preschooler (p. 482)	☒▤ PPT slides 40-44 𝑒 EILR IC images 6, 7 𝑒 EILR OBQ question 8 𝑒 EILR TB questions 8, 16-18, 25, 27 𝑒 ESLR IRQ question 7 SG Learning Activities, questions 20, 22 (p. 171) SG Review Questions, 2, 8, 10, 15 (pp. 172-173) SG Case Study, question 1 (pp. 174-175) SG Applying Knowledge, questions 1, 3 (p. 175) **BOOK RESOURCES** Figure 21-6, Liberal visiting hours enable the parent to meet the needs of the hospitalized infant (p. 481) Box 21-2, Nursing Goals in the Care of Hospitalized Toddlers (p. 481) Figure 21-7, A, CNS Approaches the Child Calmly. B, Infant Shows Apprehension. C, Beginning Trust Is Established. D, General Assessment Can Begin (p. 482) Nursing Tip (p. 482) Table 21-1, Words to Avoid and Words to Use (p. 483) Review Questions for the NCLEX® Examination, question

OBJECTIVES	CONTENT	TEACHING RESOURCES
		5 (p. 486)
		▶ Discuss various strategies to achieve the nursing goals in the care of the hospitalized toddler.
		▶ Discuss the nurse's role in supporting the child has need for mastery and control when distressed.
		Class Activity Divide the class into groups and assign each group one of the following age groups: infant, toddler, preschool, school-age, and adolescent. Have each group identify several psychosocial developmental milestones and discuss how the milestones affect the child's adjustment to hospitalization. Conversely, how does hospitalization affect development? Have each group present its findings to the class for discussion.
Contrast the problems of the preschool child and the school-age child facing hospitalization.	☐ The hospitalized preschooler (p. 482) ☐ The hospitalized school-age child (p. 483) ☐ The hospitalized adolescent (p. 483) – Early adolescence (p. 484) – Middle adolescence (p. 484) – Late adolescence (p. 484) – Adjustment to illness (p. 484) – Roommate selection (p. 484)	▣ PPT slides 45-50 *e* EILR OBQ question 9 *e* EILR TB questions 3, 5, 10, 11, 19 SG Learning Activities, questions 3, 21-26 (pp. 169, 172) SG Review Questions, questions 10, 12, 13 (pp. 173-174) SG Thinking Critically, question 2 (p. 175) SG Applying Knowledge, questions 1, 3 (p. 175) **BOOK RESOURCES** Safety Alert (p. 483) Review Questions for the NCLEX® Examination, questions 4, 5 (p. 486) ▶ Discuss how the nurse can engage the parents in determining how to approach preschool and school-age patients. *Class Activity Divide the board into two columns and write the headings "preschool child" and "school-age child" at the top of each. Have students identify problems of each hospitalized child, then compare and contrast their needs.*
List three strengths of the adolescent that the nurse might use when formulating	■ Confidentiality and legality (p. 484)	▣ PPT slide 51 *e* EILR TB question 28 SG Learning Activities, questions 1, 3 (p. 169)

Leifer

OBJECTIVES	CONTENT	TEACHING RESOURCES
nursing care plans.		**SG** SG Review Questions, question 6 (p. 173)
		SG SG Applying Knowledge, question 5 (p. 175)
		▸ Discuss the ways an adolescent's care plan can be designed to incorporate choice, privacy, and understanding.
		Class Activity Divide the class into groups and assign each group one of the following age groups: early adolescence, middle adolescence, late adolescence. Have each group discuss the strengths and weaknesses of its age group regarding hospitalization and present its findings to the class for discussion.
		Class Activity Divide the class into groups and assign each group one of the following scenarios:
		– *A high-school dropout with sickle cell anemia*
		– *A pregnant teenager with gestational diabetes*
		– *A teenager who is abusing drugs or alcohol*
		– *An honor student scheduled for a tonsillectomy*
		Have each group list the challenges each scenario presents during hospitalization and discuss effective nursing interventions for addressing the challenges. Also, discuss how the patient can be involved in formulating the care plan and adhering to its goals. Have each group present its findings to the class.
Recognize the steps in discharge planning for infants, children, and adolescents.	■ Discharge planning (p. 484) ■ Home care (p. 485)	PPT slides 52-56 **e** EILR OBQ question 10 **e** EILR TB question 23 **e** ESLR IRQ question 4 **SG** SG Learning Activities, questions 1, 27, 28 (pp. 169, 172) **BOOK RESOURCES** Legal and Ethical Considerations, Discharge Documentation (p. 485)

OBJECTIVES	CONTENT	TEACHING RESOURCES
Performance Evaluation		⊠▤ PPT slides 1-58
		e EILR IC images 1-7
		e EILR OBQ questions 1-10
		e EILR TB questions 1-28
		e ESLR IRQ questions 1-7
		〘SG〙 SG Learning Activities, questions 1-29 (pp. 169-172)
		〘SG〙 SG Review Questions, questions 1-15 (pp. 173-174)
		〘SG〙 SG Case Study, question 1 (p. 175)
		〘SG〙 SG Thinking Critically, questions 1, 2 (p. 175)
		〘SG〙 SG Applying Knowledge, questions 1-5 (p. 175)
		BOOK RESOURCES
		Review Questions for the NCLEX® Examination, questions 1-5 (p. 486)
		💡 GRN CTQ 1 (p. 486)

21.3 Homework/Assignments:

21.3 Instructor's Notes/Student Feedback:

21 Lecture Outline
The Child's Experience of Hospitalization

Slide 1

Chapter 21

The Child's Experience of Hospitalization

Slide 2

Objectives

- Identify various health care delivery settings.
- Describe three phases of separation anxiety.
- List two ways in which the nurse can lessen the stress of hospitalization for the child's parents.
- Discuss the management of pain in infants and children.

Slide 3

Objectives *(cont.)*

- Describe two milestones in the psychosocial development of the preschool child that contribute either positively or negatively to the adjustment to hospitalization.
- Contrast the problems of the preschool child and the school-age child facing hospitalization.
- Identify two problems confronting the siblings of the hospitalized child.

Slide 4

Objectives *(cont.)*

- List three strengths of the adolescent that the nurse might use when formulating nursing care plans.
- Organize a nursing care plan for a hospitalized child.
- Recognize the steps in discharge planning for infants, children, and adolescents.
- Interpret a clinical pathway for a hospitalized child.

Leifer

Slide 5

Health Care Delivery Settings

Slide 6

Outpatient Clinic

- Eliminates the need to separate the child from the family so that the treatment and the emotional impact of the illness are reduced
- Types
  – Private office or hospital-affiliated
  – Satellite
  – Pediatric research centers
  – Outpatient surgery centers

- Give an example of the types of patient populations that could be seen in each type of clinic.

Slide 7

Outpatient Clinic *(cont.)*

- Promoting a positive experience
  – Attitude of personnel child comes in contact with is of the utmost importance
  – For many children, the only exposure to health care is through brief clinic appointments

- Discuss positive and negative attitudes and how they can affect a child's experience.

Slide 8

Preparing the Child for a Treatment or Procedure

- Infants
  – Involve parents
  – Include familiar objects
  – Soothe, distract, and hug afterward

- Stress the importance of knowing the developmental stage of the child as it will guide the type of preparation needed.
- How would you involve the parents?

Slide 9

Preparing the Child for a Treatment or Procedure *(cont.)*

- Toddlers and preschoolers
  – Involve parents
  – Offer simple explanations
  – Give permission to express discomfort
  – Offer one direction at a time
  – Allow for choices, if possible
  – Use distraction
  – Hug after treatment or procedure

- Discuss simple terms in which to explain procedures to the toddler.
- Give an example of a preprocedure situation and how the nurse can effectively communicate with the toddler.
- Give an example of a situation in which a choice is offered to the toddler.
- What are some methods of distraction?

Slide 10

> **Preparing the Child for a Treatment or Procedure** *(cont.)*
>
> · School-age child
>   - All of the previous preparations, plus
>   · Let them examine equipment
>   · Encourage child to verbalize fears
>   · Offer small reward after treatment or procedure, a sticker, for example

- Give an example of a situation in which the nurse allows the child to examine or play with a piece of equipment prior to using it.
- What are other rewards a child might enjoy?

Slide 11

> **Preparing the Child for a Treatment or Procedure** *(cont.)*
>
> · Adolescent
>   - Provide privacy
>   - Involve teen in treatment or procedure
>   - Explain treatment or procedure and equipment
>   - Suggest coping techniques

- Discuss how the nurse can provide privacy to a teen and involve him or her in the treatment or procedure.
- What are some coping techniques that are appropriate for a teen?

Slide 12

> **Home**
>
> · Not only a matter of supplying appliances and nursing care
> · Includes assessment of the total needs of children and their families
> · Hospice care can also be provided in the home
> · Changes in health care delivery affect the role and responsibilities of the nurse
> · The various home and support groups that are available have the potential for improving life for the child and family and help reduce the cost of medical care

- Give an example of a situation in which a child might need varied home health care and discuss the impact on the family and child.
- What is the home health care nurse's role in coordinating these services?

Slide 13

> **Children's Hospital Unit**
>
> · Designed to meet the needs of the child and parents
> · Special treatment room for child to be examined or receive some form of treatment
> · Playrooms for the children are also available
> · Daily routine emphasizes parent rooming-in
> · Provision of consistent caregivers
> · Flexible schedules to meet the needs of the growing child

- How can the nurse assist the child and parents in maintaining their normal routine?

Slide 14

> **The Child's Reaction to Hospitalization**
>
> · Depends on
>   - Age
>   - Amount of preparation given
>   - Security of home life
>   - Previous hospitalizations
>   - Support of family and medical personnel
>   - Child's emotional health

- Discuss the varied reactions to hospitalization of an infant, toddler, preschooler, school-age child, and an adolescent.
- How can the nurse prepare the child for hospitalization?
- Discuss the issue of previous hospitalizations and how they will affect the child during this hospitalization.

Introduction to Maternity & Pediatric Nursing, 6th ed.
Leifer

Slide 15

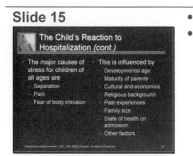

- Discuss the nurse's role in attempts to decrease the child's stress.
- How can the nurse involve the parents in decreasing the amount of stress the child is experiencing?

Slide 16

Slide 17

- Discuss nursing interventions which can assist the child through these stages.

Slide 18

Slide 19

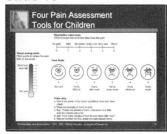

- Discuss Figure 21-2, page 474.

Audience Response Question #1
A 7-year-old is in the hospital following an appendectomy. The nurse assesses him for pain using the face scale. He points to the 0 face indicating no hurt, but the nurse notices he is grimacing and guarding the operative site. What would be the best action for the nurse to take?
  1. Note that the child is pain free.
  2. Reposition the child.
  3. Attempt assessment using another tool.
  4. Medicate immediately for pain as ordered.

Slide 20

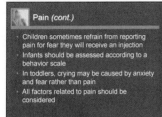

Two Additional Pain Assessment Scales

- PICIC (Pain Indicator for Communicatively Impaired Children)
  - Crying with or without tears
  - Screaming or groaning
  - Distressed facial expression
  - Tense body
  - Irritability to touch
- FLACC
  - Face: grimace
  - Legs: restless to kicking
  - Activity: quiet to arched
  - Crying: moan to scream
  - Consolability: touch to inconsolable

Slide 21

Pain *(cont.)*

- Children sometimes refrain from reporting pain for fear they will receive an injection
- Infants should be assessed according to a behavior scale
- In toddlers, crying may be caused by anxiety and fear rather than pain
- All factors related to pain should be considered

Slide 22

Managing Pain

- Nonpharmacological techniques
  - Drawing
  - Distraction
  - Imagery
  - Relaxation
  - Cognitive (thinking) strategies
  - Backrub or hand massage

- What are examples of distraction, imagery, and relaxation techniques?

Slide 23

Drug Physiology

- Elimination of the drug may be prolonged because of an immature liver enzyme system
- Dosages are influenced by weight and differences in expected absorption, metabolism, and clearance

Slide 24

Drugs Used for Pain Relief

- Acetaminophen—mild to moderate pain
  - Can lead to liver failure if not dosed correctly
- Nonsteroidal antiinflammatory drugs (NSAIDs)—mild to moderate pain
- Opioids—moderate to severe pain
  - Used for long periods of time
  - Tolerance and respiratory depression can occur

- Discuss the importance of proper dosage calculations for the pediatric patient.

Leifer

Slide 25

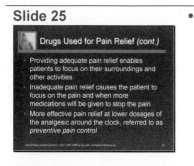

Drugs Used for Pain Relief *(cont.)*

- Providing adequate pain relief enables patients to focus on their surroundings and other activities
- Inadequate pain relief causes the patient to focus on the pain and when more medications will be given to stop the pain
- More effective pain relief at lower dosages of the analgesic around the clock, referred to as *preventive pain control*

- Discuss the nurse's role in monitoring and relieving pain.

Slide 26

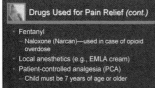

Drugs Used for Pain Relief *(cont.)*

- Fentanyl
  - Naloxone (Narcan)—used in case of opioid overdose
- Local anesthetics (e.g., EMLA cream)
- Patient-controlled analgesia (PCA)
  - Child must be 7 years of age or older

- Discuss the proper administration method for naloxone.
- How is EMLA cream used?
- Discuss the use of PCAs and signs/symptoms to monitor in the child.

Slide 27

Conscious Sedation

- The administration of IV drugs to a patient to impair consciousness but retain protective reflexes, the ability to maintain a patent airway, and the ability to respond to physical and verbal stimuli
- A 1:1 nurse-patient ratio is continued until there are stable vital signs, age-appropriate motor and verbal abilities, adequate hydration, and a presedation level of responsiveness and orientation

Slide 28

Fear

- Intrusive procedures are fear-provoking
- Disrupts child's trust level
- Threatens self-esteem and self-control
- May require restriction of activity

Slide 29

Regression

- The loss of an achieved level of functioning to a past level of behavior that was successful during earlier stages of development
- Can be minimized by an accurate nursing assessment of the child's abilities and the planning of care to support and maintain growth and development
- When the child is free from the stress that caused the regression, praise will motivate the achievement of appropriate behavior

- Give examples of regressive behavior.

Leifer

Slide 30

Cultural Needs

- Showing cultural sensitivity decreases anxiety
- Effective utilization of health care service and compliance with treatment plans are enhanced when the nurse's approach is compatible with cultural needs and beliefs
- Nonverbal cues and body language are important in intercultural communication

- How might the nurse adjust his or her approach when caring for the cultural needs of the child?
- Discuss positive and negative body language cues.

Slide 31

Cultural Needs *(cont.)*

- Crying may be interpreted by some cultures as a signal of an organic upset of illness
- One cultural group may prize autonomy and initiative while others may tolerate only complete obedience
- Respecting cultural and religious beliefs will enhance compliance
- Assess family through the eyes of its culture to avoid labeling a family who is "different" as dysfunctional

Slide 32

Fostering Intercultural Communication

- Approaches to various cultures involve knowing what is and is not acceptable as it relates to
  - Personal space
  - Smiling
  - Eye contact
  - Touch
  - Focus
- It is important for the nurse to take the time to become familiar with culturally acceptable behaviors

Slide 33

The Parents' Reactions to the Child's Hospitalization

- May believe they are to blame for their child's illness
- Immunizations may have been neglected
- Guilt, helplessness, and anxiety
- Parents are seldom the direct cause for hospital admission
- The nurse listens carefully to parental concerns and acknowledges the legitimacy of their feelings
- Encourages and supports parents and other family members, stresses their importance to the child's recovery
- Encourages their participation in the care of the child

- In what ways can a nurse support the family and involve them in the care of the hospitalized child?

Slide 34

The Parents' Reactions to the Child's Hospitalization *(cont.)*

- Parents may ventilate their feelings and stresses through anger, crying, or body language
- Behavior often involves attitudes resulting from early childhood experiences
- An understanding and acceptance of people and their problems is essential for the successful pediatric nurse
- Poor communication can result in unnecessary fear

- Discuss communication techniques that can be used by the nurse to manage parents who exhibit anger or avoidance.

Introduction to Maternity & Pediatric Nursing, 6th ed.

Leifer

Slide 35

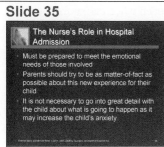

The Nurse's Role in Hospital Admission

- Must be prepared to meet the emotional needs of those involved
- Parents should try to be as matter-of-fact as possible about this new experience for their child
- It is not necessary to go into great detail with the child about what is going to happen as it may increase the child's anxiety

- Give an example of a scenario in which a parent is providing too much and too detailed information to a child and how the nurse can manage this situation.

Slide 36

Developmental History

- Family relationships and support systems
- Cultural needs that may affect care and hospital routine
- Nicknames, rituals, routines
- Developmental level and abilities
- Communication skills
- Personality, adaptability, coping skills
- Past experiences, divorces, new siblings, extended family
- Previous separation experiences
- Impact of current health problem on growth and development
- Preparation given to the child
- Previous contact with health care personnel

- Discuss the nurse's role and rationale for obtaining this information.

Slide 37

Developing a Pediatric Nursing Care Plan

- Result of nursing process
- States specifically what is to be done for each child
- Keeps the focus on the child and not on the condition or therapy
- Involves growth and development process; evaluation of the primary caregiver, who has a direct role in the safety and maintenance of the child's health

Slide 38

Clinical Pathways

- Interdisciplinary plan of care
- Displays progress of entire treatment plan
- Nursing care plan focuses on the nurse's role
- Clinical pathway focuses on the team's approach to outcomes of care

- Discuss which disciplines can be involved in the clinical pathway.

Slide 39

Developmental Nursing Tips

- Play is an important part of a nursing care plan for children
- The achievement of developmental tasks should be part of the plan of care for the hospitalized child

- Give an example of a nursing intervention involving play.

Slide 40

Needs of the Hospitalized Child

Slide 41

The Hospitalized Infant

- Can be frustrating for the infant
- Used to getting what they want when they want it
- May miss continuous affection of their parents
- Daily schedules are disrupted
- Nurse must try to meet the needs of the infant while preventing excess frustration
- Major goal is to assist parent-infant attachment process and promote sensorimotor activities
- Liberal visiting hours are essential
- Consistency in caregivers is important at this stage of development

- Discuss nursing interventions in which the nurse assists the parents and infant in sensorimotor activities.
- Discuss the importance and rationale for liberal visiting hours.
- What is the rationale for consistency of caregivers for this population?

Slide 42

The Hospitalized Toddler

- Their world revolves around their parents, especially their primary caregiver
- Cannot understand why they are separated from their caregiver and become distressed
- Cohesive staff is essential to meet the needs of the children and their parents

- Give an example of the difference between how a toddler might perceive a hospitalization versus a school-age child.

Slide 43

Nursing Goals of the Hospitalized Toddler

- Reassure parents, particularly the child's primary caregiver
- Maintain the toddler's sense of trust
- Incorporate home habits into care plans
- Allow the child to work through or master threatening experiences through soothing techniques and play
- Provide individualized, flexible nursing care plans in accordance with the child's development and diagnosis

- How can the nurse obtain the toddler's trust?
- Give an example of a soothing technique and play intervention for a toddler who has experienced a threatening situation.

Slide 44

Nursing Goals of the Hospitalized Toddler (cont.)

- Children should be forewarned about any unpleasant or new experience that they may need to undergo
- Preparation and explanation are done immediately before the procedure
  - Crying and protestations are healthy expressions and relieve tension
- When restraint is indicated (splints, IV therapy, large dressings), increased emotional support should be provided

- Discuss the rationale for preparing and explaining the procedure just prior to performing it.
- How can a toddler's emotions be supported when restrained for a procedure?

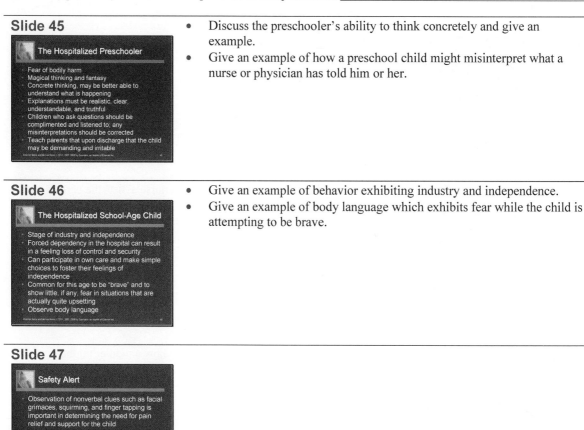

Slide 45

The Hospitalized Preschooler

- Fear of bodily harm
- Magical thinking and fantasy
- Concrete thinking, may be better able to understand what is happening
- Explanations must be realistic, clear, understandable, and truthful
- Children who ask questions should be complimented and listened to; any misinterpretations should be corrected
- Teach parents that upon discharge that the child may be demanding and irritable

- Discuss the preschooler's ability to think concretely and give an example.
- Give an example of how a preschool child might misinterpret what a nurse or physician has told him or her.

Slide 46

The Hospitalized School-Age Child

- Stage of industry and independence
- Forced dependency in the hospital can result in a feeling loss of control and security
- Can participate in own care and make simple choices to foster their feelings of independence
- Common for this age to be "brave" and to show little, if any, fear in situations that are actually quite upsetting
- Observe body language

- Give an example of behavior exhibiting industry and independence.
- Give an example of body language which exhibits fear while the child is attempting to be brave.

Slide 47

Safety Alert

- Observation of nonverbal clues such as facial grimaces, squirming, and finger tapping is important in determining the need for pain relief and support for the child

Slide 48

The Hospitalized Adolescent

- Experience feelings of loss of control during hospitalization
- May cause adolescent to withdraw, be noncompliant, or display anger
- May be concerned with how the illness will affect their appearance
- Incorporating choice, privacy, and the opportunity for peer visitors is important

- Discuss how body image is very important to this population.

Slide 49

Adjustment to Illness

- Can understand the implications of their disease
- Are capable of participating in decisions related to treatment and care
- The nurse who recognizes these skills and encourages their practice helps the adolescent gain confidence

Slide 50

> **Roommate Selection**
> - Adolescents usually do better with one or more roommates
> - It is not a good choice to have a senile patient or infant as a roommate for the adolescent patient
> - Location of adolescent's room is important

- Discuss a situation in which an adolescent is in a room with a toddler and the issues this could cause.

Slide 51

> **Confidentiality and Legality**
> - Many problems can be avoided if the confidentiality of the relationship is clearly defined during initial meetings
> - An emancipated minor is no longer under the parent's authority
> - Be familiar with state law as it applies to adolescent patients

- How might the nurse approach an adolescent and obtain his or her confidence?
- Discuss laws in your region regarding parental authority which might affect this population.

Slide 52

> **Discharge Planning**
> - Ideally begins at the moment of admission to hospital
> - Written instructions should be given for any home treatments
> - Parents also must be prepared for behavioral problems that may arise after hospitalization

Slide 53

> **Guidance for Parents**
> - Anticipating behaviors such as clinging or regression
> - Allowing the child to become a participating family member as soon as possible
> - Taking the focus off the illness
> - Being kind, firm, and consistent with misbehavior
> - Building trust by being truthful
> - Allowing time for free play

Slide 54

> **Legal and Ethical Considerations**
> - Discharge charting should include who accompanied the child (and identification given), time of discharge, behavior and condition of the child, method of transportation, vital signs and weight, medications, and instructions given to the parents or caregiver

- Discuss the rationale for documenting this information.

Slide 55

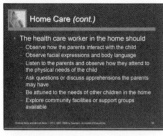

Home Care

- Children with acute or chronic conditions are cared for in the home
- Home health care and other community agencies work with the family to provide holistic care
- Respite care can be provided for the primary caregivers

Slide 56

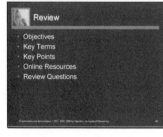

Home Care *(cont.)*

- The health care worker in the home should
  - Observe how the parents interact with the child
  - Observe facial expressions and body language
  - Listen to the parents and observe how they attend to the physical needs of the child
  - Ask questions or discuss apprehensions the parents may have
  - Be attuned to the needs of other children in the home
  - Explore community facilities or support groups available

Slide 57

Question for Review

- What is the difference between a nursing care plan and a clinical pathway?

Slide 58

Review

- Objectives
- Key Terms
- Key Points
- Online Resources
- Review Questions

TEACHING FOCUS

In this chapter, students will have the opportunity to learn the procedures to follow when admitting a child to the pediatric unit and the method used for data collection concerning the pediatric patient. Students will be shown methods for collecting specimens and will be introduced to nursing responsibilities in administering medications to infants and children. Students also will have the opportunity to learn about selected procedures, including management of airway obstruction, along with preoperative and postoperative care.

MATERIALS AND RESOURCES

- ☐ Child mannequin (all lessons)
- ☐ Computer and PowerPoint projector (all lessons)
- ☐ Dolls (all lessons)
- ☐ Flash cards (all lessons)
- ☐ Infant blanket (all lessons)
- ☐ Infant blood pressure cuff (Lesson 22.1)
- ☐ Medibottle (Lesson 22.2)
- ☐ Newborn/infant urine collection kit (Lesson 22.1)
- ☐ Poster board (Lesson 22.1)
- ☐ Syringe and cup for administering medication (Lesson 22.2)
- ☐ Videotape of child assessment (Lesson 22.1)

LESSON CHECKLIST

Preparations for this lesson include:

- Lecture
- Guest speaker: Pediatric specialist (child life specialist, nurse practitioner, or pediatrician)
- Evaluation of student knowledge and skills needed to perform all entry-level activities related to health care adaptations for the child and family, including:
  - ○ Admitting patients to the pediatric unit
  - ○ Data collection and survey tools
  - ○ Collecting specimens
  - ○ Administering medications

KEY TERMS

auscultation (p. 493)
body surface area (BSA) (p. 515)
Broviac catheter (p. 508)
dimensional analysis (p. 517)
fever (p. 495)
gastrostomy (p. 519)
hyperthermia (p. 494)

informed consent (p. 487)
intramuscular (IM) injection (p. 505)
low-flow oxygen (p. 524)
lumbar puncture (p. 500)
mist tent (p. 522)
mummy restraint (p. 489)
nomogram (p. 515)
parenteral (p. 509)

phototoxicity (p. 517)
saline lock (p. 507)
subcutaneous (SQ) injection (p. 504)
total parenteral nutrition (TPN) (p. 508)
tracheostomy (p. 519)
tympanic thermometer (p. 495)

ADDITIONAL RESOURCES

TEACH PPT slide(s) Chapter 22, 1-61
EILR IC image(s) Chapter 22, 1-22
EILR OBQ question(s) Chapter 22, 1-10
EILR TB question(s) Chapter 22, 1-30
ESLR IRQ question(s) Chapter 22, 1-5
SG Chapter 22, pp. 177-184

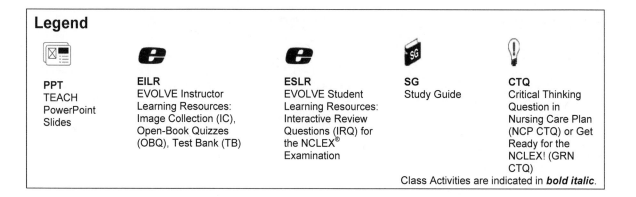

Legend

PPT
TEACH
PowerPoint
Slides

EILR
EVOLVE Instructor
Learning Resources:
Image Collection (IC),
Open-Book Quizzes
(OBQ), Test Bank (TB)

ESLR
EVOLVE Student
Learning Resources:
Interactive Review
Questions (IRQ) for
the NCLEX®
Examination

SG
Study Guide

CTQ
Critical Thinking
Question in
Nursing Care Plan
(NCP CTQ) or Get
Ready for the
NCLEX! (GRN
CTQ)

Class Activities are indicated in **_bold italic_**.

Leifer

LESSON 22.1

PRETEST

1. Which of the following is a major cause of death among infants and children?
   a. cancer
   b. heart defects
   c. accidents
   d. lack of current immunizations

2. The history survey includes
   a. a physical survey.
   b. teaching parents about injury and illness prevention.
   c. obtaining vital signs.
   d. medication administration.

3. What is the most useful method for measuring blood pressure in newborns?
   a. auscultation
   b. palpation
   c. an electronic blood pressure monitor
   d. Blood pressure is unobtainable in newborns.

4. When a child is discharged and sent home with medications, which instruction is correct?
   a. Mix all medications with food.
   b. Do not mix medications with food.
   c. Never apply a mummy restraint when administering nosedrops, eardrops, or eyedrops to an infant.
   d. Do not shake medication before administering.

5. If an infant has an airway obstruction but it cannot be visualized, the next step is to
   a. perform abdominal thrusts.
   b. perform conventional cardiopulmonary resuscitation (CPR).
   c. apply forceful back blows between the shoulder blades while the infant is positioned prone with head lower than trunk.
   d. deliver thrusts to the infant's midsternal region while the infant is on his or her back with head lower than trunk.

6. The nurse must check the ID bracelet
   a. before medications are given or treatments are carried out.
   b. after medications are given or treatments are carried out.
   c. every time the nurse enters the room.
   d. before leaving the room.

7. How should the nurse who is giving a 4-year-old child a tub bath respond to another nurse who asks for help? The nurse should
   a. stay with the child.
   b. tell the child he or she will be right back and help the nurse.
   c. leave the child alone for privacy.
   d. show the child how to use the call light to notify the nurse if he or she needs help.

8. The *first* sign of shock or body stress in infants or children is an elevated
   a. temperature.
   b. blood pressure.
   c. pulse rate.
   d. respiratory rate.

9. A sunken anterior fontanel indicates
   a. an increased intracranial pressure.
   b. normal development.
   c. dehydration.
   d. a decreased level of consciousness.

10. After a blood specimen is obtained from the femoral or jugular vein of an infant or child, the patient should be monitored frequently for
    a. bleeding.
    b. pruritus.
    c. movement.
    d. crying.

Answers

1. c	3. b	5. c	7. a	9. c
2. b	4. b	6. a	8. c	10. a

ELSEVIER

BACKGROUND ASSESSMENT

Question: What data is collected about a pediatric patient admission?

Answer: Data collection is conducted to determine the level of wellness, the response to medication or treatment, and the need for specific nursing interventions for the child. Required data include the child's age, developmental level, general appearance, responsiveness, interactions with parent, vital signs, height, and weight. For an infant, also include head circumference and fontanel appearance.

Question: A child is admitted with a tympanic temperature of 102.2° F (39° C). How should the nurse focus the data collection?

Answer: The nurse's assessment should include the response of the child to cuddling, alertness, hydration, sociability, quality of cry, and skin turgor. A quiet, lethargic child who does not respond readily to the environment may be acutely ill. Fever is managed more aggressively in a neonate than in the older infant or child because high temperatures can increase oxygen consumption, cardiac output, and the risk of seizure.

CRITICAL THINKING QUESTION

A nurse is admitting a 3-year-old boy with a very high temperature who is restless and crying. What safety measures should the nurse institute on admission of this child?

Guidelines: Safety is one of the key factors to address in the care of a child in a health care facility. Keeping the child safe in this environment must be a priority for the nurse. To protect the child from injury, the nurse should keep the side rails of the crib raised when the child is in it. Most 3-year-old children could probably climb over the side rails, and because this boy is also restless, the nurse should supply a crib with a bubble-top. When the child is out of the crib, the nurse must never leave him unattended. In addition, the nurse should be on the lookout for seizures related to high fevers.

OBJECTIVES	CONTENT	TEACHING RESOURCES
List five safety measures applicable to the care of the hospitalized child.	■ Admission to the pediatric unit (p. 487) □ Informed consent (p. 487) □ Identification (p. 487) □ Essential safety measures in the hospital setting (p. 488) □ Preparation steps for performing procedures (p. 489)	PPT slides 6-12 EILR IC images 1-3 EILR OBQ questions 1, 3 EILR TB questions 2, 18, 23 SG Learning Activities, questions 2-6 (pp. 177-178) SG Review Questions, question 17 (p. 183) SG Thinking Critically, question 1 (p. 184) **BOOK RESOURCES** Figure 22-1, Identification (ID) Bracelet (p. 488) Safety Alert (p. 488) Figure 22-2, The Nurse Should Maintain Hand Contact (p. 489) Figure 22-3, A Hard Plastic "Bubble Top" or a Soft Plastic Crib Extender (p. 489) Review Questions for the NCLEX® Examination, question 5 (p. 528) ▶ Discuss the dos and don'ts of safety measures in the hospital setting and how various situations can contribute to accidents. Accidents are a major cause of death among

OBJECTIVES	CONTENT	TEACHING RESOURCES
		infants and children.
		Class Activity **Divide the class into groups. Assign a safety measure applicable to the care of a child in a hospital to each group. Have each group explain the importance of its assigned safety measure and describe its performance to the class.**
		Class Activity **Invite a pediatric specialist to speak to the class about safety measures for a hospitalized child. Have students formulate appropriate questions to ask.**
Illustrate techniques of transporting infants and children.	☐ Transporting, positioning, and restraining (p. 489)	⊠▪ PPT slides 13, 14
		e EILR IC image 4
		e EILR OBQ question 2
		e EILR TB question 9
		e ESLR IRQ question 1
		SG Learning Activities, questions 7, 8 (p. 178)
		SG Review Questions, question 15 (p. 183)
		BOOK RESOURCES
		Figure 22-4, A, The Cradle Position. B, The Football Position. C, The Upright Position. D, The Colic Position (p. 490)
		Skill 22-1, The Mummy Restraint (Swaddling) (p. 490)
		▸ Discuss various safe methods for holding an infant, and the positions to avoid.
		Class Activity **Divide the class into small groups, and give each group a doll and a blanket. Have the groups practice safe transportation and positioning of an infant and child. Then have each group demonstrate its techniques to the class. Have the others evaluate their peers' implementation of the techniques.**
Plan the basic daily data collection for hospitalized infants and children.	▪ Assessment and Basic Data Collection (p. 491) ☐ Organizing the infant assessment (p. 491) ☐ Basic data collection (p. 491) ☐ The history survey (p. 491)	⊠▪ PPT slides 15-18
		SG Learning Activities, question 9 (p. 178)
		SG Applying Knowledge, question 1 (p. 184)
		BOOK RESOURCES
		▸ Discuss at least five steps in organizing an infant assessment.
		▸ Discuss the various stages of child development, including the activities and behaviors associated with each stage, and the knowledge nurses need to determine

OBJECTIVES	CONTENT	TEACHING RESOURCES
		what is age-appropriate.
		Class Activity Have groups of students list the type of basic information a nurse can obtain about a patient through observation. Answers may include bruises, has the child mastered age-appropriate milestones, and lack of body cleanliness. Then, have the entire class compare notes and devise a comprehensive list of observations.
		Class Activity Show a videotape of a child undergoing assessment. Have the students observe the nurse and the child. Discuss assessment techniques and what information should be noted in the chart.
Identify the normal vital signs of infants and children at various ages.	☐ The physical survey (p. 491) — Pulse and respirations (p. 492) — Blood pressure (p. 493) — Temperature (p. 493) — Pain (p. 495) — Weight (p. 495) — Height (p. 498) — Head circumference (p. 498)	⊞ PPT slides 19-29 *e* EILR IC image 5 *e* EILR OBQ questions 4, 5 *e* EILR TB questions 1, 7, 25 *e* ESLR IRQ question 2 SG Learning Activities, questions 10-17 (pp. 178-179) SG Review Questions, questions 1, 6, 8-10 (p. 182) SG Applying Knowledge, question 1 (p. 184) **BOOK RESOURCES** Figure 22-5, Positioning the Child for an Ear Examination. A, Infant. B, Child (p. 492) Table 22-1, Average Pulse Rates at Rest (p. 492) Table 22-2, Normal Respiratory Ranges for Children (p. 492) Skill 22-2, Blood Pressure Measurement in Children (p. 494) Table 22-3, Normal Temperature Ranges for Children (p. 495) ▸ Discuss the advantages and disadvantages of the various techniques used to measure blood pressure in a child. ▸ Discuss the various approaches to measuring temperature in a child. Discuss the different types of thermometers available in the pediatric unit of a hospital. ▸ Discuss the importance of accurately measuring the weight of a child. Be sure to address how weight is used to determine correct dosages for select medications.

OBJECTIVES	CONTENT	TEACHING RESOURCES
		Class Activity **In small groups, have students determine how to obtain the heights and weights of children in various age groups. Have students also practice measuring head circumference on a mannequin and noting it in the patient record.**
		Class Activity **Divide the class into small groups, and give each group a doll. Have students use the doll to identify the anatomic sites used to obtain various pulses and blood pressures.**
Devise a nursing care plan for a child with a fever.	■ Pathogenesis of fever and the use of antipyretics (p. 493) − Temperature measurement (p. 495)	PPT slides 22-25 *e* EILR OBQ question 5 *e* EILR TB question 7 SG Learning Activities, questions 14, 16 (p. 179) SG Applying Knowledge, question 1 (p. 184) **BOOK RESOURCES** Table 22-3, Normal Temperature Ranges for Children (p. 495) Skill 22-3, Axillary Temperature Technique (p. 496) Skill 22-4, Tympanic Temperature Technique (p. 496) Nursing Care Plan 22-1: The Child with a Fever (p. 497) ▸ Discuss nursing interventions that can be performed on a child who has a fever. Identify the rationale for each intervention. (See Nursing Care Plan 22-1, p. 497.) *Class Activity* **Lead students in a discussion of their responsibilities as a nurse implementing a care plan. Then ask students to summarize their responsibilities when following a nursing care plan for a febrile child.**

Discuss the technique of obtaining urine and stool specimens from infants.	■ Specimen collection (p. 498)
	
	  □ Urine specimens (p. 498)
	
	  − Obtaining a clean-catch specimen (p. 498)
	
	  − Obtaining a 24-hour specimen (p. 498)
	
	  − Testing for albumin (p. 498)
	
	  □ Stool specimens (p. 498)
		PPT slides 30, 31
		
		e EILR IC image 6
		
		e EILR OBQ question 6
		
		e EILR TB questions 3, 20, 21
		
		e ESLR IRQ question 3
		
		SG Learning Activities, question 18 (p. 179)
		
		SG Review Questions, question 3 (p. 182)
		
		SG Applying Knowledge, question 1 (p. 184)
		
		BOOK RESOURCES

OBJECTIVES	CONTENT	TEACHING RESOURCES
	☐ Blood specimens (p. 500) – Positioning the child (p. 500)	Table 22-4, Average Daily Excretion of Urine (p. 498) Skill 22-5, Collecting a Urine Specimen in Infants (p. 499) Figure 22-6, An Infant Positioned for Femoral Venipuncture (p. 500) ▶ Discuss the proper technique for obtaining a clean-catch urine specimen for infants and children. Class Activity *Divide the class into small groups. Give each group an anatomically correct doll and a newborn/pediatric urine collection kit. Have groups practice using the kit.* Class Activity *Divide the class into groups. Ask students to discuss urine specimens (clean-catch and 24-hour sample) and stool samples, along with the techniques necessary to collect each specimen from an infant. The groups should list techniques for obtaining these samples, as well as labeling and sending specimens to the lab. Then, have groups present their lists to the class.*
Position an infant for a lumbar puncture.	☐ Lumbar puncture (p. 500)	🅮 EILR IC image 7 🅮 EILR TB question 19 📗 SG Learning Activities, questions 19-21 (p. 179) **BOOK RESOURCES** Figure 22-7, A Child Positioned for a Lumbar Puncture (p. 500) ▶ Discuss the clinical conditions that would require performing a lumbar puncture on a child. Class Activity *Divide the class into small groups, and give each group a doll. Using the doll, students should practice how to position and hold an infant or child for lumbar puncture.*

Leifer

22.1 Homework/Assignments:

22.1 Instructor's Notes/Student Feedback:

Introduction to Maternity & Pediatric Nursing, 6th ed.

Leifer

LESSON 22.2

CRITICAL THINKING QUESTION

An infant, who still wears a diaper, was admitted to the pediatric unit with diarrhea that has lasted for several days. The physician has ordered the application of hydrocortisone cream to the infant's reddened buttocks. Should the nurse be concerned about this order? Explain your answer.

Guidelines: Yes. Hydrocortisone may produce adverse systemic responses when applied to the buttocks and covered with a plastic diaper. Plastic can cause an increase in absorption of the medication.

OBJECTIVES	CONTENT	TEACHING RESOURCES
Calculate the dosage of a medicine that is in liquid form.	■ Physiological responses to medications in infants and children (p. 501) ☐ Absorption of medication in infants and children (p. 501) – Gastric influences (p. 501) – Intestinal influences (p. 501) – Topical medications (p. 501) – Parenteral medications (p. 501) ☐ Metabolism of medications in infants and children (p. 501) ☐ Excretion of medications in infants and children (p. 501)	▣ PPT slides 32-40 *e* EILR OBQ question 8 *e* EILR TB questions 25, 26 SG Learning Activities, questions 22, 23 (pp. 179-108) **BOOK RESOURCES** Review Questions for the NCLEX® Examination, question 3 (p. 528) ▸ Discuss the steps required to determine whether a specific dose of a particular medication in liquid form is safe for an infant. *Class Activity Divide the class into two groups. Have one student from the first group pose a hypothetical dosing situation, and have a student from the other group solve the dosing problem in front of the class. Give each student a turn at presenting or solving a dosing scenario.*
Demonstrate techniques of administering oral, eye, and ear medications to infants and children.	■ Nursing responsibilities in administering medications to infants and children (p. 501) ☐ Parent teaching (p. 502) ☐ Administering oral medications (p. 502) ☐ Administering parenteral medications (p. 503) – Nosedrops, eardrops, and eyedrops (p. 503) – Rectal medications (p. 503)	▣ PPT slides 36-39 *e* EILR IC image 8 *e* EILR OBQ question 10 *e* EILR TB questions 4-6, 10, 24, 29 SG Learning Activities, questions 1, 24, 25 (pp. 177, 180) SG Review Questions, questions 2, 16 (pp. 182-183) **BOOK RESOURCES** Figure 22-8, The Medibottle Is Attached to the Syringe so the Infant Can Suck on the Nipple to Consume the Medication (p. 502) Skill 22-6, Administering Oral Medications to Infants and Children (p. 503)

Introduction to Maternity & Pediatric Nursing, 6th ed.

Elsevier items and derived items © 2011, 2007, 2006 by Saunders, an imprint of Elsevier Inc.

Leifer

OBJECTIVES	CONTENT	TEACHING RESOURCES
		Skill 22-7, Procedure for Administering Nosedrops to the Small Child (p. 504)
		Skill 22-8, Administering Eardrops (p. 504)
		Review Questions for the NCLEX® Examination, question 1 (p. 528)
		▶ Discuss techniques that can be used to administer oral medications to infants or children. What issues relate to the use of various foods to disguise a medication that has a bitter or unpalatable taste?
		Class Activity **Using a mannequin, ask students to demonstrate how to apply ophthalmic medications to an infant's and a child's eyes. Students should discuss general principles of the application of ophthalmic creams. Ask students to explain how the application differs between children and infants.**
		Class Activity **Ask for volunteers to use a doll to demonstrate the following techniques for administering medications:**
		1. Oral medication to an infant
		2. Oral medication to a toddler
		3. Eardrops to a child under the age of 3
		4. Eardrops to a child older than 3
		5. Eyedrops to an infant when there is only one nurse
		6. Eyedrops to an older child
		7. Use of a Medibottle or syringe
Compare the preferred sites for intramuscular injection for infants and adults.	– Subcutaneous and intramuscular injections (p. 504) – Reducing the pain of injections (p. 505)	**e** EILR IC images 9-14 **e** EILR TB questions 11, 14, 15 **sg** SG Learning Activities, questions 26, 27 (p. 180) **sg** SG Review Questions, questions 11, 12 (p. 183) **BOOK RESOURCES** Figure 22-9, Appropriate Sites for IM Injection in Children (p. 505) Medication Safety Alert, (p. 505) Figure 22-10, This Syringe Has a Plastic Sleeve (p. 506) Figure 22-11, The Hug Restraining Position (p. 506) Figure 22-12, The Graduated Control (Burette) Chamber Delivers Microdrops (p. 507) Figure 22-13, Sites for IV Infusion in Children (p. 507)

OBJECTIVES	CONTENT	TEACHING RESOURCES
		Figure 22-14, The Armboard Immobilizes the Arm During IV Therapy and Permits Movement (p. 507)
		Skill 22-9, Removal of a Peripheral Intravenous Catheter (p. 508)
		Review Questions for the NCLEX® Examination, question 2 (p. 528)
		▶ Discuss the advantages of using the thigh, ventrogluteal, and deltoid as intramuscular injection sites in children.
		Class Activity **Divide the class into small groups. Have them use a doll to practice locating the proper injection sites for infants and children. What sites are most appropriate for the medication being administered? Have students explain how injections for children differ from administering injections to adults.**
Discuss two nursing responsibilities necessary when a child is receiving parenteral fluids and the rationale for each.	– Intravenous medications (p. 506) – Long-term peripheral venous access devices (p. 507) – Central venous access devices (p. 507) – Long-term central venous access devices (p. 508) – Total parenteral nutrition (p. 508) – Nursing care of a child receiving parenteral fluids (p. 509) ■ Preventing medication errors (p. 509) ☐ Calculating pediatric drug dosages (p. 515) – Body surface area (p. 515) ☐ Calculating the safe drug dose (p. 516) – Milligrams per kilogram (mg/kg)	▣ PPT slides 40-48 𝒆 EILR IC images 15-17 𝒆 EILR OBQ questions 8, 9 𝒆 EILR TB questions 22, 27-28 𝒆 ESLR IRQ question 5 SG Learning Activities, questions 1, 28-30 (pp. 177, 180) SG Review Questions, question 5 (p. 182) SG Thinking Critically, questions 2, 3 (p. 184) SG Applying Knowledge, questions 2, 5 (p. 184) **BOOK RESOURCES** Figure 22-15, Catheter Placement for Total Parenteral Nutrition (TPN) (p. 509) Table 22-5, Nursing Guidelines for Pediatric IVs at Various Stages of Development (pp. 510-514) Figure 22-16, Pedi-Slide Chart (p. 515) Medication Safety Alert, (p. 515) Figure 22-17, Nomogram for Estimating Surface Area (p. 515) Box 22-1, Selected Age-Appropriate Techniques of Giving Medications to Children, (p. 516) Table 22-6, Drug-Environment Interactions (p. 517)

OBJECTIVES	CONTENT	TEACHING RESOURCES
	(p. 516) – Dimensional analysis (p. 517) – Determining whether a dose is safe for an infant (p. 517) ☐ Preventing drug interactions (p. 517) – Selected drug-environment interactions (p. 517) – Selected drug-drug interactions (p. 517) – Selected drug-food interactions (p. 517)	Box 22-2, Formula for Dimensional Analysis (p. 517) Table 22-7, Selected Drug-Drug Interactions (p. 518) Table 22-8, Selected Drug-Food Interactions (p. 518) ▶ Discuss adverse effects that can result from administration of total parenteral nutrition (TPN), including hypoglycemia, hyperglycemia, and electrolyte imbalances. *Class Activity Ask each student to name a nursing responsibility associated with the care of a pediatric patient who requires an IV. What nursing guidelines for pediatric IVs are used at the various stages of child development? (See Table 22-5, pp. 510-514)*
Demonstrate appropriate technique for gastrostomy tube feeding.	■ Adaptation of selected procedures to children (p. 519) ☐ Nutrition, digestion, and elimination (p. 519) – Gavage feedings (p. 519) – Gastrostomy (p. 519) – Enema (p. 519)	PPT slides 49-51 SG Learning Activities, question 31 (p. 180) SG Review Questions, question 14 (p. 183) SG Applying Knowledge, question 4 (p. 184) **BOOK RESOURCES** Nursing Tips, (p. 519) Skill 22-10, Gastrostomy Tube Feeding (p. 520) ▶ Discuss how the gastrointestinal tract of an infant affects the absorption of various medications. How would it differ between oral and gastrostomy tube administration?
Summarize the care of a child receiving oxygen.	☐ Respiration (p. 519) – Tracheostomy care (p. 519) – Oxygen therapy (p. 522) – Management of airway obstruction (p. 524)	PPT slides 52-56 EILR IC images 18-21 EILR OBQ question 10 EILR TB questions 12, 30 SG Learning Activities, questions 32-35 (p. 181) SG Review Questions, questions 4, 7, 14 (p. 182) SG Applying Knowledge, question 3 (p. 184) **BOOK RESOURCES** Figure 22-18, Tracheostomy (p. 521)

OBJECTIVES	CONTENT	TEACHING RESOURCES
		Box 22-3, Selected Considerations for the Child Receiving Oxygen (p. 523)
		Figure 22-19, This Infant Is in an Infant Seat to Maintain Fowler's Position While in a Mist Tent (p. 524)
		Figure 22-20, Child Receiving Blow-By Oxygen Therapy Via Nasal Catheter (p. 524)
		Figure 22-21, Procedures for Clearing an Airway Obstruction (p. 524)
		Safety Alerts, (pp. 524-525)
		Review Questions for the NCLEX® Examination, question 4 (p. 528)
		▸ Discuss safety considerations and indications for various methods of oxygen administration. What materials should be avoided? What infection-control measures should be employed?
		*Class Activity **Have students present safety measures that are used during oxygen therapy.***
Recall the principles of tracheostomy care.	☐ Tracheostomy care (p. 519) – Tracheostomy tube (p. 521) – Suctioning (p. 521) – Tracheal stoma (p. 521) – Observing for complications (p. 521) – Additional nursing measures (p. 522) – Discharge (p. 522) – Management of airway obstruction (p. 524)	PPT slides 52-57 EILR TB questions 12, 13 SG Learning Activities, questions 32-35 (p. 181) SG Review Questions, questions 4, 7, 14 (p. 182) SG Applying Knowledge, questions 3, 4 (p. 184) **BOOK RESOURCES** ▸ Demonstrate the correct techniques to be used during tracheostomy care to the class. Ask students to offer rationales for each step as you move from one step to the next.
List the adaptations necessary when preparing a pediatric patient for surgery.	☐ Preoperative and postoperative care (p. 525) ☐ Surgery and body piercing, body jewelry, and tattoos (p. 525)	PPT slides 58, 59 EILR IC image 22 EILR TB question 26 SG Learning Activities, question 36 (p. 181) **BOOK RESOURCES** Figure 22-22, Preparing the Child for the Sights and Sounds of Surgery (p. 525)

OBJECTIVES	CONTENT	TEACHING RESOURCES
		Table 22-9, Comparative Summary of Preparation of the Adult and Child for Surgery (p. 526)
		Table 22-10, Comparative Summary of Postoperative Care of the Adult and Child After Surgery (p. 527)
		▶ Discuss the similarities and differences in preoperative and postoperative care for a child and an adult.
		Class Activity Referring to Table 22-9, have students list the typical nursing procedures that are performed before surgery. Students should describe—and when possible, demonstrate—how these procedures are performed on infants and children. In addition, have students describe how preparing children for surgery differs from preparing adults.
Performance Evaluation		⊠▪ PPT slides 1-61
		e EILR IC images 1-22
		e EILR OBQ questions 1-10
		e EILR TB questions 1-30
		e ESLR IRQ questions 1-5
		SG Learning Activities, questions 1-36 (pp. 177-181)
		SG Review Questions, questions 1-17 (pp. 181-183)
		SG Thinking Critically, questions 1-3 (p. 184)
		SG Applying Knowledge, questions 1-5 (p. 184)
		BOOK RESOURCES
		NCP CTQ 1 (p. 497)
		Review Questions for the NCLEX® Examination, questions 1-5 (p. 528)

22.2 Homework/Assignments:

22.2 Instructor's Notes/Student Feedback:

22 | Lecture Outline
Health Care Adaptations for the Child and Family

Slide 1

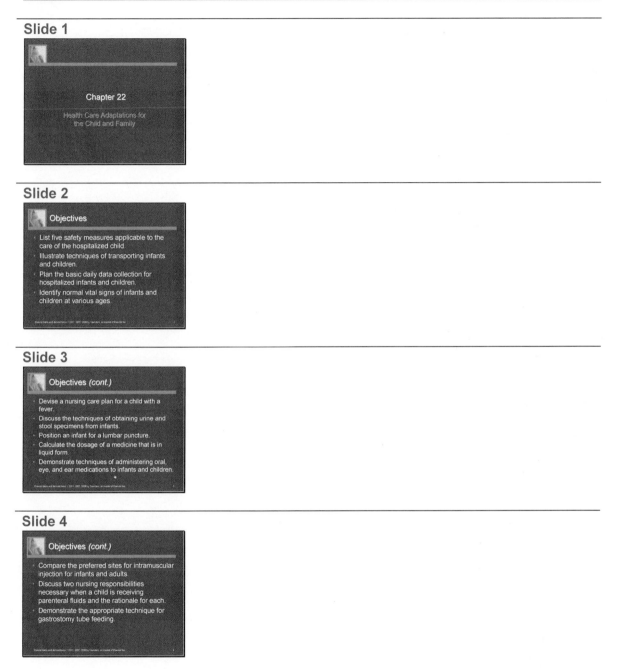

Chapter 22

Health Care Adaptations for
the Child and Family

Slide 2

Objectives

- List five safety measures applicable to the care of the hospitalized child.
- Illustrate techniques of transporting infants and children.
- Plan the basic daily data collection for hospitalized infants and children.
- Identify normal vital signs of infants and children at various ages.

Slide 3

Objectives *(cont.)*

- Devise a nursing care plan for a child with a fever.
- Discuss the techniques of obtaining urine and stool specimens from infants.
- Position an infant for a lumbar puncture.
- Calculate the dosage of a medicine that is in liquid form.
- Demonstrate techniques of administering oral, eye, and ear medications to infants and children.

Slide 4

Objectives *(cont.)*

- Compare the preferred sites for intramuscular injection for infants and adults.
- Discuss two nursing responsibilities necessary when a child is receiving parenteral fluids and the rationale for each.
- Demonstrate the appropriate technique for gastrostomy tube feeding.

Slide 5

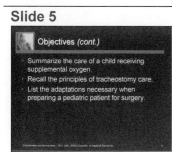

Slide 6

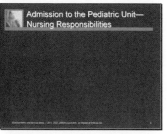

Slide 7

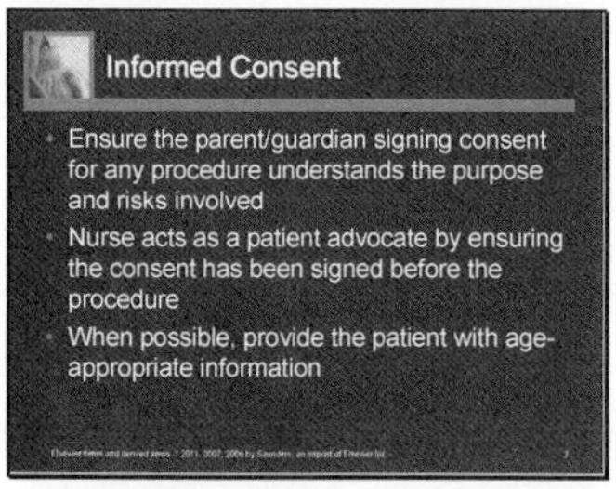

- Give an example of a situation in which informed consent is necessary and communicate the information to a child.

Slide 8

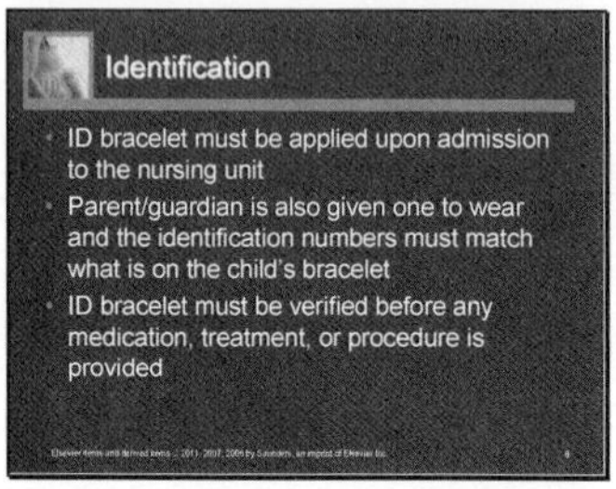

- Discuss the importance of verifying ID bracelets on the child and the parent/guardian.
- Discuss safety measures while applying the bands and for discharge.

Leifer

Slide 9 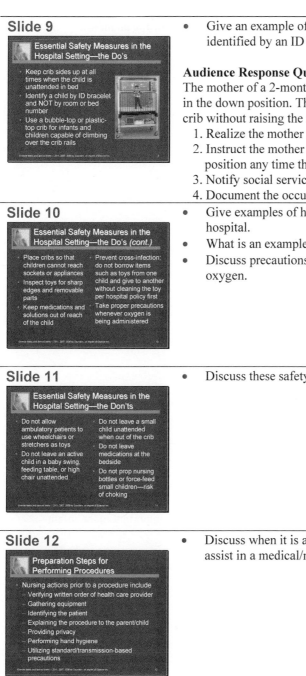	• Give an example of a potentially dangerous situation if a child is not identified by an ID bracelet.

Audience Response Question #1

The mother of a 2-month-old patient is changing his diaper with the crib rail in the down position. The nurse observes the mother walk away from the crib without raising the rail. The nurse should:

1. Realize the mother feels comfortable regarding the safety of her child.
2. Instruct the mother that crib rails must be returned to the upward position any time the child is unattended in the crib.
3. Notify social services and the pediatrician.
4. Document the occurrence in the medical record.

Slide 10

• Give examples of how to minimize unsafe conditions within the hospital.
• What is an example of a cross-infection situation?
• Discuss precautions that should be instituted when administering oxygen.

Slide 11

• Discuss these safety measures.

Slide 12

• Discuss when it is and is not appropriate for a parent or caregiver to assist in a medical/nursing procedure.

Slide 13

Transporting, Positioning, and Restraining the Infant

- Method depends on age, level of consciousness, and how far the child must travel
- Older children are transported as adults are
- Young children—cribs, wagons, pediatric-sized wheelchair, or gurney
- Side rails are up
- ID bracelet has been checked to ensure the correct child is being transported
- The nurse documents time, method of transport, where child is transported, and who is accompanying child

- What are some improper methods of transporting an infant?

Slide 14

Transporting, Positioning, and Restraining the Infant *(cont.)*

- Discuss Figure 22-4, A-D, on page 490.

Slide 15

Verifying the Child Assessment

- Children are different from adults.
- Data collection is done to determine the level of wellness, the response to medication or treatment, or the need for referral.

Slide 16

Organizing the Infant Assessment

- Select a warm, non-stimulating room
- Expose only areas of body to be examined
- Observe without touching first, with minimal touching next, and with invasive touch last to assess reflexes and blood pressure
- Talk softly
- Utilize pacifier to comfort infant
- Swaddle/hold after assessment complete
- Utilize parent teaching opportunities
- Document findings

- Discuss why these organizational steps are important in the infant assessment process.

Slide 17

Basic Data Collection

- Observation
  - How does the child look?
- Growth and development
  - Are child's size and actions age-appropriate?
- Level of interaction between child and environment
  - Is child's behavior withdrawn, normal for age and development, or inappropriate?
- Is the child tipping his head or rubbing his ears?
- Is child maintaining a rigid body posture in order to breathe?
- Are there any obvious bruises (especially in various stages of healing) or cuts?
- How clean is the child?

- Give examples of situations in which the nurse must assess and observe growth and development.

ELSEVIER

Slide 18	
The History Survey Allows the nurse to teach parents about child's needs as well as injury and illness prevention Should include questions about complementary and alternative medicine, over-the-counter medications, and immunization history · Should also include Child's health and eating habits Sleeping Toileting Activity patterns Use of special words or gestures in order to communicate with others	• Give an example of information gained during the history in which the nurse can teach the parents injury prevention. • What is the rationale for the nurse obtaining eating, toileting, sleeping, and activity patterns?

Slide 19	

The Physical Survey
 	
· Head-to-toe review upon admission and then at least once per shift or clinic visit
· Vital signs
  Temperature
  Weight
  Blood pressure
  Pulse
  Respiration rate
 	
· Hydration status
· Heart sounds
· Lung sounds
· Bowel sounds
· Skin—rashes/lesions
	• Tachycardia is often the first sign of shock or body stress in infants and children.
	• Hypotension could be a late sign of shock because of a compensatory mechanism that is activated early—this is an emergency!
	• Mottled skin on the extremities is not unusual.
	• Infants have a large body surface area and high metabolic rate that are prone to fluid loss and hypothermia as well as cold stress.
	• Hydration status:
	  – Sunken fontanel could indicate dehydration.
	  – Bulging fontanels could indicate increased intracranial pressure (ICP). In an older child and adult, increased ICP is manifested by increased systolic BP, widening pulse pressure, irregular respirations, and bradycardia. In an infant, increased ICP might only be manifested by a decreased level of consciousness.

Audience Response Question #2

A child's weight is 57 pounds upon admission. The nurse converts this to _____ kilograms.
1. 23
2. 26
3. 28.5
4. 114

Slide 20	
Pulse Rate · Apical pulse advised for children younger than 5 years of age · Radial pulse used for children older than 5 years of age · Pulse rate increases as temperature increases	• Discuss the importance of obtaining an apical pulse for one full minute.

Slide 21	
Blood Pressure (BP) · The width of the cuff should be of the upper arm · Electronic BP machines do not require auscultation with stethoscope · Normal BP is lower in children than in adults · Can secure BP cuff over brachial, popliteal, or femoral artery · A BP reading taken when an infant is crying may not be accurate	• What methods are used to obtain a BP of the brachial, popliteal, or femoral arteries? • Discuss the reason for inaccurate BP readings of children who are crying.

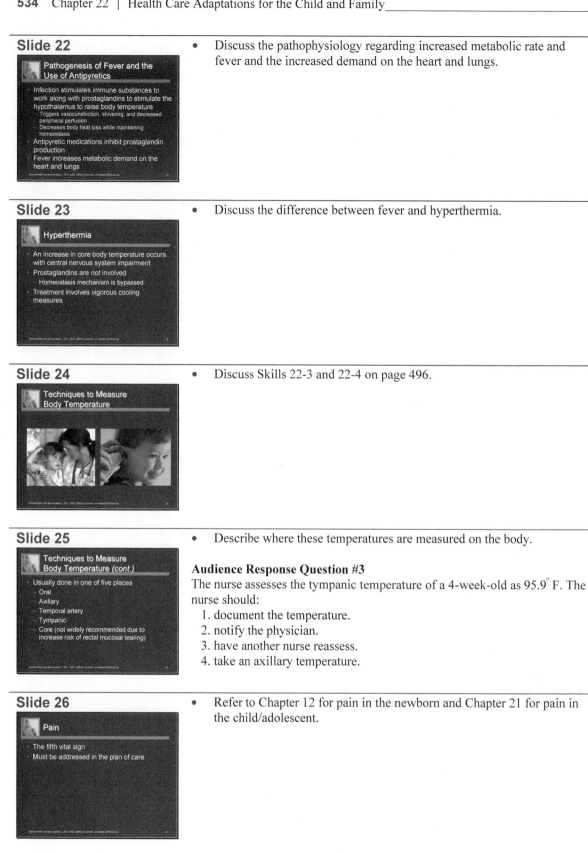

Slide 22

Pathogenesis of Fever and the Use of Antipyretics

- Infection stimulates immune substances to work along with prostaglandins to stimulate the hypothalamus to raise body temperature
  - Triggers vasoconstriction, shivering, and decreased peripheral perfusion
  - Decreases body heat loss while maintaining homeostasis
- Antipyretic medications inhibit prostaglandin production
- Fever increases metabolic demand on the heart and lungs

- Discuss the pathophysiology regarding increased metabolic rate and fever and the increased demand on the heart and lungs.

Slide 23

Hyperthermia

- An increase in core body temperature occurs with central nervous system impairment
- Prostaglandins are *not* involved
  - Homeostasis mechanism is bypassed
- Treatment involves vigorous cooling measures

- Discuss the difference between fever and hyperthermia.

Slide 24

Techniques to Measure Body Temperature

- Discuss Skills 22-3 and 22-4 on page 496.

Slide 25

Techniques to Measure Body Temperature *(cont.)*

- Usually done in one of five places
  - Oral
  - Axillary
  - Temporal artery
  - Tympanic
  - Core (not widely recommended due to increase risk of rectal mucosal tearing)

- Describe where these temperatures are measured on the body.

Audience Response Question #3
The nurse assesses the tympanic temperature of a 4-week-old as 95.9° F. The nurse should:
  1. document the temperature.
  2. notify the physician.
  3. have another nurse reassess.
  4. take an axillary temperature.

Slide 26

Pain

- The fifth vital sign
- Must be addressed in the plan of care

- Refer to Chapter 12 for pain in the newborn and Chapter 21 for pain in the child/adolescent.

Slide 27 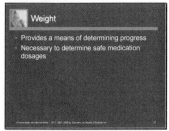	• Review techniques to use based on the age of the infant or child.

Slide 28 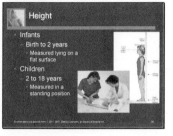	• Discuss proper procedures to measure height of infants and children.

Slide 29 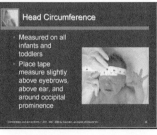	• What is the importance of head circumference measurement?

Slide 30 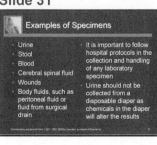	• What is the importance of proper documentation when obtaining and sending a specimen to the lab?

Slide 31	• Review the techniques for obtaining specimens listed.

Slide 32

Physiological Responses to Medications in Infants and Children

- Understanding the differences in drug absorption, distribution, metabolism, and excretion between children and adults is essential to provide safe pediatric medication administration
- Age is the most important variable in predicting response to any drug therapy

Slide 33

Absorption of Medications in Infants and Children

- Gastric influences
- Intestinal influences
- Topical medications (ointments)
- Parenteral medications

- How might medications be absorbed differently when administered by these various routes?
- What factors need to be considered in the pediatric patient prior to administering any medications?

Slide 34

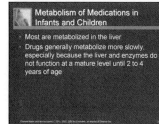

Metabolism of Medications in Infants and Children

- Most are metabolized in the liver
- Drugs generally metabolize more slowly, especially because the liver and enzymes do not function at a mature level until 2 to 4 years of age

Slide 35

Excretion of Medications in Infants and Children

- Many medications depend on the kidney for excretion
- If younger than 1 year of age, the immature kidney function prevents effective excretion of drugs from the body
- Combination of
  - Slow stomach emptying
  - Rapid intestinal transmit time
  - Unpredictable liver function
  - Inability to effectively excrete medications via the kidney
- Can result in altered responses and places the child at risk for toxicity

- Discuss the pathophysiology regarding excretion of medications via the renal system.

Slide 36

Administering Medications to Infants and Children

ELSEVIER

Slide 37

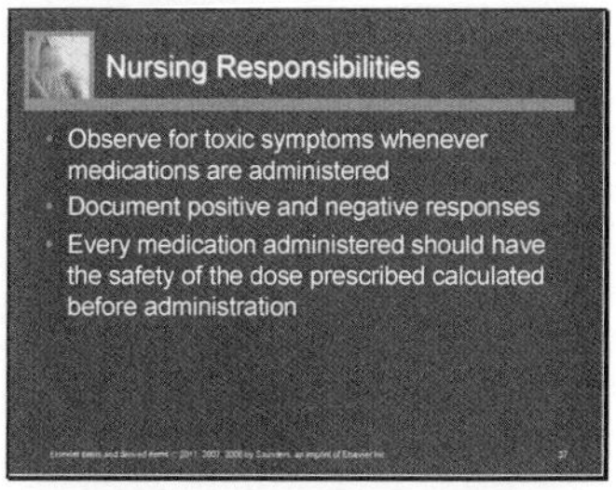

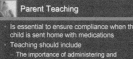

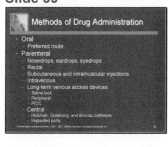

- Give an example of toxic symptoms the nurse might assess in a child.
- What are some examples of negative responses to medications?

Slide 38

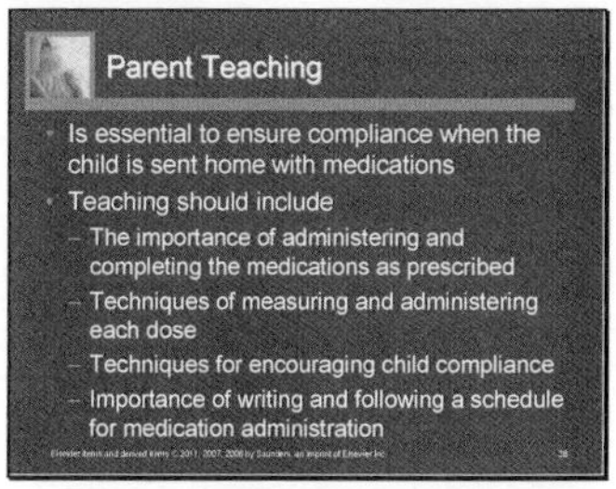

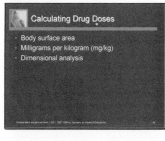

Slide 39

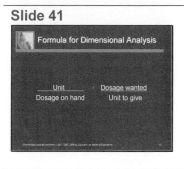

- Review the various techniques and safety measures for each method and for each age group.

Slide 40

Calculating Drug Doses

- Body surface area
- Milligrams per kilogram (mg/kg)
- Dimensional analysis

Slide 41

Formula for Dimensional Analysis

| Unit | Dosage wanted |
| Dosage on hand | Unit to give |

- Provide measurements and allow students to calculate medication using the dimensional analysis method.

Slide 42

Safety Alert

Maximum volume for IM administration
- Infants—0.5 mL
- Toddlers—1 mL
- School-age/adolescent
  - Deltoid—1 mL
  - Vastus lateralis—2 mL

- Discuss why this is important to follow.

Slide 43

Total Parenteral Nutrition

- Also known as *hyperalimentation*
- Provides nutritional needs to those who cannot use the gastrointestinal tract for nourishment for a prolonged period of time

- Allows highly concentrated solutions of protein, glucose, and other nutrients to infuse into a large vessel
- It is important for the nurse to monitor and report the following
  - Hypoglycemia
  - Hyperglycemia
  - Electrolyte imbalances

- Give an example of a child's situation that requires TPN.
- Discuss the pathophysiology regarding hyperglycemia, hypoglycemia, and electrolyte imbalances.

Slide 44

Nursing Care of a Child Receiving Parenteral Fluids

- Observe the child hourly for
  - Low volume in the bag or the need to refill the burette
  - The rate of flow of the solution
  - Pain, redness, or swelling at the needle insertion site
  - Moisture at or around the needle insertion site
- Accurate I&O is kept for all children receiving IV fluids

- Discuss the importance of monitoring the child every hour.

Slide 45

Nursing Care of a Child Receiving Parenteral Fluids *(cont.)*

- Key components to remember when providing intravenous therapies
  - The developmental level of the child
  - IV placement
  - Preparation of the child prior to insertion
  - Related nursing actions
  - Protection of the IV site
  - Mobility considerations
  - Safety needs

- Review nursing guidelines for IV therapy at various stages of development in Table 22-5, pages 510-514.

Slide 46

Preventing Medication Errors

- 6 Rights of Medication Administration
  - Patient
  - Drug
  - Dose
  - Time
  - Route
  - Documentation

ELSEVIER

Slide 47

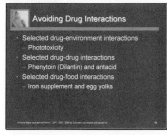

Factors to Consider for Pediatric IVs

- Developmental characteristics
- Site where IV is to be inserted
- Preparation of child
- Family Involvement
- Related nursing actions
- Protection of IV site
- Mobility Considerations
- Safety needs

Slide 48

Avoiding Drug Interactions

- Selected drug-environment interactions
  - Phototoxicity
- Selected drug-drug interactions
  - Phenytoin (Dilantin) and antacid
- Selected drug-food interactions
  - Iron supplement and egg yolks

Slide 49

- What is the proper technique when administering a gavage feeding?

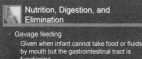

Nutrition, Digestion, and Elimination

- Gavage feeding
  - Given when infant cannot take food or fluids by mouth but the gastrointestinal tract is functioning
  - Places nutrients directly into the stomach so that natural digestion can occur

Slide 50

Nutrition, Digestion, and Elimination *(cont.)*

- Gastrostomy
  - Tube surgically placed through the abdominal wall into the stomach
  - Used in infants or children who cannot have food by mouth because of anomalies or strictures of the esophagus, severe debilitation, or coma
- Brown or green drainage may indicate that the tube has slipped from the stomach into the duodenum. This can cause an obstruction and is reported immediately.

Slide 51

- Give examples of isotonic solutions.
- What is a potential complication when administering a tap-water enema? *Fluid overload*

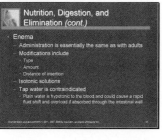

Nutrition, Digestion, and Elimination *(cont.)*

- Enema
  - Administration is essentially the same as with adults
  - Modifications include
    - Type
    - Amount
    - Distance of insertion
  - Isotonic solutions
  - Tap water is contraindicated
    - Plain water is hypotonic to the blood and could cause a rapid fluid shift and overload if absorbed through the intestinal wall

Slide 52

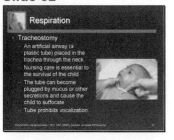

- Discuss Figure 22-18 on page 521.

Slide 53

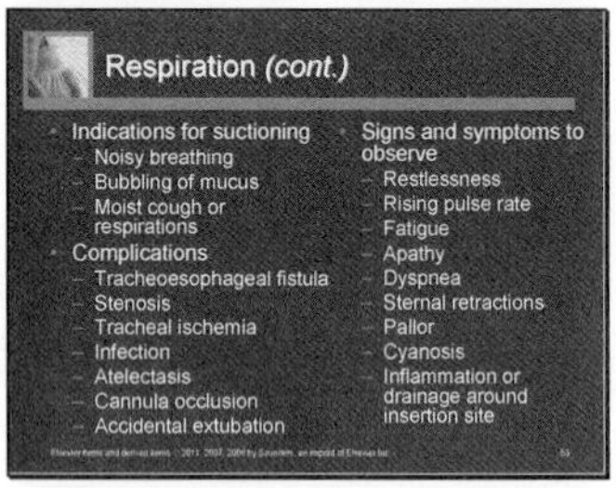

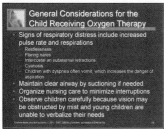

- Review the technique for correctly performing suctioning.

Slide 54

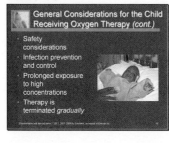

Slide 55

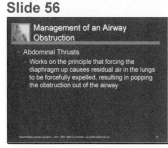

- Discuss Figure 22-20 on page 524.
- Review safety considerations when administering oxygen.

Slide 56

Management of an Airway Obstruction

- Abdominal Thrusts
  - Works on the principle that forcing the diaphragm up causes residual air in the lungs to be forcefully expelled, resulting in popping the obstruction out of the airway

Leifer

Slide 57

- Discuss the proper procedure for treating a child/infant with an airway obstruction.

Slide 58

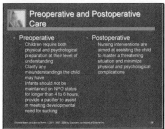

Slide 59

Slide 60

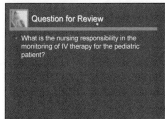

Slide 61

Leifer

TEACHING FOCUS

This chapter introduces students to eye and ear conditions that are often found in infants and children, including the pathophysiology, symptoms, treatment, and nursing care. Students are introduced to the challenges involved with caring for the hearing-impaired child. The second part of this chapter gives an overview of neurological conditions, including meningitis, developmental disabilities, cerebral palsy, seizure disorders, and head injuries. Students will have the opportunity to learn appropriate and effective nursing care of the pediatric patient and the patient's family and how to educate the family regarding home care.

MATERIALS AND RESOURCES

- ☐ 3-D models of the ear and eye (Lesson 23.1)
- ☐ 3-D model of the brain and CNS (Lesson 23.2)
- ☐ Computer and PowerPoint (all lessons)
- ☐ List of online resources for more information on specific conditions (all lessons)

LESSON CHECKLIST

Preparations for this lesson include:

- Lecture
- Guest speaker: A nurse currently working with infants or children with cerebral palsy, a representative from the Epilepsy Foundation, a parent, or member of a local support group on mental retardation
- Evaluation of student knowledge and skills needed to perform all entry-level activities related to the child with a sensory or neurological condition, including:
  - ○ Knowledge of the key terms related to common sensory or neurological conditions found in children
  - ○ Familiarity with the physiology of the ear, eye, and nervous system and their corresponding functions
  - ○ Developing an appropriate nursing care plan for pediatric patients and their families
  - ○ Understanding effective nursing interventions in head injury cases
  - ○ Performing a neurological check

KEY TERMS

amblyopia (p. 535)
athetosis (p. 548)
aura (p. 544)
barotrauma (p. 534)
clonic movement (p. 543)
cognitive impairment (p. 551)
concussion (p. 553)
conjunctivitis (p. 536)
dyslexia (p. 535)
encephalopathy (p. 539)
enucleation (p. 537)
epicanthal folds (p. 535)
extensor posturing (p. 554)

flexor posturing (p. 554)
generalized seizures (p. 544)
grand mal (p. 544)
hyperopia (p. 536)
idiopathic (p. 544)
intracranial pressure (ICP) (p. 540)
ketogenic diet (p. 546)
mental retardation (p. 551)
myringotomy (p. 532)
neurological check (p. 538)
nystagmus (p. 543)
opisthotonos (p. 541)

papilledema (p. 543)
paroxysmal (p. 544)
partial seizures (p. 544)
petit mal (p. 544)
postictal (p. 544)
posturing (p. 554)
sepsis (p. 540)
shaken baby syndrome (p. 554)
sign language (p. 533)
status epilepticus (p. 547)
strabismus (p. 536)
tonic movement (p. 543)
tympanometry (p. 533)

ADDITIONAL RESOURCES

TEACH PPT slide(s) Chapter 23, 1-82
EILR IC image(s) Chapter 23, 1-14
EILR OBQ question(s) Chapter 23, 1-10
EILR TB question(s) Chapter 23, 1-31
ESLR IRQ question(s) Chapter 23, 1-6
SG Chapter 23, pp. 185-194

Leifer

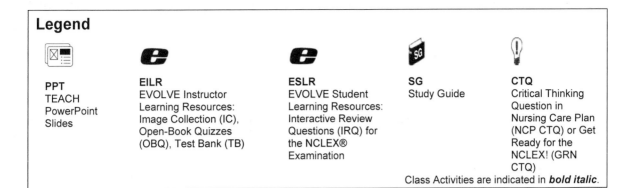

Legend

PPT
TEACH
PowerPoint
Slides

EILR
EVOLVE Instructor
Learning Resources:
Image Collection (IC),
Open-Book Quizzes
(OBQ), Test Bank (TB)

ESLR
EVOLVE Student
Learning Resources:
Interactive Review
Questions (IRQ) for
the NCLEX®
Examination

SG
Study Guide

CTQ
Critical Thinking
Question in
Nursing Care Plan
(NCP CTQ) or Get
Ready for the
NCLEX! (GRN
CTQ)

Class Activities are indicated in ***bold italic***.

LESSON 23.1

PRETEST

1. The nurse is preparing to instill eardrops into a 9-month-old baby's ear. What should she gently do to the pinna of the ear?
   a. Pull it up and back.
   b. Pull it down and back.
   c. Pull it toward the face.
   d. Pull it straight back.

2. An early sign that a 2-month-old infant may be hearing impaired is
   a. a lack of crying.
   b. a lack of response to parents' touch.
   c. a lack of startle response.
   d. frequent pulling on the ears.

3. A reading disability involving a defect in the way the brain processes graphic symbols is
   a. dyslexia.
   b. amblyopia.
   c. strabismus.
   d. hyphema.

4. A 7-year-old child was given baby aspirin when she exhibited flu-like symptoms. This puts the child at risk for
   a. salicylate poisoning.
   b. sepsis.
   c. Reye's syndrome.
   d. meningitis.

5. Prior to assisting with the lumbar puncture of a 10-month-old infant, the nurse applies EMLA cream to his spinal area to
   a. calm the infant.
   b. reduce discomfort during needle insertion.
   c. disinfect the area.
   d. prevent swelling following the procedure.

6. An 8-year-old child has a blank stare, then rapidly starts blinking. He starts to chew but has nothing in his mouth. These behaviors last 7 seconds. What type of seizure is he most likely experiencing?
   a. general (grand mal)
   b. partial (Jacksonian)
   c. atonic (drop attack)
   d. absence (petit mal)

7. A nurse caring for a hospitalized 4-year-old boy with cerebral palsy should
   a. avoid discussing religious affiliation with his parents.
   b. give the child a complete bed bath.
   c. be sure that his head is not tilted back when eating or drinking.
   d. allow him to apply his new leg braces himself.

8. How should the nurse address a 12-year-old child with an IQ of 67?
   a. focus on and praise his strengths
   b. speak loudly and slowly so that he will understand
   c. assume that he needs to be dressed and fed
   d. direct questions about the child only to his parents, family, or guardian

9. A nurse sees a 5-year-old child fall and bump his head in the parking lot. What question should the nurse ask the child in order to assess the child's level of consciousness?
   a. What day is it?
   b. What is your address?
   c. What city is this?
   d. What is your name?

10. In the United States, the fourth leading cause of death for children less than 19 years of age is
    a. child abuse.
    b. drowning.
    c. motor vehicle accidents.
    d. falls.

Answers

1. b	3. a	5. b	7. c	9. d
2. c	4. c	6. d	8. a	10. b

BACKGROUND ASSESSMENT

Question: What are five factors that can lead to mental retardation? How could each be prevented?
Answer: Congenital rubella and measles encephalitis can be prevented by antibody screening and immunization. Head trauma can be prevented by child safety restraints in vehicles and helmets. Child neglect and abuse can be prevented by parenting classes and family life education in school. Fetal alcohol syndrome can be prevented by abstinence from alcohol intake during pregnancy and public education. Neural tube defects

can be prevented by taking folic acid supplements before and during pregnancy. Mental retardation caused by prematurity can be prevented by neonatal intensive care units. Mental retardation as a result of lead poisoning can be prevented by screening for lead levels, improving the environment, and through chelation.

Question: Name three diseases that could cause an altered state of consciousness in a 6-year-old child. Define each condition and identify the symptoms. How does the mental status of the child differ for each disease?

Answer: (1) Reye's syndrome is an acute non-inflammatory encephalopathy and hepatopathy following a viral infection. Nausea and vomiting precede a sudden change in mental status. These changes may vary from mild amnesia and lethargy to disorientation and agitation that progress to coma. Seizures, flaccidity, and fixed dilated pupils can occur. (2) Sepsis is the presence of bacteria in the bloodstream. It may follow an infection or result from a primary infection. Symptoms include fever, rapid breathing and heart rate, and hypotension. The child becomes lethargic and could go into shock. (3) Encephalitis is an acute inflammation of the brain caused by a virus. It may be secondary to rubella, mumps, chickenpox, or a reaction to a smallpox vaccination. Symptoms can include fever, cramps, abdominal pain, neck stiffness, and muscle twitching. Headache followed by drowsiness can progress to coma. The child could also experience delirium. In a seizure disorder, there are sudden, intermittent periods of altered consciousness lasting anywhere from a few seconds to several minutes, possibly accompanied by involuntary clonic and tonic movements. The length and severity of the seizures depend on the type and cause.

CRITICAL THINKING QUESTION

A nurse has been assigned to care for a 2-year-old boy who has been scheduled for a myringotomy with tube insertion. How should the nurse explain this surgical intervention and its indications to the child's parents? What instructions should the nurse provide the patient's parents prior to discharge?

Guidelines: During a myringotomy, a small incision is made into the child's eardrum and a small tube is inserted to drain fluid from the middle ear. This intervention is performed for children who experience any of the following: repeated ear infections that do not improve with antimicrobials; fluid in the ears and loss of hearing for more than 3 months or changes in the actual structure of the eardrum from ear infections. The nurse should provide the parents with the following instructions: call the physician if the tube falls out; the correct way to administer prescribed ear drops and analgesics; to use a cold compress to reduce swelling and pressure; keep water out of the ear canal until the eardrum is intact; avoid inserting cotton swabs into the ears; and not to allow the child to play with anything small enough to be inserted into the ears.

OBJECTIVES	CONTENT	TEACHING RESOURCES

Discuss the prevention and treatment of ear infections.	■ The ears (p. 529)
	
	■ Disorders and dysfunction of the ear (p. 531)
	
	  □ Otitis externa (p. 531)
	
	  □ Acute otitis media (p. 531)
		⊠ PPT slides 6-15
		
		𝒆 EILR IC images 1, 2
		
		𝒆 EILR OBQ question 1
		
		𝒆 EILR TB questions 1, 2, 25
		
		SG Learning Activities, questions 2-8 (pp. 185-186)
		
		SG Review Questions, question 1 (p. 191)
		
		SG Case Study, question 2 (p. 193)
		
		BOOK RESOURCES
		
		Figure 23-1, Summary of Ear, Eye, and Neurological Differences Between the Child and the Adult (p. 530)
		
		Figure 23-2, Anatomy of the Ear (p. 530)
		
		Nursing Tip (p. 531)
		
		Nursing Tip (p. 532)

Introduction to Maternity & Pediatric Nursing, 6th ed.

OBJECTIVES	CONTENT	TEACHING RESOURCES
		Review Questions for the NCLEX® Examination, question 1 (p. 560)
		Class Activity Using a 3-D model of the ear, describe the ear's anatomy, and point out the differences between the ear of a child and that of an adult.
		Class Activity Have students call out the differences between otitis externa and otitis media. Lead a class discussion on how these conditions can be prevented. Ask the class to list appropriate nursing interventions. Have a volunteer demonstrate on another student who is role-playing a child the correct way of instilling eardrops. Have the student role-playing the child portray ear infection symptoms.
Outline the nursing approach to caring for the hearing-impaired child.	☐ Hearing impairment (p. 532) ☐ Barotrauma (p. 534)	⊞ PPT slides 16-21 *e* EILR OBQ question 2 *e* EILR TB questions 3-5, 26, 27 SG Learning Activities, questions 1, 9-12 (pp. 185-186) SG Review Questions, question 11 (p. 193) **BOOK RESOURCES** Nursing Tip (p. 532) ▸ Discuss how temporary hearing loss may affect development and socialization of the child. *Class Activity Have one student role-play a hearing-impaired child and another student role-play the nurse giving the child a flu shot. Have the student demonstrate how the nurse should approach the child to administer the vaccine. The class should evaluate the nurse and his or her approach and offer additional ideas or corrections.*
Discuss the cause and treatment of amblyopia.	■ The eyes (p. 534) ☐ Visual acuity tests (p. 535) ☐ Dyslexia (p. 535) ☐ Amblyopia (p. 535)	⊞ PPT slides 22-26 *e* EILR IC images 3, 4 *e* EILR OBQ question 3 *e* EILR TB question 7 SG Learning Activities, questions 13-16 (pp. 186-187) SG Applying Knowledge, question 2 (p. 193) **BOOK RESOURCES** Figure 23-3, The Normal Eye (p. 534)

Introduction to Maternity & Pediatric Nursing, 6th ed.

OBJECTIVES	CONTENT	TEACHING RESOURCES
		Figure 23-4, Various Types of Visual Acuity Charts (p. 535) Nursing Tips (p. 535) ▶ Discuss the challenges in testing visual acuity in toddlers and preschoolers. Invite students to share creative alternatives to the traditional testing of adults. *Class Activity **Point out parts of the eye on a 3-D model. Have the class refer to Figure 23-3 (p. 534) and identify the parts of the eye. Discuss changes in the eye associated with amblyopia. Ask the class to explain how an eye patch would strengthen the weakened eye.***
Compare the treatment of paralytic and nonparalytic strabismus.	☐ Strabismus (p. 536)	⊞ PPT slides 27-29 *e* EILR OBQ question 4 *e* EILR TB question 6 SG Learning Activities, questions 1, 17 (pp. 185, 187) **BOOK RESOURCES** Nursing Tip (p. 536) ▶ Discuss the common symptoms of strabismus. What are some of the nurse's challenges in postoperative care? *Class Activity **Have a student role-play a child with strabismus (e.g., squinting or frowning to focus, missing objects reached for, tilting head to one side to see, covering one eye to see). Ask the class to identify treatments for this child (e.g., surgery, eye patch, glasses, eye exercises).***
Review the prevention of eyestrain in children.	☐ Conjunctivitis (p. 536) ☐ Hyphema (p. 537) ☐ Retinoblastoma (p. 537)	⊞ PPT slides 30-34 *e* EILR IC image 5 *e* EILR TB questions 8, 20 *e* ESLR IRQ questions 2, 6 SG Learning Activities, questions 1, 18-20 (pp. 185, 187) **BOOK RESOURCES** Figure 23-5, Acute Bacterial Conjunctivitis (p. 537) *Class Activity **Ask the class to call out myths concerning eyestrain (e.g., sitting too close to the television, reading in the dark, crossing eyes intentionally). Have the students compare these myths to actual causes of eyestrain (e.g., heredity, weak muscles, sneezing, blow to eye, irritants).***

23.1 Homework/Assignments:

23.1 Instructor's Notes/Student Feedback:

LESSON 23.2

CRITICAL THINKING QUESTION

A 3-year-old boy is a new patient with a diagnosis of seizure disorder. What possible types of seizures might the child be experiencing and how are they characterized? What aspects of the boy's seizure activity should the nurse observe and document? What instructions regarding the seizures should the nurse provide to his parents?

Guidelines: A febrile seizure occurs when a child's illness is accompanied by fever. Partial (Jacksonian) seizures involve only one portion of the body. Generalized seizures are convulsive (grand mal) or absence (petit mal). Status epilepticus is a seizure lasting 30 minutes or longer, or repeated seizures without a return to normal between them. The nurse would observe the patient and document the length of occurrence of any of the following characteristics of a seizure: clonic and tonic movements; loss of awareness; repetitive movements, such as chewing, clapping, or lip-smacking followed by confusion; rolling back of the eyes; evidence of an aura; and jerking of one area of the body. The boy's parents should be instructed to take the following actions if a seizure occurs: call 911 if he is not breathing; help him lie down as soon as a seizure is apparent; do not put anything into his mouth; remove any harmful objects on or around him; do not give him anything by mouth immediately after the seizure; and use prescribed suppositories.

OBJECTIVES	CONTENT	TEACHING RESOURCES
Discuss the functions of the 12 cranial nerves and nursing interventions for dysfunction.	■ The nervous system (p. 537)	▣▤ PPT slides 35-37 𝒆 EILR IC images 6, 7 𝒆 EILR OBQ questions 6, 10 𝒆 ESLR IRQ question 5 📕 SG Learning Activities, question 21 (p. 187) **BOOK RESOURCES** Figure 23-6, A, Functional Areas of the Brain. B, The Nervous System (p. 538) Figure 23-7, The Cranial Nerves and Their Functions (p. 539) Box 23-1, Causes of Altered Level of Consciousness (p. 539) Safety Alert (p. 539) Table 23-1, The 12 Cranial Nerves: Selected Dysfunctions and Nursing Interventions (p. 540) ▸ Discuss the brain and nervous system. Allow students to examine 3-D models of the brain and nervous system and discuss the functional areas and pathways. *Class Activity Divide the class into three groups and assign each group one of the following: olfactory, optic, oculomotor, and trochlear nerves; trigeminal, abducens, facial, and acoustic nerves; the glossopharyngeal, vagus, spinal accessory, and hypoglossal nerves. Each group is to explain the function of its assigned nerves to the class.* *Class Activity Name an intervention (e.g., change position, provide visually attractive food, protect eyes*

OBJECTIVES	CONTENT	TEACHING RESOURCES
		from glaring lights, have suction ready, assess for aspiration, provide soft foods). Members of the group (see preceding Class Activity) that were assigned the nerve that relates to the intervention should respond by identifying the correct nerve.
Outline the prevention, treatment, and nursing care for the child with Reye's syndrome.	☐ Reye's syndrome (p. 539) ☐ Sepsis (p. 540)	PPT slides 38-42 *e* EILR OBQ question 5 *e* EILR TB questions 9, 10 *e* ESLR IRQ question 1 SG Learning Activities, questions 22, 23 (p. 187) SG Review Questions, question 2 (p. 191) **BOOK RESOURCES** Medication Safety Alert (p. 540) Review Questions for the NCLEX® Examination, question 3 (p. 560) *Class Activity Present the following scenario: a 10-year-old boy is hospitalized with Reye's syndrome following a period of varicella. Have the class discuss how this could have been prevented (immunization, avoid salicylates), how it can be treated (ICP, patent airway), and appropriate nursing care (assess vital signs and neurological status, perform parental education, observe for signs of bleeding and hypoglycemia).*
Discuss the symptoms of meningitis in a child.	☐ Meningitis (p. 541) ☐ Encephalitis (p. 542) ☐ Brain tumors (p. 542)	PPT slides 43-48 *e* EILR IC images 8, 9 *e* EILR TB questions 18, 22-28, 31 *e* ESLR IRQ question 3 SG Learning Activities, questions 1, 24-30 (pp. 185, 187-188) SG Review Questions, questions 3, 6, 12, 13 (pp. 191, 193) SG Case Study, question 1 (p. 193) **BOOK RESOURCES** Figure 23-8, The Opisthotonos Position (p. 541) Safety Alert (p. 541) Nursing Tip (p. 542)

OBJECTIVES	CONTENT	TEACHING RESOURCES
		Figure 23-9, Signs of Increased ICP in Infants and Children (p. 543) Nursing Tip (p. 543) *Class Activity **Describe a 6-month-old infant with meningitis. Ask the class to call out the symptoms they would observe in this baby (e.g., poor feeding, drowsiness, vomiting, restlessness and irritability, fever, stiff neck, high-pitched cry, convulsions).***
Discuss the various types of seizures and the nursing responsibilities.	☐ Seizure disorders (p. 543) – Febrile seizures (p. 544) – Epilepsy (p. 544)	PPT slides 49-55 *e* EILR IC image 10 *e* EILR OBQ question 6 *e* EILR TB questions 11-16, 29 *e* ESLR IRQ question 4 SG Learning Activities, questions 1, 31-35 (pp. 185, 188-189) SG Review Questions, questions 5, 7, 9, 10 (p. 192) SG Thinking Critically, question 1 (p. 193) SG Applying Knowledge, question 1 (p. 193) **BOOK RESOURCES** Box 23-2, Causes of Seizures in Children (p. 543) Table 23-2, Seizure Recognition and First Aid Response (pp. 545-546) Table 23-3, Properties of Selected Anticonvulsant Drugs (p. 547) Figure 23-10, Phenytoin-Induced Gum Hyperplasia (p. 547) Medication Safety Alerts (pp. 546-547) Nursing Tip (p. 548) Review Questions for the NCLEX® Examination, question 5 (p. 560) ▸ Discuss some of the common triggering factors for seizures. Have students role-play what to do when a child has a seizure. *Class Activity **Invite a representative from the Epilepsy Foundation to talk to the class about the current management of the disease.***

OBJECTIVES	CONTENT	TEACHING RESOURCES
		Class Activity *Divide the class into three groups. Have one group explain a grand mal seizure. Have the second group explain a petit mal seizure. Have the third group explain partial seizures.* **Class Activity** *Have two students role-play a child having a grand mal seizure and a nurse who demonstrates care for the child in a postictal state. The class is to evaluate the role-play.*

23.2 Homework/Assignments:

23.2 Instructor's Notes/Student Feedback:

Leifer

LESSON 23.3

CRITICAL THINKING QUESTION

A 6-year-old boy has developed cerebral palsy (CP) from a near-drowning 16 months ago. His parents would like to know what they should expect of the child regarding his education and future. Why would a near-drowning cause CP? What should the nurse tell the parents about realistic goals for their son?

Guidelines: In a near-drowning event, the child is deprived of oxygen while underwater. His brain suffers anoxia. The asphyxia causes the CP. In terms of expectations for the future, the parents need to maintain an optimistic, yet realistic, outlook. The parents should understand the boy's present and future abilities. The nurse should ask the parents about their goals for the boy, and tactfully point out those objectives that are unrealistic. The boy should be allowed and encouraged to function at the maximum level of his ability. Future expectations are usually more important in the teenage years and beyond, when function is better defined and the future looks clearer to all of those involved in his care. School counselors should be consulted for the best type of schools for the child based on his personal needs and abilities.

OBJECTIVES	CONTENT	TEACHING RESOURCES
Formulate a nursing care plan for the child with a decreased level of consciousness.	☐ Other conditions causing decreased level of consciousness (p. 548) – Benign paroxysmal vertigo (p. 548) – Night terrors (p. 548) – Breath-holding spells (p. 548) – Cough syncope (p. 548) – Prolonged QT syndrome (p. 548) – Rage attacks, or episodic dyscontrol syndrome (p. 548)	☒ PPT slide 56 *Class Activity Present the following scenarios: A 4-year-old child, hospitalized for asthma, has a cough syncope. Ask the class when this might happen, what would result, and how to avoid it.* *Second scenario: A 3-year-old child is holding his breath until he becomes cyanotic because he does not get a toy that he wanted. Ask the class what they would counsel the parent (e.g., do not become alarmed, avoid reinforcing behavior, ignore child). When should the child be given attention?*
Describe four types of cerebral palsy and the nursing goals involved in care.	☐ Cerebral palsy (p. 548)	☒ PPT slides 57-61 𝓮 EILR IC images 11, 12 𝓮 EILR OBQ question 9 𝓮 EILR TB question 17 📗 SG Learning Activities, questions 36-38 (p. 185) 📗 SG Review Questions, questions 4, 17 (pp. 191, 193) 📗 SG Applying Knowledge, question 3 (p. 193) **BOOK RESOURCES** Figure 23-11, A Child with Spastic Cerebral Palsy (p. 549)

Introduction to Maternity & Pediatric Nursing, 6^(th) ed.

Elsevier items and derived items © 2011, 2007, 2006 by Saunders, an imprint of Elsevier Inc.

Leifer

OBJECTIVES	CONTENT	TEACHING RESOURCES
		Table 23-4, Types of Cerebral Palsy (p. 549)
		Skill 23-1, General Modifications/Precautions in Pediatric Feeding Techniques for Children with Cerebral Palsy (p. 550)
		Figure 23-12, Feeding the Disabled Child (p. 550)
		Box 23-3, Treatment Protocol for Cerebral Palsy (p. 551)
		Review Questions for the NCLEX® Examination, question 2 (p. 560)
		Class Activity **Invite a nurse currently working with infants or children with cerebral palsy to discuss this specialty and its challenges. Include a discussion of the impact on the family and the nurse's role in education and supportive care.**
		Class Activity **Divide the class into four groups, one for each type of cerebral palsy (spastic, athetoid, ataxic, and mixed cerebral palsy). Each group is to research its type in the textbook, with a focus on nursing goals, and report its findings to the class for discussion and comparison.**
Prepare a plan for success in the care of a mentally retarded child.	☐ Cognitive impairment (p. 551) – Mental retardation (p. 551)	PPT slides 62-69 SG Learning Activities, question 39 (p. 189) SG Review Questions, question 15 (p. 193) **BOOK RESOURCES** Box 23-4, American Association on Mental Retardation (AAMR) Definition of Mental Retardation (p. 551) Box 23-5, Elements Involved in Mental Functioning (p. 552) Nursing Tip (p. 552) Nursing Tip (p. 553) Table 23-5, Interventions Currently Available to Prevent Mental Retardation (p. 553) Review Questions for the NCLEX® Examination, question 4 (p. 560) ▸ Discuss the importance of a sense of accomplishment in a child. How can a nurse foster this quality in the care of a mentally retarded child? What are some of the other challenges likely to be encountered in the care of a mentally retarded child? *Class Activity* **Request a parent or member of a local support group on mental retardation to attend and speak to the class about his or her mentally retarded child.**

ELSEVIER

Introduction to Maternity & Pediatric Nursing, 6th ed.
Leifer

23.3 Homework/Assignments:

23.3 Instructor's Notes/Student Feedback:

LESSON 23.4

CRITICAL THINKING QUESTION

A 7-month-old baby girl is brought into the emergency department by her mother's boyfriend, who was babysitting for her. The baby is in an irritable state. The nurse overhears the physician say that he suspects shaken baby syndrome. What might cause the physician to state this suspicion? What signs should the nurse look for that might indicate that the infant has suffered a head injury?
Guidelines: The physician will examine the infant for retinal hemorrhages, subdural hematoma, and fluid in the brain tissue. Signs of spinal cord damage and broken ribs could also indicate shaken baby syndrome. The baby may have bruising on her upper arms, in the axilla, or on her sides, indicating she was grasped too hard. The physician may also have seen the baby in the emergency department in the past with poor feeding, afebrile vomiting, or flu-like symptoms, lethargy, and irritability over a period of time. The nurse should watch this infant for convulsions and seizures, vomiting, drowsiness or loss of consciousness, increased fussiness, swelling of the head, fixed pupils, difficulty breathing, and decerebrate or decorticate posturing.

OBJECTIVES	CONTENT	TEACHING RESOURCES
Describe signs of increased intracranial pressure in a child.	☐ Head injuries (p. 553)	⊠▣ PPT slides 70-73 *e* EILR TB question 24 SG Learning Activities, questions 1, 43 (pp. 185, 190) SG Review Questions, question 8 (p. 192) **BOOK RESOURCES** Safety Alert (p. 554) Nursing Care Plan 23-1, The Child with Altered Level of Consciousness (pp. 558-559) *Class Activity Present the following scenario:* *A 3-year-old child is thrown from his improperly secured car seat when his mother rear-ends another car. The child hits his head on the door.* *Ask the class to identify the signs of increased intracranial pressure they should watch for in this child (e.g., drowsiness, pupillary reaction, dyspnea, blurred vision, vomiting, headache, change in alertness, etc.).*
Describe three types of posturing that may indicate brain damage.	☐ Head injuries (p. 553)	⊠▣ PPT slides 74-76 *e* EILR IC image 13 *e* EILR TB question 30 SG Learning Activities, questions 1, 40 (pp. 185, 190) **BOOK RESOURCES** Figure 23-13, Posturing (p. 554) Nursing Tip (p. 554) *Class Activity Choose three volunteers from the class to demonstrate decerebrate, decorticate, and opisthotonos*

ELSEVIER

OBJECTIVES	CONTENT	TEACHING RESOURCES
		posturing. Ask the class to identify each posturing and what type of brain injury may be involved that would cause such posturing.
Describe the components of a "neurological check."	□ Head injuries (p. 553)	🖳 PPT slides 77, 78 *e* EILR IC image 14 *e* EILR OBQ question 10 *e* EILR TB question 21 📖 SG Learning Activities, question 41 (p. 190) 📖 SG Review Questions, question 14 (p. 193) **BOOK RESOURCES** Figure 23-14, The Response of the Pupil of the Eye to a Flashlight Beam (p. 555) Box 23-6, Neurological Monitoring of Infants and Children (p. 555) Safety Alert (p. 555) *Class Activity **Have the class identify and discuss the components involved in a neurological check (e.g., motor function, muscle mass, pupillary check, orientation, cranial nerve dysfunction, etc.).*** *Class Activity **Have students work in pairs to perform a neurological check on each other. Be sure all aspects of the check are properly performed.***
Discuss neurological monitoring of infants and children.	□ Head injuries (p. 553)	🖳 PPT slides 77, 78 *e* EILR IC images 13, 14 **BOOK RESOURCES** Figure 23-13, Posturing (p. 554) Figure 23-14, The Response of the Pupil of the Eye to a Flashlight Beam (p. 555) Safety Alert (p. 555) Box 23-6, Neurological Monitoring of Infants and Children (p. 555)
State a method of determining level of consciousness in an infant.	□ Head injuries (p. 553) – Level of consciousness (p. 555)	📖 SG Learning Activities, question 42 (p. 190) 📖 SG Review Questions, question 16 (p. 193) **BOOK RESOURCES** Table 23-6, The Glasgow Coma Scale Modified for Infants (p. 557)

OBJECTIVES	CONTENT	TEACHING RESOURCES
		Safety Alert (p. 558)
		Nursing Care Plan 23-1, The Child with Altered Level of Consciousness (pp. 558-559)
		Class Activity **Set up three scenarios: a conscious, verbal child; a conscious, nonverbal child; and a nonresponsive, unconscious child. Have the class identify ways to determine each child's level of consciousness.**
Identify the priority goals in the care of a child who experienced near-drowning.	☐ Near-drowning (p. 558)	⊠▪ PPT slides 79, 80
		📖 SG Learning Activities, question 44 (p. 190)
		BOOK RESOURCES
		Safety Alert (p. 558)
		Nursing Care Plan 23-1, The Child with Altered Level of Consciousness (pp. 558-559)
		▸ Discuss the priority of care for a child who has experienced near-drowning. Include the prevention of hypoxia, aspiration, and hypothermia. When is hospitalization necessary?
		Class Activity **Present the following scenario: a 2-year-old toddler falls into his grandmother's swimming pool. The grandmother finds him face down and pulls him out. Have the class work in groups to identify and describe the priority of goals (e.g., open patient airway, breathing, call 911, reflexes, etc.). Students should then present their goals, in order of priority, to the class.**
Performance Evaluation		⊠▪ PPT slides 1-82
		𝒆 EILR IC images 1-14
		𝒆 EILR OBQ questions 1-10
		𝒆 EILR TB questions 1-31
		𝒆 ESLR IRQ questions 1-6
		📖 SG Learning Activities, questions 1-44 (p. 185-190)
		📖 SG Review Questions, questions 1-17 (pp. 192-193)
		📖 SG Case Study, questions 1, 2 (p. 193)
		📖 SG Thinking Critically, question 1 (p. 193)
		📖 SG Applying Knowledge, questions 1-3 (p. 194)
		BOOK RESOURCES

OBJECTIVES	CONTENT	TEACHING RESOURCES
		Review Questions for the NCLEX® Examination, questions 1-5 (p. 560)
		💡 GRN CTQ 1 (p. 560)

23.4 Homework/Assignments:

23.4 Instructor's Notes/Student Feedback:

23 Lecture Outline
The Child with a Sensory or Neurological Condition

Slide 1

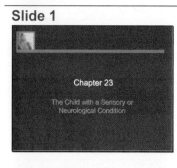

Chapter 23

The Child with a Sensory or
Neurological Condition

Slide 2

Objectives

- Discuss the prevention and treatment of ear infections.
- Outline the nursing approach to serving the hearing-impaired child.
- Discuss the cause and treatment of amblyopia.
- Compare the treatment of paralytic and nonparalytic strabismus.
- Review the prevention of eyestrain in children.

Slide 3

Objectives *(cont.)*

- Discuss the functions or the 12 cranial nerves and nursing interventions for dysfunction.
- Describe the components of a "neurological check."
- Outline the prevention, treatment, and nursing care for the child with Reye's syndrome.
- Describe the symptoms of meningitis in a child.
- Describe three types of posturing that may indicate brain damage.

Slide 4

Objectives *(cont.)*

- Discuss the various types of seizures and the nursing responsibilities.
- Prepare a plan for success in the care of a mentally retarded child.
- Describe four types of cerebral palsy and the nursing goals involved in care.
- State a method of determining level of consciousness in an infant.

Leifer

Slide 5

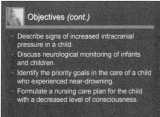

Objectives *(cont.)*

- Describe signs of increased intracranial pressure in a child.
- Discuss neurological monitoring of infants and children.
- Identify the priority goals in the care of a child who experienced near-drowning.
- Formulate a nursing care plan for the child with a decreased level of consciousness.

Slide 6

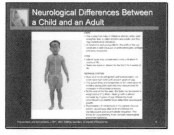

Neurological Differences Between a Child and an Adult

- Discuss the differences between the nervous system of a child and an adult.

Slide 7

Ears

- Contains the receptors of the eighth cranial (acoustic) nerve
- Two main functions
  - Hearing
  - Balance
- Three divisions
  - External
  - Middle
  - Internal

Newborn
- Tympanic membrane almost horizontal
- More vascular
- Inconsistent light reflex
- Eustachian tube is shorter and straighter than in adult
- Eustachian tube functions
  - Ventilation
  - Protection
  - Drainage

- Discuss the differences of the newborn's ear versus an adult's ear.
- Discuss how the eustachian tube functions.

Audience Response Question #1
Breastfed infants are less likely to get middle ear infections than formula fed infants.
1. True
2. False

Slide 8

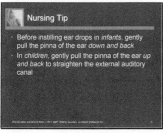

Ears *(cont.)*

- Ear alignment is observed
- Top of ear should cross imaginary line drawn from outer canthus of eye to the occiput
- Low-set ears may be associated with kidney disorders

- Demonstrate how to measure ear alignment.
- What is the significance of ear alignment?

Slide 9

Nursing Tip

- Before instilling ear drops in *infants*, gently pull the pinna of the ear *down and back*
- In *children*, gently pull the pinna of the ear *up and back* to straighten the external auditory canal

Slide 10

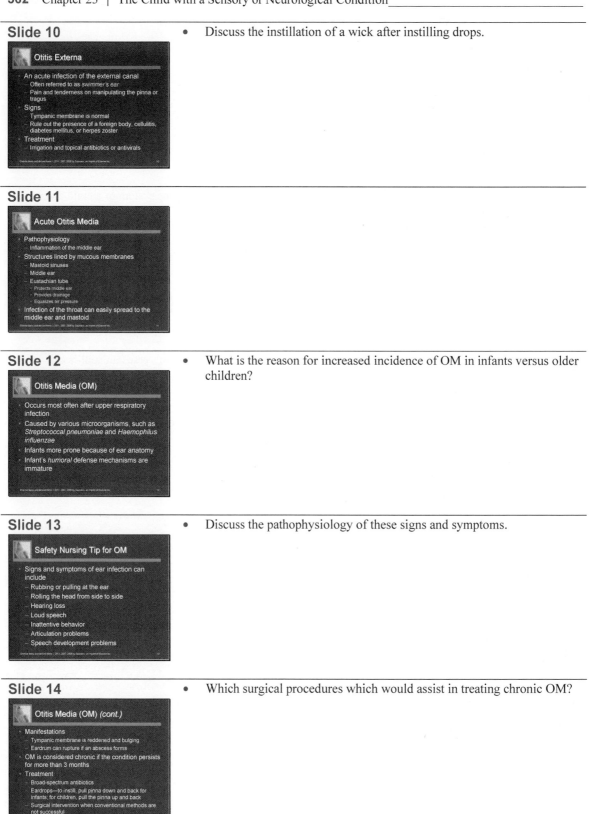

> **Otitis Externa**
>
> - An acute infection of the external canal
>   - Often referred to as *swimmer's ear*
>   - Pain and tenderness on manipulating the pinna or tragus
> - Signs
>   - Tympanic membrane is normal
>   - Rule out the presence of a foreign body, cellulitis, diabetes mellitus, or herpes zoster
> - Treatment
>   - Irrigation and topical antibiotics or antivirals

- Discuss the instillation of a wick after instilling drops.

Slide 11

> **Acute Otitis Media**
>
> - Pathophysiology
>   - Inflammation of the middle ear
> - Structures lined by mucous membranes
>   - Mastoid sinuses
>   - Middle ear
>   - Eustachian tube
>   - Protects middle ear
>   - Provides drainage
>   - Equalizes air pressure
> - Infection of the throat can easily spread to the middle ear and mastoid

Slide 12

> **Otitis Media (OM)**
>
> - Occurs most often after upper respiratory infection
> - Caused by various microorganisms, such as *Streptococcal pneumoniae* and *Haemophilus influenzae*
> - Infants more prone because of ear anatomy
> - Infant's *humoral* defense mechanisms are immature

- What is the reason for increased incidence of OM in infants versus older children?

Slide 13

> **Safety Nursing Tip for OM**
>
> - Signs and symptoms of ear infection can include
>   - Rubbing or pulling at the ear
>   - Rolling the head from side to side
>   - Hearing loss
>   - Loud speech
>   - Inattentive behavior
>   - Articulation problems
>   - Speech development problems

- Discuss the pathophysiology of these signs and symptoms.

Slide 14

> **Otitis Media (OM)** *(cont.)*
>
> - Manifestations
>   - Tympanic membrane is reddened and bulging
>   - Eardrum can rupture if an abscess forms
> - OM is considered chronic if the condition persists for more than 3 months
> - Treatment
>   - Broad-spectrum antibiotics
>   - Eardrops—to instill, pull pinna down and back for infants; for children, pull the pinna up and back
>   - Surgical intervention when conventional methods are not successful

- Which surgical procedures which would assist in treating chronic OM?

Slide 15

> **Teaching Nursing Tip**
>
> - Instruct caregivers that the child's condition may improve dramatically after antibiotics are taken for a few days
> - To prevent recurrence, caregivers must continue to administer the medication until the prescribed amount has been completed

Slide 16

> **Hearing Impairment**
>
> - Can affect speech, language, social and emotional development, behavior, and academic achievement
> - Two types: congenital deafness or acquired
>   - Can acquire it from common colds, medications, exposure to loud noise levels, certain infectious diseases
>   - Hearing loss can also be from cerumen (earwax) accumulation or from a foreign body being inserted in the ear canal

- Discuss how chronic ear infections could cause hearing impairment.
- Discuss how cerumen can safely be removed from the ear canal.

Slide 17

> **Hearing Impairment** *(cont.)*
>
> - Hearing loss can result from
>   - Defects in the transmission of sound to the middle ear
>   - Damage to the auditory nerve or ear structures
>   - A mixed loss involving both a defect in nerve pathways and interference with sound transmission
> - Behavior problems may arise because these children do not understand verbal directions

- What behaviors might a child with hearing impairment exhibit?

Slide 18

> **Hearing Impairment** *(cont.)*
>
> - Diagnosis
>   - Routine newborn hearing screens are performed before discharge
>   - Lack of a response by the infant to sounds or music, or the lack of a startle reflex in infants under 4 months of age are the first signs that a hearing impairment may exist
> - Medical or surgical treatment
>   - Hearing aids
>   - Cochlear implants

- Give an example of situations in which a nurse or parent can assess hearing response in an infant.
- Discuss the method of insertion and function of cochlear implants.

Slide 19

> **Hearing Impairment** *(cont.)*
>
> - Nursing care
> - Some means of communicating with the hearing-impaired include
>   - Lip reading, sign language, writing, visual aids
>   - Body language communicates a lot

- What are examples of visual aids that could enhance communication?
- Give examples of body language that an infant and toddler could understand.

Slide 20

Patient Teaching

When addressing a hearing-impaired child, the nurse should do the following
- Be at eye level with the child
- Be face-to-face with the child
- Establish eye contact
- Talk in short sentences
- Avoid using exaggerated face or lip movements

- Discuss the rationale for communicating at eye level and face-to-face with the child.
- Why might exaggerated face or lip movements hinder communication?

Slide 21

Barotrauma

An injury that occurs when the pressure in the atmosphere between a closed space and the surrounding area changes
- Airplane descent
- Underwater diving

- Yawning, chewing gum, or sucking on a bottle will help prevent this from occurring when descending in an airplane.
- Decongestants can also be taken, but must be taken at a time to ensure they are at their peak effect when needed for descent.
- Discuss how underwater diving can cause organisms to migrate to the middle ear due to the pressure.
- Descent should be slow to allow for equalization of pressure.
- Sensory hearing loss and vertigo with nausea and vomiting may be an early sign of decompression sickness when it occurs during the ascent phase of diving.
- Diver should be referred for medical care.

Slide 22

The Eyes

- Begin to develop in the 4-week-old embryo
- Newborn sight is not mature
- Shape of eye is less spherical in the newborn
- Tears are not present until 1 to 3 months of age
- Depth perception does not begin to develop until about 9 months of age

- Discuss how objects might appear to a newborn.
- Discuss depth perception.

Slide 23

Health Promotion

- At birth, the quiet alert infant will respond to visual stimuli by cessation of movement
- Visual responsiveness to the mother during feeding is noted
- The infant's ability to focus and follow objects in the first months of life should be documented
- Coordination of eye movements should be achieved by 3 to 6 months of age

Slide 24

Visual Acuity Tests • Ability of an infant to fixate and focus on an object can be demonstrated by 6 weeks of age • The object should not emit a sound • Testing should begin at 2 to 3 years of age	• Discuss the Snellen "E" chart. • How is the Timus machine used?

Slide 25

Dyslexia • Reading disability • Involves a defect in the cortex of the brain that processes graphic symbols • Treatment involves remedial instruction	• Discuss signs and symptoms that a child with dyslexia might exhibit. • How could remedial instruction assist the child with dyslexia?

Slide 26

Amblyopia
 	
• Reduction or loss of vision that usually occurs in children who strongly favor one eye
• Treatment
  – Glasses, opaque contact lens, or patching the good eye
    · Forces the weaker eye to be used
	• Discuss strabismus.
	• When abnormal binocular interaction occurs (in strabismus), the prognosis depends on how long the eye has been affected and the age of the child when treatment begins.
	• Occurs as a result of sensory deprivation of the affected eye, children are at risk for developing the problem until visual stability occurs, usually around 9 years of age.
	• Discuss the nurse's role in assisting the child and family with this disorder.

Slide 27

Strabismus

• Also known as *cross-eye*
• Child is not able to direct both eyes in same direction
  – Lack of coordination between the eye muscles that direct movement of the eyes
  – When coordination does not occur, the brain will disable one eye to provide a clear image
  – The disabled eye can develop permanent visual impairment due to sensory deprivation
• Several types: nonparalytic and paralytic

Slide 28

Health Promotion

• Symptoms of strabismus include the following
  – Eye "squinting" or frowning to focus
  – Missing objects that are reached for
  – Covering one eye to see
  – Tilting the head to see
  – Dizziness and/or headache

Leifer

Slide 29

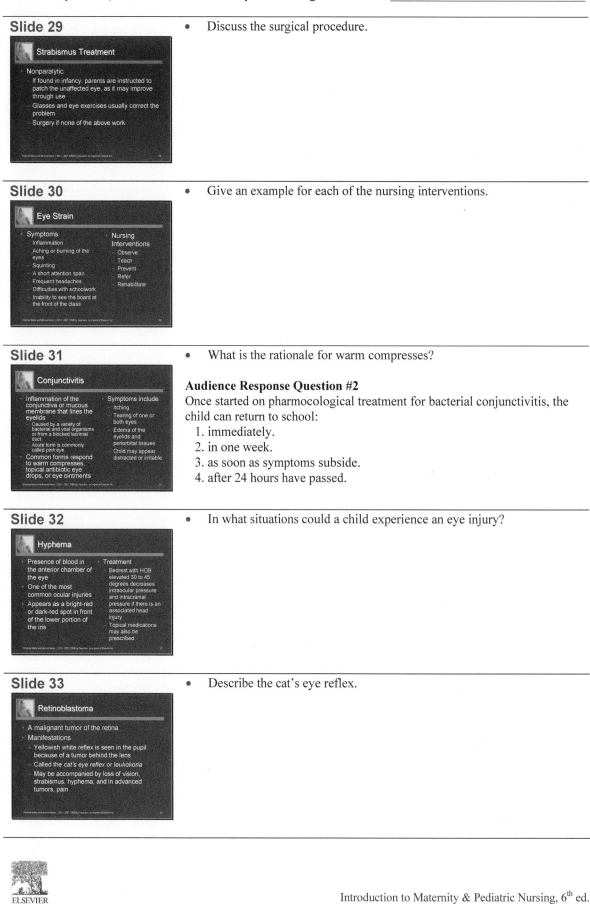

Strabismus Treatment

- Nonparalytic
  - If found in infancy, parents are instructed to patch the unaffected eye, as it may improve through use
  - Glasses and eye exercises usually correct the problem
  - Surgery if none of the above work

- Discuss the surgical procedure.

Slide 30

Eye Strain

- Symptoms
  - Inflammation
  - Aching or burning of the eyes
  - Squinting
  - A short attention span
  - Frequent headaches
  - Difficulties with schoolwork
  - Inability to see the board at the front of the class
- Nursing Interventions
  - Observe
  - Teach
  - Prevent
  - Refer
  - Rehabilitate

- Give an example for each of the nursing interventions.

Slide 31

Conjunctivitis

- Inflammation of the conjunctiva or mucous membrane that lines the eyelids
  - Caused by a variety of bacterial and viral organisms or from a blocked lacrimal duct
  - Acute form is commonly called *pink eye*
- Common forms respond to warm compresses, topical antibiotic eye drops, or eye ointments
- Symptoms include
  - Itching
  - Tearing of one or both eyes
  - Edema of the eyelids and periorbital tissues
  - Child may appear distracted or irritable

- What is the rationale for warm compresses?

Audience Response Question #2
Once started on pharmocological treatment for bacterial conjunctivitis, the child can return to school:
1. immediately.
2. in one week.
3. as soon as symptoms subside.
4. after 24 hours have passed.

Slide 32

Hyphema

- Presence of blood in the anterior chamber of the eye
- One of the most common ocular injuries
- Appears as a bright-red or dark-red spot in front of the lower portion of the iris
- Treatment
  - Bedrest with HOB elevated 30 to 45 degrees decreases intraocular pressure and intracranial pressure if there is an associated head injury
  - Topical medications may also be prescribed

- In what situations could a child experience an eye injury?

Slide 33

Retinoblastoma

- A malignant tumor of the retina
- Manifestations
  - Yellowish white reflex is seen in the pupil because of a tumor behind the lens
  - Called the *cat's eye reflex* or *leukokoria*
  - May be accompanied by loss of vision, strabismus, hyphema, and in advanced tumors, pain

- Describe the cat's eye reflex.

Slide 34

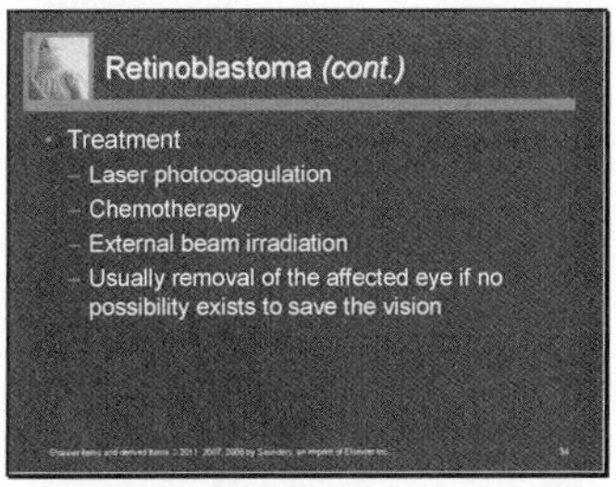

Retinoblastoma *(cont.)*

- Treatment
  - Laser photocoagulation
  - Chemotherapy
  - External beam irradiation
  - Usually removal of the affected eye if no
    possibility exists to save the vision

Slide 35

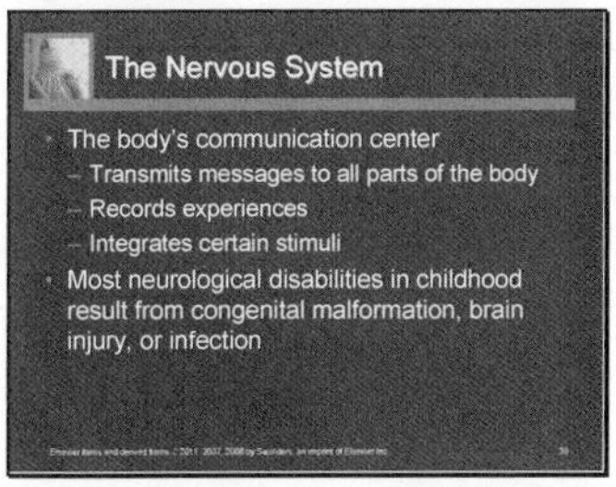

The Nervous System

- The body's communication center
  - Transmits messages to all parts of the body
  - Records experiences
  - Integrates certain stimuli
- Most neurological disabilities in childhood
  result from congenital malformation, brain
  injury, or infection

Slide 36

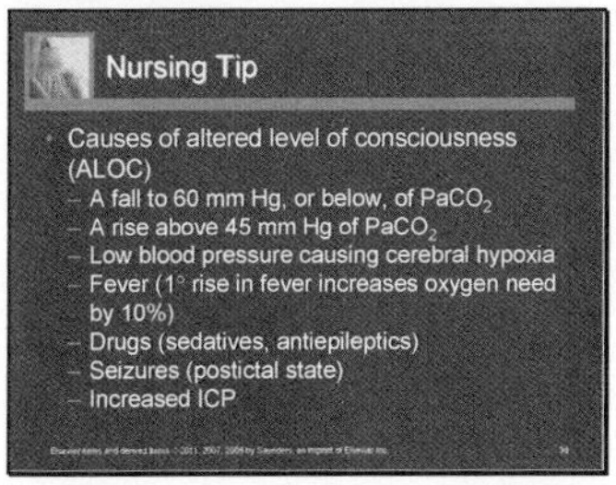

Nursing Tip

- Causes of altered level of consciousness
  (ALOC)
  - A fall to 60 mm Hg, or below, of PaCO$_2$
  - A rise above 45 mm Hg of PaCO$_2$
  - Low blood pressure causing cerebral hypoxia
  - Fever (1° rise in fever increases oxygen need
    by 10%)
  - Drugs (sedatives, antiepileptics)
  - Seizures (postictal state)
  - Increased ICP

- Discuss the pathophysiology which causes ALOC in the postictal state.

Slide 37

Neurological Clock

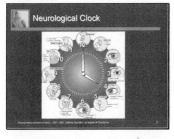

Slide 38

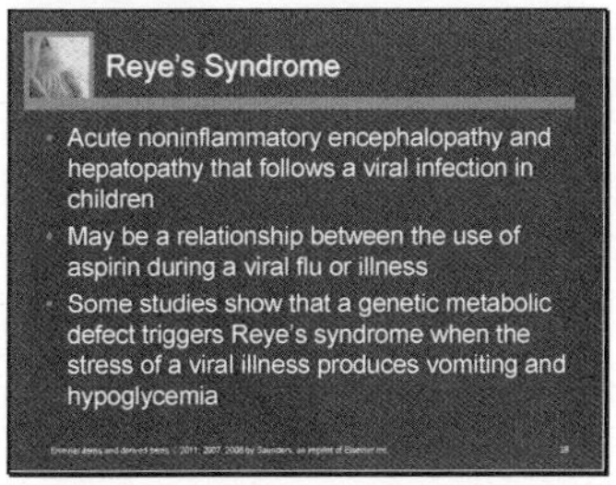

Reye's Syndrome

- Acute noninflammatory encephalopathy and
  hepatopathy that follows a viral infection in
  children
- May be a relationship between the use of
  aspirin during a viral flu or illness
- Some studies show that a genetic metabolic
  defect triggers Reye's syndrome when the
  stress of a viral illness produces vomiting and
  hypoglycemia

Slide 39

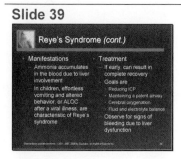

Reye's Syndrome *(cont.)*

Manifestations
- Ammonia accumulates in the blood due to liver involvement
- In children, effortless vomiting and altered behavior, or ALOC after a viral illness, are characteristic of Reye's syndrome

Treatment
- If early, can result in complete recovery
- Goals are
  - Reducing ICP
  - Maintaining a patent airway
  - Cerebral oxygenation
  - Fluid and electrolyte balance
- Observe for signs of bleeding due to liver dysfunction

- Discuss methods to maintain a patent airway.
- Discuss typical diagnostic and routine labs to obtain for a child with this condition.
- Toxic levels of ammonia cause cerebral manifestations, such as ALOC, behavioral changes, seizures, and coma.

Slide 40

Safety Nursing Tip

- Discourage the use of aspirin and other medications that contain salicylates in children with flulike symptoms
- Advise parents to read medication labels carefully to determine their ingredients

Slide 41

Sepsis

- Systemic response to infection with bacteria; also results from viral or fungal infections
- Causes a systemic inflammatory response syndrome (SIRS) due to the endotoxin of the bacteria that causes tissue damage
- Untreated can lead to septic shock, multiorgan dysfunction syndrome (MODS), and death

- What are signs and symptoms of multiorgan dysfunction syndrome?

Slide 42

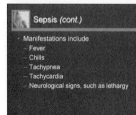

Sepsis *(cont.)*

- Manifestations include
  - Fever
  - Chills
  - Tachypnea
  - Tachycardia
  - Neurological signs, such as lethargy

- In infants, septic shock is not diagnosed by a decrease in BP because initially the infant's body compensates for the poor circulation and tissue perfusion by increasing the heart rate and vasoconstriction of peripheral blood vessels.
- Hypotension in an infant is an ominous sign that may indicate the body is no longer able to compensate adequately and cardiorespiratory arrest is about to occur.

Slide 43

Meningitis

- An inflammation of the meninges (the covering of the brain and spinal cord)
- Caused by bacterial, viral, or fungal (rare in immune-competent person) infection, Haemophilus influenzae most common
- Invades the meninges indirectly by way of the bloodstream (sepsis)
- Bacterial meningitis often referred to as purulent because of pus-forming that can occur

- What methods help prevent or limit a child's exposure to these organisms?
- Peak incidence for bacterial meningitis is 6 to 12 months of age.
- Less common in children older than 4 years of age.

ELSEVIER

Leifer

Slide 44

> ### Meningitis *(cont.)*
>
> **Manifestations**
> - If bacterial, symptoms are a result of intracranial irritation from the purulent toxins released by the bacteria
> - The presence of petechiae suggests meningococcal infection
>
> **Symptoms**
> - Severe headache
> - Drowsiness
> - Delirium
> - Irritability
> - Restlessness
> - Fever
> - Vomiting
> - Stiffness of the neck (nuchal rigidity)
> - High-pitched cry in infants
> - Seizures are common
> - Coma may occur

- Discuss the pathophysiology behind the signs and symptoms.

Slide 45

> ### Meningitis *(cont.)*
>
> - Diagnosis confirmed by examination of the CSF
> - Treatment
>   - The child is placed in droplet isolation until 24 hours after the appropriate antibiotics have been initiated
> - Nursing care
>   - Neurological checks as ordered by physician
>   - Report findings such as weakness of the limbs, speech difficulties, mental confusion, and behavior problems
>   - Maintaining an accurate recording of vital signs and intake/output
>   - Maintain a quiet environment to help decrease stimuli

- Discuss neurological assessment.
- What is the rationale of decreasing environmental stimuli?

Slide 46

> ### Encephalitis
>
> - Inflammation of the brain
>   - Also known as *encephalomyelitis* when the spinal cord is also infected
> - Symptoms result from the CNS's response to irritation
>   - Headache followed by drowsiness
>   - May proceed to coma
>   - Convulsions are seen, especially in infants
>   - Fever, cramps, abdominal pain, vomiting, nuchal rigidity, delirium, muscle twitching, abnormal eye movements

- Discuss the difference between meningitis and encephalitis.

Slide 47

> ### Encephalitis *(cont.)*
>
> - Treatment
>   - Supportive
>   - Provide relief from specific symptoms
>   - Sedatives and antipyretics may be ordered
>   - Seizure precautions are taken
>   - Provide for adequate fluid and nutrition
>   - Supplemental oxygen may be needed

- Discuss nursing interventions which are supportive and relieve symptoms.
- What are some examples of seizure precautions?

Introduction to Maternity & Pediatric Nursing, 6th ed.

Leifer

Slide 48
 	
Brain Tumors
- Second most common type of neoplasm in children
- Most occur in lower part of the brain and commonly in school-age children
- Signs and symptoms directly related to location and size of tumor
- Diagnosis is made by clinical presentation, laboratory tests, head CT or MRI, EEG
- Surgical intervention in some cases, chemotherapy and/or radiation therapy in others
	• Discuss nystagmus and papilledema.
	• Discuss signs and symptoms:
	  – Intracranial pressure (ICP)
	  – Headache
	  – Vomiting
	  – Drowsiness
	  – Seizures
	  – Nystagmus
	  – Strabismus
	  – Papilledema
	  – Ataxia
	  – Head tilt
	  – Behavioral changes
	  – In infants, cerebral enlargement

Slide 49
 	
Seizure Disorders
- Most commonly observed neurological dysfunction in children
- Etiology varies
- Sudden, intermittent episodes of ALOC that last seconds to minutes and may include involuntary tonic and clonic movements
	Audience Response Question #3
	If the nurse witnesses a child begin to seize, the first action should be to:
	  1. note the start time.
	  2. assess vital signs.
	  3. ensure safety.
	  4. insert tongue blade.

Slide 50
 	
Causes of Seizures in Children
- Intracranial
  - Epilepsy
  - Congenital anomaly
  - Birth injury
  - Infection
  - Trauma
  - Degenerative disease
  - Vascular disorder
- Extracranial
  - Fever
  - Heart disease
  - Metabolic disorders
  - Hypocalcemia
  - Hypoglycemia
  - Dehydration and malnutrition
- Toxic
  - Anesthetics
  - Drugs
  - Poisons
	• With which potential drugs and poisons might a child come into contact?

Slide 51
 	
Types of Seizures
- Febrile
- Epilepsy
- Classified as
  - Generalized
    - Tonic-clonic or grand mal
    - Three distinct phases
  - Partial
    - Account for 40%
    - Consciousness may be intact or slightly impaired
    - Can have simple or complex seizures
	• Discuss and give examples of the difference between generalized and partial seizures.
	• Describe the three phases of generalized seizures.
	  – Aura
	  – Tonic/clonic seizure
	  – Postictal
	
	Audience Response Question #4
	The higher the fever the increased risk of febrile seizure.
	  1. True
	  2. False

Slide 52

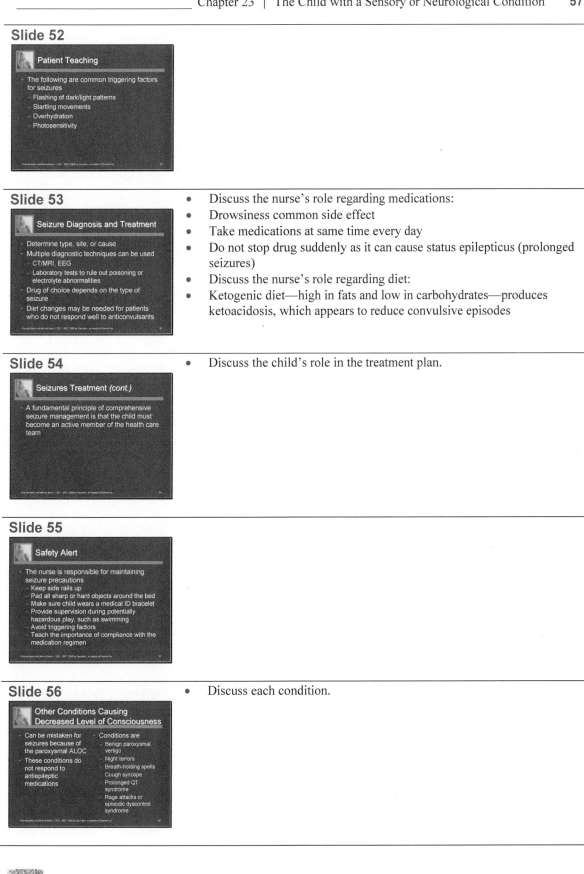

Patient Teaching

- The following are common triggering factors for seizures
  - Flashing of dark/light patterns
  - Startling movements
  - Overhydration
  - Photosensitivity

Slide 53

Seizure Diagnosis and Treatment

- Determine type, site, or cause
- Multiple diagnostic techniques can be used
  - CT/MRI, EEG
  - Laboratory tests to rule out poisoning or electrolyte abnormalities
- Drug of choice depends on the type of seizure
- Diet changes may be needed for patients who do not respond well to anticonvulsants

- Discuss the nurse's role regarding medications:
- Drowsiness common side effect
- Take medications at same time every day
- Do not stop drug suddenly as it can cause status epilepticus (prolonged seizures)
- Discuss the nurse's role regarding diet:
- Ketogenic diet—high in fats and low in carbohydrates—produces ketoacidosis, which appears to reduce convulsive episodes

Slide 54

Seizures Treatment *(cont.)*

- A fundamental principle of comprehensive seizure management is that the child must become an active member of the health care team

- Discuss the child's role in the treatment plan.

Slide 55

Safety Alert

- The nurse is responsible for maintaining seizure precautions
  - Keep side rails up
  - Pad all sharp or hard objects around the bed
  - Make sure child wears a medical ID bracelet
  - Provide supervision during potentially hazardous play, such as swimming
  - Avoid triggering factors
  - Teach the importance of compliance with the medication regimen

Slide 56

Other Conditions Causing Decreased Level of Consciousness

- Can be mistaken for seizures because of the paroxysmal ALOC
- These conditions do not respond to antiepileptic medications

- Conditions are
  - Benign paroxysmal vertigo
  - Night terrors
  - Breath-holding spells
  - Cough syncope
  - Prolonged QT syndrome
  - Rage attacks or episodic dyscontrol syndrome

- Discuss each condition.

Leifer

Slide 57

Cerebral Palsy (CP)

- A group of motor disorders caused by dysfunction of various motor centers in the brain and often related to antenatal or developmental factors
- Can be precipitated by many factors, such as birth injuries, congenital anomalies, neonatal anoxia, prematurity, subdural hemorrhage, and prenatal infection

- Discuss precipitating factors and the pathophysiology which contributes to CP.

Slide 58

Cerebral Palsy (CP) *(cont.)*

- Manifestations
  - Vary with each child
  - May range from mild to severe
  - Mental retardation sometimes seen
- Suspected during infancy if
  - There are feeding problems
  - Convulsions not associated with high fevers
  - Developmental milestones are not being achieved at expected age level

- Give examples of mild and severe forms.
- What milestones might be delayed for an infant and toddler with this condition?

Slide 59

Types of CP

Spastic	Athetoid
Involves damage to the cortex of the brain	Involves damage to the basal nuclei ganglion
Spasms occur with movement	Continuous involuntary writhing movements
Related to cerebral asphyxia	Often associated with hyperbilirubinemia
Ataxic	**Mixed**
Uncoordinated movements and ataxia from a lesion in the cerebellum	Usually a combination of spastic and athetoid

Audience Response Question #5
Complete the analogy. Ataxic : cerebral palsy as _____ : seizure
1. absence
2. clonic
3. neurological
4. intracranial pressure

Slide 60

Treatment of CP

- Botulinum toxin has been used to manage spasticity problems
- Levodopa has helped to control some of the athetoid problems
- Specific treatment is highly individualized
  - Good skin care is essential
  - All precautions taken to prevent contractures
    - Braces are often used to treat these
    - Orthopedic surgery is sometimes indicated

- Discuss the pathophysiology regarding botulinum toxin to manage spasticity.
- Discuss criteria which would provide a supportive environment for a child with CP.

Slide 61

Treatment Protocol for CP

- Establish communication
- Establish locomotion
- Use and optimize existing motor functions
- Provide intellectual stimulation
- Promote socialization
- Provide technology to encourage self-care and promote growth and development
- Provide multidisciplinary approach to care

- Give examples of technological devices which can promote growth and development.

Slide 62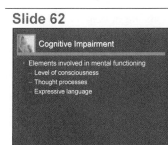

Cognitive Impairment

- Elements involved in mental functioning
  - Level of consciousness
  - Thought processes
  - Expressive language | • What is the typical IQ of a child with mental retardation?
• Discuss the particular aspects of each element involved in mental functioning.
• Level of consciousness:
 – Attention
 – Short-term memory
 – Long-term memory
 – Perceptions
 – Thought processes
 – Insight
 – Judgment
 – Affect
 – Mood
 – Expressive language
 – Vocabulary
 – Abstract thinking
 – Intelligence |
| **Slide 63**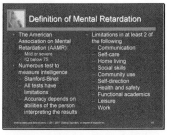

Definition of Mental Retardation

- The American Association on Mental Retardation (AAMR):
  - Mild or severe
  - IQ below 75
- Numerous test to measure intelligence
  - Stanford-Binet
  - All tests have limitations
  - Accuracy depends on abilities of the person interpreting the results

Limitations in at least 2 of the following
  - Communication
  - Self-care
  - Home living
  - Social skills
  - Community use
  - Self-direction
  - Health and safety
  - Functional academics
  - Leisure
  - Work | • Discuss the Stanford-Binet test. |
| **Slide 64**

Some Causes of Cognitive Impairment

- Neonatal period
  - PKU
  - Hypothyroidism
  - Fetal alcohol syndrome
  - Down syndrome
  - Malformations of the brain
  - Maternal infections
- Birth injuries or anoxia during or shortly after delivery
- Heredity

- During childhood
  - Meningitis
  - Lead poisoning
  - Neoplasms
  - Encephalitis
  - Living in a physically or emotionally deprived environment | • Discuss the pathophysiology regarding these causes. |
| **Slide 65**

Health Promotion

- Cognitively impaired children have the same psychosocial needs as all other children but cannot express or respond as other children do | • What are some situations in which a cognitively impaired child's psychosocial needs might not be met?
• Discuss methods to meet the impaired child's needs. |

Slide 66

> **Success in the Approach to the Mentally Retarded Child**
>
> - The nurse must assist the parents to understand that providing experiences that the child can be successful in, and concentrating on his or her strengths rather than on weaknesses, are the keys to dealing with a child who is developmentally different
> - A child who experiences constant failure becomes angry
>   - The anger causes behavior difficulties that can cloud the problem and therapy

- Give an example of a situation in which parents might help their child to become successful.

Slide 67

> **Management and Nursing Goals**
>
> - Individualized plan of care
>   - Initial step is to present the findings to the family
>   - Provide emotional support
>   - The child's competence and adaptive behaviors should be discussed along with the deficiencies
> - If child is in the hospital, the nurse needs to obtain
>   - The child's stage of maturation and ability
>   - Self-help activities
>   - Home routines

- Discuss how the nurse can assess the child's stage of maturation and ability.
- Discuss self-help activities which the nurse can promote in a child with this disorder.

Slide 68

> **Health Promotion**
>
> - Nursing responsibilities to disabled children
>   - Emphasize the *strengths* present
>   - Maintain communication with the family
>   - Avoid labels; use simple terms
>   - Contact the school nurse; plan for school needs
>   - Provide daily experiences in which the child can succeed
>   - Refer to local, state, and national support groups

- Discuss labels that should be avoided.

Slide 69

> **Nursing Tip**
>
> - Many mentally retarded children have a normal facial appearance
> - Many children with unusual faces are not mentally retarded

- Review Table 23-5 on page 553.

Slide 70

> **Head Injuries**
>
> - Major cause of death in children older than 1 year of age
> - A concussion is a temporary disturbance of the brain that is usually followed by a period of unconsciousness
> - A child's response to a head injury may differ from that of an adult

- Give examples of situations that could cause head injuries in the infant.
- How could a child's response differ from an adult who has experienced a head injury?

Slide 71

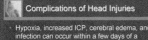

Safety Alert

- A concussion with resulting amnesia and confusion can be more serious than the presence of a fractured skull with no clinical symptoms

- Discuss the pathophysiology.

Slide 72

Complications of Head Injuries

- Hypoxia, increased ICP, cerebral edema, and infection can occur within a few days of a head injury
  - Hypoxia causes the brain to need increased energy, which increases cerebral blood flow
    - Increased blood flow causes cerebral edema
    - If ICP rises too high, cerebral perfusion diminishes, brain damage or death results

- Discuss signs and symptoms of increased ICP and cerebral edema.

Slide 73

Shaken Baby Syndrome

- Infants who are roughly shaken can sustain retinal, subarachnoid, and subdural hemorrhages in the brain, as well as high-level cervical spine injuries
- Can result in permanent brain injury or death

- Symptoms
  - Headache (manifested as fussiness in a toddler)
  - Drowsiness
  - Blurred vision
  - Vomiting
  - Dyspnea
- In severe cases child may be completely unconscious

Slide 74

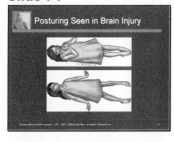

Posturing Seen in Brain Injury

- Discuss these postures and the area of injury in the brain.

Slide 75

Nursing Care of a Brain-Injured Child

- Observe child for signs of increased ICP
  - Four components of a cranial or neurological check
    - LOC
    - Pupil and eye movement
    - Vital signs
    - Motor activity

- Discuss assessment of each of these components.

Slide 76

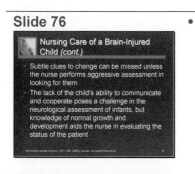

Nursing Care of a Brain-Injured Child *(cont.)*

- Subtle clues to change can be missed unless the nurse performs aggressive assessment in looking for them
- The lack of the child's ability to communicate and cooperate poses a challenge in the neurological assessment of infants, but knowledge of normal growth and development aids the nurse in evaluating the status of the patient

- Give examples of subtle changes the nurse might miss in a child who shows improvement.

Slide 77

Neurological Monitoring of Infants and Children

- Pain stimuli response
- LOC
- Arousal awareness
- Cranial nerve response
- Motor response
- Posturing
- Pupil response of the eyes
- Bulging fontanels
- Scalp vein distention
- Ataxia; spasticity of lower extremities
- Moro/tonic neck with withdrawal reflexes

- Discuss methods for assessing each component.

Slide 78

Safety Alert

- The presence of asymmetrical pupils after a head injury is a medical emergency

Slide 79

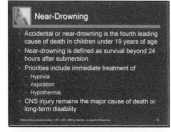

Near-Drowning

- Accidental or near-drowning is the fourth leading cause of death in children under 19 years of age
- Near-drowning is defined as survival beyond 24 hours after submersion
- Priorities include immediate treatment of
  - Hypoxia
  - Aspiration
  - Hypothermia
- CNS injury remains the major cause of death or long-term disability

Slide 80

Near-Drowning *(cont.)*

- Submersion for more than 10 minutes with failure to regain consciousness at the scene or within 24 hours is an ominous sign and indicates severe neurological deficits if the child survives

- What neurological deficits might this child exhibit?

Slide 81

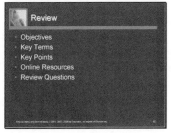

Question for Review

- What is the difference in technique of instilling eardrops in an infant and in a child?

Slide 82

Review

- Objectives
- Key Terms
- Key Points
- Online Resources
- Review Questions

Lesson Plan

24 The Child with a Musculoskeletal Condition

TEACHING FOCUS

In this chapter, students will be provided an overview of the musculoskeletal system, with emphasis on the differences between the child and adult skeletal and muscular systems. Students will have the opportunity to learn assessment skills to determine normal and abnormal findings. In addition, students will be introduced to the various types of fractures, as well as a wide variety of abnormal musculoskeletal conditions and treatment devices for each. Finally, family violence and child abuse and neglect issues will be addressed, stressing the important role of nursing care and interventions in their identification, reporting, and prevention.

MATERIALS AND RESOURCES

☐ Child abuse reporting guidelines
  (Lesson 24.2)
☐ Computer and PowerPoint projector
  (all lessons)
☐ Ice and compression bandages (Lesson 24.1)

☐ Sample x-rays of children at various ages
  (Lesson 24.1)
☐ Sample x-rays of multiple fracture types in
  children (Lesson 24.1)

LESSON CHECKLIST

Preparations for this lesson include:

- Lecture
- Guest speakers: Orthopedic surgeon, radiologist, or orthopedic technician; child abuse expert
- Evaluation of student knowledge and skills needed to perform all entry-level activities related to the child with a musculoskeletal condition, including:
  ○ Assessment of the musculoskeletal system of the growing child
  ○ Understanding the different traumatic fractures and appropriate treatments
  ○ Developing an appropriate nursing care plan for children immobilized by traction
  ○ Understanding the legal requirements related to child abuse reporting, as well as recognizing situations of abuse and neglect

KEY TERMS

arthroscopy (p. 563)
Bryant's traction (p. 563)
Buck extension (p. 563)
cast (p. 568)
compartment syndrome
  (p. 568)
compound fracture (p. 564)
contusion (p. 563)
epiphysis (p. 564)
gait (p. 562)

genu valgum (p. 563)
genu varum (p. 563)
greenstick fracture (p. 564)
hematoma (p. 563)
Legg-Calvé-Perthes
  Disease (Coxa Plana)
  (p. 573)
Milwaukee brace (p. 575)
neurovascular checks
  (p. 568)

osteomyelitis (p. 571)
Russell traction (p. 564)
shin splint (p. 577)
slipped femoral capital
  epiphysis (p. 572)
spiral fracture (p. 564)
sprain (p. 563)
strain (p. 563)

ADDITIONAL RESOURCES

TEACH PPT slide(s) Chapter 24, 1-67
EILR IC image(s) Chapter 24, 1-14
EILR OBQ question(s) Chapter 24, 1-10
EILR TB question(s) Chapter 24, 1-32
ESLR IRQ question(s) Chapter 24, 1-5
SG Chapter 24, pp. 195-202

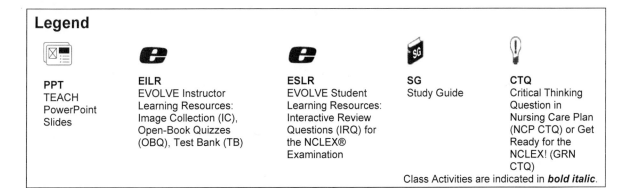

Legend

PPT
TEACH
PowerPoint
Slides

EILR
EVOLVE Instructor
Learning Resources:
Image Collection (IC),
Open-Book Quizzes
(OBQ), Test Bank (TB)

ESLR
EVOLVE Student
Learning Resources:
Interactive Review
Questions (IRQ) for
the NCLEX®
Examination

SG
Study Guide

CTQ
Critical Thinking
Question in
Nursing Care Plan
(NCP CTQ) or Get
Ready for the
NCLEX! (GRN
CTQ)

Class Activities are indicated in **bold italic**.

Leifer

LESSON 24.1

PRETEST

1. Compared with other children with disabilities, those with muscular dystrophy tend to be
   a. more outgoing and assertive.
   b. aggressive and angry.
   c. passive and withdrawn.
   d. more intelligent and arrogant.

2. The type of traction that could be used for a 24-pound, 17-month-old toddler with a fractured femur is
   a. Buck skin traction.
   b. Bryant's traction.
   c. Russell traction.
   d. 90-degree skeletal traction.

3. When checking for capillary refill, the nurse should
   a. have the patient wiggle his toes.
   b. check for quality of pulses in the extremities.
   c. squeeze tips of the fingers or toes.
   d. compress the nail bed and observe for original color return.

4. To assess motor function in an 8-year-old with a fractured radius, ask him to
   a. touch his thumb to the tip of his little finger.
   b. hyperextend his thumb.
   c. spread his fingers.
   d. make a fist.

5. One hour ago, the nurse gave an analgesic to a 22-month-old toddler with fractured ribs. Which of the following would indicate that the medication was effective?
   a. The patient verbalizes pain relief.
   b. He has stopped crying and has fallen asleep.
   c. His mother says that his pain is better.
   d. He refuses a Popsicle.

6. Scoliosis is
   a. progressive and does not stop with maturity.
   b. also known as "hunchback."
   c. always congenital and develops in utero.
   d. corrected with the use of a Madison brace.

7. A 12-year-old wide receiver suddenly develops muscle cramps during the fourth quarter of his school's football game. This sports injury may have been caused by
   a. running too fast to catch a pass.
   b. his touchdown celebration dance in the end-zone.
   c. dehydration and electrolyte imbalance.
   d. wearing shoes that were too tight.

8. A 24-year-old mother leaves her 5-year-old son at home alone when she goes to work a 10-hour shift at a coffee shop. This is an indication of
   a. emotional abuse.
   b. emotional neglect.
   c. physical abuse.
   d. physical neglect.

9. An appropriate anxiety-reducing technique for a 6-year-old girl would be
   a. spanking her doll.
   b. running around a playground.
   c. screaming and yelling.
   d. kicking a stuffed dog.

10. A toddler beginning to walk
    a. has a wide, unstable gait.
    b. swings his arms with the walking motion.
    c. can easily fracture a bone when he falls.
    d. has high arches of his feet.

Answers

1. c	3. d	5. b	7. c	9. b
2. b	4. a	6. a	8. d	10. a

BACKGROUND ASSESSMENT

Question: What are different types of bone fractures sustained by children? Briefly describe each one.

Answer: A list of bone fracture types may include any of the following: a. greenstick (one side of the bone breaks and the other just bends); b. complete (fracture runs across the entire width of the bone); c. simple (the bone is broken and the skin is not); d. compound (a broken bone protrudes out of a wound in the skin); e. epiphyseal separation (a fracture in the region of the epiphyseal growth plate); f. comminuted (a breach in the continuity of a bone that is broken into multiple pieces); g. longitudinal (fracture runs the length of the bone); h. pathological (break in a bone weakened by disease such as cancer, infection, or bone cyst); i. spiral (angular break resulting in displacement of the bone, usually from twisting); j. transverse (clean square break that divides a bone cleanly across).

Question: A 15-year-old track team member has shin splints. What are these? What are the symptoms? How can this problem be prevented?

Answer: Shin splints result from the tearing of fibers that connect muscle to bone. They are characterized by pain in the front and sides of the lower leg that develops or worsens during exercise. Tenderness over the shin and edema of the surrounding tissues may occur. Shin splints are a common problem for runners and can be reduced or avoided by wearing well-fitting shoes with plenty of impact-absorbing material in the forefoot and heel area. Running shoes should be replaced before they lose shock absorbency, usually around 500 miles. Runners should warm up before running by first walking, then gradually increasing the speed to their running speed. In addition, they should stop and stretch their calf muscles and Achilles tendons. Finally, the running surface should be grass, dirt, cinder, or rubberized.

CRITICAL THINKING QUESTION

A nurse is jogging on a trail. Suddenly, a 10-year-old boy swerves his bicycle around her, loses control of the bike, and falls eight feet in front of her. Initially he denies sustaining any injury, but the nurse notices that he limps slightly when he goes to retrieve his bicycle. How should the nurse handle this situation?

Guidelines: The nurse should get a quick medical history from the boy to determine if this is a new limp. She should determine if the boy might have sustained a sprain or strain when he fell. If the boy guards or protects the area, this may indicate an injury. The nurse should observe for swelling, warmth, bruising, or redness in the injured area. If she or the boy has a cell phone, she should call his parents or guardian. She should instruct the boy and his parent or guardian that the best immediate treatments for a soft tissue injury are rest (stay off the foot completely for 48 hours), ice (apply ice pack or package of frozen vegetables wrapped in towel to injured area 20 minutes four times a day), compression (elastic wrap to reduce swelling), and elevation (elevate limb above the level of the heart). The nurse should advise the parent or guardian to notify their physician for further direction.

OBJECTIVES	CONTENT	TEACHING RESOURCES
Discuss the musculoskeletal differences between the child and adult and how they influence orthopedic treatment and nursing care.	■ Musculoskeletal system: differences between the child and adult (p. 562)	▦ PPT slides 7, 13 𝒆 EILR IC image 1 **BOOK RESOURCES** Figure 24-1, Some Musculoskeletal System Differences Between the Child and the Adult (p. 562) ▸ Discuss the major, age-specific changes that occur in the developing child's musculoskeletal system.
Demonstrate an understanding of age-specific changes that occur in the musculoskeletal	■ Observation and Assessment of the musculoskeletal system in the growing child (p. 562)	▦ PPT slides 5-12 𝒆 EILR TB questions 9, 20 𝒆 ESLR IRQ question 1

Leifer

OBJECTIVES	CONTENT	TEACHING RESOURCES

system during growth and development.	☐ Observation of gait (p. 562)
	
	☐ Observation of muscle tone (p. 563)
	
	☐ Diagnostic tests and treatments (p. 563)
	
	  – Radiographic studies (p. 563)
	
	  – Laboratory tests and treatments (p. 563)
		SG Learning Activities, questions 1-5, 8, 10 (p. 195)
		
		SG Review Questions, question 13 (p. 200)
		
		SG Applying Knowledge, question 3 (p. 202)
		
		▶ Discuss the changes in a child's gait that occur between 18 months and 6 years. What might toe walking indicate?
		
		Class Activity Show the class sample x-rays of children in various age groups from infancy though adolescence. Have the class compare changes in each age group.
		
		Class Activity As a class, discuss the musculoskeletal differences between children and adults. Have students identify specific characteristics of the child's bones, such as ability to heal, rapid growth, flexibility, and rich blood supply, as well as the health benefits and problems that are often related to these features.

Describe the management of soft tissue injuries.	☐ Pediatric trauma (p. 563)
	
	  – Soft tissue injuries (p. 563)
	
	  – Prevention of pediatric trauma (p. 564)
		PPT slides 14, 16
		
		EILR OBQ question 2
		
		EILR TB question 7
		
		SG Learning Activities, questions 8, 9, 11, 12 (p. 196)
		
		BOOK RESOURCES
		
		Memory Jogger (p. 564)
		
		Review Questions for the NCLEX® Examination, question 3 (p. 582)
		
		▶ Discuss the principles of managing soft tissue injuries. What are risks or complications associated with them?
		
		Class Activity Have students pair up and take turns applying "RICE" to each other's ankles, as if they had soft tissue injuries.

Discuss the types of fractures commonly seen in children and their effect on growth and development.	■ Traumatic fractures (p. 564)	PPT slides 16, 17 EILR IC image 2 EILR TB question 21 SG Learning Activities, questions 9, 10, 13-15 (p. 196) SG Review Questions, question 3 (p. 199) **BOOK RESOURCES** Safety Alert (p. 564) Figure 24-2, Types of Fractures, Reduction, Methods of

Leifer

OBJECTIVES	CONTENT	TEACHING RESOURCES
		Internal Fixations (p. 565) ▸ Discuss the different fractures that are most likely to affect the growth and development of children. *Class Activity **Bring in x-rays of different types of fractures in children and show them to the class. For each x-ray, have students call out what type of fracture is shown. Ask them to discuss how each fracture could have occurred. After each scenario is presented, ask the class how this child's growth and development could be affected by the fracture.***
Differentiate between Buck extension and Russell traction.	■ Treatment of fractures with traction (p. 564) ☐ Traction in the younger child (p. 564)	PPT slides 18-26 𝒆 EILR IC images 3, 4 𝒆 EILR TB questions 2, 3, 8, 15, 22, 25, 28 SG Learning Activities, questions 6, 11, 14, 16, 17 (p. 196) SG Review Questions, questions 2, 8, 11 (pp. 199-200) SG Case Study, question 1 (p. 201) **BOOK RESOURCES** Figure 24-3, Bryant's Traction (p. 565) Nursing Tip (p. 566) Figure 24-4, Russell Skin Traction (p. 566) Safety Alert (p. 566) Review Questions for the NCLEX® Examination, question 3 (p. 582) ▸ Discuss the differences and similarities between Buck extension and Russell traction. *Class Activity **Ask half the class to roughly sketch a child in Buck extension and the other half of the class to do the same for Russell traction. Students should label the parts of the traction (e.g., weights, knots, pulleys, and frame) in their drawings. Next, as a class, have the students discuss the different types of injuries that require each type of traction.***
Compile a nursing care plan for the child who is immobilized by traction.	■ Nursing responsibilities for traction (p. 566)	PPT slides 21-26 𝒆 EILR IC images 5-8 𝒆 EILR OBQ question 3 𝒆 EILR TB question 19

OBJECTIVES	CONTENT	TEACHING RESOURCES
		SG Learning Activities, questions 13, 15, 17-20 (p. 196)
		SG Review Questions, question 11 (p. 200)
		SG Thinking Critically, question 2 (p. 201)
		SG Applying Knowledge, question 4 (p. 202)
		BOOK RESOURCES
		Nursing Tip (p. 566)
		Figure 24-5, Forces Involved in Traction (p. 566)
		Figure 24-6, 90 Degree–90 Degree Skeletal Traction (p. 567)
		Figure 24-7, Cervical Traction (p. 567)
		Figure 24-8, Overcoming the Effects of Traction on a Child (p. 567)
		Nursing Tip (p. 568)
		Nursing Care Plan 24-1, The Child in Traction (pp. 570-571)
		GRN CTQ 1 (p. 582)
		Class Activity Divide the class into small groups and present the following scenario. A 10-month-old baby is in Bryant's traction with a fractured femur. Have each group discuss nursing interventions for the following potential problems for the infant: immobility, confinement, circulation, skin breakdown, pain, constipation, and anorexia. Have each group share their results with the class.
Describe a neurovascular check.	■ Traumatic fractures (p. 564)	PPT slide 27
		EILR IC images 9, 10
		EILR OBQ question 4
		EILR TB questions 9, 12, 26, 31
		SG Learning Activities, questions 5, 12, 18, 21 (pp. 195-196)
		SG Review Questions, question 17 (p. 201)
		SG Applying Knowledge, question 1 (p. 202)
		BOOK RESOURCES

OBJECTIVES	CONTENT	TEACHING RESOURCES
		Figure 24-9, Checking Circulation to the Toes or Fingers (p. 567)
		Skill 24-1, Neurovascular Checks (p. 568)
		Nursing Tip (p. 568)
		Safety Alert (p. 568)
		Figure 24-10, Checking for Nerve Damage (p. 569)
		▸ Discuss the aspects of a neurovascular check, including pain, pulse, sensation, color, capillary refill, and movement.
		Class Activity **Divide the class into pairs and have each pair take turns role-playing the following nurse-patient interaction: a nurse performing a neurovascular check on a 14-year-old boy in a long arm cast for a fractured ulna. The nurse should include pain, pulse, sensation, color, and circulation checks. Have students discuss any questions or observations with the rest of the class.**
Discuss nursing care of a child in a cast	▪ Treatment of fractures with casts (p. 568) □ Nursing care of a child in a cast (p. 568) ▪ Disorders and dysfunction of the musculoskeletal system (p. 571) □ Osteomyelitis (p. 571)	⊠▪ PPT slides 24-34 𝓮 EILR OBQ question 5 𝓮 EILR TB questions 10, 11 𝓮 ESLR IRQ question 2 SG Learning Activities, questions 1, 19 (p. 195) SG Review Questions, question 9 (p. 200) **BOOK RESOURCES** Review Questions for the NCLEX® Examination, question 2 (p. 582) Nursing Care Plan 24-1, The Child in Traction (pp. 570-571) ▸ Discuss the signs and symptoms of osteomyelitis. ▸ Discuss the nursing care and responsibilities associated with caring for a child in traction, including the traction apparatus checklist from Nursing Tip (p. 566) and the patient checklist from Nursing Tip (p. 568).

24.1 Homework/Assignments:

24.1 Instructor's Notes/Student Feedback:

LESSON 24.2

CRITICAL THINKING QUESTION

A mother gets a call from her 12-year-old daughter's school nurse. The nurse informs her that her daughter has scoliosis, which was detected during a routine school testing. The mother has never heard of scoliosis and is concerned that her daughter will be "crippled for life." What should the school nurse tell her?

Guidelines: The nurse should tell the mother that scoliosis is a lateral curvature of the spine that is not uncommon in adolescent girls. The mother should consult her pediatrician for confirmation of the diagnosis. X-rays can determine the degree of curvature. If it is less than 20 degrees, no treatment is generally required. As the daughter's scoliosis was not found earlier, she probably has functional scoliosis, which is easily corrected by bracing for curves up to 45 degrees. The mother did not notice the curve, so it is unlikely that it is severe enough to warrant surgery. Typically, scoliosis is not painful and should not interfere with the daughter's normal activities.

OBJECTIVES	CONTENT	TEACHING RESOURCES
List two symptoms of Duchenne's muscular dystrophy.	■ Duchenne's or Becker's (pseudohypertrophic) muscular dystrophy (p. 572) ■ Slipped femoral capital epiphysis (p. 572)	PPT slides 35-39 *e* EILR OBQ question 6 *e* EILR TB questions 5, 10-12, 30 SG Learning Activities, questions 20-22 (p. 197) SG Review Questions, questions 1, 3, 6, 9 (p. 199) **BOOK RESOURCES** ▶ Discuss the nursing interventions required for Duchenne's muscular dystrophy. *Class Activity As a class, discuss the signs and symptoms of Duchenne's muscular dystrophy. Have students identify as many signs and symptoms as possible and list them on the board. Next, discuss the complications associated with each sign or symptom (i.e., falling, depression) and nursing interventions.*
Describe the symptoms, treatment, and nursing care for the child with Legg-Calvé-Perthes disease.	■ Legg-Calvé-Perthes disease (coxa plana) (p. 573) ■ Osteosarcoma (p. 573) ■ Ewing's sarcoma (p. 573)	PPT slides 40-44 *e* EILR TB questions 1, 4, 29 *e* ESLR IRQ question 5 SG Learning Activities, questions 1, 23, 24 (pp. 195, 198) SG Review Questions, questions 6, 7, 12 (p. 200) **BOOK RESOURCES** Review Questions for the NCLEX® Examination, question 1 (p. 582) ▶ Discuss the symptoms, treatment, and nursing care of osteosarcoma. ▶ Discuss the symptoms, treatment, and nursing care of

OBJECTIVES	CONTENT	TEACHING RESOURCES
		Ewing's sarcoma.
		Class Activity Divide the class into small groups. Ask each group to develop a nursing care plan for a 7-year-old boy with Legg-Calvé-Perthes disease. Have each group present its plan to the class, describing typical symptoms and nursing interventions.
Describe two topics of discussion applicable at discharge for the child with juvenile idiopathic arthritis.	■ Juvenile idiopathic arthritis (juvenile rheumatoid arthritis) (p. 574) ■ Torticollis (wry neck) (p. 574)	PPT slides 45-53 *e* EILR OBQ question 7 *e* EILR TB questions 6, 16 SG Learning Activities, questions 1, 2, 5 (pp. 195, 198) SG Review Questions, questions 10, 14 (pp. 200-201) ▸ Discuss the symptoms, treatment, and nursing care of juvenile idiopathic arthritis. ▸ Discuss the symptoms, treatment, and nursing interventions for torticollis. *Class Activity Have each student write two discharge topics to be covered for a child with juvenile idiopathic arthritis. Next, divide the class into groups of three and have each group take turns role-playing a nurse/patient/parent interaction in which the student playing the nurse gives discharge instructions to the patient and parent based on his or her identified discharge topics.*
Describe three nursing care measures required to maintain skin integrity in an adolescent child in a cast for scoliosis.	■ Scoliosis (p. 575) ■ Sports injuries (p. 576)	PPT slides 54-58 *e* EILR IC images 11-13 *e* EILR OBQ questions 8, 9 *e* EILR TB questions 13, 14, 17 *e* ESLR IRQ question 3 SG Learning Activities, questions 26-32 (pp. 198-199) SG Review Questions, questions 4, 5, 17 (p. 199) SG Applying Knowledge, questions 2, 5 (p. 202) **BOOK RESOURCES** Review Questions for the NCLEX® Examination, question 4 (p. 582) Figure 24-11, Abnormal Spinal Curvatures (p. 575)

OBJECTIVES	CONTENT	TEACHING RESOURCES
		Figure 24-12, The Milwaukee Brace (p. 575)
		Figure 24-13, Halo Traction (p. 576)
		Table 24-1, Common Sports Injuries (p. 577)
		Health Promotion: Selected Recreational Activities and Their Risks (p. 577)
		▶ Discuss the most common sports injuries for children and adolescents, as well as preventive measures.
		Class Activity Present the following scenario to the class: A 14-year-old girl is in a plaster cast from her neck to her mid-thigh following surgery for scoliosis. As a class, discuss nursing measures that will be necessary to prevent this patient's skin from breaking down.
Describe three types of child abuse.	■ Family violence (p. 578) ■ Child abuse (p. 578) ☐ Federal laws and agencies (p. 578)	⊠ PPT slide 59-64 𝒆 EILR OBQ question 10 𝒆 EILR TB question 18 𝒆 ESLR IRQ question 4 SG Learning Activities, questions 33, 34 (p. 199) SG Review Questions, questions 15, 16 (p. 201) SG Thinking Critically, question 1 (p. 201) **BOOK RESOURCES** Health Promotion, Factors that May Contribute to or Trigger Child Abuse (p. 578) Box 24-1, Nursing Interventions for abused and neglected children and adolescents (p. 579) Legal and Ethical Considerations, Reporting Suspected Abuse or Neglect (p. 579) ▶ Discuss the different types of child abuse and neglect, including emotional abuse, emotional neglect, sexual abuse, physical neglect, and physical abuse. *Class Activity Divide the class into four groups and assign each group one of the following topics: emotional abuse, emotional neglect, sexual abuse, and physical abuse. Have each group discuss and identify examples of its assigned type of abuse and present its findings to the class.* *Class Activity Divide the class into small groups and have students write down as many symptoms of childhood abuse and neglect as possible in 5 minutes. Have each group share its list with the class. Discuss the types of*

Introduction to Maternity & Pediatric Nursing, 6th ed.

OBJECTIVES	CONTENT	TEACHING RESOURCES
		abuse associated with the various symptoms.
Identify symptoms of abuse and neglect in children.	☐ Nursing care and intervention (p. 579)	PPT slides 63, 64 e EILR IC image 14 e EILR OBQ question 10 e EILR TB questions 18, 23, 24 SG Thinking Critically, question 1 (p. 201) **BOOK RESOURCES** Box 24-1, Nursing Interventions for Abused and Neglected Children and Adolescents (p. 579) Safety Alert (p. 580) Figure 24-14, Assessing for Child Abuse (p. 581) Review Questions for the NCLEX® Examination, question 5 (p. 582) ▶ Discuss the nursing interventions for child abuse and neglect listed in Box 24-1 (p. 579). Identify situations in which these interventions would be most applicable. *Class Activity Invite an expert on child abuse from a hospital or state agency to speak to the class about the most common types of abuse, current statistics, and mandated reporting laws. Ask the speaker to provide an overview of child abuse reporting guidelines, forms, and contact numbers to the class.* *Class Activity As a class, identify nursing interventions for the following scenario:* *A 5-year-old child presents with bruising on his arms ranging in color from red/purple to brown. The child's forearms are also swollen and tender. The child's mother says the child's injuries are the result of falling off his bike the previous day.*
State two cultural or medical practices that may be misinterpreted as child abuse.	☐ Cultural and medical issues (p. 580)	PPT slide 65 e EILR TB question 32 ▶ Discuss the importance of cultural practices when assessing children for possible child abuse. *Class Activity As a class, discuss different cultural practices that could be mistaken for child abuse, such as coining. Discuss the process by which the nurse should discern cultural practice from abuse, and the types of information the nurse should document in an assessment. Ask the question, "Should all potential abuse be investigated, regardless of cultural practices?"*

OBJECTIVES	CONTENT	TEACHING RESOURCES
Performance Evaluation		PPT slides 1-67
		EILR IC images 1-14
		EILR OBQ questions 1-1
		EILR TB questions 1-32
		ESLR IRQ questions 1-5
		SG Learning Activities, questions 1-34 (pp. 195-199)
		SG Review Questions, questions 1-17 (pp. 199-201)
		SG Case Study, question 1 (p. 201)
		SG Thinking Critically, questions 1, 2 (p. 201)
		SG Applying Knowledge, questions 1-5 (p. 202)
		BOOK RESOURCES
		Review Questions for the NCLEX® Examination, questions 1-5 (p. 582)
		GRN CTQ 1 (p. 582)

24.2 Homework/Assignments:

24.2 Instructor's Notes/Student Feedback:

24 Lecture Outline
The Child with a Musculoskeletal Condition

Slide 1

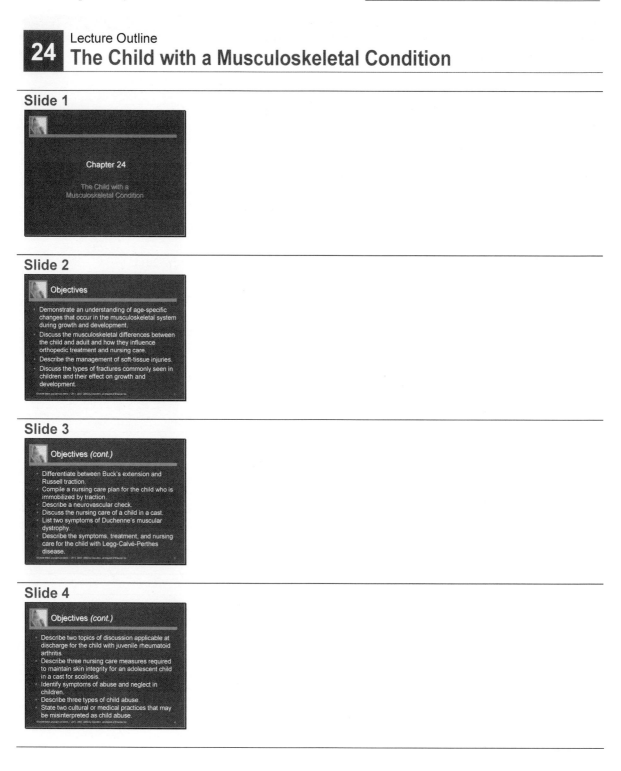

Chapter 24

The Child with a
Musculoskeletal Condition

Slide 2

Objectives

- Demonstrate an understanding of age-specific changes that occur in the musculoskeletal system during growth and development.
- Discuss the musculoskeletal differences between the child and adult and how they influence orthopedic treatment and nursing care.
- Describe the management of soft-tissue injuries.
- Discuss the types of fractures commonly seen in children and their effect on growth and development.

Slide 3

Objectives *(cont.)*

- Differentiate between Buck's extension and Russell traction.
- Compile a nursing care plan for the child who is immobilized by traction.
- Describe a neurovascular check.
- Discuss the nursing care of a child in a cast.
- List two symptoms of Duchenne's muscular dystrophy.
- Describe the symptoms, treatment, and nursing care for the child with Legg-Calvé-Perthes disease.

Slide 4

Objectives *(cont.)*

- Describe two topics of discussion applicable at discharge for the child with juvenile rheumatoid arthritis.
- Describe three nursing care measures required to maintain skin integrity for an adolescent child in a cast for scoliosis.
- Identify symptoms of abuse and neglect in children.
- Describe three types of child abuse.
- State two cultural or medical practices that may be misinterpreted as child abuse.

Leifer

Slide 5

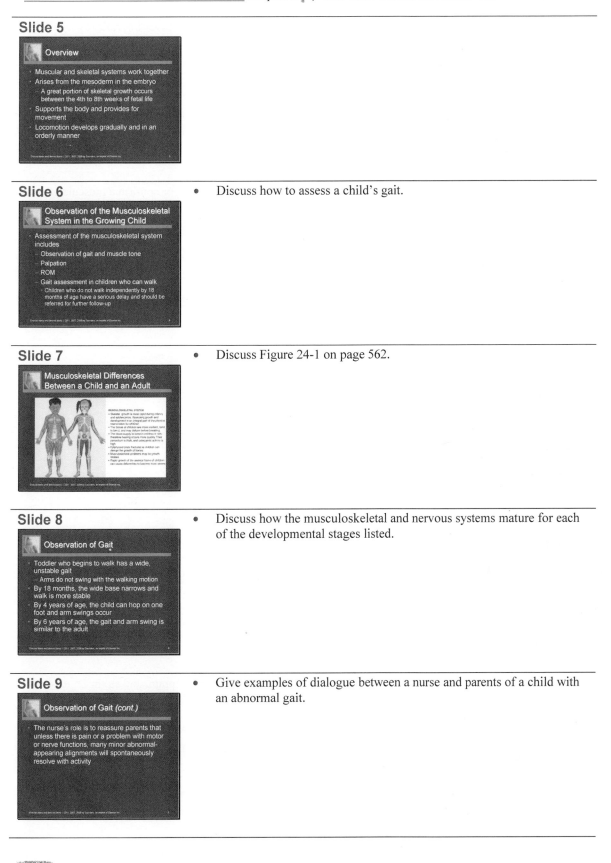

Overview

- Muscular and skeletal systems work together
- Arises from the mesoderm in the embryo
  - A great portion of skeletal growth occurs between the 4th to 8th weeks of fetal life
- Supports the body and provides for movement
- Locomotion develops gradually and in an orderly manner

Slide 6

Observation of the Musculoskeletal System in the Growing Child

- Assessment of the musculoskeletal system includes
  - Observation of gait and muscle tone
  - Palpation
  - ROM
  - Gait assessment in children who can walk
    - Children who do not walk independently by 18 months of age have a serious delay and should be referred for further follow-up

- Discuss how to assess a child's gait.

Slide 7

Musculoskeletal Differences Between a Child and an Adult

- Discuss Figure 24-1 on page 562.

Slide 8

Observation of Gait

- Toddler who begins to walk has a wide, unstable gait
  - Arms do not swing with the walking motion
- By 18 months, the wide base narrows and walk is more stable
- By 4 years of age, the child can hop on one foot and arm swings occur
- By 6 years of age, the gait and arm swing is similar to the adult

- Discuss how the musculoskeletal and nervous systems mature for each of the developmental stages listed.

Slide 9

Observation of Gait *(cont.)*

- The nurse's role is to reassure parents that unless there is pain or a problem with motor or nerve functions, many minor abnormal-appearing alignments will spontaneously resolve with activity

- Give examples of dialogue between a nurse and parents of a child with an abnormal gait.

ELSEVIER

Leifer

Slide 10 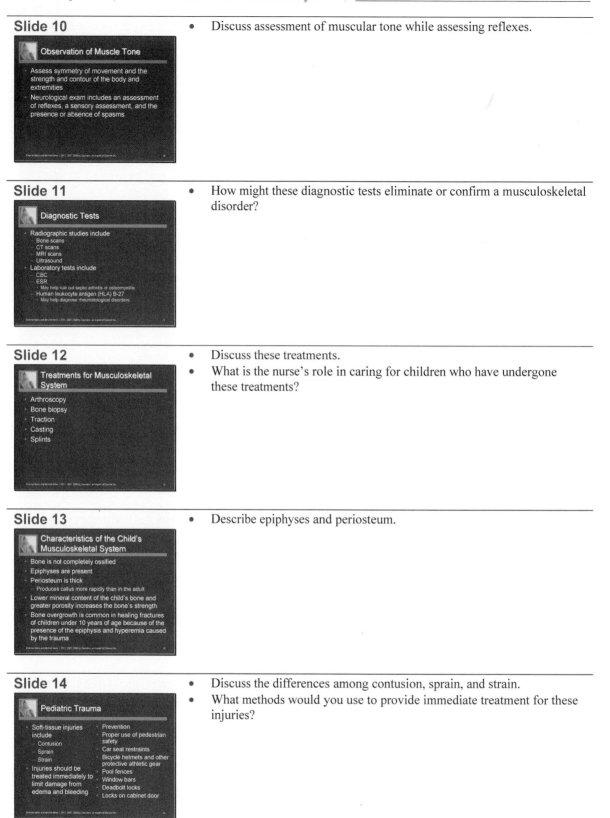 **Observation of Muscle Tone** - Assess symmetry of movement and the strength and contour of the body and extremities - Neurological exam includes an assessment of reflexes, a sensory assessment, and the presence or absence of spasms	• Discuss assessment of muscular tone while assessing reflexes.

Slide 11
Diagnostic Tests
- Radiographic studies include
  – Bone scans
  – CT scans
  – MRI scans
  – Ultrasound
- Laboratory tests include
  – CBC
  – ESR
    · May help rule out septic arthritis or osteomyelitis
  – Human leukocyte antigen (HLA) B-27
    · May help diagnose rheumatological disorders
	• How might these diagnostic tests eliminate or confirm a musculoskeletal disorder?

Slide 12 **Treatments for Musculoskeletal System** - Arthroscopy - Bone biopsy - Traction - Casting - Splints	• Discuss these treatments. • What is the nurse's role in caring for children who have undergone these treatments?
Slide 13 **Characteristics of the Child's Musculoskeletal System** - Bone is not completely ossified - Epiphyses are present - Periosteum is thick – Produces callus more rapidly than in the adult - Lower mineral content of the child's bone and greater porosity increases the bone's strength - Bone overgrowth is common in healing fractures of children under 10 years of age because of the presence of the epiphysis and hyperemia caused by the trauma	• Describe epiphyses and periosteum.

Slide 14
Pediatric Trauma
- Soft-tissue injuries include
  – Contusion
  – Sprain
  – Strain
- Injuries should be treated immediately to limit damage from edema and bleeding
 	
- Prevention
- Proper use of pedestrian safety
- Car seat restraints
- Bicycle helmets and other protective athletic gear
- Pool fences
- Window bars
- Deadbolt locks
- Locks on cabinet door
	• Discuss the differences among contusion, sprain, and strain.
	• What methods would you use to provide immediate treatment for these injuries?

Slide 15

Health Promotion

- Principles of managing soft-tissue injuries include
  - Rest
  - Ice
  - Compression
  - Elevation

Slide 16

Traumatic Fractures and Traction

- A fracture is a break in a bone and is mainly caused by accident
- Characterized by
  - Pain, tenderness on movement, and swelling
  - Discoloration, limited movement, and numbness may also occur
- Fractures heal more rapidly in children
- The child's periosteum is stronger and thicker, less stiffness on mobilization
- Injury to the cartilaginous epiphysis is serious if it happens during childhood
  - May interfere with longitudinal growth of the bone

- Discuss and provide the rationale regarding fractures that affect the cartilaginous epiphysis (growth plate) in children.

Slide 17

Types of Fractures

- Discuss the fractures listed in Figure 24-2 on page 565.
- Give an example of how each might occur.

Slide 18

Bryant's Traction

- Used for the young child who has a fractured femur
- Note that the buttocks are slightly off the bed to facilitate countertraction
- Active infants may require a jacket restraint to maintain body alignment

- Discuss the nursing care and assessment of a child in Bryant's traction.
- Refer to Figure 24-6 on page 565.

Audience Response Question #1
Complete the analogy. Bryant's traction : Volksmann ischemia as
_____ : compartment syndrome
  1. Buck's traction
  2. casts
  3. splints
  4. surgery

Slide 19

Buck's Extension

- A type of skin traction used in fractures of the femur and in hip and knee contractures
  - It pulls the hip and leg into extension
  - Countertraction is supplied by the child's body
- Essential that the child not slip down in bed
- Bed should not be placed in high-Fowler's position
- Used to reduce pain and muscle spasm associated with slipped capital femoral epiphysis

- Discuss the nursing care and assessment of a child in Buck's extension.

Slide 20

Russell Skin Traction
Similar to Buck's extension traction
A sling is positioned under the knee, which suspends the distal thigh above the bed
Pulls in two directions
Prevents posterior subluxation of the tibia on the femur
Two sets of weights, one at the head and one at the foot of the bed

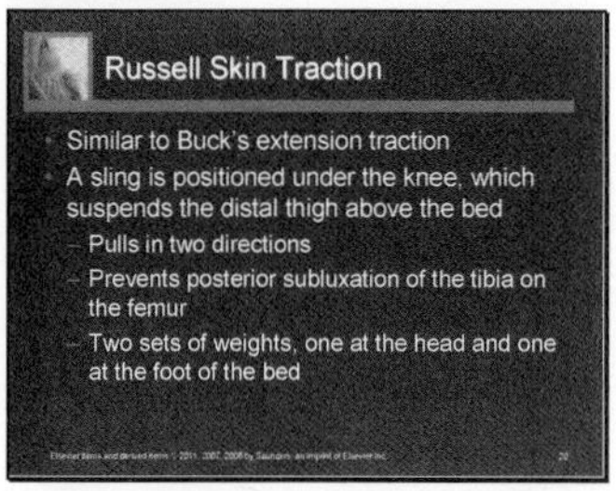

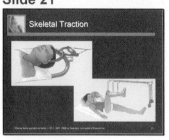

- When would this type of traction be preferred to Buck's extension traction?
- Refer to Figure 24-4 on page 566.

Slide 21

Skeletal Traction

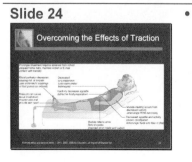

- What methods are used to prevent infection with these types of traction?

Slide 22

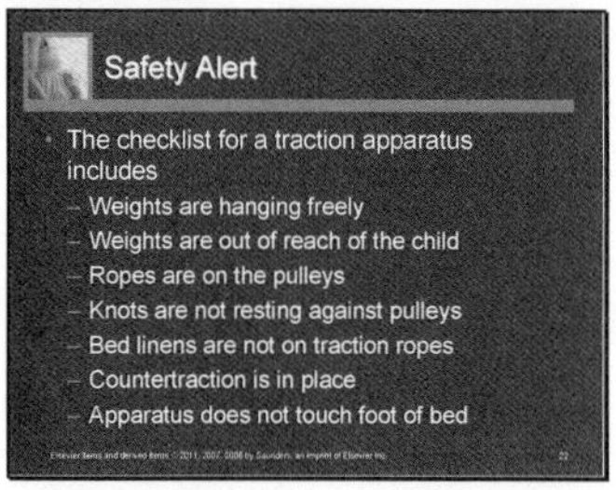

Safety Alert
The checklist for a traction apparatus includes
Weights are hanging freely
Weights are out of reach of the child
Ropes are on the pulleys
Knots are not resting against pulleys
Bed linens are not on traction ropes
Countertraction is in place
Apparatus does not touch foot of bed

Slide 23

Forces of Traction

Slide 24

Overcoming the Effects of Traction

- Discuss Figure 24-8 on page 567.

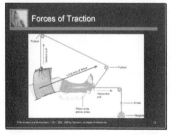

Slide 25

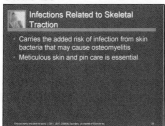

Safety Alert

- Checklist for the patient in traction
  - Body in alignment
  - HOB no higher than 20 degrees
  - Heels of feet elevated from bed
  - ROM of unaffected parts at regular intervals
  - Antiembolism stockings or foot pumps as ordered
  - Neurovascular checks performed regularly and recorded
  - Skin integrity monitored regularly and recorded
  - Pain relieved by medication is recorded
  - Measures to prevent constipation are provided
  - Use of trapeze for change of position is encouraged

- Discuss techniques to assess the neurovascular status of the extremity.
- Discuss the rationale for antiembolic measures in these types of patients.
- How is constipation prevented?

Slide 26

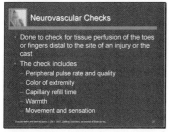

Infections Related to Skeletal Traction

- Carries the added risk of infection from skin bacteria that may cause osteomyelitis
- Meticulous skin and pin care is essential

Slide 27

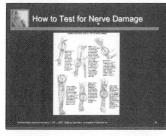

Neurovascular Checks

- Done to check for tissue perfusion of the toes or fingers distal to the site of an injury or the cast
- The check includes
  - Peripheral pulse rate and quality
  - Color of extremity
  - Capillary refill time
  - Warmth
  - Movement and sensation

Slide 28

How to Test for Nerve Damage

- Discuss Figure 24-10 on page 569.

Slide 29

Casts and Splints

- Can be made from a variety of materials
- Child is at increased risk for
  - Impaired skin integrity
  - Compartment syndrome
    - Progressive loss of tissue perfusion because of an increase in pressure caused by edema or swelling that presses on the vessels and tissues
    - If not carefully monitored, significant complications can occur

- Discuss assessment of an extremity to rule out compartment syndrome.

ELSEVIER

Introduction to Maternity & Pediatric Nursing, 6th ed.

Leifer

Slide 30

Nursing Care of a Child in a Cast

- Material used determines positioning of effected extremity for up to 72 hours
- Elevate effected extremity on a pillow
- Perform frequent neurovascular checks
- Teach cast care and how to support cast, safe transfers to/from chair/bed, how to use crutches safely, when a cast is too loose or too tight

- If fiberglass, the child can bathe and go in water.
- If plaster, child cannot get cast wet.

Slide 31

Osteomyelitis

- An infection of the bone that generally occurs in children younger than 1 year of age and in those between 5 and 14 years of age
  - Long bones contain few phagocytic cells to fight bacteria that may come to the bone from another part of the body
  - Inflammation produces an exudate that collects under the marrow and cortex of the bone

- In what situation might a child be prone to osteomyelitis?

Slide 32

Osteomyelitis *(cont.)*

- Common organisms
  - *Staphylococcus aureus* in children older than 5 years of age
    - Accounts for 75% to 80% of cases
  - *Haemophilus influenzae* most common cause in young children
- May be preceded by a local injury to the bone

- What methods are used to prevent transmission of these organisms to the injury?

Slide 33

Osteomyelitis *(cont.)*

- Vessels in affected area are compressed
  - Thrombosis occurs
    - Leads to ischemia and pain
  - Collection of pus under the periosteum of the bone can elevate the periosteum
    - Can result in necrosis of that part of the bone
    - Local inflammation and increased pressure can cause pain
  - Associated muscle spasms can cause limited active ROM

Slide 34

Osteomyelitis *(cont.)*

- Diagnostics
  - Elevated WBC and ESR
  - X-ray may initially fail to reveal infection
  - Bone scan may be more reliable
- Treatment
  - Intravenous antibiotics for several weeks
  - If pus is present, it is drained and bone is immobilized
  - Early passive ROM once splint is removed may be ordered
  - Pain relief
  - Diversional and physical therapy

- Discuss the difference between an x-ray and a bone scan.
- What methods are used to remove purulent drainage from the bone?
- Give examples of diversional activities.

Slide 35

Duchenne's or Becker's Muscular Dystrophy (MD)
- Group of disorders in which progressive muscle degeneration occurs
  - Duchenne's MD is most common
    - Onset is generally between 2 and 6 years of age
    - A history of delayed motor development during infancy may be evidenced

- How might a parent detect delayed motor development?

Slide 36

Duchenne's or Becker's Muscular Dystrophy (MD) (cont.)
- Additional signs and symptoms
  - Calf muscles in particular become hypertrophied
  - Progressive weakness as evidenced by
    - Frequent falling
    - Clumsiness
    - Contractures of the ankles and hips
    - Gower's maneuver to rise from the floor
  - Intellectual impairment is common

Slide 37

Duchenne's or Becker's Muscular Dystrophy (MD) (cont.)
- Diagnostics
  - Marked increase in blood creatine phosphokinase level
  - Muscle biopsy reveals a degeneration of muscle fibers replaced by fat and connective tissue
    - Myelogram shows decreases in the amplitude and duration of motor unit potentials
  - ECG abnormalities are also common

- Discuss the nurse's role in preparing and caring for children who will have these procedures.

Slide 38

Duchenne's or Becker's Muscular Dystrophy (MD) (cont.)
- Disease progressively worsens
- Death usually from cardiac failure or respiratory infection
- Nursing care is primarily supportive to prevent complications and maintain quality of life
- Child may experience depression because he or she cannot compete with peers

- Give examples of supportive care for these children.
- What is the nurse's role in educating the parents of a child with MD?

Slide 39

Slipped Femoral Capital Epiphysis
- Also known as coxa vera
- Spontaneous displacement of the epiphysis of the femur
- Occurs most often during rapid growth of the preadolescent and is not related to trauma
- Symptoms include thigh pain and a limp or the inability to bear weight on the involved leg
- Buck's extension traction is used to minimize further slippage until surgical intervention can take place

- How does Buck's traction assist children with this condition?

Slide 40

Legg-Calvé-Perthes Disease (Coxa Plana)

- One of a group of disorders called the osteochondroses in which the blood supply to the epiphysis, or end of the bone, is disrupted
  - Tissue death that results from inadequate blood supply is termed avascular necrosis
  - Affects the development of the head of the femur
- More common in boys 5 to 12 years of age
- Healing occurs spontaneously over 2 to 4 years

Slide 41

Legg-Calvé-Perthes Disease (Coxa Plana) (cont.)

- Symptoms include
  - Painless limp
  - Limitation of motion
- X-ray films and bone scans confirm the diagnosis
- Self-limiting, heals spontaneously with the use of ambulation-abduction casts or braces that prevent subluxation
  - Some may require hip joint replacement

- Discuss the nurse's role regarding the child with a cast or braces.

Slide 42

Osteosarcoma

- Primary malignant tumor of the long bones
  - Mean age of onset is 10 to 15 years of age
  - Children who have had radiation therapy for other types of cancer and children with retinoblastoma have a higher incidence of this disease
- Metastasis occurs quickly because of the high vascularity of bone tissue
  - Lungs are primary site of metastasis

Audience Response Question #2

Complete the analogy. Osteosarcoma : long bones as _____ : bone marrow.

    1. Ewing's sarcoma
    2. osteomyelitis
    3. leukemia
    4. sepsis

Slide 43

Osteosarcoma (cont.)

- Manifestations
  - Experiences pain and swelling at the site
  - May be lessened by flexing the extremity
  - Pathologic fractures can occur
- Diagnosis
  - Confirmed by biopsy
  - Radiological studies help to confirm
- Treatment
  - Radical resection or amputation surgery
  - Phantom limb pain can occur because nerve tracts continue to "report" pain

- What is phantom pain?

Slide 44

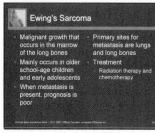

Ewing's Sarcoma

- Malignant growth that occurs in the marrow of the long bones
- Mainly occurs in older school-age children and early adolescents
- When metastasis is present, prognosis is poor
- Primary sites for metastasis are lungs and long bones
- Treatment
  - Radiation therapy and chemotherapy

ELSEVIER

Introduction to Maternity & Pediatric Nursing, 6th ed.

Leifer

Slide 45

Juvenile Idiopathic Arthritis (JIA)

- Formerly known as *juvenile rheumatoid arthritis (JRA)*
- Most common arthritic condition of childhood
- Systemic inflammatory disease involving joints, connective tissues, and viscera
- No specific tests or cures for JIA
- Duration of symptoms is important, particularly if they have lasted longer than 6 weeks

- How does JIA affect the child's joints?

Slide 46

Juvenile Idiopathic Arthritis (JIA)
(cont.)

- Three distinct methods of onset
  - Systemic (or acute febrile)
  - Polyarticular
  - Pauciarticular

- Discuss manifestations for each type of JIA.

Slide 47

Juvenile Idiopathic Arthritis (JIA)
(cont.)

- Systemic
  - Occurs most often in children 1 to 3 years of age and 8 to 10 years of age
  - Intermittent spiking fever (above 103° F) persisting for over 10 days
  - Nonpruritic macular rash
  - Abdominal pain
  - Elevated ESR and C-reactive protein

Slide 48

Juvenile Idiopathic Arthritis (JIA)
(cont.)

- Polyarticular
  - Involves five or more joints
    - Often hands and feet
    - Become swollen, warm, and tender
  - Occurs throughout childhood and adolescence
  - Predominantly seen in girls

Slide 49

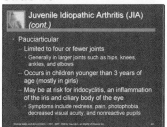

Juvenile Idiopathic Arthritis (JIA)
(cont.)

- Pauciarticular
  - Limited to four or fewer joints
    - Generally in larger joints such as hips, knees, ankles, and elbows
  - Occurs in children younger than 3 years of age (mostly in girls)
  - May be at risk for iridocyclitis, an inflammation of the iris and ciliary body of the eye
    - Symptoms include redness, pain, photophobia, decreased visual acuity, and nonreactive pupils

Slide 50

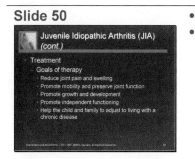

Juvenile Idiopathic Arthritis (JIA) *(cont.)*

- Treatment
  - Goals of therapy
    - Reduce joint pain and swelling
    - Promote mobility and preserve joint function
    - Promote growth and development
    - Promote independent functioning
    - Help the child and family to adjust to living with a chronic disease

- What methods can reduce joint pain and swelling?
- Give examples of how joint function can be preserved.

Slide 51

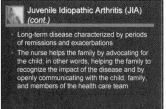

Juvenile Idiopathic Arthritis (JIA) *(cont.)*

- Long-term disease characterized by periods of remissions and exacerbations
- The nurse helps the family by advocating for the child; in other words, helping the family to recognize the impact of the disease and by openly communicating with the child, family, and members of the health care team

Slide 52

Torticollis (Wry Neck)

- Neck motion is limited because of shortening of the sternocleidomastoid muscle
- Can be congenital (most common) or acquired
  - Acute or chronic
  - Associated with breech and forceps delivery
    - May be seen in conjunction with other birth defects, such as congenital hip dysplasia

- Discuss the pathophysiology regarding breech and/or forceps delivery leading to this condition.

Slide 53

Torticollis (Wry Neck) *(cont.)*

- Symptoms are present at birth
  - Infant holds head to the side of the muscle involved with chin tilted in opposite direction
  - Hard, palpable mass of dense fibrotic tissue (fibroma), not fixed to the skin
  - Resolves by 2 to 6 months of age
  - Passive stretching, ROM, and physical therapy may be indicated
- Acquired is seen in older children, may be associated with injury, inflammation, neurological disorders, and other causes

- Discuss ROM for a child with this disorder.

Slide 54

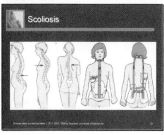

Scoliosis

- Discuss Figures 24-11 and 24-12 on page 575.

Slide 55

Scoliosis *(cont.)*

- More common in girls
- Two types
  - Functional—caused by poor posture
  - Structural—caused by changes in the shape of the vertebrae or thorax
    - Usually accompanied by rotation of the spine
    - Hips and shoulders may appear to be uneven

- Discuss poor posture and this disorder.

Slide 56

Scoliosis *(cont.)*

- Treatment
  - Aimed at correcting curvature and preventing severe scoliosis
    - Curves up to 20 degrees do not require treatment
    - Curves 20 degrees to 40 degrees require the use of a brace
    - Curves greater than 40 degrees and patients in whom conservative therapy were not successful require hospitalization
      - Spinal fusion is performed

- Review use of the Milwaukee brace on page 575.

Slide 57

Sports Injuries

- Sports-specific examinations are given for those involved in strenuous activity on entry into middle school or high school

- Common injuries include
  - Concussion
  - "Stingers" or "burners"
  - Injured knee
  - Sprain or strained ankle
  - Muscle cramps
  - Shin splints

- Discuss each of the common injuries and types of sports which could cause these injuries.

Slide 58

Sports Injuries *(cont.)*

- Sports at higher risk for injury include
  - Gymnastics
  - Wrestling
  - Football/Soccer
  - Hockey
  - Basketball
  - Volleyball
  - Running
  - Skiing or snowboarding

- Review the Health Promotion box on page 577.

Slide 59

Family Violence

- Affects children of all social classes
- Includes
  - Spousal and child abuse
  - Neglect
  - Maltreatment

- What is the difference between neglect and maltreatment?

Introduction to Maternity & Pediatric Nursing, 6th ed.

Elsevier items and derived items © 2011, 2007, 2006 by Saunders, an imprint of Elsevier Inc.   Leifer

Slide 60

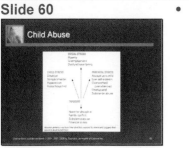

- Discuss the factors that could trigger child abuse.

Slide 61

Child Abuse *(cont.)*

- Types of child abuse
  - Emotional abuse
  - Emotional neglect
  - Sexual abuse
  - Physical neglect
  - Physical abuse

- Describe each of the types of child abuse listed.

Slide 62

Legal

- Reporting suspected abuse or neglect
  - All persons who report suspected abuse or neglect are given immunity from criminal prosecution and civil liability if the report is made in good faith
- Know what your state laws mandate for health care providers

Slide 63

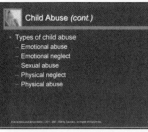

Nursing Interventions for Abused and Neglected Children and Adolescents

- Teach child anxiety-reducing techniques
- Assist child in managing his or her feelings
- Teach child assertiveness skills
- Assist child in developing problem-solving skills
- Assist child in value-building and clarification
- Assist child in enhancing his or her coping mechanisms

- Give examples of anxiety-reducing techniques.
- What are some examples of assertive skills?
- How could you enhance a child's coping mechanisms?

Slide 64

Assessing for Child Abuse

- Discuss Figure 24-14 on page 581.

Leifer

Slide 65

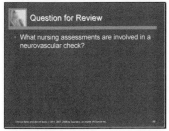

Cultural and Medical Issues

- A culturally sensitive history is essential in assessing children suspected to be victims of abuse
- Some cultural practices can be interpreted as physical abuse if the nurse is not culturally aware of folk-healing and ethnic practices
- Document all signs of abuse and interactions as well as verbal comments between the child and parent
- Child protective services should oversee any investigation that is warranted

- What are some examples of cultural practices that could be misconstrued as physical abuse?
- Give an example of documentation of suspected abuse.

Slide 66

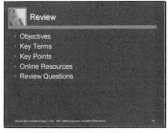

Question for Review

- What nursing assessments are involved in a neurovascular check?

Slide 67

Review

- Objectives
- Key Terms
- Key Points
- Online Resources
- Review Questions

Introduction to Maternity & Pediatric Nursing, 6th ed.
Leifer

TEACHING FOCUS

In this chapter, students will have the opportunity to learn about the skills required to care for children admitted to the pediatric unit with respiratory disorders. Methods for creating nursing care plans for pediatric patients with diagnoses of respiratory conditions will be discussed. Students will also have the opportunity to learn about treatments for respiratory patients, including nebulizer treatments and metered-dose inhalers.

MATERIALS AND RESOURCES

☐ Computer and PowerPoint projector (all lessons)

LESSON CHECKLIST

Preparations for this lesson include:

- Lecture
- Demonstration
- Guest speaker: Nurse with experience in dealing with SIDS
- Evaluation of student knowledge and skills needed to perform all entry-level activities related to respiratory conditions in children, including:
  ○ Emergency measures for patients with a diagnosis of croup, and techniques to communicate with parents
  ○ Respiratory distress and acute and chronic respiratory conditions in infants and children
  ○ Pathophysiology and manifestations of cystic fibrosis

KEY TERMS

alveoli (p. 591)
atelectasis (p. 602)
carbon dioxide narcosis
  (p. 584)
clubbing of fingers (p. 602)
coryza (p. 585)

dysphagia (p. 586)
laryngeal spasm (p. 588)
meconium ileus (p. 603)
orthopnea (p. 588)
pursed-lip breathing
  (p. 603)

reactive airway disease
  (RAD) (p. 591)
stridor (p. 587)
surfactant (p. 583)
tachypnea (p. 590)
ventilation (p. 584)

ADDITIONAL RESOURCES

TEACH PPT slide(s) Chapter 25, 1-67
EILR IC image(s) Chapter 25, 1-11
EILR OBQ question(s) Chapter 25, 1-10
EILR TB question(s) Chapter 25, 1-26
ESLR IRQ question(s) Chapter 25, 1-5
SG Chapter 25, pp. 203-209

Legend

PPT	**EILR**	**ESLR**	**SG**	**CTQ**
TEACH PowerPoint Slides	EVOLVE Instructor Learning Resources: Image Collection (IC), Open-Book Quizzes (OBQ), Test Bank (TB)	EVOLVE Student Learning Resources: Interactive Review Questions (IRQ) for the NCLEX® Examination	Study Guide	Critical Thinking Question in Nursing Care Plan (NCP CTQ) or Get Ready for the NCLEX! (GRN CTQ)

Class Activities are indicated in ***bold italic***.

LESSON 25.1

PRETEST

1. What type of hernia causes the abdominal contents to protrude into the chest?
   a. umbilical
   b. esophageal
   c. ventral
   d. diaphragmatic

2. A child diagnosed with streptococcal pharyngitis has been started on penicillin therapy. Which instructions should the nurse provide to the patient's mother?
   a. The child should avoid taking acetaminophen.
   b. The child should complete the course of antibiotics even if symptoms improve.
   c. Because the child has a viral infection, antibiotics may not help.
   d. The child is infectious even after antibiotics have begun.

3. The nurse should place a tracheotomy kit at the bedside when examining a child with
   a. epiglottitis.
   b. laryngotracheobronchitis.
   c. asthma.
   d. bronchiolitis.

4. Which condition is characterized by bronchospasm, mucosal edema, and mucus plugging that results in narrowing of the airways and impaired gas exchange?
   a. pneumonia
   b. asthma
   c. bronchiolitis
   d. croup

5. The defect in cystic fibrosis is due to
   a. endocrine gland dysfunction.
   b. adrenal gland dysfunction.
   c. exocrine gland dysfunction.
   d. thyroid gland dysfunction.

6. Which of the following causes atelectasis if the airway is blocked?
   a. bronchiolitis
   b. bronchitis
   c. pneumonia
   d. respiratory syncytial virus

7. What prevents carboxyhemoglobin (CoHb) from forming?
   a. bronchiolitis
   b. carbon monoxide poisoning
   c. cystic fibrosis
   d. bronchopulmonary dysplasia

8. What type of transmission-based precaution should be implemented in a patient with SARS?
   a. droplet
   b. contact
   c. protective
   d. airborne infection isolation

9. What should parents and children be taught to prevent the spread of infection in the immediate family?
   a. Always wear a mask.
   b. Wash drinking cup with water.
   c. Perform hand hygiene.
   d. Dust off countertops.

10. What should a parent do before bedtime to aid with sleep of a toddler with an upper respiratory illness?
    a. Increase humidity in the home.
    b. Give a bottle to suck on in bed.
    c. Bulb suction congested nasal passages.
    d. Let toddler play until bedtime.

Answers

1. d	3. a	5. c	7. b	9. c
2. b	4. b	6. a	8. d	10. c

BACKGROUND ASSESSMENT

Question: What are the symptoms of respiratory distress?

Answer: Signs of respiratory distress in infants and children include grunting and crowing sounds on respirations, pallor around the mouth, tachypnea, restlessness and apprehension, flaring nostrils, sternal retractions, and coughing. Symptoms of chronic respiratory distress are wheezing, retractions, cyanosis on exertion, use of accessory respiratory muscles, club fingers, irritability, and exhaustion. These symptoms are late indications for intervention.

Elsevier items and derived items © 2011, 2007, 2006 by Saunders, an imprint of Elsevier Inc.

Leifer

Question: Describe the pathology of respiratory syncytial virus (RSV). How is RSV transmitted, and what are its symptoms?

Answer: Fifty percent of respiratory syncytial virus (RSV) cases cause bronchiolitis. RSV is also the cause of most viral pneumonias in infants and children. RSV is prevalent during the winter months and causes epidemics worldwide. Respiratory illness involving RSV is common in children who attend day care centers. Most children are infected with RSV during their first 4 years, and reinfection is common. Infants between the ages of 2 months and 7 months who contract RSV may become severely ill because they have small airways. They are also prone to bronchiole obstruction by thick mucus. Carriers of the virus, usually individuals who are infected but continue to attend work and school, are responsible for the spread of RSV. Hospital cross-infection is a major problem because caregivers of an infected child may carry the organism and not realize it. The infant with severe illness from RSV may have symptoms of tachypnea, tachycardia, hypoxemia, and abnormal lung sounds, including wheezing, rales, or rhonchi.

CRITICAL THINKING QUESTION

A 2-year-old girl with acute croup is extremely restless and is admitted to the pediatric unit. The child's mother is concerned that her daughter's chest hurts from coughing so much and requests that she be given pain medication and sedatives to help her sleep. Are these appropriate treatments for croup? What are other treatments of the condition?

Guidelines: Croup is a viral condition that results from respiratory obstruction and is characterized by a barking or brassy cough, followed by symptoms of respiratory distress. Restlessness is a primary sign of increased respiratory obstruction; sedatives can mask the signs of restlessness and worsening respiratory obstruction. Pain medications (opiates), such as morphine, cannot be given because they depress respirations, which will also worsen the respiratory distress. Appropriate treatments are nebulized epinephrine, which alleviates symptoms of respiratory obstruction, and corticosteroids, which reduce edema caused by inflammation and prevent further destruction of ciliated epithelium. Other treatments include placing the child in a Croupette, administering intravenous fluids, placing the child on a cardiorespiratory monitor, and delivering oxygen to reduce hypoxia.

OBJECTIVES	CONTENT	TEACHING RESOURCES
Distinguish the differences between the respiratory tract of the infant and that of the adult.	■ The respiratory system (p. 583) □ Development of the respiratory tract (p. 583) □ Normal respirations (p. 584) □ Ventilation (p. 584)	⊠▤ PPT slides 6-10 𝒆 EILR IC image 1 𝒆 EILR OBQ question 1 ▦ SG Learning Activities, question 1 (p. 203) **BOOK RESOURCES** Figure 25-1, Summary of Respiratory Tract in Children (p. 584) Table 25-1, Differences in the Respiratory Tracts of the Growing Child and the Adult (p. 585) ▸ Discuss the differences the nurse should recognize when performing an assessment for a child who is suffering from a respiratory condition compared with an adult assessment. ▸ Discuss how pulmonary structures allow health care professionals to determine the location of specific defects. ▸ Discuss the function of surfactant in the respiratory system. When is it produced? ▸ Discuss the roles of the intercostal muscles, the brain,

OBJECTIVES	CONTENT	TEACHING RESOURCES
		and chemoreceptors in breathing.
		Class Activity Lead a class discussion on the normal processes of respiration. Ask students to identify which processes are affected by various respiratory conditions (such as asthma, croup, tonsillitis, sinusitis, RSV, etc.) Write the processes on the board for comparison.
		Class Activity Divide the class into groups, and assign each group a different respiratory organ or structure (lungs, alveoli, surfactant, esophagus, trachea, etc.). Have groups identify how their structure functions in the respiratory system and compare its functions in children and adults. Have each group present its findings to the class.
		Class Activity Divide the class into two groups. Have one group discuss the physiology of the infant/child respiratory system and the other group discuss the physiology of the adult respiratory system. Have each group present its findings to the class. Then, have the class identify how the adult and child respiratory tracts differ, and discuss how certain illnesses or conditions affect the adult and child systems.
Compare bed rest for a toddler with bed rest for an adult.	■ Disorders and dysfunction of the respiratory system (p. 585) □ Nasopharyngitis (p. 585) □ Acute pharyngitis (p. 586)	☒ PPT slides 11-14 𝒆 EILR OBQ question 2 𝒆 EILR TB questions 1, 12 𝗌𝗀 SG Learning Activities, questions 1-4 (p. 203) **BOOK RESOURCES** Medication Safety Alert (p. 586) Nursing Tip (p. 586) ▶ Discuss the rationale for preventing fatigue when a patient suffers from a common cold (coryza). ▶ Discuss treatment options for a pediatric patient with a common cold. ▶ Discuss why the common cold is the most common respiratory tract infection. How is it spread? *Class Activity Lead a class discussion on acute coryza. Ask students to identify signs and symptoms of the common cold, identify effective treatments for children, and compare its signs, symptoms, and treatments to those of allergic rhinitis. Write these on the board for comparison.* *Class Activity Divide the class into groups and have students identify 10 ways to prevent the spread of infection among children. Have each group share its*

Leifer

OBJECTIVES	CONTENT	TEACHING RESOURCES
		list with the class for discussion.
		Class Activity *Present the following scenario to the class for students to discuss:*
		A 3-year-old girl has an upper respiratory tract infection. She has a fever of 102° F, vomiting and diarrhea, coughing, nasal discharge, and is irritable. The physician has ordered bed rest for the child.
		Divide the class into groups and have each group identify three nursing interventions for the above scenario. Then have each group share its findings with the class.
Discuss how sinusitis in children is different from that in adults.	☐ Sinusitis in children (p. 587)	▣ PPT slide 15
		▣ SG Learning Activities, question 5 (p. 203)
		▸ Discuss the causes of sinusitis in children. What treatment options are available?
		▸ Discuss side effects that may accompany medications deemed appropriate for treating pediatric patients suffering from sinusitis.
		Class Activity *Present the following scenario to the class for students to discuss:*
		A 9-year-old boy has had an upper respiratory tract infection for the past 2 weeks, is coughing, and has developed a toothache.
		Divide the class into groups. Have each group discuss the child's signs and symptoms and identify appropriate nursing interventions. Then have each group share its findings with the class for discussion. What could happen if the illness goes untreated?
		Class Activity *Draw a time line on the board. Have student volunteers fill in the time line by identifying the developmental stages of the sinus cavities, one at a time. Then lead a class discussion about the symptoms and manifestations of sinusitis in children compared with adults.*
Discuss the nursing care of a child with croup, Respiratory Syncytial Virus (RSV), and pneumonia.	☐ Croup syndromes (p. 587) – Benign crouplike conditions (p. 587) – Acute croup (p. 588) ☐ Respiratory syncytial virus (p. 589) ☐ Pneumonia (p. 591)	▣ PPT slides 16-23, 27-32 𝒆 EILR IC image 2 𝒆 EILR TB questions 2, 5, 16, 17, 25 𝒆 ESLR IRQ question 1 ▣ SG Learning Activities, questions 1, 6, 8, 13-18 (pp. 203-205)

Introduction to Maternity & Pediatric Nursing, 6th ed.
Leifer

OBJECTIVES	CONTENT	TEACHING RESOURCES

		SG Review Questions, questions 4, 8, 40 (pp. 208-209)
		
		 SG Applying Knowledge, questions 1, 2 (p. 209)
		
		BOOK RESOURCES
		
		Figure 25-2, Signs of Respiratory Distress in Infants and Children (p. 587)
		
		Safety Alert (p. 588)
		
		Figure 25-3, A Child Receiving Aerosol Therapy (p. 588)
		
		Medication Safety Alert (p. 590)
		
		Pictorial Pathway 25-1, Care of a Child with Pneumonia (pp. 593-594)
		
		Review Questions for the NCLEX® Examination, question 5 (p. 610)
		
		▶ Discuss the nurse's role in providing patient education for patients diagnosed with acute croup.
		
		▶ Discuss the treatment strategies for a hospitalized patient with acute croup. What are some prevention strategies for croup syndromes?
		
		▶ Discuss ways to prevent the onset of RSV in infants and children.
		
		▶ Discuss signs and symptoms seen in adults and children who have pneumonia.
		
		▶ Discuss the nurse's role in the care of a patient with pneumonia who also has a fever.
		
		Class Activity *Divide the class into three groups and present one of the following scenarios to each group:*
		
		   1. A 1-year-old girl with a fever of 101° F, runny nose, sore throat, and a persistent cough
		
		   2. An 18-month-old child has a brassy cough, usually at night, accompanied by tachypnea, restlessness, and wheezing.
		
		   3. A 3-month-old girl with tachypnea, tachycardia, and high-pitched wheezing
		
		Have students identify the condition each patient is presenting and discuss nursing interventions and treatments for each. Which conditions can be treated at home, and which require hospitalization?
		
		Class Activity *Divide the class into two groups. Assign one group to discuss the signs of RSV. Assign the second group to discuss the symptoms of RSV. Then*

OBJECTIVES	CONTENT	TEACHING RESOURCES
		have each group share its findings with the class and discuss the importance of identifying signs and symptoms of RSV to allow for proper treatment and nursing care.
		Class Activity **Divide the class into three groups and assign each group one of the following scenarios:**
		1. A 5-year-old boy with a fever of 104° F, dry cough, respiratory rate of 34/min, and a poor appetite
		2. A 7-year-old girl with a fever of 102° F, productive cough, respiratory rate of 40/min, and cyanosis
		3. A 3-year-old girl who is listless, lying on her left side, has shallow respirations, productive cough, chest pain, and a fever of 103° F
		Have each group identify three nursing interventions for its assigned scenario and present its findings to the class for discussion.
Recognize the precautions involved in the care of a child diagnosed with epiglottitis.	– Epiglottitis (p. 588) – Bronchitis (p. 589) – Bronchiolitis (p. 589)	☒ PPT slides 24-26 *e* EILR OBQ question 3 *e* EILR TB question 5 SG Learning Activities, questions 1, 7, 9-12 (pp. 203-204) SG Review Questions, questions 1, 5, 8, 12 (pp. 207-208) **BOOK RESOURCES** Safety Alert (p. 589) Review Questions for the NCLEX® Examination, question 4 (p. 610) ▸ Discuss illnesses and conditions that may affect the epiglottis. ▸ Discuss why some parents refuse to vaccinate their children with routine immunizations. What ramifications and legal issues could stem from this choice? *Class Activity* **Present the following scenario to the class for students to discuss:** *A father calls the physician's office and tells the nurse that his toddler is drooling, croaking, anxious, and will not lie down. The nurse consults the physician, who determines that the child is displaying signs of epiglottitis.*

OBJECTIVES	CONTENT	TEACHING RESOURCES
		Have students identify appropriate instructions to give to the father, and discuss the care and treatment of a child with epiglottitis. Class Activity *Divide the class into groups, and assign each group one of the following conditions: epiglottitis, bronchitis, and bronchiolitis. Have each group discuss its assigned condition and identify the condition's pathophysiology, signs and symptoms, treatment, nursing interventions, and home care. Then have each group present its findings to the class.*
Describe smoke inhalation injury as it relates to delivery of nursing care.	☐ Smoke inhalation injury (p. 592)	⊠ PPT slide 33 *e* EILR TB question 19 *e* ESLR IRQ question 5 **BOOK RESOURCES** Safety Alerts (p. 592) ▸ Discuss the three stages of inhalation injury. ▸ Discuss why pulse oximetry readings are of little value in carbon monoxide poisoning.

25.1 Homework/Assignments:

25.1 Instructor's Notes/Student Feedback:

ELSEVIER

LESSON 25.2

CRITICAL THINKING QUESTION

An 8-year-old child has a history of asthma and lives with her mother and younger sister. In assessing the home environment, the nurse learns that the family lives in a townhouse and has one cat and two dogs. The mother smokes two packs of cigarettes a day, the child shares a room with her younger sister, and the house is carpeted. How could the mother modify the home environment to better control her daughter's asthma?

Guidelines: Asthma attacks can be triggered by dust, animal dander, wool, feathers, pollen, mold, cigarette smoke, and strong odors. To prevent exacerbations and avoid triggering attacks, the home environment should be carefully controlled to minimize allergens. The child should not be exposed to smoke or chemical irritants. Humidity in the living areas should be kept between 25% and 50%. Using dehumidifiers to control humidity and HEPA filters to limit allergens can help. The house should be kept free from dust and mold, and carpeting should be removed from the child's bedroom. If the carpeting cannot be removed, it should be sprayed every 3 months with Arcarosan to kill dust mites. Other dust collectors should be removed from the bedroom, including stuffed toys, upholstered furniture, and fabric curtains. Mattress and pillow covers that prevent the release of dust mites and their byproducts should be used. Bedding should be washed often in hot water. It is best if animals are removed from the home as well.

OBJECTIVES	CONTENT	TEACHING RESOURCES
Discuss the postoperative care of a 5-year-old who has had a tonsillectomy.	☐ Tonsillitis and adenoiditis (p. 592)	PPT slides 34, 35 *e* EILR OBQ question 4 *e* EILR TB questions 3, 4 *e* ESLR IRQ question 2 SG Learning Activities, questions 19, 20 (p. 205) SG Review Questions, questions 2, 6, 9, 13 (p. 208) **BOOK RESOURCES** Nursing Tip (p. 592) Review Questions for the NCLEX® Examination, question 2 (p. 610) ▸ Discuss the types of information the nurse should include in the teaching plan for a postoperative tonsillectomy patient. ▸ Discuss why milk and milk products are avoided after a tonsillectomy. ▸ Discuss signs and symptoms that may indicate bleeding after a tonsillectomy. ▸ Discuss the postoperative recovery period for children and adults after a tonsillectomy. Who is most at risk for complications? Class Activity *Present the following scenario to the class: A 5-year-old girl is in the postoperative recovery room after having a tonsillectomy. Have students discuss a*

OBJECTIVES	CONTENT	TEACHING RESOURCES
		postoperative care plan for the patient and identify appropriate nursing interventions.
Recall the characteristic manifestations of allergic rhinitis.	☐ Allergic rhinitis (p. 594)	PPT slides 36-38 EILR IC image 4 EILR OBQ question 5 EILR TB question 20 SG Learning Activities, questions 1, 21 (pp. 203, 205) **BOOK RESOURCES** Figure 25-4, The Allergic Salute (p. 595) ▶ Discuss the symptoms of allergic rhinitis and how these symptoms impact the patient's lifestyle. ▶ Discuss data collection for allergic rhinitis. *Class Activity **Present the following characteristics to the class and have students determine if the characteristics are manifestations of allergic rhinitis:*** *– yellowish-green nasal discharge* *– darkened circles under eyes* *– watery and itchy eyes* *– nasal congestion* *Class Activity **Divide the class into two groups. Assign one group to discuss the signs of allergic rhinitis, and assign the second group to discuss the symptoms of allergic rhinitis. Then have each group share its findings with the class and discuss the importance of identifying signs and symptoms of allergic rhinitis to allow for proper treatment and nursing care.***
Assess the control of environmental exposure to allergens in the home of a child with asthma.	☐ Asthma (p. 595)	PPT slides 39-47 EILR IC image 5 EILR OBQ question 6 EILR TB questions 6, 14 SG Learning Activities, questions 22-27 (pp. 205-206) SG Case Study, question 1 (p. 209) SG Applying Knowledge, question 3 (p. 209) **BOOK RESOURCES**

OBJECTIVES	CONTENT	TEACHING RESOURCES
		Figure 25-5, The Four Main Components of Asthma (p. 595)
		Figure 25-6, An Asthmatic Airway Compared to a Normal Airway (p. 596)
		Safety Alert (p. 596)
		▸ Discuss the manifestations of asthma.
		▸ Discuss why some patients develop asthma as children and others as adults.
		*Class Activity **Present the following items to the class and have students discuss how each item can be controlled to avoid environmental exposure to allergens in the home of a child with asthma.***
		– *dust*
		– *animal dander*
		– *mold*
		– *smoke*
		– *odor*
		– *upholstery*
		– *carpet*
		– *furniture*
Interpret the role of sports and physical exercise for the asthmatic child.	☐ Asthma (p. 595)	𝒆 EILR TB question 21 SG Case Study, question 1 (p. 209) **BOOK RESOURCES** Review Questions for the NCLEX® Examination, questions 1-5 (p. 610) ▸ Discuss the level of physical exercise that a child with asthma can safely engage in. *Class Activity **Divide the class into small groups and assign each group a different sport or physical activity (swimming, dancing, gymnastics, running, baseball, etc.). Have each group discuss whether or not its assigned sport would be acceptable for an asthmatic child to take part in. Have each group share its findings with the class.***
Express five goals of asthma therapy.	☐ Asthma (p. 595) – Status asthmaticus (p. 601)	PPT slides 46, 47 𝒆 EILR IC images 7, 8 𝒆 EILR OBQ question 7 𝒆 EILR TB questions 6-8, 13, 14, 18, 23, 24, 26

OBJECTIVES	CONTENT	TEACHING RESOURCES
		SG Learning Activities, questions 1, 22-27 (pp. 203, 206)
		SG Review Questions, questions 7, 9 (p. 208)
		SG Case Study, question 1 (p. 209)
		BOOK RESOURCES
		Figure 25-7, Management of Asthma (p. 597)
		Table 25-2, Asthma Drug Interactions (p. 598)
		Skill 25-1, Using the Peak Flow meter (p. 598)
		Medication Safety Alert (p. 599)
		Figure 25-8, The Asthma Diary (p. 600)
		Medication Safety Alert (p. 601)
		Skill 25-2, Using a Metered-Dose Inhaler (p. 601)
		Nursing Tip (p. 601)
		Review Questions for the NCLEX® Examination, questions 1, 3 (p. 610)
		▶ Discuss how status asthmaticus differs from an asthma attack. Why is status asthmaticus considered a medical emergency?
		▶ Discuss approaches nurses can use to manage episodes of status asthmaticus.
		▶ Discuss how the patient can manage asthma.
		Class Activity Divide the class into five groups and assign each group one of the goals of asthma therapy. Have each group discuss its assigned goal and list the goal's benefits for the asthma patient. Have each group share its findings with the class.
		Class Activity Present the following list of goals to the class and have students identify which pertain to asthma therapy and discuss the nurse's role for each:
		– Limit activity.
		– Maintain near-normal pulmonary function.
		– Prevent chronic signs and symptoms.
		– Prevent adverse reactions to medications.
		– Promote self-care and monitoring consistent with developmental level.

Leifer

25.2 Homework/Assignments:

25.2 Instructor's Notes/Student Feedback:

LESSON 25.3

CRITICAL THINKING QUESTION

A 10-year-old boy who has cystic fibrosis (CF) attends a local school and wants to participate in sports. What information should be provided to his teachers and to the coaching staff?

Guidelines: CF is a serious chronic lung disease that affects the exocrine glands. It is a multisystem disease that impacts the respiratory, digestive, and reproductive systems and the skin. This disease causes increased viscosity (thickness) of mucus gland secretion and loss of electrolytes due to sweating. It is important the boy slowly warm up before participating in a sport activity. He should also perform breathing exercises to help with air exchange and have free access to water and salt throughout the activity. Prior to any meal, he must take pancreatic enzymes to replace the enzymes his body is unable to produce. The meal should contain high protein and calories.

OBJECTIVES	CONTENT	TEACHING RESOURCES
Recall four nursing goals in the care of a child with cystic fibrosis.	☐ Cystic fibrosis (p. 601)	▣▤ PPT slides 48-54
		e EILR IC images 9, 10
		e EILR OBQ questions 8, 9
		e EILR TB questions 9-11, 22
		📖 SG Learning Activities, questions 28-35 (pp. 206-207)
		📖 SG Review Questions, questions 3, 10 (p. 208)
		📖 SG Case Study, question 2 (p. 209)
		📖 SG Thinking Critically, question 1 (p. 209)
		📖 SG Applying Knowledge, question 4 (p. 209)
		BOOK RESOURCES
		Figure 25-9, Manifestations of Cystic Fibrosis (p. 602)
		Figure 25-10, Clubbing of the Fingers, a Sign of Chronic Hypoxia (p. 602)
		▸ Discuss how and why cystic fibrosis impacts organs of the body other than the lungs.
		▸ Discuss meconium ileus. Why does it occur, and how does it lead to cystic fibrosis?
		Class Activity ***Present the following goals to the class and have students determine which pertain to caring for a child with cystic fibrosis:***
		– Decreasing nutritional demands
		– Minimizing pulmonary complications
		– Assisting the family to adjust to the chronic care of the patient
		– Promoting growth and development

OBJECTIVES	CONTENT	TEACHING RESOURCES
		Class Activity **Divide the class into groups and have each group discuss the pathophysiology of cystic fibrosis, its manifestations, and its treatments. Have each group share its findings with the class.**
Devise a nursing care plan for the child with cystic fibrosis, including family interventions.	☐ Cystic fibrosis (p. 601)	▣ PPT slides 55-57 𝒆 EILR IC image 11 𝒆 EILR TB questions 9-11 𝒆 ESLR IRQ question 4 ▦ SG Learning Activities, questions 34, 35 (p. 207) **BOOK RESOURCES** Nursing Care Plan 25-1, The Pediatric Patient with Cystic Fibrosis (pp. 604-605) Nursing Tip (p. 605) Figure 25-11, Postural Drainage (p. 606) Nursing Tip (p. 607) 💡 GRN CTQ 1 (p. 610) ▸ Discuss nursing interventions for a child with cystic fibrosis. ▸ Discuss strategies the nurse can use to help parents and children cope with cystic fibrosis. ***Class Activity*** **Present the following scenario to the class:** *A 7-year-old boy admitted to the hospital with a persistent cough, chest retractions, and nasal retractions* ***In groups, have students identify three nursing interventions for the patient and present their findings to the class for discussion.***
Review the signs and symptoms of respiratory distress in infants and children.	☐ Bronchopulmonary dysplasia (p. 608)	▣ PPT slides 58-61 𝒆 EILR IC image 2 𝒆 EILR TB question 20 𝒆 ESLR IRQ question 3 **BOOK RESOURCES** Figure 25-2, Signs of Respiratory Distress in Infants and Children (p. 587) ▸ Discuss the diagnostic procedures used to assess respiratory conditions. ▸ Discuss the signs of respiratory distress in infants and children. How do they differ from those in adults?

OBJECTIVES	CONTENT	TEACHING RESOURCES
		Class Activity Divide the class into two groups. Assign one group signs of respiratory distress in infants and children. Have this group determine what characteristics are considered signs. Assign the second group symptoms of respiratory distress in infants and children. Have this group determine what characteristics are considered symptoms. Then have each group share its findings with the class.
Review the prevention of bronchopulmonary dysplasia (BPD).	☐ Bronchopulmonary dysplasia (p. 608)	SG Learning Activities, question 36 (p. 207) **BOOK RESOURCES** Safety Alert (p. 609) ▸ Discuss preventive mechanisms used for patients with respiratory distress associated with BPD. ▸ Discuss techniques the nurse can use to educate the patient and family about BPD. *Class Activity Divide the class into groups. Ask each group to outline how BPD is transmitted, what age group it affects, and what its signs and symptoms are. Then have each group share its findings with the class. What are the complications if BPD is left untreated?* *Class Activity Present the following characteristics to the class:* — *mother who smokes* — *premature newborn* — *placing an infant to sleep on its stomach* — *high ventilator pressures* *Have the class determine which characteristics can cause BPD. Then lead a discussion on additional causes of BPD and its treatments.*
Examine the prevention of sudden infant death syndrome (SIDS).	☐ Sudden infant death syndrome (p. 609)	PPT slides 62-65 *e* EILR OBQ question 10 *e* EILR TB question 15 SG Learning Activities, question 37 (p. 207) **BOOK RESOURCES** Safety Alert (p. 609) ▸ Discuss SIDS. Why is it difficult to isolate a specific cause? ▸ Discuss ways parents can prevent SIDS from occurring.

OBJECTIVES	CONTENT	TEACHING RESOURCES
		Class Activity *Present the following scenario to the class for students to discuss:*
		A mother who is 3 weeks postpartum says that she lost a baby 2 years ago to SIDS, and is worried that it will happen again to her second child.
		Have the class identify methods of preventing SIDS and discuss ways to provide patient education to new mothers.
		Class Activity *Invite a nurse to speak to the class about SIDS.*
Performance Evaluation		⊠ PPT slides 1-67
		e EILR IC images 1-11
		e EILR OBQ questions 1-10
		e EILR TB questions 1-26
		e ESLR IRQ questions 1-5
		SG Learning Activities, questions 1-37 (pp. 203-207)
		SG Review Questions, questions 1-10 (pp. 207-209)
		SG Case Study, questions 1, 2 (p. 209)
		SG Thinking Critically, questions 1, 2 (p. 209)
		SG Applying Knowledge, questions 1-4 (p. 209)
		BOOK RESOURCES
		Review Questions for the NCLEX® Examination, questions 1-5 (p. 610)
		GRN CTQ 1 (p. 610)

25.3 Homework/Assignments:

25.3 Instructor's Notes/Student Feedback:

25 Lecture Outline
The Child with a Respiratory Disorder

Slide 1

Chapter 25

The Child with a
Respiratory Disorder

Slide 2

Objectives

- Distinguish the differences between the respiratory tract of the infant and that of the adult.
- Review the signs and symptoms of respiratory distress in infants and children.
- Discuss the nursing care of a child with croup, pneumonia, and respiratory syncytial virus (RSV).
- Recognize the precautions involved in the care of a child diagnosed with epiglottitis.

Slide 3

Objectives *(cont.)*

- Compare bedrest for a toddler with bedrest for an adult.
- Describe smoke inhalation injury as it relates to delivery of nursing care.
- Discuss the postoperative care of a 5-year-old who has had a tonsillectomy.
- Recall the characteristic manifestations of allergic rhinitis.

Slide 4

Objectives *(cont.)*

- Discuss how sinusitis in children is different from that in adults.
- Assess the control of environmental exposure to allergens in the home of a child with asthma.
- Express five goals of asthma therapy.
- Interpret the role of sports and physical exercise for the asthmatic child.

Slide 5

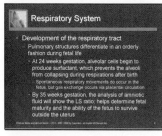

Objectives *(cont.)*

- Recall four nursing goals in the care of a child with cystic fibrosis.
- Devise a nursing care plan for the child with cystic fibrosis, including family interventions.
- Review the prevention of bronchopulmonary dysplasia.
- Examine the prevention of sudden infant death syndrome.

Slide 6

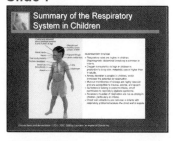

Respiratory System

- Development of the respiratory tract
  - Pulmonary structures differentiate in an orderly fashion during fetal life
    - At 24 weeks gestation, alveolar cells begin to produce surfactant, which prevents the alveoli from collapsing during respirations after birth
      - Spontaneous respiratory movements do occur in the fetus, but gas exchange occurs via placental circulation
    - By 35 weeks gestation, the analysis of amniotic fluid will show the LS ratio; helps determine fetal maturity and the ability of the fetus to survive outside the uterus

Slide 7

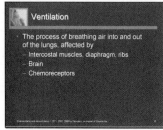

Summary of the Respiratory System in Children

- Review Figure 25-1 on page 584.

Slide 8

Ventilation

- The process of breathing air into and out of the lungs, affected by
  - Intercostal muscles, diaphragm, ribs
  - Brain
  - Chemoreceptors

- Discuss the pathophysiology of each body system that is part of the ventilation process.

Slide 9

Ventilation and Chronic Lung Disease

- High CO_2 level in blood and low O_2 saturation stimulate the brain to increase respiratory rate
- In chronic lung disease, receptors become tolerant to high CO_2 and low O_2 concentrations
- Administration of supplemental oxygen increases the O_2 saturation level
  - May result in decreased respiratory effort (carbon dioxide narcosis), leading to respiratory failure

- How do CO_2 levels affect the respiratory effort?

Leifer

Slide 10

Procedures that Can Be Done

- Throat and nasopharyngeal cultures
- Bronchoscopy
- Lung biopsy
- Arterial blood gas
- pH analysis
- Pulse oximetry
- Pulmonary function tests
- Chest X-ray
- CT scan
- Radioisotope scan
- Bronchogram
- Angiography

- Discuss how each procedure is performed.

Slide 11

Nasopharyngitis

- Upper respiratory tract infection
  - A cold, also known as coryza, most common infection of the respiratory tract
  - Nasal discharge, irritability, sore throat, cough, and general discomfort
  - Complications include bronchitis, pneumonitis, and ear infections
- Allergic rhinitis
  - Is not the same as a cold
  - Child will not have a fever, purulent nasal discharge, or reddened mucous membranes
  - Will have sneezing and itchy, watery eyes

- Discuss the nurse's role regarding preventing the spread of respiratory infections.
- What is the difference between allergic rhinitis and a viral upper respiratory infection?
- Principal cause is rhinovirus—spread from person to person by sneezing, coughing, or direct contact.
- Hand hygiene helps prevent the spread of this virus.

Slide 12

Nasopharyngitis (cont.)

- Treatment and Care
  - Rest
  - Clear airways
    - Moist air soothes the inflamed nose and throat
    - Avoid nosedrops with an oily base
  - Adequate fluid intake
  - Prevention of fever
- Skin care

- Discuss these nursing interventions and how they assist in the treatment of nasopharyngitis.
- What are some nursing interventions regarding skin care for the child who has nasopharyngitis?

Slide 13

Acute Pharyngitis

- Inflammation of the structures of the throat
- Common in children 5 to 15 years old
- Virus most common cause
- *Haemophilus influenzae* most common in children younger than 3 years
- Symptoms: fever, malaise, dysphagia, and anorexia, conjunctivitis, rhinitis, cough, and hoarseness with gradual onset, lasts no longer than 5 days
- In child older than 2 years, streptococcal pharyngitis may include fever of 104° F
- May require antibiotics if cause is bacterial

Slide 14

Acute Pharyngitis (cont.)

- Prompt treatment is necessary in strep throat to avoid serious complications such as
  - Rheumatic fever
  - Glomerulonephritis
  - Peritonsillar abscess
  - Otitis media
  - Mastoiditis
  - Meningitis
  - Osteomyelitis
  - Pneumonia

- Discuss the pathophysiology of each complication listed.

Slide 15

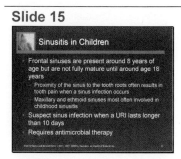

Sinusitis in Children

- Frontal sinuses are present around 8 years of age but are not fully mature until around age 18 years
  - Proximity of the sinus to the tooth roots often results in tooth pain when a sinus infection occurs
  - Maxillary and ethmoid sinuses most often involved in childhood sinusitis
- Suspect sinus infection when a URI lasts longer than 10 days
- Requires antimicrobial therapy

- What nursing interventions and home therapies would assist the child with a sinus infection?

Slide 16

Croup Syndromes

- Also referred to as subglottic croup because edema occurs below the vocal cords
- Can lead to airway obstruction, acute respiratory failure, and hypoxia
- Six types of syndromes
- "Barking" cough
- Inspiratory stridor
  - Acute spasmodic laryngitis is milder form
  - Acute laryngotracheobronchitis most common

- Discuss airway obstruction and nursing interventions when managing this urgent condition.

Slide 17

Croup Syndromes (cont.)

- Congenital laryngeal stridor (laryngomalacia)
  - Weakness in airway walls, floppy epiglottis that causes stridor on inspiration
  - Symptoms lessen when infant is placed prone or propped in side-lying position
  - Usually clears spontaneously as child grows and muscles strengthen

- Discuss the pathophysiology of lessening the symptoms by positioning an infant prone or side-lying.

Slide 18

Croup Syndromes (cont.)

- Spasmodic laryngitis (spasmodic croup)
  - Occurs in children 1 to 3 years of age
- Causes: viral, allergic, psychological
  - Trigger can be gastroesophageal reflux
- Sudden onset, usually at night
- Characterized by barking, brassy cough and respiratory distress; lasts a few hours
- Treatment: increasing humidity and providing fluids

- What methods would you use to increase the humidity in the infant's environment?
- Discuss methods to prevent gastroesophageal reflux.

Slide 19

Croup Syndromes (cont.)

- Laryngotracheobronchitis
  - Viral condition manifested by edema, destruction of respiratory cilia, and exudate, resulting in respiratory obstruction
  - Mild URI followed by barking cough, then stridor develops and leads to respiratory distress; crying and agitation worsen symptoms
- Child prefers to be in upright position (orthopnea)

Slide 20

Croup Syndromes *(cont.)*

· Treatment
  – Cold water humidifier
  – Helps relieve respiratory distress and laryngeal spasm
  – If hospitalized, may be placed in a mist tent or croupette
  – Cool air saturated in microdroplets enter small airway of child, cooling and vasoconstriction occurs, relieving the respiratory obstruction and distress
  – Opiates are contraindicated, as are sedatives

• Discuss the rationale to avoid opiates and sedatives in infants with croup.

Slide 21

Croup Syndromes *(cont.)*

· Epiglottitis
  – Swelling of the tissues above the vocal cords
    · Narrows airway inlet
  – Caused by H. influenzae type B
  – Most often seen in children 3 to 6 years of age
    · Can occur in any season
  – Course is rapid, progressive, and life-threatening

• Discuss the nurse's role in managing a child with epiglottitis.

Slide 22

Croup Syndromes *(cont.)*

· Onset of epiglottitis is abrupt
· Child insists on sitting up, leaning forward with mouth open, drools saliva because of difficulty in swallowing
· Cough is absent
· Examining the throat with a tongue blade could trigger laryngospasms; therefore, a tracheotomy set should be at the bedside before examination of the throat takes place

• What are laryngospasms?

Slide 23

Croup Syndromes *(cont.)*

· Treatment of choice is immediate tracheotomy or endotracheal intubation and oxygen
  – Prevents hypoxia, brain damage, and sudden death
· Parenteral antibiotics show dramatic improvements within a few days
· Prevention: HIB vaccine beginning at 2 months of age

Slide 24

Croup Syndromes *(cont.)*

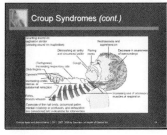

Slide 25

Bronchitis

- Infection of bronchi
  - Seldom primary infection
  - Caused by variety of microorganisms
- Unproductive "hacking" cough
  - Cough suppressants prior to bedtime so child can sleep
- OTC agents such as antihistamines, cough expectorants, and antimicrobial agents are normally not helpful

Slide 26

Bronchiolitis

- Viral infection of small airways
- Infants and children (6 months to 2 years)
  - Obstruction of airway leads to atelectasis
  - Increased respiratory rate
    - Can lead to irritability and dehydration
- RSV primary cause in 50% of cases
- Treat symptoms and place in semi-Fowler's position

Slide 27

Respiratory Syncytial Virus (RSV)

- Responsible for 50% of cases of bronchiolitis in infants and young children
- Spread by direct contact with respiratory secretions
- Survives more than 6 hours on countertops, tissues, and bars of soap
- Incubation approximately 4 days
- If hospitalized, place in contact isolation precautions

- Discuss educating the child's parents about contact isolation.
- RSV is the most common cause of viral pneumonia.
- Infants between 2 and 7 months of age can become seriously ill because of their small airways.

Slide 28

Respiratory Syncytial Virus (RSV) (cont.)

- Infant should be assigned to personnel who are not caring for patients at high risk for adverse response to RSV
- Adults who have RSV can shed the virus for up to 1 week after the infection; therefore, precautions should be taken if that adult is caring for infants
- Strict adherence to isolation precautions and hand hygiene are essential
- Symptomatic care is provided and can include
  - Supplemental oxygen
  - Intravenous hydration
  - Antiviral medication, such as ribavirin
  - IV immune globulin (RespiGam)

- Discuss types of nursing interventions to provide symptomatic care.

Audience Response Question #1
A child diagnosed with RSV will be placed on:
1. enteric precautions.
2. reverse isolation.
3. respiratory isolation.
4. no special precautions.

Slide 29

Safety Alert

- Caregivers who are pregnant or wear contact lenses should not give direct care to infants who are receiving ribavirin aerosol therapy
- *Routine immunizations may have to be postponed for 9 months after RespiGam has been given*

- Discuss the contraindication for a health care provider who is pregnant or wears contacts.
- What is the rationale regarding postponement of routine immunizations?

Slide 30

Pneumonia

- Inflammation of lungs in which the alveoli become filled with exudate and surfactant may be reduced
- Breathing shallow, resulting in decreased oxygenated blood
- Many types, classified according to causative organism (i.e., bacterial, viral)
- Group B streptococci most common cause in newborns
- Chlamydia most common cause in infants 3 weeks to 3 months of age

Slide 31

Pneumonia *(cont.)*

- Toddlers can aspirate small objects that can result in pneumonia
- *Lipoid pneumonia* occurs when infants inhale an oil-based substance
- *Hypostatic pneumonia* occurs if patients who have poor circulation in their lungs remain in one position for too long

- What objects might a toddler aspirate?
- Discuss nursing interventions when caring for a child with hypostatic pneumonia.

Slide 32

Pneumonia *(cont.)*

- Symptoms vary with age and causative organism/agent
  - Dry cough, fever, increased respiratory rate
  - Respirations shallow to reduce chest pain typically caused by coughing or from pleural irritation
  - Child is listless, poor appetite, tends to lie on affected side
- Chest X-ray confirms diagnosis
- Elevated WBC
- Cultures may be obtained from nose, throat, or sputum

- Discuss the rationale as to why a child might prefer one side to another when lying down.

Slide 33

Smoke Inhalation Injury

- May cause carbon monoxide poisoning
  - Prevents oxygen from combining with Hgb so carboxyhemoglobin cannot be formed
- Has three stages
  - Pulmonary insufficiency in first 6 hours
  - Pulmonary edema from 6 to 72 hours
  - Bronchopneumonia after 72 hours
    - Can lead to atelectasis

Slide 34

Tonsillitis and Adenoiditis

- Tonsils and adenoids are made of lymph tissue and are part of body's defense against infection
- Tonsillitis and adenoiditis
  - Difficulty swallowing and breathing
  - Provide cool mist vaporizer, salt-water gargles, throat lozenges (if age-appropriate), cool liquid diet, acetaminophen
  - Removal of tonsils and adenoids not recommended if under 3 years of age
  - Tonsillectomy done only if persistent airway obstruction or difficulty breathing occurs

Leifer

Slide 35

Safety Alert

- Frequent swallowing while the child is sleeping is an early sign of bleeding after a tonsillectomy
- Milk and milk products may coat the throat and cause the child to "clear" the throat, further irritating the operative site

- Give examples of a proper diet for a child who has had a tonsillectomy.

Slide 36

Allergic Rhinitis

- Inflammation of nasal mucosa caused by an allergic response
- Often occurs during specific seasons
- Not a life-threatening condition
- Accounts for many lost school days

- What triggers could contribute to allergic rhinitis?

Slide 37

Allergic Rhinitis (cont.)

- History shows seasonal occurrence and absence of fever or purulent drainage
- Mast cells respond to antigen by releasing mediators, such as histamine, which cause edema and increased mucus secretion
- Characteristic signs
  - Nasal congestion
  - Clear, watery nasal discharge
  - Sneezing
  - Itching of the eyes

- Discuss the pathophysiology regarding release of histamine and clinical manifestations.
- See Figure 25-4 on page 595.

Slide 38

Allergic Rhinitis (cont.)

- Symptomatic treatment
  - Antihistamines and decongestants to reduce edema
- Nursing goals
  - Help parent identify the difference between allergy and a cold
  - Provide referral for medical care and support
  - Dust control, prevention of contact with animal dander, use of HEPA filters, and planning of vacation locales are examples of parent teaching the nurse can provide

Slide 39

Asthma

- Syndrome caused by increased responsiveness of the tracheobronchial tree to various stimuli
- Leading cause of school absenteeism, emergency department visits, and hospitalization
- Recurrent and reversible obstruction of airways in which bronchospasms, mucosal edema, secretions, and plugging by mucus contribute to significant narrowing of airways and subsequent impaired gas exchange

Slide 40

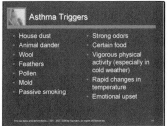

- Discuss Figure 25-5 on page 595.

Slide 41

Asthma Triggers

- House dust
- Animal dander
- Wool
- Feathers
- Pollen
- Mold
- Passive smoking
- Strong odors
- Certain food
- Vigorous physical activity (especially in cold weather)
- Rapid changes in temperature
- Emotional upset

- Discuss methods to avoid or alleviate exposure to these triggers.

Slide 42

Asthma (cont.)

- Rarely diagnosed in infancy
- Increased susceptibility of infants to respiratory obstruction and dyspnea may result from
  - Decreased smooth muscle of an infant's airway
  - Presence of increased mucus glands in the bronchi
  - Normally narrow lumen of the normal airway
  - Lack of muscle elasticity in the airway
  - Fatigue-prone and overworked diaphragmatic muscle on which infant respirations depend

---

Slide 43

Asthma (cont.)

- Manifestations
  - Obstruction most severe during expiration
  - During acute episodes, patient coughs, wheezes, and has difficulty breathing, particularly during expiration
  - Signs of air hunger, such as flaring of the nostrils, and use of accessory muscles may be evident; orthopnea appears
- Chronic asthma is manifested by discoloration beneath the eyes (allergic shiners), slight eyelid eczema, and mouth breathing

- Discuss and describe nasal flaring and accessory muscles used during these episodes.
- What are allergic shiners?

Slide 44

Asthma (cont.)

- Treatment and long-term management
  - Maintain near-normal pulmonary function and activity level
  - Prevent chronic signs and symptoms as well as exacerbations that require hospital treatment
  - Prevent adverse responses to medications
  - Promote self-care and monitoring consistent with developmental level

- Discuss methods to enhance near-normal pulmonary function.

Slide 45 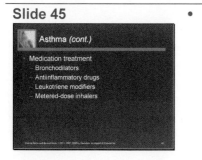 **Asthma** *(cont.)* Medication treatment – Bronchodilators – Antiinflammatory drugs – Leukotriene modifiers – Metered-dose inhalers	• Discuss the actions each medication classification provides in treating asthma.
Slide 46 **Status Asthmaticus** • Continued severe respiratory distress that is not responsive to drugs, including epinephrine and aminophylline • **This is a medical emergency** • ICU admission, supplemental oxygen, IV medications, and frequent vital signs (including pulse oximetry readings) are essential	• Give a scenario in which a child is experiencing status asthmaticus and discuss the nurse's role in managing this child.
Slide 47 **Safety Alert** • Oxygen is a drug, and administration should be correlated with monitoring of oxygen saturation levels – Too little oxygen can result in hypoxia – Too much oxygen can result in lung damage	• Discuss methods to assess adequate and inadequate oxygenation.

Slide 48
 Cystic Fibrosis
 • Major cause of serious chronic lung disease
 • Occurs 1 in 3000 live births of Caucasian infants
 • Occurs 1 in 17,000 live births of African Americans
 • Inherited recessive trait, with both parents carrying a gene for the disease
	Audience Response Question #2
	 Complete the analogy. RSV : nasal washing as cystic fibrosis : _____.
	     1. white blood cell count
	     2. echocardiogram
	     3. glucose tolerance test
	     4. sweat test

Slide 49 **Cystic Fibrosis** *(cont.)* • Basic defect is an exocrine gland dysfunction that includes – Increased viscosity (thickness) of mucus gland secretions – A loss of electrolytes in sweat because of an abnormal chloride movement	• Discuss the exocrine glands and the physiology regarding this disease.

Slide 50

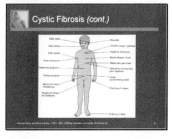

Cystic Fibrosis *(cont.)*

- Multisystem disease in which thick, viscid secretions affect
  - Respiratory system—obstructed by secretions
  - Digestive system—secretions prevent digestive enzymes from flowing to GI tract; results in poor absorption of food
    - Bulky, foul-smelling stools that are frothy because of the undigested fat content
  - Skin—loss of electrolytes in sweat causes "salty" skin surface
  - Reproductive system—secretions decrease sperm motility; thick cervical mucus can inhibit sperm from reaching fallopian tubes

Slide 51

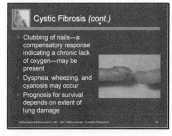

Cystic Fibrosis *(cont.)*

- • Discuss Figure 25-9 on page 602.

Slide 52

Cystic Fibrosis *(cont.)*

- Lung involvement
- Air passages become clogged with mucus
- Widespread obstruction of bronchioles
- Expiration is difficult, more air becomes trapped, small areas collapse (atelectasis)
- Right ventricle of heart, which supplies the lungs, may become strained and enlarged

- • What clinical manifestations would indicate an enlarged right ventricle?

Slide 53

Cystic Fibrosis *(cont.)*

- Clubbing of nails—a compensatory response indicating a chronic lack of oxygen—may be present
- Dyspnea, wheezing, and cyanosis may occur
- Prognosis for survival depends on extent of lung damage

Slide 54

Cystic Fibrosis *(cont.)*

- Pancreatic involvement
  - Thickened secretions block flow of pancreatic digestive enzymes
  - Newborn may experience meconium ileus
  - Infant stools may be loose
- Sweat glands
  - Sweat, tears, saliva abnormally salty due to increased chloride levels
  - Analysis of sweat is a major aid in diagnosing the condition

- • Review in more detail respiratory involvement and nursing implications.

Slide 55

> **Nursing Care for Cystic Fibrosis**
>
> · Oxygen therapy
> · Antibiotic therapy
> · Aerosol therapy
> · Use of inhalers
> · Postural drainage
> · Breathing exercises
> · Prevention of infection is essential
>
> · Oral pancreatic preparations are given to help child to digest and absorb food
> · Diet should be high in protein and calories
> · Free access to salt

- What is the nurse's role in providing each of the therapies?
- Discuss the rationale for increasing salt in the diet.

Slide 56

> **Nursing Care for Cystic Fibrosis** *(cont.)*
>
> · General hygiene
>   - Care should be given to diaper area
>   - Frequent changes of position help prevent development of pneumonia
>   - Child wears light clothing to prevent overheating
>   - Teeth may be in poor condition due to dietary deficiencies
>
> · Long-term care
>   - Goals include minimizing pulmonary complications, ensuring adequate nutrition, promoting growth and development, and assisting family to adjust to chronic care required

- Discuss the pathophysiology of frequent position changes and decreasing the risk of pneumonia.
- How can the nurse assist the family in managing a child with cystic fibrosis?

Slide 57

> **Nursing Care for Cystic Fibrosis** *(cont.)*
>
> · Parents need explicit instructions regarding
>   - Diet
>   - Medication
>   - Postural drainage
>   - Prevention of infection
>   - Rest
>   - Continued medical support
>   - Parents and child will also need emotional support

- What are some methods to prevent infection?

Slide 58

> **Bronchopulmonary Dysplasia**
>
> · A fibrosis, or thickening, of alveolar walls and bronchiolar epithelium caused by oxygen concentration above 40% or by mechanical pressure ventilation given to newborns for prolonged period of time
> · Swelling of tissues causes edema, respiratory cilia paralyzed by high oxygen concentration, and loss of ability to clear mucus
> · Respiratory obstruction, mucus plugs, and atelectasis follow

- Discuss methods to prevent or minimize this disorder.

Slide 59

> **Bronchopulmonary Dysplasia** *(cont.)*
>
> · Respiratory distress syndrome (RDS) in the newborn is major reason why oxygen and ventilators are used
> · Main cause of RDS in the newborn is prematurity
> · Goal of treatment
>   - Administer only the amount of oxygen required to prevent hypoxia at the minimum ventilator pressures needed to prevent tissue trauma
>   - Antenatal steroids hasten lung development during preterm labor
>   - Administration of surfactant within 15 minutes of delivery may also be helpful

---

Slide 60

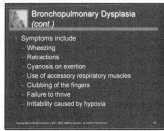

- Describe each symptom listed.

Slide 61

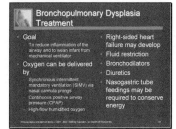

- Discuss signs and symptoms which indicate right ventricular failure.

Slide 62

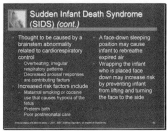

Slide 63

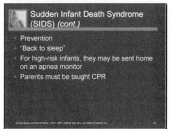

Slide 64

- Discuss methods to prevent SIDS.
- Discuss the nurse's role in educating the parents about CPR and using an apnea monitor.

Slide 65

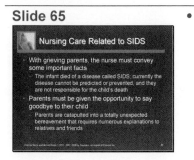

Nursing Care Related to SIDS

- With grieving parents, the nurse must convey some important facts
  - The infant died of a disease called SIDS; currently the disease cannot be predicted or prevented, and they are not responsible for the child's death
- Parents must be given the opportunity to say goodbye to their child
  - Parents are catapulted into a totally unexpected bereavement that requires numerous explanations to relatives and friends

- What resources and support systems might assist parents in dealing with their grief?

Slide 66

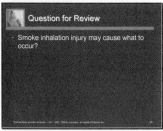

Question for Review

- Smoke inhalation injury may cause what to occur?

Slide 67

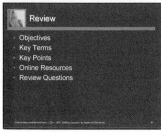

Review

- Objectives
- Key Terms
- Key Points
- Online Resources
- Review Questions

TEACHING FOCUS

In this chapter, students will have the opportunity to learn about the skills required to care for children admitted to the pediatric unit with cardiovascular disorders. Methods for creating nursing care plans for pediatric patients with diagnoses of cardiovascular conditions will be discussed. Students will also have the opportunity to learn about treatments for cardiovascular patients, including nebulizer treatments and metered-dose inhalers.

MATERIALS AND RESOURCES

☐ Computer and PowerPoint projector (all lessons)

LESSON CHECKLIST

Preparations for this lesson include:

- Lecture
- Demonstration
- Guest speaker: Nurse with experience in dealing with children with cardiovascular disease
- Evaluation of student knowledge and skills needed to perform all entry-level activities related to cardiovascular conditions in children, including:
  - Emergency measures for patients with a diagnosis of heart failure, and techniques to communicate with parents
  - Acute and chronic cardiovascular conditions in infants and children
  - Pathophysiology and manifestations of cardiomyopathy
  - Nursing diagnoses and interventions for infants with congenital heart defect complicated by congestive heart failure

KEY TERMS

carditis (p. 620)
chorea (p. 620)
hemodynamics (p. 612)
hypothermia (p. 612)
modified Jones criteria
   (p. 620)

polyarthritis (p. 619)
polycythemia (p. 615)
pulse pressure (p. 615)
shunt (p. 612)
stenosis (p. 615)
stroke volume (p. 618)

tachycardia (p. 618)
"tet" spells (p. 615)
thoracotomy (p. 612)

ADDITIONAL RESOURCES

TEACH PPT slide(s) Chapter 26, 1-54
EILR IC image(s) Chapter 26, 1-5
EILR OBQ question(s) Chapter 26, 1-10
EILR TB question(s) Chapter 26, 1-25
ESLR IRQ question(s) Chapter 26, 1-7
SG Chapter 26, pp. 211-217

Legend

PPT
TEACH
PowerPoint
Slides

EILR
EVOLVE Instructor
Learning Resources:
Image Collection (IC),
Open-Book Quizzes
(OBQ), Test Bank (TB)

ESLR
EVOLVE Student
Learning Resources:
Interactive Review
Questions (IRQ) for
the NCLEX®
Examination

SG
Study Guide

CTQ
Critical Thinking
Question in
Nursing Care Plan
(NCP CTQ) or Get
Ready for the
NCLEX! (GRN
CTQ)

Class Activities are indicated in ***bold italic***.

Leifer

LESSON 26.1

PRETEST

1. Which of the following is *not* a component of the modified Jones criteria?
   a. carditis
   b. chorea
   c. subcutaneous nodules
   d. "tet" spells

2. Which is *not* a way to treat high blood pressure in a child or adolescent?
   a. aerobic exercise
   b. increase sedentary activity
   c. weight reduction
   d. avoid smoking

3. This acquired disease often results from
   a. Kawasaki disease.
   b. kwashiorkor disease.
   c. rheumatic fever
   d. congestive heart failure.

4. Which cardiac defect can be diagnosed prior to birth?
   a. tetralogy of Fallot
   b. hypoplastic left heart syndrome
   c. coarctation of the aorta
   d. ventral septal defect

5. Cyanotic and acyanotic are two classification of what type of heart disease?
   a. restrictive
   b. congestive
   c. congenital
   d. murmur

6. Which body system develops between the third and eighth week of gestation and is the first functional system in fetal life?
   a. cardiovascular system
   b. gastrointestinal system
   c. renal system
   d. neurological system

7. The diagnostic test that produces sound wave images of the heart is referred to as a(n)
   a. aortography.
   b. echocardiography.
   c. electrocardiogram.
   d. cardiac catheterization.

8. The congenital heart disease comprising four defects is
   a. patent ductus arteriosus.
   b. atrial septal defect.
   c. coarctation of the aorta.
   d. tetralogy of Fallot.

9. Administering prophylactic antibiotics to children with heart defects before surgical or dental procedures helps to prevent
   a. pneumonia.
   b. respiratory distress.
   c. bacterial endocarditis.
   d. congestive heart failure.

10. Which autoimmune disorder is caused by a beta-hemolytic streptococcus infection and affects the heart, joints, central nervous system, skin, and subcutaneous tissues?
    a. bronchopulmonary dysplasia
    b. Kawasaki disease
    c. rheumatic fever
    d. cystic fibrosis

Answers

1. d	3. a	5. c	7. b	9. c
2. b	4. b	6. a	8. d	10. c

BACKGROUND ASSESSMENT

Question: What are the most common symptoms found in infants with congenital heart problems?
Answer: Signs of congenital health problems in infants include failure to thrive and/or poor weight gain; cyanosis, pallor; visible pulsations in the neck veins; tachypnea, dyspnea; irregular pulse rate; clubbing of fingers; fatigue during feeding or activity; and, excessive perspiration, especially over the forehead. Infants with suspected or confirmed congenital heart problems require close monitoring and rapid intervention.

CRITICAL THINKING QUESTION

A 1-year-old boy who attends day care has been diagnosed with tetralogy of Fallot. What is this condition, and what information should be provided to his parents and to the childcare staff?
Guidelines: Tetralogy of Fallot is a congenital heart defect that decreases pulmonary blood flow by allowing unoxygenated blood to enter the aorta and general circulation. There are four defects involved: stenosis of the pulmonary artery, hypertrophy of the right ventricle, dextroposition of the aorta, and ventricular septal defect.

ELSEVIER

The child will develop feeding problems, frequent respiratory infections, severe dyspnea, clubbing of the fingers and toes, growth retardation, and cyanosis. Iron deficiency is also common. Polycythemia develops, which can lead to cerebral thrombosis, and congestive heart failure will also occur. Antibiotic therapy is needed to prevent bacterial endocarditis. Open-heart surgery with total correction is usually performed on older children with excellent results. The parents and childcare staff should be informed that the child will often rest in a squatting position. This will enable him to breathe more easily by increasing systemic venous return. During the next year or so, he will experience paroxysmal hypercyanotic episodes ("tet" spells). These spells include spontaneous cyanosis, respiratory distress, weakness, and syncope, and can last anywhere from a few minutes to several hours. Episodes are followed by lethargy and sleep. When a tet spell occurs, the caretaker should place the child in a knee-chest position (the tet position) until the attack subsides. When the child is older, he may assume this position on his own.

OBJECTIVES	CONTENT	TEACHING RESOURCES
Distinguish the differences between the cardiovascular system of the infant and that of an adult.	■ The cardiovascular system (p. 611)	☒ PPT slide 5 *e* EILR IC image 1 **BOOK RESOURCES** Figure 26-1, Summary of Some Cardiovascular System Differences Between the Child and the Adult (p. 612) ▸ Discuss the physiology of the cardiovascular system.
List the general signs and symptoms of congenital heart disease.	☐ Signs related to suspected cardiac pathology (p. 611) ☐ Congenital heart defects (p. 611)	☒ PPT slides 6-13 *e* EILR IC image 2 *e* EILR OBQ question 1 *e* EILR TB questions 2, 8 [SG] SG Learning Activities, questions 2-4 (p. 211) [SG] SG Review Questions, questions 1, 8 (pp. 214-215) **BOOK RESOURCES** Table 26-1, Diagnostic Tests Used in Congenital Heart Defects (p. 613) Safety Alert (p. 613) Figure 26-2, The Normal Heart and Various Congenital Cardiac Defects (p. 614) ▸ Discuss approaches used to detect congenital heart disease. ▸ Discuss why cyanosis is not considered a definite clinical sign of congenital heart disease. *Class Activity Present the following signs and symptoms to the class and have students determine which are indications of congenital heart disease:* *– cyanosis/pallor* *– irregular pulse rate* *– normal heart and respiratory rate*

Introduction to Maternity & Pediatric Nursing, 6th ed.

Leifer

OBJECTIVES	CONTENT	TEACHING RESOURCES
		– failure to thrive or gain weight
		– wheezing with watery eyes and nasal discharge
Differentiate between patent ductus arteriosus, coarctation of the aorta, atrial septal defect, ventricular septal defect, and tetralogy of Fallot.	– Defects that increase pulmonary blood flow (p. 612) – Defects that restrict ventricular blood flow (p. 615) – Defects that decrease pulmonary blood flow (p. 615) – Defects that cause mixed pathology (p. 616)	PPT slides 14-25 EILR IC images 2, 3 EILR OBQ questions 2, 3 EILR TB questions 1, 3-5, 14, 20-24 ESLR IRQ questions 1, 6, 7 SG Learning Activities, questions 1, 5-12 (pp. 211-212) SG Review Questions, questions 2, 7, 9, 10 (pp. 214-215) **BOOK RESOURCES** Figure 26-2, The Normal Heart and Various Congenital Heart Defects (p. 614) Safety Alert (p. 615) Figure 26-3, Tet Position (p. 616) Nursing Tip (p. 616) Review Questions for the NCLEX® Examination, question 2 (p. 624) ▸ Discuss how the physiology of the cardiovascular system can lead to congenital heart defects. How can the changes that occur at birth lead to defects? ▸ Discuss diagnostic techniques used to identify atrial septal defect. ▸ Discuss the rationale for using antibiotic prophylaxis for dental procedures in patients with a ventricular septal defect. *Class Activity* **Present the following characteristics to the class and have students identify which defect each characteristic represents:** *– increased pulmonary flow* *– wide pulse pressures* *– narrowing of the aortic arch* *– dextroposition* *Class Activity* **Divide the class into four groups and assign each group one of the following topics:** *1. Defects that increase pulmonary blood flow*

OBJECTIVES	CONTENT	TEACHING RESOURCES
		2. Obstructive defects
		3. Defects that decrease pulmonary blood flow
		4. Defects that cause mixed pathology
		Have each group identify common defects within its assigned topic and explain their pathophysiology and treatments to the class.

26.1 Homework/Assignments:

26.1 Instructor's Notes/Student Feedback:

LESSON 26.2

CRITICAL THINKING QUESTION

Differentiate between primary and secondary hypertension. How is hypertension treated in children, and how can the incidence of hypertension be decreased?

Guidelines: The cause of primary hypertension, or essential hypertension, is unknown; there is no underlying disease present. Secondary hypertension is attributable to a specific disease process usually involving the renal, vascular, and endocrine systems as well as congenital problems. Other contributory factors to both types of hypertension include obesity, stress, poor diet, and inadequate exercise. Treatment and prevention of hypertension require patient education regarding modifiable risk factors, such as weight control and blood pressure assessment with routine physical examinations. Treatment should also include nutritional counseling and age-appropriate exercise programs as well as treatment for the underlying conditions in secondary hypertension. Drug therapy may not be effective for adolescents due to medication noncompliance. Community awareness and education regarding risk factors and preventive measures of hypertension are important. The school nurse can provide information to school personnel and involve the parent-teacher association in disseminating information to parents.

OBJECTIVES	CONTENT	TEACHING RESOURCES
Discuss six nursing goals relevant to the child with acquired heart disease.	– General treatment and nursing care of children with congenital heart defects (p. 616) ☐ Acquired heart disease (p. 617) – Congestive heart failure (p. 617)	⊠▪ PPT slides 26-33 𝒆 EILR OBQ questions 4-6 𝒆 EILR TB questions 6, 10, 11, 13, 19 𝒆 ESLR IRQ questions 2, 4 SG Learning Activities, questions 12-19 (pp. 212-213) SG Review Questions, questions 2-5 (p. 214) SG Thinking Critically, question 1 (p. 217) SG Applying Knowledge, questions 1-3 (p. 217) **BOOK RESOURCES** Safety Alert (p. 617) Medication Safety Alert (p. 618) Review Questions for the NCLEX® Examination, question 5 (p. 624) GRN CTQ 2 (p. 624) ▸ Discuss precautionary measures used for cardiac surgery performed in children with congenital heart defects. ▸ Discuss procedures used to diagnose congestive heart failure. *Class Activity Divide the class into six groups. Assign each group one of the nursing goals relevant to the child with heart disease. Ask each group to discuss its assigned goal and its intended effect on a child with heart disease. Then have each group share its findings with the class*

Leifer

OBJECTIVES	CONTENT	TEACHING RESOURCES
		and discuss the nurse's role in reaching these goals.

List the symptoms of rheumatic fever.	☐ Rheumatic fever (p. 619)	PPT slides 34-37
		
		EILR IC image 4
		
		EILR OBQ question 7
		
		EILR TB questions 7, 12, 15, 25
		
		ESLR IRQ questions 3, 5
		
		SG Learning Activities, question 20 (p. 213)
		
		BOOK RESOURCES
		
		Figure 26-4, Manifestations of Rheumatic Fever (p. 619)
		
		Box 26-1, Modified Jones Criteria (p. 620)
		
		▸ Discuss the levels of severity of rheumatic fever.
		
		▸ Discuss the Jones criteria for the diagnosis of acute rheumatic fever.
		
		▸ Discuss the major manifestations of rheumatic fever.
		
		Class Activity **Divide the class into two groups. Assign one group symptoms of rheumatic fever. Have this group determine what characteristics are considered symptoms. Assign the second group signs of rheumatic fever. Have this group determine what characteristics are considered signs. Then have each group present its findings to the class.**
		
		Class Activity **Present the following characteristics to the class and have students determine whether each is a sign or a symptom of rheumatic fever:**
		
		   – *polyarthritis*
		
		   – *chorea*
		
		   – *carditis*
		
		   – *fever*

Discuss the prevention of rheumatic fever.	☐ Rheumatic fever (p. 619)	PPT slides 38-40 EILR OBQ question 8 EILR TB question 16 SG Learning Activities, question 21 (p. 213) **BOOK RESOURCES** Nursing Tip (p. 621) Review Questions for the NCLEX® Examination, question 3 (p. 624)

OBJECTIVES	CONTENT	TEACHING RESOURCES
		▸ Discuss the role of streptococcal infections in developing rheumatic fever. *Class Activity **Lead a class discussion about the etiology, manifestations, treatments, signs and symptoms, and complications of rheumatic fever. Have students identify nursing interventions for a child with rheumatic fever and discuss methods of patient teaching and prevention.***
Discuss hypertension in childhood.	☐ Systemic hypertension (p .621)	PPT slides 41-44 **BOOK RESOURCES** Nursing Tip (p. 621) ▸ Discuss why the incidence of hypertension is rising among children and adolescents. ▸ Discuss the factors that contribute to hypertension in children. *Class Activity **As a class, discuss childhood hypertension, and ask students to identify why there is increasing incidence of this condition. Then have students identify nursing interventions and methods of early detection and prevention of childhood hypertension.*** *Class Activity **Divide the class into groups and ask each group to develop an education awareness advertisement for hypertension in childhood. Have each group share its ad with the class.***
Differentiate between primary and secondary hypertension.	☐ Systemic hypertension (p. 621)	PPT slides 41-43 SG Learning Activities, question 22 (p. 214) ▸ Discuss the different types of hypertension. *Class Activity **Divide the class into two groups. Assign one group primary hypertension and the other group secondary hypertension. Have each group discuss the characteristics of its assigned topic as well as the topic's causes and treatments. Then have each group share its findings with the class.***
Identify factors that can prevent hypertension.	☐ Systemic hypertension (p. 621)	PPT slide 44 EILR OBQ question 9 SG Review Questions, question 6 (p. 215) SG Thinking Critically, question 2 (p. 217) SG Applying Knowledge, question 5 (p. 217) ▸ Discuss the role of patient education in preventing hypertension in children.

OBJECTIVES	CONTENT	TEACHING RESOURCES
		Class Activity **Present the following factors to the class and have students identify which factors play a role in hypertension. Then discuss additional factors and methods of patient teaching for each.** – *obesity* – *education* – *active lifestyle* – *diet*
Describe a heart-healthy diet for a child over 2 years of age.	☐ Hyperlipidemia (p. 622)	PPT slides 45, 46 EILR TB questions 17, 18 SG Applying Knowledge, question 4 (p. 217) **BOOK RESOURCES** Table 26-2, Average Lipid Profile Levels in Childhood (p. 622) Health Promotion: Nonpharmacological methods for preventing and treating high blood pressure (p. 622) Health Promotion , Heart-Healthy Guidelines for Children (pp. 622-623) Nursing Tip (p. 623) ▸ Discuss why restricting fat from the diets of children younger than 2 years of age is not recommended. ▸ Discuss conditions that can result from a poor nutritional history in children. *Class Activity* **Divide the class into groups. Have each group develop a heart-healthy menu for children older than 2 years of age that covers all meals and snacks for 2 days. Have each group share its diet with the class and discuss the importance of establishing a heart-healthy diet early in life.**
Recognize the manifestation of Kawasaki disease and the related nursing care.	☐ Kawasaki disease (p. 623)	PPT slides 47-52 EILR IC image 5 EILR OBQ question 10 EILR TB question 9 SG Learning Activities, questions 23, 24 (p. 214) **BOOK RESOURCES** Review Questions for the NCLEX® Examination, question 4 (p. 624)

OBJECTIVES	CONTENT	TEACHING RESOURCES
		💡 GRN CTQ 1 (p. 624)
		Figure 26-5, Peeling of the Fingertips (p. 623)
Performance Evaluation		⊠ PPT slides 1-54
		𝒆 EILR IC images 1-5
		𝒆 EILR OBQ questions 1-10
		𝒆 EILR TB questions 1-25
		𝒆 ESLR IRQ questions 1-7
		📓 SG Learning Activities, questions 1-24 (pp. 211-214)
		📓 SG Review Questions, questions 1-10 (pp. 214-215)
		📓 Crossword Puzzle (p. 216)
		📓 SG Thinking Critically, questions 1, 2 (p. 217)
		📓 SG Applying Knowledge, questions 1-5 (p. 217)
		BOOK RESOURCES
		Review Questions for the NCLEX® Examination, questions 1-5 (p. 624)
		💡 GRN CTQ 1, 2 (p. 624)

26.2 Homework/Assignments:

26.2 Instructor's Notes/Student Feedback:

26 Lecture Outline
The Child with a Cardiovascular Disorder

Slide 1

Chapter 26

The Child with a
Cardiovascular Disorder

Slide 2

Objectives

- Distinguish the difference between the cardiovascular system of a child and an adult.
- List the general signs and symptoms of congenital heart disease.
- Differentiate among patent ductus arteriosus, coarctation of the aorta, atrial septal defect, ventricular septal defect, and tetralogy of Fallot.
- Discuss six nursing goals relevant to the child with heart disease.

Slide 3

Objectives *(cont.)*

- List the symptoms of rheumatic fever.
- Discuss the prevention of rheumatic fever.
- Discuss hypertension in childhood.
- Differentiate between primary and secondary hypertension.

Slide 4

Objectives *(cont.)*

- Identify factors that can prevent hypertension.
- Recognize the manifestation of Kawasaki disease and the related nursing care.
- Describe heart-healthy guidelines for children older than 2 years.

Leifer

Slide 5

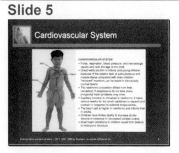

• Discuss Figure 26-1 on page 612.

Slide 6

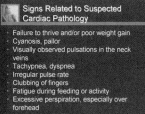

Slide 7

Slide 8

Slide 9

Slide 10

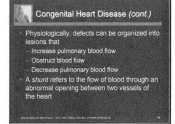

- Give examples of locations of lesions for the listed defects.

Slide 11

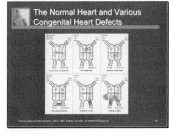

- Discuss Figure 26-2 on page 614.

Slide 12

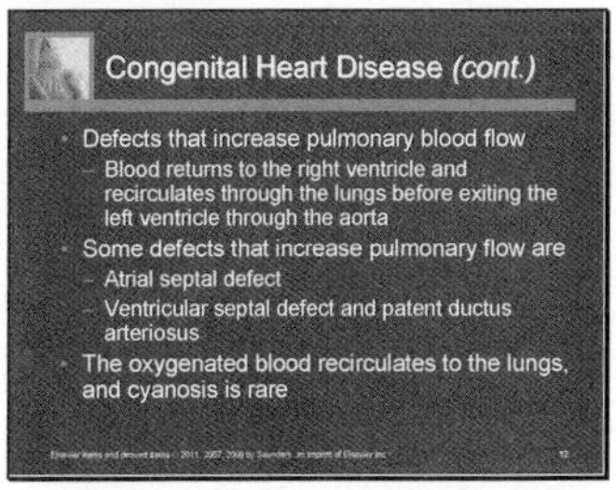

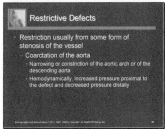

Slide 13

Nursing Tip

In congenital heart disease, cyanosis is *not* always a clinical sign

- Give examples of conditions in which a congenital heart defect does not cause cyanosis.

Audience Response Question #1
Complete the analogy. Patent ductus arteriosus : acyanotic defect as tetralogy of Fallot : _____.
   1. mixed
   2. cyanotic
   3. acyanotic
   4. obstructive

Slide 14

Restrictive Defects

- Restriction usually from some form of stenosis of the vessel
  - Coarctation of the aorta
    - Narrowing or constriction of the aortic arch or of the descending aorta
    - Hemodynamically, increased pressure proximal to the defect and decreased pressure distally

---

Slide 15

Coarctation of the Aorta

- Characteristic symptoms
- Marked difference in the blood pressure and pulses of the upper and lower extremities
- May not develop symptoms until late childhood
- Treatment is dependent upon type and severity of the defect
- Best time for surgical intervention is between 2 and 4 years of age

• What is the rationale for delaying surgical intervention until the child is 2 to 4 years old?

Slide 16

Coarctation of the Aorta *(cont.)*

- If left untreated
  - Hypertension
  - Congestive heart failure
  - Infective endocarditis may occur
- After surgery, the nurse should observe for
  - Hypertension
  - Abdominal pain associated with nausea and vomiting
  - Leukocytosis
  - GI bleeding or obstruction
- Treatment includes
  - Antihypertensive drugs
  - Steroids
  - NG tube for decompression of the stomach

• Discuss the rationale for steroid treatment.

Slide 17

Defects that Decrease Pulmonary Blood Flow

- Occurs when a congenital heart anomaly allows blood that has not passed through the lungs (unoxygenated blood) to enter the aorta and general circulation
- Cyanosis caused by the presence of unoxygenated blood in the circulation is a characteristic feature of this type of congenital heart anomaly

Slide 18

Tetralogy of Fallot

- Four defects
  - Stenosis or narrowing of the pulmonary artery
    - Decreases blood flow to the lungs
  - Hypertrophy of the right ventricle
    - Enlarges because it must work harder to pump blood through the narrow pulmonary artery
  - Dextroposition of the aorta
    - The aorta is displaced to the right and blood from both ventricles enters it
  - Ventral septal defect (VSD)

• Discuss this condition while referring to Figure 26-3 on page 616.

Slide 19

Tetralogy of Fallot *(cont.)*

- Cyanosis increases with age
- Clubbing of fingers and toes
  - Due to chronic hypoxia
- Child rests in a "squatting" position to breathe more easily by altering systemic venous return
- Prevalent symptoms include
  - Feeding problems
  - Failure to thrive
  - Frequent respiratory infections
  - Severe dyspnea on exertion
  - Polycythemia develops to compensate for the lack of oxygen

• How does the squatting position relieve dyspnea?

Leifer

Slide 20

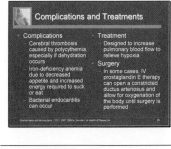

Paroxysmal Hypercyanotic
Episodes

- Known as *Tet spells*
- Occur during the first 2 years of life
- Spontaneous cyanosis, respiratory distress, weakness, and syncope occur
- They can last up to a few hours and are followed by lethargy and sleep
- Place child in knee-chest position when Tet spell occurs

- Describe Tet spells.
- Discuss the pathophysiology of the need for rest after a Tet spell.

Slide 21

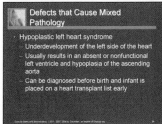

Tet Position

- Discuss Figure 26-3 on page 616.

Slide 22

Diagnosis

- Diagnosis confirmed by chest X-ray that shows a typical boot-shaped heart
- Additional tests include
  - EKG
  - 3-D echocardiography
  - Cardiac catheterization

- Discuss the boot shape and how it relates to the condition.

Slide 23

Complications and Treatments

- Complications
  - Cerebral thrombosis caused by polycythemia, especially if dehydration occurs
  - Iron-deficiency anemia due to decreased appetite and increased energy required to suck or eat
  - Bacterial endocarditis can occur
- Treatment
  - Designed to increase pulmonary blood flow to relieve hypoxia
- Surgery
  - In some cases, IV prostaglandin E therapy can open a constricted ductus arteriosus and allow for oxygenation of the body until surgery is performed

---

Slide 24

Defects that Cause Mixed
Pathology

- Hypoplastic left heart syndrome
  - Underdevelopment of the left side of the heart
  - Usually results in an absent or nonfunctional left ventricle and hypoplasia of the ascending aorta
  - Can be diagnosed before birth and infant is placed on a heart transplant list early

---

Slide 25

Defects that Cause Mixed Pathology *(cont.)*

- Hypoplastic left heart syndrome *(cont.)*
  - Initial survival depends on a patent foramen ovale and ductus arteriosus to provide a pathway for oxygenated blood to the general body system
  - Symptoms include
    - A grayish-blue color of the skin and mucous membranes
    - Signs of CHF
    - Dyspnea
    - Weak pulses
    - Cardiac murmur

Slide 26

General Treatment and Nursing Care

- Assorted medical and surgical treatments are currently available
- After the procedure, the nursing care involves
  - Monitoring vital signs
  - Observing for thrombosis formation
  - Neurovascular checks of the limb
  - Emotional support to child and family

- Discuss various medical and surgical treatments available for this condition.
- What methods can determine thrombosis formation?
- How can you provide emotional support to the child and family?

Slide 27

General Treatment and Nursing Care *(cont.)*

- Instruct parents that competitive sports are avoided in children with congenital heart disease, because the pressure for a team win can interfere with the child's need to stop activity if specific symptoms arise
- Nutritional guidance aimed at preventing anemia and promoting optimal growth and development
- Vacations to high altitudes or very cold environments may cause adverse responses in a child who is already hypoxic or has cardiac problems

- Discuss alternative physical activities a child might participate in instead of competitive sports.
- What foods prevent anemia?
- Discuss the pathophysiology regarding high altitudes and this disorder.

Slide 28

Acquired Heart Disease

- Occurs after birth
- May be a complication of a congenital heart disease or a response to respiratory infection, sepsis, hypertension, or severe anemia
- *Heart failure* is a decrease in cardiac output necessary to meet the metabolic needs of the body

Slide 29

Congestive Heart Failure (CHF)

- Manifestations depend on the side of the heart affected
  - Right side of the heart moves unoxygenated blood to the pulmonary circulation
    - A failure results in the backup of blood in the systemic venous system
  - Left side of heart moves oxygenated blood from the pulmonary circulation to the systemic circulation
    - Failure results in backup into the lungs

- Discuss in detail the physiology related to right- and left-sided heart failure.

Slide 30

> **CHF** *(cont.)*
>
> · When body tries to compensate
> – Peripheral vasoconstriction occurs
> – Results in cold and/or blue hands and feet
> – Tachycardia
> – Tachypnea

- What is peripheral vasoconstriction?

Slide 31

> **Safety Alert**
>
> · Early signs of CHF in infants that should be reported
> – Tachycardia at rest
> – Fatigue during feedings
> – Sweating around scalp and forehead
> – Dyspnea
> – Sudden weight gain

- Discuss the reason regarding the urgency of each sign.

Slide 32

> **CHF Goals of Treatment**
>
> · Goals
> – Reduce the work of the heart
> – Improve respiration
> – Maintain proper nutrition
> – Prevent infection
> – Reduce the anxiety of the patient
> – Support and instruct the parents

- Discuss methods to reduce the risk of infection.
- What methods can be used to reduce anxiety in the child?

Slide 33

> **CHF and Nursing Care**
>
> · Organize care so that infant is not unnecessarily disturbed
> · Feed early if crying and late if asleep
> · Feedings are small and frequent
> · Oxygen is administered to relieve dyspnea
> · Medications are given as prescribed, after dosages are checked for safety
> · Accurate recording of intake and output

- What is the rationale regarding small and frequent feedings?
- Discuss the importance of accurate intake and output.

Slide 34

> **Rheumatic Fever (RF)**
>
> · Systemic disease involving the joints, heart, central nervous system, skin, and subcutaneous tissues
> – Belongs to a group of disorders known as *collagen diseases*
> · Common feature is destruction of connective tissue
> – Scars mitral valve in the heart
> · Peak incidence is 5 to 15 years of age
> – More prevalent in winter and spring
> · Autoimmune disease occurring as a complication of an untreated group A beta hemolytic streptococcus infection of the throat

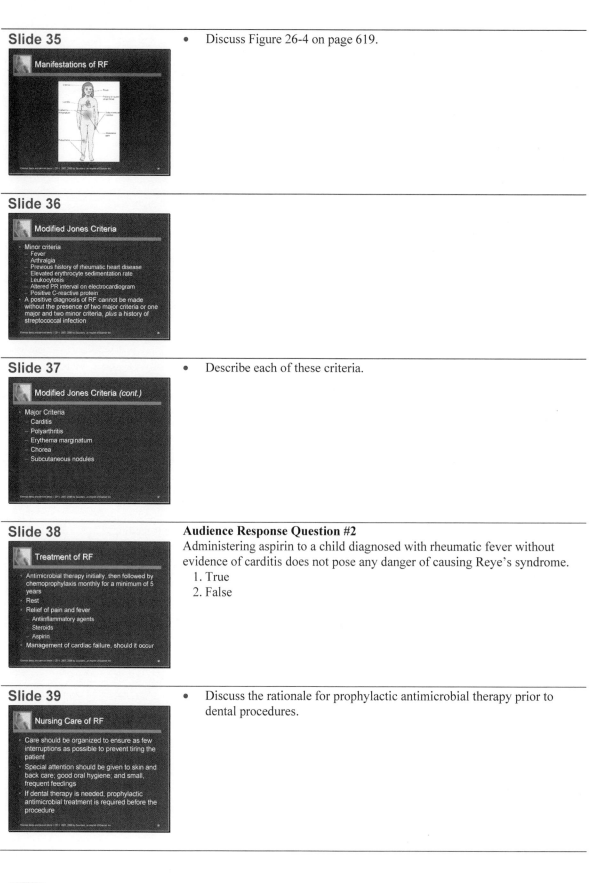

Slide 35

Manifestations of RF

- Discuss Figure 26-4 on page 619.

Slide 36

Modified Jones Criteria

- Minor criteria
  - Fever
  - Arthralgia
  - Previous history of rheumatic heart disease
  - Elevated erythrocyte sedimentation rate
  - Leukocytosis
  - Altered PR interval on electrocardiogram
  - Positive C-reactive protein
- A positive diagnosis of RF cannot be made without the presence of two major criteria or one major and two minor criteria, *plus* a history of streptococcal infection

Slide 37

Modified Jones Criteria *(cont.)*

- Major Criteria
  - Carditis
  - Polyarthritis
  - Erythema marginatum
  - Chorea
  - Subcutaneous nodules

- Describe each of these criteria.

Slide 38

Treatment of RF

- Antimicrobial therapy initially, then followed by chemoprophylaxis monthly for a minimum of 5 years
- Rest
- Relief of pain and fever
  - Antiinflammatory agents
  - Steroids
  - Aspirin
- Management of cardiac failure, should it occur

Audience Response Question #2
Administering aspirin to a child diagnosed with rheumatic fever without evidence of carditis does not pose any danger of causing Reye's syndrome.
   1. True
   2. False

Slide 39

Nursing Care of RF

- Care should be organized to ensure as few interruptions as possible to prevent tiring the patient
- Special attention should be given to skin and back care; good oral hygiene; and small, frequent feedings
- If dental therapy is needed, prophylactic antimicrobial treatment is required before the procedure

- Discuss the rationale for prophylactic antimicrobial therapy prior to dental procedures.

Leifer

Slide 40

> **Prevention of RF**
>
> · Prevention of infection and prompt treatment of group A beta-hemolytic streptococcal infections
> · Nurse stresses importance of completing all antimicrobial therapy as prescribed

- Discuss the rationale for completion of antimicrobial therapy.

Slide 41

> **Systemic Hypertension**
>
> · More prevalent during childhood and adolescence
> · Significant hypertension (HTN) is considered when measurements are persistently at or above the 95th percentile for patient's age and sex
> · Primary, or essential, HTN implies that no known underlying disease is present
> · When the cause of hypertension can be explained by a disease process, it is known as secondary
>   - Renal, congenital, vascular, and endocrine

- Blood pressure is a product of peripheral vascular resistance and cardiac output.
- An increase in cardiac output or peripheral resistance results in an increase in blood pressure.
- Discuss the increased incidence of HTN in children and adolescents.

Slide 42

> **Systemic Hypertension** *(cont.)*
>
> · Heredity, obesity, stress, and poor diet and exercise patterns are some of the contributing factors to the development of HTN
> · HTN more prevalent in children whose parents have high blood pressure

- What are modifiable risk factors concerning HTN?

Slide 43

> **Systemic Hypertension** *(cont.)*
>
> · Treatment and nursing care involve
>   - Nutritional counseling
>   - Weight reduction
>   - Age-appropriate program of aerobic exercise
>   - Adolescents should be counseled concerning the adverse effects of drugs, alcohol, and tobacco on blood pressure
> · Focus of treatment of secondary HTN is the underlying disease causing the elevated blood pressure

- Give examples of nutrition and weight reduction counseling.
- How do drugs, alcohol, and tobacco affect HTN?

Slide 44

> **Nonpharmacological Approach to HTN**
>
> · Aerobic exercise
> · Reduce sedentary activities
> · Weight reduction
> · Dietary management
> · Adequate intake of potassium and calcium
> · Avoid smoking and those who smoke

Slide 45
 	
Hyperlipidemia
- Refers to excess lipids (fat and fatlike substances in the blood)
- Lipoproteins contain lipids and proteins and include
  - *Low-density lipoproteins* (LDL) contain low amounts of triglycerides, high levels of cholesterol, and some protein
    - Carries cholesterol to the cells, which aids in cellular metabolism and steroid production
  - *High-density lipoproteins* (HDL) contain low amounts of triglycerides, little cholesterol, and high levels of protein
    - Carries cholesterol to the liver for excretion
	• Discuss Table 26-6 on page 622.

Slide 46
 	
Hyperlipidemia *(cont.)*
- Children with two consecutive blood cholesterol levels exceeding 170 mg/dL should be followed closely and offered nutritional guidance
  - Parental history of cholesterol levels exceeding 240 mg/dL or a family history of early cardiac death (under age 55 years) should have their cholesterol levels tested
- Dietary intake of no more than 300 mg of cholesterol per day and no more than 30% total dietary calories from fat are recommended
  - Children younger than 2 years of age should not have a fat-restricted diet, because calories and fat are necessary for CNS growth and development
	• Review the Health Promotion boxes on pages 622-623.

Slide 47 **Kawasaki Disease (KD)** - Also known as *mucocutaneous lymph node syndrome* - Leading cause of acquired cardiovascular disease in the U.S. - Usually affects children younger than 5 years of age - May be a reaction to toxins produced by a previous infection with an organism such as Staphylococci - Not spread from person to person	

Slide 48
 	
Kawasaki Disease (KD) *(cont.)*
- Diagnosis is made by clinical signs and symptoms, no specific lab studies
- KD causes inflammation of the vessels in the cardiovascular system
  - Weakens the walls of the vessels
- Often results in an aneurysm (an abnormal dilation of the wall of a blood vessel)
  - Aneurysms can cause thrombi (blood clots) to form, which can be life-threatening
	• Discuss clinical signs and symptoms.

Slide 49
 	
Kawasaki Disease (KD) *(cont.)*
- Manifestations
  - Onset is abrupt with a sustained fever
    - As high as 104° F (40° C)
    - Does not respond to antipyretics or antimicrobials
    - Fever lasts for more than 5 days
  - Conjunctivitis without discharge
  - Fissured lips
  - A "strawberry tongue"
  - Inflamed mouth and pharyngeal membranes
  - Enlarged nontender lymph nodes
	• Describe fissured lips and strawberry tongue.

Leifer

Slide 50

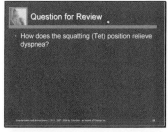

- What are some cardiac complications?

Slide 51

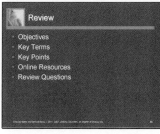

- Discuss the pathophysiology of gamma globulin and this disorder.

Slide 52

Kawasaki Disease (KD) *(cont.)*

- Nursing care
  - Symptomatic and supportive
  - Parent teaching should be reinforced concerning need to postpone active routine immunizations for several months after the administration of immune globulin, which is an immunosuppressant
  - Long-term, low-dose aspirin therapy may be prescribed
    - Compliance may be a problem for any long-term regimen in which medications must be taken when the child feels "well."

- What are some symptomatic and supportive measures for this disorder?
- Discuss the rationale regarding postponement of immunizations.

Slide 53

Question for Review

- How does the squatting (Tet) position relieve dyspnea?

Slide 54

Review

- Objectives
- Key Terms
- Key Points
- Online Resources
- Review Questions

27 The Child with a Condition of the Blood, Blood-Forming Organs, or Lymphatic System

TEACHING FOCUS

This chapter provides students the opportunity to learn about the pathophysiology, manifestations, and treatment of children who have conditions of the blood, blood-forming organs, and lymphatic system. Students have the opportunity to learn how to care for the child who has a chronic illness and how to help families adjust to the condition and to care for the child. The chapter also covers nursing care of the dying child and ways nurses can help patients and family progress through the stages of death and grief.

MATERIALS AND RESOURCES

☐ Computer and PowerPoint projector (all lessons)

LESSON CHECKLIST

Preparations for this lesson include:

- Lecture
- Evaluation of student knowledge and skills needed to perform all entry-level activities related to health care and adaptations for the child and family of the child who has a condition of the blood, blood-forming organs, or the lymphatic system, including:
  - ○ Pathophysiology, signs and symptoms, treatment, prevention, and patient education
  - ○ Assessment and monitoring of treatments, including transfusions
  - ○ Appropriate nursing interventions for transfusion or other treatment reactions
  - ○ Support of patients who are chronically ill or dying and their families
  - ○ Patient and parent teaching about treatments and home care

KEY TERMS

alopecia (p. 636)
Christmas disease (p. 633)
ecchymosis (p. 634)
erythropoietin (p. 625)
hemarthrosis (p. 633)
hematoma (p. 634)

hematopoiesis (p. 625)
hemosiderosis (p. 631)
lymphadenopathy (p. 626)
oncologists (p. 635)
petechiae (p. 626)
purpura (p. 627)

respite care (p. 641)
sickle cell crises (p. 629)
sickledex (p. 631)
splenomegaly (p. 626)

ADDITIONAL RESOURCES

TEACH PPT slide(s) Chapter 27, 1-86
EILR IC image(s) Chapter 27, 1-7
EILR OBQ question(s) Chapter 27, 1-10
EILR TB question(s) Chapter 27, 1-33
ESLR IRQ question(s) Chapter 27, 1-7
SG Chapter 27, pp. 219-227

Legend

PPT
TEACH
PowerPoint
Slides

EILR
EVOLVE Instructor
Learning Resources:
Image Collection (IC),
Open-Book Quizzes
(OBQ), Test Bank (TB)

ESLR
EVOLVE Student
Learning Resources:
Interactive Review
Questions (IRQ) for
the NCLEX®
Examination

SG
Study Guide

CTQ
Critical Thinking
Question in
Nursing Care Plan
(NCP CTQ) or Get
Ready for the
NCLEX! (GRN
CTQ)

Class Activities are indicated in ***bold italic***.

LESSON 27.1

PRETEST

1. Erythropoietin production after birth is controlled by the
   - a. heart.
   - b. liver.
   - c. kidneys.
   - d. spleen.

2. Lymphadenopathy may indicate
   - a. infection.
   - b. bleeding.
   - c. hematoma.
   - d. anemia.

3. The largest organ in the lymphatic system is the
   - a. pancreas.
   - b. liver.
   - c. heart.
   - d. spleen.

4. Screening for iron-deficiency anemia is recommended at ages
   - a. 6 and 12 months.
   - b. 9 and 24 months.
   - c. 8 and 15 months.
   - d. 36 and 48 months.

5. Sickle cell trait is different from sickle cell anemia in that the child with sickle cell trait
   - a. is only a carrier and is free from disease.
   - b. eventually develops sickle cell anemia.
   - c. has the same symptoms of sickle cell anemia.
   - d. requires ongoing treatment.

6. Deposition of iron into organs and tissues is termed
   - a. hematoma.
   - b. hematopoiesis.
   - c. hemolytic.
   - d. hemosiderosis.

7. In which of the following disorders does the body produce large amounts of fetal hemoglobin because it cannot produce adult hemoglobin?
   - a. chronic anemia
   - b. iron-deficiency anemia
   - c. thalassemia
   - d. hemophilia

8. The test used to determine the level of factor VIII in patients with hemophilia A is the
   - a. prothrombin time (PT).
   - b. partial thromboplastin time (PTT).
   - c. platelet count.
   - d. complete blood count.

9. The most common form of childhood leukemia is
   - a. lymphoma.
   - b. acute lymphocytic lymphoma (ALL).
   - c. acute non-lymphocytic lymphoma (ANLL).
   - d. acute myelocytic lymphoma (AML).

10. A malignant disease of the lymph system characterized by Reed-Sternberg cells is
    - a. sickle cell anemia.
    - b. lymphoma.
    - c. leukemia.
    - d. Hodgkin's disease.

Answers

1. c	3. d	5. a	7. c	9. b
2. a	4. b	6. d	8. b	10. d

BACKGROUND ASSESSMENT

Question: How does having a chronic illness affect the growth and development of a child? What role can the nurse play?

Answer: Chronic illness affects a child's social as well as physical development. Some diseases or conditions may cause growth retardation and interrupt development. Other factors involve the child's emotional health, including peer group acceptance. For example, adolescents may feel isolated and less in control. They may develop a negative self-image because they cannot engage in some activities with their classmates. Compliance with therapy may present difficulties for adolescents who are unable to accept that illness interferes with life activities. The nurse must be aware of the child or adolescent's growth and developmental stage and understand the issues the patient faces. The nurse can help the ill child cope with problems, learn to accept the condition, encourage adherence to treatment regimens, and suggest appropriate family and community support resources.

Question: What complications can occur as a result of frequent blood transfusion in a child who has thalassemia? What treatment is given to counteract the problems that develop? What monitoring is required, and what treatment is given if transfusion reaction occurs?

Answer: To maintain an adequate hemoglobin level, children with thalassemia require frequent blood transfusions, which can cause excessive amounts of iron to be deposited in the spleen, liver, heart, pancreas, and lymph glands. Medications may be prescribed to counteract the effect of excess iron deposits. Severe splenomegaly can occur, and the child may require a splenectomy. The patient is monitored for any untoward effects of the transfusion, such as fever, chills, itching, rash, headache, or back pain. If any of these symptoms occur, the transfusion must be stopped immediately and the remainder of the blood and the tubing returned to the blood bank. Reactions generally occur within the first 10 minutes of the start of the blood transfusion, but the child must be closely monitored throughout the infusion. Treatment of transfusion reactions can include antihistamines, medication for wheezing, and oxygen for dyspnea or cyanosis. The child also must be monitored for symptoms of circulatory overload, which include dyspnea, precordial pain, rales, cyanosis, dry cough, and distended neck veins.

CRITICAL THINKING QUESTION

During a routine clinic visit, the nurse notes that an 18-month-old child has pallid skin, appears lethargic, and is overweight. The mother says the child has become less active and increasingly irritable. What condition should the nurse suspect? What patient education is appropriate?

Guidelines: The child's symptoms indicate the need for further testing to determine if the child has iron-deficiency anemia, which can occur when iron stores become depleted. Further assessment involves analysis of red blood cells, hemoglobin, hematocrit, morphological cell changes, and iron concentration. Iron-deficiency anemia in young children typically occurs due to poor dietary intake as the child experiences rapid growth. Excess weight may be caused by the child receiving too much milk as a result of the mother trying to ease the child's irritability. The nurse should explain to the parent that iron supplements, given either orally or by injection, can treat the condition initially. The nurse should emphasize that iron supplements and maintaining sufficient iron intake through proper diet are key to eliminating the iron deficiency and maintaining the child's health. Parent education requires explicit instruction regarding types of foods that the child should eat. The nurse should consider financial, ethnic, and food preference factors in helping to develop an eating plan for the child. Iron supplementation should be given between meals to increase absorption. Milk interferes with iron absorption, whereas vitamin C improves absorption. If liquid iron is used, this should be given using a straw to prevent tooth discoloration. The nurse should inform parents that the child's stool color may change to tarry green, which is an effect of iron supplementation. The nurse can inform parents that leaving anemia untreated will slow a child's growth and can affect cognitive development. In addition, in severe cases, the heart muscle becomes weak and heart failure may result. Parents should be encouraged to bring the child back for periodic evaluation.

OBJECTIVES	CONTENT	TEACHING RESOURCES
Summarize the components of the blood.	■ Introduction (p. 625)	PPT slides 7-11
		EILR IC images 1, 2
		EILR OBQ question 1
		SG Learning Activities, question 2 (p. 219)
		BOOK RESOURCES
		Figure 27-1, Summary of Lymphatic System Differences Between the Child and the Adult (p. 626)
		Figure 27-2, The Formed Elements of the Blood (p. 626)

OBJECTIVES	CONTENT	TEACHING RESOURCES
		▶ Discuss the formation of blood disorders. ▶ Discuss the function of the lymphatic system. *Class Activity **Have students identify all the components of the blood. Group the elements as follows: formed elements, granular leukocytes, and nongranular leukocytes. Review the function of each component relative to abnormal conditions of the blood.***
List two laboratory procedures commonly performed on children with blood disorders.	■ Introduction (p. 625)	▶ Discuss the role of bone marrow aspiration in determining blood disorders. ▶ Discuss the blood count procedure used to determine blood disorders. *Class Activity **Lead a class discussion in which students describe two laboratory procedures commonly performed on children who have blood disorders: bone marrow aspiration and hemoglobin electrophoresis. Why is each procedure performed? What are possible complications?***
List the symptoms, prevention, and treatment of iron-deficiency anemia.	■ Anemias (p. 627) ☐ Iron-deficiency anemia (p. 627)	⊠ PPT slides 12-17 𝒆 EILR TB questions 2, 3 𝒆 ESLR IRQ question 5 SG Learning Activities, questions 3, 5-8 (pp. 219-220) **BOOK RESOURCES** Nursing Tip (p. 627) Medication Safety Alert (p. 628) Review Questions for the NCLEX® Examination, question 3 (p. 646) ▶ Discuss hemoglobin content in anemia. ▶ Discuss lifestyle changes that influence hemoglobin concentration. *Class Activity **Divide the class into small groups. Assign each group one of the following topics relative to iron-deficiency anemia:*** *– pathophysiology* *– manifestations* *– treatment* *– prevention/parent education* ***Have students summarize key points for each topic in a brief report to the class. Each group should describe the role of the nurse as appropriate.***

OBJECTIVES	CONTENT	TEACHING RESOURCES
Review the effects of severe anemia on the heart.	■ Anemias (p. 627)	⊠ PPT slide 15 SG Learning Activities, question 1 (p. 219) *Class Activity Lead a discussion in which students describe how anemia can lead to congestive heart failure if left untreated. Why is this dangerous?*
Recommend four food sources of iron for a child with iron-deficiency anemia.	☐ Iron-deficiency anemia (p. 627)	⊠ PPT slides 14-17 *e* EILR TB question 1 SG Learning Activities, questions 4, 9 (pp. 219-220) SG Review Questions, questions 2, 3 (p. 224) **BOOK RESOURCES** Nursing Care Plan 27-1, The Child with Iron-Deficiency Anemia (p. 628) ▸ Discuss the pathophysiology, manifestations, treatment, and prevention of iron-deficiency anemia. ▸ Discuss normal blood values for the formed elements in the blood for infants and children. *Class Activity Ask student volunteers to role-play a nurse teaching parents of a child recently diagnosed with iron-deficiency anemia about proper diet and nutrition. The nurse should identify four food sources of iron and explain how these can be incorporated into meal planning. The parents should present cultural considerations, family preferences, and the child's eating habits.*
Examine the pathology and signs and symptoms of sickle cell disease.	☐ Sickle cell disease (p. 628)	⊠ PPT slides 18-24 *e* EILR IC images 3, 4 *e* EILR TB questions 12, 31, 32 SG Learning Activities, questions 11-13 (p. 220) SG Review Questions, question 10 (p. 225) SG Thinking Critically, questions 1, 2 (p. 227) **BOOK RESOURCES** Figure 27-3, Scanning Electron Micrograph of Erythrocytes (p. 629) Figure 27-4, Transmission of Sickle Cell Disease from Parents to Children (p. 630)

OBJECTIVES	CONTENT	TEACHING RESOURCES
		▶ Discuss the difference between the two types of sickle cell disease.
		▶ Discuss the role of the gene that is the cause of sickle cell anemia.
		*Class Activity **Divide students into three groups. Have one group discuss sickle cell pathology, including genetic transmission of the disease. The second group should discuss the signs and symptoms of sickle cell crises. Group three should discuss the nursing care for a child with sickle cell crises. Each group should review the nurse's role in providing patient and parent education. What key points should the nurse discuss with parents? Have each group make a brief presentation to the class for feedback and discussion.***
Describe four types of sickle cell crises.	☐ Sickle cell disease (p. 628)	*e* EILR OBQ question 2
		e EILR TB question 10
		[SG] SG Learning Activities, questions 11, 14 (pp. 220-221)
		BOOK RESOURCES
		Table 27-1, Types of Sickle Cell Crises (p. 630)
		Nursing Tip (p. 631)
		Review Questions for the NCLEX® Examination, question 2 (p. 646)
		▶ Discuss why immunizations are important for children with sickle cell crises.
		*Class Activity **Divide students into four groups. Assign each group a sickle cell crisis: vasoocclusive, splenic sequestration, aplastic, or hyperhemolytic. Have each group make a brief presentation to the class on the signs and symptoms of its assigned crisis. What are the child's needs, and what are appropriate nursing interventions?***
Devise a nursing care plan for a child with sickle cell disease.	☐ Sickle cell disease (p. 628)	*e* EILR TB questions 10, 11
		[SG] SG Learning Activities, questions 15-18 (p. 221)
		[SG] SG Review Questions, question 11 (p. 225)
		[SG] SG Thinking Critically, question 1 (p. 227)
		[SG] SG Applying Knowledge, question 2 (p. 227)
		BOOK RESOURCES

OBJECTIVES	CONTENT	TEACHING RESOURCES
		Medication Safety Alert (p. 631)
		Nursing Tip (p. 631)
		▸ Discuss the procedures used to identify sickle cell disease.
		▸ Discuss approaches that the nurse should incorporate into the care plan for a patient diagnosed with sickle cell disease.
		*Class Activity **Provide students with this clinical situation: a 4-year-old boy is admitted to the hospital with vasoocclusive sickle cell crisis. As a class, develop a nursing care plan for the child. Include nursing outcomes, interventions, and rationales. When the episode is brought under control, what key elements should be included in a discharge plan?***

27.1 Homework/Assignments:

27.1 Instructor's Notes/Student Feedback:

LESSON 27.2

CRITICAL THINKING QUESTION

The parents of a 9-year-old boy are confused about their son's diagnosis and treatment for hemophilia A. They don't want to excessively limit their child's activities, but they are concerned about how to prevent bleeding and how to treat it if it occurs. What information and counseling should the nurse provide?

Guidelines: The nurse can explain that their son's condition is due to a deficiency in factor VIII, or antihemophilic globulin (AHG), in the blood. This causes the child to be at risk for severe bleeding from even minor injuries such as cuts or bruises. Bleeding tendencies may be mild or severe, depending on the level of factor VIII in the blood plasma. A treatment goal is to increase the level of factor VIII to improve blood clotting. In the past, blood transfusions were the primary treatment, but these placed the patient at risk for blood-borne pathogens such as HIV and hepatitis. More recently, development of synthetic recombinant antihemophilic factor, which can be administered at home, eliminates the need for transfusions. A nasal spray can be used to stop mild bleeding, while an antifibrinolytic can be used to control bleeding that may result from dental care or oral bleeding. The nurse can explain to the child and parents how to administer the medication and under what circumstances. The nurse also should inform the child and his parents about safety measures to prevent bleeding. The child should wear protective padding in play outfits when appropriate, and sports activities should be chosen that avoid undue risk of injury. Whenever possible, to increase their son's independence, he should participate in decision-making. The child should wear an identification band at all times. When bleeding does occur, the traditional RICE approach (rest, ice, compression, and elevation) should be used.

OBJECTIVES	CONTENT	TEACHING RESOURCES
Recognize the effects on the bone marrow of increased red blood cell production caused by thalassemia.	☐ Thalassemia (p. 631)	⊠ PPT slides 25-34 𝒆 EILR IC image 5 𝒆 EILR OBQ questions 3, 4 𝒆 EILR TB questions 13, 27 SG Learning Activities, questions 19, 20 (p. 221) **BOOK RESOURCES** Figure 27-5, Appearance of Child with Thalassemia Major (p. 632) Review Questions for the NCLEX® Examination, question 4 (p. 646) ▸ Discuss how chronic anemia is developed. ▸ Discuss the beta-thalassemia trait. *Class Activity **Lead a discussion in which students describe the physical changes in bony structures due to bone marrow expansion secondary to hematopoiesis in a child who has thalassemia.***
Recall the pathology and signs and symptoms of hemophilia A and B.	■ Bleeding disorders (p. 632) ☐ Hemophilia (p. 632)	⊠ PPT slides 35-44 𝒆 EILR OBQ question 5 𝒆 EILR TB questions 4, 24, 28 SG Learning Activities, questions 21-26 (pp. 221-

OBJECTIVES	CONTENT	TEACHING RESOURCES
		222) SG Review Questions, questions 4, 9 (p. 224) SG Thinking Critically, question 3 (p. 227) **BOOK RESOURCES** Nursing Tip (p. 633) ▸ Discuss how the patient's joints are affected by hemophilia. ▸ Discuss interventions patients can use to help manage their condition. *Class Activity **Divide the class into two groups. Assign one group hemophilia A and the other hemophilia B. Have each group review the pathophysiology and signs and symptoms. Then as a class, compare and contrast the two conditions.***
Identify the nursing interventions necessary to prevent hemarthrosis in a child with hemophilia.	☐ Hemophilia (p. 632)	𝓮 EILR TB question 5 𝓮 ESLR IRQ question 7 SG Learning Activities, question 1 (p. 219) SG Review Questions, questions 9, 12 (p. 225) **BOOK RESOURCES** Medication Safety Alert (p. 634) ▸ Discuss the role of wound care in patients with hemophilia. ▸ Discuss activities nurses can suggest to patients to help ease fear of hemophilia. *Class Activity **Have volunteer students role-play a nurse teaching a school-age child who has hemophilia and the child's parents how to prevent hemarthrosis, both when the child is hospitalized and at home. The instructor should play the role of the parents and express concerns about the child's safety and ability to participate in age-appropriate physical activities. The student playing the child should ask appropriate questions about the condition and what he or she is supposed to do.***
Compare and contrast four manifestations of bleeding into the skin.	☐ Platelet disorders (p. 634)	🖥 PPT slides 45 **BOOK RESOURCES** Nursing tip (p. 634) Medication Safety Alert (p. 634) ▸ Discuss the function of platelets in the body.

OBJECTIVES	CONTENT	TEACHING RESOURCES
		▸ Discuss the disorder thrombocytopenia.
		Class Activity Have students describe each of the following pairs of conditions: petechiae and purpura; ecchymosis and hematoma. What are the similarities and differences? What can each indicate?
Recall normal blood values of infants and children.	☐ Idiopathic (immunological) thrombocytopenia purpura (p. 634)	PPT slides 46-49
		EILR TB question 19
		ESLR IRQ question 4
		SG Learning Activities, questions 1, 27 (pp. 219, 222)
		SG Review Questions, questions 5, 13 (pp. 224-225)
		▸ Discuss the term *purpura*.
		▸ Discuss treatment options used for platelet disorders.
		Class Activity Lead a class discussion about the normal and abnormal blood values for a child with a blood disorder. Have the students identify which blood components are abnormal in the following disorders:
		– hemophilia
		– thalassemia
		– sickle cell anemia
		– idiopathic thrombocytopenic purpura (ITP)
		– leukemia

27.2 Homework/Assignments:

27.2 Instructor's Notes/Student Feedback:

Leifer

LESSON 27.3

CRITICAL THINKING QUESTION

The mother of a 13-year-old boy notices a painless lump on her son's neck. The physician diagnoses early stage Hodgkin's disease. What anticipatory guidance should be given to the child and his parents regarding the effects of chemotherapy and radiation on the developing adolescent?

Guidelines: The nurse should explain that aftereffects of treatment include malaise, fatigue, irritability, skin itching, sensitivity to sun, diarrhea, and hair loss. Changes in self-image due to hair loss may occur, and adolescents typically express anger, often directed at health care providers. The school nurse should be involved in the child's care and the child's schedule should be altered as necessary. The child should use sunblock to prevent burning, but not to the area treated with radiation unless recommended by the physician. The child will not be radioactive during or after the therapy. If a splenectomy is performed, the patient is at increased risk for infection, so temperature must be closely monitored. The development of secondary sexual characteristics may be delayed and treatment also may cause sterility. The adolescent may choose sperm banking before treatment. The nurse should recommend the adolescent participate in decision-making regarding his care and activities as appropriate to maintain a feeling of control. The nurse should provide empathetic support and encourage the adolescent and parents to contact the health care provider at any time with concerns and questions.

OBJECTIVES	CONTENT	TEACHING RESOURCES
Plan the nursing care of a child with leukemia.	■ Disorders of white blood cells (p. 634) ☐ Leukemia (p. 634) ☐ Hodgkin's disease (p. 638)	PPT slides 50-69 *e* EILR IC image 6 *e* EILR OBQ questions 6-8 *e* EILR TB questions 6, 8-9, 14, 16, 17, 20, 22, 26, 29, 30 *e* ESLR IRQ questions 1-3 SG Learning Activities, questions 1, 28-33 (pp. 219, 222-223) SG Review Questions, questions 6-8, 14-16 (pp. 224-225) SG Case Study, question 1 (p. 226) SG Applying Knowledge, questions 1, 3 (p. 227) **BOOK RESOURCES** Figure 27-6, The Mouth Lesions of Leukemia (p. 635) Figure 27-7, Bone Marrow Aspiration (p. 636) Nursing Tip (p. 636) Table 27-2, Criteria for Staging Hodgkin's Disease (p. 638) Nursing Care Plan 27-2, The Adolescent Receiving Cancer Chemotherapy (pp. 639-640) Review Questions for the NCLEX® Examination, question 5 (p. 646)

OBJECTIVES	CONTENT	TEACHING RESOURCES
		▸ Discuss the challenges of treating pediatric patients diagnosed with leukemia.
		▸ Discuss the four priority challenges of a child with leukemia.
		▸ Discuss how practitioners determine the diagnosis of leukemia.
		Class Activity As a class, describe physical manifestations and treatment protocols associated with leukemia. Identify desired outcomes, nursing interventions, and rationales.
Review the nursing care of a child receiving a blood transfusion.	☐ Leukemia (p. 634) ☐ Hodgkin's disease (p. 638)	⊞ PPT slides 62, 63 **𝒆** EILR TB questions 7, 15, 33 SG Learning Activities, questions 34, 35 (p. 223) SG Review Questions, question 17 (p. 225) **BOOK RESOURCES** Nursing Tip (p. 638) Review Questions for the NCLEX® Examination, question 1 (p. 646) ▸ Discuss why hemolytic reactions caused by mismatched blood are rare. *Class Activity Have students work in pairs to develop a checklist of important steps to follow when administering a blood transfusion. Students should include the following:* — *verification of correct patient and blood type* — *examining the blood for abnormalities* — *setting up the transfusion* — *checking vital signs* — *watching for and treating transfusion reactions* — *providing suitable diversion activities for the child*
Discuss the effects of chronic illness on the growth and development of children.	■ Nursing care of the chronically ill child (p. 641) ☐ Chronic illness (p. 641) ☐ Developmental disabilities (p. 641) ☐ Home care (p. 641) ☐ The chronically ill	⊞ PPT slides 70-75 **BOOK RESOURCES** Table 27-3, The Effects of Chronic Illness on Growth and Development (p. 641) Nursing Tip (p. 642) ▸ Discuss approaches nurses can use to help patients accept their bodies.

OBJECTIVES	CONTENT	TEACHING RESOURCES
	child as family member (p. 642)	▸ Discuss the teaching nurses provide to parents prior to discharge of their chronically ill child.
		▸ Discuss critical information to include on a nursing care plan designed for pediatric patients receiving chemotherapy.
		*Class Activity **Divide the class into small groups. Assign half of the groups' leukemia and the other half sickle cell anemia. Ask each group to briefly describe the pathophysiology, signs and symptoms, and treatment that may be involved long-term for a child who has the disease. How does each disease affect the child's growth and development? Ask volunteer groups for each condition to make a brief presentation. Then as a class, compare and contrast the diseases. What role can the nurse play in helping patients and their families cope?***

27.3 Homework/Assignments:

27.3 Instructor's Notes/Student Feedback:

LESSON 27.4

CRITICAL THINKING QUESTION

The parents of a toddler who has terminal leukemia anticipate that her 7-year-old brother will be troubled when his sister dies. What counseling can the nurse provide regarding the older child's possible responses to his sister's death?

Guidelines: The nurse can function as an advocate for all family members and can support and facilitate the grieving process. The nurse can advise the parents that school-age children are typically aware of the finality of death and will need to grieve over the loss of a loved one. Their child may express concerns about losing parents or other family members, too. He may be fearful and anxious and want to take care of his parents. The nurse should explain that parents should use accurate terms when discussing death with the child and that they should provide security and reassurance. The child should be allowed to say good-bye to his sister and to participate in the funeral or memorial service. Parents should encourage communication and enable the child to talk about his concerns and feelings. Maintaining a normal routine within the household such as attending a sports event together provides reassurance and stability within the family system. The nurse should take cultural factors into account when counseling the grieving family.

OBJECTIVES	CONTENT	TEACHING RESOURCES
Formulate techniques the nurse can use to facilitate the grieving process.	■ Nursing care of the dying child (p. 642) ☐ Facing death (p. 642) ☐ Self-exploration (p. 642)	PPT slides 76-84 *e* EILR OBQ question 10 *e* EILR TB question 18 ▸ Discuss why the nurse should understand the grieving process. *Class Activity As a class, discuss ways in which the nurse can help families cope with the death of a child. What are the steps of the grieving process and how can the nurse identify appropriate counseling and support for each stage? What cultural beliefs and practices may be involved?*
Contrast age-appropriate responses to a sibling's death and the nursing interventions required.	☐ The child's reaction to death (p. 642) ☐ The child's awareness of his or her condition (p. 643) ☐ Physical changes of impending death (p. 643)	PPT slides 76-84 *e* EILR OBQ question 9 *e* EILR TB questions 21, 25 SG Learning Activities, questions 37-39 (p. 223) SG Review Questions, question 1 (p. 224) **BOOK RESOURCES** Health Promotion, A Child's Response to a Sibling's Death (p. 643) Nursing Care Plan 27-3, The Dying Child (pp. 644-645) ▸ Discuss resources the nurse can use to learn how to handle situations involving death of a child. ▸ Discuss specific nursing interventions for a dying child. Why is it important to be honest with the dying child about his or her condition? What kinds of support are

OBJECTIVES	CONTENT	TEACHING RESOURCES
		appropriate for the nurse to provide?
		*Class Activity **Divide the class into small groups and assign each group one of the following age categories: infant and preschooler; and school-age child and adolescent. Ask students to discuss typical responses each age category has to the death of a child in the family. What counseling can the nurse provide to parents about anticipated responses? How can parents help their children through the grieving process? Ask groups to present to the class for discussion and feedback.***
Recall the stages of dying.	☐ Stages of dying (p. 643)	PPT slide 84 *e* EILR OBQ question 10 *e* EILR TB question 23 *e* ESLR IRQ question 6 ▸ Discuss the importance of understanding the stages of dying. ▸ Discuss observable signs in children regarding home life or family that indicate the nurse may need to provide intervention. *Class Activity **Have students discuss the stages of dying as outlined by Kübler-Ross. Provide an example of each stage.***

Discuss the nurse's role in helping families deal with the death of a child.	☐ Stages of dying (p. 643)	PPT slide 84
		
		e EILR OBQ questions 9, 10
		
		e EILR TB question 23
		
		BOOK RESOURCES
		
		Box 27-1, The Nurse's Role in Helping the Family Cope with the Dying Child (p. 643)
		
		Health Promotion, A Child's Response to a Sibling's Death (p. 643)
		
		Nursing Tip (p. 645)
		
		▸ Discuss techniques and resources the nurse can use to improve listening skills.
		
		▸ Discuss coping techniques the nurse can utilize as well as teach to the patient or the patient's family.
		
		*Class Activity **Have students describe how the following approaches by the nurse can help the family cope with a child who is dying:***
		
		   – *Listen*
		
		   – *Provide privacy*

OBJECTIVES	CONTENT	TEACHING RESOURCES
		– *Provide therapeutic intervention*
		– *Provide information*
		– *Use appropriate phrases and open-ended statements*
		In what ways can these techniques be applied in the scenario described in Nursing Care Plan 27-3 (pp. 644-645)?
Performance Evaluation		PPT slides 1-86
		e EILR IC images 1-7
		e EILR OBQ questions 1-10
		e EILR TB questions 1-33
		e ESLR IRQ questions 1-7
		SG Learning Activities, questions 1-39 (p. 219-223)
		SG Review Questions, questions 1-17 (pp. 224-225)
		Crossword Puzzle (p. 226)
		SG Case Study, question 1 (p. 226)
		SG Thinking Critically, questions 1-3 (p. 227)
		SG Applying Knowledge, questions 1-3 (p. 227)
		BOOK RESOURCES
		NCP CTQ 1 (p. 628)
		NCP CTQ 1 (p. 640)
		NCP CTQ 1 (p. 645)
		Review Questions for the NCLEX® Examination, questions 1-5 (p. 646)

27.4 Homework/Assignments:

27.4 Instructor's Notes/Student Feedback:

Introduction to Maternity & Pediatric Nursing, 6th ed.

Elsevier items and derived items © 2011, 2007, 2006 by Saunders, an imprint of Elsevier Inc.

Leifer

Lecture Outline

27 The Child with a Condition of the Blood, Blood-Forming Organs, or Lymphatic System

Slide 1

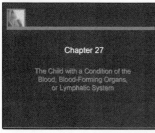

Chapter 27

The Child with a Condition of the
Blood, Blood-Forming Organs,
or Lymphatic System

Slide 2

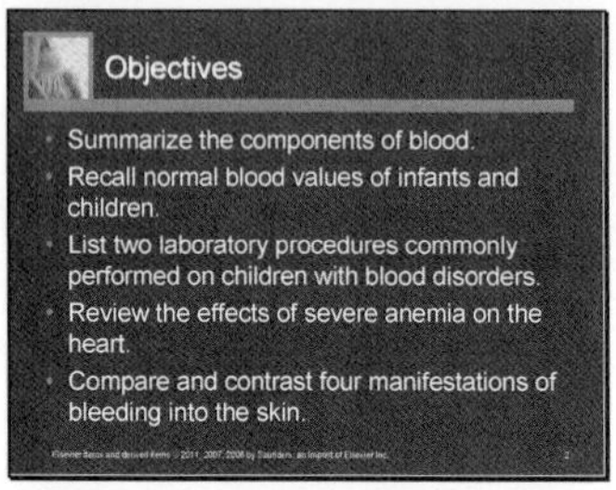

Objectives

- Summarize the components of blood.
- Recall normal blood values of infants and children.
- List two laboratory procedures commonly performed on children with blood disorders.
- Review the effects of severe anemia on the heart.
- Compare and contrast four manifestations of bleeding into the skin.

Slide 3

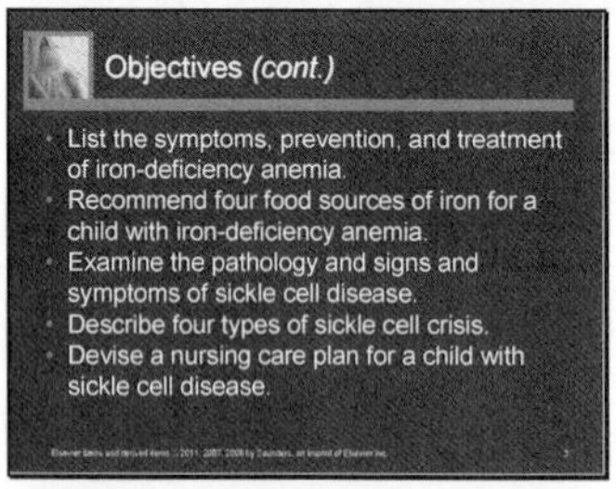

Objectives *(cont.)*

- List the symptoms, prevention, and treatment of iron-deficiency anemia.
- Recommend four food sources of iron for a child with iron-deficiency anemia.
- Examine the pathology and signs and symptoms of sickle cell disease.
- Describe four types of sickle cell crisis.
- Devise a nursing care plan for a child with sickle cell disease.

Slide 4

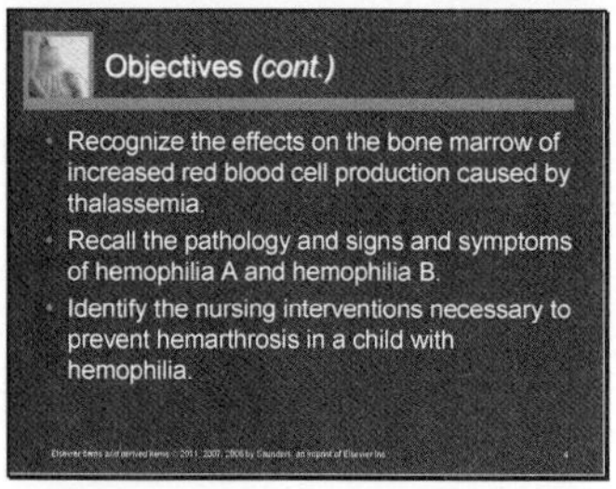

Objectives *(cont.)*

- Recognize the effects on the bone marrow of increased red blood cell production caused by thalassemia.
- Recall the pathology and signs and symptoms of hemophilia A and hemophilia B.
- Identify the nursing interventions necessary to prevent hemarthrosis in a child with hemophilia.

Slide 5

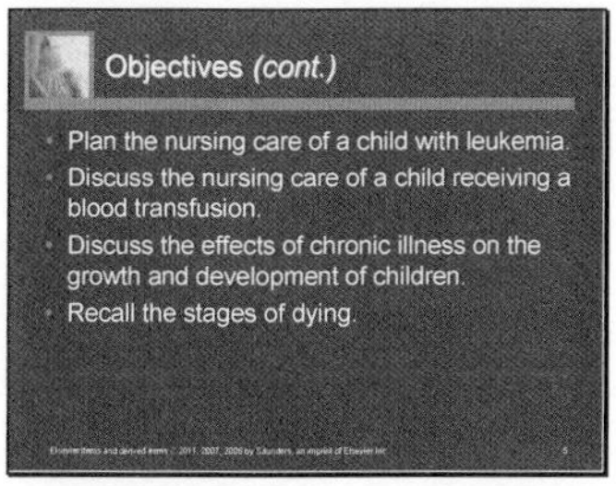

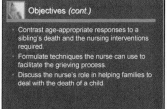

Objectives *(cont.)*

- Plan the nursing care of a child with leukemia.
- Discuss the nursing care of a child receiving a blood transfusion.
- Discuss the effects of chronic illness on the growth and development of children.
- Recall the stages of dying.

Slide 6

Objectives *(cont.)*

- Contrast age-appropriate responses to a sibling's death and the nursing interventions required.
- Formulate techniques the nurse can use to facilitate the grieving process.
- Discuss the nurse's role in helping families to deal with the death of a child.

Slide 7

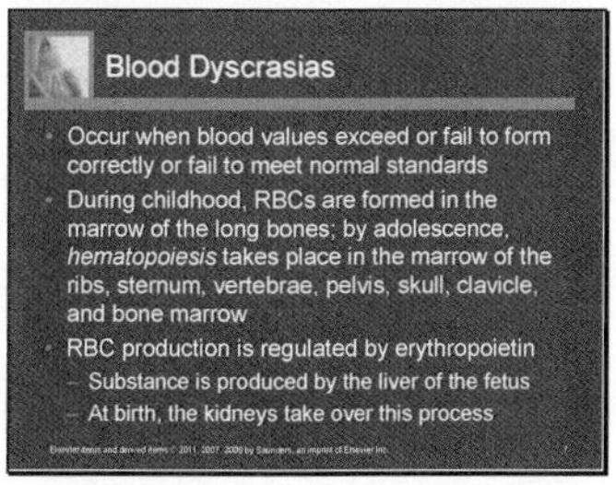

- Define hematopoiesis.

Blood Dyscrasias

- Occur when blood values exceed or fail to form correctly or fail to meet normal standards
- During childhood, RBCs are formed in the marrow of the long bones; by adolescence, *hematopoiesis* takes place in the marrow of the ribs, sternum, vertebrae, pelvis, skull, clavicle, and bone marrow
- RBC production is regulated by erythropoietin
  - Substance is produced by the liver of the fetus
  - At birth, the kidneys take over this process

Slide 8

- Discuss Figure 27-1 on page 626.

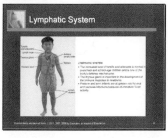

Lymphatic System

Slide 9

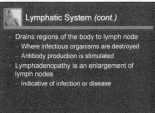

Lymphatic System *(cont.)*

- Drains regions of the body to lymph node
  - Where infectious organisms are destroyed
  - Antibody production is stimulated
- Lymphadenopathy is an enlargement of lymph nodes
  - Indicative of infection or disease

Leifer

Slide 10

Lymphatic System *(cont.)*

- Spleen is largest organ of the lymphatic system
- One of the main functions is to bring blood into contact with lymphocytes
- Most common pathological condition is enlargement (splenomegaly)
- Enlarges during infections, congenital and acquired hemolytic anemias, and liver malfunction

Slide 11

Circulating Blood

- Consists of two portions
- Plasma
- Formed elements
  - Erythrocytes
  - Leukocytes (white blood cells [WBCs])
  - Thrombocytes (platelets)
- Erythrocytes
  - Transport oxygen and carbon dioxide to and from the lungs and tissues
- Leukocytes act as the body's defense against infection
- Lymphocytes are produced in the lymphoid tissues of the body

- Refer to Figure 27-2 on page 626.

Slide 12

Anemias

- Can result from many different underlying causes
  - A reduction in the amount of circulating hemoglobin (Hgb) reduces the oxygen-carrying ability of the blood
    - An Hgb below 8 g/dl results in an increased cardiac output and a shunting of blood from the periphery to the vital organs
    - Can result in pallor, weakness, tachypnea, SOB, CHF

- What are the signs and symptoms of anemia?

Slide 13

Iron-Deficiency Anemia

- Most common nutritional deficiency of children
  - Incidence is highest during infancy (from 9th to 24th month) and adolescence
- May be caused by severe hemorrhage, inability to absorb iron received, excessive growth requirements, or an inadequate diet
  - Giving whole cow's milk to infants can lead to GI bleeding, leading to anemia

- Discuss the reasons this age group is more susceptible to iron-deficiency anemia.

Slide 14

Iron-Deficiency Anemia *(cont.)*

- Manifestations
  - Pallor
  - Irritability
  - Anorexia
  - Decrease in activity
    - Infants may be overweight due to excessive milk consumption
- Blood tests
  - RBC count
  - Hgb and hematocrit
  - Morphological cell changes
  - Iron concentrations
- Stool may be tested for occult blood

Leifer

Slide 15

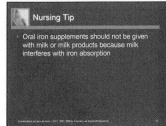

Slide 16

Nursing Tip

· Oral iron supplements should not be given with milk or milk products because milk interferes with iron absorption

Slide 17

· Refer to Nursing Care Plan 27-1 on page 628.

Parent Education

· Nurse stresses importance of breastfeeding for the first 6 months and the use of iron-fortified formula throughout the first year of life
· Stools of infants taking oral iron supplements are tarry green
· Do not give iron with milk
· To increase absorption, give the iron between meals when digestive acid concentration is at its highest

Slide 18

· Discuss the pathophysiology of the causes of sickling.
· Discuss the complications of hemosiderosis.

Sickle Cell Disease

· Inherited defect in the formation of hemoglobin
· Sickling (clumping) caused by decreased blood oxygen levels may be triggered by dehydration, infection, physical or emotional stress, or exposure to cold
  · Membranes of these cells are fragile and easily destroyed.
  · Their crescent shape makes it difficult for them to pass through the capillaries, causing a pileup of cells in the small vessels.
  · May lead to thrombosis, can be very painful
· Hemosiderosis (iron deposits into body organs) is a complication of the disease

Audience Response Question #1
A 12-month-old child is admitted to the emergency department in sickle cell crisis. Her symptoms might include:
   1. severe itching, vomiting.
   2. fever, seizures, coma.
   3. abdominal pain, swollen painful joints.
   4. polycythemia, tachycardia.

Slide 19

· Discuss the chances of a child inheriting sickle cell disease.

Transmission of Sickle Cell Disease from Parents to Children

Slide 20

Two Types of Sickle Cell Disease

Sickle cell trait (asymptomatic)
- Blood of the patient contains a mixture of Hgb A and sickle (Hgb S)
- Proportions of Hgb S are low because the disease is inherited from only one parent
- Hgb and RBC counts are normal

Sickle cell anemia (more severe)
- Clinical symptoms do not appear until the last part of the first year of life
  - May be an unusual swelling of the fingers and toes
  - Symptoms caused by enlarging bone marrow sites that impair circulation to the bone and the abnormal sickle cell shape that causes clumping, obstruction in the vessel, and ischemia to the organ the vessel supplies

---

Slide 21

Manifestations

- Hgb level ranges 6 to 9 g/dL or lower
  - Child is pale, tires easily, and has little appetite
- Sickle cell crises are painful and can be fatal
  - Symptoms: severe abdominal pain, muscle spasms, leg pain, or painful swollen joints may be seen
    - Fever, vomiting, hematuria, convulsions, stiff neck, coma, or paralysis can result
    - Risk for stroke as a complication of a vaso-occlusive sickle cell crisis

- Discuss the pathophysiology of the pain the child experiences.

Slide 22

Types of Sickle Cell Crises

- Vaso-occlusive (painful crises)
- Splenic sequestration
- Aplastic crises
- Hyperhemolytic

- Describe each crisis listed.

Slide 23

Health Promotion

- During sickle cell crisis, anticipate the child's need for tissue oxygenation, hydration, rest, protection from infection, pain control, blood transfusion, and emotional support for this life-threatening illness

- Discuss how these nursing interventions assist the child with a sickle cell crisis.

Slide 24

Therapies and Goals

- Erythropoietin and some chemotherapy regimens can increase the production of fetal Hgb and reduce complications
- Routine splenectomy is *not* recommended because the spleen generally atrophies on its own because of fibrotic changes that take place in patients with sickle cell disease
- Prevent infection, dehydration, hypoxia, and sickling

- Discuss methods which could prevent sickling, dehydration, hypoxia, and infection.

Slide 25

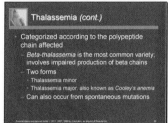

Thalassemia

- Group of hereditary blood disorders in which the patient's body cannot produce sufficient adult Hgb
- RBCs are abnormal in size and shape and are rapidly destroyed; results in chronic anemia
- Body attempts to compensate by producing large amounts of fetal Hgb

- What ethnic population is mainly affected by thalassemia?
  Mediterranean

Slide 26

Thalassemia *(cont.)*

- Categorized according to the polypeptide chain affected
  - *Beta-thalassemia* is the most common variety; involves impaired production of beta chains
  - Two forms
    - Thalassemia minor
    - Thalassemia major, also known as *Cooley's anemia*
  - Can also occur from spontaneous mutations

Slide 27

Thalassemia Minor

- Also termed beta-thalassemia trait, occurs when the child inherits a gene from only one parent
  - Heterozygous inheritance
- Associated with mild anemia
- Often misdiagnosed as having iron-deficiency anemia
- Symptoms minimal
  - Pale
  - Possible splenomegaly
- May lead a normal life with the illness going undetected
- Of genetic importance, particularly if both parents are carriers of the trait

- Define milk anemia.
- What are symptoms of thalassemia minor?

Slide 28

Thalassemia Major (Cooley's Anemia)

- Child is born with a more serious form of the disease when two thalassemia genes are inherited (homozygous inheritance)
- Progressive, severe anemia
- Evident within the second 6 months of life
- Child is pale, hypoxic, poor appetite, and may have a fever

Slide 29

Thalassemia Major (Cooley's Anemia) *(cont.)*

- Jaundice that progresses to a muddy bronze color resulting from hemosiderosis
- Liver enlarges and the spleen grows enormously
- Abdominal distention is great
- Increases pressure on the chest organs
- Cardiac failure caused by profound anemia is a constant threat

ELSEVIER

Leifer

Slide 30

Thalassemia Major
(Cooley's Anemia) *(cont.)*
- Bone marrow space enlarges to compensate for an increased production of blood cells
  - Hematopoietic defects and a massive expansion of the bone marrow in the face and skull result in changes in the facial contour
  - Teeth protrude due to an overgrowth of the upper jawbone
  - Bone becomes thin and is subject to fracture

- Discuss Figure 27-5 on page 632.

Slide 31

Thalassemia Major
(Cooley's Anemia) *(cont.)*
- Diagnosis
  - Family history of thalassemia
  - Radiographic bone growth studies
  - Blood test
  - Hemoglobin electrophoresis is helpful in diagnosing type and severity

- What is the rationale for radiographic studies of the bones?
- Discuss types of blood tests which would be ordered for a child with thalassemia major.
- Describe electrophoresis.

Slide 32

Thalassemia Major
(Cooley's Anemia) *(cont.)*
- Goals of therapy
  - Maintain hemoglobin levels to prevent overgrowth of bone marrow and resultant deformities
  - Provide for normal growth and development and physical activity
  - Prevention or early treatment of infection is important
  - Some may require a splenectomy due to degree of splenomegaly

- What activities would promote growth and development for this child?

Slide 33   ·

Thalassemia Major
(Cooley's Anemia) *(cont.)*
- Mainstay of treatment
  - Frequent blood transfusions to maintain Hgb above 10 g/dL
  - Because of the number of transfusions, hemosiderosis is seen in the spleen, liver, heart, pancreas, and lymph glands
    - Deferoxamine mesylate (Desferal), an iron-chelating agent is given to counteract this side effect
  - A splenectomy may be needed to increase comfort, increase ability to move about, and to allow for more normal growth

Slide 34

Thalassemia Major
(Cooley's Anemia) *(cont.)*
- Nursing measures
  - Adhere to the principles of long-term care
  - Whenever possible, have the same nurse assigned to the child
  - Observing the patient during blood transfusions for any adverse reactions
  - Monitoring vital signs
  - Providing for the emotional health of the child and family is essential

- Discuss signs and symptoms of a child reacting to a blood transfusion.
- What nursing interventions would promote emotional health of the child and the family?

Slide 35

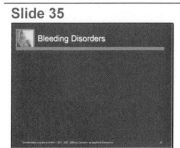

Bleeding Disorders

Slide 36

Hemophilia

- One of the oldest hereditary diseases known to man
- Blood does not clot normally
- Congenital disorder confined almost exclusively to males
  - Is transmitted by symptom-free females

Slide 37

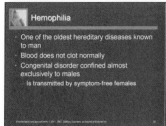

Hemophilia *(cont.)*

- Inherited sex-linked recessive trait
  - Defective gene is located on the X, or female, chromosome
  - Fetal blood samples detect hemophilia
- Two most common types
  - *Hemophilia B* (Christmas disease [a factor IX deficiency])
  - *Hemophilia A* (a deficiency in factor VIII)
- A deficiency in any one of the factors will interfere with normal blood clotting

Slide 38

- Discuss how PTT can detect this disorder.

Hemophilia A

- Caused by a deficiency of coagulation factor VIII, or antihemophilic globulin (AHG)
- Severity dependent on level of factor VIII in the plasma
- Some patients' lives can be endangered by a minor scratch, while others may simply bruise more easily than the average person
- Aim of therapy is to increase level of factor VIII to ensure clotting
- This is checked by a blood test call *partial thromboplastin time (PTT)*

Slide 39

Manifestations of Hemophilia

- Can be diagnosed at birth because factor VIII cannot cross the placenta and be transferred to the fetus
  - Usually not apparent in the newborn unless abnormal bleeding occurs at the umbilical cord or after circumcision
- Normal blood clots in 3 to 6 minutes
  - In severe hemophilia, it can take up to 1 hour or longer

Slide 40

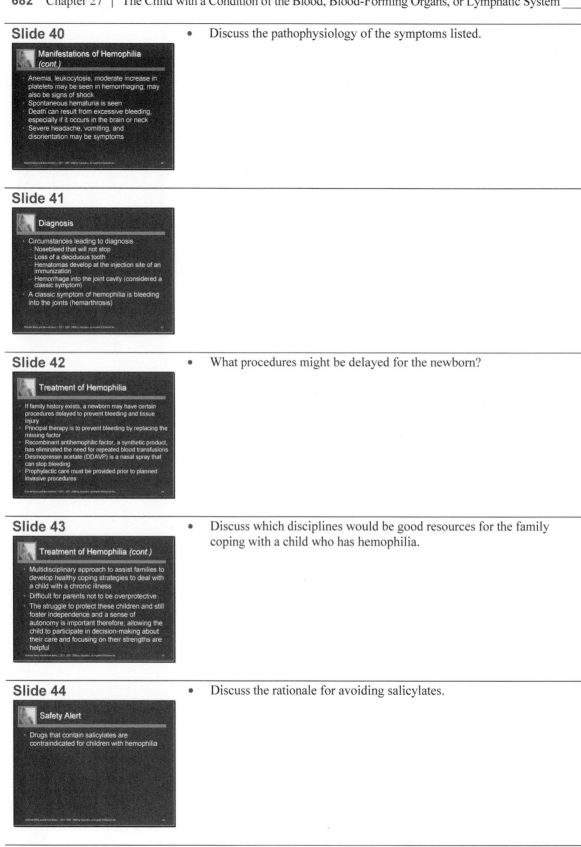

Manifestations of Hemophilia *(cont.)*

- Anemia, leukocytosis, moderate increase in platelets may be seen in hemorrhaging; may also be signs of shock
- Spontaneous hematuria is seen
- Death can result from excessive bleeding, especially if it occurs in the brain or neck
- Severe headache, vomiting, and disorientation may be symptoms

- Discuss the pathophysiology of the symptoms listed.

Slide 41

Diagnosis

- Circumstances leading to diagnosis
  - Nosebleed that will not stop
  - Loss of a deciduous tooth
  - Hematomas develop at the injection site of an immunization
  - Hemorrhage into the joint cavity (considered a classic symptom)
- A classic symptom of hemophilia is bleeding into the joints (hemarthrosis)

Slide 42

Treatment of Hemophilia

- If family history exists, a newborn may have certain procedures delayed to prevent bleeding and tissue injury
- Principal therapy is to prevent bleeding by replacing the missing factor
- Recombinant antihemophilic factor, a synthetic product, has eliminated the need for repeated blood transfusions
- Desmopressin acetate (DDAVP) is a nasal spray that can stop bleeding
- Prophylactic care must be provided prior to planned invasive procedures

- What procedures might be delayed for the newborn?

Slide 43

Treatment of Hemophilia *(cont.)*

- Multidisciplinary approach to assist families to develop healthy coping strategies to deal with a child with a chronic illness
- Difficult for parents not to be overprotective
- The struggle to protect these children and still foster independence and a sense of autonomy is important therefore; allowing the child to participate in decision-making about their care and focusing on their strengths are helpful

- Discuss which disciplines would be good resources for the family coping with a child who has hemophilia.

Slide 44

Safety Alert

- Drugs that contain salicylates are contraindicated for children with hemophilia

- Discuss the rationale for avoiding salicylates.

Slide 45

> **Platelet Disorders**
>
> · Reduction or destruction of platelets in the body interferes with the clotting mechanisms
> · Skin lesions common to this type of disorder
>   – Petechiae
>   – Purpura
>   – Ecchymosis
>   – Hematoma

- Describe petechiae, purpura, ecchymosis, and hematoma.

Slide 46

> **Idiopathic (Immunological) Thrombocytopenic Purpura (ITP)**
>
> · Acquired platelet disorder that occurs in childhood
> · Most common of the purpuras
> · Cause is unknown but is thought to be an autoimmune reaction to a virus
> · Platelets become coated with antiplatelet antibody, seen as "foreign" and are eventually destroyed by the spleen
> · ITP occurs in all age groups, with main incidence between 2 and 4 years of age

Audience Response Question #2
Complete the analogy. Hemophilia : actor VIII as ITP : _____.
  1. WBCs
  2. RBCs
  3. hemoglobin
  4. platelets

Slide 47

> **Manifestations of ITP**
>
> · Classic symptom is easy bruising
>   – Results in petechiae and purpura
> · May have recent history of rubella, rubeola, or viral respiratory infection
>   – Interval between exposure and onset is about 2 weeks
> · Platelet count below 20,000/mm³ (normal range is between 150,000 and 400,000/mm³)
>   – Diagnosis confirmed by bone marrow aspiration

- Discuss the procedure for bone marrow aspiration.

Slide 48

> **Treatment of ITP**
>
> · Neurological assessments are a priority of care
> · Treatment is not indicated in most cases
> · If indicated, prednisone, IV gamma globulin, and anti-D antibody are some of the treatment options
> · In cases of chronic ITP, a splenectomy may be required
>
> · Drugs to avoid
>   – Aspirin
>   – Phenylbutazone
>   – Phenacetin
>   – Caffeine
> · Activity is limited during acute states to avoid bruising
> · Platelets are usually not given because they are destroyed by the disease process

- Discuss a proper neurological assessment.
- What is the rationale for a splenectomy?

Slide 49

> **Complications of ITP**
>
> · Bleeding from the GI tract
> · Hemarthrosis
> · Intracranial hemorrhage
> · Prevention may be helped by immunizing all children against the viral diseases of childhood

---

Introduction to Maternity & Pediatric Nursing, 6th ed.

Leifer

Slide 50

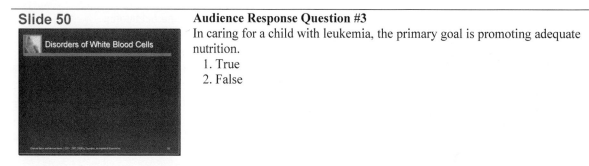

Disorders of White Blood Cells

Audience Response Question #3
In caring for a child with leukemia, the primary goal is promoting adequate nutrition.
   1. True
   2. False

Slide 51

Risk for Development of Cancer

- Genetic and environmental factors play a role
- Exposure of the fetus to diagnostic X-rays or therapeutic irradiation for brain tumors, the use of fluoroscopy, ultraviolet (sun) exposure, and some drugs have been associated with the increase in cancer

Slide 52

Leukemia

- Most common form of cancer in childhood
- Refers to a group of malignant diseases of the bone marrow and lymphatic system
- Classified according to what type of WBC affected
- Two most common
  - Acute lymphoid leukemia (ALL)
  - Acute non-lymphoid (myelogenous) leukemia (AMLL or AML)
    - Cytochemical markers, chromosome studies, and immunological markers differentiate the two types

Slide 53

Leukemia *(cont.)*

- A malignant disease of the blood-forming organs that results in an uncontrolled growth of immature WBCs
- Involves a disruption of bone marrow function caused by the overproduction of immature WBCs in the marrow
  - These immature WBCs take over the centers that are designed to form RBCs, and anemia results
- Platelet counts are also reduced
- Invasion of the bone marrow causes weakening of the bone, and pathological fractures can occur

Slide 54

Leukemia *(cont.)*

- Leukemia cells can infiltrate the spleen, liver, and lymph glands, resulting in fibrosis and diminished function
- Cancerous cells invade the CNS and other organs
  - Drain the nutrients
  - Lead to metabolic starvation of the body

- Discuss the pathophysiology of fibrosis and its effects on these organs.

Slide 55

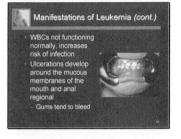

- Discuss the pathophysiology of the symptoms listed.

Slide 56

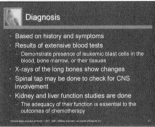

- Discuss Figure 27-6 on page 635.

Slide 57

Diagnosis

- Based on history and symptoms
- Results of extensive blood tests
  - Demonstrate presence of leukemic blast cells in the blood, bone marrow, or their tissues
- X-rays of the long bones show changes
- Spinal tap may be done to check for CNS involvement
- Kidney and liver function studies are done
  - The adequacy of their function is essential to the outcomes of chemotherapy

- Discuss what changes could be seen upon X-ray of the long bones.
- What are the effects of chemotherapy on the kidneys and the liver?

Slide 58

Treatment of Leukemia

- Long-term care given whenever possible in an outpatient setting
- Bone marrow suppression in chemotherapy requires family teaching for infection prevention
- Adequate hydration to minimize kidney damage
- Active routine immunizations must be delayed while receiving immunosuppressive drugs
- Nausea and vomiting are common side effects of chemotherapy; can lead to decreased appetite, weight loss, and generalized weakness
- Meticulous oral care is necessary

- Discuss who would be involved in the care of a child with leukemia.
- Discuss the education of parents and family in preventing infection.
- What is the rationale for avoiding immunizations during the treatment regimen? *The body will not be able to manufacture antigens as expected.*
- Give an example of why oral care is important.

Slide 59

Treatment of Leukemia *(cont.)*

- Components of chemotherapy include
  - Induction period
  - Central nervous system prophylaxis for high-risk patients
  - Maintenance
  - Reinduction therapy (if relapse occurs)
  - Extramedullary disease therapy
- Bone marrow transplant

- Discuss each of these stages of the treatment regimen.

Slide 60

Side Effects of Chemotherapy

- Steroids can mask signs of infection, cause fluid retention, induce personality changes, and cause the child's face to appear moon-shaped
- Certain chemotherapy agents can cause nausea, diarrhea, rash, hair loss, fever, anuria, anemia, and bone marrow depression
- Peripheral neuropathy may be signaled by severe constipation caused by decreased nerve sensations to the bowel

Audience Response Question #4

Which intervention is best to help prevent or reduce nausea and vomiting during chemotherapy?

1. Encourage increased fluid intake.
2. Administer an antiemetic immediately following treatment.
3. Promote diversional activities.
4. Administer an antiemetic 30 minutes before treatment.

Slide 61

Nursing Care of the Child with Leukemia

- Encourage the child to verbalize feelings
  - Giving permission to discuss their concerns will help clear up misconceptions and to decrease feelings of isolation
- Frequently observe child for infection
- Monitor vital signs and for symptoms of thrombocytopenic bleeding (a common complication of leukemia)
- Meticulous mouth and skin care

- What are ways to assess for infection?
- Discuss nursing interventions to provide good hygiene.

Slide 62

Child Receiving a Blood Transfusion

- Hemolytic reactions caused by mismatched blood are rare
- Blood is slowly infused through blood filter to avoid impurities
- Medications are **never** added to blood
- Monitor the child for signs of transfusion reaction (most occur within the first 10 minutes of the transfusion)
- Circulatory overload is a danger in children

- What are some signs of a transfusion reaction? *Chills, itching, rash, fever, headache, and pain in the back*
- What should the nurse do if a transfusion reaction occurs? *The transfusion is immediately stopped, a normal saline line is immediately opened, and the primary caregiver and hospital blood bank are notified.*
- What are signs of circulatory overload? *Dyspnea, precordial pain, rales, cyanosis, dry cough, and distended neck veins*
- If circulatory overload occurs, what are the appropriate actions? *Be prepared to administer medications and supplemental oxygen.*

Slide 63

Safety Alerts

- If a blood transfusion reaction occurs, stop the infusion, keep the vein open with normal saline solution, and notify the charge nurse
- Take the patient's vital signs and observe closely

Slide 64

Hodgkin's Disease

- A malignancy of the lymph system that primarily involves the lymph nodes
  - May metastasize to the spleen, liver, bone marrow, lungs, or other parts of the body
- Presence of giant multinucleated cells called *Reed-Sternberg cells* is diagnostic of the disease
- Rarely seen before 5 years of age, incidence increases during adolescence and early adulthood
  - Twice as common in boys as in girls

Slide 65

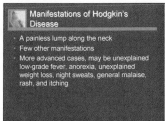

Manifestations of Hodgkin's Disease

- A painless lump along the neck
- Few other manifestations
- More advanced cases, may be unexplained low-grade fever, anorexia, unexplained weight loss, night sweats, general malaise, rash, and itching

Slide 66

Criteria for Staging Hodgkin's Disease

Stage	Criteria
I	Restricted to single site or localized in a group of lymph nodes; asymptomatic
II	Involves two or more lymph nodes in area or on same side of diaphragm
III	Involves lymph node regions on both sides of diaphragm; involves adjacent organ or spleen
IV	Is diffuse disease; least favorable prognosis

Slide 67

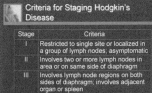

Treatment of Hodgkin's Disease

- Both radiation and chemotherapy are used in accordance with the clinical stage of the disease
- Cure is primarily related to the stage of disease at diagnosis
- Long-term prognosis is excellent

Slide 68

Nursing Care of Patients with Hodgkin's Disease

- Mainly directed toward symptomatic relief of the side effects of radiation and chemotherapy
- Education of patient and family
- Malaise is common after radiation therapy, tires easily and child may be irritable and anorexic
- Skin in treated area may be sensitive and must be protected against exposure to sunlight and irritation
- The patient *does not* become radioactive during or after therapy

- What information will parents and the family need in caring for this child?
- Discuss Nursing Care Plan 27-2 on pages 639-640.

Slide 69

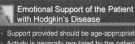

Emotional Support of the Patient with Hodgkin's Disease

- Support provided should be age-appropriate
- Activity is generally regulated by the patient
- Appearance of secondary sexual characteristics and menstruation may be delayed in pubescent patients
- Sterility is often a side effect of treatment

Leifer

Slide 70

Nursing Care of the Chronically Ill Child

Slide 71

Chronic Illness

- Behavior problems are lessened when patients can verbalize specific concerns with persons sensitive to their problems
- If they feel rejected by and different from their peers, they may be prone to depression
- Nurses must develop an awareness of the adolescent's particular fears of forced dependence, body invasion, mutilation, rejection, and loss of face, especially within peer groups
- Important to recognize the adolescent's need for self-determination

- Discuss the nurse's role in managing a child and family when dealing with a chronic illness.

Slide 72

Developmental Disabilities

- Children with developmental disabilities may often be overprotected, unable to break away from supervision, and deprived of necessary peer relationships
- The pubertal process with its emerging sexuality concerns parents and may precipitate a family crisis

Slide 73

Home Care

- Home health care and other community agencies work together to provide holistic care
- Respite care is sometimes provided to relieve parents of the responsibility of caring for the child

- Why is respite care for the family important?

Slide 74

Providing Home Health Care

- Observe how the parents interact with the child
- Do not wait for the child to cry out for attention
- Watch for facial expression and body language
- Post signs above the bed denoting special considerations, such as "never position on left side"
- Listen to the parents and observe how they attend to the physical needs of the child
- Don't be afraid to ask questions or discuss apprehensions
- Be attuned to the needs of other children in the home

- Discuss issues the nurse would assess regarding home management of the child's care.

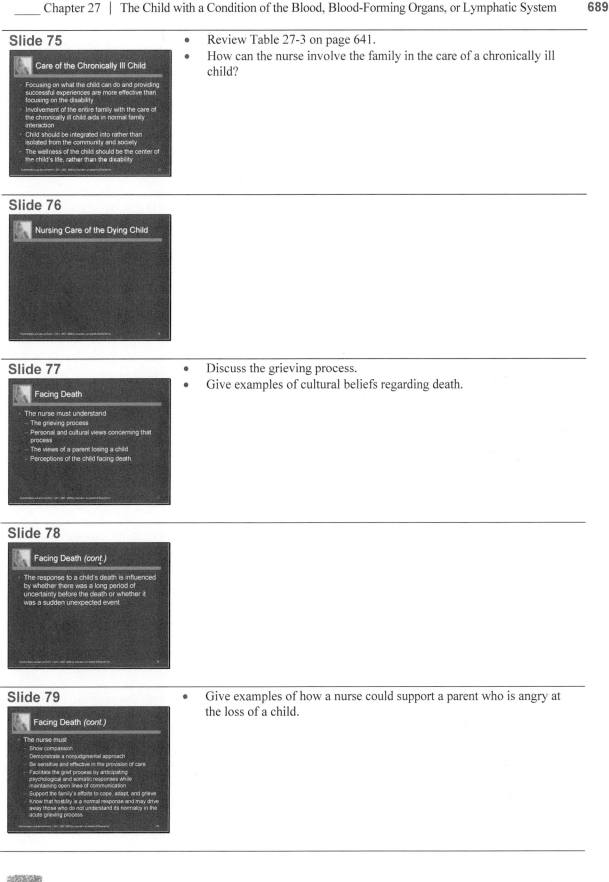

Slide 75

Care of the Chronically Ill Child

- Focusing on what the child can do and providing successful experiences are more effective than focusing on the disability
- Involvement of the entire family with the care of the chronically ill child aids in normal family interaction
- Child should be integrated into rather than isolated from the community and society
- The wellness of the child should be the center of the child's life, rather than the disability

- Review Table 27-3 on page 641.
- How can the nurse involve the family in the care of a chronically ill child?

Slide 76

Nursing Care of the Dying Child

Slide 77

Facing Death

- The nurse must understand
  - The grieving process
  - Personal and cultural views concerning that process
  - The views of a parent losing a child
  - Perceptions of the child facing death

- Discuss the grieving process.
- Give examples of cultural beliefs regarding death.

Slide 78

Facing Death *(cont.)*

- The response to a child's death is influenced by whether there was a long period of uncertainty before the death or whether it was a sudden unexpected event

Slide 79

Facing Death *(cont.)*

- The nurse must
  - Show compassion
  - Demonstrate a nonjudgmental approach
  - Be sensitive and effective in the provision of care
  - Facilitate the grief process by anticipating psychological and somatic responses while maintaining open lines of communication
  - Support the family's efforts to cope, adapt, and grieve
  - Know that hostility is a normal response and may drive away those who do not understand its normalcy in the acute grieving process

- Give examples of how a nurse could support a parent who is angry at the loss of a child.

Leifer

Slide 80

Self-Exploration

- How nurses have or have not dealt with their own losses affects present lives and the ability to relate to patients
- Nurses must recognize that *coping is an active and ongoing process*
- An active support system consisting of nonjudgmental people who are not threatened by natural expression of feeling is crucial

Slide 81

The Child's Reaction to Death

- Cognitive development, rather than chronological age, affects the response to death
- Children younger than 5 years of age are mainly concerned with separation from their parents and abandonment
- Preschool children respond to questions about death by relying on their experience and by turning to fantasy
- Children do not develop a realistic concept of death as a permanent biological process until 9 or 10 years of age

- Review the Health Promotion box on page 643 and Nursing Care Plan 27-3 on pages 644-645.

Slide 82

The Child's Awareness of His or Her Condition

- Failure to be honest with children leaves them to suffer alone, unable to express their fears and sadness or even to say goodbye

Slide 83

Physical Changes of Impending Death

- Cool, mottled, cyanotic skin and the slowing of all body processes
- Loss of consciousness, but hearing may still be intact
- Rales in the chest may be heard, which are caused by increased pooling of secretions in the lungs
- Movement and neurological signs lessen

- How would the nurse explain the dying process to the parents?
- How will you know if your teaching was effective?

Slide 84

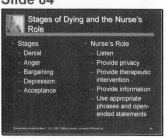

Stages of Dying and the Nurse's Role

- Stages
  - Denial
  - Anger
  - Bargaining
  - Depression
  - Acceptance
- Nurse's Role
  - Listen
  - Provide privacy
  - Provide therapeutic intervention
  - Provide information
  - Use appropriate phrases and open-ended statements

- Discuss and provide examples of how the nurse can assist an individual through each stage.

Slide 85

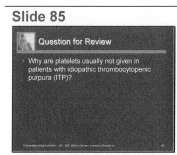

Question for Review

- Why are platelets usually not given in patients with idiopathic thrombocytopenic purpura (ITP)?

Slide 86

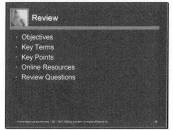

Review

- Objectives
- Key Terms
- Key Points
- Online Resources
- Review Questions

28 Lesson Plan
The Child with a Gastrointestinal Condition

TEACHING FOCUS

In this chapter, students will have the opportunity to learn about gastrointestinal conditions that affect children along with nursing management guidelines for these conditions. This chapter will examine the dangers of dehydration for infants and young children and practical ways to prevent and treat conditions such as pinworm, thrush, and poisoning. Students also will have the opportunity to consider the role nurses fulfill in educating parents about appropriate types of preventive measures for these conditions.

MATERIALS AND RESOURCES

☐ Chart listing the various sources of lead poisoning (Lesson 28.3)

☐ Computer and PowerPoint projector (all lessons)

☐ Diagram of gastrointestinal system (Lesson 28.1)

☐ Doll for demonstration of incision care (Lesson 28.1)

☐ Model of an infant to demonstrate the proper burping method with gastroesophageal reflux (Lesson 28.1)

☐ Sling to demonstrate on model of infant the technique of Fowler's sling (Lesson 28.2)

LESSON CHECKLIST

Preparations for this lesson include:

- Lecture
- Demonstration
- Guest speakers: Pediatric nurse, nutritionist, public health nurse, poison control official
- Evaluation of student knowledge and skills needed to perform all entry-level activities related to the child with a gastrointestinal condition, including:
  - Conducting parent education on poison prevention and treatment, proper hygiene, and proper hydration of infants during sickness
  - Identifying potential anomalies of the gastrointestinal system
  - Implementing appropriate interventions for conditions such as dehydration, pinworm, roundworm, or thrush
  - Instructing on sources of lead poisoning and nutritional deficiencies and their effects on children

KEY TERMS

anasarca (p. 663)
anthelmintics (p. 667)
colitis (p. 655)
colonoscopy (p. 648)
currant jelly stools (p. 654)
encopresis (p. 657)
endoscopy (p. 648)
enterocolitis (p. 653)
guarding (p. 666)
herniorrhaphy (p. 655)

homeostasis (p. 661)
hypertonic (p. 662)
hypotonic (p. 662)
incarcerated (p. 654)
isotonic (p. 662)
McBurney's point (p. 666)
parenteral fluids (p. 660)
peritoneal dialysis (p. 669)
pica (p. 670)
plumbism (p. 669)

polyhydramnios (p. 649)
projectile vomiting (p. 650)
pruritus (p. 648)
rebound tenderness (p. 666)
reflux (p. 656)
sigmoidoscopy (p. 648)
stenosis (p. 650)

ADDITIONAL RESOURCES

TEACH PPT slide(s) Chapter 28, 1-83
EILR IC image(s) Chapter 28, 1-10
EILR OBQ question(s) Chapter 28, 1-10
EILR TB question(s) Chapter 28, 1-38
ESLR IRQ question(s) Chapter 28, 1-6
SG Chapter 28, pp. 229-236

Elsevier items and derived items © 2011, 2007, 2006 by Saunders, an imprint of Elsevier Inc.

Leifer

Legend

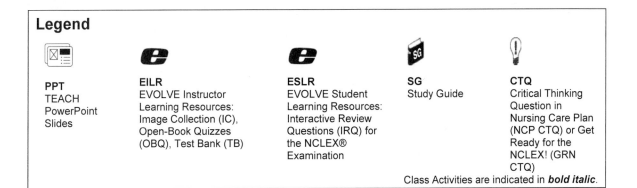

PPT
TEACH
PowerPoint
Slides

EILR
EVOLVE Instructor
Learning Resources:
Image Collection (IC),
Open-Book Quizzes
(OBQ), Test Bank (TB)

ESLR
EVOLVE Student
Learning Resources:
Interactive Review
Questions (IRQ) for
the NCLEX®
Examination

SG
Study Guide

CTQ
Critical Thinking
Question in
Nursing Care Plan
(NCP CTQ) or Get
Ready for the
NCLEX! (GRN
CTQ)

Class Activities are indicated in **bold italic**.

LESSON 28.1

PRETEST

1. Which laboratory test can reveal anemia and infections?
   a. liver function tests (LFT)
   b. complete blood count (CBC)
   c. sequential multiple analysis (SMA 12)
   d. basic metabolic panel (BMP)

2. Direct visualization of the GI tract through a flexible lighted tube is called
   a. telescopy.
   b. endoscopy.
   c. ultrasonography.
   d. computed tomography.

3. The outstanding symptom of celiac disease is
   a. nausea.
   b. diarrhea.
   c. frothy stools.
   d. constipation.

4. Nursing diagnoses for a child with pyloric stenosis includes
   a. Imbalanced nutrition: more than body requirements related to persistent vomiting.
   b. Deficient fluid volume related to effects of persistent vomiting.
   c. Increased knowledge related to treatments, surgery, and postoperative care.
   d. Chronic pain related to incision, muscle cutting, and manipulation during surgery.

5. In the newborn, failure to pass meconium stools within 24 to 48 hours may be a symptom of
   a. celiac disease.
   b. Meckel's diverticulum.
   c. hernias.
   d. Hirschsprung's disease.

6. Treatment for gastroenteritis in a child is focused on
   a. identifying and eradicating the cause.
   b. a watch and wait attitude.
   c. administering the right antibiotic.
   d. pain medication.

7. The Greek word "chalasia" means
   a. stimulation.
   b. manifestation.
   c. relaxation.
   d. dehydration.

8. Outcomes in a nursing care plan for children with gastroenteritis include
   a. urine output below 1ml/kg/hr.
   b. keeping the child cool.
   c. preventing a fluid and electrolyte imbalance.
   d. the child showing signs of secondary infection.

9. Parenteral fluids are those given by
   a. some route other than the digestive tract.
   b. mouth.
   c. a straw.
   d. a bottle.

10. Characteristic tenderness in the right lower quadrant in appendicitis is known as
    a. Epstein's pearls.
    b. pyloric stenosis.
    c. hypotonia.
    d. McBurney's point.

Answers

1. b	3. c	5. d	7. c	9. a
2. b	4. b	6. a	8. c	10. d

BACKGROUND ASSESSMENT

Question: What should be the focus of nursing interventions for a child with a gastrointestinal condition?
Answer: Children with gastrointestinal disorders become dehydrated in a short amount of time. This is true especially when the child experiences vomiting and diarrhea, which lead to an electrolyte imbalance. Nurses should assess the child for signs of dehydration, which include dry mucous membranes and poor skin turgor. The parents should be asked how frequently the child has been experiencing vomiting and diarrhea, and how often the child has voided in the preceding 24 hours. The child's weight should be measured and compared to previous weight measurements. Diagnostic studies, such as an abdominal X-ray, are usually ordered as well as lab values to assess any possible electrolyte imbalance. Patient and family teaching should be done, especially if treatment for the disorder requires an alternate method of feeding, such as use of a feeding tube.

Question: Why does dehydration occur more quickly in infants than in adults?
Answer: Infants do not concentrate urine as well as adults and therefore they have a greater water loss in their urine. In an infant, the body surface area compared to the body mass causes more fluid loss from evaporation in the skin, lungs, and saliva. When an infant is sick he may be unable to take in enough fluid because of nausea or vomiting. With diarrhea, fluid intake (with oral hydration therapy) should be increased. Infants have a higher exchange rate of ingestion and excretion of fluids, so their fluid balance is more affected when they are sick. Infants who don't eat or drink for a day are prone to dehydration.

CRITICAL THINKING QUESTION

A nurse is conducting teaching and discharge planning for the parents of a child who is scheduled to undergo surgery for a gastrointestinal disorder. What should the nurse tell them?
Guidelines: The nurse should teach them about preoperative care routines, surgical routines, and postoperative care. The nurse should educate the parents on the methods of pain assessment and management, reintroducing feedings, and providing care of the incision, including a discussion of the supplies that will be needed at home and where the parent can obtain them. Also, the nurse should evaluate the parents' ability to assess and manage the child's pain, feed the child, and care for the child's incision.

OBJECTIVES	CONTENT	TEACHING RESOURCES
Discuss three common gastrointestinal anomalies in infants.	■ The gastrointestinal tract (p. 647) ■ Disorders and dysfunction of the gastrointestinal tract (p. 648) ■ Congenital disorders (p. 648) □ Esophageal atresia (tracheoesophageal fistula) (p. 648) □ Imperforate anus (p. 649) □ Pyloric stenosis (p. 650) □ Celiac disease (p. 650) □ Hirschsprung's disease (aganglionic megacolon) (p. 652)	PPT slides 5-34 EILR IC images 1-7 EILR OBQ questions 1-4 EILR TB questions 1, 6, 11-13, 19, 31, 32 ESLR IRQ question 1 SG Learning Activities, questions 1, 2-5, 7-16 (p. 229-230) SG Review Questions, questions 1, 5, 9, 12, 15 (pp. 233-235) SG Applying Knowledge, questions 1, 2 (p. 236) **BOOK RESOURCES** Figure 28-1, Some of the Gastrointestinal System Differences Between the Child and Adult (p. 648) Figure 28-2, Esophageal Atresia (p. 649) Nursing Tip (p. 649) Figure 28-3, Pyloric Stenosis (p. 650)

ELSEVIER

OBJECTIVES	CONTENT	TEACHING RESOURCES
	☐ Intussusception (p. 653) ☐ Meckel's diverticulum (p. 654) ☐ Hernias (p. 654)	Figure 28-4, A Child with Celiac Disease (p. 652) Safety Alert (p. 652) Figure 28-5, Hirschsprung's Disease (p. 653) Figure 28-6, Intussusception (p. 653) Figure 28-7, Umbilical Hernia in Infant Boy (p. 654) Review Questions for the NCLEX® Examination, question 2 (p. 673) ▸ Discuss the prevalence of imperforate anus and the importance of observing a meconium stool. What are the potential consequences if the child is sent home without ensuring the patency of the anal canal? ▸ Discuss the various types of hernias and their manifestations. Class Activity *Divide the class into three groups and assign each group a gastrointestinal anomaly to discuss. Students should present a summary of their discussion to the class.* Class Activity *Have each group choose one nursing diagnosis for each gastrointestinal anomaly and include the rationales for the diagnosis, nursing interventions, and expected outcomes.*
Discuss dietary management of celiac disease.	☐ Celiac disease (p. 650)	▣▪ PPT slides 20, 21 𝒆 EILR IC image 4 𝒆 EILR TB questions 1, 6, 13, 20 🆂🅶 SG Learning Activities, questions 7-9 (p. 230) 🆂🅶 SG Review Questions, questions 1, 5, 9, 15 (pp. 229-235) **BOOK RESOURCES** Figure 28-4, A Child with Celiac Disease (p. 652) Review Questions for the NCLEX® Examination, question 2 (p. 673) ▸ Discuss the dietary restrictions required for this disease.
Understand the symptoms, treatments, and nursing care of a child with Hirschprung's disease.	☐ Hirschsprung's disease (aganglionic megacolon) (p. 652)	▣▪ PPT slides 23-27 𝒆 EILR IC image 5 𝒆 ESLR IRQ question 3 🆂🅶 SG Learning Activities, questions 1-12 (pp. 229-230)

Introduction to Maternity & Pediatric Nursing, 6th ed.

Elsevier items and derived items © 2011, 2007, 2006 by Saunders, an imprint of Elsevier Inc.

Leifer

OBJECTIVES	CONTENT	TEACHING RESOURCES
		SG Review Questions, question 12 (p. 234)
		BOOK RESOURCES
		Figure 28-5, Hirschsprung's Disease (p. 653)
		Review Questions for the NCLEX® Examination, question 2 (p. 673)
		▸ Discuss the symptoms, treatments, and nursing care for this disease.
Understand the treatment and nursing care of a child with intussusception.	☐ Intussusception (p. 653)	PPT slides 28-30
		e EILR IC image 6
		e ESLR IRQ question 2
		SG Learning Activities, questions 13, 14 (p. 230)
		SG Review Questions, question 5 (pp. 233)
		BOOK RESOURCES
		Figure 28-6, Intussusception (p. 653)
		▸ Discuss the various types of hernias and their manifestations.
		*Class Activity **Divide the class into three groups. One group discusses the pathophysiology of intussusceptions, another group discusses how the disease manifests, and the last group discusses nursing interventions. Have all present to class.***
Discuss the postoperative nursing care of an infant with pyloric stenosis.	☐ Pyloric stenosis (p. 650)	PPT slides 17-19
		e EILR OBQ questions 3, 4
		e EILR TB question 29
		SG Learning Activities, questions 1, 2, 6 (p. 229)
		BOOK RESOURCES
		Clinical Pathway 28-1, An Interdisciplinary Plan of Care for the Infant with Pyloric Stenosis (pp. 651-652)
		Review Questions for the NCLEX® Examination, questions 1, 3 (p. 673)
		▸ Discuss ways to manage and educate parents who lack confidence in their ability to assess and manage the infant's pain and discomfort following surgery.
		*Class Activity **Have pairs of students take turns role-playing a nurse providing parent teaching about postoperative care of the infant. Have students focus on the following points:***

OBJECTIVES	CONTENT	TEACHING RESOURCES
		– *wound care (especially when the wound is in close proximity to the diaper area)*
		– *nutrition*
		– *fluid volume (deficit)*
		Class Activity Have volunteers demonstrate incision care on a doll. Discuss important steps in postoperative nursing care, including:
		– *observation of vital signs*
		– *administration of IV fluids*
		– *inspection of the wound site*
		– *parent education about feeding techniques*
		– *avoiding wound contamination*

28.1 Homework/Assignments:

28.1 Homework/Assignments:

CRITICAL THINKING QUESTION

An infant is admitted to the hospital for dehydration related to gastroenteritis and vomiting. The nurse observed the infant's mother immediately place the child flat in the crib after a feeding. How should the nurse respond?

Guidelines: The nurse should explain to the mother that the child must be burped and placed on its right side after being fed to prevent vomiting or aspiration of vomitus. Furthermore, the infant should be handled as little as possible, and treatments should be avoided immediately after feedings.

OBJECTIVES	CONTENT	TEACHING RESOURCES
Interpret the nursing management of an infant with gastro-esophageal reflux.	■ Disorders of motility (p. 655) ☐ Gastroenteritis (p. 655) ☐ Vomiting (p. 655) ☐ Gastroesophageal reflux (p. 656) ☐ Diarrhea (p. 657) ☐ Constipation (p. 657)	⊠▪ PPT slides 35-46 *e* EILR IC image 8 *e* EILR OBQ questions 5, 6 *e* EILR TB question 2, 5, 10, 21, 22, 30, 34, 37, 38 SG Learning Activities, questions 16-26 (pp. 230-231) SG Review Questions, question 11 (p. 234) SG Thinking Critically, question 1 (p. 235) SG Applying Knowledge, question 4 (p. 236) **BOOK RESOURCES** Table 28-1, Clarifying Food Labels (p. 655) Nursing Tip (p. 655) Figure 28-8, Fowler's Sling (p. 656) Nursing Tip (p. 657) Nursing Care Plan 28-1, The Child with Gastroenteritis (Diarrhea and Vomiting) (pp. 658-659) ▸ Discuss the importance of burping a child with gastroesophageal reflux. Why is this practice along with avoidance of overfeeding an essential part of the treatment plan? *Class Activity **Divide the class into three groups to discuss gastroesophageal reflux. Have one group address the pathophysiology, one the manifestations, and one the treatment and nursing care. Then have each group present its findings to the class.*** *Class Activity **Have students work in pairs and develop a patient or parent teaching plan for gastroesophageal reflux. As a class, discuss the plans and the important patient education steps.***
Explain why infants and	☐ Fluid and electrolyte imbalance (p. 659)	⊠▪ PPT slides 47-54

OBJECTIVES	CONTENT	TEACHING RESOURCES
young children become dehydrated more easily than do adults.	– Principles of fluid balance in children (p. 659) – Oral fluids (p. 660) – Parenteral fluids (p. 660) ☐ Dehydration (p. 661) ☐ Overhydration (p. 662)	*e* EILR IC image 9 *e* EILR OBQ question 7 *e* EILR TB questions 3, 4, 14, 27, 33, 35 *e* ESLR IRQ question 4 SG Learning Activities, questions 27, 47 (p. 231) SG Review Questions, questions 6-8, (pp. 233-234) **BOOK RESOURCES** Safety Alert (p. 659) Figure 28-9, Relationship of body water and body solids (p. 660) Table 28-2, Signs of Isotonic, hypertonic, and hypotonic dehydration (p. 661) Table 28-3, Average daily excretion of urine (p. 662) Nursing Tip (p. 662) Safety Alert (p. 662) Table 28-4, Estimation of dehydration (p. 662) ▸ Discuss the differences in water loss between infants and adults. Detail specific physiological processes in the infant such as metabolic rate, heat production, and surface area and how these processes can contribute to dehydration. *Class Activity **Divide the class into small groups. Have each group discuss a different body regulatory mechanism with regard to fluid balance. Then have each group report its findings to the class.*** *Class Activity **Ask for three volunteers. Using Figure 28-9 (p. 660), ask each student to explain the relationship of body water and body solids to the body weight. One student should explain this relationship for the adult man, another for the adult woman, and the third student for a child.***
Differentiate between three types of dehydration.	☐ Dehydration (p. 661) ☐ Overhydration (p. 662)	PPT slides 51-54 *e* EILR IC image 9 *e* EILR OBQ question 8 *e* EILR TB questions 3, 4, 28, 33 SG Learning Activities, questions 1, 28, 43, 44 (pp. 229, 231, 233) SG Review Questions, questions 6-8, 17 (pp. 233-235)

OBJECTIVES	CONTENT	TEACHING RESOURCES
		BOOK RESOURCES
		Figure 28-9, Relationship of Body Water to Body Solids (p. 660)
		Table 28-2, Signs of Isotonic, Hypertonic, and Hypotonic Dehydration (p. 661)
		Table 28-3, Average Daily Excretion of Urine (p. 662)
		Table 28-4, Estimation of Dehydration (p. 662)
		Nursing Tip (p. 662)
		Table 28-5, Interpreting ABG Values (p. 663)
		▸ Discuss creative ways to entice small children to take fluids orally to keep them hydrated during sickness.
		Class Activity Choose three students. Have each student define one of the following three terms: isotonic, hypotonic, and hypertonic. Discuss examples of each type of dehydration and the signs that are associated with them.
		Class Activity Ask the class to define intracellular fluid and to distinguish it from extracellular fluid. What are the compartments for each? Discuss factors that affect fluid balance in children and adults. What aspects are unique to children?
Understand how nutritional deficiencies influence growth and development.	■ Nutritional deficiencies (p. 664) ☐ Failure to thrive (p. 664) ☐ Kwashiorkor (p. 665) ☐ Rickets (p. 665) ☐ Scurvy (p. 665)	PPT slides 55-64 EILR IC image 10 EILR OBQ question 9 EILR TB questions 23-25, 28, 36 SG Learning Activities, questions 29-33, 46 (p. 231-232) SG Review Questions, question 2, 3, 16 (pp. 233, 235) SG Case Study, question 1 (p. 235) **BOOK RESOURCES** Figure 28-10, Failure to Thrive (p. 664) ▸ Discuss the nursing interventions and teaching that would be required for failure to thrive, kwashiorkor, rickets, and scurvy.

28.2 Homework/Assignments:

28.2 Instructor's Notes/Student Feedback:

LESSON 28.3

CRITICAL THINKING QUESTION

A father brings his 2-year-old child to the emergency department. He is holding an empty bottle of aspirin and tells the nurse that there were ten 325 mg tablets in the bottle. How should the nurse respond?

Guidelines: The nurse recognizes that salicylate acts rapidly and is excreted slowly, and that ingestion of 150 mg/kg causes symptoms. The child, who weighs 19 pounds (8.63 kg) might have ingested as much as 3,250 mg of aspirin. Therefore, this situation must be treated as an emergency. The nurse anticipates that the emergency department physician will order administration of vitamin K to control bleeding, because aspirin acts as an anticoagulant. The physician might also order peritoneal dialysis, a therapeutic measure used in acute renal failure to remove toxic substances from the blood, or hemodialysis, which is used for a similar purpose. Most importantly, the nurse must constantly practice and teach safety measures to help prevent emergencies caused by ingestion of over-the-counter medications.

OBJECTIVES	CONTENT	TEACHING RESOURCES
Review the prevention of the spread of thrush in infants and children.	■ Infections (p. 665) ☐ Appendicitis (p. 665) ☐ Thrush (oral candidiasis) (p. 666)	⊠▪ PPT slides 65-68 *e* EILR OBQ question 10 *e* EILR TB question 26 **SG** SG Learning Activities, questions 34, 35 (p. 232) **BOOK RESOURCES** Nursing Tip (p. 666) ▸ Discuss the importance and types of proper hygiene for both the mother and attending health care workers to prevent the spread of thrush. *Class Activity* **Divide the class into three groups. Have one group discuss manifestations, one group discuss pathophysiology, and one group discuss treatment and nursing care of thrush in infants and children. Have groups present their findings to the class.**
Trace the route of the pinworm lifecycle and describe how reinfection takes place.	☐ Worms (p. 667) – Enterobiasis (pinworms) (p. 667) – Ascariasis (roundworms) (p. 667)	⊠▪ PPT slides 69, 70 *e* EILR TB questions 7-9, 18 **SG** SG Learning Activities, questions 36, 37 (p. 232) **SG** SG Review Questions, questions 4, 10 (pp. 233-234) **BOOK RESOURCES** Review Questions for the NCLEX® Examination, question 4 (p. 673) ▸ Discuss the common causes of pinworms and how a nurse might educate parents on preventive measures. *Class Activity* **Have a student draw the lifecycle of the pinworm on the board and explain it to the class. Ask the class to add any necessary points to the description.**

ELSEVIER

Introduction to Maternity & Pediatric Nursing, 6ᵗʰ ed.

Elsevier items and derived items © 2011, 2007, 2006 by Saunders, an imprint of Elsevier Inc.   Leifer

OBJECTIVES	CONTENT	TEACHING RESOURCES
		Class Activity **Have students research the Enterobius vermicularis (pinworm) and present some of its characteristics to the class, along with pictures. Have students determine the prevalence in the United States as well as in other countries.** *(For students to prepare for this activity, see Homework/Assignments #1.)*
Prepare a teaching plan for the prevention of poisoning in children.	■ Poisoning (p. 667) ☐ General concepts (p. 667) ☐ Poisonous plants (p. 668)	▣ PPT slides 71-74 𝓮 EILR TB question 17 SG Learning Activities, questions 38, 39 (p. 232) SG Thinking Critically, question 2 (p. 235) SG Applying Knowledge, question 3 (p. 236) **BOOK RESOURCES** Table 28-6, Detecting the Poison by Specific Odor of Vomitus (p. 668) Health Promotion, Common Household Plants that Are Poisonous (p. 668) Box 28-1, Poisons Commonly Encountered in Pediatrics (p. 670) ▸ Discuss the cardinal signs that indicate the type of agent and course of action once poisoning is suspected. Suggest ways parents could prevent accidental poisoning in the home environment. *Class Activity* **Divide the class into three groups and assign each group one of the following topics: poisonous plants, poisonous drugs, and lead poisoning. Have each group research its topic on the Internet and then present its findings to the class.** *(For students to prepare for this activity, see Homework/Assignments #2.)*
List two measures to reduce acetaminophen poisoning in children.	☐ Drugs (p. 668) – Acetaminophen poisoning (p. 668) – Salicylate poisoning (p. 669)	▣ PPT slides 75-77 𝓮 EILR TB question 15 𝓮 ESLR IRQ question 5 SG Learning Activities, question 40 (p. 232) SG Review Questions, question 13 (p. 234) **BOOK RESOURCES** Table 28-7, Selected Over-the-Counter Drugs that Are Deadly to Toddlers (p. 669)

Introduction to Maternity & Pediatric Nursing, 6th ed.

Leifer

OBJECTIVES	CONTENT	TEACHING RESOURCES
		Box 28-1, Poisons Commonly Encountered in Pediatrics (p. 670)
		Table 28-8, Anticipated Care for Poisoning (p. 671)
		▶ Discuss the specific precautions that must be communicated to parents when giving small children acetaminophen. Outline how this could be communicated in a clear manner so there is no misunderstanding.
		Class Activity Discuss the manifestations, pathophysiology, treatment, and nursing care of acetaminophen poisoning. Why has this condition become more common? What steps can be taken to reduce the frequency of acetaminophen poisoning in children?
		Class Activity Have a student discuss the difference between rapid-acting and timed-release aspirin. Ask a student to demonstrate safety packaging. Discuss other measures that could reduce the frequency of acetaminophen poisoning in children.
Indicate the primary source of lead poisoning.	☐ Lead poisoning (p. 669) ■ Foreign body ingestion (p. 672)	PPT slides 78-81 EILR TB question 16 ESLR IRQ question 6 SG Learning Activities, questions 1, 41, 42 (pp. 232-233) SG Review Questions, question 14 (p. 235) **BOOK RESOURCES** Box 28-1, Poisons Commonly Encountered in Pediatrics (p. 670) Safety Alert (p. 671) Nursing Tip (p. 671) Review Questions for the NCLEX® Examination, question 5 (p. 673) ▶ Discuss questions a nurse might ask parents to determine whether lead may be in the child's environment and thus responsible for the symptoms suggesting lead poisoning. *Class Activity Discuss potential sources of lead poisoning in the environment, and specific sources associated with lead poisoning of children in particular ethnic or cultural groups. What measures can be taken to minimize the risk of lead poisoning?*
Performance		PPT slides 1-83

OBJECTIVES	CONTENT	TEACHING RESOURCES
Evaluation		*e* EILR IC images 1-10
		e EILR OBQ questions 1-10
		e EILR TB questions 1-38
		e ESLR IRQ questions 1-6
		SG Learning Activities, questions 1-44 (pp. 229-233)
		SG Review Questions, questions 1-17 (pp. 233-235)
		SG Case Study, question 1 (p. 235)
		SG Thinking Critically, questions 1, 2 (p. 235)
		SG Applying Knowledge, questions 1-4 (p. 235-236)
		BOOK RESOURCES
		NCP CTQ 1 (p. 659)
		Review Questions for the NCLEX® Examination, questions 1-5 (p. 673)

28.3 Homework/Assignments:

1. Have students research the *Enterobius vermicularis* (pinworm) and present some of its characteristics to the class, along with pictures. Have students determine the prevalence in the United States as well as in other countries.

2. Divide the class into three groups, and assign each group one of the following topics: poisonous plants, poisonous drugs, and lead poisoning. Have each group research its topic on the Internet and then present its findings to the class.

28.3 Instructor's Notes/Student Feedback:

28 | Lecture Outline
The Child with a Gastrointestinal Condition

Slide 1

Chapter 28

The Child with a
Gastrointestinal Condition

Slide 2

Objectives

- Define each key term listed.
- Discuss three common gastrointestinal anomalies in infants.
- Discuss the postoperative nursing care of an infant with pyloric stenosis.
- Discuss the dietary management of celiac disease.
- Understand the symptoms, treatment, and nursing care of a child with Hirschprung's disease.

Slide 3

Objectives *(cont.)*

- Understand the treatment and nursing care of a child with intussusception.
- Interpret the nursing management of an infant with gastroesophageal reflux.
- Differentiate among three types of dehydration.
- Explain why infants and young children become dehydrated more easily than adults.
- Understand how nutritional deficiencies influence growth and development.

Slide 4

Objectives *(cont.)*

- Review the prevention of the spread of thrush in infants and children.
- Trace the route of the pinworm cycle and describe how reinfection takes place.
- Prepare a teaching plan for the prevention of poisoning in children.
- List two measures to reduce acetaminophen poisoning in children.
- Indicate the primary source of lead poisoning.

ELSEVIER

Introduction to Maternity & Pediatric Nursing, 6th ed.
Leifer

Slide 5

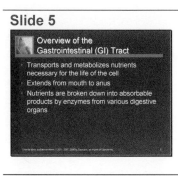

Slide 6

- Discuss Figure 28-1 on page 648.

Slide 7

- Discuss the x-ray and endoscopic procedures listed.

Slide 8

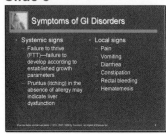

- Give an example of an infant who is diagnosed with "failure to thrive."
- Discuss the pathophysiology regarding pruritus in relation to liver dysfunction.

Slide 9

- What are nursing interventions for each topic listed?

Leifer

Slide 10

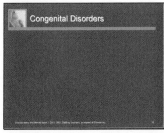

Congenital Disorders

Slide 11

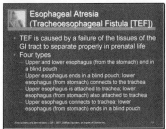

Esophageal Atresia
(Tracheoesophageal Fistula [TEF])

- TEF is caused by a failure of the tissues of the GI tract to separate properly in prenatal life
- Four types
  - Upper and lower esophagus (from the stomach) end in a blind pouch
  - Upper esophagus ends in a blind pouch; lower esophagus (from stomach) connects to the trachea
  - Upper esophagus is attached to trachea; lower esophagus (from stomach) also attached to trachea
  - Upper esophagus connects to trachea; lower esophagus (from stomach) ends in a blind pouch

• Refer to Figure 28-2 on page 649.

Slide 12

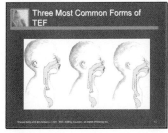

Three Most Common Forms of TEF

Slide 13

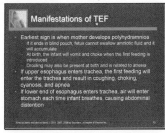

Manifestations of TEF

- Earliest sign is when mother develops polyhydramnios
  - If it ends in blind pouch, fetus cannot swallow amniotic fluid and it will accumulate
  - At birth, the infant will vomit and choke when the first feeding is introduced
  - Drooling may also be present at birth and is related to atresia
- If upper esophagus enters trachea, the first feeding will enter the trachea and result in coughing, choking, cyanosis, and apnea
- If lower end of esophagus enters trachea, air will enter stomach each time infant breathes, causing abdominal distention

Slide 14

Nursing Care of TEF

- Prevent pneumonia, choking, and apnea in the newborn
  - Assessment of the newborn during the first feeding for signs/symptoms of TEF is essential
  - Feeding usually is with clear water or colostrum to minimize seriousness of aspiration
- Surgical repair is essential for survival

ELSEVIER

Introduction to Maternity & Pediatric Nursing, 6th ed.
Leifer

Slide 15

Imperforate Anus

- Lower GI and anus arise from two different types of tissue during fetal development
- Once the two meet, perforation occurs allowing for a passageway
- When perforation does not take place, the lower end of the GI tract and anus end in a blind pouch
- Four types ranging from stenosis to complete separation or failure of the anus to form

Slide 16

Imperforate Anus (cont.)

- Manifestations
  - Failure to pass meconium in the first 24 hours must be reported
  - Infant should not be discharged home until a meconium stool has passed
- Treatment
  - Once established, infant is NPO and prepared for surgery
  - Initial surgical procedure may be a colostomy
  - Subsequent surgeries will reestablish patency of anal canal

- What is the rationale for a colostomy?

Slide 17

Pyloric Stenosis

- Obstruction of the lower end of the stomach caused by overgrowth of the circular muscles of the pylorus or spasms of the sphincter
- Commonly classified as a congenital anomaly
- Symptoms usually do not appear until the infant is 2 or 3 weeks old
  - Most common surgical condition of GI tract in infancy
- Incidence is higher in boys

Slide 18

Manifestations of Pyloric Stenosis

- Projectile vomiting is outstanding symptom from force or pressure being exerted on the pylorus
  - Vomitus contains mucus and ingested milk
  - Infant is constantly hungry and will eat again immediately after vomiting
- Dehydration and olive-shaped mass may be felt in upper right quadrant of abdomen

- Describe the symptom of projectile vomiting.
- Discuss the significance of an olive-shaped mass.
- Refer to Figure 28-3 on page 650.

Slide 19

Treatment of Pyloric Stenosis

- Surgery is called pyloromyotomy
- Preoperative nursing care
  - Intravenous fluids to treat or prevent dehydration
  - Thickened feedings may be given by a teaspoon or through a nipple with a large hole
  - Burped before and during feedings to remove any gas accumulated in the stomach
  - Place on right side (preferably Fowler's position) after feeding to facilitate stomach drainage into the intestines
  - If infant vomits, nurse is instructed to refeed the infant
- Postoperative nursing care
  - Monitor intravenous fluids, provide feedings as prescribed by surgeon, document intake and output, monitor surgical site

- Review Clinical Pathway 28-1 on pages 651-652.

Slide 20

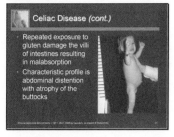

Celiac Disease

- Also known as *gluten enteropathy* and *sprue*
- Leading malabsorption problem in children
  - Thought to be caused by inherited disposition with environmental triggers
- Symptoms not evident until 6 months to 2 years of age when foods containing gluten are introduced
  - Wheat, barley, oats, and rye

Slide 21

- What is the role of the villi in the intestines?

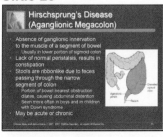

Celiac Disease *(cont.)*

- Repeated exposure to gluten damage the villi of intestines resulting in malabsorption
- Characteristic profile is abdominal distention with atrophy of the buttocks

Slide 22

Celiac Disease *(cont.)*

- Infant presents with failure to thrive
- Infant is irritable
- Stools are large, bulky, and frothy
- Diagnosis confirmed by serum immunoglobin A (IgA) and small bowel biopsy

- Treatment
  - Lifelong diet restricted in wheat, barley, oats, and rye
  - Detailed parent teaching is essential
    - A professional nutritionist or dietitian can aid in identifying foods that are gluten-free

Slide 23

- Refer to Figure 28-5 on page 653.

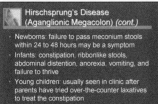

Hirschsprung's Disease (Aganglionic Megacolon)

- Absence of ganglionic innervation to the muscle of a segment of bowel
  - Usually in lower portion of sigmoid colon
- Lack of normal peristalsis, results in constipation
- Stools are ribbonlike due to feces passing through the narrow segment of colon
  - Portion of bowel nearest obstruction dilates, causing abdominal distention
  - Seen more often in boys and in children with Down syndrome
- May be acute or chronic

Slide 24

Hirschsprung's Disease (Aganglionic Megacolon) *(cont.)*

- Newborns: failure to pass meconium stools within 24 to 48 hours may be a symptom
- Infants: constipation, ribbonlike stools, abdominal distention, anorexia, vomiting, and failure to thrive
- Young children: usually seen in clinic after parents have tried over-the-counter laxatives to treat the constipation

Leifer

Slide 25

Hirschsprung's Disease
(Aganglionic Megacolon) *(cont.)*

If untreated, other signs
of intestinal obstruction
and shock may be seen
- Enterocolitis
(inflammation of the
small bowel and colon)
is a serious condition
  - Fever, explosive stools,
  and depletion of strength

Diagnostics
- Barium enema
- Rectal biopsy
- Anorectal manometry
  - Measures pressure in
  anal sphincter

- Discuss the barium enema and the nurse's role in educating the parents about this procedure.
- Describe how anorectal manometry is performed.

Slide 26

Hirschsprung's Disease
(Aganglionic Megacolon) *(cont.)*

- Treatment
  - Surgery to remove
  impaired part of colon
  and an anastomosis
  of intestine is
  performed
  - In newborns, a
  colostomy may be
  needed until 12 to 18
  months of age, when
  more extensive repair
  may be performed

- Nursing Care
  - Dependent upon age of
  child
  - In newborns, detection is
  high-priority
  - As child grows, careful
  attention to a history of
  constipation and diarrhea
  is important
  - Signs of undernutrition,
  abdominal distention, and
  poor feedings are suspect

- Relate the signs and symptoms with the pathophysiology of this disease.

Slide 27

Hirschsprung's Disease
(Aganglionic Megacolon) *(cont.)*

- Enemas
  - Due to increased size of mucous membranes'
  surface area, an increased absorption of the
  fluid can be anticipated
    - Therefore, normal saline solution should be used to
    prevent water intoxication and death
  - Parents should check with the pediatrician to
  see how much saline should be administered
  with each enema

- What is water intoxication?

Slide 28

Intussusception

- A slipping of one part of the
intestine into another part just
below it
  - Often seen at the ileocecal valve
  The mesentery, a double fan-shaped
  fold of peritoneum that covers most of
  intestine and is filled with blood vessels
  and nerves, is also pulled along
- Edema occurs
- At first, intestinal obstruction
occurs, but then strangulation of
the bowel occurs as peristalsis
occurs
- Affected portion may burst, leading
to peritonitis

- Discuss the severity of this condition and the need for urgent medical treatment.

Slide 29

Intussusception *(cont.)*

- Generally occurs in boys between
3 months and 6 years
  - Frequency decreases after
  age 36 months
- Can have spontaneous reduction
- Onset is usually sudden
  - May have a fever as high as
  106° F (41.1° C)
  - As it progresses, child may
  show signs of shock,
  sweating, weak pulse, shallow,
  grunting respirations;
  abdomen is rigid

- In infants, severe pain in
abdomen, loud cries, straining
efforts, and kicking and drawing
of legs toward abdomen
- Child vomits green or greenish-
yellow fluid (bilious)
- Bowel movements diminish, little
flatus is passed
- Blood and mucus with no feces
are common about 12 hours
after onset of obstruction, called
currant jelly stools

- Currant jelly stools are the hallmark symptom of this condition.

Leifer

Slide 30

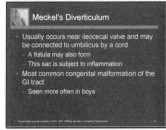

Treatment of Intussusception

- This condition is an emergency
- Diagnosis is determined by history and physical findings
- May feel a sausage-shaped mass in right upper abdomen
- Barium enema is treatment of choice, with surgery if reduction does not occur

- What is the rationale for a barium enema as a treatment option for this condition?

Slide 31

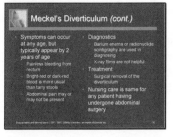

Meckel's Diverticulum

- Usually occurs near ileocecal valve and may be connected to umbilicus by a cord
  - A fistula may also form
  - This sac is subject to inflammation
- Most common congenital malformation of the GI tract
  - Seen more often in boys

Slide 32

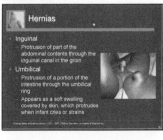

Meckel's Diverticulum *(cont.)*

- Symptoms can occur at any age, but typically appear by 2 years of age
  - Painless bleeding from rectum
  - Bright-red or dark-red blood is more usual than tarry stools
  - Abdominal pain may or may not be present
- Diagnostics
  - Barium enema or radionuclide scintigraphy are used in diagnosing
  - X-ray films are not helpful
- Treatment
  - Surgical removal of the diverticulum
  - Nursing care is same for any patient having undergone abdominal surgery

- Give examples of nursing interventions for a patient having surgical repair of a Meckel's diverticulum.

Slide 33

Hernias

- Inguinal
  - Protrusion of part of the abdominal contents through the inguinal canal in the groin
- Umbilical
  - Protrusion of a portion of the intestine through the umbilical ring
  - Appears as a soft swelling covered by skin, which protrudes when infant cries or strains

- Discuss the difference between inguinal versus umbilical hernias.

Slide 34

Hernias *(cont.)*

- May be present at birth (congenital) or acquired
- Is reducible if it can be put back into place by gentle pressure
- If it cannot be put back, it is irreducible or incarcerated
- Strangulated hernia is when intestine becomes caught in the passage and the blood supply is diminished
- Child may vomit and have severe abdominal pain
- Emergent surgery is indicated in this type of situation
- In most cases, same-day surgery is performed

- Define incarcerated and strangulated hernias.

Leifer

Slide 35 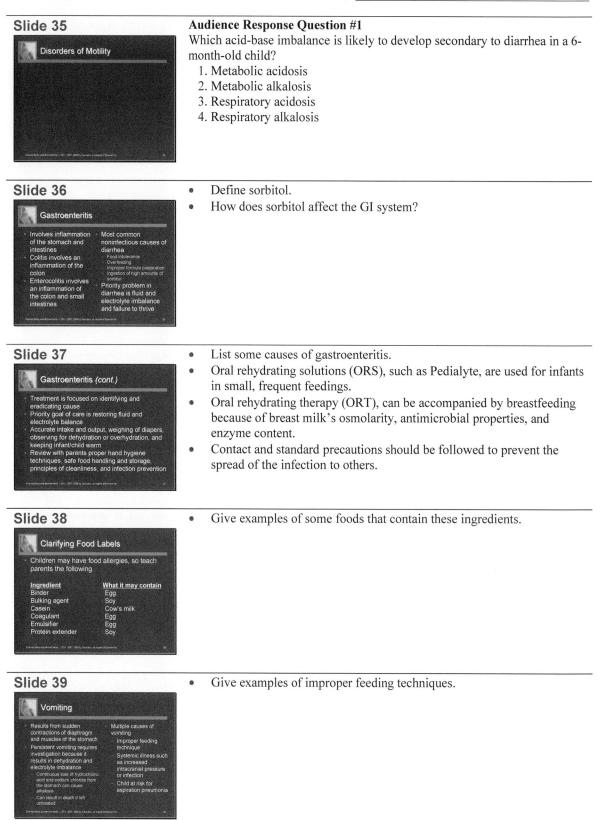Disorders of Motility	**Audience Response Question #1** Which acid-base imbalance is likely to develop secondary to diarrhea in a 6-month-old child? 1. Metabolic acidosis 2. Metabolic alkalosis 3. Respiratory acidosis 4. Respiratory alkalosis

Slide 36
Gastroenteritis
• Involves inflammation of the stomach and intestines
• Colitis involves an inflammation of the colon
• Enterocolitis involves an inflammation of the colon and small intestines
• Most common noninfectious causes of diarrhea
  Food intolerance
  Overfeeding
  Improper formula preparation
  Ingestion of high amounts of sorbitol
• Priority problem in diarrhea is fluid and electrolyte imbalance and failure to thrive
	• Define sorbitol.
	• How does sorbitol affect the GI system?

Slide 37 Gastroenteritis *(cont.)* • Treatment is focused on identifying and eradicating cause • Priority goal of care is restoring fluid and electrolyte balance • Accurate intake and output, weighing of diapers, observing for dehydration or overhydration, and keeping infant/child warm • Review with parents proper hand hygiene techniques, safe food handling and storage, principles of cleanliness, and infection prevention	• List some causes of gastroenteritis. • Oral rehydrating solutions (ORS), such as Pedialyte, are used for infants in small, frequent feedings. • Oral rehydrating therapy (ORT), can be accompanied by breastfeeding because of breast milk's osmolarity, antimicrobial properties, and enzyme content. • Contact and standard precautions should be followed to prevent the spread of the infection to others.
Slide 38 Clarifying Food Labels • Children may have food allergies, so teach parents the following **Ingredient** — **What it may contain** Binder — Egg Bulking agent — Soy Casein — Cow's milk Coagulant — Egg Emulsifier — Egg Protein extender — Soy	• Give examples of some foods that contain these ingredients.

Slide 39
Vomiting
• Results from sudden contractions of diaphragm and muscles of the stomach
• Persistent vomiting requires investigation because it results in dehydration and electrolyte imbalance
  Continuous loss of hydrochloric acid and sodium chloride from the stomach can cause alkalosis
  Can result in death if left untreated
• Multiple causes of vomiting
  Improper feeding technique
  Systemic illness such as increased intracranial pressure or infection
  Child at risk for aspiration pneumonia
	• Give examples of improper feeding techniques.

Slide 40	
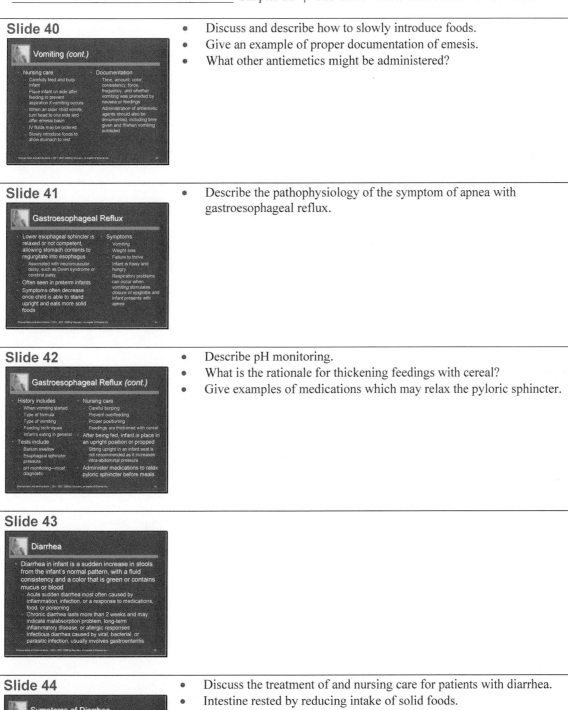	• Discuss and describe how to slowly introduce foods. • Give an example of proper documentation of emesis. • What other antiemetics might be administered?

Slide 41

• Describe the pathophysiology of the symptom of apnea with gastroesophageal reflux.

Slide 42

• Describe pH monitoring.
• What is the rationale for thickening feedings with cereal?
• Give examples of medications which may relax the pyloric sphincter.

Slide 43

Slide 44

• Discuss the treatment of and nursing care for patients with diarrhea.
• Intestine rested by reducing intake of solid foods.
• ORS solutions, such as Pedialyte or Infalyte, in liquid or frozen form are given with gradual introduction of a soft, bland diet.
• Clear fluids, fruit juice (without pulp), gelatin, and carbonated drinks have a low electrolyte content and should be avoided.
• Caffeinated beverages act as a diuretic and worsen dehydration.
• Chicken broth is high in sodium and not advised.
• BRAT diet is not nutritionally sound enough to support growth and development.

Slide 45

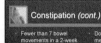

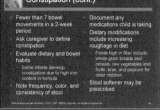

Constipation

- Difficult or infrequent defecation with the passage of hard, dry fecal material
  - May be periods of diarrhea or encopresis (constipation with fecal soiling)
- May be a symptom of other disorders
- Diet, culture, and social, psychological, and familial patterns may also influence occurrence
- Daily use of laxatives or enemas should be discouraged

- Give an example of other disorders that could cause constipation.
- Why should enemas and laxatives not be used daily for constipation?

Audience Response Question #2
A child is considered constipated if he or she does not have a bowel movement at least every 3 days.
  1. True
  2. False

Slide 46

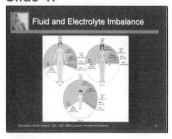

Constipation *(cont.)*

- Fewer than 7 bowel movements in a 2-week period
- Ask caregiver to define constipation
- Evaluate dietary and bowel habits
  - Some infants develop constipation due to high iron content in formula
- Note frequency, color, and consistency of stool
- Document any medications child is taking
- Dietary modifications include increasing roughage in diet
  - Foods high in fiber include whole-grain breads and cereals, raw vegetables and fruits, bran, and popcorn for older children
- Stool softener may be prescribed

Slide 47

Fluid and Electrolyte Imbalance

- Discuss Figure 28-9 on page 660.

Slide 48

Fluid and Electrolyte Imbalance *(cont.)*

- In children under 2 years of age, surface area is important because more water is lost through the skin than through the kidneys
- Metabolic rate and heat production are also 2 to 3 times greater in infants per kg of body weight
  - Produces more waste products, which must be diluted to be excreted
  - Stimulates respirations, which increase evaporation through the lungs
  - Greater percentage of body water in children under 2 years is contained in extracellular compartment

- Discuss surface area, metabolic rate, and heat production.
- Surface area of the infant is from 2 to 3 times greater than the adult.

Slide 49

Fluid and Electrolyte Imbalance *(cont.)*

- Fluid turnover is rapid, and dehydration occurs more quickly in infants than in adults
- A sick infant does not adapt as readily to shift in intake and output
- Less able to concentrate urine and require more water than an adult's kidneys to excrete a given amount of solute

Leifer

Slide 50	
Fluid and Electrolyte Imbalance *(cont.)* · Electrolyte balance depends on fluid balance and cardiovascular, renal, adrenal, pituitary, parathyroid, and pulmonary regulatory mechanisms · Signs of dehydration may not be evident until the fluid loss reaches 4%, and severe dehydration may not be evident until the fluid loss reaches 10% · Can treat with oral fluids or parenteral fluids	• Describe the signs and symptoms of dehydration in infants and children.

Slide 51	

Dehydration
 	
· Causes fluid and electrolyte disturbances
· Evaluation of type and severity, including clinical observation and chemical analysis of the blood
 	
· Types of dehydration are classified according to level of serum sodium, which depends on the relative losses of water and electrolytes
  - Isotonic
  - Hypotonic
  - Hypertonic
	• Isotonic dehydration: equal amounts of fluids and electrolytes have been lost
	• Hypotonic dehydration: more electrolytes than fluid have been lost
	• Hypertonic dehydration: More fluid than electrolytes have been lost
	• Each form of dehydration is associated with different relative losses from intracellular fluid (ICF) and extracellular fluid (ECF).
	• Each requires specific modifications of treatment.

Slide 52	

Dehydration *(cont.)*
 	
· *Maintenance fluid therapy* replaces normal water and electrolyte losses
· Deficit therapy restores preexisting body fluid and electrolyte deficiencies
  - Shock is greatest threat to life in isotonic dehydration
  - Children with hypotonic dehydration are at risk for water intoxication
· Potassium is lost in almost all degrees of dehydration and is replaced only after normal urinary excretion is confirmed
	• Give an example of maintenance and deficit IV fluids.

Slide 53	

Overhydration
 	
· The body receives more fluid than it can excrete
· Manifests as edema (excess fluid in interstitial spaces)
  - Interstitial fluid is similar to plasma, but contains little protein
  - Any factor causing sodium retention can cause edema
· Flow of blood out of the interstitial compartments depends on adequate circulation of blood and lymph
· Low protein levels disturb osmotic cellular pressure
· Anasarca is severe generalized edema
	• Discuss areas in which edema might be present.
	
	Audience Response Question #3
	What is an indication of overhydration of a 1-month-old infant on intravenous fluids?
	  1. Heart rate of 100
	  2. Lethargy
	  3. Bulging fontanel
	  4. Increased urine output

Slide 54	

Overhydration *(cont.)*
 	
· Treatment
  - IV therapy is ordered and child is monitored
  - Is dependent upon type of electrolyte imbalance child has
  - If child has a hypertonic type of dehydration, tomato juice should *not* be offered
  - If child has a hypotonic type of dehydration, plain water should *not* be offered
 	
· Nursing care
  - Early detection and management of edema are essential
  - Accurate daily weight, vital signs, observing physical appearance, and noting changes in urine output
  - Important for nurse to monitor clinical laboratory results and adjust fluids and foods offered to the child
	• Discuss the rationale for IV therapy for overhydration.
	• Why should tomato juice be avoided when a child is experiencing hypertonic dehydration?
	• Discuss laboratory results the nurse should monitor for a child who is dehydrated.

Slide 55

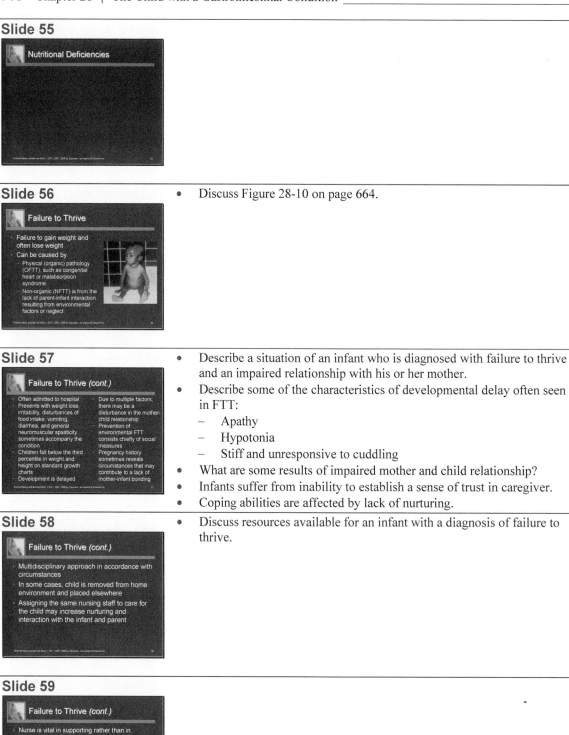

Slide 56

- Discuss Figure 28-10 on page 664.

Slide 57

- Describe a situation of an infant who is diagnosed with failure to thrive and an impaired relationship with his or her mother.
- Describe some of the characteristics of developmental delay often seen in FTT:
  – Apathy
  – Hypotonia
  – Stiff and unresponsive to cuddling
- What are some results of impaired mother and child relationship?
- Infants suffer from inability to establish a sense of trust in caregiver.
- Coping abilities are affected by lack of nurturing.

Slide 58

- Discuss resources available for an infant with a diagnosis of failure to thrive.

Slide 59

Slide 60

Kwashiorkor

- Severe deficiency of protein in the diet despite the fact that the number of calories consumed may be nearly adequate
- Belongs to a class of disorders termed *protein-energy malnutrition*
- Seen most often in third-world countries

- Discuss Figure 28-10 on page 664.

Slide 61

Kwashiorkor *(cont.)*

- Occurs in children 1 to 4 years of age who have been weaned from the breast
  - Oral intake is deficient in protein
  - Child fails to grow normally
  - Muscles become weak and wasted
  - Edema of abdomen
  - Diarrhea, skin infections, irritability, anorexia, and vomiting may be present
  - Hair thins and is dry and may contain a white streak
  - Child looks apathetic and weak

- Discuss the pathophysiology regarding abdominal edema, diarrhea, and skin infections.
- Protein is basis of melanin, a substance that provides color to hair.
- A white streak in the hair of the child is a sign of this protein malnutrition.

Slide 62

Kwashiorkor *(cont.)*

- Treatment is mainly preventive
- Simple protein powder sprinkled on the culturally prepared meal will alleviate the problem

Slide 63

Rickets

- Caused by deficient amounts of vitamin D
  - Exposure to sunshine is necessary for proper absorption and metabolism of calcium and phosphorus
- Classic symptoms are bow-legs; knock-knees; beading of the ribs, called rachitic rosary; and, improper formation of teeth
  - Vitamin supplements along with exercise and exposure to outdoor sunlight is primary form of treatment

- Describe rachitic rosary.

Slide 64

Scurvy

- Caused by insufficient fruits and vegetables that contain vitamin C
- Symptoms include joint pain, bleeding gums, loose teeth, lack of energy
- Vitamin C
  - Easily destroyed by heat and exposure to air
  - Not stored in the body and daily intake of the vitamin is necessary
- Vitamin supplements and dietary intake such as citrus fruits and raw leafy vegetables

- Give examples of foods which are rich in vitamin C.

Audience Response Question #4
Complete the analogy. Rickets : vitamin D as scurvy : _____.
1. vitamin C
2. iron
3. vitamin K
4. vitamin B$_6$

ELSEVIER

Leifer

Slide 65

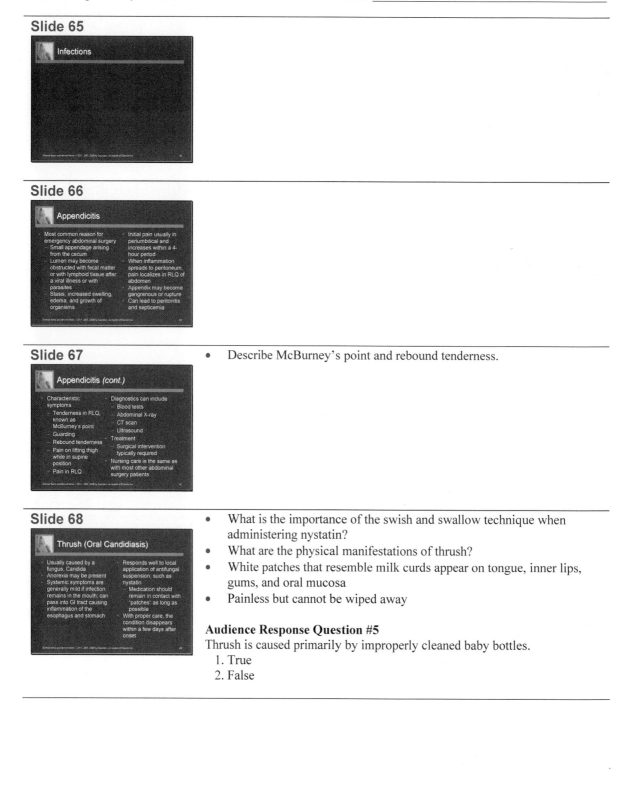

Slide 66

Slide 67

- Describe McBurney's point and rebound tenderness.

Slide 68

- What is the importance of the swish and swallow technique when administering nystatin?
- What are the physical manifestations of thrush?
- White patches that resemble milk curds appear on tongue, inner lips, gums, and oral mucosa
- Painless but cannot be wiped away

Audience Response Question #5
Thrush is caused primarily by improperly cleaned baby bottles.
   1. True
   2. False

Slide 69

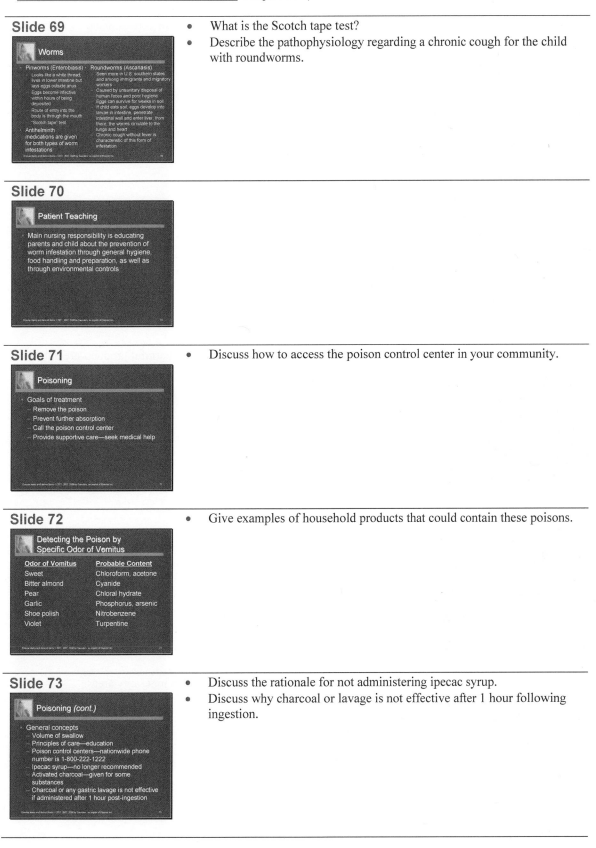

- What is the Scotch tape test?
- Describe the pathophysiology regarding a chronic cough for the child with roundworms.

Slide 70

Patient Teaching

- Main nursing responsibility is educating parents and child about the prevention of worm infestation through general hygiene, food handling and preparation, as well as through environmental controls

Slide 71

Poisoning

- Goals of treatment
  - Remove the poison
  - Prevent further absorption
  - Call the poison control center
  - Provide supportive care—seek medical help

- Discuss how to access the poison control center in your community.

Slide 72

Detecting the Poison by Specific Odor of Vomitus

Odor of Vomitus	Probable Content
Sweet	Chloroform, acetone
Bitter almond	Cyanide
Pear	Chloral hydrate
Garlic	Phosphorus, arsenic
Shoe polish	Nitrobenzene
Violet	Turpentine

- Give examples of household products that could contain these poisons.

Slide 73

Poisoning *(cont.)*

- General concepts
  - Volume of swallow
  - Principles of care—education
  - Poison control centers—nationwide phone number is 1-800-222-1222
  - Ipecac syrup—no longer recommended
  - Activated charcoal—given for some substances
  - Charcoal or any gastric lavage is not effective if administered after 1 hour post-ingestion

- Discuss the rationale for not administering ipecac syrup.
- Discuss why charcoal or lavage is not effective after 1 hour following ingestion.

Slide 74

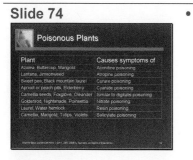

Poisonous Plants

Plant	Causes symptoms of
Azalea, Buttercup, Marigold	Aconitine poisoning
Lantana, Jimsonweed	Atropine poisoning
Sweet pea, Black mountain laurel	Curare poisoning
Apricot or peach pits, Elderberry	Cyanide poisoning
Camellia seeds, Foxglove, Oleander	Similar to digitalis poisoning
Goldenrod, Nightshade, Poinsettia	Nitrate poisoning
Laurel, Water hemlock	Resin poisoning
Camellia, Marigold, Tulips, Violets	Salicylate poisoning

• Discuss poisonous plants that are common in your climate.

Slide 75

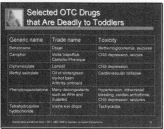

Selected OTC Drugs that Are Deadly to Toddlers

Generic name	Trade name	Toxicity
Benzocaine	Orajel	Methemoglobinemia, seizures
Camphor	Vicks VapoRub Campho-Phenique	CNS depression, seizure
Diphenoxylate	Lomotil	CNS depression
Methyl salicylate	Oil of wintergreen Icy-hot balm Arthritis ointment	Cardiovascular collapse
Phenylpropanolamine	Many decongestants such as Afrin and Sudafed	Hypertension, intracranial bleeding, cardiac arrhythmia, CNS depression, seizures
Tetrahydrozoline hydrochloride	Visine eye drops	Tachycardia

Slide 76

Safety Alert

- Many over-the-counter medications are considered harmless by parents but can be deadly to the toddler or small child
- Keep all medications (prescription or otherwise), including herbal supplements, out of reach of small children

• How can a parent ensure these potentially harmful products are out of reach of children?

Slide 77

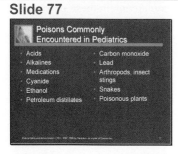

Poisons Commonly Encountered in Pediatrics

- Acids
- Alkalines
- Medications
- Cyanide
- Ethanol
- Petroleum distillates
- Carbon monoxide
- Lead
- Arthropods, insect stings
- Snakes
- Poisonous plants

Slide 78

Lead Poisoning (Plumbism)

- Results when a child repeatedly ingests or absorbs substances containing lead
- Incidence higher in inner-city tenements
- Children who chew on window sills and stair rails ingest flakes of paint, putty, or crumbled plaster
- Eating nonfood items is called pica
- Can have a lasting effect on the CNS, especially the brain
- Mental retardation occurs in severe cases of lead poisoning

• Discuss the issue of increased incidence in inner-city areas.

Leifer

Slide 79

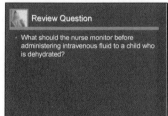

Lead Poisoning (Plumbism) *(cont.)*

- Symptoms occur gradually
  - Lead settles in soft tissues and bones
  - Is excreted in urine
- Beginning stages, signs may be weakness, weight loss, anorexia, pallor, irritability, vomiting, abdominal pain, and constipation
- Later stages, signs may be anemia and nervous system involvement

Slide 80

Lead Poisoning (Plumbism) *(cont.)*

- Lead is toxic to the synthesis of heme in the blood, which is necessary for hemoglobin formation and renal tubule functioning
- Blood lead levels are primary screening test
- X-ray films of bones may show further lead deposits
- History may reveal pica
- Treatment is aimed at reducing concentration of lead in blood
  - Chelating agents may be taken for several months
- Prognosis depends on extent of poisoning

Slide 81

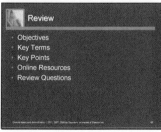

Foreign Bodies

- 80% of all ingestions occur in children between 6 months and 3 years of age
  - About 80% of items ingested pass through the GI tract without difficulty
  - May take up to 6 days to occur
- Caution parents not to use laxatives and to maintain a normal diet to avoid intestinal spasms

- If an object is small enough to pass through a standard, cardboard roll of toilet paper, children should not be allowed to play with it.

Slide 82

Review Question

- What should the nurse monitor before administering intravenous fluid to a child who is dehydrated?

Slide 83

Review

- Objectives
- Key Terms
- Key Points
- Online Resources
- Review Questions

ELSEVIER

29 Lesson Plan
The Child with a Genitourinary Condition

TEACHING FOCUS

In this chapter, students have the opportunity to learn about genitourinary conditions that affect children, along with nursing management guidelines. The chapter covers the functions of the kidney, diagnostic procedures for detecting genitourinary conditions, and practical ways to manage conditions such as nephrosis, acute glomerulonephritis, and Wilms' tumor. Students also have the opportunity to learn about the nurse's role in educating parents about managing these conditions.

MATERIALS AND RESOURCES

☐ Computer and PowerPoint projector (all lessons)
☐ Anatomical diagram of kidney (Lesson 29.1)

LESSON CHECKLIST

Preparations for this lesson include:

- Lecture
- Evaluation of student knowledge and skills needed to perform all entry-level activities related to the care of the child who has a genitourinary condition, including:
  - ○ Parent education about the function of the kidney and genitourinary system
  - ○ Potential anomalies of the genitourinary system.
  - ○ Appropriate interventions for conditions such as nephrosis, acute glomerulonephritis, and Wilms' tumor
  - ○ Genitourinary surgery, undescended testes, and coping aids for families
  - ○ Parent education for child care at home

KEY TERMS

chordee (p. 677)
cryptorchidism (p. 685)
cystometrogram (p. 676)
dysuria (p. 676)
encopresis (p. 676)
enuresis (p. 676)
epispadias (p. 677)
frequency (p. 676)
glomeruli (p. 680)
hydrocele (p. 684)

hydronephrosis (p. 678)
hyperkalemia (p. 683)
hypoalbuminemia (p. 681)
hypospadias (p. 677)
micturition (p. 676)
nephron (p. 674)
neutropenia (p. 681)
nocturia (p. 676)
oliguria (p. 677)
orchiopexy (p. 686)

paraphimosis (p. 677)
phimosis (p. 677)
polyuria (p. 677)
pyelonephritis (p. 678)
testicular torsion (p. 686)
ureteritis (p. 678)
urethritis (p. 678)
urgency (p. 676)
vesicoureteral reflux
(p. 678)

ADDITIONAL RESOURCES

TEACH PPT slide(s) Chapter 29, 1-34
EILR IC image(s) Chapter 29, 1-8
EILR OBQ question(s) Chapter 29, 1-10
EILR TB question(s) Chapter 29, 1-29
ESLR IRQ question(s) Chapter 29, 1-6
SG Chapter 29, pp. 237-243

Leifer

Legend

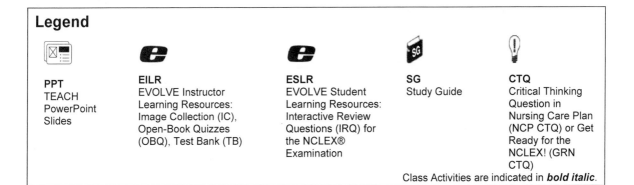

PPT	**EILR**	**ESLR**	**SG**	**CTQ**
TEACH PowerPoint Slides	EVOLVE Instructor Learning Resources: Image Collection (IC), Open-Book Quizzes (OBQ), Test Bank (TB)	EVOLVE Student Learning Resources: Interactive Review Questions (IRQ) for the NCLEX® Examination	Study Guide	Critical Thinking Question in Nursing Care Plan (NCP CTQ) or Get Ready for the NCLEX! (GRN CTQ)

Class Activities are indicated in ***bold italic***.

LESSON 29.1

PRETEST

1. The primary function of the kidney is
   a. to make white blood cells.
   b. to rid the body of waste products.
   c. to metabolize lipids.
   d. oxygen exchange.

2. Fecal soiling beyond 4 years of age is called
   a. encopresis.
   b. cryptorchidism.
   c. epispadias.
   d. micturition.

3. Dysuria is described as
   a. increased urine output.
   b. decreased urine output.
   c. uncontrolled voiding after established bladder control.
   d. difficulty in urination.

4. The distention of the renal pelvis because of an obstruction is called
   a. hydronephrosis.
   b. urethritis.
   c. pyelonephritis.
   d. exstrophy.

5. What factor indicates that a urinary tract infection (UTI) is present?
   a. frequent urination
   b. acidic urine
   c. bacterial growth on a urine specimen
   d. 7-day course of antibiotics

6. The working unit of the kidneys is called
   a. tubule.
   b. glomeruli.
   c. ureter.
   d. urethra.

7. Which of the following points should the nurse emphasize to a female child who has a UTI?
   a. wearing silk underwear
   b. maintaining the alkalinity of urine
   c. encouraging bubble baths
   d. perineal cleansing from front to back

8. Hyperkalemia is
   a. excessive potassium in the blood.
   b. excessive sodium in the blood.
   c. too little potassium in the blood.
   d. too little sodium in the blood.

9. Ascites is a(n)
   a. serious congenital defect in which the bladder lies exposed.
   b. urethral opening on the underside of the penis.
   c. abnormal collection of fluid in the peritoneal cavity.
   d. excessive amount of fluid in the sac that surrounds the testicles.

10. Undescended testes in a male is called
    a. cryptorchidism.
    b. hypospadias.
    c. testicular torsion.
    d. phimosis.

Answers

1. b	3. d	5. c	7. d	9. c
2. a	4. a	6. b	8. a	10. a

BACKGROUND ASSESSMENT

Question: What does the urinary system consist of and what is its function?
Answer: The urinary system consists of two kidneys, two ureters, the urinary bladder, and the urethra. The function of the kidneys is to rid the body of waste products and to maintain body fluid homeostasis. The kidneys produce substances that stimulate red blood cell formation in the bone marrow. The kidneys also produce renin, which helps regulate blood pressure.

Question: What patient education, including parent teaching, is indicated for pediatric patients of various ages who undergo urinary diversion procedures? What role can the nurse play?

Answer: This type of surgery can be a source of apprehension for children and parents. The physical care of the child with a urinary stoma presents hygiene and skin problems. The parent can also experience increased stress when leaving the child, especially an infant, in the care of others. In addition, a great deal of time must be allotted to the child because of frequent trips to health care providers. Stress for the child from this type of procedure is age-related. Parents of newborns grieve for the loss of a perfect child and experience concerns about the length and quality of the infant's life. The toddler may have difficulty in achieving toilet independence. The school-age child is aware of being different and may have a distorted body image. Adolescents may develop lower self-esteem and be concerned about sexuality. The nurse can anticipate how the diagnosis and treatment may affect the family and can provide appropriate teaching about infection prevention and skin care, as well as postsurgical care. The nurse also can provide emotional support and information about community resources.

CRITICAL THINKING QUESTION

The parents of a 4-year-old boy explain to the clinic nurse that for weeks the child has been irritable and listless and even though he has developed a poor appetite, has gained weight. What signs and symptoms should the nurse look for, and what condition should the nurse suspect? What nursing interventions and parent education are appropriate?

Guidelines: If the nurse notes the child's skin appears pale, swelling of the ankles and around the perimeter of the eyes, and abdominal distention, then the nurse should suspect nephrotic syndrome, or nephrosis. This kidney condition is most commonly seen in boys 2 to 7 years old. The nurse should inform the parents that the physician may order tests to make a specific diagnosis based on blood, urine, and other diagnostic procedures. The nurse should explain that treatment goals are to minimize edema, prevent infection, and reduce the loss of protein in the urine. Treatment may be long-term but can be accomplished at home with periodic hospitalization for special therapy. The nurse should inform parents that they will need to record the child's weight, urinary proteins, and medications daily. They must also report signs of infection, abnormal weight gain, and increased protein in the urine and should provide good skin care when the child is edematous. The nurse can tell the parents that the boy will most likely be able to continue with normal childhood activities when the acute stage of the illness subsides.

OBJECTIVES	CONTENT	TEACHING RESOURCES
Name the functional unit of the kidney.	■ Development of the urinary tract (p. 674) ■ Development of the reproductive systems (p. 675)	PPT slides 4-6 *e* EILR IC images 1-3 *e* EILR OBQ questions 1-3 *e* EILR TB questions 27, 29 SG Learning Activities, question 3 (p. 237) SG Review Questions, questions 14, 17 (pp. 241) SG Applying Knowledge, question 1 (p. 243) **BOOK RESOURCES** Figure 29-1, Summary of Some Urinary System Differences Between the Child and the Adult (p. 675) Figure 29-2, The Urinary System's Chief Function (p. 675) Figure 29-3, Summary of Some Reproductive System Differences Between the Child and the Adult Male and

OBJECTIVES	CONTENT	TEACHING RESOURCES
		Female (p. 676) ▸ Discuss the structure, function, and development of the urinary tract and the reproductive systems. *Class Activity Provide students with an anatomical diagram of the kidney and have students point out the nephron. Lead a discussion in which students describe how the urinary system works, including the specific function of the nephron.*
List four urological diagnostic procedures.	■ Assessment of urinary function (p. 676)	PPT slides 7, 8 *e* EILR OBQ questions 3-7 *e* EILR TB questions 13-14, 18, 26 SG Learning Activities, questions 1, 2, 5, 7 (pp. 237-238) SG Review Questions, questions 14, 17, 19 (p. 241) SG Applying Knowledge, questions 2, 4 (p. 243) **BOOK RESOURCES** Nursing Tip, (p. 676) Table 29-1, Common Laboratory Tests for Urinary Tract Function (p. 677) ▸ Discuss the pathophysiology, treatment, and nursing care of anomalies of the urinary tract: phimosis, hypospadias and epispadias, exstrophy of the bladder, and obstructive uropathy. *Class Activity Divide the class into small groups or pairs, and assign each group or pair one of the following diagnostic procedures:* *– urinalysis* *– ultrasonography* *– intravenous (IV) pyelogram* *– computed tomography (CT) kidney scan* *– renal biopsy* *– uroflow* *– cystoscopy* *– voiding cystourethrography* *– cystometrogram and urethral pressure profile* *Have students research how the procedure is performed, what conditions the procedure is intended to assess, and what information it provides. Then have students make a brief report to the class. (For students to prepare for this activity, see Homework/Assignments #1.)*
Recognize urinary tract	■ Anomalies of the urinary tract (p. 677)	PPT slides 9-18

OBJECTIVES	CONTENT	TEACHING RESOURCES
anomalies in infants.	☐ Phimosis (p. 677) ☐ Hypospadias and epispadias (p. 677) ☐ Exstrophy of the bladder (p. 678) ☐ Obstructive uropathy (p. 678) ■ Acute urinary tract infection (p. 679)	*e* EILR IC images 4-7 *e* EILR OBQ questions 5-7 *e* EILR TB questions 1-2, 5, 7, 18, 22, 28 *e* ESLR IRQ questions 1, 4-6 SG Learning Activities, questions 1, 3, 5, 8 (pp. 237-238) SG Review Questions, questions 3, 7, 8, 11 (pp. 240-241) **BOOK RESOURCES** Figure 29-4, Phimosis (p. 677) Figure 29-5, Paraphimosis (p. 678) Figure 29-6, Epispadias, Hypospadias, Chordee (p. 678) Table 29-2, Surgical Procedures Used in Urinary Diversion (p. 679) Nursing Tip (p. 679) Figure 29-7, Vesicoureteral Reflux (p. 680) Nursing Tip, (p. 680) Nursing Care Plan 29-1, The Child with a Urinary Tract Infection (pp. 681-682) ▸ Discuss the pathophysiology, signs and symptoms, treatment, and nursing care of UTIs.

29.1 Homework/Assignments:

1. Divide the class into small groups or pairs and assign each group or pair one of the following diagnostic procedures: urinalysis, ultrasonography, intravenous (IV) pyelogram, computed tomography (CT) kidney scan, renal biopsy, uroflow, cystoscopy, voiding cystourethrography, cystometrogram, and urethral pressure profile. Have students research how the procedure is performed, what conditions the procedure is intended to assess, and what information it provides. Then have students make a brief report to the class.

29.1 Instructor's Notes/Student Feedback:

Introduction to Maternity & Pediatric Nursing, 6th ed.

Elsevier items and derived items © 2011, 2007, 2006 by Saunders, an imprint of Elsevier Inc.

Leifer

LESSON 29.2

CRITICAL THINKING QUESTION

An 11-year-old girl has been diagnosed with a UTI. What key points should the nurse teach the patient and her parents about treatment of the condition?

Guidelines: Instruct parents to administer medication as prescribed and continue for the length of time recommended by the physician. The typical course of antibiotics is 7 to 10 days. The nurse should emphasize the importance of completing the prescribed dose, even if symptoms subside. Tell the child and her parents that she should avoid hot baths and whirlpools because they can be potential sources of infection. Emphasize that the perineal area should cleansed from front to back to minimize the spread of bacteria. Advise parents to ensure that the child has adequate fluid intake because children dehydrate quickly. Explain that the child should come to the office for a follow-up urine culture 1 week after medication has been discontinued to determine if bacteria have been eradicated. Advise parents that recurrence is common within 3 to 12 months, but may be asymptomatic, so routine office visits for follow-up urine cultures are recommended.

OBJECTIVES	CONTENT	TEACHING RESOURCES
Discuss the skin care pertinent to the child with nephrosis.	■ Nephrotic syndrome (nephrosis) (p. 680)	▣ PPT slides 19-23 𝒆 EILR OBQ question 8 𝒆 EILR TB questions 15, 16 SG Learning Activities, questions 4, 12 (p. 237) SG Review Questions, questions 1, 2, 15 (pp. 239-240) SG Case Study, question 1 (p. 242) **BOOK RESOURCES** Review Questions for the NCLEX® Examination, question 3 (p. 688) ▸ Discuss the pathophysiology, manifestations, treatment, and nursing care for a child who has nephrosis. *Class Activity Lead a class discussion about the skin care necessary for a child who has nephrosis and the role of the nurse in patient education. During what periods is good skin care especially important? Why? What skin assessments should be performed and what nursing interventions are appropriate?*
Explain any alterations in diet applicable to the child with nephrosis.	■ Nephrotic syndrome (nephrosis) (p. 680)	𝒆 EILR TB questions 16, 25 SG Review Questions, question 13 (p. 241) SG Case Study, question 1 (p. 242) SG Thinking Critically, question 2 (p. 243) **BOOK RESOURCES** Review Questions for the NCLEX® Examination, question 2 (p. 688) ▸ Discuss the role nurses play in educating parents about dietary considerations for a child who has nephrotic syndrome.

ELSEVIER

OBJECTIVES	CONTENT	TEACHING RESOURCES
		Class Activity Develop a role-play in which the instructor plays the nurse teaching parents who ask challenging questions about dietary considerations for a child with nephritis. The role-play should explain the relationship between salt and edema; the reasons a child may lack an appetite; how to prepare a balanced, attractive-looking meal; and the appropriate amount of fluids required. Have student volunteers play the role of the parents. Next, have students summarize the key points of dietary considerations for nephrotic syndrome.
Differentiate between nephrosis and acute glomerulo-nephritis.	■ Nephrotic syndrome (nephrosis) (p. 680) ■ Acute glomerulonephritis (p. 683)	⊠▪ PPT slides 19-24 𝒆 EILR OBQ question 9 𝒆 EILR TB questions 3, 4, 6, 8-10, 17, 23 SG Learning Activities, questions 9, 10, 13-17 (p. 238) SG Review Questions, questions 4, 5, 9, 10, 16 (pp. 241) SG Thinking Critically, question 1 (p. 243) SG Applying Knowledge, question 3 (p. 243) **BOOK RESOURCES** Table 29-3, Comparison between Nephrosis and Acute Glomerulonephritis (p. 683) Review Questions for the NCLEX® Examination, question 5 (p. 688) ▸ Discuss the pathophysiology, signs and symptoms, treatment, and nursing care for a child who has acute glomerulonephritis. What supportive role can the nurse play and what parent education is appropriate? *Class Activity Present this clinical situation to the class:* *Two 5-year-old boys present with periorbital edema upon awakening in the morning. One recently had strep throat and now has blood in the urine.* *Ask students which child is likely to have nephrosis and which is likely to have acute glomerulonephritis. Ask students to explain their rationale for the conclusion.*

29.2 Homework/Assignments:

29.2 Instructor's Notes/Student Feedback:

LESSON 29.3

CRITICAL THINKING QUESTION

During routine monitoring of a 6-year-old child who underwent renal surgery 24 hours earlier, the nurse notes a temperature of 102° F. What should the nurse suspect, and what interventions are appropriate?

Guidelines: The nurse should suspect a postsurgical infection and observe for signs of infection, including fever, incisional tenderness, redness, drainage from the incision, and lethargy. The nurse should observe and record the patency, color, amount, and consistency of any drainage. The nurse also should check the catheter to ensure it is not obstructed by mucus shreds, blood clots, or chemical sediment. Obstruction of the catheter can lead to UTI, urine stasis, and possibly to hydronephrosis. The nurse also should obtain urine cultures as ordered because pathogens in the urine, determined by a culture, can indicate infection. In addition to routine assessments and monitoring of vital signs, the nurse continues to administer any medications or other treatments that are ordered. The desired outcome is for the child's temperature to maintain a level at or below 100.4° F and to treat and prevent infections.

OBJECTIVES	CONTENT	TEACHING RESOURCES
Outline the nursing care for a child who is diagnosed as having Wilms' tumor.	■ Wilms' tumor (p. 684) ■ Hydrocele (p. 684)	▣ PPT slides 25-28 🅮 EILR IC image 8 🅮 EILR TB questions 11, 21 🅮 ESLR IRQ question 3 🆂🅶 SG Learning Activities, questions 1, 18-21 (pp. 237, 239) 🆂🅶 SG Review Questions, questions 6, 18 (pp. 240-241) **BOOK RESOURCES** Review Questions for the NCLEX® Examination, question 4 (p. 688) Safety Alert (p. 684) Figure 29-8, Hydrocele (p. 684) Nursing Care Plan 29-2, Child Undergoing Surgery of the Renal System (pp. 685-686) ▸ Discuss the role nurses can play in helping children and parents cope with concerns about surgery and other treatments for Wilms' tumor and hydrocele. What are some key teaching points? *Class Activity **Divide the class into small groups, and ask each group to review a nursing care plan for a child who is diagnosed with Wilms' tumor and undergoes renal surgery. Students may refer to Nursing Care Plan 29-2 (pp. 685-686). What is one key factor pertinent to Wilms' tumor that is omitted from the nursing care plan? Why? Reconvene the class and ask for volunteer groups to present their plans. The class should evaluate the plans for completeness and accuracy.***
Discuss the impact of undescended	■ Cryptorchidism (p. 684)	▣ PPT slides 29-31 🅮 EILR OBQ question 10

OBJECTIVES	CONTENT	TEACHING RESOURCES
testes on fertility.		*e* EILR TB question 12
		e ESLR IRQ question 2
		‣ Discuss ways a nurse can help parents discuss concerns about their child's possible infertility due to undescended testes. Identify some key points that could be asked to initiate discussion with parents.
		Class Activity Lead a discussion in which students describe the structure and function of the testes and also the pathophysiology of undescended testes. What treatments are commonly performed and what is the potential impact on the child's fertility?
Discuss the impact of genitourinary surgery on the growth and development of children at various ages.	■ Impact of urinary or genital surgery on growth and development (p. 687)	▨ PPT slide 32
		e EILR OBQ question 10
		e EILR TB questions 7, 19, 20, 24
		▣ SG Review Questions, questions 12, 19 (p. 241)
		BOOK RESOURCES
		Nursing Care Plan 29-2, Child Undergoing Surgery of the Renal System (pp. 685-686)
		Review Questions for the NCLEX® Examination, question 1 (p. 687)
		‣ Discuss ways nurses can explain the effects of genitourinary surgery on growth and development to children and adolescents. How can parents be involved in these discussions?
		Class Activity Divide the class into three sections, and assign each section one age group: toddler/preschool, school-age, and adolescent. Have each group develop questions that the parents and the child may have about the particulars of genitourinary surgery. They should address facts about the procedure, how the child may perceive the surgery, and what effects can be anticipated on the child's growth and development. The questions and answers should be challenging and age-appropriate. Have volunteer groups present to the class for evaluation and feedback. What did students learn from the role-play?
Performance Evaluation		▨ PPT slides 1-34
		e EILR IC images 1-8
		e EILR OBQ questions 1-10
		e EILR TB questions 1-29
		e ESLR IRQ questions 1-6
		▣ SG Learning Activities, questions 1-21 (pp. 237-239)

OBJECTIVES	CONTENT	TEACHING RESOURCES
		SG Review Questions, questions 1-19 (pp. 239-241)
		SG Crossword Puzzle (p. 242)
		SG Case Study, question 1 (p. 242)
		SG Thinking Critically, questions 1, 2 (p. 243)
		SG Applying Knowledge, questions 1-4 (p. 243)
		BOOK RESOURCES
		NCP CTQ 1 (p. 682)
		NCP CTQ 1 (p. 686)
		Review Questions for the NCLEX® Examination, questions 1-5 (pp. 687-688)

29.3 Homework/Assignments:

29.3 Instructor's Notes/Student Feedback:

Leifer

29 | Lecture Outline
The Child with a Genitourinary Condition

Slide 1

Chapter 29

The Child with a
Genitourinary Condition

Slide 2

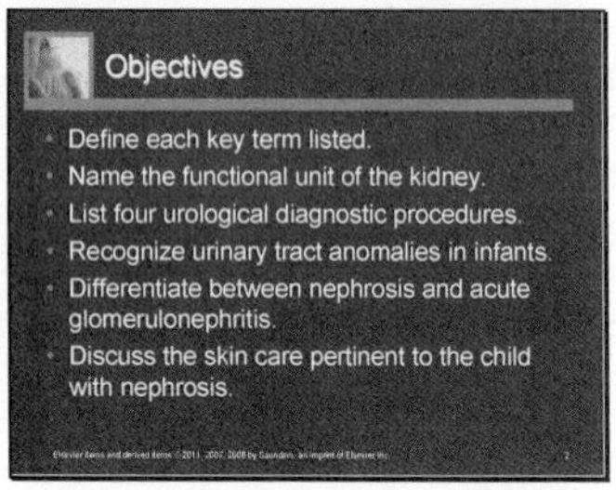

Objectives

- Define each key term listed.
- Name the functional unit of the kidney.
- List four urological diagnostic procedures.
- Recognize urinary tract anomalies in infants.
- Differentiate between nephrosis and acute glomerulonephritis.
- Discuss the skin care pertinent to the child with nephrosis.

Slide 3

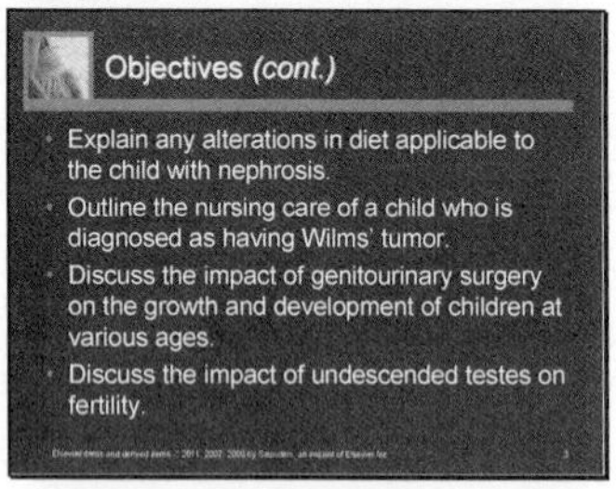

Objectives *(cont.)*

- Explain any alterations in diet applicable to the child with nephrosis.
- Outline the nursing care of a child who is diagnosed as having Wilms' tumor.
- Discuss the impact of genitourinary surgery on the growth and development of children at various ages.
- Discuss the impact of undescended testes on fertility.

Slide 4

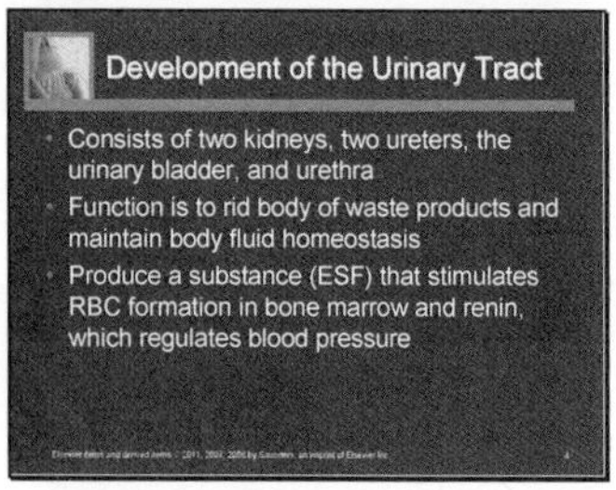

Development of the Urinary Tract

- Consists of two kidneys, two ureters, the urinary bladder, and urethra
- Function is to rid body of waste products and maintain body fluid homeostasis
- Produce a substance (ESF) that stimulates RBC formation in bone marrow and renin, which regulates blood pressure

- Refer to Figure 29-1 on page 675.

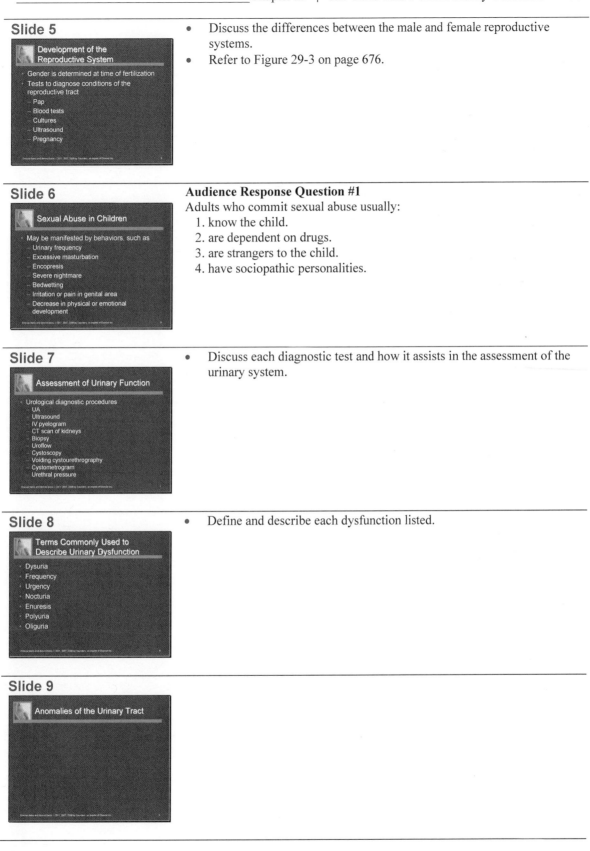

Slide 5

Development of the Reproductive System
- Gender is determined at time of fertilization
- Tests to diagnose conditions of the reproductive tract
  - Pap
  - Blood tests
  - Cultures
  - Ultrasound
  - Pregnancy

- Discuss the differences between the male and female reproductive systems.
- Refer to Figure 29-3 on page 676.

Slide 6

Sexual Abuse in Children
- May be manifested by behaviors, such as
  - Urinary frequency
  - Excessive masturbation
  - Encopresis
  - Severe nightmare
  - Bedwetting
  - Irritation or pain in genital area
  - Decrease in physical or emotional development

Audience Response Question #1
Adults who commit sexual abuse usually:
1. know the child.
2. are dependent on drugs.
3. are strangers to the child.
4. have sociopathic personalities.

Slide 7

Assessment of Urinary Function
- Urological diagnostic procedures
  - UA
  - Ultrasound
  - IV pyelogram
  - CT scan of kidneys
  - Biopsy
  - Uroflow
  - Cystoscopy
  - Voiding cystourethrography
  - Cystometrogram
  - Urethral pressure

- Discuss each diagnostic test and how it assists in the assessment of the urinary system.

Slide 8

Terms Commonly Used to Describe Urinary Dysfunction
- Dysuria
- Frequency
- Urgency
- Nocturia
- Enuresis
- Polyuria
- Oliguria

- Define and describe each dysfunction listed.

Slide 9

Anomalies of the Urinary Tract

Slide 10

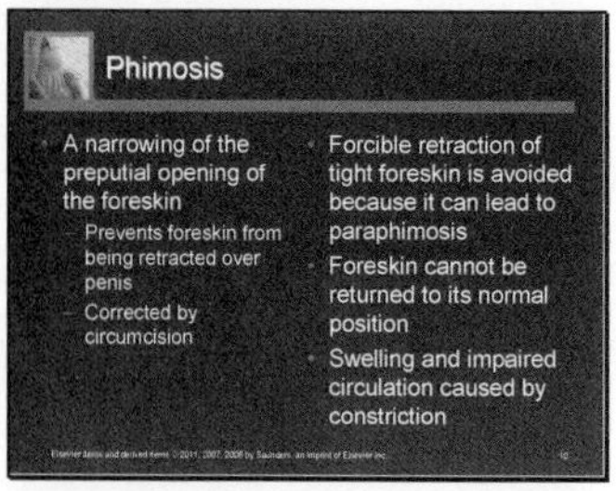

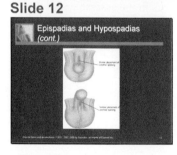

- Refer to Figure 29-5 on page 678.

Slide 11

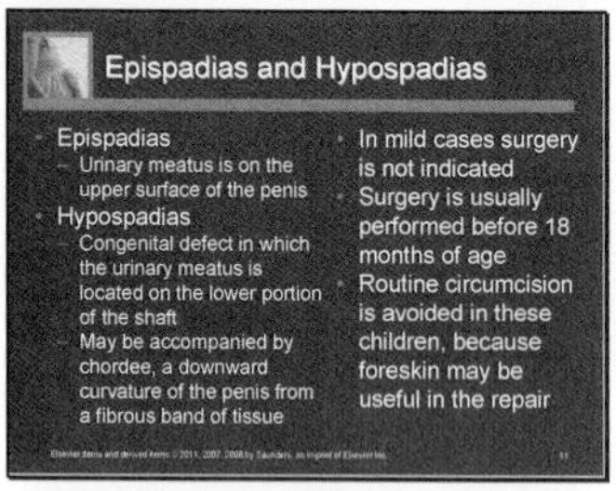

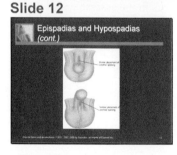

- Refer to Figure 29-6 on page 678.
- Surgery may be indicated if the child cannot stand to void, which may cause psychological issues, or if there may be difficulties in future sexual relationships.

Audience Response Question #2
Hypospadias must be surgically corrected to preserve proper genitourinary function.
   1. True
   2. False

Slide 12

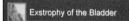

- Refer to Figure 29-6 on page 678.

Slide 13

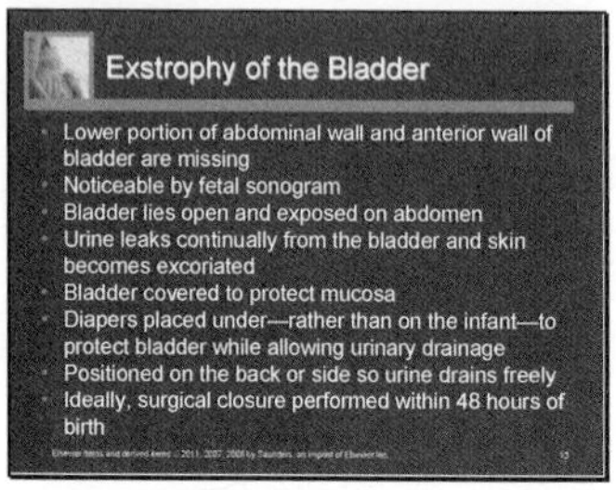

Slide 14
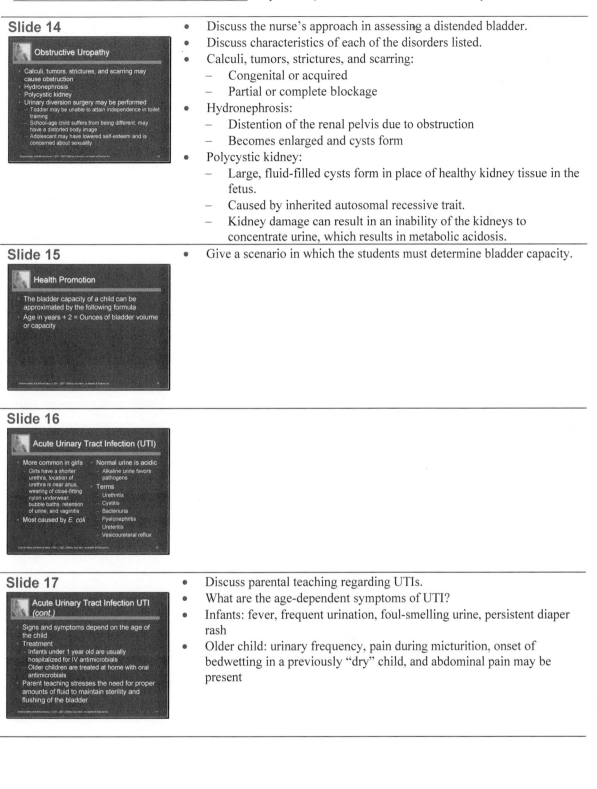
	• Discuss the nurse's approach in assessing a distended bladder.
	• Discuss characteristics of each of the disorders listed.
	• Calculi, tumors, strictures, and scarring:
	  – Congenital or acquired
	  – Partial or complete blockage
	• Hydronephrosis:
	  – Distention of the renal pelvis due to obstruction
	  – Becomes enlarged and cysts form
	• Polycystic kidney:
	  – Large, fluid-filled cysts form in place of healthy kidney tissue in the fetus.
	  – Caused by inherited autosomal recessive trait.
	  – Kidney damage can result in an inability of the kidneys to concentrate urine, which results in metabolic acidosis.

Slide 15	• Give a scenario in which the students must determine bladder capacity.
Slide 16	
Slide 17	• Discuss parental teaching regarding UTIs. • What are the age-dependent symptoms of UTI? • Infants: fever, frequent urination, foul-smelling urine, persistent diaper rash • Older child: urinary frequency, pain during micturition, onset of bedwetting in a previously "dry" child, and abdominal pain may be present

Slide 18

Health Promotion

- Interventions to prevent UTI
  - Cleanse perineum with each diaper change
  - Wipe perineum front to back
  - Avoid bubble baths
  - Have child urinate immediately after a bath
  - Use white cotton underwear
  - Use loose-fitting pants
  - Offer adequate fluid intake

Slide 19

Nephrotic Syndrome (Nephrosis)

- A number of different types of kidney conditions distinguished by the presence of marked amounts of protein in the urine, edema, and hypoalbuminemia
  - More common in boys
  - Seen more in children 2 to 7 years of age
  - May be related to a thymus T-cell dysfunction
  - Prognosis is good in steroid-responsive patients

Slide 20

Nephrotic Syndrome (Nephrosis) (cont.)

- Generalized edema
- Weight gain
- Pale, irritable, listless
- Poor appetite
- Blood pressure usually normal
- Urine exam reveals massive albumin and a few RBCs
- Prone to infection when absolute granulocyte counts fall below 1000 cells/mm³ (neutropenia)

- Discuss the pathophysiology regarding normal blood pressure in children with nephrosis.
- How can medication toxicity occur with this disorder?
- Working units of the kidneys that filter the blood become damaged and allow albumin and blood cells in the urine.
- Level of protein in blood falls, called hypoalbuminemia.

Slide 21

Nephrotic Syndrome (Nephrosis) (cont.)

- Treatment
  - Steroids to reduce proteinuria and edema
    - Steroids mask infection; therefore, it is important to monitor the child for signs of infection
  - Prevent medication toxicity
  - Diuretics have not been effective in reducing nephrotic edema
  - Avoid adding salt to foods whenever edema is present
  - Fluids generally are not restricted except when massive edema is present

- Provide a reason for the ineffectiveness of diuretics with this disorder.

Slide 22

Nephrotic Syndrome (Nephrosis) (cont.)

- Nursing care
  - Supportive care to parents and child
  - Parent instructed to keep daily record of the child's weight, urinary protein levels, and medications
  - No vaccinations or immunizations should be administered while the disease is active or during immunosuppressive therapy
  - Positioning
  - Strict monitoring of I&O
  - Daily weight and protection from infection

- Discuss the rationale for monitoring and recording weight, urine protein levels, and medications.

Leifer

Slide 23

Safety Alert

- A child recovering from nephrotic syndrome should not receive any vaccinations or immunizations while the disease is active and during immunosuppressive therapy.

Slide 24

Acute Glomerulonephritis

- Allergic reaction (antigen-antibody) to group A beta-hemolytic streptococcal infection
- Antibodies produced to fight invading organisms also react against glomerular tissue
- Both kidneys usually affected
- Mild cases generally recover within a couple of weeks

- Discuss the pathophysiology of manifestations:
- Periorbital edema upon wakening in the morning
- Urine is smoky brown or bloody
- Urine output may be decreased
- Urine specific gravity is high; albumin, RBC, WBC, and casts may be found on exam
- Hyperkalemia, BUN, creatinine, and sedimentation rate are elevated
- Hypertension may occur

Audience Response Question #3
Complete the analogy. Nephrosis : generalized edema as acute glomerulonephritis : _____.
   1. pedal edema
   2. increased abdominal girth
   3. periorbital edema
   4. hypotension

Slide 25

Wilms' Tumor (Nephroblastoma)

- Embryonal adenosarcoma is thought to have a genetic basis
- Most discovered before age 3 years
- One of the most common malignancies of early life
- Few or no symptoms during the early stages of growth
- Abdominal mass usually found by parent or during routine health checkup

Audience Response Question #4
The most common symptom noted in children with Wilms' tumor is:
   1. abdominal pain.
   2. hematuria.
   3. hypertension.
   4. abdominal mass.

Slide 26

Wilms' Tumor *(cont.)*

- IV pyelogram reveals a growth, tumor compresses kidney tissue, usually encapsulated
- May cause hypertension
- Until the tumor has been surgically removed, abdominal palpation must not be performed
- A sign above the bed and a notation on the chart must clearly state no abdominal palpation

ELSEVIER

Introduction to Maternity & Pediatric Nursing, 6th ed.
Leifer

Slide 27

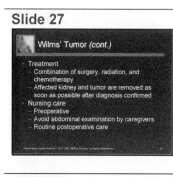

Wilms' Tumor *(cont.)*

- Treatment
  - Combination of surgery, radiation, and chemotherapy
  - Affected kidney and tumor are removed as soon as possible after diagnosis confirmed
- Nursing care
  - Preoperative
  - Avoid abdominal examination by caregivers
  - Routine postoperative care

- Discuss the rationale regarding combination therapy of radiation and chemotherapy.
- Discuss Nursing Care Plan 29-2 on pages 685-686.

Slide 28

Hydrocele

- Excessive amount of fluid in sac that surrounds the testicle
- Causes scrotum to swell
- Chronic hydrocele that persists beyond 1 year is corrected by surgery

- Discuss the difference between a simple hydrocele and a hydrocele with herniation.

Slide 29

Cryptorchidism

- Testes fail to descend into the scrotum
- Unilateral form is more common
- Testes are warmer in abdomen, sperm cells begin to deteriorate
- If both testes are involved, sterility can result
- Often accompanied by inguinal hernia
- Testes continue to secrete hormones directly into the bloodstream, so secondary sex characteristics are not affected

Slide 30

Cryptorchidism *(cont.)*

- Treatment
  - Hormonal management before surgery consists of the administration of human chorionic gonadotropin (hCG)
  - May precipitate descent of the testes into the scrotal sac
  - Orchiopexy improves the condition, fertility rate among these patients may be reduced
  - Increased risk of testicular tumors as the child reaches adulthood

- What is the importance of a monthly testicular self-exam?

Slide 31

Cryptorchidism *(cont.)*

- Nursing care
  - Scrotal support
  - Prevent contamination of suture line
  - Teach testicular self-exam
  - Psychological and emotional support
  - Surgery on "private parts" can be embarrassing
  - Nurse assures the child that his penis will not be affected

- Discuss the rationale for scrotal support following an orchiopexy.
- What is a possible result of orchiopexy?

Leifer

Slide 32

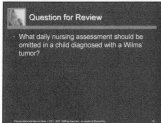

- Give examples of growth and development issues that could occur for children between the ages of 3 and 10.
- Give examples of growth and development issues that could occur for and adolescents.

Slide 33

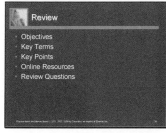

Slide 34

30 The Child with a Skin Condition

TEACHING FOCUS

In this chapter, the two main topics are identification and treatment of various skin conditions, and the classification and treatment of burns. Various skin conditions and their symptoms, common therapies, and the differences between child and adult responses to burns are presented. Emergency burn treatment is also highlighted, including nursing interventions specific to children suffering burn injuries.

MATERIALS AND RESOURCES

- ☐ Atlas of burns and their classification (Lesson 30.2)
- ☐ Atlas of skin disorders (Lesson 30.1)
- ☐ Computer and PowerPoint projector (all lessons)
- ☐ Pictures of frostbite victims (Lesson 30.3)
- ☐ Samples of cream, ointment, lotion, aerosol spray, gel, and oil (Lesson 30.1)

LESSON CHECKLIST

Preparations for this lesson include:

- Lecture
- Demonstration
- Guest speakers: Dermatologist, burn treatment center nurse, school nurse
- Evaluation of student knowledge and skills needed to perform all entry-level activities related to the care of the child with a skin condition, including:
  - ○ Identification of various common skin disorders and infections
  - ○ Emergency burn treatment
  - ○ Understanding how the response of the child's body to burns differs from that of an adult
  - ○ Nursing interventions in the care of a child burn patient

KEY TERMS

allergens (p. 695)
alopecia (p. 699)
autograft (p. 704)
chilblain (p. 707)
comedo (p. 694)
crust (p. 691)
Curling's ulcer (p. 704)
debridement (p. 704)
dermabrasion (p. 694)
ecchymosis (p. 691)
emollient (p. 696)
eschar (p. 703)

exanthem (p. 690)
frostbite (p. 707)
heterografts (p. 704)
hives (p. 690)
homografts (p. 704)
ileus (p. 704)
isograft (p. 704)
macule (p. 691)
methicillin-resistant
    Staphylococcus aureus
    (MRSA) (p. 698)
papule (p. 691)

pediculosis (p. 700)
pruritus (p. 692)
pustule (p. 691)
sebum (p. 694)
stye (p. 691)
total body surface area
    (TBSA) (p. 701)
vesicle (p. 691)
wheal (p. 691)
xenografts (p. 704)

ADDITIONAL RESOURCES

TEACH PPT slide(s) Chapter 30, 1-62
EILR IC image(s) Chapter 30, 1-18
EILR OBQ question(s) Chapter 30, 1-10
EILR TB question(s) Chapter 30, 1-35
ESLR IRQ question(s) Chapter 30, 1-5
SG Chapter 30, pp. 245-252

Legend

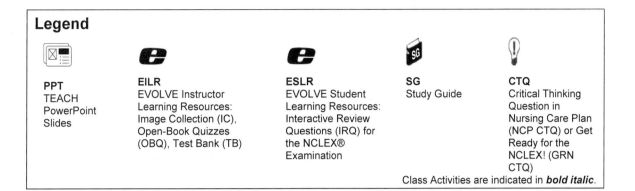

PPT
TEACH
PowerPoint
Slides

EILR
EVOLVE Instructor
Learning Resources:
Image Collection (IC),
Open-Book Quizzes
(OBQ), Test Bank (TB)

ESLR
EVOLVE Student
Learning Resources:
Interactive Review
Questions (IRQ) for
the NCLEX®
Examination

SG
Study Guide

CTQ
Critical Thinking
Question in
Nursing Care Plan
(NCP CTQ) or Get
Ready for the
NCLEX! (GRN
CTQ)

Class Activities are indicated in ***bold italic***.

LESSON 30.1

PRETEST

1. Which test is especially useful in screening for tuberculosis?
   a. purified protein derivative (PPD) test
   c. complete blood count
   b. serum electrolyte level
   d. exanthem

2. Which of the following skin disorders for very young children might be most disturbing for parents in terms of the reaction of others to the disorder?
   a. strawberry nevus
   c. diaper dermatitis
   b. intertrigo
   d. acne

3. The nurse realizes the adolescent needs more education about acne when he makes the statement
   a. "I can eat chocolate and drink coke."
   b. "I'll try and get out in the sun a little more."
   c. "I'll squeeze these pimples to get the juice out as soon as they appear."
   d. "I won't clean my face more than is normally recommended."

4. Treatment for infantile eczema includes
   a. washing the hair with shampoo.
   c. using Dial soap.
   b. avoiding use of bath oils.
   d. an emollient bath.

5. The skin disorder that is characterized by patches of alopecia is called
   a. tinea capitis.
   c. tinea pedis.
   b. tinea corporis.
   d. tinea cruris.

6. The most common form of pediculosis seen in children is
   a. pediculosis capitis.
   c. pediculosis pubis.
   b. pediculosis corporis.
   d. pediculosis pedis.

7. An appropriate nursing diagnosis for a child who has been burned on a large body surface is
   a. Ineffective health maintenance.
   c. Risk for infection.
   b. Risk for injury.
   d. Social isolation.

8. For what degree burn would the treatment include immersion in cold water and covering with a sterile dressing?
   a. first-degree burn
   c. deep-dermal burn
   b. second-degree burn
   d. third-degree burn

9. In the case of exposure to freezing temperatures, what part(s) of the body should be warmed first?
   a. hands
   c. legs
   b. feet
   d. head and torso

10. One way a nurse can prevent infection in a child with a new burn is to
    a. apply a moisturizer to maintain skin moisture.
    b. use sterile technique when in contact with the wound.
    c. provide bicarbonate soda baths prn.
    d. allow the child to sleep instead of waking the child to take his or her vital signs.

Answers

1. a	3. c	5. a	7. c	9. d
2. a	4. d	6. a	8. c	10. b

BACKGROUND ASSESSMENT

Question: What are the differences between the integumentary system of the adult and the child?
Answer: An infant has a thin epidermis that will blister easily, and infections may occur more readily. An infant's skin is alkaline, which can increase susceptibility to infection. A skin infection in a child is more likely to lead to a systemic disease. A child's sebaceous glands do not begin producing until the age of 8 to 10 years; until then the skin is dry and chaps easily. The ability to perspire through the skin matures by the age of 3 years and axillary perspiration begins near puberty; therefore, thermoregulation is altered until this occurs. Preterm infants and newborns have less subcutaneous body fat and a greater sensitivity to heat and cold.

Introduction to Maternity & Pediatric Nursing, 6th ed.

Elsevier items and derived items © 2011, 2007, 2006 by Saunders, an imprint of Elsevier Inc.

Leifer

Question: What are the nursing diagnoses for a child with third-degree (full-thickness) burns?
Answer: The priority nursing diagnosis for all burn patients involves potential for Ineffective airway clearance caused by airway edema. The goals of treatment are to prevent airway edema and assure air exchange. The nurse should expect that the patient undergoes endotracheal intubation and mechanical ventilation. The risk for decreased fluid volume loss leading to dehydration and oliguria should be the next priority; renal function also needs to be continually assessed. Hydration through IV fluids must be initiated. Hypothermia is also a likely diagnosis. Risk for infection could increase due to the loss of intact skin and the possibility of infection. Additional nursing diagnoses might include Anxiety or fear related to pain from treatments; Disturbed body image; Impaired skin integrity; Ineffective tissue perfusion; and Acute pain related to injury and treatments.

CRITICAL THINKING QUESTION

A female adolescent has had a port-wine nevus since early childhood and now has severe acne. She doesn't understand why she is susceptible to these skin disorders, and she asks whether she has done something wrong. How should the nurse respond and what advice should the nurse give her?
Guidelines: Explain to the patient that she did not do anything wrong related to her skin disorders—these conditions are common to children and adolescents. The nurse could show the patient pictures that are documented in textbooks about each of the conditions, and then discuss available treatment options. If the patient can wear makeup, it may be helpful to cover up the port-wine nevus, or she can simply explain to people that it is a type of birthmark. The nurse should tell the patient that the acne problem can be helped by seeking treatment from a dermatologist, and it is a condition that can change with time and medication. The nurse should provide the patient with resources in treating the acne and give her a list of referrals for dermatologists. Most of all, the nurse should listen to the patient's concerns, as adolescents are very sensitive about their physical appearance.

OBJECTIVES	CONTENT	TEACHING RESOURCES
Recall the differences between the skin of the infant and that of the adult.	■ Skin development and functions (p. 689) ■ Skin disorders and variations (p. 690)	⊠ PPT slides 5-10 *e* EILR IC images 1, 2 *e* EILR OBQ question 1 *e* EILR TB question 1 SG Learning Activities, questions 1-7 (pp. 1-3) SG Review Questions, questions 1, 2 (pp. 249) **BOOK RESOURCES** Figure 30-1, Summary of Some Integumentary System Differences Between the Child and the Adult (p. 690) Box 30-1, Terms Used to Describe Skin Conditions (p. 691) Figure 30-2, A Stye or Hordeolum (p. 691) ▸ Discuss the main function of the skin. ▸ Discuss the distinguishing characteristics of the various manifestations of skin conditions: macule, papule, vesicle, pustule, crust, ecchymosis, and wheal. *Class Activity Lead a class discussion about skin function, characteristics of skin conditions, and consequences of infections in adults versus children. Then ask students to create a table listing the differences between the skin of*

ELSEVIER

OBJECTIVES	CONTENT	TEACHING RESOURCES
		an infant and the skin of an adult. *Class Activity **Invite a dermatologist to speak to the class regarding skin disorders commonly seen in children and how they are treated.***
Identify common congenital skin lesions and infections.	■ Congenital lesions (p. 691) □ Strawberry nevus (p. 691) □ Port wine nevus (p. 692) ■ Infections (p. 692) □ Miliaria (p. 692) □ Intertrigo (p. 692) □ Seborrheic dermatitis (p. 693) □ Diaper dermatitis (p. 693) – Treatment and nursing care (p. 693)	PPT slides 11-21 *e* EILR IC images 3-8 *e* EILR OBQ question 2 *e* EILR TB questions 1, 15, 17, 28 *e* ESLR IRQ question 4 SG Learning Activities, questions 1-7 (pp. 245-246) SG Case Study, question 2 (p. 252) SG Applying Knowledge, question 1 (p. 252) **BOOK RESOURCES** Figure 30-3, Strawberry Nevus (p. 692) Figure 30-4, Port Wine Stain (p. 692) Figure 30-5, Miliaria (p. 692) Figure 30-6, Intertrigo (p. 693) Figure 30-7, Seborrheic Dermatitis (Cradle Cap) (p. 693) Figure 30-8, Diaper Rash (Diaper Dermatitis) (p. 693) Review Questions for the NCLEX® Examination, question 4 (p. 708) ▶ Discuss why skin infections can have more severe consequences in the child than in the adult. ▶ Discuss the characteristics of two congenital lesions— the strawberry nevus and the port wine nevus. ▶ Discuss the treatment for diaper dermatitis.

Describe two topical agents used to treat acne.	□ Acne vulgaris (p. 694)
	  – Pathophysiology (p. 694)
	  – Treatment (p. 694)
	□ Herpes simplex type 1 (p. 695)
	  – Pathophysiology (p. 695)
	  – Treatment and nursing care
		PPT slides 22-24
		
		e EILR IC images 9, 10
		
		e EILR OBQ question 3
		
		e EILR TB questions 7, 19, 22, 29, 31
		
		SG Learning Activities, questions 1, 8-11 (pp. 245-246)
		
		SG Review Questions, questions 9, 12, 18 (pp. 250-251)

OBJECTIVES	CONTENT	TEACHING RESOURCES
	(p. 695)	SG Case Study, question 1 (p. 251) **BOOK RESOURCES** Figure 30-9, Acne (p. 694) Nursing Tip (p. 695) Figure 30-10, Herpes Simplex (p. 695) ▸ Discuss the factors that cause or affect acne. ▸ Discuss the treatment for acne, including care of the skin, over-the-counter medications, diet, and prescription medications. ▸ Discuss which drugs are likely to cause drug-induced acne. ▸ Discuss the characteristics of herpes simplex type 1 and explain its causative factors. ▸ Discuss measures for avoiding the spread of this virus. *Class Activity Lead a class discussion about acne, its causes, treatment, dietary considerations, and medications that can cause drug-induced acne. Then have students work in pairs to role-play a patient education session between a nurse and a teen who has acne. The nurse should describe to the patient how to apply a topical agent to treat the acne and explain other factors that could affect the teen's acne.* *Class Activity Have the students research over-the-counter drugs available for treating acne. Be sure the students identify the active ingredients in each product. Then have the students take turns presenting their findings in class. (For students to prepare for this activity, see Homework/Assignments #1.)* *Class Activity Divide the class into small groups and have each group formulate questions about herpes, including its characteristics, treatment, and preventive care. Have groups exchange questions, and then answer the set of questions they received. In addition, students should identify nursing interventions for patients with herpes simplex type 1. Have groups share their questions and answers with the class.*

30.1 Homework/Assignments:

1. Have the students' research over-the-counter drugs available for treating acne. Be sure the students identify the active ingredients in each product.

30.1 Instructor's Notes/Student Feedback:

CRITICAL THINKING QUESTION

A mother comes to the clinic with her 1-year-old child who has visible infantile eczema on his face. She remarks that she can't have his picture taken due to the visible lesions and asks how long they will last or what she can do to eliminate them. What would be an appropriate nursing response to her concerns and questions?

Guidelines: Explain to the mother that this is a genetic hypersensitivity that the child should outgrow. The etiology is unclear, but it is usually caused by an allergy. Most infants' symptoms subside by age 2, when breastfeeding has stopped, or when the weather is warmer. If itching is causing irritability and sleep disruption, the physician might prescribe an antihistamine. Provide her with resources that suggest treatments, such as using a mild soap and bath oils in the bath. Inform the mother that topical medications are available, and after discussing it with her physician, she may want to try one of them. Explain that this condition is usually temporary and should improve.

OBJECTIVES	CONTENT	TEACHING RESOURCES
Summarize the nursing care for a child who has infantile eczema. State the rationale for each nursing measure.	☐ Infantile eczema (p. 695) – Pathophysiology (p. 695) – Manifestations (p. 695) – Treatment and nursing care (p. 695)	PPT slides 25-28 EILR IC image 11 EILR OBQ questions 4, 5 EILR TB questions 2, 3, 18, 30 SG Learning Activities, questions 12-14 (p. 246) SG Review Questions, questions 1, 11, 17 (pp. 245, 250) SG Applying Knowledge, question 1 (p. 252) **BOOK RESOURCES** Figure 30-11, Infantile Eczema (Atopic Dermatitis) (p. 695) Nursing Care Plan 30-1: The Child with Eczema (pp. 696-697) Nursing Tip (p. 698) Review Questions for the NCLEX® Examination, questions 2, 5 (p. 708) ▸ Discuss the pathophysiology of infantile eczema. ▸ Discuss the nursing interventions that are taken to relieve and prevent itching, including environmental factors (clothing, soap, food, supervision, elbow restraints, etc.). Why is itch control so essential? *Class Activity **Divide the class into small groups to discuss the pathophysiology of infantile eczema, its manifestations, and appropriate treatment. Have each group create a summary of these topics and share it with the class.***

OBJECTIVES	CONTENT	TEACHING RESOURCES
		Class Activity ***Working in small groups, ask students to identify appropriate nursing interventions for infantile eczema and provide a rationale for each nursing intervention. Groups should then share their conclusions with the class.***
Differentiate four types of topical medication.	– Treatment and nursing care (p. 695)	☒ PPT slides 28, 29 🅮 EILR OBQ questions 6, 7 🅮 EILR TB questions 11, 13, 33 🆂🅶 SG Review Questions, question 17 (p. 251) **BOOK RESOURCES** Table 30-1, Types of Topical Medications (p. 698) ▸ Discuss the different types of topical medications that are available and the advantages and disadvantages of each. *Class Activity* ***Divide the class into four groups, and assign a topical medication to each group. Have the group research the medication and list its benefits and side effects, including its advantages and disadvantages compared to the other three medications. (For students to prepare for this activity, see Homework/Assignments #1.)***
Discuss the nursing care of various microbial infections of the skin.	☐ Staphylococcal infection (p. 698) – Pathophysiology (p. 698) – Treatment and nursing care (p. 698) ☐ Impetigo (p. 698) – Pathophysiology (p. 698) – Manifestations (p. 698) – Treatment and nursing care (p. 699) ☐ Fungal infections (p. 699) – Pathophysiology (p. 699)	☒ PPT slides 30-33 🅮 EILR IC images 12, 13 🅮 EILR TB questions 4, 16, 26 🆂🅶 SG Learning Activities, questions 15-18 (pp. 246-247) 🆂🅶 SG Review Questions, question 8 (p. 250) **BOOK RESOURCES** Figure 30-12, Impetigo (p. 699) Figure 30-13, Tinea Corporis (p. 699) ▸ Discuss possible complications of skin infections such as septicemia and other infections that may result. ▸ Discuss the characteristics and treatment of scalded skin syndrome. *Class Activity* ***Divide the class into three groups. Assign each group one of the types of infection discussed (staphylococcal, impetigo, or fungal). Have each group discuss the pathophysiology and manifestations of its assigned infection. Groups should also discuss the appropriate treatment and nursing interventions. Then***

OBJECTIVES	CONTENT	TEACHING RESOURCES
		each group will present its description to the class.
Discuss the prevention and care of pediculosis and scabies.	☐ Pediculosis (p. 700) – Pediculosis capitis (p. 700) ☐ Scabies (p. 700) – Pathophysiology (p. 700) – Treatment and nursing care (p. 700)	▣ PPT slides 34, 35 *e* EILR IC image 14 *e* EILR OBQ question 8 *e* EILR TB questions 5, 6, 25, 35 *e* ESLR IRQ question 3 SG Learning Activities, questions 19-24 (pp. 246-247) SG Review Questions, questions 2, 10, 16 (pp. 249, 250) **BOOK RESOURCES** Figure 30-14, Pediculosis (p. 700) ▸ Discuss the pathophysiology of pediculosis and its treatment. ▸ Discuss the pathophysiology and treatment of scabies. Why is it important for all family members, and other persons who have had close contact with the patient, to receive treatment? Class Activity *Divide the class into three groups, and assign each group one of the three types of pediculosis. Groups should design an informative poster that educates the reader about type of infestation, including its pathophysiology and manifestations. Groups should then discuss interventions and nursing care. Finally, groups should present their poster and summarize nursing interventions for the class.* Class Activity *Lead a discussion of the pathophysiology, treatment, and nursing interventions associated with scabies, including an explanation of how scabies can be spread and methods to minimize risk.* Class Activity *Have students work in small groups to create an educational brochure for families describing scabies, along with prevention and treatment recommendations. Have groups present their brochures to the class.*

30.2 Homework/Assignments:

1. Divide the class into four groups and assign a topical medication to each group. Have the group research the medication and list its benefits and risks, including advantages and disadvantages compared to the other three medications.

30.2 Instructor's Notes/Student Feedback:

LESSON 30.3

CRITICAL THINKING QUESTION

The school nurse for an elementary school must prepare an educational program for the school children on emergency responses for a burn injury. How could the nurse educate the children on this process?
Guidelines: The nurse could create several brightly colored posters discussing the relevant topics, which would include "stop the burning process," "evaluate the injury," "cover the burn," and "transport to a hospital." Key points to describe for each poster would include the following:
Stop the burning process: Stop, drop, roll; roll in a blanket; brush off powder before washing
Evaluate the injury: Check ABCs (airway, breathing, circulation)
Cover the burn: Cover with clean cloth; remove burned clothing or metal
Transport to hospital: Call 911; do not give fluids; provide comfort
Then the nurse could ask several children to volunteer to come in front of the group and act out the process.

OBJECTIVES	CONTENT	TEACHING RESOURCES
Differentiate among first-, second-, and third-degree burns in anatomical structures involved, appearance, level of sensation, and first-aid required.	■ Injuries (p. 701) □ Burns (p. 701) – Pathophysiology (p. 701) – Classification (p. 701) – Treatment (p. 702)	☒ PPT slides 36-41 *e* EILR IC images 15, 16 *e* EILR OBQ questions 9, 10 *e* EILR TB questions 8-11, 34 *e* EILR IRC question 5 SG Learning Activities, questions 1, 25-37 (pp. 246-249) SG Review Questions, questions 3-7 (pp. 249-250) SG Applying Knowledge, question 1 (p. 252) **BOOK RESOURCES** Safety Alert (p. 701) Nursing Tips (p. 703) Figure 30-15, Body Surface Area (BSA) Charts (p. 701) Table 30-2, Classification and First-Aid Treatment of Burns (p. 702) Table 30-3, Response to Burn Injury in Children (p. 702) Figure 30-16, Mechanism of Electrical Injury (p. 703) Box 30-2, Topical Agents Used to Treat Burn Patients (p. 706) ▶ Discuss the four different types of burns based on the causal agent. ▶ Discuss the differences between first-, second-, and third-degree burns in terms of anatomy and depth, appearance and sensation, and treatment. *Class Activity **Divide the class into small groups. Have each group create a display of the body surface chart and***

OBJECTIVES	CONTENT	TEACHING RESOURCES
		the types of burns based on the causal agent. Have each group present its display to the class. *Class Activity In the same small groups, have students create posters on the differences between first-, second-, and third-degree burns, along with depth, appearance, sensation and treatment information. Then have students present their posters to the class.*
Identify the principles of topical therapy.	– Treatment (p. 702)	SG Review Questions, question 13 (pp. 250) **BOOK RESOURCES** Review Questions for the NCLEX® Examination, question 3 (p. 708) Box 30-2, Topical Agents Used to Treat Burn Patients (p. 706)
Describe how the response of the child with burns differs from that of the adult.	– Treatment (p. 702) – Nursing care of the burned child (p. 706)	PPT slides 42-44 **BOOK RESOURCES** Table 30-3, Response to Burn Injury in Children (p. 702) Nursing Tip (p. 706) Review Questions for the NCLEX® Examination, questions 1 (p. 708) ▶ Discuss the role that total body surface area plays in the evaluation of burns. ▶ Discuss the child's physiological response to burn injury and how it differs from that of an adult. *Class Activity Each student should write out one way that a child responds differently to a burn than an adult, and why that occurs. Write out each response on the board until all eight have been identified.*
Examine the emergency treatment of three types of burns.	– Treatment (p. 702) – Nursing care of the burned child (p. 706)	PPT slides 43-50 EILR IC image 16 EILR OBQ question 10 EILR TB question 21 ESLR IRQ question 1 **BOOK RESOURCES** Figure 30-16, Mechanism of Electrical Injury (p. 703) ▶ Discuss various methods of burn dressing. ▶ Discuss the various types of temporary and permanent skin grafts that are used for burns. *Class Activity Divide the class into small groups, and assign half of the groups electrical burns, and the other*

Leifer

OBJECTIVES	CONTENT	TEACHING RESOURCES
		half thermal burns. Have each group discuss the emergency care of its assigned type of burn. Under what conditions would an airway need to be established? What laboratory tests are performed? Have each group share its findings with the class for discussion.
		Class Activity Ask students to work in small groups and create a chart that explains the emergency treatment of the three types of burns. Each group will present its chart for a particular age group: elementary, middle school, high school, or adults/parents. Students can use pictures or graphics in the chart. The entire class should critique each presentation.
		Class Activity Invite an RN from a burn center to class to discuss emergency treatment procedures for a burn victim, as well as interesting clinical experiences.
List five objectives of the nurse caring for the burned child.	– Nursing care of the burned child (p. 706)	PPT slides 51-57 *e* EILR IC images 17, 18 *e* EILR TB questions 12, 14, 23, 27 SG Thinking Critically, question 1 (p. 251) SG Review Questions, questions 14, 15 (p. 251) **BOOK RESOURCES** Figure 30-17, Collage of Burn Dressing Change (p. 705) Figure 30-18, Scald burns (p. 707) ▸ Discuss the importance of assessing for signs of infection and fluid overload, as well as providing emotional support to the child with burns. *Class Activity Divide the class into five groups. Assign each group one of the following considerations that a nurse must take into account when treating a burned child: (1) protective isolation, (2) infection, (3) fluid overload, (4) metabolism demands, and (5) unaffected parts. Each group should explain how each consideration affects care.* *Class Activity A 10-year-old child with deep thermal burns and blisters requires treatment. In order of priority, list the nursing interventions that would be implemented.*
Discuss the prevention and treatment of sunburn and frostbite.	☐ Sunburn (p. 707) ☐ Frostbite (p. 707)	PPT slides 58-60 *e* EILR IC image 18 *e* EILR TB questions 20, 24, 32 *e* ESLR IRQ question 2

OBJECTIVES	CONTENT	TEACHING RESOURCES
		SG Learning Activities, questions 38, 39 (p. 249)
		BOOK RESOURCES
		▸ Discuss the differences between sunblock and sunscreen.
		▸ Discuss the signs of frostbite. What nursing interventions are used for frostbitten extremities?
		▸ Discuss how to educate parents in the prevention of frostbite.
		*Class Activity **Lead a class discussion about the clinical manifestations of frostbite. Display pictures that illustrate the manifestations.***
		*Class Activity **Ask students to work in small groups to create a nursing care plan appropriate for a child with frostbite that includes nursing diagnosis, interventions, rationale, and outcomes that would be expected. Include physical, social, and emotional nursing diagnoses.***
Performance Evaluation		PPT slides 1-62
		e EILR IC images 1-18
		e EILR OBQ questions 1-10
		e EILR TB questions 1-35
		e ESLR IRQ questions 1-5
		SG Learning Activities, questions 1-39 (pp. 245-249)
		SG Review Questions, questions 1-18 (pp. 249-251)
		SG Case Study, questions 1, 2 (p. 251-252)
		SG Thinking Critically, question 1 (p. 251)
		SG Applying Knowledge, question 1 (p. 252)
		BOOK RESOURCES
		NCP CTQ 1 (p. 697)
		Review Questions for the NCLEX® Examination, questions 1-5 (p. 708)

Leifer

30.3 Homework/Assignments:

30.3 Instructor's Notes/Student Feedback:

30 Lecture Outline
The Child with a Skin Condition

Slide 1

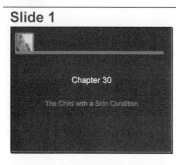

Chapter 30

The Child with a Skin Condition

Slide 2

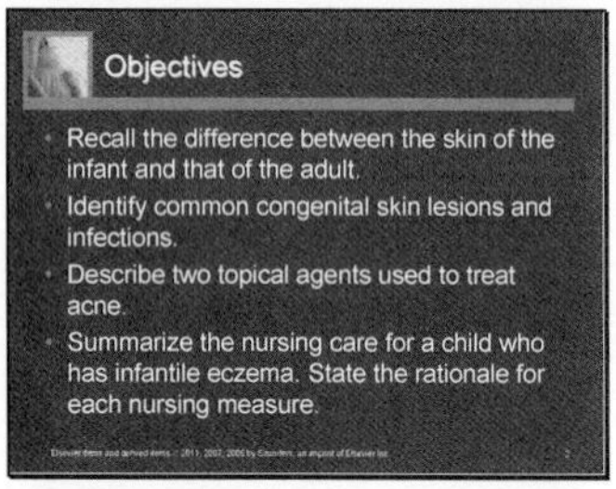

Objectives

- Recall the difference between the skin of the infant and that of the adult.
- Identify common congenital skin lesions and infections.
- Describe two topical agents used to treat acne.
- Summarize the nursing care for a child who has infantile eczema. State the rationale for each nursing measure.

Slide 3

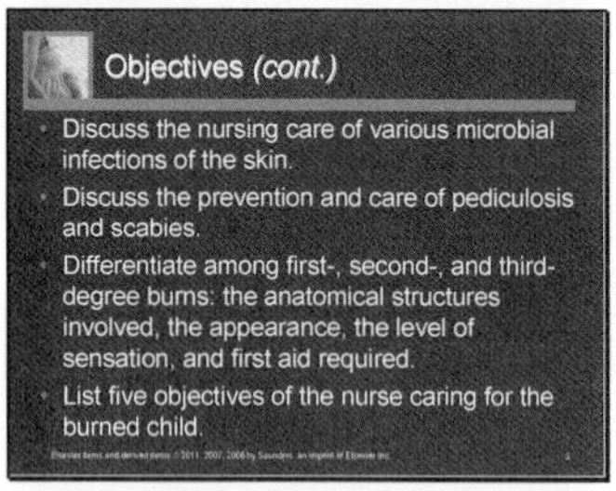

Objectives *(cont.)*

- Discuss the nursing care of various microbial infections of the skin.
- Discuss the prevention and care of pediculosis and scabies.
- Differentiate among first-, second-, and third-degree burns: the anatomical structures involved, the appearance, the level of sensation, and first aid required.
- List five objectives of the nurse caring for the burned child.

Slide 4

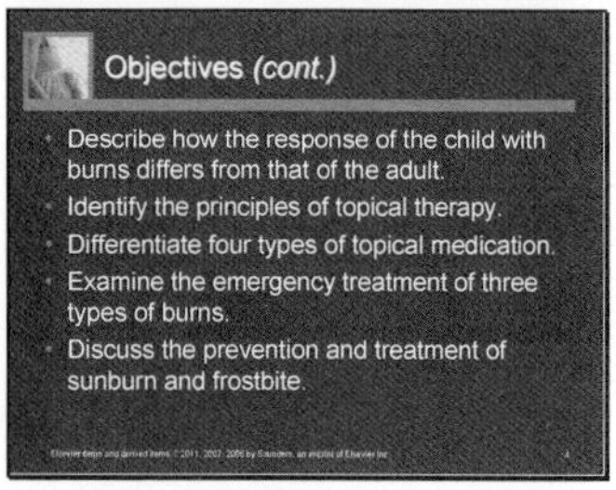

Objectives *(cont.)*

- Describe how the response of the child with burns differs from that of the adult.
- Identify the principles of topical therapy.
- Differentiate four types of topical medication.
- Examine the emergency treatment of three types of burns.
- Discuss the prevention and treatment of sunburn and frostbite.

Leifer

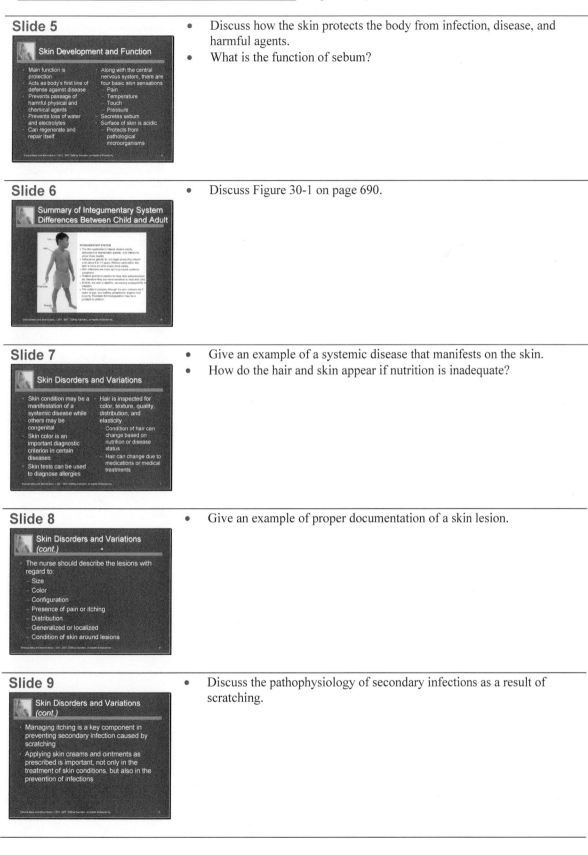

Slide 5

Skin Development and Function

Main function is protection
Acts as body's first line of defense against disease
Prevents passage of harmful physical and chemical agents
Prevents loss of water and electrolytes
Can regenerate and repair itself

Along with the central nervous system, there are four basic skin sensations
- Pain
- Temperature
- Touch
- Pressure
Secretes sebum
Surface of skin is acidic
- Protects from pathological microorganisms

- Discuss how the skin protects the body from infection, disease, and harmful agents.
- What is the function of sebum?

Slide 6

Summary of Integumentary System Differences Between Child and Adult

INTEGUMENTARY SYSTEM

- Discuss Figure 30-1 on page 690.

Slide 7

Skin Disorders and Variations

Skin condition may be a manifestation of a systemic disease while others may be congenital
Skin color is an important diagnostic criterion in certain diseases
Skin tests can be used to diagnose allergies

Hair is inspected for color, texture, quality, distribution, and elasticity
- Condition of hair can change based on nutrition or disease status
- Hair can change due to medications or medical treatments

- Give an example of a systemic disease that manifests on the skin.
- How do the hair and skin appear if nutrition is inadequate?

Slide 8

Skin Disorders and Variations (cont.)

The nurse should describe the lesions with regard to:
- Size
- Color
- Configuration
- Presence of pain or itching
- Distribution
- Generalized or localized
- Condition of skin around lesions

- Give an example of proper documentation of a skin lesion.

Slide 9

Skin Disorders and Variations (cont.)

Managing itching is a key component in preventing secondary infection caused by scratching
Applying skin creams and ointments as prescribed is important, not only in the treatment of skin conditions, but also in the prevention of infections

- Discuss the pathophysiology of secondary infections as a result of scratching.

Leifer

Slide 10

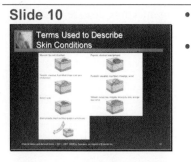

- Discuss what each term means and have students given examples of each.
- Refer to Box 30-1 on page 691.

Slide 11

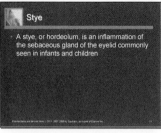

Stye

A stye, or hordeolum, is an inflammation of the sebaceous gland of the eyelid commonly seen in infants and children

- Discuss Figure 30-2 on page 691.

Slide 12

Strawberry Nevus

- Common hemangioma
- Consists of dilated capillaries in the dermal space
- Usually disappears without treatment
- May not be apparent until a few weeks after birth
- Begins flat, but becomes raised, bright red, elevated, and sharply demarcated

- Discuss Figure 30-3 on page 692.

Slide 13

Port Wine Nevus

- Present at birth
- Caused by dilated dermal capillaries
- Lesions are flat, sharply demarcated, and purple to pink
- Different from strawberry nevus in that the lesion darkens as child gets older, it does not disappear

- What can make port wine nevi disappear?
- Discuss Figure 30-3 on page 692.

Slide 14

Skin Manifestations of Illness

- Café au lait macules
  - Light brown, oval patches
  - Multiple macules are associated with neurofibromatosis (a chromosomal abnormality) and tuberous sclerosis
- Hypopigmented macules
  - Whitish oval- or leaf-shaped
  - Multiple macules associated with tuberous sclerosis

Leifer

Slide 15

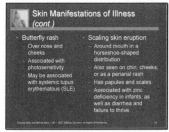

Skin Manifestations of Illness *(cont.)*

- Butterfly rash
  - Over nose and cheeks
  - Associated with photosensitivity
  - May be associated with systemic lupus erythematous (SLE)
- Scaling skin eruption
  - Around mouth in a horseshoe-shaped distribution
  - Also seen on chin, cheeks, or as a perianal rash
  - Has papules and scales
  - Associated with zinc deficiency in infants, as well as diarrhea and failure to thrive

Slide 16

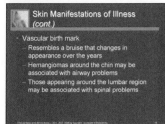

Skin Manifestations of Illness *(cont.)*

- Vascular birth mark
  - Resembles a bruise that changes in appearance over the years
  - Hemangiomas around the chin may be associated with airway problems
  - Those appearing around the lumbar region may be associated with spinal problems

Audience Response Question #1
Congenital birth marks could be caused by foods the mother ingests during pregnancy.
    1. True
    2. False

Slide 17

Infections

Slide 18

Miliaria

- "Prickly heat" or a rash caused by excess body heat and moisture
- Sweat is retained in the sweat glands, which become blocked or inflamed
- Rupture or leakage causes the skin to appear inflamed
- Appears suddenly as tiny, pinhead-sized, reddened papules
  - May be itchy
  - Often appears in diaper area or skin folds
  - Remove extra clothing, bathing, skin care, frequent diaper changes

- Discuss Figure 30-5 on page 692.

Slide 19

Intertrigo

- "Chafing"
- Dermatitis in skin folds
  - Patches are red and moist
  - Aggravated by urine, feces, heat and moisture
- Prevention consists of keeping affected area clean and dry

- Discuss Figure 30-6 on page 693.

ELSEVIER

Introduction to Maternity & Pediatric Nursing, 6th ed.
Leifer

Slide 20

Seborrheic Dermatitis

- "Cradle cap"
  - Inflammation of the skin that involves the sebaceous glands
  - Characterized by thick, yellow, oily, adherent, crustlike scales on the scalp and forehead
  - Resembles eczema, but does not itch
- Seen in newborns, infants, and at puberty
- Treatment is shampooing hair on consistent basis

- Discuss Figure 30-7 on page 693.

Slide 21

Diaper Dermatitis

- Skin irritated by prolonged contact with urine, feces, retained laundry soaps, and friction
- May be seen in response to addition of solid foods, feeding, chemicals, contact with household substances
- Beefy red rash may be indicative of a *Candida* infection
- Prevented by frequent diaper changes with meticulous skin care

- Discuss frequent diaper changes, cleansing of the skin, and allowing air to assist in the healing process.
- Discuss Figure 30-8 on page 693.

Slide 22

Acne Vulgaris

- Inflammation of the sebaceous glands and hair follicles
  - Sebaceous follicles enlarge at puberty
  - Secrete increased amounts of sebum (a fatty substance)
- Comedo is a plug of keratin, sebum, or bacteria
  - Open—blackhead
  - Closed—whitehead and are responsible for the inflammatory process of acne

- Discuss Figure 30-9 on page 694.

Slide 23

Acne Vulgaris (cont.)

- Routine skin cleansing
- Greasy hair products and cosmetics should be avoided
- Excessive cleansing can irritate skin
- Multiple topical and oral treatments available
- Important to stress to teenager to follow medication treatments as prescribed

- Discuss the pathophysiology regarding skin care and the treatment of acne vulgaris.

Slide 24

Herpes Simplex Type I

- Known as a *cold sore* or *fever blister*
- May feel a tingling, itching, or burning on the lip
- Vesicles and crusts form, takes up to 10 days to heal
- Most communicable in the early phase of the outbreak
- Recurrence is common as virus lays dormant until activated by stress, sun, menstruation, fever, or other causes
- Treatment is with antiviral medications, both oral and topical

- Discuss the pathophysiology regarding the role of stress, sun, menstruation, and other causes of the manifestation of fever blisters/cold sores.

Slide 25

Infantile Eczema

- Atopic dermatitis is an inflammation of genetically hypersensitive skin
  - Local vasodilation in affected areas
- Spongiosis or breakdown of dermal cells and formation of intradermal vesicles
  - Rarely seen in breastfed infants until they begin to eat additional food
  - It is a symptom rather than a disorder
  - Infant is oversensitive to certain substances
- Worse in winter

- What is the reason for the occurrence of increased incidence during the winter months?

Slide 26

Infantile Eczema (cont.)

- Lesions easily infected by bacterial or viral agents
- Infants/children with eczema should not be exposed to adults with cold sores because they may develop a systemic reaction with high fever and multiple vesicles on the eczematous skin
- May flare up after immunizations
- Lab studies show increased IgE and eosinophil levels

- Discuss the pathophysiology regarding a flare-up of eczema following administration of immunizations.

Slide 27

Treatment for Infantile Eczema

- Aimed at relieving pruritus, hydrating the skin, relieving inflammation, and preventing infection
- Emollient bath, such as a mixture of cornstarch and baking soda or oatmeal is sometimes ordered
- Bath oil helps keep skin moist and should be added to bath after the child has soaked for a while and skin is hydrated; the oil will help hold the moisture in the skin
- Medications
  - Corticosteroids
  - Antibiotics
  - Anti-itching medications

Slide 28

Parent Teaching

- Ointments should be completely washed off between applications
- Cortisone creams should be avoided because they do not resolve the underlying cause
- How to apply topical medications
  - Best absorbed after a warm bath
  - Applied by stroking in direction of hair growth
  - Use proper amount of ointment
  - Elbow restraints can prevent an infant from scratching while allowing freedom of movement
  - Topical steroids should not be used when a viral infection is present

Slide 29

Nursing Tip

- Parents should be taught that kissing a wound to "make it better" can introduce organisms that can cause infection

- What is a more sanitary option to kissing a wound to "make it better"?

Leifer

Slide 30

Staphylococcal Infection

- Primary infection may develop in the newborn in the umbilicus or circumcision wound
- May occur while in hospital or after discharge
- Infection spreads readily from one infant to another
- Small pustules on the newborn must be reported immediately
- Antibiotic ointments are used in some situations while in others, intravenous antibiotics are required
- If an infant has MRSA, the child is placed in contact isolation if hospitalized

- Give examples of how *staphylococcus* is spread from one infant to another.

Slide 31

Scalded Skin Syndrome

- Caused by *S. aureus*
- Lesions begin with a mild erythema with a sandpaper texture
- Vesicles appear and rupture and peeling occurs, exposing a bright-red surface
- Skin appears scalded and child abuse is often suspected

- Discuss why the use of disposable individual equipment is important in the prevention of infection on the nursing unit or clinic setting.

Slide 32

Impetigo

- Caused by *staphylococci* or group a beta-hemolytic *streptococci*
  - Bullous form seen in infants usually staphylococcal
  - Nonbullous form is seen in children and young adults
  - Newborns susceptible because resistance to skin bacteria is low
- **Very contagious**
- Treatment is either oral or parenteral antibiotics

- Discuss the treatment options for impetigo.
- Refer to Figure 30-12 on page 699.

Slide 33

Fungal Infections

- Invade stratum corneum, hair and nails
- Fungi are larger than bacteria
- Tinea capitis—alopecia
- Tinea corporis—oval scaly inflamed ring with clear center
- Tinea pedis—lesions are between toes, on instep and soles; pruritic
- Tinea cruris—"jock itch"

- Discuss Figure 30-13 on page 699.
- What precautions should the nurse take when caring for a patient with a fungal infection?

Audience Response Question #2

A fungal infection of the skin that can occur on the scalp, body, and feet is:
1. Ringworm
2. Pediculosis
3. Herpes Simplex II
4. Urticaria

Slide 34

Pediculosis

- Three types
  - Pediculosis capitis—head lice
  - Pediculosis corporis—body lice
  - Pediculosis pubis—pubic lice, known as *crabs*
- Survival of lice depends on blood extracted from infected person

- How is pediculosis treated?
- Refer to Figure 30-14 on page 700.

Leifer

Slide 35

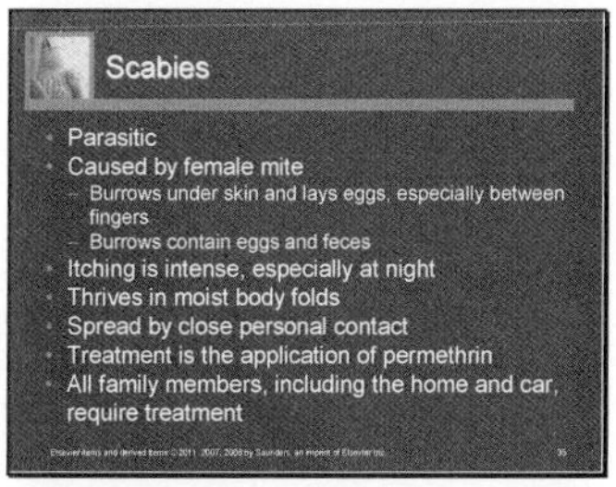

Scabies

- Parasitic
- Caused by female mite
  - Burrows under skin and lays eggs, especially between fingers
  - Burrows contain eggs and feces
- Itching is intense, especially at night
- Thrives in moist body folds
- Spread by close personal contact
- Treatment is the application of permethrin
- All family members, including the home and car, require treatment

Slide 36

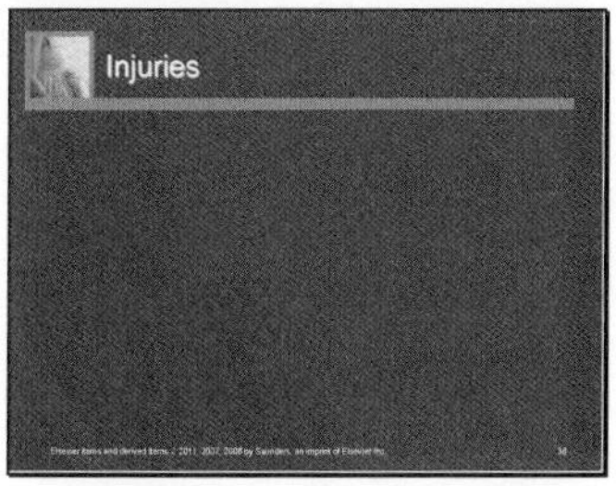

Injuries

Slide 37

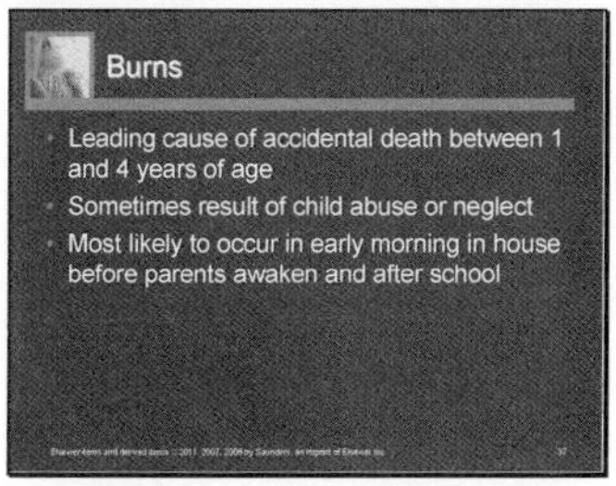

Burns

- Leading cause of accidental death between 1 and 4 years of age
- Sometimes result of child abuse or neglect
- Most likely to occur in early morning in house before parents awaken and after school

- Discuss the reason for the increased incidence of burns in children ages 1 to 4 years.

Slide 38

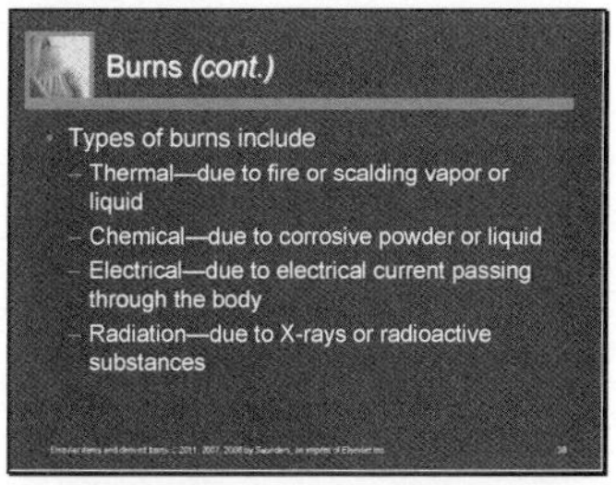

Burns *(cont.)*

- Types of burns include
  - Thermal—due to fire or scalding vapor or liquid
  - Chemical—due to corrosive powder or liquid
  - Electrical—due to electrical current passing through the body
  - Radiation—due to X-rays or radioactive substances

- Give an example of situations that result in a thermal, chemical, electrical, or radiation burn.

Slide 39

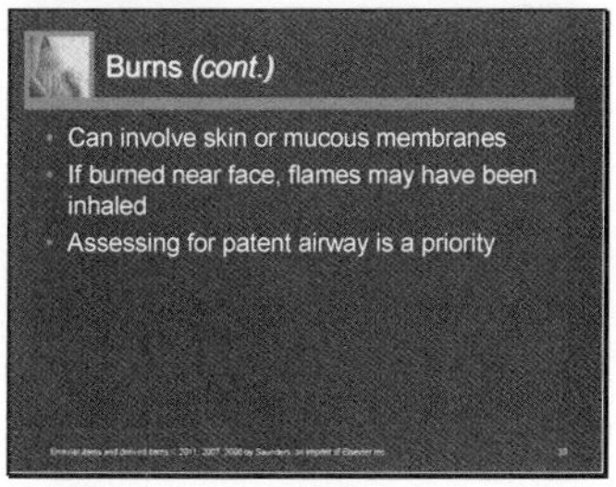

Burns *(cont.)*

- Can involve skin or mucous membranes
- If burned near face, flames may have been inhaled
- Assessing for patent airway is a priority

Audience Response Question #3

Complete the analogy. First degree burn : epidermal as third degree burn : _____.

1. epidermal and dermal
2. dermal
3. subdermal
4. partial thickness

Slide 40

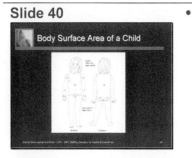

- Discuss Figure 30-15, page 701.

Slide 41

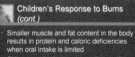

- Discuss Figure 30-15, page 701.
- Give an example of a situation in which this tool would be used.

Slide 42

Children's Response to Burns

- Skin is thinner, leads to more serious depth of burn with lower temperatures and shorter exposures
- Immature response systems in young children can cause shock and heart failure
- Large body surface area of child results in greater fluid, electrolyte, and heat loss
- Increased BMR results in increased protein and calorie needs

Slide 43

Children's Response to Burns
(cont.)

- Smaller muscle and fat content in the body results in protein and caloric deficiencies when oral intake is limited
- Skin more elastic, causing pulling on the scarring areas and resulting in formation of a larger scar

Slide 44

Children's Response to Burns
(cont.)

- Immature immune system predisposes child to developing infections that complicate burn treatment
- Prolonged immobilization and treatment required for burns adversely affects growth and development

Leifer

Slide 45

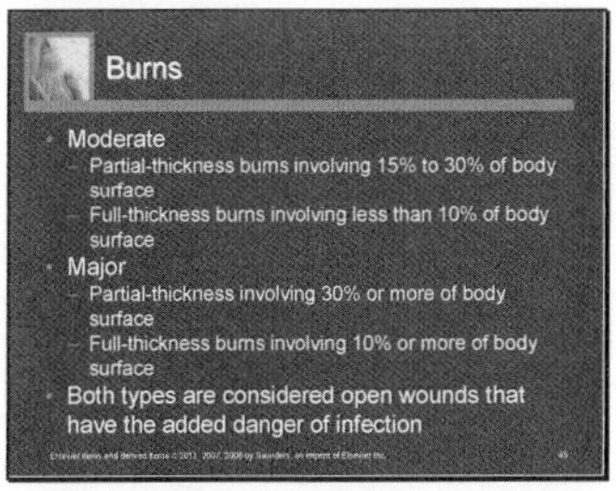

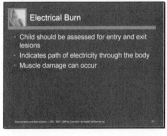

Burns

- Moderate
  - Partial-thickness burns involving 15% to 30% of body surface
  - Full-thickness burns involving less than 10% of body surface
- Major
  - Partial-thickness involving 30% or more of body surface
  - Full-thickness burns involving 10% or more of body surface
- Both types are considered open wounds that have the added danger of infection

- Give an example of a moderate versus a major burn.

Slide 46

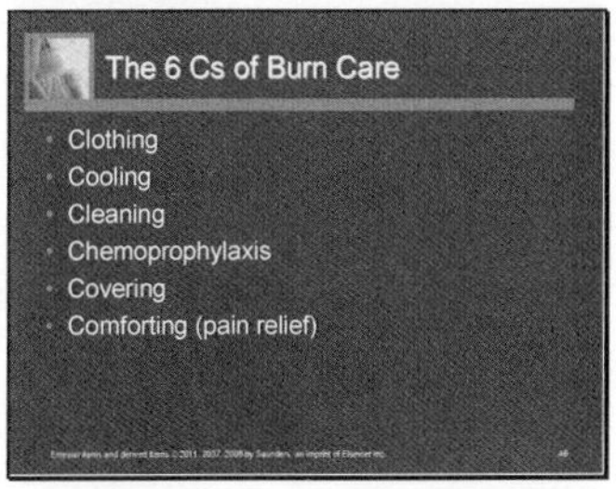

The 6 Cs of Burn Care

- Clothing
- Cooling
- Cleaning
- Chemoprophylaxis
- Covering
- Comforting (pain relief)

Slide 47

Electrical Burn

- Child should be assessed for entry and exit lesions
- Indicates path of electricity through the body
- Muscle damage can occur

Slide 48

Mechanism of Electrical Injury

- Discuss Figure 30-16 on page 703.

Slide 49

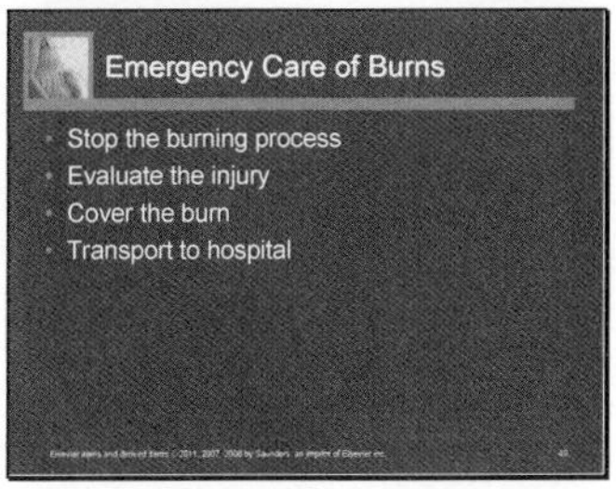

Emergency Care of Burns

- Stop the burning process
- Evaluate the injury
- Cover the burn
- Transport to hospital

- How do you stop the burning process?
- Discuss the assessment process of a burn injury.
- Give examples of various materials which might be appropriate to apply to a burn.

Introduction to Maternity & Pediatric Nursing, 6th ed.

Leifer

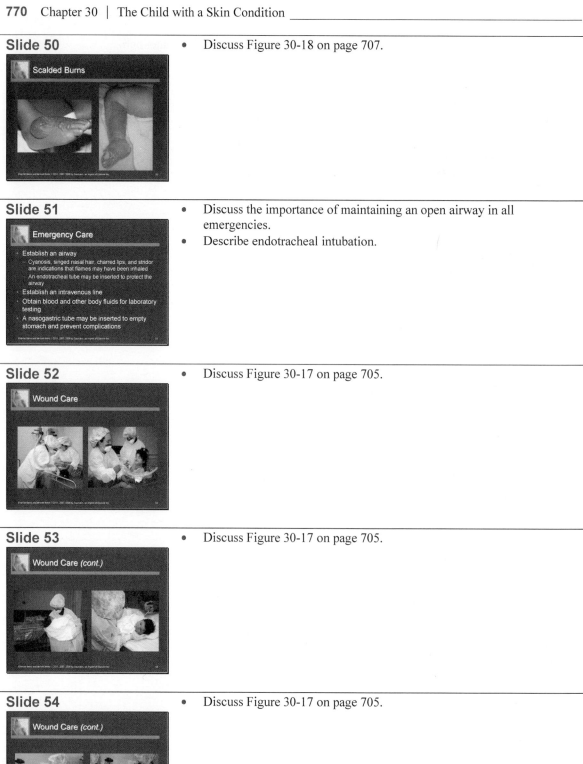

Slide 50

Discuss Figure 30-18 on page 707.

Slide 51

- Discuss the importance of maintaining an open airway in all emergencies.
- Describe endotracheal intubation.

Slide 52

Discuss Figure 30-17 on page 705.

Slide 53

Discuss Figure 30-17 on page 705.

Slide 54

Discuss Figure 30-17 on page 705.

Leifer

Slide 55

Wound Care *(cont.)*

- Can be painful; pain medications should be given in advance of the treatments to ensure adequate pain control is achieved
- Cleansing and debridement
- Loss of skin increases threat of infection and fluid loss caused by evaporation can be significant

- What is the rationale for cleansing and debriding wounds?

Slide 56

Nursing Care

- Protective isolation is instituted
- All instruments are sterile
- Ointments are applied with a sterile gloved hand or sterile tongue depressor
- Care must be taken to avoid injury to granulating tissue

- Discuss the rationale for isolation and sterile procedures.
- What is the importance of granulated tissue in the healing process?

Slide 57

Nursing Care *(cont.)*

- Immediately report signs of infections
- Observe for fluid overload
- Burn victims have an increased demand on metabolism, require high-protein diet; additional vitamins and minerals may also be required
- Prevention of contractures is important
- Providing emotional support to the child and family is essential

- Give examples of signs and symptoms to report immediately.
- Discuss the pathophysiology regarding the increased metabolic rate of burn victims.
- What nursing interventions can prevent contractures?

Slide 58

Sunburn

- Common skin injury due to overexposure to sun
- Can be minor epidermal burn to serious partial-thickness burn with blisters
- Goal of treatment
  - Stop exposure
  - Treat inflammation
  - Rehydrate skin

Slide 59

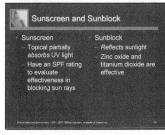

Sunscreen and Sunblock

Sunscreen	Sunblock
- Topical partially *absorbs* UV light	- *Reflects* sunlight
- Have an SPF rating to evaluate effectiveness in blocking sun rays	- Zinc oxide and titanium dioxide are effective

Introduction to Maternity & Pediatric Nursing, 6th ed.
Leifer

Slide 60

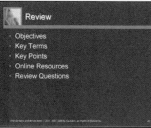

Frostbite

- Results from freezing of a body part
  - Chilblain: a cold injury with erythema and formation of vesicles and ulcerative lesions that occur as a result of vasoconstriction
  - In exposure to extreme cold, warmth is lost in the periphery of the body before the core temperature drops
- In extreme cases, the head and torso should be warmed before the extremities to ensure survival
  - A deep purple flush appears with the return of sensation, which is accompanied by extreme pain
- Can result in necrosis and may require amputation of the affected extremity

Slide 61

Question for Review

- What safety measures must the nurse take when providing wound care management to a child with severe burns?

Slide 62

Review

- Objectives
- Key Terms
- Key Points
- Online Resources
- Review Questions

Leifer

31 Lesson Plan
The Child with a Metabolic Condition

TEACHING FOCUS

The focus of this chapter is to discuss the care of the child with a metabolic condition. Students will have the opportunity to learn about various metabolic disorders with emphasis on management of the diabetic child. Diabetic nursing care is discussed as well as the myriad of family education issues that exist for the family with a diabetic child. Techniques such as glucose monitoring and insulin injection are discussed in detail. Students will also have the opportunity to learn about nutrition, exercise, skin care, and the psychosocial impact of diabetes on daily life.

MATERIALS AND RESOURCES

☐ Computer and PowerPoint projector (all lessons)
☐ Glucose meters (Lesson 31.2)
☐ Insulin pump (Lesson 31.2)

☐ Mannequin (Lesson 31.2)
☐ Syringes and vials of fluid to simulate short- and long-acting insulin (Lesson 31.2)

LESSON CHECKLIST

Preparations for this lesson include:

- Lecture
- Demonstration
- Guest speakers: Nutritionist, endocrinologist, technical sales representative for glucose meters or insulin pumps
- Evaluation of student knowledge and skills needed to perform all entry-level activities related to metabolic conditions in children, including:
  ○ A description and diagnosis of various metabolic disorders
  ○ Identifying types of diabetes and their distinguishing characteristics
  ○ Care of the child with diabetes mellitus, type 1 insulin-dependent
  ○ Family and child education
  ○ National and local diabetes organizations

KEY TERMS

antidiuretic hormone (p. 711)
dawn phenomenon (p. 722)
gestational diabetes mellitus (GDM) (p. 714)
glucagon (p. 722)
glycosuria (p. 714)

glycosylated hemoglobin test (HgbA1c) (p. 714)
hormones (p. 709)
hyperglycemia (p. 714)
hypoglycemia (p. 721)
hypotonia (p. 711)
ketoacidosis (p. 715)

lipoatrophy (p. 721)
polydipsia (p. 714)
polyphagia (p. 714)
polyuria (p. 714)
Somogyi phenomenon (p. 722)
target organ (p. 709)
vasopressin (p. 711)

ADDITIONAL RESOURCES

TEACH PPT slide(s) Chapter 31, 1-58
EILR IC image(s) Chapter 31, 1-8
EILR OBQ question(s) Chapter 31, 1-10
EILR TB question(s) Chapter 31, 1-30
ESLR IRQ question(s) Chapter 31, 1-6
SG Chapter 31, pp. 253-259

Legend

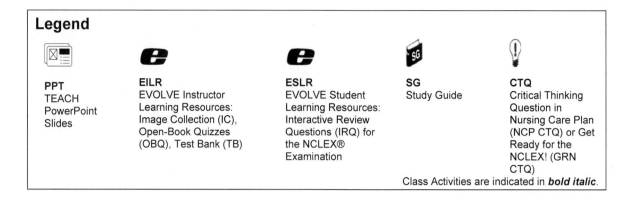

PPT
TEACH
PowerPoint
Slides

EILR
EVOLVE Instructor
Learning Resources:
Image Collection (IC),
Open-Book Quizzes
(OBQ), Test Bank (TB)

ESLR
EVOLVE Student
Learning Resources:
Interactive Review
Questions (IRQ) for
the NCLEX®
Examination

SG
Study Guide

CTQ
Critical Thinking
Question in
Nursing Care Plan
(NCP CTQ) or Get
Ready for the
NCLEX! (GRN
CTQ)

Class Activities are indicated in ***bold italic***.

LESSON 31.1

PRETEST

1. Which of the following diseases displays a clinical manifestation of elevated calcium?
   a. hypopituitarism
   b. hyperpituitarism
   c. hypoparathyroidism
   d. hyperparathyroidism

2. A nursing diagnosis of Deficient fluid volume might be appropriate for which particular disorder?
   a. Tay-Sachs
   b. hypothyroidism
   c. diabetes insipidus
   d. diabetes mellitus

3. A 7-year-old child has been diagnosed with diabetes mellitus. The correct classification would likely be
   a. type 1 diabetes.
   b. type 2 diabetes.
   c. maturity-onset diabetes of youth.
   d. gestational diabetes.

4. What blood test reflects glycemic levels over several months?
   a. random blood glucose
   b. fasting blood glucose
   c. glucose tolerance test
   d. glycosylated hemoglobin test

5. The patient calls out and states he is sweating and shaky. Knowing that he is diabetic, what would be the first action taken by the nurse?
   a. Check his glycosylated hemoglobin test.
   b. Give him some orange juice.
   c. Give him his scheduled insulin.
   d. Notify the physician.

6. A 16-year-old diabetic girl has been admitted with a blood sugar of 800. In addition to the usual nursing interventions for patients who have elevated blood sugar, what other considerations for this age group should the nurse be aware of when discussing the patient's diabetic condition with her?
   a. how many carbohydrates the patient is eating
   b. how often the patient checks her blood sugar
   c. rebellion can be a factor in adolescents
   d. compliance with wearing her medical identification bracelet

7. The nurse is aware that the patient requires more teaching about diet management related to diabetes mellitus when the patient states
   a. "I will restrict all carbohydrates from my diet."
   b. "I bring my lunch to school."
   c. "I eat some raw fruit and vegetables every day."
   d. "I've switched from Frosted Flakes to Raisin Bran cereal."

8. Insulin is usually administered
   a. orally.
   b. by intramuscular injection.
   c. by subcutaneous injection.
   d. by IV.

9. If a patient is injected with NPH insulin at 8 AM, when will its action peak?
   a. 31-90 minutes
   b. 2-3 hours
   c. 4-12 hours
   d. 10-31 hours

10. What time of day does the Somogyi phenomenon occur?
    a. late morning
    b. noon
    c. late afternoon
    d. night

Answers

1. d	3. a	5. b	7. a	9. c
2. c	4. d	6. c	8. c	10. d

BACKGROUND ASSESSMENT

Question: What system is influential in controlling metabolism? Which glands are involved in the process of metabolism and which hormones are associated with each gland?

Answer: The endocrine system regulates the body's metabolic process by the use of hormones that are secreted directly into the bloodstream. The anterior pituitary secretes the growth hormone, the posterior pituitary secretes antidiuretic hormone, the parathyroid secretes parahormone and parathormone, and the adrenal gland secretes steroids, epinephrine, and cortisol.

Question: What is the cause of diabetes mellitus and how can it be managed?

Answer: Type 1 diabetes mellitus is considered an autoimmune disease in which the beta cells in the islets of Langerhans of the pancreas are destroyed and can't release insulin into the bloodstream. Type 2 diabetes mellitus occurs when the beta cells release insufficient amounts of insulin, body cells are resistant to insulin, or both. When the body has an insufficient amount of insulin, the intake of carbohydrates causes the blood glucose level to rise. Diabetes mellitus can be managed in several ways, depending on the extent of the disease. For some, diet modifications can maintain the blood glucose level within normal ranges. For others, a combination of diet modifications and medication in the form of pills may be needed. For the client whose pancreas secretes very little or no insulin, a combination of diet, pills, or insulin may be required. Individuals must check their blood glucose levels to determine if their management is successful.

CRITICAL THINKING QUESTION

A nursing student is considering working for a pediatric endocrinologist after graduation and is concerned about her ability to gain sufficient knowledge to respond to questions from patients and their parents about various metabolic disorders. What could the student do to acquire more knowledge in this field, and what will the student discover in terms of the role of the endocrine system?

Guidelines: In addition to studying material in the textbook, the student could search the Internet for information about metabolic disorders. Based on the data that he or she accumulates, the student could make charts that compare and contrast the pathophysiology, manifestations, and interventions associated with metabolic disorders prevalent in children. The student would learn that different endocrine glands have different functions related to child development, and a decrease or increase in hormones secreted by the glands can cause life-changing problems. The student will also discover that monitoring growth parameters is of vital importance to a child's health. In addition, the student could locate national and local support groups for various metabolic disorders and talk with them about disease management. Asking other nurses about their experiences with children who have diabetes mellitus and other metabolic disorders could also help the student remember the signs and symptoms associated with each endocrine disorder.

OBJECTIVES	CONTENT	TEACHING RESOURCES
Relate why growth parameters are of importance to patients with a family history of endocrine disease.	■ Integration of the nervous and endocrine systems (p. 709)	⊠ PPT slides 5-10 *e* EILR IC image 1 *e* EILR OBQ question 1 *e* EILR TB question 25 SG SG Learning Activities, question 2 (p. 253) **BOOK RESOURCES** Figure 31-1, Summary of Some Endocrine System Differences Between the Child and the Adult (p. 710) Nursing Tip (p. 710) ▸ Discuss the interrelationship of the nervous system and the endocrine system.

OBJECTIVES	CONTENT	TEACHING RESOURCES
		▸ Discuss why endocrine dysfunction in the mother may affect the fetus and how endocrine disease can arise. Why is it important to monitor body functions? ▸ Discuss the significance of clinical signs such as failure to thrive, poor feeding, lethargy, vomiting, or an enlarged liver in the infant. Discuss the significance of developmental delay, convulsions, or odors in the urine or body in older children. *Class Activity* **Invite a pediatric nurse practitioner to speak on the effects of endocrine disease and explain growth parameters and charts.**

List the symptoms of hypothyroidism in infants.	■ Disorders and dysfunction of the endocrine system (p. 710)
	
	  ☐ Inborn errors of metabolism (p. 710)
	
	  ☐ Tay-Sachs disease (p. 710)
	
	■ Endocrine disorders (p. 711)
	
	  ☐ Hypothyroidism (p. 711)
		⊠▪ PPT slides 11-20
		
		𝑒 EILR IC image 2
		
		𝑒 EILR OBQ question 2
		
		𝑒 EILR TB questions 1, 10, 14, 15, 26
		
		𝑒 ESLR IRQ questions 1, 2, 5
		
		SG Learning Activities, questions 2-7, 30 (pp. 253-254, 256)
		
		SG Review Questions, questions 12, 14, 15 (p. 258)
		
		BOOK RESOURCES
		
		Figure 31-2, An Infant with Hypothyroidism (p. 711)
		
		▸ Discuss the pathophysiology responsible for hypothyroidism.
		
		▸ Discuss circumstances under which hypothyroidism commonly occurs. What are the symptoms of hypothyroidism?
		
		Class Activity **Divide the class into three small groups. Ask one group to discuss and then present the pathophysiology of Tay-Sachs disease. Assign another group the manifestations of the disease, and another group the treatment and nursing care for the disease. Have each group present its material to the class for discussion.**
		
		Class Activity **Divide the class into small groups and assign each group one of the following topics: pathophysiology of hypothyroidism, juvenile hypothyroidism, manifestations of hypothyroidism, and treatment and nursing interventions. Have each group present its material to the class for discussion.**

Leifer

OBJECTIVES	CONTENT	TEACHING RESOURCES
Discuss the dietary adjustment required for a child with diabetes insipidus.	☐ Common metabolic dysfunctions (p. 711) ☐ Diabetes insipidus (p. 711)	☒▣ PPT slides 21-25 *e* EILR TB questions 11, 16, 17 *e* ESLR IRQ questions 3, 4 ▣ SG Learning Activities, questions 8-10, 30 (pp. 254, 256) ▣ SG Review Questions, questions 3, 16 (pp. 257, 259) **BOOK RESOURCES** Table 31-1, Metabolic Dysfunctions (p. 712) Review Questions for the NCLEX® Examination, question 1 (p. 726) ▸ Discuss the cause and symptoms of diabetes insipidus. Discuss treatment for diabetes insipidus. ▸ Discuss fluid requirements of the child with diabetes insipidus and adjustments that need to be made at school to accommodate the child with this disorder. *Class Activity **Divide the class into small groups to identify and discuss the pathophysiology, manifestations, treatment, and nursing interventions related to diabetes insipidus. Have each group present a summary of its findings to the class for discussion.***
Differentiate between type 1 and type 2 diabetes mellitus.	☐ Diabetes mellitus (p. 713) – Type 1 diabetes mellitus (p. 714) – Diagnostic blood tests (p. 714)	☒▣ PPT slides 26-34 *e* EILR IC image 3 *e* EILR OBQ questions 3-9 *e* EILR TB questions 2, 3, 12, 18, 29, 30 *e* ESLR IRQ question 6 ▣ SG Learning Activities, questions 1, 11-18, 30 (pp. 253-255) ▣ SG Review Questions, questions 2, 6-11 (pp. 257-258) **BOOK RESOURCES** Table 31-2, Classification of Diabetes Mellitus (p. 713) Table 31-3, Clinical Features of Type 1 and Type 2 Diabetes (p. 713) Nursing Tip (p. 714) Figure 31-3, The Glucose Tolerance Test (p. 715) ▸ Discuss the two types of diabetes mellitus and list the

OBJECTIVES	CONTENT	TEACHING RESOURCES
		characteristics of each. What are the older names used for these disorders?
		▶ Discuss the clinical characteristics of type 1 and type 2 diabetes. How do they differ?
		▶ Discuss the etiology, pathophysiology, and treatment of diabetes mellitus. What are the risk factors for diabetes mellitus?
		▶ Discuss the difference between maturity-onset diabetes of youth and type 1 diabetes mellitus.
		Class Activity Divide the class into four groups. Assign one of the following topics to each group for discussion: the pathophysiology of diabetes, the etiology of diabetes, type 1 diabetes, and type 2 diabetes. Ask each group to present a description of its topic to the entire class.
		Class Activity Divide the class into two groups. Assign type 1 diabetes to one group and type 2 to the other group. Ask each group to discuss and characterize its assigned type of diabetes, including incidence, manifestations, and treatment. Have a volunteer from each group present the group's findings to the class. Then create a chart reflecting the information presented by the groups.

31.1 Homework/Assignments:

31.1 Instructor's Notes/Student Feedback:

LESSON 31.2

CRITICAL THINKING QUESTION

A 10-year-old boy has been diagnosed with type 1 diabetes mellitus. What should the nurse recommend that he do to learn about his condition?

Guidelines: The child and his parents would benefit from attending a class on diabetes mellitus and learning about the distinction between type 1 and type 2 diabetes. Written handouts and audiovisual aids are helpful. The parents should be informed about diabetes organizations that provide a variety of support materials free of charge. The child has to be taught how to check his own blood glucose levels by operating a personal glucose meter. He will require education about the signs and symptoms of hypoglycemia and hyperglycemia and what actions to take in response. The nurse should inform the boy and his parents of how exercise, medications, and diet work together to affect his glucose levels. A nutritionist would be helpful in explaining how to manage the child's diet. The nurse should inform the parents and the child that education about the disorder will be ongoing. The nurse should show the child the many new products that can be substituted for products that contain sugar. He will need to learn how to administer his own insulin—he can practice on a doll at first. The nurse should introduce him to other children who are already proficient at insulin administration and allow him to talk to and watch them. The parents will have to be responsible for most of the child's diabetic management at first, but the child will take over as he feels more comfortable. Encouragement and support from the nursing staff are vital. The nurse can suggest national and local diabetes organizations and clinics at local children's hospitals that offer support groups for children and family.

OBJECTIVES	CONTENT	TEACHING RESOURCES
List three precipitating events that might cause diabetic ketoacidosis.	– Diabetic ketoacidosis (p. 715)	PPT slides 35, 36 EILR TB question 9 SG Learning Activities, question 1 (p. 253) SG Review Questions, question 5 (p. 257) **BOOK RESOURCES** Table 31-4, Hyperglycemia and Hypoglycemia (p. 716) ▸ Discuss the circumstances under which diabetic ketoacidosis commonly occurs. What are the symptoms of ketoacidosis? *Class Activity Working in pairs, ask students to take turns role-playing instructions that a nurse would give a client about diabetic ketoacidosis. Topics could include pathophysiology, signs and symptoms, and how to treat symptoms of hyperglycemia.* *Class Activity Lead a discussion about sick-day rules for children and how they can prevent an episode of diabetic ketoacidosis. Ask the class why an infection can lead to ketoacidosis.*
Compare the signs and symptoms of hyperglycemia and hypoglycemia.	– Diabetic ketoacidosis (p. 715)	PPT slide 37 EILR OBQ question 7 EILR TB questions 4, 5, 20

OBJECTIVES	CONTENT	TEACHING RESOURCES
		SG SG Learning Activities, questions 1, 25, 29 (pp. 253, 256)
		SG SG Review Questions, question 8 (p. 258)
		BOOK RESOURCES
		Table 31-4, Hyperglycemia and Hypoglycemia (p. 716)
		Review Questions for the NCLEX® Examination, questions 3, 5 (p. 726)
		▸ Discuss the signs and symptoms of hyperglycemia and hypoglycemia and the possible underlying causes of each.
		*Class Activity **In small groups, have students discuss the differences and similarities in the symptoms of hyperglycemia and hypoglycemia. Which complication must be recognized and treated right away?***
		*Class Activity **Lead an activity in which some students take a turn stating a sign or symptom of hyperglycemia or hypoglycemia, while other students state the correct condition.***
List a predictable stress that the disease of diabetes mellitus has on children and families during the following periods of life: infancy, toddlerhood, preschool age, elementary school age, puberty, and adolescence.	– Treatment and nursing care (p. 715)	**PPT** slides 37-40
		e EILR OBQ questions 3-10
		e EILR TB question 27
		SG SG Learning Activities, questions 19, 23, 27, 28, 31, and 37 (p. 255)
		SG SG Review Questions, question 9 (p. 258)
		BOOK RESOURCES
		Nursing Care Plan 31-1, The Child with Diabetes Mellitus (p. 717)
		Table 31-7, Nursing Interventions for Predictable Types of Stress on a Child with Type 1 Diabetes and on the Family (p. 724)
		▸ Discuss three general goals of treatment for children with type 1 diabetes. What are the roles of the family financial situation, cultural background, and educational status in the management of this disorder?
		▸ Discuss the special impact this disease has on the patient and his or her family in terms of learning to accept the disease and its therapy during the following stages of life: infancy, toddlerhood, preschool age, elementary school age, puberty, and adolescence.

OBJECTIVES	CONTENT	TEACHING RESOURCES
		Class Activity **Divide the class into small groups and assign each group one of the following periods of life: infancy, toddlerhood, preschool age, elementary school age, puberty, or adolescence. Ask each group to discuss and then present to the class some age-related factors in the treatment of diabetes.**
Outline the educational needs of the parents and the child with diabetes mellitus in the following areas: nutrition and meal planning, exercise, blood tests, glucose monitoring administration of insulin, and skin care.	– Teaching plan for children with diabetes mellitus (p. 716) – Blood glucose self-monitoring (p. 716) – Continuous glucose monitoring (p. 718) – Diet therapy for children with diabetes mellitus (p. 718)	▦ PPT slides 40-44 𝒆 EILR IC images 4-7 𝒆 EILR OBQ questions 8-10 𝒆 EILR TB questions 4, 6-8, 21-24, 28 SG Learning Activities, questions 20, 27, 28, 30, 33 (p. 255-256) SG Review Questions, questions 1, 2, 13 (pp. 257-258) **BOOK RESOURCES** Nursing Care Plan 31-1, The Child with Diabetes Mellitus (p. 717) Table 31-5, Glycemic Index of Selected Foods (p. 719) Medication Safety Alert (p. 719) Nursing Tip (p. 719) Figure 31-4, Subcutaneous Injection of Insulin (p. 719) Figure 31-5, The Accu-Chek Insulin Pump (p. 720) Figure 31-6, Self-Injection of Insulin (p. 720) Figure 31-7, Sites of Injection of Insulin (p. 720) Medication Safety Alert (p. 721) Review Questions for the NCLEX® Examination, question 4 (p. 726) ▸ Discuss nutritional management for the diabetic child. What other factors play a role in achieving glycemic control? ▸ Discuss options for glucose monitoring. How would you present monitoring of glucose levels to a toddler and his parents? At what point will the child be able to monitor his or her glucose independently? Describe a teaching pathway for achieving this goal. ▸ Discuss the role of exercise in glycemic control. ▸ Discuss how to choose injection sites and measures you would take to prevent tissue damage at injection sites.

OBJECTIVES	CONTENT	TEACHING RESOURCES
		List the various kinds of insulin and their advantages and disadvantages. Which ones are most commonly used for children?
		▸ Discuss the role of foot care in the diabetic child. Discuss care of the diabetic child in special circumstances such as travel or surgery.
		*Class Activity **Divide the class into small groups. Have each group create a teaching plan for a child and family about such procedures as blood tests, insulin administration, and skin care. Have the groups make presentations to the class and evaluate which teaching plan is most informative.***
		*Class Activity **Invite a nutritionist to discuss diet therapy for the diabetic child.***
		*Class Activity **Ask pairs of students to role-play a nurse instructing a young patient who has diabetes and his or her mother about dietary management. The nurse should explain the following topics, and patient and mother should pose challenging questions:***
		– *meal planning*
		– *consistency in amounts of food and meal timing*
		– *exchange lists*
		– *the role of fiber*
		– *food processing*
		– *artificial sweeteners*
Discuss the preparation and administration of insulin to a child, highlighting any differences between pediatric and adult administration.	– Home management of children with diabetes mellitus (p. 723)	▣ PPT slides 45-49
		🄴 EILR IC image 8
		🄴 EILR OBQ question 10
		🄴 EILR TB question 19
		📙 SG Learning Activities, questions 21-23, 30 (pp. 255-256)
		📙 SG Review Questions, question 16 (p. 259)
		BOOK RESOURCES
		Medication Safety Alert (p. 721)
		Table 31-6, Types of Insulin (p. 721)
		Figure 31-8, Mixing Insulin (p. 722)
		Review Questions for the NCLEX® Examination, question 4 (p. 726)

OBJECTIVES	CONTENT	TEACHING RESOURCES
		▸ Discuss the types of insulin that are not commonly administered to children and why. Why are children more prone to insulin shock than adults?
		Class Activity Divide the class into small groups to create a teaching poster on the types of insulin that could be administered to a child. The posters should include the reasons some insulin is not administered to children. The posters should also include drawings of insulin administration, drawings of injection sites on a body, and charts for the child to document injection sites.
		Class Activity Have students observe a demonstration of insulin being administered to various sites on a mannequin. Then have students draw up insulin and practice administering it.
List three possible causes of insulin shock.	– Home management of children with diabetes mellitus (p. 723)	PPT slides 50-52
		EILR OBQ question 10
		SG Learning Activities, questions 23-25 (p. 256)
		SG Review Questions, questions 4, 8, 9 (pp. 257-258)
		▸ Discuss the pathophysiology of insulin shock. What are the symptoms of insulin shock and what immediate treatment should be implemented?
		Class Activity Conduct a class discussion about the causes and contributing factors of insulin shock. Ask students to identify the lifestyle and dietary factors that might contribute to insulin shock.
		Class Activity Have students work in small groups to prepare a patient education booklet for parents and children that explains the role of insulin in the body and how insulin shock can be prevented in people who have diabetes. Each group should present its booklet to the class for evaluation.
Explain the Somogyi phenomenon.	– Home management of children with diabetes mellitus (p. 723)	PPT slides 53-56
		EILR TB question 13
		SG Learning Activities, questions 26, 34 (p. 256)
		BOOK RESOURCES
		Table 31-7, Nursing Intervention for Predictable Types of Stress on a Child with Type 1 Diabetes and on the Family (p. 724)
		Nutrition Considerations, Diet Therapy in Pediatric Metabolic Disorders (p. 725)

OBJECTIVES	CONTENT	TEACHING RESOURCES
		▸ Discuss the common symptoms of the Somogyi phenomenon. How does it differ from the "dawn phenomenon"?
		▸ Discuss the benefits and effects of exercise for the diabetic adolescent. What is the role of exercise in glycemic control? Identify special considerations in terms of the timing of exercise and food intake around exercise time.
		*Class Activity **Divide the class into small groups. Each group should create an exercise plan for a child with type 1 diabetes and explain to the class why its plan is appropriate.***
		*Class Activity **In small groups, have students create a booklet for children and parents that explains the benefits of exercise, types of exercise, how exercise can lower blood sugar, and what foods or items should be carried with them at all times. Each group should present its booklet to the class for discussion of teaching effectiveness.***
		*Class Activity **Each student should research specifics of the Somogyi phenomenon. On the board, have each student write a fact about the phenomenon, including causes, clinical manifestations, and treatments. Each student should research specifics about the "dawn phenomenon" and compare it to the Somogyi phenomenon.*** (For students to prepare for this activity, see Homework/Assignments #1.)
Performance Evaluation		▣ PPT slides 1-58
		𝒆 EILR IC images 1-8
		𝒆 EILR OBQ questions 1-10
		𝒆 EILR TB questions 1-30
		𝒆 ESLR IRQ questions 1-6
		SG Learning Activities, questions 1-30 (p. 253-257)
		SG Review Questions, questions 1-16 (pp. 257-259)
		SG Case Study, question 1 (p. 259)
		SG Thinking Critically, question 1 (p. 259)
		SG Applying Knowledge, questions 1-3 (p. 259)
		BOOK RESOURCES

OBJECTIVES	CONTENT	TEACHING RESOURCES
		NCP CTQ 1 (p. 717) Review Questions for the NCLEX® Examination, questions 1-5 (p. 726)

31.2 Homework/Assignments:

1. Each student should research the specifics about the Somogyi phenomenon. On the board, have each student write a fact about the phenomenon, including causes, clinical manifestations, and treatments. Each student will research the specifics about the "dawn phenomenon" and compare it to the Somogyi phenomenon.

31.2 Instructor's Notes/Student Feedback:

31 Lecture Outline
The Child with a Metabolic Condition

Slide 1

Chapter 31

The Child with a
Metabolic Condition

Slide 2

Objectives

- Relate why growth parameters are of importance to patients with a family history of endocrine disease.
- List the symptoms of hypothyroidism in infants.
- Discuss the dietary adjustment required for a child with diabetes insipidus.
- Compare the signs and symptoms of hyperglycemia and hypoglycemia.

Slide 3

Objectives *(cont.)*

- Differentiate between type 1 and type 2 diabetes.
- List three precipitating events that might cause diabetic ketoacidosis.
- List a predictable stress that the disease of diabetes has on children and families during the following periods of life: infancy, toddlers, preschool age, elementary school-age, puberty, and adolescence.

Slide 4

Objectives *(cont.)*

- Outline the educational needs of the diabetic child and parents in the following areas: nutrition and meal planning, exercise, blood tests, administration of insulin, and skin care.
- List three possible causes of insulin shock.
- Explain the Somogyi phenomenon.
- Discuss the preparation and administration of insulin to a child, highlighting any differences between pediatric and adult administration.

Slide 5 **Endocrine System** Two major control systems that monitor the functions of the body are the — Nervous system — Endocrine system These systems are interdependent Endocrine (ductless) glands regulate the body's metabolic processes Primary responsibilities — Growth — Maturation — Reproduction — Response of the body to stress	• Briefly discuss the manner in which the CNS controls the body versus the endocrine system.
Slide 6 **Endocrine System** *(cont.)*	• Discuss Figure 31-1 on page 710.
Slide 7 **Endocrine System** *(cont.)* • Hormones — Chemical substances produced by the glands — Secreted directly into the blood — An organ specifically influenced by a certain hormone is called a *target organ* — Too much or too little can result in disease	• Give an example of a disease in which too much of a hormone has caused the disease. • Give an example of a disease in which too little of a hormone has caused the disease.
Slide 8 **Endocrine System** *(cont.)* • The absence or deficiency of an enzyme that has a role in metabolism causes a defect in the metabolic process • Most inborn errors of metabolism can be detected by clinical signs or screening tests that can be performed in utero • Lethargy, poor feeding, failure to thrive, vomiting, and an enlarged liver may be early signs of an inborn error of metabolism in the newborn	• In what metabolic disorder is an enzyme lacking? • Discuss newborn screenings which are performed prior to discharge from the hospital.
Slide 9 **Endocrine System** *(cont.)* • If clinical signs are not manifested in the neonatal period, an infection or body stress can precipitate symptoms of a latent defect in the older child • Unexplained mental retardation, developmental delay, convulsions, an odor to the body or urine, or episodes of vomiting may be subtle signs of a metabolic dysfunction	• Give an example of a disorder which was caused by an infection.

Slide 10

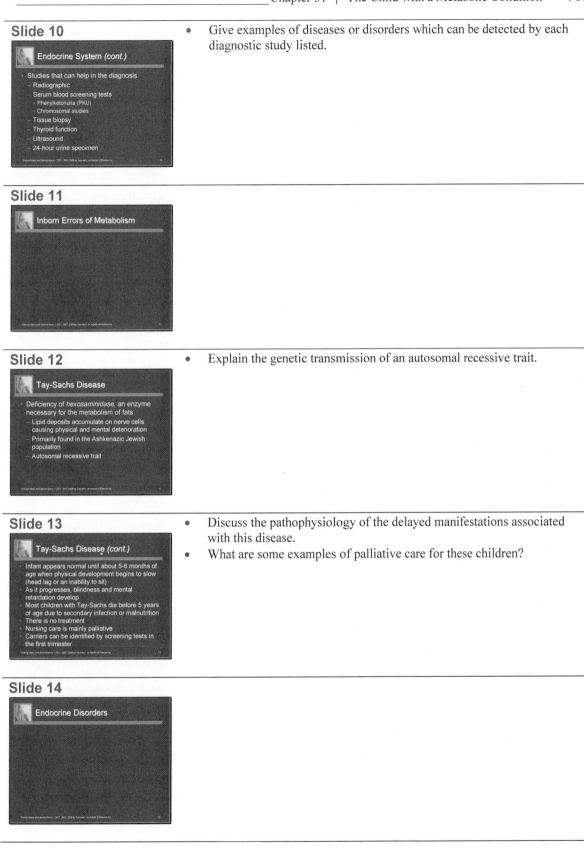

Endocrine System *(cont.)*

· Studies that can help in the diagnosis
  - Radiographic
  - Serum blood screening tests
    · Phenylketonuria (PKU)
    · Chromosomal studies
  - Tissue biopsy
  - Thyroid function
  - Ultrasound
  - 24-hour urine specimen

- • Give examples of diseases or disorders which can be detected by each diagnostic study listed.

Slide 11

Inborn Errors of Metabolism

Slide 12

Tay-Sachs Disease

· Deficiency of *hexosaminidase*, an enzyme necessary for the metabolism of fats
  - Lipid deposits accumulate on nerve cells causing physical and mental deterioration
  - Primarily found in the Ashkenazic Jewish population
  - Autosomal recessive trait

- • Explain the genetic transmission of an autosomal recessive trait.

Slide 13

Tay-Sachs Disease *(cont.)*

· Infant appears normal until about 5-6 months of age when physical development begins to slow (head lag or an inability to sit)
· As it progresses, blindness and mental retardation develop
· Most children with Tay-Sachs die before 5 years of age due to secondary infection or malnutrition
· There is no treatment
· Nursing care is mainly palliative
· Carriers can be identified by screening tests in the first trimester

- • Discuss the pathophysiology of the delayed manifestations associated with this disease.
- • What are some examples of palliative care for these children?

Slide 14

Endocrine Disorders

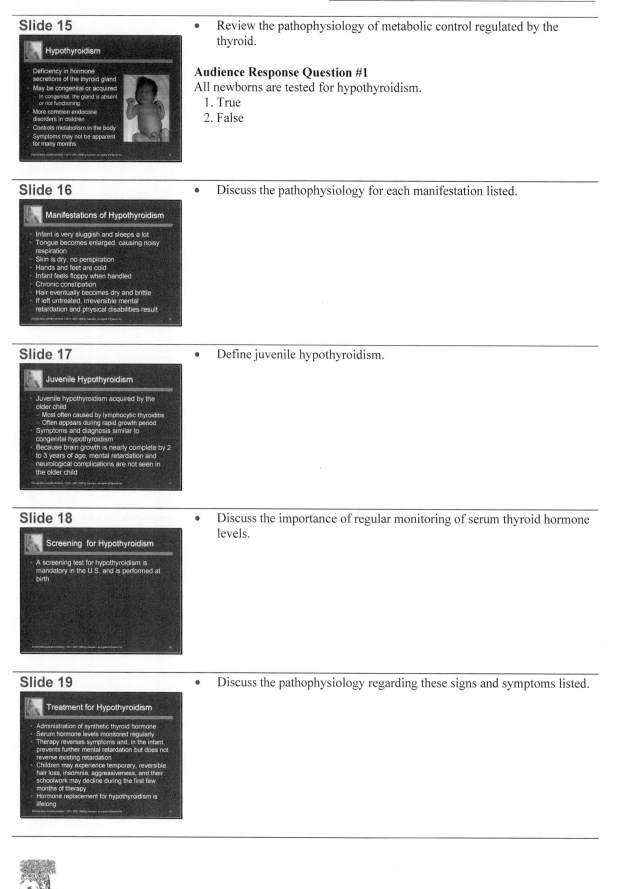

Slide 15

Review the pathophysiology of metabolic control regulated by the thyroid.

Audience Response Question #1
All newborns are tested for hypothyroidism.
1. True
2. False

Slide 16

Discuss the pathophysiology for each manifestation listed.

Slide 17

Define juvenile hypothyroidism.

Slide 18

Discuss the importance of regular monitoring of serum thyroid hormone levels.

Slide 19

Discuss the pathophysiology regarding these signs and symptoms listed.

Slide 20

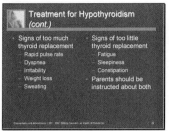

- How would you educate parents about these signs?

Slide 21

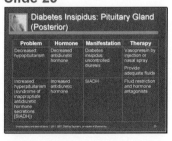

Slide 22

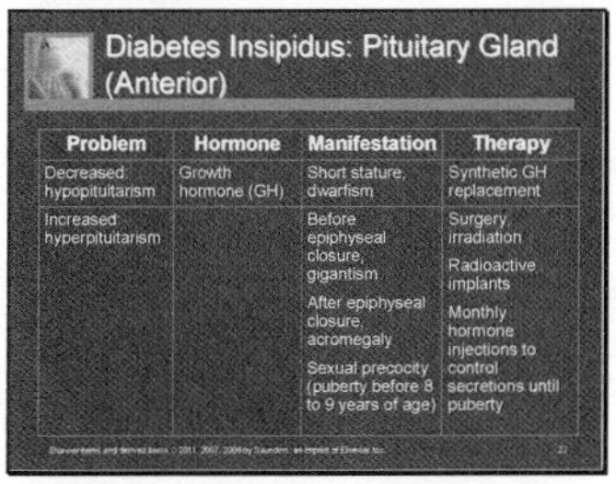

- Discuss the difference between hypopituitarism and hyperpituitarism.

Slide 23

- What is the difference between diabetes insipidus and diabetes mellitus?

Slide 24

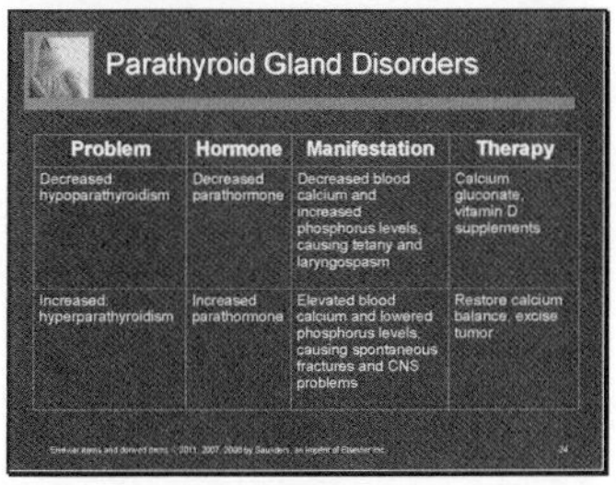

- Discuss the role of the parathyroid gland.

Slide 25

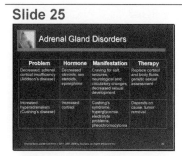

- What is the function of the adrenal glands?

Audience Response Question #2
Complete the analogy. Adrenalcortical insufficiency : Addison's disease as hyperadrenalism : _____.
1. Diabetes mellitus
2. Perthe's disease
3. Cushing's disease
4. Turner's syndrome

Slide 26

Diabetes Mellitus (DM)

- Chronic metabolic syndrome—the body is unable to use carbohydrates properly
  - Leads to impairment of glucose transport
- Body unable to store and use fats properly
- Decrease in protein synthesis
- When blood glucose level becomes dangerously high
  - Glucose spills into the urine
  - Diuresis occurs

- Discuss the effects of hyperglycemia on the kidneys.

Slide 27

Diabetes Mellitus (DM) *(cont.)*

- Incomplete fat metabolism produces ketone bodies that accumulate in the blood
  - Known as ketonemia
    - Serious complication
- DM impacts physical and psychological growth and development of children
- Treatment designed to
  - Optimize growth and development
  - Minimize complications

Slide 28

Diabetes Mellitus (DM) *(cont.)*

- Long-term complications related to hyperglycemia
  - Blindness
  - Circulatory problems
  - Kidney disease
  - Neuropathy

Slide 29

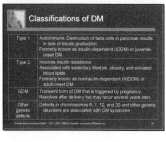

- Discuss each classification of diabetes mellitus and give examples of patients with each disorder.

Slide 30

Type 1 Diabetes Mellitus (DM)

- Can occur at any time in childhood; new cases highest among
  - 5- and 7-year-olds: Stress of school and increased exposure to infectious diseases may be a triggering factor
  - 11- to 13-year-olds: During puberty, rapid growth, increased emotional stress, and insulin antagonism of sex hormones may be implicated
- More difficult to manage in childhood because of growing, energy expenditure, varying nutritional needs
- Initial diagnosis may be determined when the child develops ketoacidosis

- Discuss the effects of growth and development and the difficulties in managing this disease.
- Give a rationale for the child in a ketoacidotic state and this incident being the initial diagnosis.

Slide 31

Manifestations of Type 1 DM

- Classic triad of symptoms
  - Polydipsia
  - Polyuria
  - Polyphagia
- Symptoms appear more rapidly in children
- Insidious onset with lethargy, weakness, and weight loss also common
- Skin becomes dry
- Vaginal yeast infections may be seen in the adolescent girl

- Define each symptom listed.
- Discuss the pathophysiology of the increased incidence of vaginal yeast infections and type 1 diabetes mellitus.

Slide 32

Laboratory Findings in Type 1 DM

- Glucose in urine (glycosuria)
- Hyperglycemia
  - Occurs because glucose cannot enter the cells without the help of insulin; glucose stays in bloodstream
- Cells use protein and fat for energy
  - Protein stores in body are depleted
  - Lack of glucose in cells triggers polyphagia
- Increase in glucose intake further increases glucose levels in the blood

Slide 33

Honeymoon Period of Type 1 DM

- After initially diagnosis, the child is stabilized by insulin dosage and condition may appear to improve
  - Insulin requirements decrease, child feels well
  - Supports parents' phase of "denial"
- Lasts a short time; therefore, parents must closely monitor blood glucose levels to avoid complications

- Give an example of a situation in which an adolescent and parents experience this stage.

Slide 34

Diagnostic Tests for DM

- Random blood glucose
  - Blood is drawn at any time; no preparation; results should be within normal limits for both diabetic and nondiabetic patients
- Fasting blood glucose
  - If greater than 126 mg/dL on two separate occasions, and the history is positive, patient is considered as having DM and requires treatment
- Glucose tolerance test
  - Blood glucose level above 200 mg/dl is considered positive
- Glycosylated hemoglobin (HbA1c):
  - Values of 6% to 9% represent very good metabolic control
  - Values above 12% indicate poor control

- Discuss each test and patient education required for each.
- Discuss the accuracy of glycosylated hemoglobin.

Leifer

Slide 35

Diabetic Ketoacidosis (DKA)

- Also referred to as *diabetic coma*, even though patient may not be in one
- May results from a secondary infection and patient does not follow proper self-care
- May also occur if disease proceeds unrecognized
- Ketoacidosis is the end result of the effects of insulin deficiency

- What are the manifestations of ketoacidosis?

Audience Response Question #3
Diabetic ketoacidosis (DKA) results from an excessive accumulation of:
1. Ketone bodies from fat metabolism
2. Sodium bicarbonate from renal compensation
3. Glucose from carbohydrate metabolism
4. Potassium from insulin reaction

Slide 36

Diabetic Ketoacidosis (DKA)
(cont.)

- Signs and symptoms include
  - Ketonuria
  - Decreased serum bicarbonate concentration (decreased CO_2 levels) and low pH
  - Hypertonic dehydration
  - Fruity odor to breath
  - Nausea
  - ALOC
- Symptoms range from mild to severe
  - Occur within hours to days

- Discuss the pathophysiology of decreased bicarbonate levels and ketoacidosis.
- How do the renal and respiratory systems compensate for DKA?

Slide 37

Treatment Goals of DM

- Ensure normal growth and development through metabolic control
- Enable child to cope with a chronic illness, have a happy and active childhood, and be well-integrated into the family
- Prevent complications through tight blood glucose control

- Discuss methods to ensure control of DM.

Slide 38

Nursing Care of a Child with DM

- Parent and child education
  - Patient's age, financial, educational, cultural, and religious situations must be considered when developing a teaching plan
    - For example, pork-based insulin may not be accepted by some religions; therefore, compliance with treatment may be reduced

- What other cultural obstacles might the nurse encounter?

Slide 39

Nursing Care of a Child with DM
(cont.)

- Children with DM are growing, additional dimensions of the disorder and its treatment become evident
  - Growth is not steady
  - Occurs in spurts and plateaus that affect treatment
  - Infants and toddlers may have hydration problems
  - Preschool children have irregular activity and eating patterns
  - School-age children may grieve over the diagnosis
  - May use illness to gain attention or to avoid responsibilities
  - Onset of puberty may require insulin adjustments
  - Adolescents often resent this condition and may have more difficulty in resolving conflict between dependence and independence; may lead to rebellion against parents and treatment regimen

Leifer

Slide 40

Triad of Management for DM

- Well-balanced diet
- Precise insulin administration
- Regular exercise

- Give an example of a child whose DM is well-controlled versus a child whose DM is not controlled.

Slide 41

Teaching Plan for a Child with DM

- Physiology of the pancreas and its function
- Function of insulin
- Blood glucose self-monitoring
- Diet therapy (glycemic index of foods and cholesterol intake)
- Insulin management
- Exercise
- Skin care
- Foot care
- Infections
- Emotional upsets
- Urine check
- Glucose-insulin imbalances
- Travel
- Follow-up care
- Illness or surgery

- Discuss the glycemic index and give examples of foods which are high on the glycemic index.
- Discuss the pathophysiology of exercise and how it assists the transport of insulin into the cells.
- What is the rationale for good skin and foot care?

Slide 42

Nutritional Management of DM

- Ensure normal growth and development
- Distribute food intake so that it aids metabolic control
- Individualize the diet in accordance with the child's ethnic background, age, sex, weight, activity, family economics, and food preferences
  - Total estimated caloric intake is based upon body size or surface area
  - Most carbohydrate intake should consist of complex carbohydrates that absorb slowly and do not cause sudden and wide elevation of blood glucose

- Relate complex carbohydrates and the glycemic index.

Slide 43

Dietary Fiber and DM

- Soluble fiber has been shown to
  - Reduce blood glucose levels
  - Lower serum cholesterol values
  - Sometimes reduce insulin requirements
- Fiber appears to slow the rate of absorption of sugar by the digestive tract

- Discuss the pathophysiology of fiber and its effect on glucose levels.

Slide 44

Safety Alert

- Instruct the patient and family to read food labels carefully
  - The word *dietetic* does not mean *diabetic*
  - Dietetic merely means something has been changed or replaced
    - For example, the food may contain less salt or less sugar

Introduction to Maternity & Pediatric Nursing, 6th ed.

Leifer

Slide 45

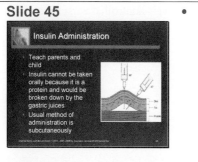

- Discuss how insulin is absorbed if accidentally administered in the muscle.

Slide 46

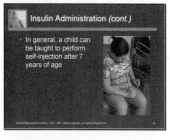

- Discuss insulin pumps and how effective they are at controlling blood glucose levels.

Slide 47

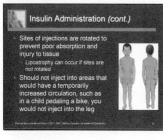

- What is the importance of site rotation?

Slide 48

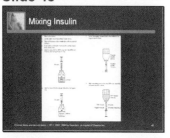

- Refer to Figure 30-8 on page 722.
- Discuss the importance of withdrawing regular insulin before the long-acting insulin.

Slide 49

- Discuss the nurse's role in monitoring the patient who is on different types of insulin.

Leifer

Slide 50

Insulin Shock

- Also known as *hypoglycemia*
- Blood glucose level becomes abnormally low
- Caused by *too much* insulin
- Factors
  - Poorly planned exercise
  - Reduced diet
  - Errors made because of improper knowledge of insulin and the insulin syringe

- Give an example of a situation in which a child with DM experiences hypoglycemia due to exercise.

Slide 51

Insulin Shock *(cont.)*

- Children are more prone to insulin reactions than adults because
  - The condition itself is more unstable in young people
  - They are growing
  - Their activities are more irregular
- Symptoms of insulin reaction
  - Irritable
  - May behave poorly
  - Pale
- May complain of feeling hungry and weak
- Sweating occurs
- CNS symptoms arise because glucose is vital to proper functioning of nerves

Slide 52

Insulin Shock *(cont.)*

- Immediate treatment
  - Administering sugar in some form, such as orange juice, hard candy, or a commercial product
  - Begins to feel better within a few minutes and then may eat a small amount of protein or starch to prevent another reaction
  - Glucagon is recommended in cases of severe hypoglycemia

Slide 53

Somogyi Phenomenon

- Rebound hyperglycemia
- Blood glucose levels are lowered to a point at which the body's counter-regulatory hormones (epinephrine, cortisol, glucagon) are released
- Glucose is released from muscle and liver cells which leads to a rapid rise in blood glucose levels

- Discuss the increased incidence of Somogyi phenomenon during the night.

Slide 54

Somogyi Phenomenon *(cont.)*

- Generally the result of chronic insulin use, especially in patients who required fairly large doses of insulin to regulate their blood sugars
- Hypoglycemia during the night and high glucose levels in the morning are suggestive of the phenomenon
- Child may need less insulin, not more, to rectify the problem

Slide 55

> **Somogyi Phenomenon** *(cont.)*
>
> · Differs from the *dawn phenomenon* in which early morning elevations of blood glucose occur *without* preceding hypoglycemia but may be a response to growth hormone secretion that occurs in the early morning hours
> · Together the Somogyi and dawn phenomena are the most common causes of instability in diabetic children

Slide 56

> **Type 2 Diabetes Mellitus (DM)**
>
> · Thought to be precipitated by
>   -- Obesity
>   -- Low physical activity
>   -- Lipid-rich diet resulting in insulin resistance
> · Diet is main emphasis of management along with exercise and other weight control measures
> · Insulin, oral hypoglycemic medications contribute to stable control of blood glucose level

- Discuss the increased incidence of type 2 DM in children in the United States.
- Discuss the role of diet and exercise in controlling this disease.

Slide 57

> **Question for Review**
>
> · What is the difference between a blood glucose level and an HgbA$_{1c}$ level, as seen in the lab report of a child with diabetes mellitus?

Slide 58

> **Review**
>
> · Objectives
> · Key Terms
> · Key Points
> · Online Resources
> · Review Questions

TEACHING FOCUS

This chapter introduces students to the common characteristics of communicable diseases, as well as detection and principles in the prevention of those diseases. Students have the opportunity to become familiar with national and international immunization programs and the nurse's role in the immunization of children. Students also have the opportunity to formulate nursing care plans and patient and parent teaching plans.

MATERIALS AND RESOURCES

☐ Computer and PowerPoint projector (all lessons)
☐ Sample consent forms, immunization education brochures, and immunization schedules (Lesson 32.2)

LESSON CHECKLIST

Preparations for this lesson include:

- Lecture
- Guest speaker: Community health professional experienced in working with patients who have STIs and HIV/AIDS
- Evaluation of student knowledge and skills needed to perform all entry-level nursing activities related to the child with a communicable disease, including:
  ○ Characteristics of communicable diseases
  ○ Detection and prevention of communicable diseases
  ○ Immunization programs, including the nurse's role
  ○ Nursing plans and patient education

KEY TERMS

acquired immunity (p. 731)
active immunity (p. 732)
body substance (p. 731)
communicable disease (p. 731)
endemic (p. 731)
epidemic (p. 731)
erythema (p. 733)
fomite (p. 731)
health care–associated
    infection (p. 731)
incubation period (p. 731)

macule (p. 733)
natural immunity (p. 731)
opportunistic infections
    (p. 731)
pandemic (p. 731)
papule (p. 733)
passive immunity (p. 732)
pathogens (p. 731)
pathognomonic (p. 733)
portal of entry (p. 731)
portal of exit (p. 731)

prodromal period (p. 731)
pustule (p. 733)
reservoir for infection (p. 731)
scab (p. 733)
standard precautions (p. 732)
transmission-based precautions
    (p. 732)
vector (p. 731)
vesicle (p. 733)

ADDITIONAL RESOURCES

TEACH PPT slide(s) Chapter 32, 1-46
EILR IC image(s) Chapter 32, 1-7
EILR OBQ question(s) Chapter 32, 1-10
EILR TB question(s) Chapter 32, 1-29
ESLR IRQ question(s) Chapter 32, 1-5
SG Chapter 32, pp. 261-265

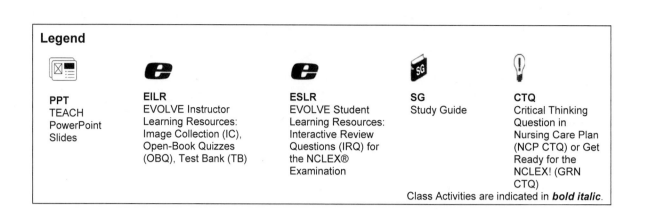

Legend

PPT
TEACH
PowerPoint
Slides

EILR
EVOLVE Instructor
Learning Resources:
Image Collection (IC),
Open-Book Quizzes
(OBQ), Test Bank (TB)

ESLR
EVOLVE Student
Learning Resources:
Interactive Review
Questions (IRQ) for
the NCLEX®
Examination

SG
Study Guide

CTQ
Critical Thinking
Question in
Nursing Care Plan
(NCP CTQ) or Get
Ready for the
NCLEX! (GRN
CTQ)

Class Activities are indicated in **_bold italic_**.

LESSON 32.1

PRETEST

1. The prodromal period of infection refers to the
   a. invasion of a pathogen.
   b. route of entry for the pathogen.
   c. initial disease stage when early symptoms appear.
   d. sudden increase in communicable disease.

2. What is a basic essential factor in the prevention of a communicable disease?
   a. use of negative-pressure rooms
   b. identification of high-risk patients
   c. proper hand hygiene
   d. autoclave sterilization

3. An elevated circular reddened area without fluid is referred to as a
   a. papule.
   b. vesicle.
   c. scab.
   d. pustule.

4. Which of the following can reduce pain at the injection site during vaccination?
   a. thimerosal
   b. acetaminophen
   c. EMLA cream
   d. epinephrine

5. Who should be notified immediately if a biological agent used as a weapon is recognized?
   a. hospital security department
   b. hospital infection control and CDC
   c. local police department
   d. news media

6. How should the varicella vaccine be stored?
   a. inside a refrigerator door compartment
   b. at room temperature
   c. in the refrigerator at 35° to 46° F
   d. in the freezer at −15° C (5° F) or lower

7. Standard infection control precautions should be observed for
   a. all patients.
   b. patients with weeping wounds.
   c. patients with compromised immune systems.
   d. patients with chickenpox.

8. A positive Mantoux intradermal PPD skin test indicates susceptibility to
   a. scarlet fever.
   b. diphtheria.
   c. tuberculosis.
   d. HIV.

9. Administration of a tetanus serum provides
   a. active immunity.
   b. passive immunity.
   c. natural immunity.
   d. inherited immunity.

10. An infection acquired in a health care setting is referred to as a(n)
    a. health care–acquired infection.
    b. chain of infection.
    c. opportunistic infection.
    d. reservoir for infection.

Answers

1. c	3. a	5. b	7. a	9. b
2. c	4. c	6. d	8. c	10. a

BACKGROUND ASSESSMENT

Question: What are the various roles nurses can play in immunizing children?

Answer: Educating the public about the value of immunizations is an important nursing role. Nurses also ensure proper storage and administration procedures for a wide variety of vaccines. During well-child visits, the nurse verifies the recommended vaccination schedule and immunization status. The nurse also identifies any contraindications, such as altered immune status, allergy, pregnancy, or active infection, and in addition, assesses for adverse reactions. The nurse provides patient and parent education and also documents and confirms parental consent.

Question: How do infants or children contract the human immunodeficiency virus (HIV)?
Answer: HIV is transmitted via body secretions such as blood, sexual fluids, breast milk, and saliva. Mothers infected with HIV can transmit the virus to their newborns at birth or by breastfeeding. Children can contract the virus through sexual contact with an infected carrier, intravenous drug use, or blood transfusions, although this method of transmission has been greatly reduced. Casual contact, such as going to school or living with an infected person, does not transmit the virus. Education regarding disease transmission and hygiene practices is an important nursing function in the prevention of HIV. Awareness of the clinical manifestations of HIV infection assists in early identification and intervention to slow the progression of infections associated with AIDS.

CRITICAL THINKING QUESTION

A mother tells the clinic nurse that her child was sent home from kindergarten due to a facial rash that the teacher thinks might be fifth disease. The mother wants to know if the condition is serious and if the child should be kept away from others. How does the nurse respond?

Guidelines: Fifth disease, also known as *erythema infectiosum*, is a contagious viral disease caused by the human parvovirus B19 (PV-B19) and is common among children. The virus causes a red rash on the face that looks like a slapped cheek, which can spread to the trunk and arms. Transmission occurs by respiratory secretions, so the child's classmates may have been exposed to it during the incubation period. Because the rash has already appeared, however, the child is no longer contagious, so it is unnecessary to keep the child away from school. Reassure the mother that fifth disease is a common, benign childhood illness that usually runs its course without complications. Encourage the mother to verify that classroom objects such as doorknobs, toys, and tabletops are disinfected regularly to help prevent the spread of a variety of infections transmitted in the same way as PV-B19

OBJECTIVES	CONTENT	TEACHING RESOURCES
Discuss the characteristics of common childhood communicable diseases.	■ Introduction (p. 727) ☐ Common childhood communicable diseases (p. 727) ☐ Review of terms (p. 731)	⊠▪ PPT slides 4-6 *e* EILR IC images 1-4 *e* EILR OBQ questions 1, 3, 4 *e* EILR TB questions 6, 7, 11, 16, 17, 19, 28, 29 *e* ESLR IRQ question 5 SG Learning Activities, questions 1, 2-7, 18 (pp. 261-263) SG Review Questions, questions 1-3, 5, 6, 9, 11 (pp. 264-265) **BOOK RESOURCES** Health Promotion, Communicable Diseases of Childhood (pp. 728-731) Figure 32-1, Chickenpox (p. 731) Figure 32-2, German Measles (p. 731) Figure 32-3, Measles (p. 731) Figure 32-4, The chain of infection (p. 732) ▸ Discuss the incidence of various communicable childhood diseases in the United States and worldwide today and in the past.

OBJECTIVES	CONTENT	TEACHING RESOURCES
		Class Activity **Divide the class into groups and assign each group one of the following lists of communicable diseases:**
		1. *Varicella (chickenpox), variola (smallpox), Rubella (German measles), rubeola, fifth disease, and roseola*
		2. *Mumps, pertussis (whooping cough), and polio*
		3. *Infectious mononucleosis, hepatitis A, hepatitis B, and Lyme disease*
		4. *Tuberculosis, diphtheria, and scarlet fever*
		Ask each group to make a brief report about its diseases' causes, signs and symptoms, incubation periods, prevention/treatment, and how long each disease is contagious. Students should note any common factors, important differences, or key points as appropriate for each disease. What nursing assessments and interventions are appropriate? Students may refer to Health Promotion, Communicable Diseases of Childhood (pp. 729-732).
		Class Activity **Lead a discussion in which students explain why infants and children are at greater risk of infection than adults are. Students should incorporate what they learned from the previous Class Activity. Are children more liable to contract a communicable disease at specific times of the year? If so, which diseases, and why? What parent education is important in reducing exposure and reducing the spread of infection?**
Interpret the detection and prevention of common childhood communicable diseases.	■ Host resistance (p. 732) □ Types of immunity (p. 732) □ Transmission of infection (p. 732)	PPT slides 7-9 *e* EILR IC image 4 *e* EILR OBQ question 4 *e* EILR TB questions 1, 23 SG Learning Activities, questions 11-13 (p. 262) **BOOK RESOURCES** Figure 32-4, The Chain of Infection (p. 732) ▸ Discuss natural and acquired resistance to infection. ▸ Discuss ways in which infections can be transmitted. How can a person be a carrier of a disease but not ever be sick or show symptoms? *Class Activity* **Provide students with the following list of terms and, with books closed, have them place them in the chain of infection:**

OBJECTIVES	CONTENT	TEACHING RESOURCES
		– *mode of transmission*
		– *causative agent*
		– *reservoir*
		– *portal of exit*
		– *susceptible host*
		– *portal of entry*
		Ask a student volunteer to diagram a linked chain on the board with each term located in its appropriate place, based on student responses. Correct assignments as needed.
		Class Activity *Using the previous Class Activity and Figure 32-4 (p. 733), ask students to describe the progression of the following diseases around the linked chain: measles, polio, infectious mononucleosis, and Lyme disease. At which points in the chain can parents and health professionals detect and prevent each disease, in effect, breaking a link? What role can the nurse play in patient and parent education?*
		Class Activity *Ask students to research the person known as "Typhoid Mary" and make a brief report to the class. Would her case be handled in the same way today as it was a century ago? (For students to prepare for this activity, refer to Homework/Assignments #1).*

32.1 Homework/Assignments:

1. Ask students to research the person "Typhoid Mary" and make a brief report to the class. Would her case be handled in the same way today as it was a century ago?

32.1 Instructor's Notes/Student Feedback:

LESSON 32.2

CRITICAL THINKING QUESTION

The mother of a 2-year-old child asks the nurse administering influenza vaccine at a community health fair if a person can actually contract the flu from the vaccine itself. The mother is concerned because she cares for other children in her home and wants to protect herself and her toddler. The mother states that she herself has no known allergies but says the child is allergic to peanuts, eggs, and dairy products. How should the nurse respond? Should the nurse administer the vaccine to the mother and child?

Guidelines: The nurse should explain that the influenza vaccine consists of an inactivated, or killed, form of the virus. The inactivated form does not transmit infection but it does stimulate the person's immune system to make protective antibodies against the virus. The mother may be immunized, but the child should not be, due to the allergy to eggs. This is because the flu vaccine is made with egg proteins and is contraindicated for those who have an allergy to eggs. Flu vaccine also is contraindicated for those allergic to thimerosal, a preservative used in the vaccine.

OBJECTIVES	CONTENT	TEACHING RESOURCES
Discuss three principles involved in standard precautions used to prevent the transmission of communicable diseases to children.	■ Medical asepsis, standard precautions, and transmission-based precautions (p. 733) ☐ Protective environment isolation (p. 733) ☐ Hand hygiene (p. 733) ☐ Family education (p. 734) ■ Rashes (p. 734)	PPT slides 10-19 𝑒 EILR OBQ questions 2, 5 𝑒 EILR TB questions 3, 5, 12, 13, 20, 25 𝑒 ESLR IRQ question 1 SG Learning Activities, questions 1, 8, 14-17 (pp. 261-263) SG Review Questions, questions 4, 7, 8, 10 (pp. 264-265) **BOOK RESOURCES** Safety Alerts (p. 733) Nursing Tip (p. 734) Review Questions for the NCLEX® Examination, question 3 (p. 746) Appendix A: Standard Precautions and Body Substance Precautions (p. 771) ▸ Discuss why strict adherence to aseptic techniques is important in reducing the spread of communicable diseases. Compare and contrast standard, large droplet infection, airborne infection, and contact precautions. ▸ Discuss what each of the following terms for various rashes signifies: macule, papule, erythema, vesicle, pustule, scab, and pathognomonic. How can the name and description be used to diagnose diseases? *Class Activity **Provide students with this clinical situation: An adolescent girl is following a regimen of immunosuppressant therapy following a lung transplant. Lead a discussion in which students answer the following***

OBJECTIVES	CONTENT	TEACHING RESOURCES
		questions: *1. **What type of isolation precautions are indicated?*** *2. **How does standard isolation compare and contrast to protective isolation?*** *3. **What diagnoses would indicate the need for protective isolation?*** *4. **What are developmental or psychosocial challenges related to protective isolation this patient may face?*** *5. **What nursing procedures and interventions are needed for this patient?*** *6. **What is the nurse's role in patient education and parent education?***
Discuss the national and international immunization programs.	■ Worldwide immunization programs (p. 734) □ *Healthy People 2020* (p. 734)	PPT slide 20 *e* EILR TB question 2 **BOOK RESOURCES** Table 32-1, Types of Immunization Agents (p. 734) ▶ Discuss ways in which the United States government and international immunization programs expect to reduce the incidence of communicable diseases. How does air travel affect disease transmission? *Class Activity Ask students to research CDC and WHO recommendations regarding vaccinations. How are the recommendations alike or different? How do the vaccination rates compare for the United States and other countries? What are funding sources for vaccination programs? Students should make a brief report to the class. (For students to prepare for this activity, see Homework/Assignments #1).*
Describe the nurse's role in the immunization of children.	□ The nurse's role (p. 735) – Vaccines (p. 735) – Routes of administration (p. 735) – Storage and handling (p. 735) – Emergency preparedness (p. 736) – Allergies and adverse responses	PPT slides 21-36 *e* EILR IC images 5-7 *e* EILR OBQ questions 6-9 *e* EILR TB questions 4, 10, 14, 15, 24, 26, 27 *e* ESLR IRQ questions 2, 4 SG Learning Activities, questions 18-22 (p. 261) SG Review Questions, questions 12-14 (p. 263) SG Thinking Critically, question 1 (p. 263)

OBJECTIVES	CONTENT	TEACHING RESOURCES
	(p. 736) – Refusal of vaccination (p. 736) ☐ Immunization schedule for children (p. 737) ■ The future of immunotherapy (p. 737) ■ Bioterrorism and the pediatric patient (p. 740) ☐ A new type of childhood trauma (p. 740) – Physiological effects (p. 740) – Psychological effects (p. 740) – The Nurse's Role (p. 741) ☐ Initial observation (p. 741) ☐ The pediatric patient in a disaster setting (p. 741)	[SG] SG Applying Knowledge, question 2 (p. 263) **BOOK RESOURCES** Table 32-1, Types of Immunization Agents (p. 734) Nursing Tip (p. 734) Figure 32-5, The "Hug" Restraining Position for Administering Vaccinations (p. 735) Nursing Tip (p. 736) Box 32-1, Changes to the 2010 Vaccine Recommendation Schedules (p. 737) Nursing Tip (p. 737) Figure 32-6, Immunization Schedule for Infants and Children in the United States (p. 738) Figure 32-7 Catch-up Immunization Schedule for Children (p. 739) Table 32-2, Common Diseases that can be Spread Through Bioterrorism (p. 740) Review Questions for the NCLEX® Examination, questions 4, 5 (p. 746) ▶ Discuss the research and development of new vaccines and the potential for effective immunotherapy against autoimmune conditions. ▶ Discuss the potential physiological and psychological effects of bioterrorism on children. Why are children more vulnerable? What is the nurse's role in observation and reporting? *Class Activity **Lead a class discussion in which students identify the various roles the nurse can play in immunizing children against contagious diseases.*** *Class Activity **Bring in sample consent forms, parent education brochures, and immunization cards for contagious childhood diseases. Then, have students role-play a nurse explaining to parents who are reluctant to have their children vaccinated why a routine immunization schedule is important. The parents should ask challenging questions about side effects, contracting the disease, fear of transmission, and discomfort for the child. The nurse may use the sample forms and brochures as appropriate.***

32.2 Homework/Assignments:

1. Ask students to research CDC and WHO recommendations regarding vaccinations. How are the recommendations alike or different? How do the vaccination rates compare for the United States and other countries? What are funding sources for vaccination programs? Students should make a brief report to the class.

32.2 Instructor's Notes/Student Feedback:

LESSON 32.3

CRITICAL THINKING QUESTION

During a required sports physical exam, a 15-year-old boy asks the nurse for an antibiotic to treat what he thinks is a bladder infection. He says it burns when he urinates and that he has noticed some white discharge from his penis. What should the nurse suspect and what further assessment is necessary? What patient education is appropriate?

Guidelines: The symptoms the patient describes are associated with sexually transmitted infections (STIs) such as gonorrhea and Chlamydia, although these infections may be asymptomatic in males. Maintaining a matter-of-fact, nonjudgmental manner, the nurse should attempt to determine the patient's sexual exposure and his understanding of disease transmission and risks. The physician most likely will order a urine test to determine if an infection is present. Provide the patient with information regarding prevalence and transmission of STIs and the importance of notifying partners if he is sexually active. The nurse also should explain treatment methods and ways to prevent future infection. The nurse should explain that sexual abstinence is the only 100% effective method against STI and that all forms of sexual activity can transmit infection. The nurse should advise that if abstinence is not observed, condoms may provide some protection. The nurse should review the correct way to apply a condom and explain that oil-based lubricants, which can degrade the protective barrier, should be avoided. The nurse should also encourage the boy to notify his sexual contacts if an STI is diagnosed.

OBJECTIVES	CONTENT	TEACHING RESOURCES
Demonstrate a teaching plan for preventing sexually transmitted infections (STIs) in an adolescent.	■ Sexually transmitted infections (p. 741) □ Overview (p. 741) □ Nursing care and responsibilities (p. 741)	PPT slides 37-39 EILR TB questions 8, 18, 22 SG Learning Activities, question 23 (p. 263) SG Thinking Critically, question 2 (p. 265) SG Applying Knowledge, question 1 (p. 265) **BOOK RESOURCES** Nursing Tip (p. 741) Table 32-3, Nursing Care to Prevent and Treat Sexually Transmitted Infections (p. 742) Nursing Tip (p. 742) *Class Activity **Invite a community health worker to discuss treatment and prevention of STIs and HIV/AIDS among adolescents. What messages and media are the most persuasive? What are some barriers to success? What role can a nurse play? Ask students to prepare questions in advance.*** *Class Activity **Lead a discussion in which students develop a teaching program about sex education that a community nurse can provide to adolescents in a school or other community environment. What key messages should the program deliver? To what individuals? Which individuals should be involved in the program? What are the legal or ethical considerations in providing sex education?***

OBJECTIVES	CONTENT	TEACHING RESOURCES
Formulate a nursing care plan for a child with acquired immuno-deficiency syndrome (AIDS).	■ Sexually transmitted infections (p. 741) ☐ Overview (p. 741) ☐ Nursing care and responsibilities (p. 741) ☐ HIV/AIDS in children (p. 743)	☒■ PPT slides 40-44 𝒆 EILR OBQ question 10 𝒆 EILR TB questions 9, 21 𝒆 ESLR IRQ question 3 ⬛SG SG Learning Activities, questions 24, 25 (p. 263) **BOOK RESOURCES** Nursing Tip (p. 741) Table 32-3, Nursing Care to Prevent and Treat Sexually Transmitted Infections (p. 742) Nursing Tip (p. 742) Nursing Care Plan 32-1, The Infant with HIV (pp. 744-745) Review Questions for the NCLEX® Examination, questions 1, 2 (p. 746) ▸ Discuss the incidence, pathophysiology, and manifestations of HIV/AIDS in children, the research and development of new vaccines, and the potential for effective immunotherapy against autoimmune conditions. *Class Activity **Divide the class into small groups and ask them to develop a nursing care plan for a school-age child who has HIV/AIDS. Groups should be assigned one of the selected nursing diagnoses listed in Nursing Care Plan 32-1 (pp. 745-746) and apply their plans to an older child. The plans should reflect different types of nursing interventions for a child in earlier and later stages of the illness. Groups should present their plans to the class for feedback and discussion.***
Performance Evaluation		☒■ PPT slides 1-46 𝒆 EILR IC images 1-7 𝒆 EILR OBQ questions 1-10 𝒆 EILR TB questions 1-29 𝒆 ESLR IRQ questions 1-5 ⬛SG SG Learning Activities, questions 1-25 (pp. 261-263) ⬛SG SG Review Questions, questions 1-14 (pp. 264-265) ⬛SG SG Thinking Critically, questions 1-2 (p. 265)

OBJECTIVES	CONTENT	TEACHING RESOURCES
		SG Applying Knowledge, questions 1-2 (p. 265)
		BOOK RESOURCES
		NCP CTQ 1 (p. 745)
		Review Questions for the NCLEX® Examination, questions 1-5 (p. 746)

32.3 Homework/Assignments:

32.3 Instructor's/Student Feedback:

32 Lecture Outline
The Child with a Communicable Disease

Slide 1

Chapter 32

The Child with a
Communicable Disease

Slide 2

Objectives

- Define each key term listed.
- Interpret the detection and prevention of common childhood communicable diseases.
- Discuss the characteristics of common childhood communicable diseases.
- Discuss three principles involved in standard precautions used to prevent the transmission of communicable diseases in children.

Slide 3

Objectives *(cont.)*

- Discuss national and international immunization programs.
- Describe the nurse's role in the immunization of children.
- Demonstrate a teaching plan for preventing sexually transmitted infections (STIs) in an adolescent.
- Formulate a nursing care plan for a child with acquired immunodeficiency syndrome (AIDS).

Slide 4

Communicable Disease

- Prevention and control are the key factors in managing infectious disease
- HIV, hepatitis, TB, and STIs are infections continue to occur worldwide
- The incidence of common childhood communicable disease has decreased with the use of appropriate immunizations
- The nurse must know and be alert to signs and symptoms of communicable disease because air travel enables rapid transmission around the world

- Discuss the impact of increased international mobility and how it impacts communicable diseases.

Leifer

Slide 5

Review of Terms

- Communicable disease—can be transmitted from one person to another
- Incubation period—time between exposure to pathogen and onset of clinical symptoms
- Prodromal period—time between earliest symptom and appearance of typical rash or fever
- Vector—an insect or animal that carries and spreads disease

Slide 6

Review of Terms *(cont.)*

- Pandemic—a worldwide high incidence of a communicable disease; i.e., H1N1 influenza
- Epidemic—sudden increase of disease in localized area
- Endemic—an expected continuous incidence of disease in a localized area
- Opportunistic infection—caused by organism normally present in the environment that the immune-suppressed person cannot fight
- Health care–associated infection—an infection acquired after admission to a health care facility

Slide 7

Virulence of Infection

- Host resistance to disease is influenced by
  - Age
  - Sex
  - Genetic makeup
  - Nutritional status
  - Physical/emotional health
  - Phagocytes in blood to attack/destroy pathogens
  - Intact skin and mucous membranes
  - Functioning immune system

- Discuss how each factor affects the disease process.

Slide 8

Types of Immunity

- Natural—resistance is inborn
- Acquired—not born with it; as a result of having disease or receiving vaccines or immune serum
- Active immunity—when a person produces his or her own immunity
- Passive immunity—provides the antibody to the person; does not last as long

- Give examples of each type of immunity.

Slide 9

Transmission of Infection

- Direct—transmitted by contact with an infected person
- Indirect—transmitted by contact with objects that have been contaminated by an infected person (fomites)

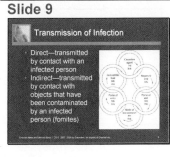

- Discuss Figure 32-4 on page 732.

Slide 10

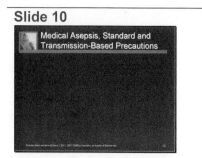

Medical Asepsis, Standard and Transmission-Based Precautions

Slide 11

Preventing the Spread of Infection

- Aseptic technique—used with all patients
- Standard precautions—involve hand hygiene and the use of appropriate personal protective equipment (PPE) based on the tasks to be performed or known infectious disease status of the patient
- Transmission-based precautions—designed according to the method of spread of a specific organism

- Give an example of a nursing intervention that applies to each technique listed.

Slide 12

Airborne Infection Isolation Precautions

- Airborne particles <5 microns in size float in the air and contaminate anything within the room
  - Particles can remain airborne for several hours
  - Used for conditions such as TB and varicella
- Use of negative pressure room and an N95 particulate respirator mask is required whenever in the room with the patient
- N95 mask is removed only upon exiting the room and hand hygiene is performed

- Explain a negative pressure room and types of diseases which require this type of precaution.

Slide 13

Contact Precautions

- When contamination is likely to occur skin to skin or through contact with a contaminated fomite
  - Used in conditions such as RSV, MRSA, VRE, or *Clostridium difficile* infections
- Private room or cohorting of patients with same type of infection is recommended
- Fluid-resistant cover gown and disposable gloves should be donned prior to entering the patient's room and removed upon leaving
- Hand hygiene is required

Slide 14

Droplet Precautions

- Droplets (>5 microns in size) from coughing or sneezing can contaminate surrounding environment up to 3 feet around the patient
  - Droplets do not stay suspended in the air, they immediately "fall"
- Use of a regular mask is required. A cover gown and gloves may also be required such as when caring for a child with RSV
- PPE is removed upon exiting the room and hand hygiene is performed

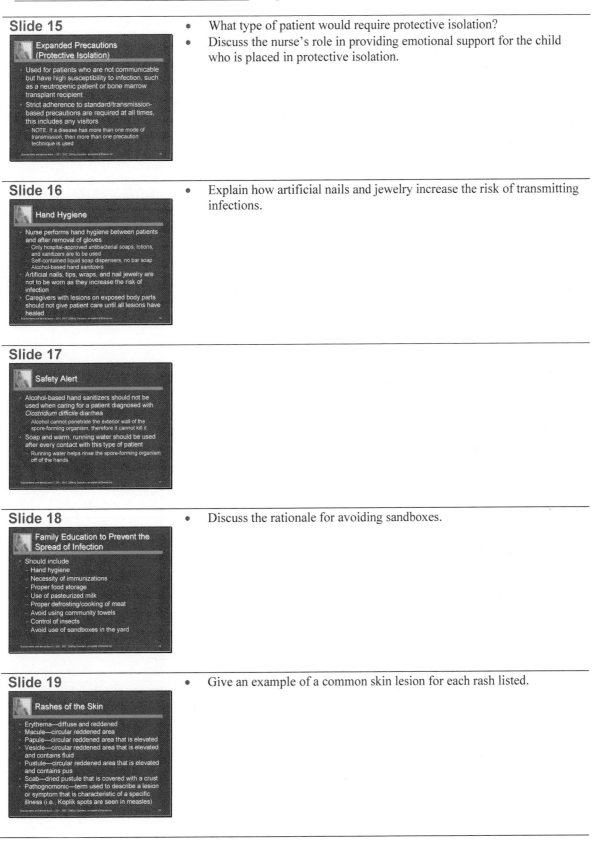

Slide 15

Expanded Precautions
(Protective Isolation)

- Used for patients who are not communicable but have high susceptibility to infection, such as a neutropenic patient or bone marrow transplant recipient
- Strict adherence to standard/transmission-based precautions are required at all times, this includes any visitors
  - NOTE: If a disease has more than one mode of transmission, then more than one precaution technique is used

- What type of patient would require protective isolation?
- Discuss the nurse's role in providing emotional support for the child who is placed in protective isolation.

Slide 16

Hand Hygiene

- Nurse performs hand hygiene between patients and after removal of gloves
  - Only hospital-approved antibacterial soaps, lotions, and sanitizers are to be used
  - Self-contained liquid soap dispensers, no bar soap
  - Alcohol-based hand sanitizers
- Artificial nails, tips, wraps, and nail jewelry are not to be worn as they increase the risk of infection
- Caregivers with lesions on exposed body parts should not give patient care until all lesions have healed

- Explain how artificial nails and jewelry increase the risk of transmitting infections.

Slide 17

Safety Alert

- Alcohol-based hand sanitizers should not be used when caring for a patient diagnosed with *Clostridium difficile* diarrhea
  - Alcohol cannot penetrate the exterior wall of the spore-forming organism, therefore it cannot kill it
- Soap and warm, running water should be used after every contact with this type of patient
  - Running water helps rinse the spore-forming organism off of the hands

Slide 18

Family Education to Prevent the Spread of Infection

- Should include
  - Hand hygiene
  - Necessity of immunizations
  - Proper food storage
  - Use of pasteurized milk
  - Proper defrosting/cooking of meat
  - Avoid using community towels
  - Control of insects
  - Avoid use of sandboxes in the yard

- Discuss the rationale for avoiding sandboxes.

Slide 19

Rashes of the Skin

- Erythema—diffuse and reddened
- Macule—circular reddened area
- Papule—circular reddened area that is elevated
- Vesicle—circular reddened area that is elevated and contains fluid
- Pustule—circular reddened area that is elevated and contains pus
- Scab—dried pustule that is covered with a crust
- Pathognomonic—term used to describe a lesion or symptom that is characteristic of a specific illness (i.e., Koplik spots are seen in measles)

- Give an example of a common skin lesion for each rash listed.

ELSEVIER

Introduction to Maternity & Pediatric Nursing, 6th ed.
Leifer

Elsevier items and derived items © 2011, 2007, 2006 by Saunders, an imprint of Elsevier Inc.

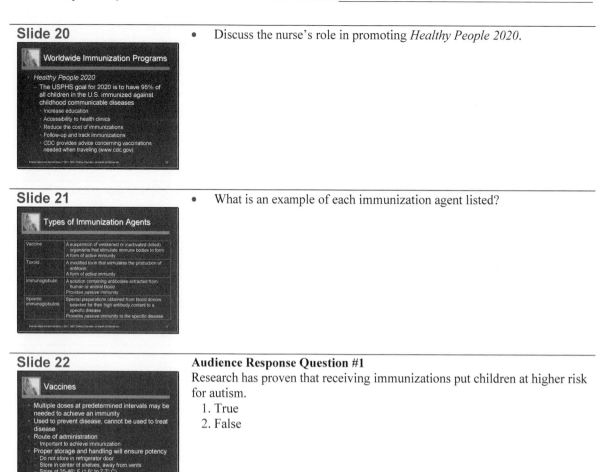

Slide 20

Worldwide Immunization Programs

• Healthy People 2020
 – The USPHS goal for 2020 is to have 95% of all children in the U.S. immunized against childhood communicable diseases
  · Increase education
  · Accessibility to health clinics
  · Reduce the cost of immunizations
  · Follow-up and track immunizations
  · CDC provides advice concerning vaccinations needed when traveling (www.cdc.gov)

• Discuss the nurse's role in promoting *Healthy People 2020*.

Slide 21

Types of Immunization Agents

Vaccine	A suspension of weakened or inactivated (killed) organisms that stimulate immune bodies to form. A form of active immunity
Toxoid	A modified toxin that stimulates the production of antitoxin. A form of active immunity
Immunoglobulin	A solution containing antibodies extracted from human or animal blood. Provides passive immunity
Specific immunoglobulins	Special preparations obtained from blood donors selected for their high antibody content to a specific disease. Provides passive immunity to the specific disease

• What is an example of each immunization agent listed?

Slide 22

Vaccines

• Multiple doses at predetermined intervals may be needed to achieve an immunity
• Used to prevent disease, cannot be used to treat disease
• Route of administration
 – Important to achieve immunization
• Proper storage and handling will ensure potency
 – Do not store in refrigerator door
 – Store in center of shelves, away from vents
 – Store at 35-46° F (1.6° to 7.7° C)

Audience Response Question #1
Research has proven that receiving immunizations put children at higher risk for autism.
   1. True
   2. False

Slide 23

Nursing Tip

• The earliest age a vaccine should be administered is the youngest age at which the infant's body can respond by developing antibodies to that illness

Slide 24

Allergies and Toxicities

• Epinephrine should be available in unit where immunizations are given
• Child should be observed for 20 minutes after immunization
• Do not administer the following vaccines if patient is allergic to
 – Baker's yeast: avoid recombinant hepatitis B vaccine
 – Eggs: avoid influenza vaccine, MMR
 – Neomycin: avoid IPV, MMR, and varicella vaccine

• Discuss the rationale for the immediate availability of epinephrine.
• Why should the child be monitored for 20 minutes post-administration?

Leifer

Slide 25

> **Allergies and Toxicities** *(cont.)*
>
> · Varicella must be given same day as MMR or no less than one month later
> · A tuberculin skin test should not be given within 6 weeks of MMR or varicella
> · Thimerosal: a mercury-containing preservative in some vaccines can cause toxicity
> · Some vaccines can be given on the same day but must be in different syringes and administered in different sites
> · Serious adverse events must be reported to the national VAERS

- Discuss the rationale for each item listed.
- Discuss the purpose of the national VAERS program and its rationale.

Slide 26

> **Contraindications to Immunizations**
>
> · Immunocompromised state
> · Pregnancy (with certain vaccines)
> · Bacteremia or meningitis
> · Immunocompromised caregiver in the home
>   – Requires individual evaluation by the health care provider
> · Corticosteroid therapy
>   – Requires individual evaluation
> · History of high fever or other reaction after previous immunization

- Give a rationale regarding the contraindication for each item listed.

Slide 27

> **Nursing Tip**
>
> · An interrupted vaccination series can usually continue without restarting the entire series

Slide 28

> **The Future of Immunotherapy**
>
> · Refining and combining vaccines continues
> · Transcutaneous immunization through intact skin
> · Recombinant DNA technology is developing vaccines for use with rheumatic fever and malaria
> · Development of RNA and DNA viruses to be used as vectors (carriers) of antigens

Slide 29

> **The Future of Immunotherapy** *(cont.)*
>
> · Development of "gene gun" to blast vaccine through intact skin
> · Development of immunotherapy for non-communicable diseases such as mucosal administration of myelin for multiple sclerosis
> · Development of tumor antigens

- Discuss the impact on your culture of these technological advances.

Slide 30

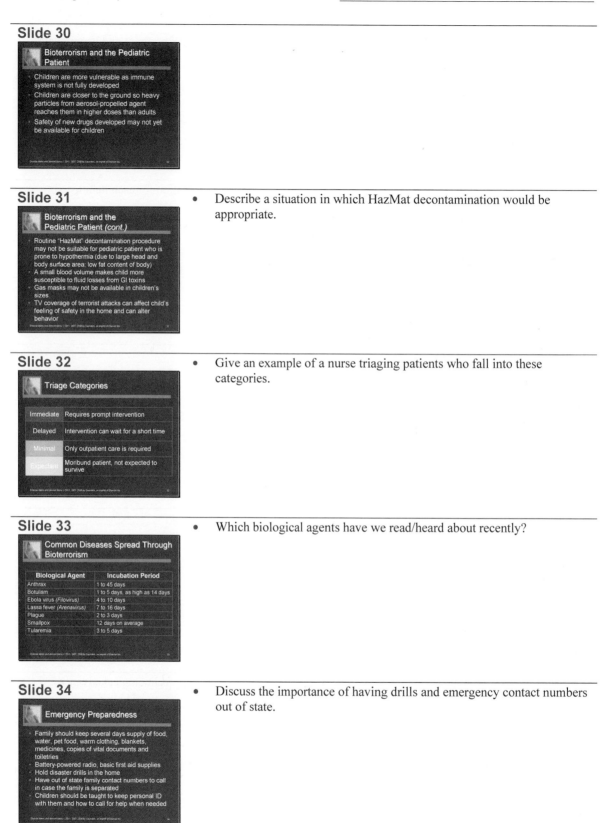

Bioterrorism and the Pediatric Patient

- Children are more vulnerable as immune system is not fully developed
- Children are closer to the ground so heavy particles from aerosol-propelled agent reaches them in higher doses than adults
- Safety of new drugs developed may not yet be available for children

Slide 31

Bioterrorism and the Pediatric Patient *(cont.)*

- Routine "HazMat" decontamination procedure may not be suitable for pediatric patient who is prone to hypothermia (due to large head and body surface area; low fat content of body)
- A small blood volume makes child more susceptible to fluid losses from GI toxins
- Gas masks may not be available in children's sizes
- TV coverage of terrorist attacks can affect child's feeling of safety in the home and can alter behavior

- Describe a situation in which HazMat decontamination would be appropriate.

Slide 32

Triage Categories

Immediate	Requires prompt intervention
Delayed	Intervention can wait for a short time
Minimal	Only outpatient care is required
Expectant	Moribund patient, not expected to survive

- Give an example of a nurse triaging patients who fall into these categories.

Slide 33

Common Diseases Spread Through Bioterrorism

Biological Agent	Incubation Period
Anthrax	1 to 45 days
Botulism	1 to 5 days, as high as 14 days
Ebola virus (Filovirus)	4 to 10 days
Lassa fever (Arenavirus)	7 to 16 days
Plague	2 to 3 days
Smallpox	12 days on average
Tularemia	3 to 5 days

- Which biological agents have we read/heard about recently?

Slide 34

Emergency Preparedness

- Family should keep several days supply of food, water, pet food, warm clothing, blankets, medicines, copies of vital documents and toiletries
- Battery-powered radio, basic first aid supplies
- Hold disaster drills in the home
- Have out of state family contact numbers to call in case the family is separated
- Children should be taught to keep personal ID with them and how to call for help when needed

- Discuss the importance of having drills and emergency contact numbers out of state.

Slide 35

Initial Observations During Disasters

- Assess the "ABCs" and mental status
- Heightened awareness by health care personnel plays critical role in facilitating early recognition of bioterror attack
- Work with emergency department, Infection Control staff, and the local public health department to help coordinate actions that are needed
- NOTE: It is imperative to follow your chain of reporting at your facility

Slide 36

The Pediatric Patient in a Disaster Setting

- Has a proportionately larger body surface area, thinner skin
- May have increased pulmonary problems compared to the adult
- Children are closer to the ground and may be exposed to more toxins
- Immature blood-brain barrier and increased CNS receptor sensitivity increases their sensitivity to nerve agents
- Use of Broselow-Luten color-coded, water-resistant tapes for drug calculations decreases risk of medication errors
- Can also use the Pediatric Antidotes for Chemical Warfare for dosage calculations

Slide 37

Sexually Transmitted Infections

- Infections spread through sexual activity
- Can be spread from pregnant mother to fetus
- Can be spread through sexual abuse of child
- Can be spread by use of contaminated needles or exposure to blood
- Nurse required to report STIs to the local Public Health Department
- Contacts of infected person will also need to be tested

Audience Response Question #2

Nurses who wish to help adolescents with STIs:
  1. need to include their parents.
  2. should let the adolescent guide the discussion.
  3. need to provide emotional support
  4. provide birth control information.

Slide 38

Nursing Care and Responsibilities

- Create environment where patient feels safe and at ease
- Listen, be nonjudgmental, and provide emotional support
- Provide privacy during examinations
- Encourage questions
- Assure confidentiality
- Assess level of knowledge and understanding
- Help patient formulate positive self-attitude

- Give an example of a nurse providing a safe, nonjudgmental environment.
- How can the nurse assist the child in formulating a positive self-attitude?

Slide 39

Nursing Tip

- Sex education is not limited to mechanics of intercourse, but rather includes the feelings involved in sexual experience, expectations, fantasies, fulfillments, and disappointments

Slide 40

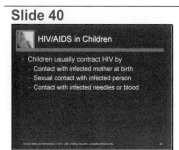

- Give examples of how a child might come in contact with infected needles or blood.

Slide 41

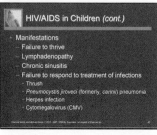

Slide 42

Slide 43

Slide 44

- What are some examples of supportive treatment?
- Give examples of resources available within a community.

Slide 45

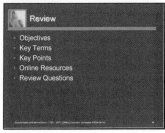

Question for Review

- What type of immunity is given to infants and children through routine vaccinations for common childhood communicable disease?

Slide 46

Review

- Objectives
- Key Terms
- Key Points
- Online Resources
- Review Questions

33 The Child with an Emotional or Behavioral Condition

TEACHING FOCUS

In this chapter, students will be introduced to the terms for various kinds of mental health disorders and the criteria for referring a patient for mental health services. Students will review the impact of early childhood experiences on their emotional and personality development. Students will have the opportunity to identify children and adolescents at risk for suicide and to learn about immediate and long-term interventions. Students will have the opportunity to learn about the diagnostic symptoms of disorders affecting children and adolescents, including attention deficit-hyperactivity disorder, eating disorders, and alcohol and substance abuse.

MATERIALS AND RESOURCES

- ☐ Computer and PowerPoint projector (all lessons)
- ☐ List of commonly abused drugs (Lesson 33.2)
- ☐ Magazines targeted at adolescent girls and boys (Lesson 33.2)
- ☐ Photocopy of Box 33-1, Summary of Disorders Usually First Evident in Infancy, Childhood, and Adolescence (Lesson 33.1)

LESSON CHECKLIST

Preparations for this lesson include:

- Lecture
- Guest speakers: Psychiatric clinical nurse specialist; educator with training in teaching children with ADHD
- Evaluation of student knowledge and skills needed to perform all entry-level activities related to the child with an emotional or behavioral condition, including:
  - ○ Understanding the causes of behavioral disorders, including the effect of early childhood experiences on adult life
  - ○ Understanding different types of behavioral disorders and their manifestations, treatment, and prognosis
  - ○ Identifying nursing interventions and implementing a nursing care plan for behavioral disorders

KEY TERMS

art therapy (p. 748)
behavior modification (p. 748)
bibliotherapy (p. 748)

Diagnostic and Statistical Manual of Mental Disorders (DSM-IV-TR) (p. 747)
dysfunctional (p. 748)
family therapy (p. 748)

intervention (p. 748)
milieu therapy (p. 748)
play therapy (p. 748)
psychosomatic (p. 748)
recreation therapy (p. 748)
sibling rivalry (p. 758)

ADDITIONAL RESOURCES

TEACH PPT slide(s) Chapter 33, 1-51
EILR IC image(s) Chapter 33, 1-3
EILR OBQ question(s) Chapter 33, 1-10
EILR TB question(s) Chapter 33, 1-29
ESLR IRQ question(s) Chapter 33, 1-5
SG Chapter 33, pp. 267-272

Legend

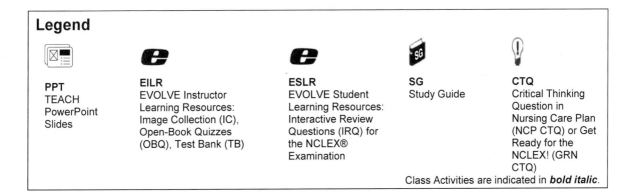

PPT
TEACH
PowerPoint
Slides

EILR
EVOLVE Instructor
Learning Resources:
Image Collection (IC),
Open-Book Quizzes
(OBQ), Test Bank (TB)

ESLR
EVOLVE Student
Learning Resources:
Interactive Review
Questions (IRQ) for
the NCLEX®
Examination

SG
Study Guide

CTQ
Critical Thinking
Question in
Nursing Care Plan
(NCP CTQ) or Get
Ready for the
NCLEX! (GRN
CTQ)

Class Activities are indicated in ***bold italic***.

PRETEST

1. Therapy that uses stories depicting children in situations similar to the patient's is called
   - a. milieu therapy.
   - b. bibliotherapy.
   - c. behavior modification.
   - d. family therapy.

2. Abusers of which drug place the user at risk for HIV or hepatitis infection?
   - a. marijuana
   - b. heroin
   - c. gateway substances
   - d. alcohol

3. An example of receptive language skills is
   - a. expression of ideas.
   - b. differentiating words that sound alike.
   - c. remembering personal information.
   - d. listening and comprehension.

4. Which of the following is part of the diagnostic criteria for ADHD?
   - a. symptoms initially occur after age 7
   - b. symptoms last less than 6 months
   - c. symptoms are linked to additional central nervous system disorders
   - d. symptoms include inattention, hyperactivity, impulsivity, and distractibility

5. A recommended strategy for managing ADHD in the classroom is
   - a. limiting teacher instructions to reduce confusion.
   - b. reminding the child to refocus his or her attention.
   - c. seating the child in the rear of the classroom.
   - d. curtailing school breaks to reduce distraction.

6. Which physical symptom is associated with anorexia nervosa?
   - a. dry skin
   - b. heavy, frequent menstruation
   - c. heat intolerance
   - d. diarrhea

7. Use of laxatives in bulimia can lead to what type of serious side effect?
   - a. paralysis
   - b. suicide
   - c. electrolyte imbalance
   - d. erosion of tooth enamel

8. The most prevalent emotional and behavioral disorder among American adolescents is
   - a. substance abuse.
   - b. depression.
   - c. bulimia.
   - d. obsessive-compulsive disorder.

9. A craving or compulsion to use a chemical substance is referred to as
   - a. tolerance.
   - b. psychological dependence.
   - c. physical dependence.
   - d. experimentation.

10. When caring for an adolescent who threatens suicide, the appropriate nursing intervention is to
    - a. take any threat seriously.
    - b. point out the adolescent's irrational thought process.
    - c. understand this is expected impulsive behavior.
    - d. minimize the threat to avoid the stigma associated with depression.

Answers

| 1. b | 3. d | 5. b | 7. c | 9. b |
| 2. b | 4. d | 6. a | 8. a | 10. a |

BACKGROUND ASSESSMENT

Question: What are the different types and settings of psychiatric treatment for children or adolescents with emotional or behavioral disorders?

Answer: Psychiatric treatment can be provided in several settings, including inpatient hospital settings, residential treatment settings, partial hospitalization treatment settings, and outpatient locations, depending on the child's or adolescent's specific needs. Each setting provides services for diagnostic and treatment interventions. Treatment interventions include individual, family, and group therapy from a cognitive behavioral approach, milieu therapy, play therapy, and art therapy. Creating an emotionally safe environment for children or adolescents and their families is paramount.

Question: What is the role of the nurse in caring for a child or adolescent with an emotional or behavioral condition?

Answer: Facilitating communication, assessing and documenting specific changes in mood and behaviors, and providing resources for mental health services are roles of the nurse working with children and adolescents with emotional or behavioral disorders. Nurses advocate for the welfare and protection of children by supporting organizations devoted to children's interests and by staying abreast of legal regulations that affect children and adolescents. Supporting parents or other family members is also a nursing role for all families. Avoiding confrontation or judgment is essential to initiate treatment, build trust, and provide security for the child. The ongoing contact a nurse has with children and their families as well as the nurse's training in assessment, therapeutic communication, anticipatory guidance, and growth and development, enable the nurse to identify at-risk children and families. Facilitating prompt treatment is critical.

CRITICAL THINKING QUESTION

The single mother of an 8-year-old boy brings her son to the clinic for an annual physical examination. She asks if he should be put on Ritalin because of increasing problems at school. According to the boy's teacher, he is fidgety during class and easily distracted from his work, and often instigates other children to talk and misbehave. The boy's grades have declined since he switched schools during the last school year. The boy's mother explains that she "can't keep taking time off from her job to discuss her son's behavioral problems at school." Is Ritalin an appropriate intervention for this child?

Guidelines: Although this child exhibits some of the symptoms associated with attention deficit-hyperactivity disorder (ADHD) such as impulsivity and inattention, he does not meet the DSM-IV criteria for diagnosis which stipulates symptoms should: (1) begin before age 7 years; (2) last longer than 6 months; and (3) be unrelated to a preexisting central nervous system illness. Based on the nurse's health history and data assessment, this child does not meet these criteria. The recent move and change in school settings, however, could be contributing factors to his difficulties at school and should be explored with his family and teacher. Emphasizing the child's strengths and how those attributes can help him improve his attention and remain focused in school is helpful. Notify the child's pediatrician about the mother's concerns. Explain that stress can cause a temporary change in a child's school performance. A referral to a family counselor may be appropriate to assist him and his mother in adjusting to the stress involved in moving, new experiences, and single parenthood. In addition, psychological testing can be completed to assist in the diagnosis of any emotional, behavioral, or learning disabilities that may be a factor.

OBJECTIVES	CONTENT	TEACHING RESOURCES
Differentiate among the following terms: *psychiatrist, psychoanalyst, clinical psychologist,* and *counselor.*	■ The nurse's role (p. 747) ■ Types and settings of treatment (p. 748)	⊠ PPT slides 5-9 𝒆 EILR OBQ question 1 𝒆 EILR TB questions 15, 16, 24, 25, 29 𝒆 ESLR IRQ questions 1, 2 📖 SG Learning Activities, questions 1-3 (p. 267) **BOOK RESOURCES**

OBJECTIVES	CONTENT	TEACHING RESOURCES
		Nursing Tip (p. 748) ▸ Discuss the ways nurses can assess a child or adolescent's behavior, including child-parent interactions. *Class Activity Have a student create a table that differentiates the educational background, clinical training, and treatment roles of the psychiatrist, psychoanalyst, clinical psychologist, social worker, and counselor.* *Class Activity Invite a psychiatric clinical nurse specialist to the class to discuss his or her educational background, scope of practice, and work settings. Allow time for students to ask questions.*
Discuss the impact of early childhood experience on a person's adult life.	■ Origins of emotional and behavioral conditions (p. 748)	PPT slide 10 *e* EILR TB questions 19, 28 **BOOK RESOURCES** Box 33-1, Summary of Disorders Usually First Evident in Infancy, Childhood, and Adolescence (p. 749) ▸ Discuss the nurse's role in the assessment of risk factors for emotional and behavioral conditions. *Class Activity Have students explain how genetics, family pattern disruption, and abuse might affect a child's emotional and personality development. What mental health disorders are suspected of having a genetic link?* *Class Activity Provide the students with a photocopy of Box 33-1, Summary of Disorders Usually First Evident in Infancy, Childhood, and Adolescence (p. 751). Assign specific disorders to designated students. For each disorder, have a student identify etiology assessment findings and related nursing interventions.*
Discuss the effect of childhood autism on growth and development.	■ Organic behavioral disorders (p. 749) ☐ Childhood autism (p. 749)	PPT slides 11, 12 *e* EILR OBQ question 2 *e* EILR TB questions 11, 12, 17 SG Learning Activities, questions 4-6 (p. 267) SG Case Study, question 1 (p. 272) ▸ Discuss nursing interventions for helping parents to accept the need for mental health services. *Class Activity Divide the class into two groups. Have one group identify five criteria that indicate the need to refer a child for mental health services. Ask the other*

OBJECTIVES	CONTENT	TEACHING RESOURCES
		group to compile a list of mental health agencies and services available in a specific demographic area.
Discuss behavioral treatments and how they are applied to obsessive-compulsive disorders and depression in children.	☐ Obsessive-compulsive disorders in children (p. 749) ■ Environmental or biochemical behavioral disorders (p. 750) ☐ Depression (p. 750)	⊠▀ PPT slides 13-18 🅮 EILR TB question 9 🆂🅶 SG Learning Activities, question 7 (p. 267) 🆂🅶 SG Applying Knowledge, questions 1, 2 (p. 272) **BOOK RESOURCES** Nursing Care Plan 33-1, The Depressed Adolescent (pp. 751-752) Review Questions for the NCLEX® Examination, question 5 (p. 759) *Class Activity Assign each student a specific psychiatric disorder. Have students research the specific psychiatric disorder as assigned, including the diagnostic criteria from DSM-IV. Have students create a case presentation meeting the criteria. Have each student present his or her findings to the class. (For students to prepare for this activity, see Homework/Assignments #1.)*
List the symptoms of potential suicide in children and adolescents.	■ Environmental or biochemical behavioral disorders (p. 750) ☐ Depression (p. 750) ☐ Suicide (p. 750)	⊠▀ PPT slides 15-22 🅮 EILR OBQ questions 3, 4 🅮 EILR TB questions 2, 4, 5 🆂🅶 SG Learning Activities, questions 1, 8-11 (pp. 267-268) 🆂🅶 SG Review Questions, questions 1, 7, 8 (pp. 270-271) **BOOK RESOURCES** Safety Alert (p. 750) Nursing Tip (p. 750) Nursing Care Plan 33-1, The Depressed Adolescent (pp. 751-752) ▶ Discuss the use of empathy and active listening skills with an adolescent patient who expresses feelings of hopelessness and worthlessness. *Class Activity Ask students to identify the symptoms of depression and probable causes of this disorder. Include the progression of symptoms that may lead to suicidal ideation. Then, as a class, discuss child and*

OBJECTIVES	CONTENT	TEACHING RESOURCES
		adolescent suicide, its prevalence, and nursing interventions.
Discuss immediate and long-range plans for the suicidal patient.	☐ Suicide (p. 750)	SG Review Questions, question 7 (pp. 271) ▸ Discuss the nurse's role in educating the parents of a suicidal child or adolescent. *Class Activity **Divide the class into small groups, and ask students to identify the nursing interventions for the treatment of an adolescent patient with suicidal ideation with plan and intent.***

33.1 Homework/Assignments:
1. Assign each student a specific psychiatric disorder. Have students research the specific psychiatric disorder as assigned, including the diagnostic criteria from DSM-IV. Have students create a case presentation meeting the criteria. Have each student present his or her findings to the class.

33.1 Instructor's Notes/Student Feedback:

LESSON 33.2

CRITICAL THINKING QUESTION

A student at a middle school was suspended from school after being caught "huffing" paints in the art studio. During a meeting with the school nurse, the child's parents explain that they feel the suspension was unwarranted because their son's behavior is typical "kids will be kids stuff." What information should the nurse provide the parents to involve them in adequately addressing the child's behavior?

Guidelines: The nurse should introduce the parents to the concept of "gateway substances," which are common household chemicals such as paint, glue, or alcohol that can be abused. Although these are legal substances, using them to achieve a sense of euphoria or altered consciousness can lead to abuse of more lethal drugs—hence the term "gateway." Early identification of drug abuse is crucial for identifying the problem underlying the child's behavior. Although experimentation is a part of adolescent development, it can lead to dependence and should be addressed with involved parenting and school support. Creating a safe and secure environment for effective communication is an important first step. The nurse should provide the parents with statistics regarding adolescent drug abuse and related problems such as accidents, failing grades, and law enforcement issues. The nurse should also give the parents information regarding counseling services and arrange for follow-up evaluations.

OBJECTIVES	CONTENT	TEACHING RESOURCES
List four behaviors that may indicate substance abuse.	☐ Substance abuse (p. 750) – Alcohol (p. 751) – Cocaine (p. 752) – Gateway substances (p. 752) – Marijuana (p. 754) – Opiates (p. 754) – Prevention and nursing goals (p. 754)	PPT slides 23-30 *e* EILR IC images 1, 2 *e* EILR OBQ question 5 *e* EILR TB questions 13, 14, 18, 20, 21, 26 *e* ESLR IRQ question 3 SG Learning Activities, questions 1, 12-16 (pp. 267, 269) SG Review Questions, questions 2-6, 9, 10, 15 (pp. 270-272) **BOOK RESOURCES** Figure 33-1, Beer and Cigarettes Used by Young Adolescents Are Considered "Gateway" Substances (p. 752) Table 33-1, Characteristics of Abused Drugs and Their Acute Reactions in Adolescents (p. 753) Table 33-2, Street Names for Commonly Abused Drugs (p. 754) Safety Alert (p. 754) Figure 33-2, Some Defense Patterns of Children of Alcoholics (p. 755) ▸ Discuss ways to determine a patient's level of substance abuse. *Class Activity **Have students identify behaviors that suggest a child or adolescent is abusing drugs.***

OBJECTIVES	CONTENT	TEACHING RESOURCES
		Discuss various types of substance abuse, including chemicals that are commonly abused. *Class Activity Provide students with a list of commonly abused chemicals and ask them to identify their street names, pharmacological names, route, physical and behavioral signs, and complications of abuse.*
Name two programs for members of families of alcoholics.	– Alcohol (p. 751)	PPT slides 31, 32 EILR OBQ question 6 ▸ Discuss the nurse's role in educating the patient and family about alcoholism. *Class Activity Have students research two programs for members of families with alcoholism. Then, have students summarize the services and treatment modalities used by the programs as well as financial fees and types of professionals who run the programs. Have students present their findings to the class. (For students to prepare for this activity, see Homework/Assignments #1.)*
Discuss the problems facing children of alcoholics.	– Children of alcoholics (p. 754)	PPT slides 32 EILR OBQ question 6 EILR TB questions 3, 6 ESLR IRQ question 4 **BOOK RESOURCES** Figure 33-2, Some Defense Patterns of Children of Alcoholics (p. 755) ▸ Discuss appropriate nursing interventions when a patient is identified as the child of an alcoholic. (Refer to Figure 33-2, p. 755) *Class Activity Divide the class into small groups to discuss the characteristics of the following types of coping behavior exhibited by children of alcoholics: flight, fight, perfection, and a super-coper or family savior. Have each group list examples of behavior for each coping mechanism and related behavioral or emotional problems. What are the treatment interventions for these individuals?*
List four symptoms of attention deficit-hyperactivity disorder.	☐ Attention deficit hyperactivity disorder (p. 755)	PPT slides 33-35 EILR OBQ question 7 EILR TB question 1 SG Learning Activities, questions 18, 19 (p. 269)

Leifer

OBJECTIVES	CONTENT	TEACHING RESOURCES
		SG SG Review Questions, questions 13, 14 (pp. 271-272)
		SG SG Thinking Critically, question 1 (p. 272)
		SG SG Applying Knowledge, question 3 (p. 272)
		BOOK RESOURCES
		Nursing Tip (p. 756)
		▶ Discuss the seven areas of learning disabilities that ADHD children may experience.
		▶ Discuss students' personal experiences with family members who have ADHD.
		*Class Activity **Have students identify at least four symptoms associated with ADHD and the DSM-IV diagnostic criteria for the disorder.***
		*Class Activity **Have students discuss medications that are used in the treatment of ADHD, including route of administration, side effects, and other pharmacological information.***
Describe techniques of helping children with attention deficit-hyperactivity disorder to adjust to the school setting.	□ Attention deficit hyperactivity disorder (p. 755)	**e** EILR OBQ question 8
		e EILR TB question 7
		BOOK RESOURCES
		Health Promotion, Strategies for Managing the Child with ADHD in the Classroom (p. 756)
		Review Questions for the NCLEX® Examination, question 4 (p. 759)
		▶ Discuss the nurse's role in educating the family of a child who is diagnosed as ADHD.
		*Class Activity **Invite an educator with training in teaching children with ADHD to discuss successful classroom techniques for children with ADHD.***
		*Class Activity **Have students identify signs of ADHD, and summarize interventions that can be used in the classroom, the home, and the health care environment for children with ADHD.***
Compare and contrast the characteristics of bulimia and anorexia nervosa.	□ Anorexia nervosa (p. 756) □ Bulimia (p. 757) ■ Minimizing the impact of behavioral disorders in children (p. 758)	PPT slides 36-49
		e EILR IC image 3
		e EILR OBQ questions 9, 10
		e EILR TB questions 8, 10, 27

Elsevier items and derived items © 2011, 2007, 2006 by Saunders, an imprint of Elsevier Inc.

OBJECTIVES	CONTENT	TEACHING RESOURCES
	□ Effect of the illness on growth and development (p. 758) □ Effect of the illness on siblings (p. 758)	*e* ESLR IRQ question 5 *SG* SG Learning Activities, questions 20-24 (pp. 269-270) *SG* SG Review Questions, question 11 (p. 271) **BOOK RESOURCES** Figure 33-3, Adolescents with Eating Disorders (p. 757) Review Questions for the NCLEX® Examination, questions 1-3 (p. 759) ▸ Discuss the nurse's role in engaging the whole family in education and counseling to address an eating disorder. *Class Activity **Instruct students to create a table that lists the symptoms of bulimia and anorexia nervosa, including a column depicting physical complications associated with each disorder. Have students present their tables to the class.*** *Class Activity **Ask students to describe a typical profile of a child or adolescent with anorexia and bulimia. Ask students to compare and contrast the characteristics of children with these disorders and identify any similar characteristics and behavior patterns.*** *Class Activity **Ask students to review magazines targeted at adolescent girls and boys and compare and contrast the body image messages. Initiate a discussion that traces societal influence on eating disorders among children and adolescents.***
Performance Evaluation		🗔 PPT slides 1-51 *e* EILR IC images 1-3 *e* EILR OBQ questions 1-10 *e* EILR TB questions 1-29 *e* ESLR IRQ questions 1-5 *SG* SG Learning Activities, questions 1-24 (pp. 267-270) *SG* SG Review Questions, questions 1-15 (pp. 270-272) *SG* SG Case Study, question 1 (p. 272)

ELSEVIER

Introduction to Maternity & Pediatric Nursing, 6ᵗʰ ed.
Leifer

OBJECTIVES	CONTENT	TEACHING RESOURCES
		SG Thinking Critically, question 1 (p. 272)
		SG Applying Knowledge, questions 1-3 (p. 272)
		BOOK RESOURCES
		Review Questions for the NCLEX® Examination, questions 1-5 (p. 759)

33.2 Homework/Assignments:

1. Have student's research two programs for members of families with alcoholism. Then have student's summarize the services and treatment modalities used by the programs as well as financial fees and types of professionals who run the programs.

33.2 Instructor's Notes/Student Feedback:

33 Lecture Outline
The Child with an Emotional or Behavioral Condition

Slide 1

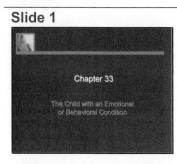

Chapter 33

The Child with an Emotional
or Behavioral Condition

Slide 2

Objectives

- Differentiate among the following terms:
  *psychiatrist, psychoanalyst, clinical
  psychologist,* and *counselor.*
- Discuss the impact of early childhood
  experience on a person's adult life.
- Discuss the effect of childhood autism on
  growth and development.

Slide 3

   Objectives *(cont.)*

- Discuss behavioral therapy and how it is
  applied to obsessive-compulsive disorders
  and depression in children.
- List the symptoms of potential suicide in
  children and adolescents.
- Discuss immediate and long-range plans for
  suicidal patient.
- List four behaviors that may indicate
  substance abuse.

Slide 4

   Objectives *(cont.)*

- Name two programs for members of families
  of alcoholics.
- Discuss the problems facing children of
  alcoholics.
- List four symptoms of attention-deficit/
  hyperactivity disorder.
- Describe techniques of helping children with
  attention-deficient/hyperactivity disorder.
- Compare and contrast the characteristics of
  bulimia and anorexia nervosa.

Slide 5

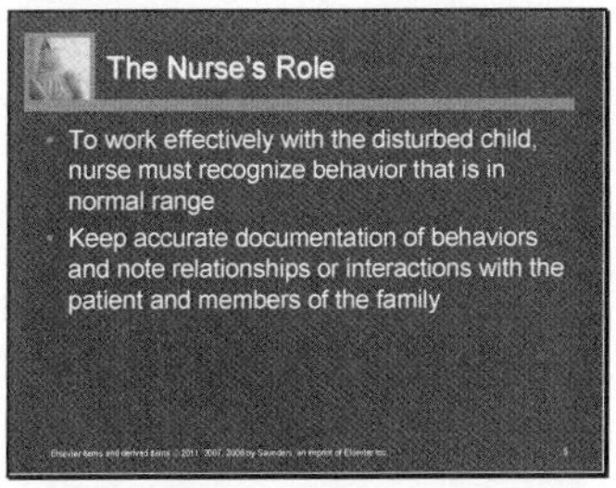

The Nurse's Role

- To work effectively with the disturbed child, nurse must recognize behavior that is in normal range
- Keep accurate documentation of behaviors and note relationships or interactions with the patient and members of the family

Slide 6

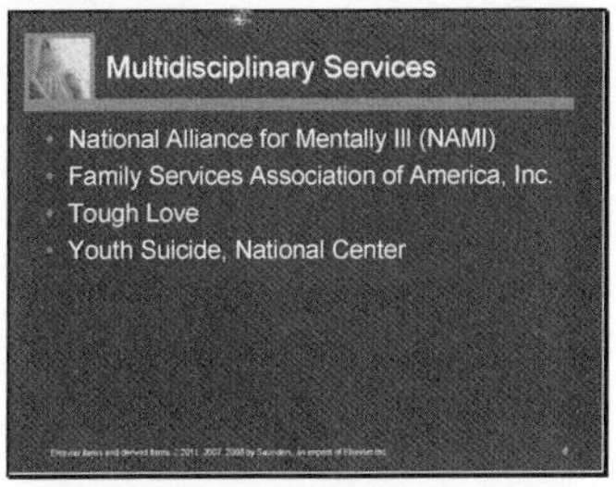

Multidisciplinary Services

- National Alliance for Mentally III (NAMI)
- Family Services Association of America, Inc.
- Tough Love
- Youth Suicide, National Center

- Discuss these services and the resources they provide.
- What is an example of tough love?

Slide 7

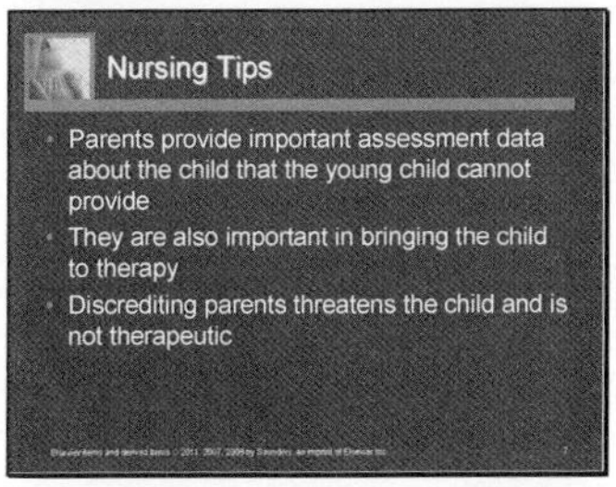

Nursing Tips

- Parents provide important assessment data about the child that the young child cannot provide
- They are also important in bringing the child to therapy
- Discrediting parents threatens the child and is not therapeutic

- Give an example of data a parent might provide because the child is unable.
- What is a situation in which a parent might be discredited?

Slide 8

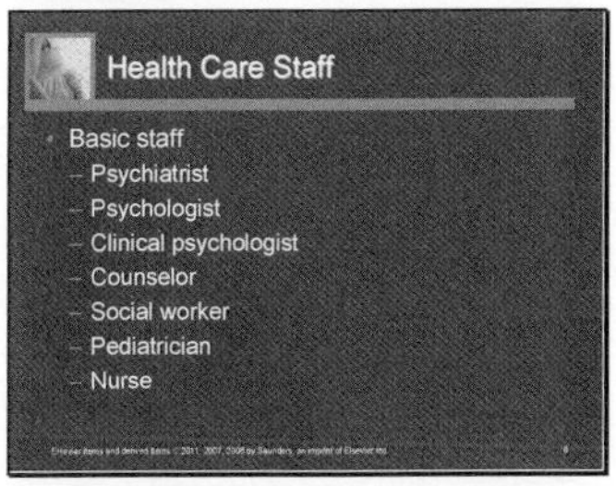

Health Care Staff

- Basic staff
  - Psychiatrist
  - Psychologist
  - Clinical psychologist
  - Counselor
  - Social worker
  - Pediatrician
  - Nurse

- Discuss the role of each discipline.

Slide 9

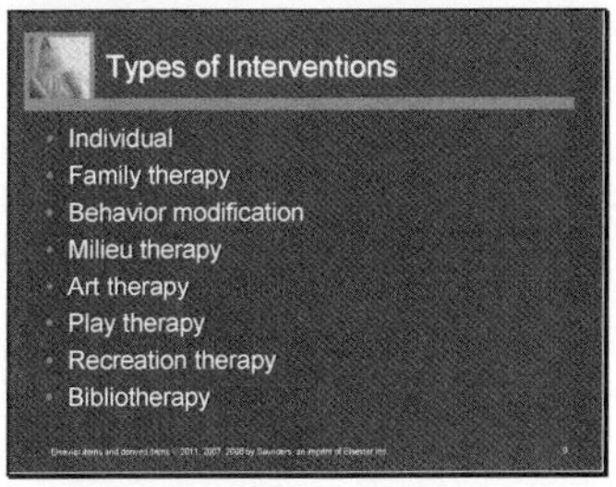

Types of Interventions

- Individual
- Family therapy
- Behavior modification
- Milieu therapy
- Art therapy
- Play therapy
- Recreation therapy
- Bibliotherapy

- Give an example of an intervention for each category.

Slide 10

Origins of Emotional and Behavioral Conditions

Dysfunctional families can have long-lasting impact on the child
- Failure to develop sense of trust
- Excessive fears
- Misdirected anger
- Feelings of lack of control over themselves and their environment
  - May feel negative about themselves
  - May experience guilt and blame themselves when confronted with disappointment and failure

- In what ways does a dysfunctional family impact a child?

Slide 11

Organic Behavioral Disorders

Slide 12

Childhood Autism

May be due to autosomal recessive inheritance
- Signs and symptoms
  - Lack of pointing or gesturing at an early age
  - Failure to make eye contact/look at others
  - Poor attention
  - Poor response to name
  - Repetitive behaviors are significant signs of dysfunction by 1 year of age
- Requires highly structured environment
- Use one request at a time

- Discuss autosomal recessive inheritance.
- Compare a structured environment versus a nonstructured environment for a child with autism.
- Discuss the appropriate methods of approach and communication that should be used with an autistic child.

Audience Response Question #1
Autism can be successfully treated with dietary management.
1. True
2. False

Slide 13

Obsessive-Compulsive Disorders in Children

Involves a recurrent, persistent, repetitive thought that invades the conscious mind (obsession) or ritual movement or activity (not related to adapting to the environment) that assumes inordinate importance (compulsion)

- Give an example of obsessive thought or activity.
- What is a compulsion?

Slide 14

Obsessive-Compulsive Disorders in Children (cont.)

- May be related to depression
- May start as early as 4 years of age and progress to interfering with daily functioning until 10 years of age or older
- No impairment in cognitive function
- Genetic origin
- Can involve family problems
- Treatment is behavior therapy and medication

- Discuss how family problems can trigger this behavior.
- How does this behavior provide a sense of comfort to the individual?

Introduction to Maternity & Pediatric Nursing, 6th ed.

Leifer

Slide 15

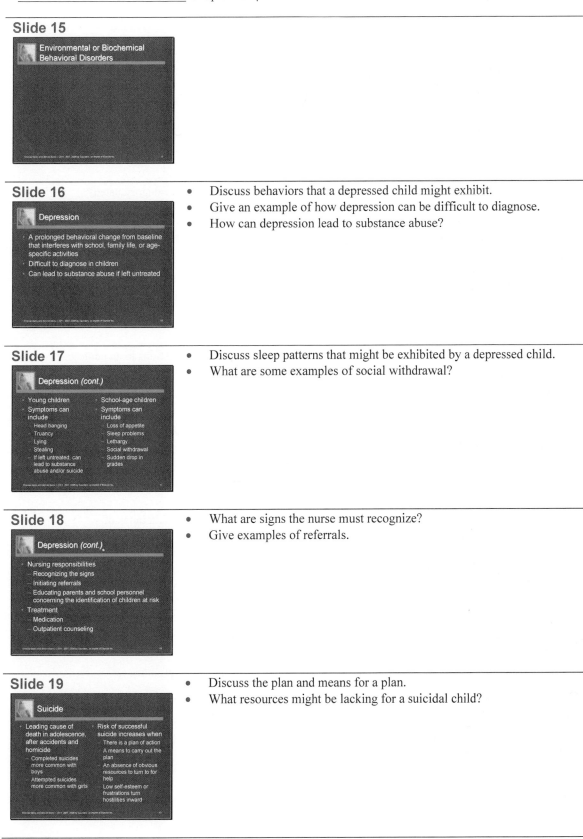

Environmental or Biochemical
Behavioral Disorders

Slide 16

Depression

- A prolonged behavioral change from baseline that interferes with school, family life, or age-specific activities
- Difficult to diagnose in children
- Can lead to substance abuse if left untreated

- Discuss behaviors that a depressed child might exhibit.
- Give an example of how depression can be difficult to diagnose.
- How can depression lead to substance abuse?

Slide 17

Depression *(cont.)*

Young children	School-age children
Symptoms can include	Symptoms can include
Head banging	Loss of appetite
Truancy	Sleep problems
Lying	Lethargy
Stealing	Social withdrawal
If left untreated, can lead to substance abuse and/or suicide	Sudden drop in grades

- Discuss sleep patterns that might be exhibited by a depressed child.
- What are some examples of social withdrawal?

Slide 18

Depression *(cont.)*

- Nursing responsibilities
  - Recognizing the signs
  - Initiating referrals
  - Educating parents and school personnel concerning the identification of children at risk
- Treatment
  - Medication
  - Outpatient counseling

- What are signs the nurse must recognize?
- Give examples of referrals.

Slide 19

Suicide

Leading cause of death in adolescence, after accidents and homicide	Risk of successful suicide increases when
Completed suicides more common with boys	There is a plan of action
	A means to carry out the plan
Attempted suicides more common with girls	An absence of obvious resources to turn to for help
	Low self-esteem or frustrations turn hostilities inward

- Discuss the plan and means for a plan.
- What resources might be lacking for a suicidal child?

Slide 20

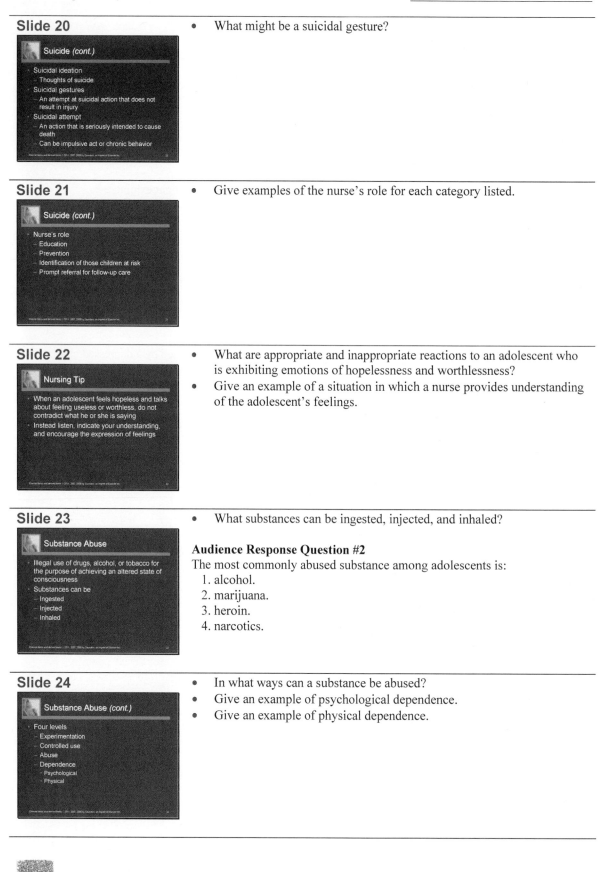

Suicide *(cont.)*

- Suicidal ideation
  - Thoughts of suicide
- Suicidal gestures
  - An attempt at suicidal action that does not result in injury
- Suicidal attempt
  - An action that is seriously intended to cause death
  - Can be impulsive act or chronic behavior

- What might be a suicidal gesture?

Slide 21

Suicide *(cont.)*

- Nurse's role
  - Education
  - Prevention
  - Identification of those children at risk
  - Prompt referral for follow-up care

- Give examples of the nurse's role for each category listed.

Slide 22

Nursing Tip

- When an adolescent feels hopeless and talks about feeling useless or worthless, do not contradict what he or she is saying
- Instead listen, indicate your understanding, and encourage the expression of feelings

- What are appropriate and inappropriate reactions to an adolescent who is exhibiting emotions of hopelessness and worthlessness?
- Give an example of a situation in which a nurse provides understanding of the adolescent's feelings.

Slide 23

Substance Abuse

- Illegal use of drugs, alcohol, or tobacco for the purpose of achieving an altered state of consciousness
- Substances can be
  - Ingested
  - Injected
  - Inhaled

- What substances can be ingested, injected, and inhaled?

Audience Response Question #2
The most commonly abused substance among adolescents is:
  1. alcohol.
  2. marijuana.
  3. heroin.
  4. narcotics.

Slide 24

Substance Abuse *(cont.)*

- Four levels
  - Experimentation
  - Controlled use
  - Abuse
  - Dependence
    - Psychological
    - Physical

- In what ways can a substance be abused?
- Give an example of psychological dependence.
- Give an example of physical dependence.

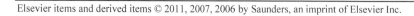

Slide 25

> **Substance Abuse** *(cont.)*
>
> - Two types of dependence
>   - Psychological and physical
> - Substances that are used/abused
>   - Alcohol
>   - Experimentation has traditionally been accepted as a normal part of growing up
>   - Cocaine ("crack")
>   - Can be snorted, smoked, or injected into a vein
>   - Can cause antisocial behavior or life-threatening response

- Discuss how different cultures accept or reject alcohol.
- Give an example of antisocial behavior when crack is abused.

Slide 26

> **Substance Abuse** *(cont.)*
>
> - Gateway substances (lead to abuse of stronger drugs)
>   - Common household products cause euphoria (high) and then CNS depression
>   - Cleaning fluid
>   - Glue
>   - Lighter fluid
>   - Paints
>   - Shoe polish

- How are these products abused?
- Discuss educating parents about signs and symptoms to assess for abuse of these products.

Slide 27

> **Substance Abuse** *(cont.)*
>
> - Marijuana (hemp plant)
>   - Smoked or ingested
> - Causes the person to experience
>   - Loss of inhibitions
>   - Euphoria
>   - Loss of coordination and direction

- Describe loss of inhibitions.
- How might coordination be affected with the use of this drug?

Slide 28

> **Substance Abuse** *(cont.)*
>
> - Opiates
>   - Heroin
> - Users are at risk for
>   - HIV
>   - Hepatitis
> - Long-term therapy is required

- Discuss why this population might be at risk for HIV and hepatitis.
- Why might this population require long-term therapy?

Slide 29

> **Substance Abuse** *(cont.)*
>
> - Prevention and nursing goals
>   - Teach parenting skills to expectant parents
>   - Develop positive self-image and feelings of self-worth
>   - Provide positive role models
>   - Develop coping skills regarding substance abuse

- What parenting skills might the nurse provide expectant parents?
- Discuss how positive self-esteem can be developed.
- Give an example of a positive and negative role model.
- What coping skills can be used instead of a drug?

ELSEVIER

Introduction to Maternity & Pediatric Nursing, 6th ed.

Leifer

Slide 30

Substance Abuse *(cont.)*
- Children of alcoholics
- Support groups available
  - Al-Anon (for adolescents)
  - Alcoholics Anonymous (AA—for adults)
- Child confused by unpredictability of family life
  - Their needs are not being met
  - May take role of parent
  - May be isolated from peers
  - Role models distorted or lacking

- How does an alcoholic parent affect his or her child?
- Discuss the different support groups and their services.
- Give examples of how a child might isolate from peers because of an issue with substance abuse in the family.

Slide 31

Children of Alcoholics

- Discuss Figure 33-2 on page 755.

Slide 32

Children of Alcoholics *(cont.)*
- Clues
  - Refusal to talk about family life
  - Poor grades or overachievement
  - Unusual need to please
  - Fatigue
  - Passive or acting-out behavior
  - Maturity beyond the child's years

- Discuss why the child might exhibit these clues.
- Discuss the immediate priorities the nurse should teach the child in an emergency.

Slide 33

Attention Deficit Hyperactivity Disorder (ADHD)
- An inappropriate degree of gross motor activity, impulsivity, and inattention in school or home setting that begins before age 7 years, lasts more than 6 months, and is not related to the existence of any other central nervous system illness
- Characterized by inattention, hyperactivity, impulsivity, and distractibility
- May be genetic

- Give an example of a situation in which a child is exhibiting ADHD.

Slide 34

Attention Deficit Hyperactivity Disorder (ADHD) *(cont.)*
- *DSM-IV-TR* lists criteria for ADHD
  - May have above-average intelligence
  - Problem may be
    - Receptive language
    - Expressive language
    - Information processing
    - Memory
    - Motor coordination
    - Orientation
    - Behavior

- Give examples of receptive and expressive language.
- How might ADHD affect memory, motor coordination, and behavior?

Slide 35

> **Attention Deficit Hyperactivity Disorder (ADHD)** *(cont.)*
> - Screening tools can enable early intervention
>   - Such as "Einstein Evaluation of School-Related Skills"
> - May have
>   - Dyslexia
>   - Dysgraphia
>   - Problem expressing themselves

- Discuss why early intervention is important.
- Give examples of: dyslexia, dysgraphia, and difficulty expressing oneself.

Audience Response Question #3
The child receiving methylphenidate (Ritalin) to treat ADHD must be carefully monitored for:
1. excessive appetite.
2. dental caries.
3. height and weight.
4. altered skin integrity.

Slide 36

> **Anorexia Nervosa**
> - A form of self-starvation seen mostly in adolescent girls

Slide 37

> **Anorexia Nervosa** *(cont.)*
> - Criteria according to the *DSM-IV-TR*
>   - Failure to maintain the minimum normal weight for age and height
>   - An intense fear of gaining weight
>   - Excess influence of body weight on self-evaluation
>   - Amenorrhea

- Discuss a scenario of a girl exhibiting anorexia nervosa.
- How is weight related to amenorrhea?

Slide 38

> **Anorexia Nervosa** *(cont.)*
> - May be genetic
> - Characteristics
>   - Average to superior intelligence
>   - Overachievers who expect to be perfect in all areas
>   - Threatened by their emerging sexuality
>   - Obedient
>   - Nonassertive and shy
> - Have a low self-esteem

- Discuss how perfection influences those with anorexia nervosa.
- Why does one with low self-esteem focus on perfection?

Slide 39

> **Anorexia Nervosa** *(cont.)*
> - On physical examination may find
>   - Dry skin
>   - Amenorrhea
>   - Lanugo hair over the back and extremities
>   - Cold intolerance
>   - Low blood pressure
>   - Abdominal pain
>   - Constipation

- Discuss the rationale and/or pathophysiology for each disorder.

Slide 40

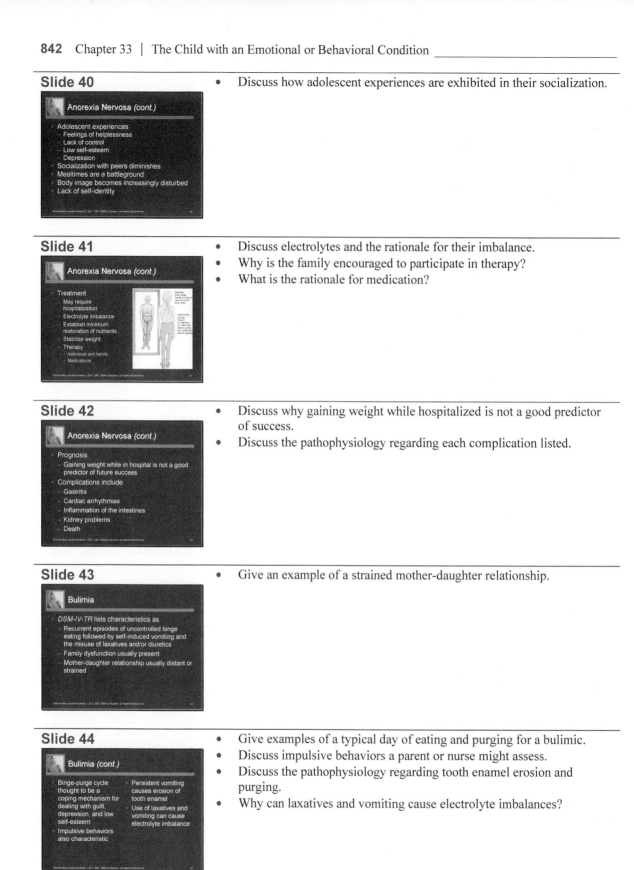

Anorexia Nervosa *(cont.)*

- Adolescent experiences
  - Feelings of helplessness
  - Lack of control
  - Low self-esteem
  - Depression
- Socialization with peers diminishes
- Mealtimes are a battleground
- Body image becomes increasingly disturbed
- Lack of self-identity

- Discuss how adolescent experiences are exhibited in their socialization.

Slide 41

Anorexia Nervosa *(cont.)*

- Treatment
  - May require hospitalization
  - Electrolyte imbalance
  - Establish minimum restoration of nutrients
  - Stabilize weight
  - Therapy
    - Individual and family
    - Medications

- Discuss electrolytes and the rationale for their imbalance.
- Why is the family encouraged to participate in therapy?
- What is the rationale for medication?

Slide 42

Anorexia Nervosa *(cont.)*

- Prognosis
  - Gaining weight while in hospital is not a good predictor of future success
- Complications include
  - Gastritis
  - Cardiac arrhythmias
  - Inflammation of the intestines
  - Kidney problems
  - Death

- Discuss why gaining weight while hospitalized is not a good predictor of success.
- Discuss the pathophysiology regarding each complication listed.

Slide 43

Bulimia

- *DSM-IV-TR* lists characteristics as
  - Recurrent episodes of uncontrolled binge eating followed by self-induced vomiting and the misuse of laxatives and/or diuretics
  - Family dysfunction usually present
  - Mother-daughter relationship usually distant or strained

- Give an example of a strained mother-daughter relationship.

Slide 44

Bulimia *(cont.)*

- Binge-purge cycle thought to be a coping mechanism for dealing with guilt, depression, and low self-esteem
- Impulsive behaviors also characteristic
- Persistent vomiting causes erosion of tooth enamel
- Use of laxatives and vomiting can cause electrolyte imbalance

- Give examples of a typical day of eating and purging for a bulimic.
- Discuss impulsive behaviors a parent or nurse might assess.
- Discuss the pathophysiology regarding tooth enamel erosion and purging.
- Why can laxatives and vomiting cause electrolyte imbalances?

Leifer

Slide 45

> **Bulimia** *(cont.)*
>
> · Nursing role
>   - Educate
>   - Prevent
>   - Identify
>   - Refer

- Give examples of how the nurse might influence the prevention of bulimia.
- What referrals might the nurse provide for a patient who is exhibiting bulimia?

Slide 46

> **Minimizing the Impact of Behavioral Disorders in Children**
>
> · Once the source of the problem is identified, a combination of mental health interventions can be implemented or the child can be referred as needed

- Give an example of a problem and a referral for the child.

Slide 47

> **Effect of the Illness on Growth and Development**
>
> · Duration and intensity of a stressful event and the child's coping skills determine the impact on the growth and development process
> · Requires a total family approach to care
> · A knowledgeable, caring, understanding, and supportive nature is valuable for any nurse caring for children with behavioral disorders

- How can a stressful situation affect a child's growth and development?
- Discuss effective and ineffective coping skills for a child who has experienced a stressful event.
- How can a family provide support?

Slide 48

> **Effect of the Illness on Siblings**
>
> · Most siblings of children with emotional disorders either suffer emotional scars or develop protective coping mechanisms to deal with their experiences
> · If long-term, the siblings are at risk for developing low self-esteem and problems with their own peer relationships

Slide 49

> **Sibling Rivalry**
>
> · A competition between siblings for the attention or love of parents
> · Is a normal part of growth and development
> · Can cause guilt on the part of the sibling who is not ill
> · Teaches interactive social skills that will be used with friends

- Why does the sibling who is not ill feel guilty?

Slide 50

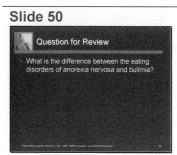

Question for Review

- What is the difference between the eating disorders of anorexia nervosa and bulimia?

Slide 51

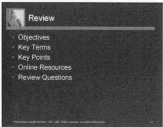

Review

- Objectives
- Key Terms
- Key Points
- Online Resources
- Review Questions

Leifer

Lesson Plan

34 Complementary and Alternative Therapies in Maternity and Pediatric Nursing

TEACHING FOCUS

In this chapter, students will be introduced to complementary and alternative medicine (CAM) therapies, including federal regulations, the impact on the nursing care of patients, the role of the nurse, and the acceptance of CAM in nursing practice. Students will have an opportunity to examine the characteristics of commonly used CAM therapies with areas of contraindications.

MATERIALS AND RESOURCES

☐ Computer and PowerPoint projector (all lessons)

LESSON CHECKLIST

Preparations for this lesson include:

- Lecture
- Guest speakers: Nursing practitioner of CAM therapy, practitioner of acupuncture and reflexology
- Evaluation of student knowledge and skills needed to perform all entry-level activities related to CAM therapies in maternity and pediatric nursing, including:
  ○ The history of involvement of the federal government in CAM therapies
  ○ The nursing care of patients using CAM therapies, the role of the nurse in CAM therapy, and acceptance of CAM therapy in nursing practice
  ○ The characteristics of specific CAM therapies
  ○ The uses, toxicities, and contraindications of herbal products used during pregnancy or menopause

KEY TERMS

alternative therapy (p. 760)
aromatherapy (p. 765)
coin-rubbing (p. 763)
complementary therapy (p. 760)

dermatomes (p. 764)
herbal medicine (p. 765)
hyperbaric oxygen therapy (HBOT) (p. 768)
meridians (p. 764)

reflexology (p. 764)
Rolfing (p. 763)
shiatsu (p. 764)

ADDITIONAL RESOURCES

TEACH PPT slide(s) Chapter 34, 1-40
EILR IC image(s) Chapter 34, 1-4
EILR OBQ question(s) Chapter 34, 1-10
EILR TB question(s) Chapter 34, 1-22
ESLR IRQ question(s) Chapter 34, 1-5
SG Chapter 34, pp. 271-276

Legend

PPT
TEACH
PowerPoint
Slides

EILR
EVOLVE Instructor
Learning Resources:
Image Collection (IC),
Open-Book Quizzes
(OBQ), Test Bank (TB)

ESLR
EVOLVE Student
Learning Resources:
Interactive Review
Questions (IRQ) for
the NCLEX®
Examination

SG
Study Guide

CTQ
Critical Thinking
Question in
Nursing Care Plan
(NCP CTQ) or Get
Ready for the
NCLEX! (GRN
CTQ)

Class Activities are indicated in ***bold italic***.

Leifer

LESSON 34.1

PRETEST

1. The use of acupuncture and opioid analgesics to treat pain is an example of
   a. alternative therapy.
   c. herbal medicine.
   b. complementary therapy.
   d. cultural competence.

2. Which of the following is a correct statement about herbal supplements?
   a. The potency of herbal supplements is not regulated by the FDA.
   b. Herbs are not classified as dietary supplements.
   c. Herbal supplements do not vary in strengths and ingredients.
   d. Proof of efficacy is required for the marketing and sale of herbs.

3. Which herbal form contains alcohol?
   a. compress
   c. extract
   b. capsule
   d. tincture

4. Which federal organization has been designated as a research and public information resource for complementary and alternative medicine?
   a. Food and Drug Administration
   b. National Center for Complementary and Alternative Medicine
   c. Department of Health and Human Services
   d. Office of Alternative Medicine

5. Cao-Gio, or coin-rubbing, can be mistaken for child abuse because it
   a. contributes to fractures in children.
   c. causes pain when performed.
   b. can leave marks on the skin.
   d. deprives a child of sleep.

6. Which of the following is a Hindu practice based on the rhythms of nature?
   a. ayurveda
   c. reflexology
   b. shiatsu
   d. acupuncture

7. Which essential oil is contraindicated during pregnancy?
   a. jasmine
   c. lavender
   b. citrus
   d. nutmeg

8. Acupuncture relates to invisible energy tracks running through the body called
   a. meridians.
   c. biofeedback.
   b. dermatomes.
   d. reiki.

9. Transcutaneous electrical nerve stimulation (TENS) can prevent what from occurring in patients receiving chemotherapy?
   a. anemia
   c. hair loss
   b. low white blood cell count
   d. nausea and vomiting

10. Which herb should a menopausal woman with uterine fibroids avoid because it contains phytoestrogens?
    a. dong quai
    c. mother wort
    b. black cohosh
    d. chasteberry

Answers

| 1. b | 3. d | 5. b | 7. d | 9. d |
| 2. a | 4. b | 6. a | 8. a | 10. a |

BACKGROUND ASSESSMENT

Question: Why should nurses be knowledgeable about complementary and alternative medicine (CAM) therapies?

Answer: It is likely that most nurses will encounter some form of CAM during their career, especially as interest in alternative therapy increases. Knowledge of CAM helps the nurse recognize potential complications and contraindications, which is necessary and valuable in establishing nursing interventions. An understanding of CAM expands a nurse's cultural competence and reflects the principle that healing is enhanced in an environment of partnership and cultural respect.

ELSEVIER

Introduction to Maternity & Pediatric Nursing, 6th ed.

Elsevier items and derived items © 2011, 2007, 2006 by Saunders, an imprint of Elsevier Inc.   Leifer

Question: What precautions should a nurse be aware of regarding complementary and alternative medicine (CAM) therapy?

Answer: CAM therapies are not regulated by federal agencies such as the FDA. Therefore, they are not standardized or proven in terms of their efficacy, mechanism of action, side effects, contraindications, and safety issues. The perception that CAM therapies are "natural" can be misleading because many naturally occurring substances can cause serious harm. Polypharmacy should be assessed to prevent drug interactions and unintended side effects. CAM can alter glucose levels and lower drug levels of other medications that have been prescribed to treat conditions such as AIDS, diabetes, or cancer. Using over-the-counter herbal supplements before surgery may contribute to bleeding irregularities or increased sedation and respiratory depression. Lack of standard dosages and ingredients should be taken into consideration, especially when used by children or older patients who have altered drug metabolism.

CRITICAL THINKING QUESTION

A massage therapist is pregnant with her first baby and asks a friend, who is a nurse, what natural remedies she should use to promote a healthy pregnancy and a positive labor and delivery experience. How should the nurse respond?

Guidelines: The nurse should explain that some CAM therapies, such as saunas or certain herbal supplements, are unsafe for a fetus and can lead to premature labor; whereas other therapies, such as TENS, are safe treatments for pregnancy-related symptoms such as nausea. Effleurage and hydrotherapy are techniques that can be used during labor to reduce the pain and anxiety associated with dilation and contractions. Encourage the massage therapist to enroll in a prenatal class. The nurse should emphasize that any CAM therapies the massage therapist considers should first be discussed with her obstetrician or nurse midwife to prevent interactions or contraindications.

OBJECTIVES	CONTENT	TEACHING RESOURCES
Define complementary and alternative medicine (CAM) therapy.	■ Complementary and alternative therapies (p. 760) ■ Pediatric use (p. 760)	⊠▦ PPT slides 5-7 *e* EILR OBQ question 1 *e* EILR TB questions 9, 17 🕮 SG Learning Activities, question 1 (p. 271) **BOOK RESOURCES** Review Questions for the NCLEX® Examination, question 3 (p. 770) ▸ Discuss how a nurse's personal opinions about CAM may affect patient compliance with traditional therapies. *Class Activity Ask students to define complementary, alternative, and conventional medicine therapy. Then ask students to list examples of each type of therapy.*
Discuss the integration of CAM therapy in nursing practice.	■ The nurse's role (p. 761)	⊠▦ PPT slides 8-13 *e* EILR IC image 1 *e* EILR OBQ question 3 *e* EILR TB questions 11, 20, 21 🕮 SG Review Questions, question 1 (p. 273) **BOOK RESOURCES**

Leifer

OBJECTIVES	CONTENT	TEACHING RESOURCES
		Figure 34-1, Alternative Health Care (p. 761)
		Cultural Considerations, Popular Cultural Folk Healers (p. 761)
		Box 34-1, Cautions in Complementary and Alternative Medicine Therapy (p. 762)
		▶ Discuss students' ideas about why the acceptance and use of CAM therapies has increased.
		*Class Activity **Invite a nurse practitioner of a particular CAM therapy to discuss his or her specialty. Invite questions from the class.***
Discuss the impact on nursing care of patients who use CAM therapy.	■ The nurse's role (p. 761)	PPT slides 11-13 **BOOK RESOURCES** Cultural Considerations, Popular Cultural Folk Healers (p. 761) ▶ Discuss students' personal experiences with CAM therapies including their reasons for use and the outcomes.
Identify the role of the nurse in CAM therapy.	■ The nurse's role (p. 761)	PPT slides 8-13 𝑒 EILR TB question 14 SG Review Questions, questions 6, 7 (p. 274) **BOOK RESOURCES** Cultural Considerations, Popular Cultural Folk Healers (p. 761) Review Questions for the NCLEX® Examination, questions 1-3, 5 (p. 770) ▶ Discuss the role of cultural competence in caring for patients who choose CAM. *Class Activity **Have students list three nursing roles in relationship to CAM. What nursing interventions related to CAM might be encountered in the field of maternity and pediatric nursing?*** *Class Activity **What patient education is appropriate for the following scenarios?*** *1. **A woman has recently given birth and now wants to use ayurvedic herbs to restore balance to her body.*** *2. **A woman who is 8 months pregnant asks about using aromatherapy during labor and delivery to relieve anxiety.*** *3. **A pregnant woman asks whether she can drink chamomile tea before bed.***

OBJECTIVES	CONTENT	TEACHING RESOURCES
		4. A postmenopausal woman asks about natural therapies for managing menopausal symptoms.
State three herbs that should be discontinued 2 weeks before surgery.	■ The nurse's role (p. 761)	▣▪ PPT slide 14
		e EILR OBQ question 2
		e EILR TB question 6
		BOOK RESOURCES
		Table 34-1, Herbs that Should Be Discontinued Two Weeks Before Surgery (p. 762)
		▸ Discuss the nurse's role in educating patients about the effects of herbs prior to surgery. (Refer to Table 34-1, p. 762)
		Class Activity Discuss specific herbs that should be discontinued at least 2 weeks before surgery and the reason for the contraindication. What herbs can be taken up to the date of surgery?
		Class Activity Have pairs of students take turns role-playing a nurse interviewing a patient about preoperative health history and assessment to identify interactions or complications with CAM therapy and the scheduled surgery. Students should include patient teaching methods and nursing interventions.
Describe the involvement of the federal government in CAM therapy.	■ Federal regulations (p. 762)	▣▪ PPT slide 15
		SG Learning Activities, question 2 (p. 271)
		SG Applying Knowledge, question 1 (p. 276)
		BOOK RESOURCES
		Review Questions for the NCLEX® Examination, question 4 (p. 770)
		▸ Discuss the health care implications of an unregulated herbal industry.
		Class Activity Divide the class into two groups. Have one group research the FDA and its role in CAM, and the other group research the National Center for Complementary and Alternative Medicine (NCCAM). Compare and contrast the goals and activities of each organization in relation to CAM. (For students to prepare for this activity, see Homework/Assignments #1.)
		Class Activity Instruct students to write a summary of one article published by the NCCAM's journal, **The Scientific Review of Alternative Medicine.** *(For students to prepare for this activity, see Homework/ Assignments #2.)*

OBJECTIVES	CONTENT	TEACHING RESOURCES
		*Class Activity **Moderate a class discussion about the herbal supplement industry and its interest in limiting the FDA's regulation of herbal products. Ask students to consider if this helps or hurts the consumer of CAM. What are dietary supplements and are they regulated by the FDA?***

34.1 Homework/Assignments:

1. Divide the class into two groups. Have one group research the FDA and its role in CAM, and the other group research the National Center for Complementary and Alternative Medicine (NCCAM). Compare and contrast the goals and activities of each organization in relation to CAM.

2. Instruct students to write a summary of one article published by the NCCAM's journal, *The Scientific Review of Alternative Medicine.*

34.1 Instructor's Notes/Student Feedback:

CRITICAL THINKING QUESTION

The mother of a patient with sickle cell anemia is concerned about her child having negative effects from chronic use of opioid narcotics. She asks the nurse whether there are other pain management methods that she can use during a sickle cell crisis. How should the nurse respond?

Guidelines: The nurse should support the mother's interest in exploring complementary methods of pain management and her goal of minimizing the negative effects related to medication. The nurse should identify comfort measures that are safe for pediatric patients, such as guided imagery; relaxation through music, art, and play therapy; and healing touch. The nurse should also inform the mother that some CAM therapies can increase bleeding and may interact negatively with other conventional therapies. Therefore, it is important for the mother to consult with her child's pediatrician regarding all treatment modalities, including natural products or therapies. The nurse should answer any questions the mother has regarding prescribed conventional therapy, such as analgesics and hydration, and reinforce the concept that giving pain medication on a schedule before the pain becomes intense will reduce the dosage necessary for relief. The nurse should also instruct the mother to keep a record of the time and doses of pain medication given to the child. A referral to a pain management center may be indicated and should be discussed with the child's pediatrician.

OBJECTIVES	CONTENT	TEACHING RESOURCES
State the use of meridians, dermatomes, and reflexology lines in CAM therapy.	■ Common alternative health care practices (p. 763) ☐ Massage (p. 763) ☐ Osteopathy (p. 763) ☐ Energy healing (p. 763) ☐ Reflexology (p. 764) ☐ Acupuncture and acupressure (p. 764)	PPT slides 16-22 *e* EILR IC images 2-4 *e* EILR TB questions 1, 2, 10, 18, 19, 22 *e* ESLR IRQ question 2 SG Learning Activities, questions 3, 4 (p. 271) SG Review Questions, questions 3-5 (pp. 273-274) **BOOK RESOURCES** Figure 34-2, "Cao-Gio" (p. 763) Figure 34-3, The ReliefBand (p. 763) Figure 34-4, (A) Meridians; (B) Dermatomes; (C) Reflexology Lines (p. 764) GRN CTQ 1, 2 (p. 770) ▸ Discuss the ways that nurses can benefit from understanding the use of meridians, dermatomes, and reflexology lines. (Refer to Figure 34-4, p. 764) *Class Activity Invite a practitioner of acupuncture and reflexology to lecture on meridians and energy flow theory and their effects on specific medical conditions. Allow students to ask questions.*
State five types of CAM therapy in common use.	■ Common alternative health care practices (p. 763) ☐ Massage (p. 763) ☐ Osteopathy (p. 763)	PPT slides 23-31 *e* EILR OBQ questions 4-8 *e* EILR TB questions 1-5, 8, 13, 16

OBJECTIVES	CONTENT	TEACHING RESOURCES
	☐ Energy healing (p. 763)	SG Learning Activities, questions 5-7 (pp. 271-272)
	☐ Reflexology (p. 764)	
	☐ Acupuncture and acupressure (p. 764)	SG Applying Knowledge, question 2 (p. 276)
	☐ Homeopathy (p. 764)	**BOOK RESOURCES**
	☐ Ayurveda (p. 765)	Figure 34-2, "Cao-Gio" (p. 763)
	☐ Aromatherapy (p. 765)	Figure 34-4, (A) Meridians; (B) Dermatomes; (C) Reflexology Lines (p. 764)
	☐ Hypnotherapy (p. 765)	Nursing Tip (p. 765)
	☐ Hydrotherapy (p. 765)	Review Questions for the NCLEX® Examination, question 3 (p. 770)
	☐ Guided imagery (p. 765)	▶ Discuss the nurse's role in educating patients about the benefits and risks of CAM for certain diagnoses.
	☐ Biofeedback (p. 765)	
	☐ Chiropractic care (p. 765)	*Class Activity Ask students to discuss anecdotal evidence related to the use of CAM therapies based on their own experiences or those of their family or friends. Did it have a positive effect on health and wellness?*

34.2 Homework/Assignments:

34.2 Instructor's Notes/Student Feedback:

CRITICAL THINKING QUESTION

The nurse is reviewing preoperative instructions with her patient who is scheduled for a hysterectomy. The nurse instructs her to take nothing by mouth beginning at midnight before her surgery and to discontinue her daily aspirin to prevent increased bleeding during surgery. The patient asks if it is OK for her to continue taking her herbal supplements with a few sips of water. What is the nurse's appropriate response?

Guidelines: The nurse should assess and document all medications, including herbs, in the patient's chart and communicate the information to the surgeon. The nurse should then instruct the patient to withhold all supplements because they may interfere with other medications given to her during and after surgery, and they could increase bleeding.

OBJECTIVES	CONTENT	TEACHING RESOURCES

State three herbal products contraindicated in pregnancy.	☐ Herbal remedies (p. 765)
	  – Herbs and obstetrics (p. 766)
	  – Herbs and pediatrics (p. 767)
	  – Herbs and menopause (p. 767)
	☐ Hyperbaric oxygen therapy (p. 768)
	☐ Sauna/heat therapy (p. 769)
		PPT slides 32-36
		
		e EILR OBQ questions 4-10
		
		e ESLR IRQ questions 3, 5
		
		SG Learning Activities, questions 5-6, 9-10 (pp. 271-273)
		
		SG Review Questions, questions 7-8 (p. 274)
		
		SG Case Study, question 1 (p. 276)
		
		BOOK RESOURCES
		
		Table 34-2, Common Herbs Contraindicated in Pregnancy and Lactation (p. 766)
		
		Box 34-2, Herbs that Promote Menstruation and May Cause Miscarriage (p. 767)
		
		Table 34-3, Herbs commonly used in pediatrics (pp. 767-768)
		
		Table 34-4 Popular herbs used in menopause (p. 769)
		
		Review Questions for the NCLEX® Examination, question 2-3 (p. 770)
		
		▸ Discuss the nurse's role in educating the patient about herbs that are contraindicated in pregnancy and lactation. (Refer to Table 34-2, p. 766)
		
		Class Activity Ask students to identify herbal products that are contraindicated in pregnancy and include the rationale.

Discuss the use of hyperbaric oxygen therapy in the care of carbon monoxide	☐ Hyperbaric oxygen therapy (p. 768)	PPT slides 37, 38 *e* EILR OBQ question 10 *e* EILR TB question 15

OBJECTIVES	CONTENT	TEACHING RESOURCES
poisoning and necrotic ulcers.		▸ Discuss the nursing care required pre- and post-hyperbaric oxygen therapy treatments.
State three herbal products commonly used in pediatrics.	– Herbs and pediatrics (p. 767)	⊠▣ PPT slide 34 𝒆 EILR TB question 12 𝒆 ESLR IRQ question 4 ▨ SG Learning Activities, questions 6, 8 (p. 272) **BOOK RESOURCES** Table 34-3, Herbs Commonly Used in Pediatrics (pp. 767-768) ▸ Discuss strategies for eliciting information about parents' use of CAM therapy for their children. *Class Activity **Have each student list three herbal products commonly used in pediatric care and three common pediatric health conditions that can be adversely affected by herbal products. Discuss the importance of patient education for parents who use herbal products.***
State popular herbs used during menopause.	– Herbs and menopause (p. 767)	⊠▣ PPT slide 36 𝒆 EILR OBQ question 9 𝒆 EILR TB question 7 𝒆 ESLR IRQ question 1 ▨ SG Learning Activities, question 11 (p. 273) ▨ SG Review Questions, question 2 (p. 273) **BOOK RESOURCES** Table 34-4, Popular Herbs Used in Menopause (p. 769) ▸ Discuss strategies for educating patients about natural approaches for managing menopausal symptoms. *Class Activity **Have students list three products used for relief of menopausal symptoms and discuss their contraindications.***
Performance Evaluation		⊠▣ PPT slides 1-40 𝒆 EILR IC images 1-4 𝒆 EILR OBQ questions 1-10 𝒆 EILR TB questions 1-22 𝒆 ESLR IRQ questions 1-5

Introduction to Maternity & Pediatric Nursing, 6th ed.

Leifer

OBJECTIVES	CONTENT	TEACHING RESOURCES
		SG Learning Activities, questions 1-11 (pp. 271-273)
		SG Review Questions, questions 1-8 (pp. 273-274)
		SG Crossword puzzle (p. 275)
		SG Case Study, question 1 (p. 276)
		SG Applying Knowledge, questions 1-2 (p. 276)
		BOOK RESOURCES
		Review Questions for the NCLEX® Examination, questions 1-5 (p. 770)
		GRN CTQ 1, 2 (p. 770)

34.3 Homework/Assignments:

34.3 Instructor's Notes/Student Feedback:

Lecture Outline

34 Complementary and Alternative Therapies in Maternity and Pediatric Nursing

Slide 1

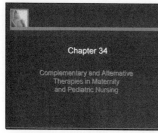

Chapter 34

Complementary and Alternative
Therapies in Maternity
and Pediatric Nursing

Slide 2

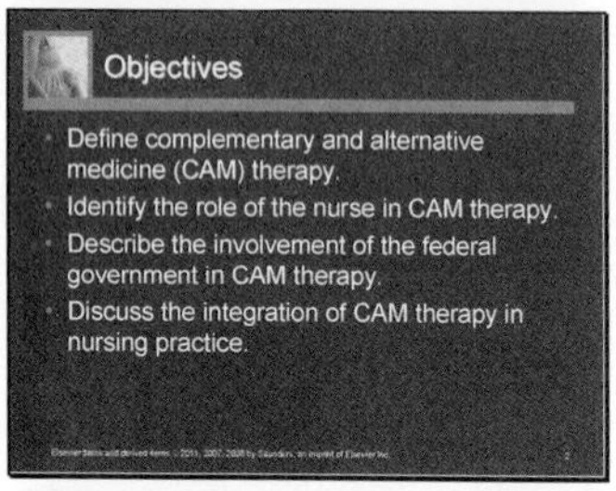

Objectives

- Define complementary and alternative medicine (CAM) therapy.
- Identify the role of the nurse in CAM therapy.
- Describe the involvement of the federal government in CAM therapy.
- Discuss the integration of CAM therapy in nursing practice.

Slide 3

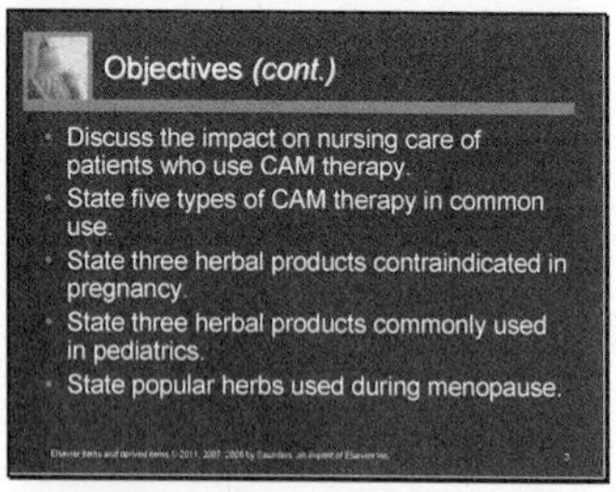

Objectives *(cont.)*

- Discuss the impact on nursing care of patients who use CAM therapy.
- State five types of CAM therapy in common use.
- State three herbal products contraindicated in pregnancy.
- State three herbal products commonly used in pediatrics.
- State popular herbs used during menopause.

Slide 4

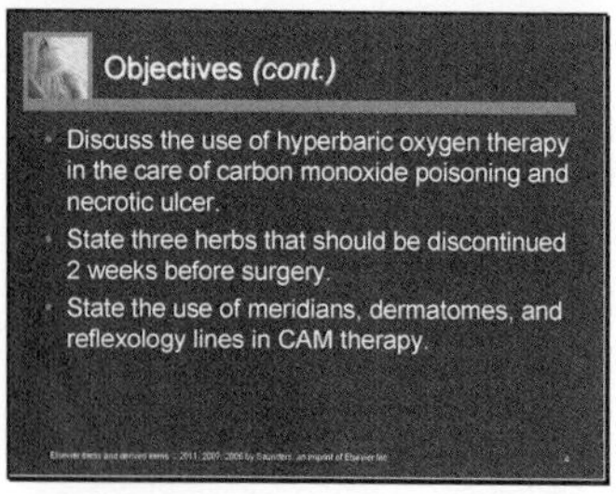

Objectives *(cont.)*

- Discuss the use of hyperbaric oxygen therapy in the care of carbon monoxide poisoning and necrotic ulcer.
- State three herbs that should be discontinued 2 weeks before surgery.
- State the use of meridians, dermatomes, and reflexology lines in CAM therapy.

Leifer

Slide 5	• Give examples of complementary therapies.
	• Give examples of alternative therapies.

Slide 5

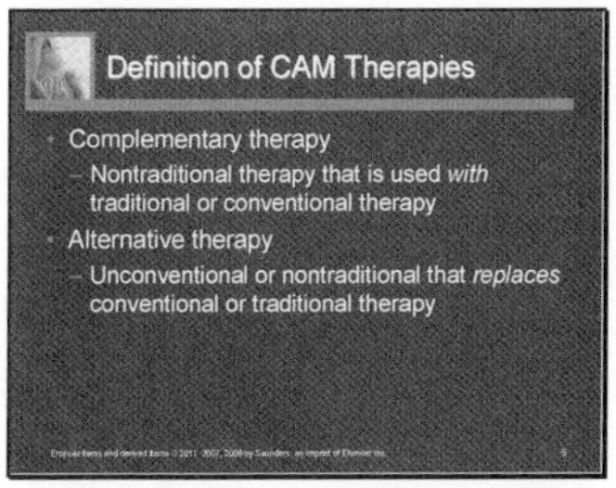

Definition of CAM Therapies

· Complementary therapy
  – Nontraditional therapy that is used *with* traditional or conventional therapy
· Alternative therapy
  – Unconventional or nontraditional that *replaces* conventional or traditional therapy

---

Slide 6

Alternative Health Care

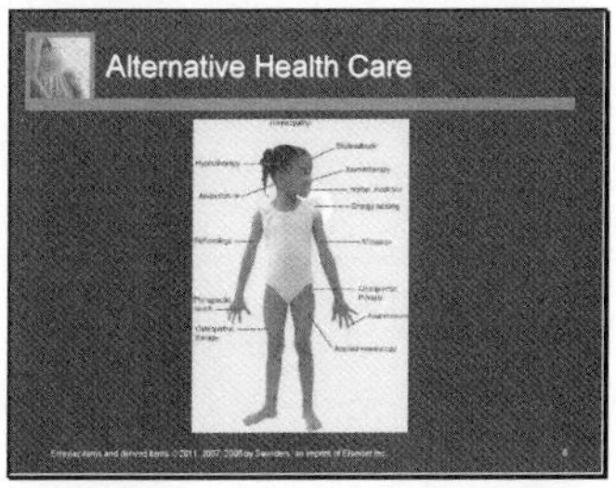

• Refer to Figure 34-1 on page 761.
• Discuss each of the alternatives listed and which body system(s) it affects.

Slide 7

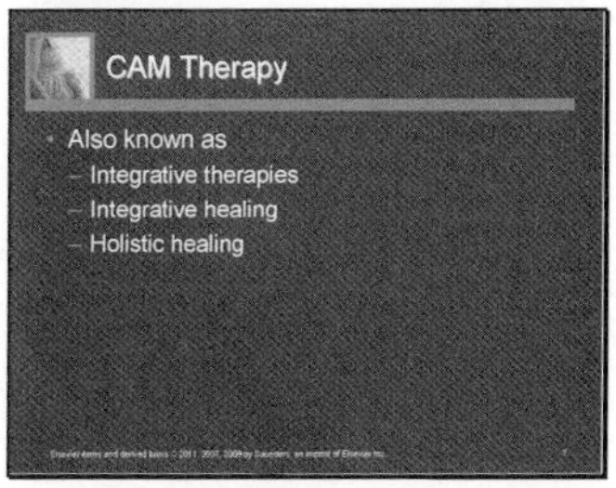

CAM Therapy

· Also known as
  – Integrative therapies
  – Integrative healing
  – Holistic healing

• Discuss the terms now classified as complementary and alternative medicine.

Slide 8

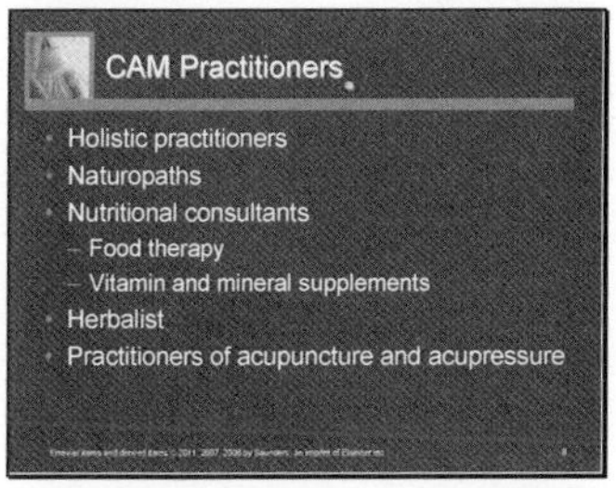

CAM Practitioners

· Holistic practitioners
· Naturopaths
· Nutritional consultants
  – Food therapy
  – Vitamin and mineral supplements
· Herbalist
· Practitioners of acupuncture and acupressure

• Describe the differences between a holistic practitioner and a naturopathic practitioner.
• What is the difference between acupuncture and acupressure?

Slide 9

Popular Cultural Folk Healers

· Mexican: *Curanderos*
· African American: Root doctor
· Asian and Chinese: Herbalist
· Puerto Rican: Espiritistas or santiguadoras
· Navajo: Singers

Slide 10

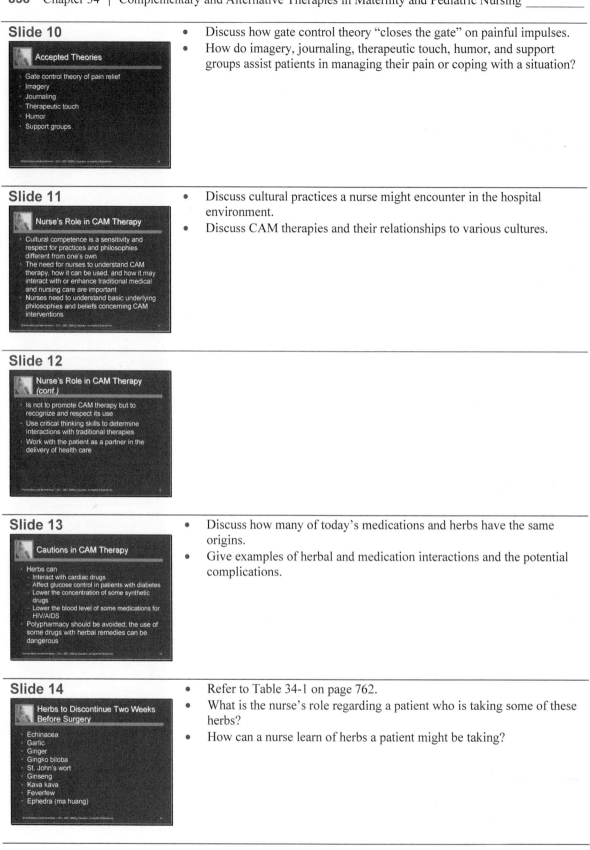

- Discuss how gate control theory "closes the gate" on painful impulses.
- How do imagery, journaling, therapeutic touch, humor, and support groups assist patients in managing their pain or coping with a situation?

Slide 11

- Discuss cultural practices a nurse might encounter in the hospital environment.
- Discuss CAM therapies and their relationships to various cultures.

Slide 12

Slide 13

- Discuss how many of today's medications and herbs have the same origins.
- Give examples of herbal and medication interactions and the potential complications.

Slide 14

- Refer to Table 34-1 on page 762.
- What is the nurse's role regarding a patient who is taking some of these herbs?
- How can a nurse learn of herbs a patient might be taking?

Slide 15

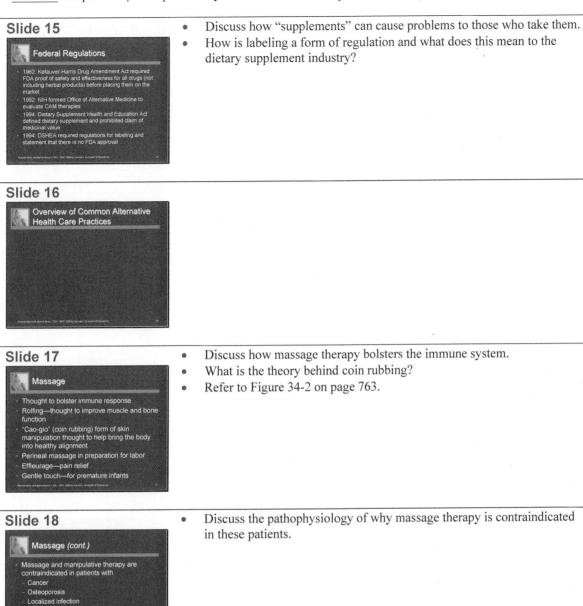

Federal Regulations

- 1962: Kefauver-Harris Drug Amendment Act required FDA proof of safety and effectiveness for all drugs (not including herbal products) before placing them on the market
- 1992: NIH formed Office of Alternative Medicine to evaluate CAM therapies
- 1994: Dietary Supplement Health and Education Act defined dietary supplement and prohibited claim of medicinal value
- 1994: DSHEA required regulations for labeling and statement that there is no FDA approval

- Discuss how "supplements" can cause problems to those who take them.
- How is labeling a form of regulation and what does this mean to the dietary supplement industry?

Slide 16

Overview of Common Alternative Health Care Practices

Slide 17

Massage

- Thought to bolster immune response
- Rolfing—thought to improve muscle and bone function
- "Cao-gio" (coin rubbing) form of skin manipulation thought to help bring the body into healthy alignment
- Perineal massage in preparation for labor
- Effleurage—pain relief
- Gentle touch—for premature infants

- Discuss how massage therapy bolsters the immune system.
- What is the theory behind coin rubbing?
- Refer to Figure 34-2 on page 763.

Slide 18

Massage *(cont.)*

- Massage and manipulative therapy are contraindicated in patients with
  - Cancer
  - Osteoporosis
  - Localized infection
  - Cardiac and circulatory disorders
- Because of the increased blood flow to the affected areas

- Discuss the pathophysiology of why massage therapy is contraindicated in these patients.

Slide 19

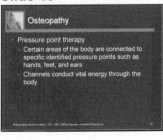

Osteopathy

- Pressure point therapy
  - Certain areas of the body are connected to specific identified pressure points such as hands, feet, and ears
  - Channels conduct vital energy through the body

Introduction to Maternity & Pediatric Nursing, 6th ed.

Leifer

Slide 20

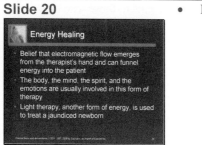

Energy Healing

- Belief that electromagnetic flow emerges from the therapist's hand and can funnel energy into the patient
- The body, the mind, the spirit, and the emotions are usually involved in this form of therapy
- Light therapy, another form of energy, is used to treat a jaundiced newborn

- How does light therapy help to relieve jaundice in the newborn?

Slide 21

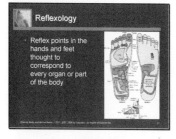

Reflexology

- Reflex points in the hands and feet thought to correspond to every organ or part of the body

- Discuss the theory regarding reflexology.

Slide 22

Acupuncture and Acupressure

- Complex meridians that are pathways to specific organs or parts of the body
- It is at these points that positive or negative energy can be realigned
- "Chi" energy is thought to regulate proper body function
- Points to avoid during pregnancy are
  - Bottom of foot
  - Inner lower leg
  - Base of thumb
  - Most areas over abdomen

- Refer to Figure 34-4 on page 764.
- Compare and contrast these areas.
- Discuss the meridians, dermatome, and reflexology lines.

Slide 23

Homeopathy

- Uses plants, herbs, and earth minerals
- Belief that disease is an energy imbalance and that prescribed remedies assist the body to reestablish correct balance
- Taken sublingually
- Don't combine with caffeine, alcohol, or traditional Western medicine
- Only one remedy is administered at a time

- Give examples of potential complications combining homeopathy with Western medicine.

Slide 24

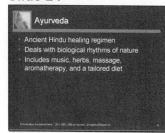

Ayurveda

- Ancient Hindu healing regimen
- Deals with biological rhythms of nature
- Includes music, herbs, massage, aromatherapy, and a tailored diet

---

ELSEVIER

Leifer